ENCYCLOPEDIA
of the
BATTLE OF FRANKLIN

◦∞ THE LOCHLAINN SEABROOK COLLECTION ∞◦
Books by award-winning author Lochlainn Seabrook

A Rebel Born: A Defense of Nathan Bedford Forrest - Confederate General, American Legend (winner of the 2011 Jefferson Davis Historical Gold Medal)

Nathan Bedford Forrest: Southern Hero, American Patriot - Honoring a Confederate Icon and the Old South

The Quotable Nathan Bedford Forrest: Selections From the Writings and Speeches of the Confederacy's Most Brilliant Cavalryman

Give 'Em Hell Boys! The Complete Military Correspondence of Nathan Bedford Forrest

Everything You Were Taught About the Civil War is Wrong, Ask a Southerner! - Correcting the Errors of Yankee "History"

Honest Jeff and Dishonest Abe: A Southern Children's Guide to the Civil War

Abraham Lincoln: The Southern View - Demythologizing America's Sixteenth President

The Unquotable Abraham Lincoln: The President's Quotes They Don't Want You To Know!

Lincolnology: The Real Abraham Lincoln Revealed in His Own Words - A Study of Lincoln's Suppressed, Misinterpreted, and Forgotten Writings and Speeches

The Quotable Jefferson Davis: Selections From the Writings and Speeches of the Confederacy's First President

The Quotable Alexander H. Stephens: Selections From the Writings and Speeches of the Confederacy's First Vice President

The Quotable Robert E. Lee: Selections From the Writings and Speeches of the South's Most Beloved Civil War General

The Old Rebel: Robert E. Lee As He Was Seen By His Contemporaries

The Constitution of the Confederate States of America: Explained

The Quotable Edward A. Pollard: Selections From the Writings of the Confederacy's Greatest Defender

Encyclopedia of the Battle of Franklin - A Comprehensive Guide to the Conflict that Changed the Civil War

Carnton Plantation Ghost Stories: True Tales of the Unexplained from Tennessee's Most Haunted Civil War House!

The McGavocks of Carnton Plantation: A Southern History - Celebrating One of Dixie's Most Noble Confederate Families and Their Tennessee Home

The Caudills: An Etymological, Ethnological, and Genealogical Study - Exploring the Name and National Origins of a European-American Family

The Blakeneys: An Etymological, Ethnological, and Genealogical Study - Uncovering the Mysterious Origins of the Blakeney Family and Name

Britannia Rules: Goddess-Worship in Ancient Anglo-Celtic Society - An Academic Look at the United Kingdom's Matricentric Spiritual Past

UFOs and Aliens: The Complete Guidebook

Christmas Before Christianity: How the Birthday of the "Sun" Became the Birthday of the "Son"

The Book of Kelle: An Introduction to Goddess-Worship and the Great Celtic Mother-Goddess Kelle, Original Blessed Lady of Ireland

The Goddess Dictionary of Words and Phrases: Introducing a New Core Vocabulary for the Women's Spirituality Movement

Aphrodite's Trade: The Hidden History of Prostitution Unveiled

Thought Provoking Books For Smart People
www.SeaRavenPress.com

ENCYCLOPEDIA of the BATTLE OF FRANKLIN

A Comprehensive Guide to the
Conflict the Changed the Civil War

LOCHLAINN SEABROOK

WINNER OF THE JEFFERSON DAVIS HISTORICAL GOLD MEDAL

Foreword by Michael Givens

SEA RAVEN PRESS, FRANKLIN, TENNESSEE, USA

ENCYCLOPEDIA OF THE BATTLE OF FRANKLIN

Published by
Sea Raven Press, P.O. Box 1054, Franklin, Tennessee 37065-1054 USA
www.searavenpress.com • searavenpress@nii.net

Copyright © 2012 Lochlainn Seabrook
in accordance with U.S. and international copyright laws and regulations, as stated and protected under the Berne Union for the Protection of Literary and Artistic Property (Berne Convention), and the Universal Copyright Convention (the UCC). All rights reserved under the Pan-American and International Copyright Conventions.

First Sea Raven Press Civil War Sesquicentennial Edition: April 2012

ISBN: 978-0-9838185-7-1
Library of Congress Catalog Number: 2012937241

This work is the copyrighted intellectual property of Lochlainn Seabrook and has been registered with the Copyright Office at the Library of Congress in Washington, D.C., USA. No part of this work (including text, covers, drawings, photos, illustrations, maps, images, diagrams, etc.), in whole or in part, may be used, reproduced, stored in a retrieval system, or transmitted, in any form or by any means now known or hereafter invented, without written permission from the publisher. The sale, duplication, hire, lending, copying, digitalization, or reproduction of this material, in any manner or form whatsoever, is also prohibited, and is a violation of federal, civil, and digital copyright law, which provides severe civil and criminal penalties for any violations.

Encyclopedia of the Battle of Franklin: A Comprehensive Guide to the Conflict the Changed the Civil War / by Lochlainn Seabrook. Foreword by Michael Givens. Includes an index and bibliographical references.

Front and back cover design, interior book design and layout, by Lochlainn Seabrook
Typography: Sea Raven Press Book Design
Cover photo: "Tennessee Battlefield" © Lochlainn Seabrook
All images are from 19th-Century public domain sources, unless otherwise indicated
(Portions of this book have been adapted from the author's other works.)

The views on the American "Civil War" documented in this book *are* those of the publisher.

The paper used in this book is acid-free and lignin-free. It has been certified by the Sustainable Forestry Initiative and the Forest Stewardship Council and meets all ANSI standards for archival quality paper.

PRINTED & MANUFACTURED IN OCCUPIED TENNESSEE, FORMER CONFEDERATE STATES OF AMERICA

Dedication

To my conservative Confederate cousins who fought for the Constitution and against Northern liberalism and despotism at the Battle of Franklin, November 30, 1864. Though they are gone their memory and honor will live on.

Tyree Harris Bell
Abraham Buford
Theodrick "Tod" Carter
Jesse Johnson Finley
Nathan Bedford Forrest
Hugh Alfred Garland Jr.
States Rights Gist
George Washington Gordon
John Bell Hood
Henry Rootes Jackson
Stephen Dill Lee
Mark Perrin Lowrey
Arthur Middleton Manigault
Edmund Winston Pettus
William Andrew Quarles
Edmund Winchester Rucker
Alexander Peter Stewart
John B. Womack

"Every man thinks less of himself
for not having been a soldier."

Samuel Johnson, 1776

ACKNOWLEDGMENTS

I would like to thank the following individuals for their kindness and generosity:

My wife Cassidy
My daughters Fiona and Dixie
Michael Givens, Commander-in-Chief, Sons of Confederate Veterans
Dr. Michael Bradley, Chaplain, Sons of Confederate Veterans
Sam Huffman, *Save The Franklin Battlefield*
Betty Jane Carl, McGavock Confederate Cemetery list

THE BATTLE OF FRANKLIN.

CONTENTS

Acknowledgments - 7
Notes to My Readers - 11
Preface, by Lochlainn Seabrook - 15
Foreword, by Michael Givens - 17
In Memoriam - 21

ENCYCLOPEDIA ENTRIES
A - 25
B - 42
C - 79
D - 125
E - 130
F - 138
G - 182
H - 204
I - 214
J - 215
K - 221
L - 225
M - 233
N - 246
O - 251
P - 259
Q - 262
R - 265
S - 276
T - 303
U - 321
V - 323
W - 325
Y - 339
Z - 340

APPENDICES

Battle Maps
Appendix A: Franklin, Columbia, Spring Hill, Nashville - 343

Military Organization
Appendix B: Personnel Organization of the C.S.A. - 354
Appendix C: C.S.A. Chain of Command - 355
Appendix D: Command Structure of Confederate Forces, November-December 1864 - 356
Appendix E: Confederate Forces Present at the Battle of Franklin - 365
Appendix F: Command Structure of Union Forces at the Battle of Franklin - 376
Appendix G: Union Forces Present at the Battle of Franklin - 381

Descriptions of the Battle of Franklin
Appendix H: Confederate General John Bell Hood - 385
Appendix I: Confederate Private Sam Rush Watkins - 391
Appendix J: Confederate Chaplain Charles Todd Quintard - 395
Appendix K: Confederate Captain Joseph Boyce - 404
Appendix L: Southern Journalist Edward Alfred Pollard - 413
Appendix M: Confederate Colonel William Dudley Gale - 419
Appendix N: Union General John McAllister Schofield - 428
Appendix O: Union Captain John K. Shellenberger - 441
Appendix P: General Stewart's Tribute to General Adams - 462
Appendix Q: Cunningham's Tribute to General Strahl - 468
Appendix R: General Stewart's Official Military Reports - 473

McGavock Confederate Cemetery Roster
Appendix S: List of the Deceased - 482

Illustrations - 541
Bibliography - 843
Index of Entries - 887
Meet the Author - 911
Meet the Foreword Writer - 915

NOTES TO MY READERS

🔫 In any study of the "Civil War" it is vitally important to keep in mind that the two major political parties were then the opposite of what they are today. The Democrats of the mid 19th Century were conservatives, akin to the Republican Party of today, while the Republicans of the mid 19th Century were liberals, akin to the Democratic Party of today. Thus the Confederacy's Democratic president, Jefferson Davis, was a conservative (with libertarian leanings); the Union's Republican president, Abraham Lincoln, was a liberal (with socialistic leanings).

🔫 What is commonly known as "the Battle of Franklin" is actually the second of three Civil War engagements that were fought in "Tennessee's handsomest town":

- The Battle of Franklin I (or First Franklin) was fought on April 10, 1863.
- The Battle of Franklin II (or Second Franklin)—the conflict that is the subject of this book—was fought on November 30, 1864.
- The Battle of Franklin III (or Third Franklin) was fought on December 17, 1864, one day after the disastrous Battle of Nashville (December 15-16, 1864)—as Yankees chased the retreating Rebels back into Franklin, and from there southward into Mississippi.

Though I have never approved of the custom of referring to the Battle of Franklin II as the "Battle of Franklin," for simplicity's sake, throughout this book I will do just that. When referring to the other two conflicts, I will use the more correct terms Battle of Franklin I and Battle of Franklin III, in order to differentiate them from the Battle of Franklin II.

🔫 As in the preceding paragraph, I will sometimes use the phrase "Civil War," just as 19th-Century Confederates like Jefferson Davis, Joseph E. Johnston, and Nathan Bedford Forrest did on occasion. Today, here in the 21st-Century South, we normally denounce and deliberately avoid the term "Civil War" as a wholly inaccurate anti-South expression. Thus, I feel the necessity of offering an explanation.

The term "Civil War" was invented by liberal Northern President Lincoln and his constituents to help obscure the truth about the conflict. What is that truth? Lincoln wanted the world to believe that his War was between states belonging to the *same* country, the true definition of "civil war."

However, we know this is not true because the South legally seceded under the Constitution's tacit guarantee of states' rights (Amendments Nine and Ten)—which include the powers of accession and secession. This means that the War was actually a conflict between two *separate* countries: the Confederate States of America and the United States of America. This is why, here in Dixie, we prefer, and typically use, such phrases as: the War for Southern Independence, the War Against Northern Aggression, the War for States' Rights, or my own personal preference, Lincoln's War; anything but the "Civil War."

Why then do I occasionally use this phrase? Sometimes—out of necessity—for commercial purposes; at other times, for literary and poetic purposes. I certainly never mean to use it in reference to historical fact, for the phrase "Civil War" is the opposite of fact. It is just another aspect of that great corpus of Northern mythology.

Concerning the encyclopedia entries, not every individual or item listed was connected to the Battle of Franklin. In such cases I have included them because they were, in some way, indirectly related. Conversely, not everyone who participated in the Battle of Franklin is listed. This is due both to space and also because not everyone who was present is known: there were over 50,000 Confederate and Union soldiers on the field that day. Lastly, Confederate figures and topics receive more attention and space than Union figures and topics.

To expedite indexing, and also to avoid confusion between identically named Union military units (there were numerous "Second Divisions" and "Third Brigades," for example), I have given my own names to such units where deemed necessary. For instance, in this encyclopedia the Fourth U.S. Army Corps' Second Division has been renamed "Wagner's Second Division" in order to identify it and set it apart from other similarly named units, such as the Second Division, Twenty-third U.S. Army Corps—here renamed "Ruger's Second Division."

For the story of what led to the Battle of Franklin, and also what happened during and after the conflict, please read the following entries in this order: The Battle of Columbia, the Battle of Spring Hill, the Battle of Franklin, and the Battle of Nashville. Also see the numerous eyewitness descriptions of the Battle of Franklin in the Appendices.

🔫 The *Encyclopedia of the Battle of Franklin* is the product of eight years of intensive research and writing, including countless hours spent in libraries around Middle Tennessee, and many more sifting through my own massive personal library. Despite the tremendous effort involved, complete accuracy concerning every fact and figure cannot be guaranteed. This is due to the near ubiquitous problem of differences in the original sources, many of which not even the most careful historians have ever agreed upon. I have done my best to mitigate the host of contradictory, questionable, and outright erroneous material that confronts every serious Civil War scholar.

🔫 In this work I have included many of the surviving historic sites that were associated with the Battle of Franklin. It is worth noting that though these were once purely Confederate, owned by Confederate families, living in a Confederate town, in the Confederate States of America, today the casual Franklin visitor will not see one vestige of the Confederacy anywhere near these structures, in particular, those open to the public.

Sadly, as an unnecessary concession to political correctness, and as a part of the ongoing movement to obliterate the South's true history, such Southern emblems as the Confederate Flag are no longer displayed at most of Franklin's historic houses and Civil War sites. This reveals an appalling ignorance of authentic Southern history and an insensitivity to the memory and honor of our Confederate soldiers, especially to those who fought and died at the Battle of Franklin in an effort to preserve the Constitution of the American Founding Fathers.

Additionally, of course, prohibiting Confederate displays in a Confederate city at Confederate sites and monuments is an insult to the descendants and relatives of all Confederate soldiers, and a grave offense to our wonderful Southern heritage and Confederate history. The South has nothing to be ashamed of and everything to be proud of, as any reader of my books will readily acknowledge.

It is hoped, by this author and thousands of other Franklinites, that this egregious violation against our Southern ancestors and the worthy Cause they supported (the Ninth and Tenth Amendments) will one day be rectified.

🔫 For those interested in the Truth about the War for Southern Independence, see my books:

Everything You Were Taught About the Civil War is Wrong, Ask a Southerner! - Correcting the Errors of Yankee "History"

Honest Jeff and Dishonest Abe: A Southern Children's Guide to the Civil War

A Rebel Born: A Defense of Nathan Bedford Forrest - Confederate General, American Legend

Nathan Bedford Forrest: Southern Hero, American Patriot - Honoring a Confederate Icon & the Old South

The Quotable Nathan Bedford Forrest: Selections From the Writings & Speeches of the Confederacy's Most Brilliant Cavalryman

Give 'Em Hell Boys! The Complete Military Correspondence of Nathan Bedford Forrest

The Quotable Robert E. Lee: Selections From the Writings & Speeches of the South's Most Beloved Civil War General

The Old Rebel: Robert E. Lee As He Was Seen By His Contemporaries

The Quotable Jefferson Davis: Selections From the Writings & Speeches of the Confederacy's First President

Abraham Lincoln: The Southern View - Demythologizing America's Sixteenth President

Lincolnology: The Real Abraham Lincoln Revealed in His Own Words - A Study of Lincoln's Suppressed, Misinterpreted, & Forgotten Writings & Speeches

The Unquotable Abraham Lincoln: The President's Quotes They Don't Want You to Know!

The Quotable Alexander H. Stephens: Selections From the Writings & Speeches of the Confederacy's First Vice President

The Constitution of the Confederate States of America: Explained

The McGavocks of Carnton Plantation: A Southern History - Celebrating One of Dixie's Most Noble Confederate Families & Their Tennessee Home

Carnton Plantation Ghost Stories: True Tales of the Unexplained from Tennessee's Most Haunted Civil War House!

(Photo © Lochlainn Seabrook)

PREFACE

The Battle of Franklin is one of the most overlooked and misunderstood conflicts of the War for Southern Independence. And yet it is arguably one of the most important and decisive struggles in American history.

Though a few books have been written on the subject, considering its stunning death toll and disastrous consequences, it has produced far less literature than other Civil War battles. Hundreds, for example, have been written on the Battle of Gettysburg alone. The total number of 20th-Century books on the Battle of Franklin can be counted on one hand, and only a few have been written in the 21st Century. With new information available today, this has left a gapping hole in the study and understanding of this conflict.

What has been missing in particular is a comprehensive resource for students, casual readers, historians, Civil War scholars, teachers, professors, tourists, public and educational libraries, and military academies interested in this calamitous conflict, one that sank the Confederacy in the Western Theater in just five hours. The *Encyclopedia of the Battle of Franklin* is a one-stop, all-in-one reference book written to fill this niche.

Additionally, most titles on the War for Southern Independence have been written by pro-North authors, giving one of America's most momentous conflicts a decidedly biased and inaccurate slant. Being both a citizen of Franklin and the descendant of Confederate ancestors (at least a dozen of my cousins fought at the Battle of Franklin, including the lead Confederate commander, General John Bell Hood), my book aims to correct this imbalance by coming from a Southern viewpoint. Why is this important?

The Battle of Franklin was a Confederate conflict that took place on Confederate soil against a foreign enemy. It was engaged in by Confederate boys and men (and some Confederate women) who fought and died for the Confederate Cause: the Constitution, self-determination, personal liberty, and states' rights. Since it was not fought between separate states, but between two separate nations, the War was never thought of as "civil" in the South. In Franklin, and all across the Southern states, it always was, and still is, rightly referred to as the War for Southern Independence.

For these reasons I feel that it is extremely important to offer the world a book on the Battle of Franklin that is seen through the eyes of the South. For the "Civil War," Lincoln's War, cannot be fully understood without a thorough knowledge of the Southern perspective.

My work provides the reader with this vital, seldom discussed material, while at the same time giving me an opportunity to overturn many of the preposterous anti-South myths that have been generated by Northern propagandists over the past 150 years. The redaction of history is never a good thing, especially when penned by the victors.

Though my book is Southern in perspective, this does not mean that it is subjective. In its pages will also be found traditionally accepted information on all of the main players at the Battle of Franklin, including important places and events related to the conflict, both Confederate and Union. Entries include such luminaries as President Jefferson Davis, President Abraham Lincoln, General Nathan Bedford Forrest, and General Ulysses S. Grant, not to mention hundreds of individuals of lesser rank, and even non-combatants, not often covered.

In addition, there are entries on the causes of the War, the issue of slavery, and the various historic homes and plantations involved in or affected by the Battle of Franklin, some completely unknown to the public. I have also included material on the closely related Battles of Columbia, Spring Hill, Nashville, and Franklin III, along with entries on the architectural styles of the period, maps of the battle, lists of the Rebel and Yankee command structures, genealogical connections, eyewitness descriptions of the battle, official reports, a complete list of the known Confederate soldiers killed at Franklin (buried at nearby McGavock Confederate Cemetery), hundreds of photos and illustrations, a detailed index, an exhaustive bibliography, and more.

This is a handbook that I hope will be enjoyed for generations to come by all those interested in not only the Battle of Franklin, but the War for Southern Independence itself.

Lochlainn Seabrook, SCV
Jefferson Davis Historical Gold Medal winner
Franklin, Tennessee
April 2012

FOREWORD

> But when ye shall hear of wars and commotions, be not terrified: for these things must first come to pass; but the end is not by and by. *Luke 21:9*

Marching through the forest we had an anxious jovial air as we approached to the edge of the open field. Snapping twigs and rustling leaves were like a drumbeat to our quiet martial refrain. Then we came into the sun and everything changed. We marched four abreast, fully exposed, into the open. No longer sheltered in the shadows of the canopy, we were marching across the field in broad daylight, into the jaws of death. Just an instant before, I had been aware of the presence of thousands of men to my right and left, the men before me and the men behind. But at that frozen moment in time, I was alone. The beat of our marching feet had silenced. Like grey ghosts, we marched on, but I could hear nothing. Slowly the sound of my own heartbeat crept up through my throat and into my ears pounding my mind with thunder. My senses awakened by the pressure of my compatriot's shoulders pressed against mine. Soon, the air was filled with the footfalls and hammering heartbeats of 10,000 men. Like a pack of mechanical wolves, marching in unison across this hecatomb field, I was not alone. These few men around me were my strength and I was theirs. When we go to war, we fight for God and country. When we go to battle, we fight for the men at our side.

This is not the recollection of a soldier of 1862, but my own impressions as a reenactor 140 years later. (I realize that the difference is like the distance of the earth to the moon, but on a clear night, from here on Earth, we can see the moon in good detail.) At the moment that we stepped onto the field mentioned above, I was overcome with an emotion I had never known. I mentioned this odd feeling to the man to my right and he informed me that we had just stepped onto the actual battlefield. This was the same battlefield that had been saturated with not only the blood of my heroes, but my very ancestors. Many of my ancestors fought in the Battle of Franklin.

In the scheme of world history, the War for Southern Independence was by no means an isolated event. There were many factors leading up to this defining moment in history. The War was a logical step in the slow walk of human liberty. Perhaps that walk began on June 15, 1215, in a meadow at Runnymede in South England when King John was pressed to sign the Magna Carta. Certainly, liberty stepped forward again when the American Colonies seceded from Great Britain in 1776 forming themselves into independent sovereign States. This act marked the genesis of the American brand of liberty that has been emulated and envied throughout the civilized world.

While the secession of the Southern States from the United States in 1860-61 was another step forward in the journey to liberty, the invasion of the newly formed Confederate States by the United States represents major steps backwards. Furthermore, the Federal victory, followed by punitive reconstruction laws, destroyed the sovereignty of the States and replaced it with a unitary state. Since the loss at Appomattox, American liberties have been steadily surrendered to the central government. Unitary state governments abound throughout the world. A few examples are: Afghanistan, Bangladesh, Cambodia, Chad, The People's Republic of China, Haiti, Libya, Saudi Arabia and The United Kingdom. One needs only to look to these governments for a glimpse of what is to come if we are to continue in this direction.

One can only speculate over what our world might look like today had the South been allowed to peaceably follow her rightful path to self-government. The game of "What if" leads us to many questions, including different outcomes of particular events. The untimely death of General Jackson or an advance on Washington after the Battle of Manassas are but two of many examples that come to mind.

The Battle of Franklin, November 30th, 1864 is another such event. It has been called the "Bloodiest five hours of the War." Never on any field did braver men tread. The Confederacy lost at least 7000 souls that fateful day and night. Among the killed was Major-General P. R. Cleburne, Brigadier-Generals Gist, John Adams, Strahl and Granbury. Major-General Brown, Brigadier-Generals Carter, Manigault, Quarles, Cockrell and Scott were wounded, and Brigadier-General Gordon was captured. Where might the Cause (and hence our own liberty) have gone, with a Confederate victory at Franklin? How might our country have benefitted from the continued talents and love of her fallen sons for just a bit longer?

It is from questions such as these that we learn from the past and work to make our lives and the lives of our children better. Thanks to the scholarly efforts of Southern historian Lochlainn Seabrook and his one-of-a-kind encyclopedia, we may more thoroughly study the events of the Battle of Franklin. It is our shared hope that more Americans will open their minds to the true history of our republic before it's too late and we might begin taking forward steps toward liberty once again. The Lord said, ". . . the end is not by and by." Indeed it is not.

Michael Givens
Commander-in-Chief, Sons of Confederate Veterans
Beaufort, South Carolina
April 2012

IN MEMORIAM

"The Confederate Soldiers were our kinfolk and our heroes. We testify to the country our enduring fidelity to their memory. We commemorate their valor and devotion. There were some things that were not surrendered at Appomattox. We did not surrender our rights and history, nor was it one of the conditions of surrender that unfriendly lips should be suffered to tell the story of that war or that unfriendly hands should write the epitaphs of the Confederate dead. We have a right to teach our children the true history of that war, the causes that led up to it and the principles involved."

Tennessee Senator Edward Ward Carmack, 1903

Gravestone of John B. Womack, McGavock Confederate Cemetery, Franklin, Tennessee. Womack, a cousin of the author and of country artist Lee Ann Womack, perished at the Battle of Franklin, November 30, 1864, fighting for the Constitution and personal freedom. (Photo copyright © Lochlainn Seabrook)

ENTRIES

ABATIS: Pronounced Á-but-ee, this word derives from the French word *abattre*, meaning a defensive barrier made from felled trees, whose branches have been sharpened and faced toward the enemy.

At the Battle of Franklin abatis was used only by the Union forces, most who were lodged in defensive positions inside five-foot deep trenches called breastworks. Out in front they had assembled abatis made from local Osage-orange trees. Osage-orange is a hard wood that perfectly sharpens into a terrifying lethal weapon. Typically, straight branches were cut and honed into needle-sharp spear points, which were then stuck into wooden hubs, like spokes without the outer wheel—a deadly barrier known as a *cheval-de-frise* (French for "horse from Friesland").

At the Battle of Franklin these bristly impenetrable instruments of death greatly interrupted the flow of the offensive Confederate troops as waves of regiments assaulted the entrenched Union forces. Many Rebels were pushed back, wounded—their hands ripped to pieces by the hedges of thorns and spiked wheels. Many even died trying to surmount or crawl under the abatis to get at the enemy.

It is no exaggeration to say that the Yankee Osage abatis was a major factor in the Union victory that day, November 30, 1864. Confederate Colonel Ellison Capers, present at the conflict, referred to the Yankee wall of pointed brambles as a "formidable and fearful obstruction."

ABERCROMBIE, ROBERT H. (CSA): Confederate Lieutenant Colonel Abercrombie led the Forty-fifth Alabama Infantry at the Battle of Franklin, where he was wounded in action.

ADAIRE, THOMAS N. (CSA): Confederate Colonel Adaire led the Fourth Mississippi Infantry at the Battle of Franklin, where he was wounded in action.

ADAMS STREET: A Franklin, Tennessee, street named in honor of Confederate Brigadier General John Adams, who fought for constitutional government at the Battle of Franklin.

ADAMS, JOHN (CSA): Adams was born July 1, 1825, in Nashville, Davidson County, Tennessee, the son of Irishman Thomas Patton Adams and Scotswoman Anne Tennant. He graduated twenty-fifth in his class from West Point Military Academy in June of 1846, and began serving as Second Lieutenant in the First Dragoons U.S. Regular Army under Captain Philip Kearny in the Mexican War. In 1851 he was breveted for meritorious conduct at the Battle of Santa Cruz de Rosales, achieving the rank of First Lieutenant.

Promoted to Captain in 1851, the Irish-Scottish-American served for five years at Fort Crook, California, where he also worked as a recruitment officer. On May 4, 1854, while serving temporarily at Fort Snelling, Minnesota, as an aide-de-camp to Governor William Gorman, Adams married an Arkansas girl of Scottish descent, Georgiana McDougall, the daughter of Charles McDougall and Maria Griffith Hanson. Adams, Georgiana, and their four sons, Charles McDougall, Thomas Patton, John, and Francis Joseph, are listed in the 1860 U.S. Census at Millville, Shasta County, California. Later, as Adams continued to be transferred around the country, two daughters, Georgiana McDougall, and Emma Portis, were born to the couple.

In 1861, with the start of Lincoln's War, Adams sided with the South and the Constitution. Resigning from the U.S. Army, he returned to Tennessee (which had seceded on May 27, 1861), where he joined the Confederate Army. He rose rapidly up in ranks, first becoming captain of cavalry (in Memphis), then colonel, then finally brigadier general in December 1862.

When Confederate Brigadier General Lloyd Tilghman passed away on May 16, 1863, Adams replaced him, taking command of Tilghman's Brigade. In May and June of

1863 Adams fought at Vicksburg under Confederate General Joseph Eggleston Johnston, and in Mississippi Adams later served with Confederate General Leonidas Polk. Throughout the first half of 1864 Adams fought gallantly throughout the entire Atlanta Campaign, beginning with the First Battle of Dalton, February 22-27.

Fatefully, Adams and his brigade were then transferred to the Army of Tennessee, headed by the hard-headed, anachronistic Confederate General John Bell Hood. On November 30, 1864, Adams rode out on to the Plain of Franklin under the famed Rebel cavalryman General Nathan Bedford Forrest. An amazing story of courage and heroism was about to begin.

As the chaos of battle commenced, Adam's Brigade band marched forward through the tall bluegrass playing *Dixie*. Thick artillery smoke filled the air and in the melee Adams was soon dangerously wounded in the shoulder. Refusing to leave the field, declaring "I'm going to see my men through," he galloped ahead toward the famed Carter family cotton gin, the site of what would become the heaviest fighting at Franklin.

Under a continual "galling fire" from the Yankees, Adams fearlessly spurred his bay horse, Old Charley, through the haze, jumped the ditch, then rode right up on to a Union embankment, yelling out encouragement to his men as he went. As he sat alone astride his mount directly in front of the Federal line by the Carter ginhouse, Union commander Colonel W. Scott Stewart ordered his men to "hold your fire." The stunned Yanks had seldom witnessed such bravery, and were hoping the dashing Tennessean would not be shot. "He was too brave to be killed," recalled a Union soldier later. Bullets and cannon fire whizzed past Adams, narrowly missing him. Another Yankee wrote that Adams "seemed to be in the hands of the Unseen."

Unfortunately at that moment, Old Charley slipped and fell, pinning Adams beneath him. As he was trying to extricate himself, Adams was hit by nine stray bullets. His noble steed died instantly from additional fire, and Adams, still conscious, was dragged by the dismayed enemy from the parapet and into a trench.

In a rare second act of

Yankee altruism, Union soldiers apologized to the severely wounded Confederate officer and gave him water, and even a cotton pillow to comfort him; but to no avail. As the sorrowful Federals gathered respectfully around Adams, he uttered his last words: "It is the fate of a soldier to die for his country." He then passed into the Great Beyond.

John Casement, one of the Union generals Adams had been fighting only minutes earlier, appropriated several of Adams' belongings—his watch, ring, saddle, and pistol—as spoils of war. (Later, perhaps realizing the magnitude of their unethical behavior, the Yanks had Adams' ring and watch sent back through the Confederate lines, under a flag of truce, so they could be returned to the general's widow, Georgiana.)

The next day, December 1, Adams' body was recovered from the field and taken to nearby Carnton Mansion, where it was laid upon the lower porch alongside the corpses of Generals Cleburne, Strahl, and Carter, all who also had perished near Columbia Pike, only yards from Adams (streets in the area have been named for all four officers). Rueful Confederate soldiers marched by throughout the day, for the last time saluting the officers they adored and had followed into the jaws of Hell at Franklin.

Adams' body was taken by horse and cart to Pulaski, Giles County, Tennessee, where he was laid to rest with his family at Maplewood Cemetery.

After the disastrous Battle of Nashville two weeks later, a routed Hood and his remaining bedraggled troops passed back south again through Franklin in an attempt to escape the pursuing Yanks—culminating in the Battle of Franklin III on December 17, 1864. It was noted by many that Adams' horse, Old Charley, still sat gruesomely astride the Federal works, its head and forelegs draped on one side, its hind legs and tail on the other; a bitter reminder of that terrible day, November 30, 1864, when Adams and dozens of other Rebel officers were wounded or killed, and where the Confederacy itself died a most ignoble death.

ADAMS' BRIGADE (CSA): This Rebel infantry brigade fought at the Battle of Franklin in Loring's Division, Stewart's Corps, C.S. Army of Tennessee.

Named after Confederate Brigadier General John Adams, it was comprised of the Sixth Mississippi, Fourteenth Mississippi, Fifteenth Mississippi, Twentieth Mississippi, Twenty-third Mississippi, and Forty-third Mississippi.

After Adams' death at Franklin the brigade was taken over by Confederate Colonel Robert Gadden Haynes Lowry.

AFRICAN-AMERICANS: Though it has been little discussed until recently, blacks played a major role in the War for Southern Independence, with about 180,000 fighting for the Union and as many as between 300,000 and 1 million fighting for the Confederacy (according to the military definition of a "private soldier").

While pro-North writers tell us that the Union enlisted blacks soldiers long before the Confederacy, the opposite is true: the South's first all-black militia was officially formed on April 23, 1861, only nine days after the first battle of the War at Fort Sumter, South Carolina. The unit, known as the "Native Guards (colored)," was "duly and legally enrolled as a part of the militia of the State, its officers being commissioned by Thomas O. Moore, Governor and Commander-in-Chief of the State of Louisiana . . ."

In contrast, the North's first all-black militia, the First South Carolina Volunteers, was not commissioned until November 7, 1862, under Yankee Colonel Thomas Wentworth Higginson.

Though official records are lacking, we know without question that Confederate blacks fought at the Battle of Franklin, for some forty-five slaves belonging to the famed Confederate cavalryman General Nathan Bedford Forrest, marched alongside him into battle throughout the entire War, which would included the bloody conflict at Franklin (twenty other blacks served with Forrest as well, making a total of at least sixty-five black Confederates present on the Franklin battlefield November 30, 1864).

Promised their freedom at war's end, Forrest's African-American soldiers fought loyally and courageously, staying with their commander for four long years—despite being freed by Forrest midway through the conflict. Contrary to Yankee myth, such emancipations were common and were practiced by thousands of white Southerners throughout the War.

Unfortunately for posterity, neither the names or the roles of black Confederates at the Battle of Franklin were chronicled. We can be certain that they were both excellent soldiers and highly dedicated to the Southern Cause, however, for Forrest would have never asked them to join his ranks, nor would they have remained by his side month after month if they had not been.

At least 565 soldiers who died at the Battle of Franklin are listed as "unknowns." There can be little doubt that a percentage of these were African-Americans, blacks who died defending the constitutional rights of their homeland, the Southern states, against Yankee liberalism and Northern tyranny.

AMERICAN BATTLEFIELD PROTECTION PROGRAM: Located in Washington, D.C., the American Battlefield Protection Program operates under the auspices of the Heritage Preservation Services, part of the U.S. National Park Service. Their goal is to identify, evaluate, protect, and promote the "preservation of significant historic battlefields associated with wars on American soil."

The core of the Franklin battlefield was never protected, and—except for a small plot of sacred battle ground only recently set aside at the corner of Cleburne Street and Columbia Avenue—what little is left has all but disappeared under urban sprawl.

ANTEBELLUM HOUSES: The word antebellum derives from the Latin words *ante* ("before") and *bellum* ("war"), thus meaning "before the war." In America the term is used chiefly in an architectural sense to indicate a structure built prior to start of the War for Southern Independence, April 12, 1861.

Though Franklin is today dotted with beautiful postwar Victorian homes and buildings, it still possesses numerous antebellum houses, magnificent structures lovingly built before Lincoln launched his illegal assault on the Constitution and the South. Among these are: Laurel Hill, the Harrison House, the Carter House, Riverside Plantation, the Lotz House, the Figuers House, River View, and Carnton Plantation.

Antebellum homes outside Franklin, but still inside Williamson County, include: Oaklawn Mansion, Isola Bella, Mooreland, the Knox-Crockett House, Forge Seat, Midway Plantation, Green Pastures, Homestead Manor, Ewell Farm, and Ferguson Hall.

Maury County, also profoundly connected to the Battle of Franklin, has its own stupendous antebellum homes, many in some way connected to Lincoln's War: Rattle and Snap, Elm Springs, the Polk House, Rippavilla, the Athenaeum, and the once beautiful Caldwell House (no longer standing).

Davidson County, where the survivors of Franklin were defeated at the Battle of Nashville, lays claim to dozens of striking antebellum homes as well, including: Belle Meade Plantation, Belmont Mansion, the Hermitage, and Travellers Rest.

ARMISTEAD, EDWARD HERBERT (CSA): Confederate Major Armistead was born January 18, 1839, at Montgomery, Alabama. He led the Twenty-second Alabama Infantry at the Battle of Franklin, where he was wounded in action. He died from his injuries a few days later, on December 7, 1864, and was buried in Montgomery's Oakwood Cemetery.

ARMSTRONG, FRANK CRAWFORD (CSA): Born on November 22, 1835, in Scullyville, Le Flore County, Oklahoma, he was the son of Frank W. Armstrong and Anne Millard. Of English heritage, he attended Holy Cross Academy at Brookline, Massachusetts.

Armstrong's affinity for the military was first evidenced at the youthful age of twenty while he was on an expedition with the U.S. Army in New Mexico in 1854. After a fight with "Indian marauders" in which he displayed remarkable valor, he was awarded the rank of lieutenant, a promotion normally reserved only for West Point graduates.

Armstrong married Maria Polk Walker in 1860, in the Choctaw Indian Territory of Oklahoma. With the start of Lincoln's War in 1861, he sided with the South and the Constitution, resigned from the U.S. Army, and joined the Confederacy.

As a staff officer for Confederate General James McQueen McIntosh, Armstrong fought at the Battle of

Chustenahlah in the Oklahoma Cherokee Nation on December 26, 1861. He then served as assistant adjutant general under Confederate General Ben McCullough.

At the Battle of Elk Tavern Armstrong received praise from Confederate General Earl Van Dorn, after which he was promoted to colonel of the Third Louisiana Infantry. Another promotion, this time to brigadier general, followed, and Armstrong was made head of the entire cavalry of the Western army.

As more battles ensued, his acclaim continued to rise. Confederate General Sterling Price, for example, commended Armstrong for his "prudence, discretion, and good sense" in the heat of battle. At the Mississippi Battles of Iuka and Corinth in September and October 1862, Armstrong helped save the day by aiding in the retreat of Price's and Van Dorn's defeated Rebel forces.

Armstrong was with Confederate cavalryman General Nathan Bedford Forrest at the Battle of Thompson's Station, Tennessee, on March 5, 1863. Here Union Colonel John Coburn and 1,220 of his men were taken prisoner in a decisive Confederate victory. After capturing a Yankee garrison at the Battle of Brentwood, March 25, 1863, Armstrong fought valiantly at the Battle of Franklin I on April 10, 1863, and later at Chickamauga on September 20.

After a promotion to major general, Armstrong accompanied Confederate General Lucius Polk throughout the Atlanta Campaign, and then served under Confederate General John Bell Hood at the Battles of Spring Hill (November 29, 1864) and Franklin II (November 30, 1864). Here he bravely led his own unit, Armstrong's Brigade, against the enemy.

Armstrong and his Mississippi Cavalry were also present at the Battles of Murfreesboro (December 5-7, 1864) and also Nashville (December 15-16, 1864), where he and Forrest added to their already celebrated fame by leading the rear guard that saved what was left of Hood's tattered Army of Tennessee, south out of the Volunteer State (Forrest was not at the Battle of Nashville).

Armstrong's final fight came on April 2, 1865, at the Battle of Selma, Alabama, where the Rebels lost against Yankee General John Harrison Wilson. Lincoln's War ended seven days later at Appomattox, Virginia.

Armstrong died on September 8, 1909, in Bar Harbor, Hancock County, Maine, to the end noted for his heroism and deep devotion to the Confederate Cause. He was buried at Rock Creek Cemetery, Washington, D.C.

ARMSTRONG'S BRIGADE (CSA): This Rebel cavalry brigade fought at the Battle of Franklin in Jackson's Division, Forrest's Cavalry Corps, C.S. Army of Tennessee.

Named after its commander Confederate Brigadier General Frank Crawford Armstrong, it was comprised of the First Mississippi Cavalry, Second Mississippi Cavalry, Twenty-eighth Mississippi Cavalry, and Ballentine's Mississippi Cavalry.

ARMY OF THE CUMBERLAND (USA): Known for its unstoppable power, unflinching regiments, and cohesive structure, during its history the Army of the Cumberland was an ominous juggernaut that bore down and annihilated many a Confederate force. The only Yankee army that was bigger and stronger was the Army of the Potomac.

Formed on May 21, 1861, just one month after Lincoln initiated his war (at Fort Sumter), like many armies, the Army of the Cumberland went through a number of structural and command changes. Originally known as the Department of Kentucky and led by Brigadier General Robert Anderson, in October 1861 the famed army was then turned over to William Tecumseh Sherman and the name was altered to the Department of the Cumberland, after the river of the same name.

In November 1861 it was renamed the Army of the Ohio with General Don Carlos Buell as its commander. In October 1862, it was renamed the Army of the Cumberland, known also as the Fourteenth Army Corps, and placed under the command of Union Major General William Starke Rosecrans. The army's right wing was led by Alexander McDowell McCook, the center by General George Henry Thomas, and the left wing by Thomas Leonidas Crittenden.

Finally, in October 1863, Thomas was placed in charge, his

command being overseen by Union General Ulysses S. Grant after March 1864.

The Army of the Cumberland fought at Mill Springs, Shiloh, Perryville, Murfreesboro, the Tullahoma Campaign, Chickamauga (where Thomas won the nickname the "Rock of Chickamauga"), Chattanooga, and the Atlanta Campaign. Most importantly, the Army of the Cumberland was responsible for sealing the fate of the Southern Cause at Nashville, December 15-16, 1864.

Early in the War, in February 1862, Buell and the Army of the Cumberland had captured and occupied the all-important capital city of Nashville, Tennessee, which remained in the possession of the Yanks for the duration of the conflict. It was this occupation that Confederate General John Bell Hood and his Army of Tennessee were hoping to overtake in November 1864.

On the way to Nashville Hood clashed with U.S. General John McAllister Schofield at Columbia and Spring Hill, finally, on November 30, ending up on the Plain of Franklin, where Hood's miscalculations cost the South the Confederacy itself.

Limping into Nashville, Hood encountered a strongly entrenched Thomas and the Army of the Cumberland, where they dealt the Army of Tennessee the final death blow. Hood, and what was left of his forces, hastily retreated south with Thomas' men on their heels. The chase lasted for several weeks, until the Army of the Cumberland had forced Hood back across the Tennessee River and into Mississippi.

To this day the Army of Tennessee's name is equated with gallant defeat in the South. In the North, however, the Army of the Cumberland is equated with the decisive victory that finished off the Confederacy on the very Tennessee river from which it derived its name.

ARMY OF NORTHERN VIRGINIA (CSA): One of the Confederacy's top military forces, and one of the world's most celebrated militias, the Army of Northern Virginia left an enduring legacy of boldness, aggressiveness, and determination in battle that has endured into the present day.

Though its regiments hailed from all over the Confederacy (as distant as

Arizona), as its name indicates, the Army's main region of operations was Virginia. It was led, consecutively, by Confederate Generals Pierre Gustav Toutant de Beauregard, Joseph Eggleston Johnston, and last, by Robert Edward Lee, considered by many to be the Confederacy's most outstanding commander.

Noted individuals who served under Lee include: Lieutenant General Thomas Jonathan "Stonewall" Jackson, Lieutenant General James Longstreet, Major General James Ewell Brown Stuart, and Brigadier General William Nelson Pendleton.

The Army of Northern Virginia fought in numerous conflicts—many against the Yankee Army of the Potomac, its primary foe. These include the Battles of Sharpsburg (Antietam to Yanks), Chancellorsville, Cold Harbor, the Crater, Fredericksburg, Gettysburg, Malvern Hill, Second Manassas (Second Bull Run to Yanks), Petersburg, Fair Oaks (Seven Pines to Yanks), and Spotsylvania.

The lead Confederate figure at the Battle of Franklin, General John Bell Hood, once served under Lee in the Army of Northern Virginia. At the Battle of Gettysburg in July 1863, Hood led his own division, losing the use of his left arm in the ensuing conflict.

A little over a year later, at the Battle of Franklin, Hood "slaughtered his own army," setting the stage for the death of the Confederacy itself. One consequence of Hood's debacle at Franklin was that a mere five months later, Lee, Hood's former commander, surrendered at Appomattox to Ulysses S. Grant and the Army of the Potomac. With this act on April 9, 1865, the Southern Cause officially became the "Lost Cause," until decades later when the banner was once again lifted up, this time by modern Southern Nationalists.

ARMY OF THE OHIO (USA): Formed in 1861, and named after the Ohio River, the Union Army of the Ohio, like many other armies, went through numerous structural changes and commanders. In 1862 it was reorganized into the Fourteenth Army Corps, also known as the famed Army of the Cumberland (River), the name by which it was known until the end of the War.

In its short existence, the

Army of the Ohio was present on the field of action at Rowlett's Station, Shiloh, Mill Springs, Corinth, and Perryville. Its chief Union commanders were Major General Don Carlos Buell, Major William Starke Rosecrans, and "the Rock of Chickamauga," Major General George Henry Thomas, the man who would deliver the death blow to the Confederate Army of Tennessee at the Battle of Nashville, December 15-16, 1864.

A separate Army of the Ohio, which served in the Atlanta campaign under General William Tecumseh Sherman, was led by Yankee General John McAllister Schofield, whose forces lost against the Rebels at the Battle of Kennesaw Mountain, June 27, 1864. It was Schofield who later, through luck, the cover of darkness, and the foolhardiness of the Rebel commander General John Bell Hood, soundly defeated the Confederates at the tragic Second Battle of Franklin, November 30, 1864.

ARMY OF THE POTOMAC (CSA): The original name of the famed Army of Northern Virginia, it was first led by Confederate General Pierre Gustave Toutant de Beauregard. It was later commanded, under the name it would retain until it surrendered at Appomattox, by Confederate General Robert Edward Lee.

(The Confederate Army of the Potomac is not to be confused with the U.S. Army of the Potomac, whose officers included Brigadier General Irvin McDowell, Major General George B. McClellan, Major General Ambrose E. Burnside, Major General Joseph Hooker, and Major General George G. Meade.)

ARMY OF TENNESSEE (CSA): In the Western Theater of operations the Confederate Army of Tennessee was the main fighting force during the War for Southern Independence. Named after the state of Tennessee, and first commanded by Confederate General Braxton Bragg, it was formed November 20, 1862, after which it spent much of the remainder of the War pitted against Union Major General William Starke Rosecrans and the U.S. Army of the Cumberland.

The Confederate Army of Tennessee (state)—which should not be confused with the Union's Army of the Tennessee (River)—fought at many of the

War's most important battles and skirmishes, including Spring Hill, Columbia, Murfreesboro, the Tullahoma Campaign, Missionary Ridge, the Atlanta Campaign, and, with the Army of Northern Virginia, at Chickamauga.

At the end of 1863 a defeated Bragg was replaced with General Joseph E. Johnston, who also failed to impress either his fellow commanders or Confederate President Jefferson Davis. In fact, up until now, the Tennessee Army had been seemingly cursed with both insurmountable command problems and just plain bad luck. Yet things were about to get worse.

In 1864, amidst ongoing bickering and divisiveness in the upper ranks, a third officer was sent in to lead the Army of Tennessee: General John Bell Hood. This was to be one of President Davis' most fateful decisions.

Hood, the epitome of the "Peter Principle" (being promoted to a level above one's abilities), began by allowing Yankee General William T. Sherman to capture Atlanta on September 2, 1864. Hood then led his army west into Tennessee, leaving Sherman free to engage in his famed eastward "March to the Sea," utterly destroying much of the South's infrastructure, culture, and people as he went.

Moving up into Tennessee, Hood soon squared off with Union commander General John McAllister Schofield at the Battle of Franklin (November 30, 1864), and with Schofield and General George Henry Thomas and the Army of the Cumberland at the Battle of Nashville (December 15-16, 1864).

At bloody Franklin, the "Gettysburg of the West," the Tennessee Army fought valiantly, both against a well-stocked and well-fed enemy and against the suicidal orders of their old-fashioned Kentucky commander. But to no avail. When it was over five short hours later, Hood had sacrificed nearly a third of his militia, the result of spite, arrogance, revenge, preposterous dreams of glory, and possibly the use of the mind-clouding painkiller laudanum. The next morning, seeing 1,750 of his men lying dead on the Plain of Franklin, Hood sat astride his horse and "wept like a baby," according to one eyewitness account.

But Hood had not yet

completed his destruction of the Army of Tennessee. Two weeks later he lost hundreds more of his faithful barefooted soldiers at Nashville in a futile attempt to regain the long Union-occupied city.

Beaten, demoralized, frozen, and exhausted, Hood and his army made a disorganized and hasty retreat, chased all the way to the southern Tennessee border by the victorious Yanks. Only the stunning maneuvers of cavalryman General Nathan Bedford Forrest, who adroitly protected the rear beginning about December 19, saved what was left of the ragtag Army of Tennessee that day in late December 1864.

Limping into Mississippi in tatters, the once proud and mighty Confederate army had been decimated. Starving and fatigued, thousands were now shoeless as they marched across the frozen ground. Many were wearing Yankee uniforms that had been desperately torn from the corpses of Union soldiers they had slaughtered defending their country that winter.

Hood resigned and went to live in New Orleans, where he died in 1879 of yellow fever. His command was taken over by Confederate General Richard Taylor, an almost symbolic gesture at that point: by January 1864 the Confederacy was, for all practical purposes, out of ammunition, food, clothing, and men, and morale was at its lowest level. Hood had done more to help bring about the death of the Army of Tennessee than any Union force, and all in less than a year.

With the Confederacy's strongest Western military force gone, Union victory was only a matter of time. Less than four months later, on April 9, 1865, Hood's former commander, General Robert E. Lee, surrendered at Appomattox.

Had President Davis replaced Joseph E. Johnston with someone like the brilliant Irish Confederate cavalryman, Patrick R. Cleburne, instead of Hood, the outcome of the war might have been quite different. Unfortunately Davis seemed to dislike Cleburne, while he adored Hood (for being an aggressive fighter). These would be remembered as two of the greatest misjudgements of character in American history.

ARMY OF THE TENNESSEE (USA): Unlike the Confederate Army of Tennessee, which was named after the state, the Union's Army of the Tennessee was named after the Tennessee River.

Originally known as the Army in the Field, and led by Union General Ulysses S. Grant (the first army he commanded), it was later called the Army of West Tennessee, and finally, the Army of the Tennessee.

Besides Grant, its U.S. officers also included Major General James B. McPherson, Major General John A. Logan, and Major General Oliver O. Howard.

The army saw action at the Battles of Vicksburg, Chattanooga, Atlanta, Ezra Church, Jonesboro, and in the Carolinas Campaign. It is most famous, however, for being part of General William Tecumseh Sherman's "March to the Sea," in which Sherman employed a scorched earth policy of harassing, robbing, and even raping and killing civilians, the burning of crops, the stealing and slaughter of livestock, pilfering family supplies, the bombing and burning of homes, office buildings, plantations, farms, and churches, and the destruction of railroads. It was also involved in numerous other violations of both the Constitution and the Geneva Convention, such as the forced conscription of captured black slaves.

Though deified by the North, in the South Sherman came to be one of the most hated men of all time. To this day his name, along with the Yank's Army of the Tennessee, still stirs strong negative emotions among the children of the Confederacy.

ASHFORD, FREDERICK A. (CSA): Confederate Colonel Ashford led the Sixteenth Alabama Infantry at the Battle of Franklin, where he was killed in action.

ASHWOOD HALL: This palatial Greek Revival house was built at a cost of $20,000 (today's equivalent of $500,000) by the renowned Confederate Bishop-General Leonidas Polk, in the town of Ashwood, located near Mount Pleasant, Maury County, Tennessee.

Across the street from Ashwood Hall, in 1840, Polk constructed the family chapel, Saint John's Episcopal Church. It was in Saint John's cemetery that the famed Irish Confederate

General Patrick R. Cleburne was originally buried after his untimely death at the Battle of Franklin, November 30, 1864 (in April 1870 his remains were reinterred at Helena, Arkansas, his adopted hometown).

The Irish-American Polk, also known as "the Fighting Bishop," is noted not only for being the second cousin of President James K. Polk, but also for being the man who, in Georgia, on May 11, 1864, the eve of the Atlanta Campaign, baptized Confederate General John Bell Hood, the commander of the Army of Tennessee at Franklin. Just thirty-three days later, on June 14, 1864, Polk would be blown in half by Yankee cannon fire while bravely serving his country at the Battle of Pine Mountain, Georgia.

In five months, on November 26, 1864, Hood himself showed up at the front door of Ashwood Hall, now owned by Leonidas' brother, Colonel Andrew Jackson Polk. Here Hood set up headquarters for the night, before marching his army to its doom four days later at Franklin.

Sadly, Ashwood Hall no longer exists, having burned to the ground in 1874 (two outbuildings and a grove of trees are all that remain). Saint John's Episcopal Church, however, still stands on the original site, one of the last surviving Southern plantation churches of its kind.

ATHENAEUM RECTORY: Designed by architect Adolphus Heiman and built by master builder Nathan Vaught, construction on the Athenaeum began in 1835 in Columbia, Tennessee, as a home for Samuel Polk Walker, a nephew of U.S. President James Knox Polk. Walker never inhabited the residence and after it was finished in 1837 it became the home of Vermonter Reverend Franklin Gillette Smith, a staunch Confederate supporter.

From 1852 to 1904 Smith ran the Columbia Athenaeum School for Young Ladies at the Athenaeum. Courses offered included mathematics, science, and business, unusual because at the time such areas of learning were considered solely "male interests." Sports (such as tennis, bowling, gymnastics, and croquet), the Bible, etiquette, art, and music was also taught, and the young women had access to the school's 16,000-book library.

During Lincoln's War the house—which combines Greek Revival, Moorish, and Gothic architectural styles—served as the temporary headquarters for Union General John McAllister Schofield in 1864. Union General James Scott Negley is also said to have used the rectory as his headquarters, and Confederate General Nathan Bedford Forrest stopped here on a number of occasions.

The home derives its name from the Greek Athenaeum, an ancient school named after the Goddess Athena (from which the city of Athens, Greece, takes its name), who governed education and the arts.

The present day 1861 Athenaeum Girls' School and the 1861 Ladies' Weekend continue the tradition begun by Reverend Smith in 1852. Here, modern young ladies (fourteen through eighteen) and women over nineteen—wearing authentic Victorian clothing—can attend studies at the Athenaeum in etiquette, penmanship, dance, music, art, and various social graces, while learning such sports as side-saddle horsemanship and archery.

The Girls' School graduation ceremony includes a formal ball at which the young ladies are escorted by members of the Jackson Cadets, a local organization of young men devoted to the study of Civil War era customs and history.

The Athenaeum Rectory is today owned by the Association for the Preservation of Tennessee Antiquities and is operated by the Maury County Chapter of the APTA. The historic house museum is open to the public for touring.

ATKINS, THOMAS M. (CSA): Confederate Lieutenant Colonel Atkins led the Forty-ninth Tennessee Infantry at the Battle of Franklin, where he was wounded in action and captured.

BADGER, EDWARD (CSA): Confederate Lieutenant Colonel Badger led the First and Fourth Florida Infantries at the Battle of Franklin, where he was wounded in action.

BAKER, EDWARD ADAMS (USA): A lieutenant colonel in the Union Army's Sixty-fifth Indiana Infantry, Casement's Brigade, Baker was one of the Yanks who aided the dying Confederate General John Adams after he was pulled from under his fallen horse, Old Charley, on the battlefield at Franklin, November 30, 1864.

Though Baker had engaged in the killing of Confederates at the Battle of Franklin, years after the War, at Webb City, Missouri, he kindly penned a letter to Adam's widow Georgiana McDougall, which was printed in the June 1897 issue of *Confederate Veteran* magazine. In it he describes the final moments of her husband's life:

"General Adams rode up to our works and, cheering his men, made an attempt to leap his horse over them. The horse fell upon the top of the embankment and the general was caught under him, pierced with bullets. As soon as the charge was repulsed, our men sprang over the works and lifted the horse, while others dragged the general from under him. He was perfectly conscious and knew his fate. He asked for water, as all dying men do in battle as the life-blood drips from the body. One of my men gave him a canteen of water, while another brought an armful of cotton from an old gin near by and made him a pillow. The general gallantly thanked them and in answer to our expressions of sorrow at his sad fate, he said, 'It is the fate of a soldier to die for his country,' and expired. Robert Baker, one of my men, took the saddle from the dead horse and threw it in General Casement's ambulance, who expressed it to his home in Ohio"

BALD HILL: During the War for Southern Independence, Bald Hill, the tallest natural elevation in Nashville, Tennessee, was a barren (hence the name) hilltop occupied by the Yankees and used by them for both defensive and observation purposes.

Containing an armed battery and earthworks, the 744 foot prominence was essential in guarding Harding Pike to the south, upon which Confederate General John Bell Hood and the tattered Army of Tennessee were expected to march northward in their effort to re-occupy Nashville two weeks after the tragic Battle of Franklin. Indeed, it was at Bald Hill, on December 15, 1864, that the Union began its attack on the Rebel left wing as it advanced toward Nashville.

With its commanding view in all directions, Bald Hill was put to good purpose by Union General George Henry "Pap" Thomas as an observation post, just as Hood had used Winstead Hill at Franklin. One of the many reasons for the ignoble defeat and rout suffered by Hood and the Confederates at Nashville must be attributed to Bald Hill and its outstanding defensive features, well utilized by the Yanks.

Forty-five years after the War, in 1910, the area was subdivided and sold as residential lots. Sixteen years later, in 1926, 8.33 acres of this land were purchased by the city of Nashville from Bald Hill residents, most significantly from John W. Love, for the construction of a reservoir (the street embracing Bald Hill is today called Love Circle). The 2 million-gallon water tank of the Love Circle Reservoir still sits inside the hill.

Now encompassed by Love Circle Park, the once famed eminence is today barely noticeable and many Nashvillians have never heard of it. This is not surprising as Bald Hill is located in a leafy but densely populated area off of busy West End Avenue near the side streets of Acklen, Orleans Drive, and 32nd Avenue. The hill—recently made even more famous by resident country artist John Rich—is marked by a large and unattractive radio tower that now perches astride it.

BALLENTINE'S MISSISSIPPI CAVALRY (CSA): This Rebel cavalry regiment fought at the Battle of Franklin in Armstrong's Brigade, Jackson's Division, Forrest's Cavalry Corps, C.S. Army of Tennessee.

BATE, WILLIAM BRIMAGE (CSA): Bate was born on October 7, 1826, at Castalian Springs, Tennessee. Like most Southerners, he was very independent minded, in his case dropping out of school to learn the Mississippi River steamboat trade.

When the Mexican-American War began in 1846, he joined the U.S. military, serving in that conflict as a lieutenant. Afterward he became an attorney and a member of the Tennessee legislature. With the start of Lincoln's War in April 1861, he sided with the South and the Constitution, and joined the Confederate army.

Starting out as the colonel of the Second Tennessee Infantry, Bate fought with distinction at the Battles of Shiloh (where he was severely injured), Chickamauga, Resaca, and Atlanta, rising to the rank of major general. He went on to serve with the Confederacy's Army of Tennessee, fighting at the Battles of Spring Hill, Nashville, and Franklin, where he led an infantry division on the far left of the battlefield.

After Lincoln's War Bate once again practiced law in the Nashville area. In 1882 he became a Democratic (the conservatives of the day) governor of Tennessee (serving two terms) and in 1886 a Tennessee state senator (serving four terms). He died on March 9, 1905 in Washington, D.C., and was buried at Mount Olivet Cemetery, Nashville, Tennessee.

BATE'S DIVISION (CSA): This Rebel division, named after Confederate Major General William Brimage Bate, was present at the Battle of Franklin. It was comprised of Tyler's Brigade, Finley's Brigade, and Jackson's Brigade.

BATES, EDWARD (USA): A Yankee captain in Colonel Emerson Opdycke's Brigade, Bates commanded the One hundred twenty-fifth Ohio Regiment at the Battle of Franklin.

BATTLE OF COLUMBIA (November 24-29, 1864): This conflict resulted from a race to see who could get to Nashville first: The Confederates or the Yankees. U.S. General John M. Schofield's plans entailed joining forces at Nashville with his superior General George H. Thomas. Confederate General John Bell Hood's goal was to destroy Schofield's army before it could get anywhere near Nashville.

Traveling north from Pulaski, Tennessee, Schofield arrived in Columbia on

November 24, 1864. Hood's cavalry, under General Nathan Bedford Forrest, arrived from Florence, Alabama, shortly thereafter, resulting in numerous skirmishes over the next two days.

Determined to get to Spring Hill before Hood, Schofield attempted a northward march, but both armies were detained due to inclement weather. The next day, November 29, Yankee troops proceeded toward Spring Hill with the Rebels following closely behind.

BATTLE OF FRANKLIN (November 30, 1864): In the early morning of November 30, 1864, Union Major General John McAllister Schofield marched into Franklin with some 25,000 men, on his way to Yankee-occupied Nashville, where he planned on reinforcing Major General George Henry Thomas' troops. Unfortunately for Schofield, he found that the bridges across the Harpeth River had been washed out, just one of the many tragic elements that would combine to create one of the world's bloodiest and most senseless battles.

Less than a day's march behind Schofield was Confederate General John Bell Hood, among the War's most controversial figures. Hood, with about 18,000 men, fully intended on catching up with Schofield before he reached Nashville. Luck was on Hood's side, for the moment. Schofield was forced to spend the day in Franklin while his troops hurriedly repaired the bridges over the Harpeth.

Utilizing ditches, breastworks, and fortifications, and even a fort (Granger), from earlier skirmishes around Franklin (1862-1863), the Yanks fortified the old works and entrenched themselves in a wide arc around the southern edge of the town, enclosing their ranks and the center of the city. Their preparation was somewhat haphazard, as it was firmly believed that they would be clear of Franklin and well on their way to Nashville before Hood and his Rebels troops arrived.

Even if Hood did catch up with them, the Yanks were not worried, for behind them spread the great Plain of Franklin, a wide-open, fairly level field several miles square. No one, they thought, not even the aggressive Hood, would be foolish enough to attack across a flat open plain. Indeed, so relaxed were the Union soldiers that as they sun passed across the sky that calm autumn day, they napped, played cards, ate lunch, and read books to each other in their trenches, never once suspecting the horrors to come.

Unlike the relaxed atmosphere that pervaded the Union side that day, Hood was highly agitated. For one thing, at Spring Hill the night before, Schofield and his 25,000-man force had managed to sneak past Hood's encampment as the Confederate army slept only yards away. Though Hood was ultimately responsible, the next morning during an officer's breakfast at Rippavilla Plantation, the infuriated and humiliated one-legged general had given his subordinates a severe dressing down. Between the yelling and cursing, a furious General Nathan Bedford Forrest stormed out, fed up with Hood's tendency to blame subordinates for his own failures.

Thinking his men were weak and may have been purposefully trying to avoid combat, the Spring Hill debacle led Hood to question the fortitude of his troops. This was compounded, in turn, by an additional problem.

By the end of 1864, a new "modern" trend in fighting had developed: military tacticians had discovered that shooting from inside trenches, called breastworks (as they were chest high when standing), could help save lives and win battles. Gone now were the days of the full frontal assault used by peoples like the ancient Celts and Romans, and even by Americans and Britons in the Revolutionary War eighty-nine years earlier.

The Union armies had by this time adopted the use of breastworks, and so, in fact, had nearly all of the other Confederate commanders. But Hood, an old-fashioned "man's man" who clung to the past, had used the full frontal assault technique to great advantage earlier in the War, and saw no reason to abandon it now. Besides, Hood reasoned, this new-fangled idea of hiding inside trenches was unmanly and the use of it contemptible. Only a coward would hide in a hole in the ground. "Real men" fight out in the open and march in formation straight at the enemy, with heads held high.

Hood's troops, of course, enthusiastically favored

the idea of breastworks and pressured their individual commanders to allow their use. All the officers agreed, except one: Hood.

On the afternoon of November 30, Hood stood at the top of Winstead Hill on Columbia Pike just south of downtown Franklin, and surveyed the wide Plain of Franklin through his field glasses. The sight of 25,000 well-entrenched blue-coated infantryman, cavalryman, and heavy artillery lined up around Franklin in a large horseshoe shape had no affect on the war-hardened Confederate general. "We will make the fight!" he barked to his stunned and angry officers.

At this, famed Irish General Patrick Cleburne, turned to one of his fellow officers and pronounced: "Well Govan, if we are to die, let us die like men!" If only the astute Irishman could have known how prophetic his words would turn out to be.

As a lonely Hood stood gazing out from Winstead Hill, he found himself facing more than just an enemy in blue coats. His own inner demons taunted him with memories of both past glories and past failures. His mind now seethed with a multitude of reasons, some bordering on psychotic, for launching his preposterous full frontal attack against a larger, more heavily fortified army:

1) Hood needed to prove to his men, his officers, his friend Jefferson Davis, his fiancee Sarah "Sally" "Buck" Preston, and to the South itself, that he was worthy of the title Major General, and that his earlier failures on the field (particularly at the Battle of Atlanta) were nothing more than minor aberrations. His past sins would all be forgiven and posterity would record him as a national hero—if only he could now win Franklin.

2) He needed to fulfill his long-held dreams of glory, in which he would seize Nashville (where he would restock his army using captured Union supplies), ford the Cumberland River and invade Kentucky, cross the Ohio River to capture Cincinnati, and then move east through the Cumberland Mountains into Virginia where he would attack and conquer Grant.

3) Hood wanted to prove once and for all that his men were

courageousness, and he would do it even if he had to force them to march into battle across the two mile Plain of Franklin. Naturally Hood got little or no support for this madness. Indeed, the more resistance he got to the idea the more determined he became to see it through.

4) He was also angry at his subordinate officers for the debacle at Spring Hill, especially Cleburne, who he thought had fought poorly there, and who had had the temerity to tell Hood that a full frontal attack at Franklin was madness. (According to one school of thought, in retaliation, Hood would treacherously order Cleburne and his cavalry into the most potentially dangerous area of the Franklin battlefield—with grave results.)

5) Schofield, the Yankee commander across the field, was Hood's former West Point roommate and they knew each other well, but no doubt shared little mutual admiration. They had graduated on the same day together in 1853, one with honor, one with dishonor. Out of a class of fifty students, Schofield had graduated fourth and was considered a military scholar. Hood graduated forty-fourth in his class with dishonors and with over 100 demerits for bad behavior, and was considered a "West Point failure." That morning it is quite probable that Hood was thinking: "Schofield may have beaten me at school, but I'm going to beat him on the battlefield—where it really counts!"

6) Physical pain was Hood's relentless companion. He had lost his right leg at Chickamauga and the use of his left arm at Gettysburg, wounds that caused him unending distress and misery. So serious were his injuries that he had to be lifted into his saddle and strapped in. At Spring Hill the day before, Hood had fallen from his horse, creating even more debilitating anguish. It has been said that to relieve the constant pain, he was accustomed to drinking alcohol or taking laudanum, a derivative of opium and a common Victorian pain killer. While there is no proof for these charges, Hood would not be the first person to use drugs to nullify pain, and since he had ready access to both liquor and laudanum, the possibility that Hood's judgement was clouded

by artificial means on November 30, must at least be considered.

7) Many inside and outside the military regarded Hood as a simpleton, lacking native intelligence and common sense. While this is a wholly subjective and no doubt biased charge, some of Hood's actions do seem to corroborate it.

In the end, while the exact motivations for Hood's decisions at Franklin are forever lost to history, he made them nonetheless. Sadly for the Southern people, they completely altered the outcome of Lincoln's War in favor of the North.

That morning, sensing disaster ahead, Hood's soldiers dubbed the spacious empty field that lay between themselves and the enemy the "valley of death." His officers, angry, baffled, and dismayed, called the looming battle a "suicide mission."

So sure were most of Hood's men that they would not live through the conflict that they dressed in their finest apparel, in order to insure that they would be prepared for burial. They also asked their army chaplains to keep their jewelry, letters, watches, and other valuables, with orders to send them home if they did not survive.

Hood's officers rode back and forth from the field to Winstead and Breezy Hills where Hood was stationed, with proposals for various alternative tactics. Forrest's couriers had returned, for example, with intelligence suggesting that a flanking attack to the east would win the day. Cleburne proposed that the infantrymen advance into battle in life-saving columns rather than in death-dealing rows (the latter being Hood's idea). Others literally begged Hood to reconsider the entire battle, hoping to stave off the certain death and destruction of the Army of Tennessee. But stubborn Hood would not listen.

At about 4:00 PM that afternoon he gave the order to "charge," and 18,000 Confederate Rebels moved slowly in long straight lines across the Plain of Franklin to meet their fate at the hands of the entrenched Union troops. To the sound of thousands of tramping feet, Rebel war whoops could be heard while the Confederate brass and drum bands played *Bonnie Blue Flag* and *Dixie*. Bayonets, swords, and knives glistened threateningly in the setting sun, as coveys of quail burst from out of the tall bluegrass just ahead of the advancing army.

Meanwhile, the Yankee troops were gazing lazily down upon the flat fields from behind their trenches in stunned amazement. Were the Rebels really going to attack or were they just practicing military maneuvers? At that point it was unclear. Union soldiers later recorded in their journals and diaries that the advance of the Confederate Army of Tennessee across the Franklin Plain that day was the most magnificent sight they had ever seen.

By the time they realized that the Rebs were attacking, not marching, it was almost too late. Against the enemy's "galling fire," thousands of sprinting, screaming Confederates swarmed across the field and up and over the Union breastworks, shooting and stabbing as they went. Hundreds of Yanks died in the initial wave of attack, as the Rebels penetrated their lines at various points. But these victories were small and, as it would turn out, temporary.

In all, the Rebs carried out between thirteen and eighteen full frontal attacks on the enemy, each one resulting in more losses. Their hearts were indeed courageous that day, but they were no match for either the sharp Osage-orange abatis that lay like barbed-wire in front of the Yankee entrenchments, or the rapidly firing repeating rifles of the Union soldiers. Thousands of Confederate men were mowed down like wooden ducks in a shooting gallery by enfilade fire as it strafed sideways across the field from Fort Granger, situated to the northeast, and from a Yankee battery of artillery on the east side of the Harpeth.

By around 9:00 PM that evening, most of the fighting had subsided, with sporadic skirmishes continuing on into the darkness of the early morning hours. One of the Civil War's few nighttime battles was over.

At 11:00 PM, under cover of darkness, Schofield's army began slipping across the now repaired bridges toward Nashville. As the massive military force ponderously squeezed single-file over the Harpeth River, Hood had one last chance to exterminate the enemy. Unfortunately, the one-legged general was miles away to the south, at Winstead Hill, still quite unaware of his own losses, let alone of the escaping Yankee forces. Schofield was in Nashville within hours. Another great missed opportunity.

The next morning, December 1, the sun rose on a grim spectacle of incomprehensible proportions. Hood rode out on to the field and, eyewitnesses report, "wept like a baby" at the sight before him. The Franklin Plain was two to three bodies deep as far as the eye could see. Trenches and breastworks were filled up to seven bodies deep. Everywhere corpses posed in hideous stances, some burned beyond recognition, some headless, some cut in half by cannon balls.

Witnesses saw row after row of dead Rebels, lying in perfect formation, as if, one said, someone had come in the night and neatly and gently laid one next to the other. Severed human arms, legs, hands, feet, and heads lay scattered in all directions amid the shredded bodies of dead and wounded horses. It sleeted that cool morning, and red blood-filled water poured off the battlefield.

The citizens of Franklin were horrified, and mournful wails and weeping could be heard as sisters, mothers, and wives searched desperately among the carnage for their loved ones. Forty-four field hospitals, forty-one Confederate, three Union, had been quickly set up throughout the town. Designated by red flags hung outside, between those being operated on and those recovering, the wounded soon filled up every available space.

Most of the Confederate dead were buried where they lay, in shallow two-foot graves, each one with a simple wooden marker (these were used for firewood by local black families the following winter).

Despite the bloodbath, Hood declared Franklin a victory, since the Union troops had hurriedly vacated the town early in the morning in order to reach Nashville before the Confederates. (Later, when Hood learned of his ghastly casualty rate, he reluctantly listed Franklin in his report as what it actually was: a decimating loss for the South.)

The tragedy of the Battle of Franklin is epitomized in the figure of a young Confederate captain named Tod Carter. He had been shot down the night before only yards from his front door on Columbia Pike, fighting for his town's emancipation from

Lincoln's despotic enslavement of the South. That morning Tod's grieving family had been led to his near-lifeless body among the dead. He was carried him back to his childhood home where he died shortly thereafter.

Worse was to come. To Hood's horror reports came in that five of his generals had been killed: Patrick R. Cleburne, Otho F. Strahl, John Adams, Hiram B. Granbury, and States Rights Gist. (A sixth general, John C. Carter, would die from his wounds a few days later, on December 10.) In addition, fifty-four lower ranked regimental commanders were missing, or had been captured, wounded, or killed.

In all, while the Yankees had suffered only 2,325 casualties (among them, only 189 dead) on November 30, 1864, Hood had suffered some 7,000 casualties: 1,750 dead, 4,500 wounded, and 702 captured, nearly one third of those who had marched against the Union that day.

While other battles would claim far more lives, few if any lost as many men in such a short time as the Battle of Franklin—also known as the "Pickett's Charge of the West" due to its appalling bloodiness.

Gettysburg, for example, a battle that took place over a period of three days (July 1-3, 1863), has long been considered the War's bloodiest conflict in terms of numbers killed. The most accurate estimates today, however, put the actual total of Confederate dead at Gettysburg at between 2,600 and 4,500 over the three-day period. Taking the mean average of these two numbers, we come up with a figure of 3,550. At once the difference between the death count at Franklin and the one at Gettysburg is striking.

Approximately 1,750 Confederates died at Franklin in five hours: around 350 men per hour, or about six men per minute. Some 3,550 Confederates died at Gettysburg in 72 hours: around 49 men per hour, or less than one man per minute. This means that if the Confederates at Gettysburg had died at the same rate as those at Franklin, 25,200 Confederates would have died at Gettysburg. Actually, however, less than 4,000 perished.

In terms of sheer numbers alone then, Franklin must lay claim to being the War's bloodiest battle, as more died in a shorter period of time than in any other conflict.

The true tragedy of the Battle of Franklin, however, entails more than just the mathematics of death. This was a conflict that was wholly unnecessary—for several reasons.

By the end of 1864, Lincoln's War was, for all intents and purposes, already over. Every major Confederate capitol had long since been captured (Nashville, for instance, had been occupied by the Yankees since February 1862, and was still occupied during the Battle of Franklin).

In addition, thanks to U.S. war criminals like Abraham Lincoln, Ulysses S. Grant, William T. Sherman, and Philip Sheridan, the infrastructure of the South lay in ruins. Railroads, communications, bridges, and roads had been incapacitated. Entire cities, like Richmond, Virginia, had been reduced to smoking rubble. Livestock, granaries, and root cellars had been plundered, after which Southern factories, sea ports, garrisons, churches, stores, shops, farms, plantations, mansions, estates, and houses, had been put to the torch by merciless Yankee troops. Without communications and production capabilities, the South had little hope of regaining strength and outlasting the Union.

Lastly, by November 1864, Confederate soldiers themselves had long since run out of clothing, food, weapons, and ammunition. A majority of Rebels by this time were barefoot and thousands more were wearing the blue uniforms of their enemy to the North, desperately stolen from the corpses of Union soldiers. General Robert E. Lee himself noted sadly that one of the main reasons he surrendered at Appomattox was because he could no longer bear to see the suffering of his starving, freezing, shoeless men.

Throughout the Rebel army desertion was now at an all-time high, while morale was at an all-time low, for the Battle of Franklin had literally destroyed any chance the Confederacy might have had to free itself from Yankee imperialism.

No army can operate without its command structure, and most of this had been destroyed at Franklin. Here, the Army of Tennessee, the last great hope of the South in the Western Theater, perished as an obstinate Hood marched his men across an open field to certain death. Hood's own officers later ruefully noted that "on November 30, 1864, Hood slaughtered his own army and killed the Confederacy—all in a single blow."

So utterly terrible, so culturally and economically catastrophic was the Battle of Franklin, that unlike other conflicts, in later years surviving veterans found it nearly impossible to return to the scene. When they did, even the most war-toughened officers could not hold back the tears. Colonel Virgil S. Murphy perfectly conveyed the sentiments of most when he wrote that the Franklin battlefield is "an unholy ground that exemplified man's inhumanity to man."

For the most part, Franklin's "unholy ground"—bounded on the north by the Carter House, to the south by Winstead and Breezy Hills, to the west by Carters Creek Pike, and to the east by the Harpeth River—has been today covered by parking lots, strip malls, fast food restaurants, and subdivisions, though a nationwide effort has begun to preserve a small green space on the outer fringes of the original battlefield that has been miraculously left undeveloped—though only because it was being used as a gold course.

The most sacred area—where the heaviest fighting and killing took place—has long been buried under great swaths of asphalt, roadways, store fronts, and track housing, leading the Civil War Preservation Trust to rank the area one of the top ten most endangered battlefields in America.

The town's seeming disregard for its own historic past is not as insensitive as it first seems. The stinging pain of that bright November day nearly a century and a half ago, when the Northern invaders snuffed out the lives of the town's flower of youth, still haunts Franklin, resurrecting memories of a dreadful moment in time, one that many, even today, would rather forget.

But forget we must not, for there are many invaluable lessons to be learned from this conflict, lessons about life and death, love and hatred, tolerance and prejudice, pride and humility, economics and culture, politics and religion. To forget the Battle of Franklin is to ignore the dark side of human nature, that place in each one of us where, uncontrolled, lust for power and money can run amuck, overriding common sense, established law, and universal spiritual precepts.

In the end the Battle of Franklin must be counted as one of the great tragedies of American if not world history. For not only were thousands of lives wasted, and not only was the Southern Cause lost, but we engaged in a conflict that should have never been fought, in a larger war that should have never been waged.

BATTLE OF NASHVILLE (December 15-16, 1864): The Battle of Nashville took place just two weeks after the Battle of Franklin, November 30, where, tragically and unnecessarily, the Confederate Army of Tennessee had been considerably weakened by poor planning on the part of its leader, General John Bell Hood.

Now at Nashville, Hood was pitted against U.S. General George Henry Thomas and elements of the U.S. Army of the Cumberland and the U.S. Army of the Ohio. Though Hood reached Nashville by December 2, defensive preparations and inclement weather delayed combat for two weeks.

In the predawn light of December 15, the Yanks attacked the Confederate right and about noon they hit the Confederate left. The Rebels being greatly outnumbered, both Union assaults were successful.

On the morning of December 16, Thomas' men charged the Confederate strongholds once again, this time with even more confidence and firepower. Hood had placed his troops on top of several hills around Nashville, a strategy that would prove fatal. These were easily overrun, sending Hood's men fleeing southward through a single opening in the Federal line.

The route led Hood and the battered remains of the Army of Tennessee back through Brentwood, Franklin (where the Battle of Franklin III took place on December 17), Spring Hill, and Columbia. The Yanks chased the bedraggled Rebels for ten days, only giving up the pursuit after Hood crossed the Tennessee River near Florence, Alabama, on Christmas Day. The pathway of this route is today indicated by historical markers captioned "Hood's Retreat."

January 13, at Tupelo, Mississippi, Hood asked to be

relieved from his command. The Army of Tennessee was then turned over to Confederate General Richard Taylor—the son of U.S. President Zachary Taylor and the brother of Sarah Knox Taylor (the first wife of President Jefferson Davis).

Confederate strength in the Western Theater was now almost nonexistent. Lincoln's War itself would be over in three months.

BATTLE OF SPRING HILL (November 29, 1864): On November 29, 1864, shortly after the Confederate victory at the Battle of Columbia, Tennessee (November 24-29), C.S. General John Bell Hood and U.S. General John M. Schofield, clashed once again, this time at Spring Hill, Tennessee.

The day before, as both sides marched north toward Spring Hill, Confederate General Nathan Bedford Forrest and his cavalry engaged Union General James H. Wilson's cavalry, though without any real progress.

The next day, November 29, Hood and his men crossed the Duck River and moved on into Spring Hill, where his troops were repulsed during an assault near the town's crossroads.

That night Schofield and his army snuck quietly past the sleeping Rebels and into Franklin on their way to Nashville. The next morning, November 30, when Hood discovered the error, he became furious, dressing down his officers during breakfast at Rippavilla Plantation. The precise reason for the fiasco, and the identity of those directly responsible, have never been definitively determined. Hood blamed it on his subordinates; Hood's subordinates blamed it on him.

This embarrassing event has understandably gone down in the history books as the "Spring Hill Debacle." Rebel General Benjamin Franklin Cheatham complained that they had "lost a brilliant opportunity to deal the enemy a crushing blow." Of the affair Hood himself said: "The best move in my career as a soldier, I was thus destined to behold come to naught."

And indeed, what a grand "missed opportunity" it was. For this turned out to be Hood's one and only chance to smash Schofield's forces before they reached Nashville.

Instead, the Union troops were already in Franklin by the time Hood woke up in Spring

Hill on November 30. Trapped in Franklin due to washed out bridges, Schofield had no choice but to stand and fight Hood and the Army of Tennessee when they arrived on the outskirts of town that afternoon. The result was a disaster far worse than Spring Hill: the Battle of Franklin.

BEATTY, SAMUEL (USA): The son of John Beatty and Christina Powell, Beatty was born December 16, 1820, at Mifflin, Pennsylvania. Later he moved to Ohio.

With the onset of Lincoln's War he sided with the North and against the Constitution. Joining the U.S. army, he served as a colonel with the Nineteenth Ohio Infantry.

In late 1862 he was promoted to brigadier general and given command of his own unit: the Third Brigade, Wood's Third Division, Fourth U.S. Army Corps, which he led at the Battle of Franklin (some sources say he was ill during the conflict, and that his brigade was led by Colonel Frederick Knefler). Over a year earlier, in 1863, he married Susan Van Lear Graham.

After the War Beatty returned to Ohio to farm, where he died May 26, 1885. He was buried in Massillon City Cemetery, Massillon, Stark County, Ohio.

BEATTY'S THIRD BRIGADE (USA): This Yankee infantry brigade fought at the Battle of Franklin in Wood's Third Division, Fourth U.S. Army Corps, probably under the command of Union Colonel Frederick Knefler.

Named after U.S. Brigadier General Samuel Beatty, it was comprised of the Seventy-ninth Indiana, Eighty-sixth Indiana, Thirteenth Ohio, and Nineteenth Ohio.

BEAUREGARD, PIERRE GUSTAVE TOUTANT (CSA): A West Point graduate (class of 1838) and a Mexican-American War veteran, Beauregard was born on May 28, 1818, in Saint Bernard Parish, Louisiana.

In 1841 Beauregard married Marie Laure Villeré and the couple bore three children: René, Henri, and Laure. Several years after Marie's premature death he married Caroline Deslonde, the sister-in-law of John Slidell, who was to become an important Confederate ambassador. Caroline, however, died within a few years of their marriage.

In April 1861, with the start of the "Civil War," Beauregard oversaw the bombing of Fort Sumter at Charleston, South Carolina, where U.S. President Abraham Lincoln craftily tricked the Confederacy into firing the first shot.

Beauregard went on to fight at such engagements as Shiloh, First Manassas, and Corinth. After his superior General Albert Sidney Johnston was killed (on April 6, 1862), Beauregard was put in command of the C.S. Army of Tennessee.

By July 17, 1864, Beauregard had fallen out of favor with Confederate President Jefferson Davis, after which Davis turned over Beauregard's command to one of his personal favorites, General John Bell Hood. This would prove to be one of the Rebel chief executive's worst decisions.

Although Davis had appointed Beauregard to be Hood's superior in the Fall of 1864, the Creole was not responsible for Hood's calamitous Tennessee campaign, for just prior to this operation Hood himself seemed confused as to his future plans, and had in fact presented Davis and Beauregard with two very different strategies. Basically operating on his own from this point on, and without any oversight to rein him in, Hood went on to wreck the Army of Tennessee (at Franklin and Nashville) before the end of the year. All that was left was for Beauregard to pick up the pieces.

On January 14, 1865, Beauregard, the designer of the Confederacy's beautiful and greatly misunderstood Battle Flag, traveled to Tupelo, Mississippi, to inspect what remained of Hood's men. What he found were about 15,000 mostly bedraggled freezing soldiers, less than half of which were still capable of proper military service. As Hood had already asked to be relieved of his command, Beauregard promptly turned over the army to Confederate General Richard Taylor.

After the War Beauregard fought valiantly against the North's cruel and illegal Reconstruction polices. In his later years the conservative Southerner and well educated civil engineer became involved with several railroads, wrote a number of books, and, like most other white Southerners, promoted black civil rights.

The two-time widower—after whom a Louisiana Parish has been named—passed away on February 20, 1893, at New Orleans, and was buried in the city's famous Metairie Cemetery.

BECKHAM, ROBERT FRANKLIN (CSA): Beckham was born May 6, 1837, in Culpeper County, Virginia. He graduated from West Point in 1859, sixth in his class, and served with the U.S. Topographical Engineers.

With the outbreak of Lincoln's War Beckham sided with the South and the Constitution, serving as a lieutenant of artillery in the Confederate army. As a major he led the Stuart Horse Artillery in General Robert E. Lee's Army of Northern Virginia.

In February 1864 he was promoted to colonel and put in command of Lieutenant General Stephen Dill Lee's Corps Artillery under General John Bell Hood, C.S. Army of Tennessee.

On November 29, 1864, on his way to the Battle of Franklin, Beckham was wounded during a skirmish near Columbia, Tennessee. His command as head of Lee's Artillery Corps was taken over by Confederate Major John W. Johnston, who led the unit at Franklin on November 30.

Beckham died from his wounds December 5, 1864, near Ashwood, Tennessee, and was buried in the town's Saint John's Episcopal Church Cemetery.

BEECHLAWN: Built in the early 1850s, during Lincoln's War Beechlawn was the residence of the Warfield family.

Located just south of the city of Columbia, Tennessee, the Greek Revival home served as Confederate General John Bell Hood's headquarters on the night of November 27, 1864, three days before the Battle of Franklin. Here Hood held an officer's meeting and planned out a number of his doomed tactics.

The grand home, named for the beech grove that surrounds it, has been put on the roster of National Register of Historic Places. It is today privately owned.

BELL, TYREE HARRIS (CSA): Though Bell was born September 5, 1815, at Covington, Kentucky, he grew up in Gallatin, Tennessee. With the onset of Lincoln's War, he sided with the South and the Constitution.

After joining the Confederate army he fought bravely at such battles as Belmont, Shiloh, Brice's Cross Roads, and Harrisburg.

In January 1864 Bell was given command of a brigade by Confederate General Nathan Bedford Forrest, which he held until the close of the War. Bell's Brigade went on to achieve everlasting fame at the Battles of Spring Hill and Franklin, while Bell himself was repeatedly praised by Forrest in his official reports for his "conduct" and "gallantry."

After the War Brigadier General Bell moved to Fresno County, California, where he became a farmer and political activist. On September 1, 1902, during a trip to New Orleans, Louisiana, Bell passed away. His body was taken back to the Fresno area, where he was buried at Bethel Cemetery, just outside the town of Sanger, California.

BELL'S BRIGADE (CSA): This Rebel cavalry brigade fought at the Battle of Franklin in Buford's Division, Forrest's Cavalry Corps, C.S. Army of Tennessee.

Named after its commander Confederate Colonel Tyree Harris Bell, it was comprised of the Second Tennessee Cavalry, Nineteenth Tennessee Cavalry, Twentieth Tennessee Cavalry, Twenty-first Tennessee Cavalry, and Nixon's Tennessee Cavalry.

BELLE MEADE PLANTATION: The "Queen of Tennessee Plantations," as Belle Meade was once known, was begun in the 1820s by John Harding of Virginia, and completed in 1853 by his son General William Giles Harding. The once 5,400 acre estate was famous for its racetrack, thoroughbred horse nursery, and horse breeding program, which produced a number of celebrated racers, including "Iroquois," the first American-bred horse to win the English Derby.

Belle Meade, French for "beautiful meadow," played an important role in Lincoln's War, serving as a Confederate headquarters for one of General Nathan Bedford Forrest's men, General James R. Chalmers, shortly after the Battle of Franklin.

General William Giles Harding was married to Elizabeth Irwin McGavock, the daughter of Randal McGavock, eleventh mayor of Nashville and the founder of Carnton Plantation in Franklin, Tennessee. Local tradition states that on January 2, 1840, Elizabeth and William married in the guest parlor at Carnton. This marriage effectually made the two estates "sister plantations," a title they both retain to this day.

After the War General Harding turned Belle Meade over to his son-in-law William Hicks "Red" Jackson, who commanded a Rebel division under General Forrest at the Battle of Franklin. Jackson further commercialized the plantation by putting in a 600 acre deer park and offering the sale of breeding ponies, Cashmere goats, Cotswold sheep, and Alderney cattle. By the early 1900s Belle Meade had become the oldest and biggest thoroughbred farm in the United States.

In 1953 the plantation was purchased by the state of Tennessee. Restored to its former glory, today Belle Meade is a thriving historical site and one of Nashville's top tourist attractions.

BELMONT MANSION: One of Nashville's most beautiful antebellum homes, and the second largest one still in existence in the U.S., Belmont Mansion is an Italianate villa that was built in 1850.

Its most famous occupant was the renowned Victorian, Adelicia Acklen. One of America's wealthiest women, with land holdings in Tennessee, Texas and Louisiana, she was the daughter of Reverend Oliver Bliss Hayes and Sarah Clements Hightower. Adelicia survived Lincoln's War, was married three times, and bore ten children.

Belmont Mansion, originally known as Bellemonte (Italian for "Beautiful mountain"), began as a 180 acre estate that included a bowling alley, an art gallery, a zoo, a deer park, a bear house, statuary, numerous gazebos, and stunning formal gardens. The interior is one of the most magnificent known, and includes both the celebrated Grand Staircase and the Grand Salon, the latter which includes Greek columns, fine art, and Victorian chandeliers.

During Lincoln's War the home was spared the wrath of the Yankee invaders, but only because, during the Battle of Nashville, its 105 foot brick water tower was needed for a Federal lookout post and because the mansion was required for the headquarters of Union General T.

J. Wood.

Adelicia died in 1887 and was buried at the Acklen Family Mausoleum at Mount Olivet Cemetery in Nashville. Her brother, Oliver Bliss Hayes, II, married Emily McGavock, the daughter of Lysander McGavock (founder of Midway Plantation in Brentwood, Tennessee) and Elizabeth Crockett (the third cousin of famed American frontiersman, Davy Crockett). Oliver and Emily built and lived in lovely Boxwood Hall in Brentwood.

After Adelicia's death, Belmont Mansion was turned into the Belmont Junior College for Girls, which became the coed school today known as Belmont University. Preserved as a National Historic Place in 1971, it is now open to the public.

BIDDLE, JAMES (USA): Biddle was a Yankee colonel who led the Second Brigade, Johnson's Sixth Division, Wilson's Cavalry Corps, at the Battle of Franklin.

BIDDLE'S SECOND BRIGADE (USA): This Yankee brigade fought at the Battle of Franklin in Johnson's Sixth Division, Wilson's Cavalry Corps.

Named after U.S. Colonel James Biddle, it was comprised of the Fourteenth Illinois Cavalry, Sixth Indiana Cavalry, Eighth Michigan Cavalry, and Third Tennessee Volunteer Infantry.

BIFFLE, JACOB BARNETT (CSA): Biffle, the son of War of 1812 veteran John Barnett Biffle and Mary M. Chambers, was born in May 31, 1830, near Ashland, Tennessee. The German-American went on to fight in the Mexican-American War.

With the outbreak of Lincoln's War, Biffle sided with the South and the Constitution. After joining the Confederate army, he helped form the Second Tennessee Cavalry Battalion, and as a lieutenant general went on to lead the Ninth (officially known as the Nineteenth) Tennessee Cavalry Regiment.

For his nontraditional approach to warfare (which greatly benefitted the Confederacy), Biffle was viciously labeled a "guerilla" by his Yankee enemies. He fought at such battles as Thompson's Station, Brentwood, and Chickamauga.

At the Battle of Franklin he commanded Biffle's Brigade,

with leadership qualities that some have compared to those of his equally unorthodox superior, Confederate General Nathan Bedford Forrest. Biffle's command served at Franklin in Chalmers' Division under Brigadier General James Ronald Chalmers.

After the War, "Jake," as he was known, moved his wife Sarah Ann Lusk (with whom he had nine children) and his family to the Confederate friendly town of Myra, Texas, where he became a cattle rancher. One day, on December 15, 1876, while working a cattle drive, he got into an argument with his cook, Scott Waters, who shot the former Confederate officer in the side.

Biffle's wound proved fatal. He passed away several weeks later on January 5, 1877, and was buried in Myra's Reed Cemetery.

BIFFLE'S BRIGADE (CSA): This Rebel cavalry brigade fought at the Battle of Franklin in Chalmers' Division, Forrest's Cavalry Corps, C.S. Army of Tennessee.

Named after its commander Confederate Brigadier General Jacob Barnett Biffle, it was comprised solely of the Tenth Tennessee Cavalry (some sources say the Ninth Tennessee Cavalry).

BISHOP, WILLIAM H. (CSA): Confederate Colonel Bishop led the Seventh Mississippi Infantry at the Battle of Franklin, where he was killed in action.

BLACK CONFEDERATES: To the unenlightened the term "black Confederate" appears to be an oxymoron. However, it is a historical fact that the vast majority of Southern blacks, at least 95 percent, sided with the Confederacy during the War for Southern Independence.

Though this truth has long been vigorously suppressed by the liberal controlled media and educational system, it is vitally important that we acknowledge the black Confederate. For not only should he be recognized for his valor and patriotism in fighting for the South and the Constitution, but without an understanding of the enormous role blacks played in aiding the Confederacy, a full understanding of the "Civil War" itself is impossible. In particular, the history of the black Confederate illuminates the issues that led to the Battle of Franklin.

Since the Confederate Congress (unwisely) did not *officially* accept blacks into its army until the War was almost over, there are no accurate records of how many African-Americans actually joined the Confederacy. The most conservative estimates put the number of Confederate blacks at about 65,000.

However, careful modern research has shown this estimate to be woefully under counted, with the true figure being somewhere between 300,000 and 1 million. This is based on the military definition of a "private soldier" as determined by German-American Union General August Valentine Kautz, in 1864:

"In the fullest sense, any man in the military service who receives pay, whether sworn in or not, is a soldier, because he is subject to military law. Under this general head, laborers, teamsters, sutlers, chaplains, etc., are soldiers."

Using Kautz's definition, it is clear to all modern objective observers that when all of the surviving records are tabulated, at least 1 million black soldiers served with the Confederacy in one capacity or another.

This number being established, the question now is why would African-Americans fight for the South, the region that allegedly invented and supported black slavery?

To begin with, it is important to understand that American slavery was not a "Southern institution," it was a Northern one: both the American slave trade (buying and selling slaves) and American slavery (owning slaves) got their start in the Yankee state of Massachusetts: the former institution in the year 1638, the latter institution in the year 1641.

Throughout the 17th and 18th Centuries, Northern ships, owned by Northern businessmen, funded by Northern money, and commanded by Northern sea captains, sailed to Africa to trade commodities for slaves—nearly all who had already been enslaved by their own native chieftains under the ancient, harsh, and pitiless indigenous African slavery system.

Boston, Providence, Philadelphia, Baltimore, and even our nation's capital city Washington, D.C., all evolved into thriving slave ports. The greatest of them all was New York City, which became not only the nation's largest slaving port, but the very heart of America's slave industry. This is, after all, the main reason New York City is today both the USA's largest metropolis and its financial capital.

In contrast, the South never traded in slaves or owned a slave ship. Every single enslaved African brought into this country was brought here under the U.S. flag, which flew atop the masts of Northern vessels. To reemphasize: no African was ever forced to come to America aboard a Southern ship, and the Confederate flag never waved from the mast of any slaver's ship.

How and why then did slavery emerge in the South?

The North's short cold summers and its rocky sandy soil proved to be incompatible with large scale farming. This, along with rampant Northern white racism, eventually made slavery unprofitable in the Northern states. And so it was pushed southward where the summers were longer, the soil was more fertile, and the whites more tolerant.

It was this very tolerance that made life far more enjoyable for Southern slaves than for Northern ones. And it was this acceptance of other races that led to the development of close bonds between Southern whites and blacks, both enslaved and free.

When Lincoln's War came, warm relationships between black slaves and their employees ("owners") took precedence over political and social issues, such as emancipation. For, after all, the American abolition movement had begun in the South (not in the North), with white Southerners—like Thomas Jefferson, George Washington, St. George Tucker, Fernando Fairfax, and George Mason—pushing for the destruction of slavery even before the formation of the United States in 1776.

Thus by the time the U.S. President Abraham Lincoln launched his illegal invasion of the South in 1861, Southern slaves were well aware that the institution was doomed, and that whether the South won or not, they would soon be freed. There was no need then, for them to leave their beloved Southern homes and flee North. In fact, there were numerous reasons for them not to.

One of these was Lincoln himself, who never hesitated to make his views on American blacks public throughout his political career: either corral all African-Americans into their own all-black state, or better yet, deport all of them to foreign countries, the racist leader repeated endlessly before and during his presidency.

On July 17, 1858, for example, in a public address at Springfield, Illinois, white separatist Lincoln told his audience:

"What I would most desire would be the separation of the white and black races."

On August 21, 1858, in a speech at Ottawa, Illinois, when asked what his future plans were for black slaves, Lincoln declared:

"My first impulse would be to free all the slaves, and send them to Liberia [Africa]—to their own native land."

Lincoln's enthusiasm for deporting all American blacks, then known as "colonization," continued not only throughout his presidency, but right up until the end of his life: a few days before his assassination, he called Union General Benjamin F. Butler to the White House to discuss his latest ideas on black deportation.

Authentic students of American history will be familiar with President Lincoln's Preliminary Emancipation Proclamation (issued September 22, 1862), as well as his District of Columbia Emancipation Act (issued April 16, 1862), both which contained a number of his shockingly bigoted, wholly anti-black, pro-colonization ideas.

In light of such overt Yankee racism, promoted by none less than the veritable leader of the United States itself, what incentive did Southern blacks, freed or enslaved, have for abandoning the racially tolerant South for the racially prejudiced North?

Added to this was another powerful incentive for Victorian blacks to defend Dixie: by the time the War opened in 1861, ten generations of blacks had been born and raised in America (the first African servants had been brought to America by the Dutch in 1619), and their population in the South had risen to 4 million (3.5 million slaves, 500,000 freemen). Ten generations were far longer than many white families had been in America at the time.

In short, the South was the only home that Southern blacks had ever known. It was their land, land they had worked for centuries and had cultivated with their very own blood, sweat, and tears. Their parents, grandparents, and great-grandparents were buried on Southern soil, and they too wanted to be buried there.

Not only was the South their homeland, in many ways it was their very identity as well. Indeed, by 1861 Southern blacks no longer considered themselves "Africans." They were now Americans.

Let us remember that, despite the preachings of pro-North writers and historians, the South *did not* go to War over slavery, a fact that President Jefferson Davis and thousands of other Southerners repeatedly emphasized. The Southern Cause, as it was called, was concerned with states rights, self-government, self-determination, and the preservation of the original Constitution of the Founding Fathers.

Above all, the South fought because it had no choice. Though it had originally sought a peaceful separation from the U.S., after the opening Battle of Fort Sumter the South had to defend itself against a foreign invader; namely, the North's despotic "King Abraham" and his new imperialistic styled Federal government.

In essence, Southern blacks supported the Confederacy because they did not want to see their homeland occupied, their families endangered, or the Southern economy interrupted. This was a people who, though they detested slavery, believed in defending their Southern heritage, their Southern history, and their Southern culture.

The 19th-Century South was not a monoracial white European society as uneducated pro-North writers contend. It was a deeply multicultural, multiracial society, a profound blend of both European and African (and also Hispanic and Asian) traditions and customs. As a result, today all true Southerners—whatever their race—continue to be proud of Dixie's multiracial heritage, just as most Victorian white and black Southerners were.

This pride is built on historical fact, not fantasy: it was blacks who farmed most of the land, ran most of the plantations, and constructed most of the homes and buildings across the South. It was black architecture, black music, black fashion, black recipes, and black religious beliefs, that helped build what we call today "Southern culture." In turn, along the way Southern blacks absorbed and embraced nearly every aspect of European culture, creating a truly homogenous society.

It can hardly be surprising then that like their white counterparts, many Victorian blacks eagerly took up arms to protect the South from the illicit Yankee invasion in 1861. And so it was that thousands of slaves and freed blacks "enlisted" in the Confederate army and navy.

Many joined the Southern military as simple laborers; others as teamsters, bodyguards, barbers, nurses, cooks, musicians, scouts, construction workers, and some as servants. Despite not being officially recognized at the time, hundreds of thousands more chose to serve as Confederate soldiers, anxiously anticipating the chance to put on uniforms, drill with their units, and hunt down and kill Yankees.

Several all-black Confederate regiments were formed at the very beginning of the War, such as the First Louisiana of Native Guards, which organized in 1861. Union soldiers reported black Confederate sharpshooters on the Rebel lines at the Battle of Seven Days (June 25-July 1, 1862). The Confederate Ordnance Department was 25 percent black, while the Confederate navy was comprised of some 1,000 black sailors.

General Stonewall Jackson's army alone contained 3,000 black soldiers. Clad "in all kinds of uniforms," and armed with "rifles, muskets, sabres, bowie-knives, dirks, etc.," to the shocked Yankee soldiers who witnessed them they were "manifestly an integral portion of the Southern Confederacy."

For indisputable proof of the black Confederate soldier we need look no further than a letter written by former Northern slave Frederick Douglass to Lincoln in 1862. In it the black civil rights leader uses the example of the overwhelming number of blacks in the Confederate army at the time to urge the president to allow blacks to officially enlist in the Union army. (Racist Lincoln, a lifelong member of the American Colonization Society and an aggressive supporter of American apartheid, had steadfastly refused up until that time.) Wrote Douglass to the president:

"There are at the present moment, many colored men in the Confederate Army doing duty not only as cooks, servants and laborers, but as real soldiers, having muskets on their shoulders and bullets in their pockets, ready to shoot down loyal [Yankee] troops, and do all that soldiers may do to destroy the Federal government and build up that of the traitors and rebels. There were such soldiers at Manassas, and they are probably there still. There is a negro in the [Confederate] army as well as in the fence, and our Government is likely to find it out before the war comes to an end. That the negroes are numerous in the rebel army, and do for that army it heaviest work, is beyond question."

Countless stories have come down to us of black Confederates fighting with honor and heroism—and thousands more, most whose names will never be known—who understandably died for the Cause of Southern Freedom.

Among those were the sixty-five loyal African-Americans who donned Confederate gray and fought the Yanks at the Battle of Franklin under General Nathan Bedford Forrest on November 30, 1864.

BLACKS: See African-Americans and Black Confederates.

BLEDSOE'S MISSOURI BATTERY (CSA): This Rebel battery fought at the Battle of Franklin in Hotchkiss' Battalion, Cheatham's Corps Artillery, C.S. Army of Tennessee.

BOSTICK HOUSE: See Everbright.

BOSTICK, JOSEPH (CSA): Bostick was born April 1, 1832, at Hardeman Cross Roads, Tennessee. He was the son of Hardin Perkins Bostick (grandson of Bethenia Perkins of Halifax County, Virginia) and Margaret Rebecca Litton.

A close cousin of the owners of Everbright (also known as the Bostick House) in Franklin, he was a successful doctor who served in the Confederate military and fought at the Battle of Franklin.

Dr. Bostick survived the War and passed away in December 1886 at South Pittsburg, Tennessee, where he labored as the town's first physician. He was buried in the town's City Cemetery.

BOSTICK, REBECCA LETITIA: Rebecca Letitia Bostick (née Cannon) was born October 11, 1810, in Tennessee. She was the wife of Richard Whitman Hyde Bostick, the first cousin of Joseph Bostick (previous entry). The couple owned Everbright, also known as the Bostick House, which played a small role in the Battle of Franklin.

Both Rebecca and her husband are buried at Resthaven Cemetery, Franklin, Tennessee. Several Franklin streets memorialize this family: Bostick Street, Cannon Street, Everbright Avenue, and Perkins Drive.

BOUANCHAUD'S LOUISIANA BATTERY (CSA): This Rebel battery fought at the Battle of Franklin in Myrick's Battalion, Stewart's Corps Artillery, C.S. Army of Tennessee.

BOXMERE: The name of the home of Hardin P. Figuers, this antebellum house is located in Franklin, Tennessee. An eyewitness at the Battle of Franklin, young Figuers sat in the trees in the front yard and watched as the conflict commenced and spread across the town.

During the battle, Boxmere was illegally occupied by U.S. Brigadier General William Grose and his staff. Afterward, the home was converted into one of Franklin's forty-one Confederate field hospitals.

Boxmere is listed on the National Register of Historic Places and is today privately owned.

BRADLEY, LUTHER PRENTICE (USA): Bradley was born December 8, 1822, at New Haven, Connecticut. With the start of Lincoln's War he sided with the North and against the Constitution.

After joining the U.S. Army, he commanded Federal units at such battles as Murfreesboro (Stones River to Yanks), Tullahoma, Dalton, Resaca, New Hope Church, Kennesaw Mountain, Peach Tree Creek, Atlanta, Chickamauga, and Jonesboro.

Later, as a brigadier general, he commanded the Third Brigade, Wagner's Second Division, Fourth U.S. Army Corps, at the Battle of Spring Hill, where he was "severely wounded." Unable to fight the next day at the Battle of Franklin, Bradley's Third Brigade was commanded by Colonel Joseph Conrad at that conflict. Bradley, however, was recuperating in Franklin during the battle and met with other wounded Union officers afterward.

Postbellum, Bradley married and had two sons. He continued to serve with the U.S. army, fighting Indians in New Mexico, Montana, Nebraska, Wyoming, Kansas, and Arizona. He was at Camp Robinson (located near present day Crawford, Nebraska) when Native-American Chief Crazy Horse was killed in September 1877.

Bradley passed away in Tacoma, Washington, on March 13, 1910, and was buried at Arlington National Cemetery.

BRADLEY'S THIRD BRIGADE (USA): This Yankee infantry brigade fought at the Battle of Franklin in Wagner's Second Division, Fourth U.S. Army Corps.

Named after Yankee Brigadier General Luther P. Bradley, who was not present at the Battle of Franklin (due to an injury he received the day before at the Battle of Spring Hill), the brigade was led at Franklin by Colonel Joseph Conrad.

Bradley's Third Brigade was comprised of the Forty-second Illinois, Fifty-first Illinois, Seventy-ninth Illinois, Fifteenth Missouri, Sixty-fourth Ohio, and Sixty-fifth Ohio.

BRAGG, BRAXTON (CSA): Bragg was born on March 22, 1817, at Warrenton, South Carolina. In 1837 he graduated fifth in his class from West Point, going on to fight in both the Seminole Wars and the Mexican-American War. In the late 1850s he took up the occupation of planter in Louisiana.

A favorite of Confederate President Jefferson Davis, during Lincoln's War Bragg was rapidly promoted. In 1862 he attained the rank of full general and was given command of the Army of Tennessee. He fought at such battles as Shiloh, Murfreesboro, Chickamauga, and Perryville.

Due to ongoing conflicts with other Confederate officers (such as Patrick R. Cleburne, William J. Hardee, and Nathan Bedford Forrest), in early 1864 Bragg asked to be relieved of his command. President Davis granted the request, replaced him with General Joseph E. Johnston, and made Bragg his military advisor at Richmond.

Johnston was soon replaced by General John Bell Hood, who went on to greatly thin the ranks of the Army of Tennessee at Franklin and Nashville in the Fall of 1864.

After Lincoln's War Bragg worked as a civil engineer. He died in Galveston, Texas, on September 27, 1876, and was buried in Magnolia Cemetery, Mobile, Alabama.

Though traditionally regarded as a cranky, difficult, and often inconsistent Confederate officer, Bragg served his country with courage and is still admired by many across the South. Indeed, this very admiration led to the naming of Fort Bragg (North Carolina) in his honor.

BRANTLEY, WILLIAM FELIX (CSA): The son of William Brantley and Marinda Jolly, Brantley was born March 12, 1830, in Green County, Alabama. In 1852 he began working as an attorney at Greensboro, Mississippi.

With the start of Lincoln's War, Brantley sided with the South and the Constitution. After joining the Confederate army, he served as captain of the Wigfall Rifles. He fought at such battles as Murfreesboro, Chickamauga, Lookout Mountain, Resaca, and Ezra Church.

As a brigadier general he led his own unit at the Battle of Franklin—Brantley's Brigade, Johnson's Division, Lee's Corps, C.S. Army of Tennessee—against Yankee General Orlando H. Moore near Carter's Creek Pike.

Brantley, who lived in one of the more dangerous and violent regions of Mississippi, married twice and bore several children. Many of his family members were killed in cold blood by outlaws, and Brantley himself died from an assassin's bullet on November 2, 1870, while traveling along a road just outside the town of Winona, Mississippi. He was buried in Greensboro Cemetery, Grady, Webster County, Mississippi.

BRANTLEY'S BRIGADE (CSA): This Rebel infantry brigade fought at the Battle of Franklin in Johnson's Division, Lee's Corps, C.S. Army of Tennessee.

Named after Confederate Brigadier General William Felix Brantley, it was comprised of the

Twenty-fourth Mississippi, Twenty-seventh Mississippi, Twenty-ninth Mississippi, Thirtieth Mississippi, and Thirty-fourth Mississippi.

BRATTON, JOHN C. (CSA): Confederate Major Bratton led the Ninth Arkansas Infantry at the Battle of Franklin, where he was wounded in action.

BREASTWORKS: A temporary fortification, so-named because it is built to the height of a man's chest for protection. A breastwork can be constructed above or below ground.

The numerous breastworks of the well entrenched Union army at the Battle of Franklin were instrumental in the Yankee victory that day. As the Confederates boldly advanced on the Federal positions across the open Plain of Franklin, they were mowed down by fire from Union troops concealed behind dozens of breastworks.

BREEZY HILL: A prominence located just to the east of Winstead Hill at Franklin, Tennessee, during the Battle of Franklin it was used as an observation post by Confederate General John Bell Hood and his staff. Civilians too gathered on the summit of Breezy Hill that day, to watch the drama unfold and cheer on the Confederate army.

Modern day Columbia Pike runs between Breezy Hill and Winstead Hill. While the latter has been beautifully preserved as part of the Franklin battlefield, Breezy Hill at present remains an untamed hilltop woodland and is not open to the public.

BRIDGES, LYMAN A. (USA): U.S. Captain Bridges commanded the Fourth U.S. Army Corps Artillery at the Battle of Franklin, November 30, 1864.

BROUGHTON, EDWARD THOMAS, JR. (CSA): The son of Edward Thomas Broughton Sr. and Rachel Winborne, Broughton was born April 3, 1834, in Monroe County, Alabama. In 1847 he moved to Texas with his family. He married Mary Elizabeth Douglas in 1856, then studied law and was admitted to the bar in 1857.

With the outbreak of Lincoln's War, Broughton sided with the South and the Constitution. He helped organize the Kaufman Light Infantry, which he led as captain. The unit was renamed the Johnson Guards, after which it was attached to the Seventh Texas Regiment in late 1861.

Broughton was captured and exchanged several times during the War. He was with the Seventh Texas at the Battle of Franklin, November 30, 1864, where he took over command of Granbury's Brigade after its leader General Hiram Bronson Granbury was killed in action.

After the War Broughton moved to Sherman, Grayson County, Texas, where he served as a senator and died February 12, 1874. He was buried in Oakwood Cemetery, Tyler, Smith County, Texas.

BROWN, JOHN CALVIN (CSA): The son of Duncan Brown and Margaret Smith, Brown was born January 6, 1827, in Giles County, Tennessee. He attended, and graduated from, Jackson College (Columbia, Tennessee) in 1846, then went on to practice law in Pulaski.

He married Anne Pointer of Spring Hill, who passed away prematurely in 1858. In 1864 Brown married his second wife, Elizabeth Childress of Murfreesboro, with whom he had four children. The Brown family mansion at Pulaski is today part of the campus of Martin Methodist College.

With the onset of Lincoln's War, Brown sided with the South and the Constitution. While serving in the Confederate army he was captured at the Battle of Fort Donelson and was imprisoned for six months at Fort Warren, Boston, Massachusetts. After he was exchanged and released, he went on to fight at such battles as Perryville, Chickamauga, and Missionary Ridge.

For his gallantry on the field of action, Brown was promoted to major general, going on to lead a division under Confederate General Benjamin F. Cheatham at the Battle of Franklin, where he was severely injured. This, along with an earlier wound he had received at the Battle of Perryville, disabled him for several months.

In 1870 the conservative Southerner was elected Tennessee governor—the first Democrat (the conservatives of the day) to serve as governor after the War—serving two consecutive terms. Afterward he resumed his law practice. In

1889 he became president of the South's largest industrial company, the Tennessee Coal, Iron, and Railroad Company.

Brown died at Red Boiling Springs, Macon County, Tennessee, on August 17, 1889, and was buried in Maplewood Cemetery, Pulaski, Giles County, Tennessee.

BROWN, JOHN W. (CSA): Confederate Captain Brown led the Seventh Texas Infantry at the Battle of Franklin, where he was captured by the enemy.

BROWN'S DIVISION (CSA): This division, named after Confederate Major General John Calvin Brown, was present at the Battle of Franklin, and is sometimes known as "Cheatham's Old Division."

Serving in Cheatham's Corps, C.S. Army of Tennessee, it was comprised of Gist's Brigade, Maney's Brigade, Strahl's Brigade, and Vaughan's Brigade. After General Brown was injured at Franklin the division was taken over by Confederate Brigadier General Mark Perrin Lowrey.

BUCKET RINGS: When Civil War doctors performed surgery on wounded soldiers, they would occasionally rinse their instruments and hands in buckets of water left near the operating table. The bloody overflow from these buckets left circular reddish-brown stains on the wooden floors known as "bucket rings." Some of these macabre spirals have been preserved in historic buildings into the present day.

One of the best examples can be found in the mansion at Carnton Plantation, which was used as a Confederate field hospital during and after the Battle of Franklin. Here surgeons amputated the limbs of countless seriously wounded men, leaving not only the stains of pools of blood on the floor, but bucket rings as well.

BUELL, DON CARLOS (USA): Buell was born on March 23, 1818, at Lowell, Ohio. He graduated from West Point in 1841, then went on to fight Indians in Florida and Mexicans in the Western Territories (Mexican-American War).

Buell helped organize the Yankees' famous Army of the Potomac, and his movement into

Nashville using the Cumberland and Tennessee Rivers expedited Union General Ulysses S. Grant's victories at the Battles of Fort Henry and Fort Donelson. Buell's capture of Nashville in February 1862 helped lead to the Battle of Franklin and was instrumental in sealing the fate of the Confederacy in the Western Theater.

At the Battle of Perryville on October 8, 1862, Buell won against Confederate General Braxton Bragg, but the Yankee brass disliked what they considered to be his inefficient tactics. Criticized from all sides, his command was handed over to Union General William Starke Rosecrans and Buell was investigated by a military committee. Though nothing came of the inquiry, the conclusion of the panel was not a positive one and Buell resigned from the military in June 1864.

After the War the Yankee Welshman ran a coal mine in Kentucky, became president of the Green River Iron Company, and worked as a pension agent at Louisville. He died on November 19, 1898, near Paradise, Kentucky, and was buried in Bellefontaine Cemetery, Saint Louis, Missouri.

BUFORD STREET: A Franklin, Tennessee, street named in honor of Confederate Brigadier General Abraham Buford, who fought for constitutional government at the Battle of Franklin.

BUFORD, ABRAHAM (CSA): Known as "Abe," Buford was born January 18, 1820, at Woodford, Kentucky. A descendant of both the European royal Beauforts (the original spelling of his surname) and the famous Lee family of Virginia (he was a cousin of Confederate General Robert E. Lee), he was the son of William B. Buford and Frances Walker Kirtley. He was named after his great-uncle Abraham Buford, a noted commander in the American Revolutionary War.

Like so many other Civil War officers, Buford started out as a West Point graduate (class of 1841) and was a participant in the Mexican-American War.

After the U.S. defeated Mexico he settled down to breed and race horses at his impressive farm, Bosque Bonita ("Beautiful Woods"), located near Versailles, Kentucky.

With the start of Lincoln's War he sided with the South and the Constitution. He joined the Confederacy, eventually serving as a brigadier general under Confederate General Nathan Bedford Forrest until the close of the War. Buford fought at the Battles of Champion Hill, Brice's Cross Roads, Spring Hill, and Nashville, among many others.

At the Battle of Franklin he led a cavalry unit, Buford's Division, Forrest's Cavalry Corps, C.S. Army of Tennessee, on the Confederates' far right, between the Harpeth River and Lewisburg Pike.

After the War Buford returned to his equine pursuits and served in the Kentucky legislature. His debts became insurmountable, however, forcing him into bankruptcy. Both his only son, twenty-three year old William, and his wife Amanda Harris, died during the same period.

By then, having lost his beautiful farm Bosque Bonita to his creditors, and overcome with depression, during a visit to his brother's house in Danville, Indiana, Buford committed suicide on June 9, 1884.

He was buried in Lexington Cemetery, Lexington, Kentucky. A street in Franklin, Tennessee, is named after Buford, memorializing his gallantry at the Battle of Franklin.

BUFORD'S DIVISION (CSA): This Rebel division fought at the Battle of Franklin in Forrest's Cavalry Corps, C.S. Army of Tennessee. Led by Confederate Brigadier General Abraham Buford, it was comprised of Bell's Brigade and Crossland's Brigade.

BULLOCK, ROBERT (CSA): The son of Richard Bullock and Mildred Walker, Bullock was born December 8, 1828, at Greenville, North Carolina. After moving to Florida in his late teens, he taught school, then became a court clerk in Marion County. In the early 1850s he married and bore four known children, then fought in the Seminole Wars.

With the start of Lincoln's War, he sided with the South and the Constitution. After joining the Confederate army, he was commissioned a captain in the Seventh Florida Infantry, fighting in such battles as Murfreesboro, Shiloh, Missionary Ridge, Chickamauga, and Atlanta.

In 1864 Bullock was made brigadier general, leading his own unit, Bullock's Brigade (originally known as Finley's Brigade), Bate's Division, Cheatham's Corps, C.S. Army of Tennessee, at the Battle of Franklin.

Postbellum, Bullock was admitted to the bar in Florida, going on to serve as a probate court judge, a Democratic (the conservatives of the day) congressman, and a judge.

He died at Ocala, Marion County, Florida, July 27, 1905, and was buried in the town's Evergreen Cemetery.

CALDWELL HOUSE AND CEMETERY: Once located on what is now Royal Park Boulevard, Spring Hill, Tennessee, the Caldwell House no longer exists, having disappeared around the year 1900.

All that remains on the property today is a small family cemetery, sad, neglected, overgrown, and nearly forgotten, encircled by a slowly deteriorating white picket fence. Encroaching in upon this tiny graveyard is an ever-growing industrial park along with fast-blossoming modern subdivisions, monuments to Spring Hill's boast of being America's fourteenth fastest growing city.

Since the five aging Caldwell gravestones are connected to the Battle of Franklin, we will chronicle them here before they too disappear. On them are crudely chiseled the following names and dates (my notes are in brackets):

St. Claire Caldwell born in East Tenn [Monroe Co.], April 22, 1793 [son of James Caldwell and Jean unknown]. Died Jan. 3, 1856 [in Maury County, TN].

Mary Moore wife of D. B. St. Claire, F. Caldwell and daughter of Henry Pointer [and Mary Ragland]. Born Aug. 28, 1809 [in Maury County, TN]. Died Jan. 9, 1878.

Martha Jane; wife of Henry Pointer [and Mary Ragland], and daughter of St. Claire F. Caldwell, born Dec. 12, 1823 [in Maury Co., TN]. Died Oct. 12, 1857. Aged 33 years and 10 months.

James Henry Caldwell died April 25th, 1843. Aged 3 years 10 months & 27 days.

Ann Elizabeth the dutiful, beloved and affectionate wife of M. L. Stockard. Born Oct. 15, 1833. Died Dec. 6, 1865.

The once thriving Caldwell House is most famous for having been the headquarters of Confederate General Nathan Bedford Forrest on November

29, 1864, just prior to the Battles of Spring Hill and Franklin.

On a historical marker at the Caldwell House and Cemetery site there is an old photo of the once lovely home (©. 1900), with the following words:

"Caldwell House, Nathan Bedford Forrest's headquarters: About 11:30 A.M. Nathan Bedford Forrest's Cavalry approached Spring Hill from the east. Approximately 2 miles east of town Forrest encountered advance skirmishes of the small Federal garrison. For the next 2.5 hours Forrest's Cavalry, well organized and heavily outnumbering the impromptu Federal covering force, drove them back to Spring Hill. The Union defenders resisted stubbornly in heavy skirmish lines, taking full advantage of the terrain and their superior fire power, which consisted of Spencer carbines, other breech-loading carbines, and Colt-revolving rifle muskets. Arriving Federal infantry and artillery repulsed Forrest's attempts to capture Spring Hill. Forrest's men were fatigued after two long days in the saddle and three hours of combat, and their ammunition was nearly exhausted. Forrest had performed his job admirably, but Hood's infantry would have to continue the work that his cavalryman had begun. That evening Forrest established his headquarters at the Caldwell home. Only the family cemetery remains today."

CALLAHAN, DENNY (CSA): Callahan was a young Irish-American soldier who fought in the Confederacy's First Missouri Brigade at the Battle of Franklin. A sergeant, he was known for his humor as well as his bravery: after three of his comrades fell during the assault, he successfully carried his unit's flag up to the Yankee front lines, where he was wounded and captured.

Callahan's brigade, commanded by General Francis Marion Cockrell, was with French's Division, Stewart's Corps, C.S. Army of Tennessee. The First Missouri fought Yankee General William T. Sherman during the Georgia Campaign, and took part in such battles as Jonesboro, Allatoona, and Tilton.

CANNIFF, PATRICK (CSA): Confederate Captain Canniff led the Third and Fifth Missouri Infantries at the Battle of Franklin, where he was killed in action.

CANTLEY'S BRIGADE (CSA): This Rebel infantry brigade fought at the Battle of Franklin in Walthall's Division, Stewart's Corps, C.S. Army of Tennessee.

Led by Confederate Brigadier General Charles Miller Shelley, it was comprised of the Seventeenth Alabama, Twenty-sixth Alabama, Twenty-ninth

Alabama, and Thirty-seventh Mississippi.

CAPERS, ELLISON (CSA): The son of William Capers and Susan McGill, Capers was born October 14, 1837, at Charleston, South Carolina. In 1857 the English-Irish-American graduated from the South Carolina Military Academy (now known as the Citadel), then became a mathematics professor.

He married Charlotte Rebecca Palmer of Cherry Grove Plantation in 1859, and in 1860 he was made major of Charleston's First Regiment of Rifles, which served with Confederate General Pierre G. T. Beauregard at the Battle of Fort Sumter.

In 1862 the First Regiment of Rifles was reorganized as the Twenty-fourth Regiment of South Carolina Volunteers, and Capers, now a lieutenant colonel, was placed in command. He was present at the Battles of Secessionville, Chickamauga, and Missionary Ridge. During the Tennessee Campaign, while serving under Confederate General Braxton Bragg, Capers was promoted to colonel.

While leading the Twenty-fourth at the Battle of Franklin, Capers was seriously wounded. At the time, the Twenty-fourth was serving in the brigade of General States Rights Gist, who died from his wounds on the night of November 30, 1864. Subsequently Capers was made brigadier general and placed in charge of Gist's Brigade.

At the opening of the Battle of Franklin, Capers made note of the "magnificent spectacle" of the advancing Confederate army, with its numerous horseback riding officers, one hundred regiments, colorful flags, and jaunty band music.

Postbellum, Capers was elected to the office of South Carolina's secretary of state, and in 1867 he entered the Christian ministry, serving as rector of numerous Episcopal churches. In 1893 he was made assistant bishop of South Carolina, in 1894 he was made bishop, and in 1904 he was elected chancellor of the University of the South.

He also served as chaplain general of the United Confederate Veterans, and contributed writings to the *Confederate Military History* (South Carolina volume).

Capers died at Columbia, Richland County, South Carolina, April 22, 1908, and was buried in the town's Trinity Episcopal Cathedral Cemetery.

CAPRON, HORACE (USA): Capron, the son of Dr. Seth Capron and Eunice Mann, was born August 31, 1804, at Attleboro, Massachusetts. He married Louisa Victoria Snowden and the couple bore six known children: Horace Jr., Nicholas, Adeline, Albert, Elizabeth, and Osmond.

After the Mexican-American War Capron was appointed to remove and resettle Indians in Texas. After his wife Louisa died in 1849 he married Margaret Baker.

With the onset of Lincoln's War, Capron sided with the North and against the Constitution. He was soon promoted to colonel, in command of the Fourteenth Regiment, Illinois Volunteer Cavalry. At the start of the conflict in April 1861 he was already fifty-seven years old, making him the oldest cavalry officer in the Union army.

Seriously wounded at Athens, Georgia, on August 3, 1864, he left active service and was breveted brigadier general of U.S. Volunteers. His brigade, however, went on to fight at the Battle of Franklin, which, in Capron's absence, was led by Union Colonel Thomas J. Harrison.

After the War Capron served as U.S. commissioner of agriculture in 1867, and in 1871 he began a nine year stint working with the Japanese at Hokkaido to improve their agricultural, road, street, and water systems.

He died at Washington, D.C. on February 22, 1885, and was buried in the District's Oak Hill Cemetery. After his death his wife sold his enormous Japanese art collection to the Smithsonian Institution. The Mansion, the magnificent antebellum home he completed in 1854, still stands at Hebron, McHenry County, Illinois.

CARNTON PLANTATION: Built in Franklin, Tennessee, sometime around 1815 by Randal McGavock, the eleventh mayor of Nashville, Carnton was home to the McGavock family for eighty-five years. It was completed in 1826, originally possessed about 1,420 acres, and included barns, paddocks, fruit orchards, great fields of cotton, hemp, tobacco, and small grains, large stands of statuesque trees, barns, a five-bay carriage house, servants quarters, sheds, a greenhouse, and corrals located across the back of the property. Nearly all of these have disappeared over the past two centuries due to modernization, human interference, and weather.

After Randal's death in 1843, Confederate Colonel John W. McGavock and his wife Caroline "Carrie" Winder—known as the "Good Samaritan of Williamson County" for her many good deeds—set about updating and modernizing Carnton Plantation, adding, among other things, the famous Greek Revival front and back porches.

One of John and Carrie's daughters, Harriet "Hattie McGavock, married George Limerick Cowan, who served as a Confederate lieutenant in General Nathan Bedford Forrest's famous Escort. Hattie and George lived at Windermere, the house at the bottom of Carnton's driveway.

Due to Lincoln's War, the McGavocks found themselves in financial trouble after the conflict ended. As the family members died off over the following decades, Carnton Plantation herself began to dissipate, and in 1911 it was sold to private owners by Susan Lee "Susie" Ewing, the widow of Winder McGavock, Randal's grandson.

Carnton's 10,000 square foot mansion played a major role in Lincoln's War, serving as one of the town's forty-four field hospitals. In the case of Carnton, it was used strictly for Confederate troops. While countless Rebel soldiers convalesced in the yards outside, hundreds more were operated on inside Carnton, with numerous amputated limbs being tossed out of the mansion's front windows into great piles in the yard. These ghastly surgeries left their mark, most which may be seen to this day: brownish red stains on some of the floors where blood dripped or pooled.

Confederate Captain William Dudley Gale, adjutant general to General Alexander P. Stewart, wrote of the awful scene at Carnton:

"[Carnton] . . . was to the rear of our line. The house is one of the large old-fashioned houses of the better class in Tennessee, two stories high, with many rooms. . . . This was taken as a hospital, and the wounded, in hundreds, were brought to it during the battle, and all the night after. Every room was filled, every bed had two poor, bleeding fellows, every spare space, niche, and corner under the stairs, in the hall, everywhere—but one room for her own family. And when the noble old house could hold no more, the yard was appropriated until the wounded and the dead filled that, and all were not yet provided for.

"Our doctors were deficient in bandages, and she [Mrs. Carrie McGavock] began by giving her old linen, then her towels and napkins, then her sheets and tablecloths, then her husband's shirts and her own undergarments. During all this time the surgeons plied their dreadful work amid the sighs and moans and death rattle. Yet, amid, it all, the noble woman . . . was very active and constantly at work. During all the night neither she nor any of the household slept, but dispensed tea and coffee and such stimulants as she had, and that, too, with her own hands."

Yankee soldiers had previously threatened to burn Carnton to the ground, unless her owner at the time, Randal's son Confederate Colonel John W. McGavock, signed the Union's illegal Oath of Allegiance to the U.S. He had little choice, of course, for if had refused to sign, his family would have been made homeless and millions of dollars of equity would have gone up in smoke.

While the decision was undoubtedly extremely agonizing for Colonel McGavock, his signature saved Carnton Plantation, preserving an important piece of American history for future generations.

Despite John's oath-taking and the Yankee's "generous" promise not to torch Carnton, Union soldiers committed numerous crimes against the family and their property anyway, such as stealing millions of dollars in livestock and lumber. After the War the McGavocks sued the U.S. government for damages, but were never repaid or compensated.

In April 1866 Colonel John and Carrie gave two acres at what is now the northwest corner of Carnton (next to the McGavock Family Cemetery) to be used as an eternal resting place for the nearly 2,000 Rebel soldiers who died during the Battle of Franklin.

John, along with various citizens of Franklin, helped raise the money to fund the reburial project. Since the remains of many of the soldiers were never found, only 1,481 ended up with graves at the site, known as the McGavock Confederate Cemetery.

When the cemetery was completed in 1866 it was dedicated and opened to the public. It is unique in that it survives as the largest privately owned Confederate cemetery in the U.S. To this day the graveyard continues to be a popular pilgrimage site for traditional Southerners and neo-Confederates, a role it took on even before the end of the 19th Century.

After Susie (Ewing) McGavock sold Carnton in 1911, it was occupied by a series of different private owners into the 1970s. In 1976, with the mansion on the verge of complete dilapidation, the Carnton Association (a group of concerned citizens) was formed as a non-profit organization to help raise money for its purchase.

Two years later, the owners at that time, Dr. and Mrs. W. D. Sugg of Bradenton, Florida, generously donated the entire ten acre estate to the private foundation, with the deed being signed on September 22, 1978.

Since then, the Association has acquired an extra thirty-eight acres from the state as a barrier to further incursion from the modern world.

Carnton, often referred to as "Tennessee's most haunted Civil War house," is today open for public tours.

CARPETBAGGERS: During the twelve years of Reconstruction many unscrupulous Northerners poured into the South to take advantage of the weakened condition of the Confederate states.

These unwanted outsiders, who got their name because they carried all of their belongings in carpetbags, tricked and plundered Confederate families out of millions of dollars, and like their Southern counterparts, the traitorous scallywags, were considered the scourge of the postwar era.

The word continues to be used today to describe a Yankee, stranger, foreigner, or newcomer to Dixie who interferes in a Southerner's affairs, in particular his or her constitutional freedoms and Southern traditions.

CARTER FAMILY COTTON GIN HOUSE: Owned by Fountain Branch Carter of Franklin, Tennessee, the family's cotton gin house is famous for having been located at the epicenter of the fiercest fighting at the Battle of Franklin, November 30, 1864.

A Yankee flank, Yankee entrenchments, and a Yankee gun battery were situated around the gin house during the conflict. Many Confederate soldiers were gunned down by the "deadly hail of lead and iron" that poured forth from the area as they were advancing north up Columbia Avenue (then known as Columbia Turnpike).

Prior to the battle Yankee soldiers pulled much of gin house apart to use its wooden boards to reinforce their trenches. What little was left of the structure completely disappeared with time over the following years.

The Carter family cotton gin house was located about 240 feet to the east of present day Cleburne Street and Columbia Avenue (around what is now 109 Cleburne Street). On the morning of December 1 the body of Confederate General Patrick R. Cleburne was discovered just south of the gin house.

Today a small parcel of land at the corner of Cleburne Street and Columbia Avenue, complete with historical markers, has been set aside to mark the site. The Cotton Gin Memorial is open to the public.

CARTER, FOUNTAIN BRANCH: Carter, the son of Francis Watkins Carter and Sarah Holcomb Anderson, was born in Halifax, Virginia, April 6, 1797. He grew up in Waddell Hollow near Natchez Trace, not far from the village of Leiper's Fork, Williamson County, Tennessee.

Carter's wife was Mary Armistead "Polly" Atkinson, with whom he bore, according to some sources, a dozen children. Among the better known were Confederate Lieutenant Colonel Moscow Branch Carter and Confederate Captain Theodrick "Tod" Carter, the latter who perished from wounds inflicted at the Battle of Franklin.

Fountain's home, known today as the Carter House, was a Union headquarters during the Battle of Franklin, and was located near the family's cotton gin house, the epicenter of the fiercest fighting.

A longtime resident of Franklin, Fountain worked as a farmer, shoe manufacturer, and surveyor, owned nearly thirty black servants, and was worth a total of about $1.5 million in today's currency. He was on the committee that oversaw the building of the second location of Franklin's First Presbyterian Church (at the corners of present day Main Street and Fifth Avenue). Fountain passed away in Franklin August 22, 1871, and was buried in the town's old City Cemetery.

CARTER, FRANCIS WATKINS (CSA): Francis, nicknamed "Wad," was born November 30, 1842, at Franklin, Tennessee. A son of Fountain Branch Carter, Francis served, with his brothers Moscow and Tod, in Company H, Twentieth Tennessee Infantry.

He did not, however, fight at the Battle of Franklin. Having been severely injured at the Battle of Shiloh (April 6-7, 1862), the eighteen year old underwent a lengthy recovery and left the Confederate military near the end of 1862 on a medical discharge.

According to local Franklin lore, later in life Francis spent five years traversing the unexplored regions of South America.

CARTER, JOHN CARPENTER (CSA): The son of Edward J. Carter and Angelina Matilda Carpenter, Carter was born December 19, 1837, at Waynesboro, Burke County, Georgia.

Carter (who is not related to the Carter family of Franklin's Carter House), was educated at the University of Virginia and later took up the study of law at Cumberland University, Lebanon, Tennessee.

In the Spring of 1859 he married Louisa D. Caruthers—the daughter of his college law professor, Judge Abram Caruthers—and bore several children: Eliza and Edward.

In 1861 Carter moved his family to Memphis, Tennessee, where he operated a successful law practice. With the opening of Lincoln's War, he sided with the South and the Constitution.

After joining the Confederate army, he rose quickly up the ranks, while fighting in such battles as Jonesboro, Atlanta, Chickamauga, Shiloh, Perryville, and Murfreesboro.

At the Battle of Franklin General Carter was shot in the stomach near the Carter House, but survived. He was taken to the William Harrison House on the other side of Winstead Hill, a few miles to the south, where he passed away from his wounds on December 10.

His burial service at Rose Hill Cemetery at Columbia, Tennessee, was given by Confederate Army Chaplain Charles Todd Quintard.

Carter's grave site can still be seen, and there is a street in Franklin named after him not far from where he fell for the last time on November 30, 1864.

CARTER HOUSE: Built in 1830 by Fountain Branch Carter on nineteen acres of land purchased from Angus McPhail and his wife Ann Sharpe, the Carter House is most famous for its role in the Battle of Franklin. The Carter family land eventually grew to nearly 300 acres, encompassing property on both sides of the Columbia Turnpike (now Columbia Avenue).

At 4:30 AM on the morning of November 30, 1864, Yankee General Jacob Dolson Cox rudely and illegally took over the Carter House for use as his Union headquarters. Immediately Federal troops began preparing for Confederate General John Bell Hood's Army of Tennessee, advancing from the south after the debacle the day before known as the Spring Hill Affair. Blue-coated soldiers tore apart several barns, including much of the Carter family's cotton gin house, for wood, to be used in the support of their entrenchments.

Sensing imminent danger, as the late afternoon approached, the following Carter family members and allied relations and friends took refuge in the Carter House basement: Fountain (father), Confederate Lieutenant Colonel Moscow (son), Mary Alice (daughter) and her three children, Orlando, Alice, and Marcus, Sarah (daughter), Annie Vick (daughter), Frances (daughter), Sally Dobbins McKinney (daughter-in-law) and her two children, Fountain McKinney Carter and Ruth Carter, two or three black servants, and finally the family of their German neighbors Albert Lotz and his wife Margaretha, and their children, Paul, Matilda, and Augustus (and possibly their seventeen year old daughter Amelia).

At 4:00 PM the battle opened, as cannon fire and bullets rained down around the Carter House. Though the main fighting was over by 9:00 PM, it was not until 12 o'clock midnight that the shooting completely ceased, and the terrified families felt safe enough to leave the basement.

Tragically, Fountain's beloved twenty-four year old son Tod was found shot not far from his family home. Still alive, he was brought home, where he died two days later from his wounds.

The Carter House, now a Registered National Historic Landmark—along with a number of outbuildings (such as the smokehouse)—has been preserved and has been open for public tours since 1953. The cruel remnants of that Autumn day in November 1864 can still be seen in the bullet holes, cannonball holes, and ricochet marks left in several surviving buildings on the property.

CARTER, MOSCOW B. (CSA): A son of Fountain Branch Carter, he was born December 5, 1825, in a house located at the corner of Church Street and Fourth Avenue, Franklin, Tennessee. He attended Franklin's Harpeth Academy, studied law, fought in the Mexican-American War, and helped run the first telegraph line across Illinois.

In 1851 he married Orlena "Callie" Dobbins of Boone's Hill, Lincoln County, Tennessee. The couple bore four children: Mary Orlena ("Lena"), Walter Fountain, Annie Josephine, and Hugh Ewing.

Orlena passed away in 1860, after which he married America Cattles in 1866. When she too died, in this case in 1876, Carter married a third time to Marmela E. Miot of South Carolina. He had children with both his second and third wives, as well.

A member of the Masons and a political conservative (a Democrat, as they were then known), with the start of Lincoln's War, Carter sided with the South and the Constitution. Joining the Confederate army, he served, with his brothers Tod and Francis, as a lieutenant colonel in Company H, Twentieth Tennessee Infantry.

Carter did not fight at the Battle of Franklin: he was captured at the Battle of Mill Springs on January 19, 1862, and was at his father Fountain's home in Franklin, a prisoner on parole, at the time.

After the War he lived in Franklin until 1898, then moved to nearby Triune for five years, then moved back to Franklin, living in a home "two miles south" of the town. He died at Franklin in 1913.

CARTER, SALLIE: Born Sarah Ewing (and nicknamed "Sallie") in 1826, she later married Boyd Sims, Joe Carter, and Judge John M. Gaut, and so is sometimes referred to as Sarah Sims Carter Gaut—but more often simply as Sallie Carter.

Sallie became famous for sewing and then flying the first Confederate Flag in Williamson County, Tennessee. The beautiful symbol was displayed at her home on Third Avenue North, at Franklin, and was raised by a group of young men that included Theodrick "Tod" Carter.

Sallie became well-known for another event: it was at her Franklin home in 1895 that the United Daughters of the Confederacy's Chapter Number Fourteen was formed. This UDC chapter thrives to this day. Sallie died a Southern heroine in 1912.

CARTER'S BRIGADE (CSA): See Maney's Brigade.

CARTER STREET: A street in Franklin, Tennessee, named in memory of Confederate General John Carpenter Carter, who died on December 10, 1864, at the Harrison House from wounds sustained at the Battle of Franklin on November 30.

CARTER, THEODRICK "TOD" (CSA): A son of Fountain Branch Carter and Mary Armistead "Polly" Atkinson, he was born March 24, 1840, at the famed Carter House, Franklin, Tennessee. The name Theodrick (misspelled on this historical marker in front of the Carter House) was a popular one among the Carter clan, appearing numerous times in the family tree all the way back to the 1600s. His family and friends, however, called him "Tod."

Tod's mother Mary died when he was only twelve, after which the influence of his father and older brothers took center stage in his life. He was probably not aware that he descended from European royalty and that he was cousins with Confederate General Robert E. Lee.

From an early age Tod exhibited literary skills, reading the Classics, and immersing himself in the study of Latin, Greek, mathematics, and philosophy, probably at nearby Harpeth Academy. He also studied law, and by 1861 was working as a Franklin attorney.

When Lincoln's War started, Tod, of course, sided with the South and the Constitution. He enlisted in the Confederate army on May 18, 1861, in what would become Company H of the Twentieth Tennessee Infantry. Joining up with him that day were his brothers Moscow and Francis.

On May 1, 1862, Tod was promoted to captain of the Quartermaster Department, and on October 24 he was made assistant quartermaster. That same year he became a correspondent for Chattanooga, Tennessee's *The Daily Rebel*, a proudly pro-South paper that helped keep Confederate soldiers abreast of the latest news. He wrote his column under the pseudonym "Mint Julep."

By the Autumn of 1863 Tod had fought in numerous conflicts. Unfortunately he was captured at the Battle of Missionary Ridge on November 25, 1863, and was to be sent to the Yankee prison on Johnson's Island, near Sandusky, Ohio.

On the way, however, the plucky Tennessean managed to escape, jumping from a moving Federal train in the dead of night. Aided by South-sympathizing Yankees, he made his way to Dalton, Georgia, where his regiment, the Twentieth Tennessee, was encamped at the time—probably around late February 1864.

From Georgia, in September, Tod and his fellow Confederate soldiers set out for Tennessee under the Army of Tennessee's new commander, General John Bell Hood. They arrived at the town of Columbia in late November, just behind Union General John M. Schofield, commanding the Army of the Ohio.

On the afternoon of November 30, 1864, while Tod's family in Franklin was huddling in the Carter House basement for safety, the two armies met on the Plain of Franklin. Although as assistant quartermaster Tod was not obliged to engage in combat, he enthusiastically joined his excited comrades as they deployed from Winstead Hill that afternoon. Nothing could keep the young captain from defending his hometown, particularly in light of the fact that the despised Yankees had illegally commandeered his family's house and destroyed much of their property.

At about 5:00 PM Tod boldly rode his horse

"Rosencrantz" into the fray, leading Bate's Division in its first charge against the enemy near Carter's Creek Pike. Tod was hit by a bullet almost immediately, and flew over the head of his horse, landing unconscious on the ground a mere 525 feet southwest of his father's home, the Carter House.

Around midnight, by which time the battle had died down, Tod's family emerged from the basement, and, hearing the tragic news of his injury, went in search of him. Aided by Confederate General Thomas Benton Smith, the family, bearing torches, picked their way through the bloody fields of deceased soldiers, the air filled with the awful shrieks of the wounded and dying.

Near daylight Tod was discovered laying near his dead horse, mumbling incoherently. He was carried the short distance to his home and placed on a bed in the war ravaged house. The regimental surgeon, Dr. Deering Roberts, did his best to find and remove the bullet from Tod's head, but to no avail. On December 2, two days after he had been shot, Tod passed away in the front parlor of the Carter House, only feet from the room in which he had been born.

He was buried with a simple headstone at Franklin's Rest Haven Cemetery, where his grave can still be seen. To this day Captain Theodrick "Tod" Carter is honored as a true Southern hero who gave his life for the Confederate Cause: states' rights, self-determination, and self-government.

CARTER, WILLIAM F. (CSA): Confederate Colonel Carter led the Second and Sixth Missouri Infantries at the Battle of Franklin, where he was wounded in action.

CASEMENT, JOHN STEPHEN (USA): Nicknamed "General Jack," Casement was born January 19, 1829, at Geneva, New York, and worked at various occupations in the railroad industry in Michigan and Ohio. In 1857 he married women's rights advocate Frances Jennings, the daughter of famed Yankee abolitionist Charles C. Jennings.

With the outbreak of Lincoln's War, Casement sided with the North and against the Constitution. After joining the U.S. army, Colonel Casement led the One hundred third Ohio Volunteer Regiment during the first half of the conflict.

At the Battle of Franklin—where his repeating rifles were responsible for the bloody slaughter of countless Confederate soldiers—he led the Second Brigade under Yankee General Jacob Dolson Cox, who credited Casement with greatly aiding in the Union victory that day. Casement ended his Civil War service as a brigadier general, fighting his last conflict at the Battle of Wilmington in February 1865.

Postbellum, Casement returned to his career in the railroad business, overseeing the building of the Transcontinental Railroad from Fremont, Nebraska, to Promontory, Utah. It is said that it was Casement who pounded in the celebrated gold spike at the railroad's opening celebration on May 10, 1869.

The aging Yankee officer passed away December 13, 1909, at Painesville, Ohio, and was buried in the town's Evergreen Cemetery.

CASEMENT'S SECOND BRIGADE (USA): This Yankee infantry brigade fought at the Battle of Franklin in Cox's Third Division, Twenty-third U.S. Army Corps.

Named after U.S. Colonel John Stephen Casement, the Second Brigade was comprised of the Sixty-fifth Illinois, Sixty-fifth Indiana, One hundred twenty-fourth Indiana, One hundred third Ohio, and Fifth Tennessee.

CASUALTY: Often misdefined solely as one who has died, the word actually applies to anyone in the military who is lost due to wounds, injury, sickness, imprisonment, capture, or, of course, death, or who is missing in action. (The word casualty can also apply to non-military persons.)

By this definition there were some 7,000 Confederate casualties at the Battle of Franklin, including 1,750 killed, 4,500 wounded, and 702 captured by the enemy.

CAVALRY: An army component mounted on horseback. (Modern cavalries ride on or in motorized vehicles.)

The Confederacy's cavalries were far superior to those of the Union, for the simple reason that Southern boys and men, being from a largely agricultural region, were more familiar with horses than their Northern foes.

Some Confederates used their cavalry in highly original and unorthodox ways. General Nathan Bedford Forrest, for example—rightly known as the "Wizard of the Saddle"—preferred sending his riders into battle as either "dismounted cavalry" or "mounted infantry."

CEDAR HILL: A small prominence in Franklin, Tennessee, it was once part of the Fort Granger complex on its southeast border. It contains a lunette earthwork and possibly other important Civil War fortifications (mainly Union). However, the site is currently privately owned and is not open to the public.

CHALMERS, JAMES RONALD (CSA): Chalmers, the son of U.S. Senator Joseph Williams Chalmers, was born on January 11, 1831, in Halifax County, Virginia. After graduating from South Carolina College (now the University of South Carolina) he worked as a lawyer and a district attorney in Mississippi. He was present at Mississippi's secession convention in early 1861.

With the start of Lincoln's War Chalmers sided with the South and the Constitution. He fought at such battles as Shiloh, Booneville, and Murfreesboro. In 1864 he was transferred to General Nathan Bedford Forrest's Cavalry Corps, during which time he led a division at the Battle of Franklin.

After Lincoln's War, Chalmers returned to Mississippi to resume his law practice. A true Southern conservative, he fought against the liberal North's cruel and illegal "Reconstruction" policies, and was elected three times as a Mississippi state representative.

After retiring in 1888, he moved to Memphis, Tennessee, where he died April 9, 1898. He was buried at the city's famous Elmwood Cemetery.

CHALMERS' DIVISION (CSA): This Rebel division fought at the Battle of Franklin in Forrest's Cavalry Corps, C.S. Army of Tennessee.

Named after its commander Confederate Brigadier General James Ronald Chalmers, it was comprised of Rucker's Brigade and Biffle's Brigade.

CHEAIRS, MARTIN TERRELL: The son of Nathaniel Cheairs III and Sarah Rush, Cheairs was born May 19, 1804, probably in Anson County, North Carolina. He was the brother of Confederate Major Nathaniel Francis Cheairs, the founder of Rippavilla Plantation, Spring Hill, Tennessee.

Martin Cheairs is known for his own historic home in Spring Hill: Ferguson Hall, site of the murder of Confederate General Earl Van Dorn.

Cheairs married Martha Ann Bond in 1837. He died at Spring Hill on May 12, 1891, and was buried in the town's Spring Hill Cemetery.

CHEAIRS, NATHANIEL FRANCIS IV (CSA): The son of Nathaniel Cheairs III and Sarah Rush, Cheairs was born on the property of future Rippavilla Plantation on December 6, 1818, at Spring Hill, Tennessee.

In 1841 he married Susan Peters McKissack, the sister of the infamous Jessie Helen McKissack, whose husband, Dr. George Boddie Peters, murdered Confederate General Earl Van Dorn in a jealous rage. Nathaniel and Susan bore four children before the year 1851: Jeanette, Thomas, Sarah, and William.

In 1852 Cheairs began construction on Rippavilla Plantation, patterned after Spring Hill's Ferguson Hall, owned by Cheairs' brother Martin, and the site of Van Dorn's death. Rippavilla was completed in 1855.

With the outbreak of Lincoln's War, Cheairs sided with the South and the Constitution. After joining the Confederate army he served as a major, surrendering the flag at the Battle of Fort Donelson in February 1862.

After his release from prison in August, he served as an aide to Confederate General Nathan Bedford Forrest. In late 1863 Cheairs was captured by the Yankees once again, this time for selling cattle to Confederate troops, and was sent to Camp Chase in Ohio.

Major Cheairs passed away January 2, 1914, in Maury County, Tennessee (some sources say Waco, McLenna County, Texas), and was buried in Rose Hill Cemetery, Columbia, Tennessee.

Cheairs' home, Rippavilla, was the center of much activity during Lincoln's War. It has been preserved into the present day and is open for public tours.

CHEATHAM, BENJAMIN FRANKLIN (CSA): The son of Leonard Pope Cheatham and Elizabeth Davis Robertson, Cheatham was born October 20, 1820, at Nashville, Tennessee. A descendant of Nashville's cofounder James Robertson (of Virginia), Cheatham served as a colonel in the Mexican-American War, pursued his dreams in the California Gold Rush, then returned home to work his farm.

At the onset of Lincoln's War, Cheatham sided with the South and the Constitution. After joining the Confederate army he was rapidly promoted, serving gallantly in the Army of Tennessee throughout all of its primary engagements.

He soon developed a reputation as a tough and aggressive fighter, his powerful physique, intense eyes, and thick mustache giving him a commanding and intimidating appearance. His incessant cursing and alleged hard drinking added to his fearsomeness, though his soldiers, who knew him affectionately as "Frank," adored him.

General Cheatham was implicated in the Spring Hill Affair (November 29, 1864) by his superior Confederate General John Bell Hood. But the charge (that Cheatham mistakenly allowed the enemy to sneak past the Confederate encampment at Spring Hill) is not overly convincing, and the circumstances surrounding (as well as the blame for) the debacle are still being debated to this day.

If Cheatham was truly "derelict in his duties" at the Battle of Spring Hill, as Hood claimed, then he was also partly responsible for the disaster that would become the Battle of Franklin the following day.

The truth will probably never be known, and, despite the best efforts of Civil War scholars, the matter remains an open-ended mystery.

Although he suffered severe losses among his officers at the Battle of Franklin due to his position at the center of the fight, Cheatham expertly commanded his own corps, Cheatham's Corps, throughout the ordeal.

Postbellum, the former Confederate officer married Anna Bell Robertson (no relation to his grandfather James Robertson) and bore five children: Benjamin Franklin Jr., Patton Robertson,

Joseph Johnston, Medora, and Alice.

General Cheatham went on to serve as both the superintendent of Tennessee state prisons and as Nashville's postmaster. He died September 4, 1886, and was buried at Mount Olivet Cemetery, Nashville.

CHEATHAM'S CORPS (CSA): This Rebel corps, led by Confederate Major General Benjamin F. Cheatham at the Battle of Franklin, was comprised of Cleburne's Division, Brown's Division, and Bate's Division.

CHEATHAM'S CORPS ARTILLERY (CSA): This Rebel artillery corps, commanded by Confederate Colonel Melancthon Smith, was present at the Battle of Franklin. It was comprised of Hoxton's Battalion, Hotchkiss' Battalion, and Cobb's Battalion.

CHICAGO BOARD OF TRADE BATTERY (USA): This Yankee artillery unit fought at the Battle of Franklin in McCook's First Division Artillery, McCook's First Division, Wilson's Cavalry Corps.

CIVIL WAR: See War for Southern Independence.

CLAYTON, HENRY DELAMAR, SR. (CSA): The son of Nelson Clayton, Clayton was born March 7, 1827, in Pulaski County, Georgia. An 1848 graduate of Virginia's Emory and Henry College, after passing his bar exam he moved to Alabama where, in 1850, he married Victoria Virginia Hunter and began practicing law. Between 1857 and 1861 he served twice as an Alabama congressman.

With the outbreak of Lincoln's War, Clayton sided with the South and the Constitution. After joining the Confederate army, he led a division under General Stephen Dill Lee's Corps at the Battle of Franklin.

Known as one of the "fightin' generals," Clayton also fought at such battles as Nashville, Murfreesboro, Chickamauga, Jonesboro, Rocky Face, and New Hope Church.

After the War Clayton was elected president of the University of Alabama in 1880, at which time he also became a law educator. He passed away at Tuscaloosa, Alabama, on October

13, 1889, and was buried in Fairview Cemetery, Eufaula, Alabama.

CLAYTON'S DIVISION (CSA): This Rebel division, named after Confederate General Henry DeLamar Clayton Sr., was present at the Battle of Franklin. It was comprised of Gibson's Brigade, Stovall's Brigade, and Holtzclaw's Brigade.

CLEBURNE STREET: A street in Franklin, Tennessee, named in honor of famed Confederate cavalryman General Patrick R. Cleburne. It is located in the vicinity of where Cleburne fell dead on the battlefield, not far from the Carter House on what is now Columbia Avenue.

CLEBURNE, PATRICK RONAYNE (CSA): Cleburne was born in County Cork, Ireland, on Saint Patrick's Day (March 17), 1828. After emigrating to the U.S. in 1849, he settled in Helena, Arkansas, where he opened a drugstore and became a successful attorney.

With the start of Lincoln's War, Cleburne sided with the South and the Constitution. In the Confederate army he achieved rapid promotion, fighting in such battles as Shiloh, Perryville, and Murfreesboro.

Fierce in combat and idolized by his troops, Major General Cleburne was also widely respected by other Confederate officers. Often justly referred to as the "Stonewall (Jackson) of the West," he received two official thanks from the Confederate Congress for his gallant service.

In early January 1864, Cleburne—only one of the two foreign Confederate officers to reach the level of major general—wrote out a brilliant plan to *officially* enlist and emancipate black servants across the South, which he sent to the Confederate brass at Richmond. (Note that hundreds of thousands of both enslaved and free blacks had been fighting *unofficially* in the Confederate ranks since the opening of Lincoln's War.)

The plan for official enlistment was, unfortunately, rejected as being premature at the time. Cleburne's suggestion became law a little over a year later (in March 1865), however, though too late to help the Confederate Cause.

Just prior to the Battle of Franklin, Cleburne had argued with his superior, the old-fashioned Kentuckian General John Bell Hood, insisting that marching the Army of Tennessee over the broad flat Plain of Franklin in front of well entrenched Yankee troops, was nothing short of a suicide mission. Instead of advancing the men in easily targeted lines, he asked, why not sent them out in lifesaving columns?

Unwisely, Hood ignored his Irish subordinate's suggestion. When Cleburne heard the news that the battle would proceed under Hood's plan, he turned to one of his own officers, Brigadier General Daniel C. Govan, and said: "Well, Govan, if we are to die, let us die like men." These were to be among his final words.

Leading a division under General Benjamin F. Cheatham that included Govan's Brigade, Granbury's Brigade, and Lowrey's Brigade, it was here, on November 30, 1864, that the noble Cleburne fell dead amidst the battle smoke after having two horses shot out from under him.

The morning following the battle, December 1, Cleburne's body was discovered about 300 feet east of Columbia Pike, and some 180 feet south of the Carter family cotton gin house. A single bullet had pierced the left side of his chest. His corpse was placed on the rear lower porch of nearby Carnton Plantation so that his melancholy soldiers could file past and pay their respects.

In Mobile, Alabama, when the general's fiancée Susan Tarlton overheard a corner paperboy yelling out the news of her lover's death, she fainted and had to be carried into her family's home and revived.

On December 2, Cleburne's body was taken south to Columbia, Tennessee, where he was buried in the town's Rose Hill Cemetery. Due to the issue of having been placed too near the graves of detested Union soldiers, his body was then reentered at Saint John's Episcopal Church, located south of Columbia.

Cleburne's journey was not over yet, however. After the War his remains were removed once more, this time to his adopted hometown, Helena, Arkansas. To this day the Irishman rests in peace at the town's Confederate Cemetery.

One of six generals to perish from wounds received at the Battle of Franklin, startled eyewitnesses continue to see and hear Cleburne's ghost pacing back and forth in his heavy officer's boots on Carnton's rear lower porch, where his corpse was laid out on December 1, 1864.

CLEBURNE'S DIVISION (CSA): This division, named after Confederate General Patrick R. Cleburne, fought at the Battle of Franklin in Cheatham's Corps, C.S. Army of Tennessee.

After Cleburne was killed at Franklin, November 30, 1864, command of the division was taken over by Confederate Brigadier General James A. Smith.

Cleburne's Division was comprised of Lowrey's Brigade, Govan's Brigade, Granbury's Brigade, and Smith's Brigade.

CLIFFE, CORNELIA STITH: The daughter of noted North Carolinian John Nichols, Mrs. Cliffe of Franklin, Tennessee, was a widow at the time of the great battle there on November 30, 1864.

Though formally she had been married to a Union captain, she had always been a staunch supporter of the Confederacy. Indeed, just prior to the battle she risked her life by running through enemy fire to burn the Nashville bridge over the Harpeth River, hoping to help slow the advance of the Yankee army into town.

After the Battle of Franklin, Mrs. Cliffe was the one of the first people on the battlefield nursing the wounded and dying soldiers, while her home was converted into one of the city's forty-four field hospitals.

A generous donator of time and money to the Southern Cause, Mrs. Cliffe made the first robes for the original Ku Klux Klan, a social-welfare organization formed to aid Southerners *of all races* after the War (note that this, the original KKK, has no connection to the modern KKK that was formed after 1900).

A true Confederate to the end—whose brothers had fought for the South—Mrs. Cliffe died in Franklin in 1928.

CLIFFE, DANIEL BONAPARTE (CSA/USA): Born at Wooster, Wayne County, Ohio, January 16, 1823, Cliffe moved to Franklin, Tennessee, as a boy in 1836 to live with his uncle Dr. Daniel McPhail.

The son of Dr. Joseph Cliffe and Isabella McPhail, he

studied medicine and in 1842 married local Southern belle Virginia Whitfield, with whom he had six children: John, Daniel, James, Joseph, Charles, and Isabella ("Belle")—the wife of Union General James P. Brownlow.

At the start of Lincoln's War, Cliffe sided with the South and the Constitution, serving in the Confederacy's Twentieth Tennessee Regiment as a brigade surgeon under General Felix Zollicoffer. After the Battle of Fishing Creek in January 1862, however, he began to lose interest in the Southern Cause and switched his allegiance to the Union.

Despite this, the prominent Franklinite continued to use his influence to assist Southerners whenever he could, even ministering to fallen Rebel soldiers after the Battle of Franklin.

Before that conflict, his tiny office on East Main Street was used as a temporary headquarters by Union General John M. Schofield. Today it is the site of Franklin's Visitors Center.

Postbellum, Dr. Cliffe, one of Williamson County's largest landowners, served as the president of the Tennessee and Alabama Railroad, mayor of Franklin, and president of the Franklin National Bank. He was also a Freemason (belonging to Franklin's Hiram Masonic Lodge No. 7) and a member of the ancient, secretive Christian order, the Knights Templar.

Though, for switching sides during Lincoln's War, he was considered a scallywag (turncoat) by many Southerners, he was generally held in high esteem, and was considered one of Franklin's most prominent individuals.

Cliffe died in Franklin January 22, 1913, and was buried in the town's Rest Haven Cemetery. His equally famous father, Dr. Joseph E. Cliffe, is buried across the street at Franklin's old City Cemetery.

CLOUSTON, ELIZABETH FIELD: The daughter of Edward Graham Clouston and Cena McCabe, Clouston was born in the early 1840s in Franklin, Tennessee. She is best known for being the live-in governess at the McGavock home, Carnton Plantation, where she gave the family's children educational instruction while the local school was closed during the Battle of

Franklin.

Clouston's room was located on the second floor of the mansion in what is now called the "children's nursery." Looking at the east side of Carnton, one can still see a "ghost" impression of the door that led from her room into what used to be the kitchen building (actually one of the original rustic homes on the property, and which was destroyed by a tornado in 1909).

Nanny "Lizzy," as she was known, helped nurse wounded Confederate soldiers that were brought to Carnton after the conflict. One of these, Mississippi officer Roland W. Jones, became her husband in December 1865.

COBB'S BATTALION (CSA): This Rebel battalion fought at the Battle of Franklin in Cheatham's Corps Artillery, C.S. Army of Tennessee. It was comprised of Ferguson's South Carolina Battery, Phillip's Tennessee Battery, and Slocumb's Louisianan Battery.

COCKRELL, FRANCIS MARION (CSA): The son of Joseph Cockrell and Nancy Ellis, Cockrell was born on October 1, 1834 at Warrensburg, Johnson County, Missouri.

After graduating from the state's Chapel Hill College in July 1853, he became a lawyer and married Anna Ewing of Richmond, Missouri—the daughter of Ephraim Brevard Ewing and Elizabeth Ann Allen.

With the outbreak of Lincoln's War, Cockrell sided with the South and the Constitution. After joining the Confederacy, he fought at such battles as Vicksburg, Elkhorn Tavern, Wilson's Creek, and Carthage. After the Atlanta Campaign his brigade became part of the C.S. Army of Tennessee under Confederate General John Bell Hood.

Cockrell's Brigade fought under French's Division, Stewart's Corps, at the Battle of Franklin on November 30, 1864, where he was severely wounded.

Brigadier General Cockrell was captured twice during the War: the first time at Vicksburg, the second at Fort Blakeley, Alabama.

Postbellum, he returned to Missouri to resume his law practice. In 1874 he was elected as a Democrat (the conservatives of the day) to the United States Senate, and was reelected four times, serving from March 4,

1875, to March 3, 1905. He also served on the Committee on Claims (Forty-sixth Congress) and the Committee on Appropriations (Fifty-third Congress).

In 1905 President Theodore Roosevelt appointed him to the Interstate Commerce Commission, and in 1911 he was appointed a United States commissioner to help reestablish the boundary line between Texas and New Mexico.

General Cockrell passed away at Washington, D.C. on December 13, 1915, and was buried in Sunset Hill Cemetery at Warrensburg, Missouri.

COCKRELL'S BRIGADE (CSA): This Rebel infantry brigade fought at the Battle of Franklin in French's Division, Stewart's Corps, C.S. Army of Tennessee.

Named after Confederate Brigadier General Francis Marion Cockrell, the brigade was comprised of the First Missouri Infantry, Second Missouri Infantry, Third Missouri Infantry, Fourth Missouri Infantry, Fifth Missouri Infantry, Sixth Missouri Infantry, First Missouri Cavalry, and Third Missouri Cavalry.

COLEMAN, DAVID (CSA): The son of William Coleman and Cynthia Swain, Coleman was born February 5, 1824, in Buncombe County, North Carolina. He was educated at Asheville's Newton Academy, served in the Mexican-American War, and became a lawyer. In 1854 and 1856 he was elected as a Democrat (the conservatives of the day) to the U.S. Senate.

At the start of Lincoln's War, Coleman sided with the South and the Constitution. After joining the Confederate navy, he quickly grew impatient over delays brought on by Lincoln's illegal naval blockade. He then entered the Confederate army and was placed in command of what would become the Thirty-ninth Regiment North Carolina.

Colonel Coleman went on to lead Confederate Brigadier General Matthew D. Ector's Brigade in the C.S. Army of Tennessee. Though the brigade was at Franklin during the battle on November 30, 1864, it was on detached duty and so was not part of the active combat forces.

Considered one of the most influential individuals in western North Carolina (next to Governor Zebulon B. Vance), after the War Coleman returned to his law profession, which he practiced until his death, March 5, 1883. A lifelong bachelor, he was buried in Riverside Cemetery at Asheville, North Carolina.

COLEMAN ROAD: A road in Franklin, Tennessee, named after Confederate Colonel David Coleman, who commanded Ector's Brigade, French's Division, Stewart's Corps, C.S. Army of Tennessee.

Coleman Road runs east and west from Columbia Pike/Route 31 to Carters Creek Pike. Its eastern end is located across from present day Henpeck Lane.

COLLINS' FARM: This famous but modest homestead, built in the common "saddlebag" style of the period, is located in Franklin, Tennessee. It was owned by William C. Collins, and was originally located on the northeastern edge of nearby Carnton Plantation.

Collins purchased the 3.5 acre property in 1867 from Carnton's owner Confederate Colonel John W. McGavock.

Portions of the Battle of Franklin were fought over and around the home when Confederate William W. Loring's Division advanced northward through its yards under heavy Union fire. After the battle, Collins' Farm served as one of the town's forty-four field hospitals, and a number of soldiers were temporarily buried in the family's garden.

In 1911 Franklin attorney Thomas P. "Captain Tom" Henderson, purchased Collins' Farm. He is best known for being a member of a World War I group whose goal was to kidnap the German Kaiser Wilhelm.

Well into the 1960s, Henderson and his wife Lucille Carter entertained numerous celebrities and politicians at Collins' Farm, which has been preserved as a historic site.

COLLINS, WILLIAM C.: Born in 1823, Collins was the manager of Carnton Plantation during Lincoln's War, and was involved in the McGavock Confederate Cemetery reburial project. His daughter Malvina C. Collins, was married to George W. Cuppet, the reburial supervisor. Collins, who passed away in 1895, owned historic Collins' Farm with his wife Lucy Ellen Birch.

COLUMBIA, TENNESSEE: Settled in the early 1800s and incorporated in 1817 in what is now Maury County, Tennessee, Columbia was the boyhood home of U.S. President James K. Polk, and is the current home base for the national headquarters of the Sons of Confederate Veterans.

The town is connected to the Battle of Franklin because Confederate General John Bell Hood skirmished with Union General John M. Schofield at the Battle of Columbia, November 24-November 29, 1864, just prior to the Battles of Spring Hill and Franklin.

There were no known casualties, and, as Hood managed to drive Schofield out of Columbia and north into Spring Hill, the conflict was considered a Confederate victory.

COLUMBIA TURNPIKE: Today a bustling, heavily traveled, two-lane highway known in Franklin as Columbia Avenue, during the Battle of Franklin, Columbia Turnpike (or more commonly Columbia Pike), as it was then known, was little more than a single-lane dirt road, traversed by the occasional pedestrian, rider, or horse and buggy.

Stretching south to north from the town of Spring Hill to Franklin, in the 1860s it served as the main artery for both Confederate and Union troops, cavalries, and artillery moving through the area.

Untold thousands were wounded or killed on and around Columbia Pike during the battles of Spring Hill and Franklin, as Rebel General Hood chased Yankee General Schofield north across Tennessee in his doomed bid to reoccupy Nashville. (Earlier, on March 5, 1863, there were an estimated 2,200 Rebel and Yankee casualties around Columbia Pike during the Battle of Thompson's Station.) As such, dozens of private homes lining the road were commandeered by officers from both sides, leaving in their wake a thirty-mile line of some of America's richest history, drama, and tragedy.

Besides hosting nearly a half dozen significant battles and dozens of skirmishes, many of the War's most important military meetings took place in houses scattered along Columbia Pike. Such meetings often included heated arguments, debates, threats, chastisements, fateful decisions, and even the murder of a Confederate general by a jealous husband.

A number of these homes (mainly mansions, estates, and plantations) have been preserved and can still be seen along Columbia Avenue (modern Highway 31). And while some are now privately owned, the majority are open to the public for touring, and are part of what was once known as Middle Tennessee's "Antebellum Trail." For anyone interested in the War for Southern Independence, driving the area's Antebellum Trail is both an educational and an awe-inspiring experience.

Today, though it is still a busy suburban road, Columbia Avenue has been replaced as the main highway in the region by I-65, the 884-mile long interstate that connects, from south to north, Alabama, Tennessee, Kentucky, and Indiana.

CONFEDERACY: See Confederate States of America.

CONFEDERATE CEMETERY: See McGavock Confederate Cemetery

CONFEDERATE FLAG: There were four official Confederate flags:

- The First National (the "Stars and Bars")
- The Second National (the "Stainless Banner")
- The Third National (the "Blood-stained Banner")
- The Battle Flag (the "Soldier's Flag")

It is the last flag, the Battle Flag, that has become a symbol of contention due to its wholly inappropriate (and sacrilegious) use by racist and anti-American groups.

Purposefully designed by South Carolina state Representative William Porcher Miles and Confederate General Pierre G. T. Beauregard to sharply distinguish it from the U.S. flag on the battlefield, the C.S. Battle Flag is a true symbol of the Southern Cause: the defense of the Constitution (in particular the Ninth and Tenth Amendments) and Dixie's wonderful multiracial, multicultural heritage. Those who try to imbue the flag with racist overtones are either uneducated or are intentionally seeking to create racial strife in an overt attempt to achieve their own radical and historically inaccurate and unjustifiable agendas.

Traditional Southerners, as well as lovers of liberty everywhere, reject such efforts to defile authentic Southern history, culture, and heritage.

It is for these reasons that the Confederate Battle Flag will continue to be proudly displayed and flown across the U.S. Not to promote racial discord, but to promote a return to the Constitution of the Founding Fathers (minus the slavery clauses) and the honorable celebration of Southern culture and her history.

CONFEDERATE MONUMENT: The beautiful and moving Confederate Monument at Franklin, Tennessee's town square was erected in 1899 by Franklin Chapter #14 of the United Daughters of the Confederacy (UDC).

The unveiling took place on November 30 to mark the thirty-fifth anniversary of the Battle of Franklin. Some 10,000 people attended the ceremony, including a number of illustrious individuals and Confederate veterans.

The primary speaker was General George W. Gordon, a Battle of Franklin vet and the probable first Grand Wizard of the Ku Klux Klan—originally a generous social-welfare organization devoted to assisting Southerners of *all races* who had been debilitated by Lincoln's War.

The six foot Carrara marble man perched atop the thirty-one foot granite shaft is nicknamed "Chip," due to the piece knocked from the brim of his hat that occurred while he was being lowered into place in 1899 by horses and pulleys. Also known as the Confederate Sentry Statue, he stands at "parade rest" over the engraved words: "Our Confederate Soldier."

On the eastern face of the Vermont granite shaft the following words are engraved:

"Erected to Confederate Soldiers by Franklin Chapter No. 14, Daughters of the Confederacy, Nov. 30, A. D. 1899."

On the western face these words are engraved:

"In honor and memory of our heroes, both private and chief, of the Southern Confederacy. No country ever had truer sons, no cause nobler champions, no people bolder defenders, than the brave soldiers to whose memory this stone is erected."

On the north face:

"Would not it be a shame for us if their memory part from our land and hearts, and a wrong them to and a shame to us. The glories they won shall not wane for us. In legend and lay, our Heroes in Grey shall ever live over again for us."

On the south face:

"We who saw them and knew them well are witnesses to the coming ages of their valor and fidelity; tried and true, glory-crowned. 1861 - 1865."

For a Southern memorial, it is indeed strange that the four cannon placed around the monument are from Massachusetts, the state where both the American slave trade and American slavery began, and the state which Jefferson Davis once called the South's most violent and irrational enemy.

Worse, modern liberals, scallywags, and transplanted Yankees have begun describing Franklin's Confederate Monument as a symbol of both the Confederate *and* the Union soldier! As the foregoing quotes from the monument's engravings show, however, it is patently clear that this is not the meaning intended by its original designers, builders, and erectors. This is, after all, why it is called "*Confederate* Monument," not "Confederate and Union Monument."

Finally, it must be noted here that at the present time the Confederate Battle Flag is not allowed to be displayed at the monument. This politically correct conciliation to the anti-South movement and the uneducated is an insult to all true Southerners, particularly those who descend from Confederate soldiers.

CONFEDERATE STATES ARMY: What began as the Provisional Army of the Confederate States in February 1861, became the official Army of the Confederate States in March 1861, authorized by the Confederate Congress.

The Confederate States War Department was in control of the operation of the Confederate States Army, while Confederate President Jefferson Davis was given control over military operations.

The exact number of men in the Confederate States Army is unknown. Estimates have ranged range from 500,000 to 1.5 million. Despite such vague calculations, based on information gathered from a variety of sources, the official number was probably close to 1.3 million at its peak, nearly two thirds less than the 3 million serving in the United States Army.

Unlike most armies, the C.S. military did not have an official general-in-chief until late in the War, when General Robert E. Lee was appointed to the position by the Confederate Congress in January 1865. This was unfortunate, for it greatly hampered the army's effectiveness against the U.S. military, headed by Yankee General Ulysses S. Grant from the middle of the War onward.

The C.S. Army was comprised of the following primary independent armies (partial alphabetized list):

Army of Central Kentucky
Army of the Kanawha
Army of Kentucky
Army of Middle Tennessee
Army of Mississippi
Army of Missouri
Army of New Mexico
Army of Northern Virginia
Army of the Northwest
Army of the Peninsula
Army of the Potomac
Army of the Trans-Mississippi
Army of Tennessee
Army of the Valley
Army of the West

On the Confederate side, the Battle of Franklin was fought by the Army of Tennessee under General John Bell Hood.

It should be noted that military departments could often quickly change name and leaders as the situation required. The Army of Tennessee, for example, had over a half dozen commanders and was originally known as the Army of Mississippi.

The Confederate military was not a "racist," monoracial, all-white army, as anti-South, pro-North historians having been preaching for decades. In actual fact it was the U.S. army that was monoracial and all-white for its first two years and nearly completely racist during the entire duration of the War.

The Confederate military was quite the opposite. This nonracist, multiracial, multicultural army was unofficially comprised of about:

• 1 million European-Americans
• 300,000 (to 1 million) African-Americans
• 70,000 Native-Americans
• 60,000 Latin-Americans

- 50,000 foreigners
- 12,000 Jewish-Americans
- 10,000 Asian-Americans

The Confederate States Army was formally disbanded on April 9, 1865, the day General Lee "surrendered" to General Grant at Appomattox, Virginia—an act that the Southern leader would come to regret.

CONFEDERATE STATES OF AMERICA: The CSA was a conservative Confederate Republic, legally formed under the Constitution's Ninth and Tenth Amendments beginning in December 1860, provisionally in February 1861, and officially in February 1862. The purpose of the secession of the Southern states? To maintain the states' rights aspects of the Constitution against the liberal anti-Constitution North.

Though it sent numerous diplomats to Washington in an attempt to avoid bloodshed, when the warmongering big government progressive, U.S. President Abraham Lincoln, tricked the South into firing the first shot at Fort Sumter on April 12, 1861, the CSA had no choice but to defend herself. And so, as Lincoln disingenuously claimed, "the War came."

Four years later Lincoln's fight to kill states' rights, and force the Southern states back into what the Founding Fathers had intended to be a "voluntary union of friendly states," came to an end when attrition and simple numerical power finally wore down the Southern armies. Starving, cold, and in many cases barefoot, to many Rebel soldiers the end seemed inevitable. Despite this, Confederate President Jefferson Davis, like most of his military officers and even many Southern troops, wanted to fight on.

The compassionate and Christ-like Confederate General Robert E. Lee, however, could not bear to see his men suffer another day. And so, on April 9, 1865, he reluctantly "surrendered" his Army of Northern Virginia to Union General Ulysses S. Grant.

Lincoln's illegal, disastrous, bloody, and unnecessary War had finally come to an end. But at what cost? At the tip of a bayonet, and at the cost of thousands of lives and the near bankruptcy of the U.S. Treasury, the conservative Southern states were coerced back into a union with a liberal neighbor who did not like or respect them. All so that, as power-hungry Lincoln snidely remarked in his July 4, 1861, Message to Congress in Special Session, he could continue to "collect the revenue" of the wealthy agrarian Southern states.

The truth is that while Lincoln may have violently forced the South back into an unwanted reunion, he was not able to kill off the Confederate States of America. Indeed, no official papers were ever signed by any Southerner or Northerner dissolving the CSA, and to this day the Confederacy lives on as a great political ideal to millions of traditional Southerners and liberty loving non-Southerners.

The desire for freedom that fueled the first American Revolutionary War in 1776 is the same desire that fueled our second Revolutionary War in 1861, and it is the same desire that knocked down the Berlin Wall in 1989. It is the same one that still fires the blood in Northern Ireland, and powers the current secession movements in Russia, Spain, Scotland, China, Wales, India, Somalia, Burma, Syria, Brazil, Indonesia, and Canada, to name but a few.

Thus, for many of us here in the United States, the dream of true self-determination, personal liberty, and self-government—that is, the Confederate Cause—did not die with Lee's "surrender" in 1865.

Such a dream cannot perish, for it is written on the hearts of the people, and it will, as certainly as the Sun rises each morning, ascend upon the world once more. This is, after all, what is meant by the expression: "The South will rise again!"

CONFEDERATION: Favored by the conservative South from the beginning, a confederation is a two-tiered political body with sovereign states loosely linked to a weak central government. In a confederation the states are considered individual nations, nearly completely independent of the central government, whose sole role—according to the U.S. Constitution—is military defense.

The confederation contrasts sharply with the federation, which is comprised of weak dependent states operating under an all-powerful central government. Unfortunately for the Victorian South, the federation, with its monolithic centralized core and dictatorial like president, was the type of government preferred by liberal Lincoln and the progressive Northern states.

The confederation is in fact nearly identical to the republic, the type of government originally created for America by the thirty-nine Founding Fathers. This is why both the Founding generation and 19th Century Southerners so often referred to the original United States as both "the Confederacy" and a "Confederate Republic."

After Lincoln's illicit four-year war upon the South, however, America's confederate-styled government was altered to a centralized government, a transition that has never been, and never will be, accepted in the traditional South. Worse still, modern day liberal presidents, from Franklin D. Roosevelt into the present, have continued Lincoln's big government, socialistic, anti-Constitution policies. Conservative Southern President Thomas Jefferson is surely turning over in his grave.

Understanding the intent of the Founding Fathers and the original confederate U.S. is vital if one is to understand the Southern Confederacy that arose in 1861. For it was nothing more than an attempt by Southerners to retain the confederate form of government and the Constitution as they were originally created by those who framed the Declaration of Independence—our nation's first and foremost secession document. This is why our country's first official national charter was not called the "U.S. Constitution," it was called the "Articles of Confederation."

Amendments Nine and Ten of the U.S. Constitution, for example, tacitly guarantee both states' rights and state sovereignty, which include the full right of both accession *and* secession. Thus, when writing out the C.S. Constitution in 1861, its authors allowed each state to act in its own "sovereign and independent character."

In 1864 famed Irishman and Confederate General Patrick R. Cleburne accurately portrayed the Confederacy's fight for freedom from the U.S. when he equated it with Northern Ireland's fight for freedom from England.

Lincoln's new federal-style government, with its substantially weakened states and strong centralized core, remains in power to this day, at odds with both the republican confederacy the Founding Fathers created and the confederation that the South so valiantly but tragically fought for.

CONRAD, JOSEPH (USA): Conrad was born May 17, 1828, at Wied-Selters, Germany. After graduating from the Hesse-Darmstadt Military Academy in 1848, he emigrated to Missouri and joined the Union army at the start of Lincoln's War, becoming captain of the Third Missouri Infantry.

He fought at such battles as Carthage, Pea Ridge, Corinth, Perryville, Chickamauga, and Missionary Ridge, as well as the Atlanta Campaign.

At the Battle of Franklin, Colonel Conrad led Brigadier General Luther Bradley's Third Brigade, Wagner's Second Division, Fourth U.S. Army Corps (Bradley had been injured the day before at the Battle of Spring Hill).

Conrad left the Civil War a brigadier general, then was posted in Texas until 1866, after which he was mustered out of service. He died July 16, 1897, at Fort Randall, South Dakota, and was buried at Arlington National Cemetery.

COON, DATUS ENSIGN (USA): The son of Luke Coon and Lois Burdick, Coon was born February 20, 1831, at De Ruyter, Madison County, New York. He attended Milton Academy at Milton, Wisconsin, then taught school for several years in Iowa. It was in Iowa that he became one of the state's first newspapermen, starting up several papers in the 1850s.

In 1855 he married Hattie A. Cummins of Delhi, Iowa. Both Hattie and their one child passed away in 1857.

At the start of Lincoln's War Coon sided with the North and against the Constitution. After joining the U.S. army he organized Company One of the Second Iowa Cavalry. As a colonel, Coon commanded his own unit at the Battle of Franklin: Coon's Second Brigade, Hatch's Fifth Division, Wilson's Cavalry Corps.

After the War Coon married Jennie E. Bailey of Davenport, Iowa, with whom he had two daughters. He then moved to Alabama, grew cotton, and was elected state senator and state representative.

In 1879 he was appointed U.S. consul to Cuba by President Rutherford B. Hayes, where he stayed for six years. While living on the island, both his wife Jennie and one of their daughters died.

Coon then moved to San Diego, California, and began working in the real estate industry. On December 17, 1893, he was killed by the accidental discharge of a revolver. He was buried at Mount Hope Cemetery, San Diego, California.

COON'S SECOND BRIGADE (USA): This Yankee cavalry brigade fought at the Battle of Franklin in Hatch's Fifth Division, Wilson's Cavalry Corps.

Named after U.S. Colonel Datus Ensign Coon, it was comprised of the Second Iowa Cavalry, Sixth Illinois Cavalry, Seventh Illinois Cavalry, Ninth Illinois Cavalry, and Twelfth Tennessee Cavalry.

COOPER, JOSEPH ALEXANDER (USA): The son of John Cooper and Hester Sage, Cooper was born November 25, 1823, in Whitley County, Kentucky. He was raised in Campbell County, Tennessee, where he married Mary Hutson in 1846.

Cooper fought in the Mexican-American War, then returned to Tennessee where he took up farming near the town of Jacksboro.

At the start of Lincoln's War, Cooper sided with the North and against the Constitution. After joining the Union army, he fought at such battles as Mill Springs, Murfreesboro, Jonesboro, Bentonville, Nashville, and Chickamauga. Though his First Brigade was assigned to Ruger's Second Division, it was on detached duty at the time of the Battle of Franklin, and so was no present. Cooper was mustered out of service in early 1866, a major general.

Postbellum, former Union general and now U.S. President Ulysses S. Grant, appointed Cooper to the office of internal revenue collector at Knoxville, Tennessee.

A longtime Baptist, Cooper then moved to Stafford County, Kansas, where he once again engaged in the occupation of farming. He died there May 20, 1910, and was buried at Knoxville National Cemetery, Knoxville, Tennessee.

COOPER, SYLVESTER C. (CSA): Confederate Major Cooper led the Forty-sixth

Tennessee Infantry at the Battle of Franklin, where he was wounded in action and captured.

COOPER'S FIRST BRIGADE (USA): This Yankee infantry brigade fought at the Battle of Franklin in Ruger's Second Division, Twenty-third U.S. Army Corps.

Named after U.S. Brigadier General Joseph Alexander Cooper, it was comprised of the One hundred thirtieth Indiana, Twenty-sixth Kentucky, Twenty-fifth Michigan, Ninety-ninth Ohio, Third Tennessee, and Sixth Tennessee.

COPLEY, JOHN M. (CSA): Copley, a Tennessean, joined the Confederate army at the age of fifteen, serving in Company B, Forty-ninth Tennessee Infantry. In 1862, while he was in a hospital in Nashville recuperating from pneumonia, he was taken prisoner when the city was captured by Union troops. A Yankee friend helped him get permission to go home for the remainder of his recovery.

After he was exchanged for a Union soldier he returned to his unit and fought at the Battle of Franklin, where has was taken captive for a second time. He spent the rest of the War at the horrid Union prison Camp Douglas, in Illinois—known to Confederate soldiers as "Eighty acres of Hell."

After the War Copley took the illegal Oath of Allegiance to the U.S., returned to civilian life, and married Corrie M. Billingslea. He wrote a book in 1893 called *A Sketch of the Battle of Franklin, Tenn.; With Reminiscences of Camp Douglas*.

CORPUT'S GEORGIA BATTERY (CSA): This Rebel battery fought at the Battle of Franklin with Johnson's Battalion, Lee's Corps Artillery, C.S. Army of Tennessee.

COURTNEY, FRANCES "FANNIE": The daughter of Robert Courtney and Eliza T. Haynes, Courtney was born January 14, 1845, at Franklin, Tennessee.

A strong Union supporter, after the Battle of Franklin the teenager and her mother tended to over 100 wounded Yankee soldiers at the Presbyterian Church, the largest of the three Union field hospitals set up around the town (the other forty-one field hospitals were dedicated to Confederate soldiers).

Nicknamed Fannie, the young girl's political position on the War, of course, was not particularly popular in Franklin; especially considering the fact that several of her family members were serving under Confederate General Nathan Bedford Forrest.

After the War Courtney moved to Wyoming with her new husband, Union Lieutenant Colonel George Washington Grummond, who was killed there shortly after by Indians at the Fort Kearney Massacre, December 21, 1866. Subsequently she married the fort's post commander, U.S. Colonel (later a brigadier general) Henry Beebee Carrington.

Frances C. Carrington, as Courtney later became known, wrote a book in 1910 entitled: *My Army Life and the Fort Phil Kearney Massacre*. She passed away at Hyde Park, Massachusetts, October 17, 1911, and appears to have been buried at the town's Fairview Cemetery, along with her second husband, General Carrington, who died in 1912. Courtney's first husband Lieutenant Colonel Grummond was buried at Rest Haven Cemetery, Franklin, Tennessee.

COURTNEY'S BATTALION (CSA): This Rebel battalion fought at the Battle of Franklin in Lee's Corps Artillery, C.S. Army of Tennessee.

Led by Confederate Captain James Postell Douglas, it was comprised of Dent's Alabama Battery, Douglas' Texas Battery, and Garrity's Alabama Battery.

COWAN, GEORGE LIMERICK (CSA): The son of Robert W. Cowan and Hannah Limerick, Cowan was one of ten children. He was born October 15, 1842, at Bally Kelly, County Derry, Ireland. The family moved to Shelbyville, Bedford County, Tennessee, in 1851 and began farming.

Cowan attended the common public schools of the day and later opened up a dry goods business in Nashville.

At the start of Lincoln's War, Cowan sided with the South and the Constitution. A staunch traditionalist, after joining the Confederate army he assisted in organizing a company of men that became an escort for Rebel General Nathan Bedford Forrest. Cowan moved up the ranks, eventually attaining second lieutenant, a position he retained until the end of the War.

The young officer fought with Forrest through all of the corps' engagements, including the Battle of Franklin, and was with his commander at the cavalry's final surrender May 10, 1865, at Gainesville, Alabama.

After the War Cowan returned to Shelbyville and resumed farming and his education. In Nashville he started up a business called Kinkade, Hanley and Company, a drug firm which he operated until 1877. Subsequently he launched another business, Cowan and Company, that lasted until 1887, after which he moved to Franklin, Tennessee.

On January 3, 1884, he married Harriet Young "Hattie" McGavock, the granddaughter of Randal McGavock (founder of Carnton Plantation) and the great-granddaughter of Felix Grundy (celebrated Tennessee senator, statesman, and attorney). On the southwest portion of the Carnton estate, Cowan built a "cottage" known as Windermere (named after Hattie's mother, Caroline Winder), where the couple lived and bore five children: Carrie, John, Leah, Samuel, and Winder.

Cowan continued farming and began breeding race horses. The various positions and occupations he held throughout the latter period of his life included: trustee of the Confederate soldiers' home in Nashville; chairman of the McGavock Confederate Cemetery; secretary of the Bivouac of Confederate Soldiers; member of Hiram Lodge Number Seven, of the Free and Accepted Masons; twenty year delegate to the Grand Lodge; grand king of the state chapter; member of the Orestes Lodge Number 10, of the Knights of Pythias; Democratic (the conservatives of the day) chairman of the county executive committee; and fifteen year superintendent of Franklin's Presbyterian Sunday School.

Cowan also ran an insurance business in Franklin for seven years and was known as an expert accountant.

An ardent conservative and Confederate to the end, the well respected Scottish-Irish Southern gentleman passed away at Windermere September 18, 1919, and was buried in the Cowan family plot, Mt. Hope Cemetery, Franklin, Tennessee.

Note: Mysteriously, Cowan's funeral service was conducted by the Knights Templar, a clandestine Christian military order that officially dates from the 12th Century, but has roots that go back to the Gnostic schools of ancient Egypt. It is not known if Cowan was a member of the Knights Templar, just as it is not known why this extremely powerful, highly secretive holy order was in charge of Cowan's funeral.

What is known is that his wife Hattie was a direct descendant of Merovée (b. about 415), the first of the famed dynastic line of long-haired kings of France, who take their name from him: the Merovingians.

According to Christian mythology, King Merovée's mother, Queen Basina of France, was impregnated by a blood descendant of Jesus and his *secret* wife Mary Magdalene (see John 2:1-2), making Merovée and all of his descendants carriers of the holy blood of Jesus (i.e., the "Holy Grail").

As one of the primary roles of the Knights Templar is to protect Jesus' bloodline, it is the author's theory that this may explain their presence at Cowan's funeral, for both the lieutenant's wife and his children were blood descendants of King Merovée.

COWAN'S MISSISSIPPI BATTERY (CSA): This Rebel battery fought at the Battle of Franklin in Myrick's Battalion, Stewart's Corps Artillery, C.S. Army of Tennessee.

COX, AARON A. (CSA): Confederate Captain Cox led the Fifth Confederate Infantry at the Battle of Franklin, where he was captured by the enemy.

COX, JACOB DOLSON (USA): The son of New Yorkers Jacob Dolson Cox Sr. and Thedia Redelia Kenyon, Cox was born at Montreal, Canada, on October 27, 1828. In 1849 he married Helen Clarissa Finney, an Ohio descendant of European royalty, with whom he bore eight children.

After graduating with a degree in theology from Oberlin College in 1851, he studied law and opened up his own practice in Warren, Ohio, in 1853. While serving as a Republican (the liberals of the day) state senator in 1858, the strongly abolitionist attorney made a number of powerful political connections.

With the opening of Lincoln's War in 1861, Cox sided with the North and against the Constitution. He was soon appointed brigadier general of Ohio troops in the U.S. army, serving under such Union commanders as George B. McClellan, John Pope, and John M. Schofield, finally attaining the rank of major general.

Under General Schofield, Cox fought at the Battle of Franklin, temporarily leading the Twenty-third U.S. Army Corps of the Army of the Ohio. It was at this conflict that Cox illegally commandeered the home of Fountain Branch Carter (the Carter House) in Franklin, which he used as his headquarters.

The act was illegal because Lincoln's War itself was illegal: President Lincoln had launched his war on the South and states' rights without the approval of Congress, an express violation of the Constitution (see Article One, Section Eight, Clause Eleven). To this day, in the eyes of Dixie, this single act makes Lincoln and all of his military officers war criminals.

After the War Cox served as governor of Ohio from 1866-1867, then secretary of the interior under U.S. President Ulysses S. Grant, a position from which he resigned due to rampant corruption in the department (a common problem throughout Grant's two administrations).

During the 1870s and 1880s Cox served variously as president of the Toledo and Wabash Railway Company, as a congressman, as dean of the Cincinnati Law School, as president of the University of Cincinnati, and as president of the American Microscopical Society.

As a postwar military historian, some of Cox's writings have been condemned as political coverups, and his lukewarm approach to black civil rights made him unpopular with many Yankee abolitionists. (Cox, like Lincoln, was squarely against giving blacks the right to vote and, also like Lincoln, campaigned to have blacks put in their own separate region or state.)

While on vacation at Magnolia, Cape Ann, Massachusetts, Cox died August 4, 1900, and was buried at Spring Grove Cemetery, Cincinnati, Ohio. The Jacob D. Cox House, his Italianate home in the Queen City, still stands, and was added to the National Register of Historic Places in the 1970s.

COX, THEODORE (USA): Born September 7, 1839, at Long Island, New York, Cox was the son of Jacob Dolson Cox Sr. and Thedia Redelia Kenyon, and the brother of Union General Jacob Dolson Cox.

Cox was a captain who served under his brother as his chief of staff and as adjutant general of the Twenty-third U.S. Army Corps during the Battle of Franklin. He delivered General Cox's famous note to Union General Schofield after the battle, seeking permission to remain in Franklin and hold the Union position against Confederate General John Bell Hood's advancing forces (Schofield denied the request and moved on to Nashville).

After the War Cox became secretary and treasurer of the Little Miami Railroad Company, a position he held until his death, February 2, 1892, at Cincinnati, Ohio.

COX'S THIRD DIVISION (USA): This Yankee division, named after U.S. Brigadier General Jacob Dolson Cox, served in the Twenty-third U.S. Army Corps at the Battle of Franklin.

The Third Division was not led by Cox at Franklin, however, for he been put in temporary charge of the Twenty-third U.S. Army Corps. Thus his position as head of the division was temporarily taken over by U.S. Brigadier General James William Reilly at the battle.

The Third Division was comprised of Reilly's First Brigade, Casement's Second Brigade, and Stiles' Third Brigade.

COX'S THIRD DIVISION ARTILLERY (USA): This Yankee artillery unit fought at the Battle of Franklin in the Twenty-third U.S. Army Corps. It was comprised of the Twenty-third Indiana Battery and the First Ohio Battery.

CRITTENDEN, ROBERT F. (CSA): Confederate Colonel Crittenden led the Thirty-third Alabama Infantry at the Battle of Franklin, where he was captured by the enemy.

CROSSLAND, EDWARD (CSA): The son of Samuel Crossland and Elizabeth Harry, he was born June 30, 1827, in Hickman County, Kentucky. He practiced law and served as both a sheriff and a Kentucky state representative.

Crossland married Mary Hess and had several children, among them: Samuel H. Crossland, Jefferson D. Crossland, and Catherine Crossland, who married Montana Governor Robert Burns Smith.

With the start of Lincoln's War, Crossland sided with the South and the Constitution. After joining the Confederate army he eventually served as colonel of the Seventh Kentucky Infantry. He was later given a brigade in Brigadier General Abraham Buford's Division of General Nathan Bedford Forrest's Cavalry, which fought at the Battle of Franklin.

After the War Crossland served as a court judge and a Kentucky congressman. He passed away at Mayfield, Graves County, Kentucky, on September 11, 1881, and was buried in the town's Maplewood Cemetery.

CROSSLAND'S BRIGADE (CSA): This Rebel cavalry brigade fought at the Battle of Franklin in Buford's Division, Forrest's Cavalry Corps, C.S. Army of Tennessee.

Named after its commander Confederate Colonel Edward Crossland, it was comprised of the Third Kentucky Mounted Infantry, Seventh Kentucky Mounted Infantry, Eighth Kentucky Mounted Infantry, Twelfth Kentucky Mounted Infantry, Twelfth Kentucky Cavalry, and Huey's Kentucky Battalion.

CROXTON, JOHN THOMAS (USA): Croxton was born November 20, 1836, at Paris, Kentucky, on a large plantation. After graduating with honors from Yale University, he studied and taught law, then became a practicing attorney in Kentucky. Like most Southerners, he was an abolitionist. Croxton married Catherine Rogers and had several children.

With the start of Lincoln's War, he sided with the North and against the Constitution. After joining the Union army, he served as lieutenant colonel of the Fourth Kentucky Mounted Infantry. As a brigadier general, he led the First Brigade in the cavalry corps of Yankee Major General James H. Wilson at the Battle of Franklin.

In early April 1865, Croxton and his troops attacked Tuscaloosa, Alabama, and were directly responsible for burning down not only much of the town, but most of the buildings belonging to the University of Alabama. Why Yankees waged war on civilians, schools, and businesses is a question that is still being asked in the South to this day.

What is known is that these war crimes, sanctioned by none other than President Abraham Lincoln, were against both universal military law and the Geneva Conventions.

After the War, at which time Croxton was breveted major general, he supported the North's brutal, illegal, and unnecessary Reconstruction policies by commanding a military district at Macon, Georgia.

After resigning from Union service in December 1865, the politically liberal general returned to his farm at Paris, Kentucky, where he once again took up the practice of law. In 1873, President Ulysses S. Grant assigned him the position of U.S. minister to Bolivia, and he moved his family to La Paz.

Croxton died at age thirty-seven in Bolivia on April 16, 1874. His remains were brought back to Paris, where he was buried at the town's Paris Cemetery.

CROXTON'S FIRST BRIGADE (USA): This Yankee cavalry brigade fought at the Battle of Franklin in McCook's First Division, Wilson's Cavalry Corps.

Named after U.S. Brigadier General John Thomas Croxton, it was comprised of the Eighth Iowa Cavalry, Fourth Kentucky Mounted Infantry, Second Michigan Cavalry, and First Tennessee Cavalry.

CUMMINGS' BRIGADE (CSA): This Rebel infantry brigade fought at the Battle of Franklin in Stevenson's Division, Lee's Corps, C.S. Army of Tennessee.

Led by Confederate Colonel Elihu P. Watkins, it was comprised of the Twenty-fourth Georgia, Thirty-sixth Georgia, Thirty-ninth Georgia, and Fifty-sixth Georgia.

CUNNINGHAM, CHARLES J. L. (CSA): Confederate Colonel Cunningham led the Fifty-seventh Alabama Infantry at the Battle of Franklin, where he was wounded in action.

CUNNINGHAM, SUMNER ARCHIBALD (CSA): Cunningham, the son of John

Washington Campbell Cunningham and Mary Ann Buchanan, was born on a farm on July 21, 1843, in Bedford County, Tennessee.

With the onset of Lincoln's War, Cunningham sided with the South and the Constitution, serving as sergeant of Company B, Forty-First Tennessee Infantry, which fought at the Battle of Franklin.

He fought earlier at the Battle of Fort Donelson, where he was captured, imprisoned, and later exchanged. After Franklin he fought at the equally doomed Battle of Nashville.

Following the War, Cunningham married Laura Davis and became a journalist. He came to own and edit several newspapers, including *The Shelbyville Commercial* and *The Chattanooga Times*.

In 1893 he founded, edited, and published the popular pro-South magazine, *Confederate Veteran*, which is in publication to this day.

He passed away on December 13, 1913, in Nashville, Tennessee, and was buried at Willow Mount Cemetery, Shelbyville, Bedford County, Tennessee. Engraved on his headstone are these wonderful words: "He gathered the history of his people, written in tears but radiant with glory."

CUPPET, GEORGE W.: Born in 1833, at Preston, Virginia (now West Virginia), he was the brother of Marcellus Cuppet, and the reburial supervisor of the McGavock Confederate Cemetery project in the Spring of 1866.

Cuppet was probably given the job due to the fact that he was married to Malvina C. Collins, the daughter of William C. Collins, the manager of Carnton Plantation—the property on which the cemetery was to be established.

CUPPET, MARCELLUS: Cuppet, the son of John Jacob Cuppet and Eva Fearer, was born January 16, 1841, in what is now West Virginia. In 1866 he was assigned the task of managing the reburial project at the McGavock Confederate Cemetery, Carnton Plantation, Franklin, Tennessee.

Cuppet got the job because he was the brother of the reburial supervisor George W. Cuppet, who was the son-in-law of William C. Collins, the manager of Franklin's Carnton Plantation during Lincoln's War.

Contrary to Carnton legend, Cuppet was not African-American or a former Carnton servant.

On April 26, 1866, during the midst of the project, Cuppet died of a heart attack, and was buried in the Texas section of the cemetery—making him the only civilian known to be interred there.

DARDEN'S MISSISSIPPI BATTERY (CSA): This Rebel battery fought at the Battle of Franklin in Myrick's Battalion, Stewart's Corps Artillery, C.S. Army of Tennessee.

DAVIDSON, FRANCIS M. (USA): At the Battle of Franklin, Union Major Davidson commanded the Fourteenth Illinois Cavalry, Biddle's Second Brigade, Hatch's Fifth Division Artillery, Wilson's Cavalry Corps.

DAVIS, JEFFERSON (CSA): First—and so far—the only president of the Southern Confederacy, Davis was born June 3, 1808, in Christian (now Todd) County, Kentucky. His father, Samuel Emory Davis, was a Revolutionary War veteran.

Raised in Mississippi, Davis later attended Kentucky's Transylvania University, after which he began schooling at West Point at the age of sixteen.

Upon graduating from the military academy in 1828, he began serving in the U.S. army. In 1831 he fought in the Black Hawk War, winning the respect of those Indians he captured on account of his kindness and mercy.

Davis resigned from the military in 1835 and, on June 17 of that year, he married Sarah Knox Taylor (the daughter of future U.S. President Zachary Taylor) near Louisville, Kentucky. During a trip to Louisiana a few months later, Sarah contracted malaria and died.

Now a cotton planter and the owner of a large farm, "Brierfield," Davis soon became involved in politics. He belonged to the traditional school of Southern conservatism, and advocated states' rights, limited government, and strict constitutionalism.

In 1845 he married his second wife, Varina Howell, and was elected a congressman. In 1846 he resigned to fight in the

Mexican-American War, gallantly commanding a Mississippi regiment.

Following that conflict, Davis was elected state senator and began campaigning for Southern rights. In 1853 he became secretary of war under Franklin Pierce, our fourteenth U.S. president and a rare Yankee leader who was sympathetic to the South.

With the secession of the Southern states Davis reluctantly accepted his selection as president of Dixie's new constitutionally formed country, the Confederate States of America, and was inaugurated on February 18, 1861.

According to Franklin, Tennessee, legend, President Davis personally authorized Confederate Colonel John W. McGavock, the owner of Carnton Plantation, to use his famous estate as a Confederate field hospital during Lincoln's War. On November 30, 1864, during, and for six months after the Battle of Franklin, it was turned over to the Confederacy for just that purpose.

Though Davis was an outstanding military man, a refined Southern gentleman, and a brilliant intellectual who led the Confederacy through four painfully difficult years, his administration was marred by favoritism, cronyism, petty quarreling among his officers, and lack of focus.

In November 1864 he began promoting the idea of emancipating slaves and enlisting them in the C.S. army. Although African-Americans had been serving unofficially in the Confederate military from the very beginning, in March 1865 he began official black enlistment. The effort, however, was too late: General Robert E. Lee surrendered only a month later.

Assuming that the remaining Confederate forces could keep the conflict alive for another year or so (he was correct), Davis and his family fled south to reassemble his armies. He was captured, shackled, jailed, and nearly died in prison. The charge against him? "Treason against the United States of America," an accusation that was as illegal as it was absurd.

Davis begged to be tried and put on the witness stand, but no lawyer would take his case. For everyone knew that under the scrutiny of a court of law, the constitutional right of secession would be upheld and the U.S.

government's many illicit actions during the Civil War would be exposed!

After release from his two year prison sentence, Davis wrote several important books, gave speeches, and traveled throughout Europe.

The great Southern statesman died at New Orleans, Louisiana, on December 6, 1889. Though he was first buried there in Metairie Cemetery, in 1893 his wife Varina had his body taken back to Virginia, where he was buried in Hollywood Cemetery at Richmond.

For his nobility, sacrifices for the Southern Cause, and his devotion to Confederate ideals, Davis will always be regarded as a hero across the South.

DAVIS, NEWTON N. (CSA): Confederate Colonel Davis led the Twenty-fourth Alabama Infantry at the Battle of Franklin, where he was wounded in action.

DAVIS' FORD: A crossing on the Duck River, located a few miles east of Columbia, Tennessee. The ford was an important transit point for Confederate troops prior to the Battle of Franklin.

DEAS, ZACHARIAH CANTEY (CSA): The son of James Sutherland Deas and Margaret Rebecca Chesnut, Deas was born October 25, 1819, at Camden, South Carolina, and was a cousin of Confederate General James Chesnut—the husband of famed Southern diarist Mary (Boykin) Chesnut.

Deas grew up in Alabama, fought in the Mexican-American War, and married Helen Gaines Lyon in 1853.

He made a fortune in the Alabama cotton brokerage business, then, siding with the South and the Constitution, joined the Confederate army at the start of Lincoln's War.

Using his own money, he outfitted the Twenty-second Alabama Infantry, and rose to the rank of brigadier general. He fought at the Battles of Shiloh, Murfreesboro, Chattanooga, and Chickamauga. At the Battle of Franklin, where he was wounded, he led his own unit: Deas' Brigade, Johnson's Division, Lee's Corps, C.S. Army of Tennessee.

After the War Deas moved to New York City, where he became a successful stock broker. He passed away there on March 6, 1882, and was buried in the Bronx's Woodlawn Cemetery.

DEAS' BRIGADE (CSA): This Rebel infantry brigade fought at the Battle of Franklin in Johnson's Division, Lee's Corps, C.S. Army of Tennessee.

Named after Confederate Brigadier General Zachariah Cantey Deas, it was comprised of the Nineteenth Alabama, Twenty-second Alabama, Twenty-fifth Alabama, Thirty-ninth Alabama, and the Fiftieth Alabama.

DENT'S ALABAMA BATTERY (CSA): This Rebel battery fought at the Battle of Franklin with Courtney's Battalion, Lee's Corps Artillery, C.S. Army of Tennessee.

DIBRELL'S BRIGADE (CSA): Named for Confederate Brigadier General George Gibbs Dibrell, several detached regiments from his brigade were present at the Battle of Spring Hill and the Battle of Franklin, serving primarily in Biffle's Brigade, Chalmers' Division, Forrest's Cavalry Corps, C.S. Army of Tennessee.

Dibrell himself was not at Franklin, having been sent to serve under Joseph E. Johnston after the Battle of First Dalton.

DIXON, M. H. (CSA): Confederate Major Dixon led the Third Confederate Infantry at the Battle of Franklin, where he was captured by the enemy.

DOUGLAS, JAMES POSTELL (CSA): The son of Alexander Douglas and Margaret T. Cowsar, Douglas was born January 7, 1836, in Lancaster County, South Carolina, and was raised at Talladega, Alabama, and later at Tyler, Texas.

As a young man his occupations included mail deliveryman, principal of the Tyler Male Academy, lawyer, and newspaperman.

With the outbreak of Lincoln's War Douglas sided with the South and the Constitution. After joining the Confederate army he advanced rapidly up the ranks, finally leading his own unit: Douglas' Battery.

He fought at such battles as Murfreesboro, Chickamauga, Chattanooga, and Atlanta. At the Battle of Franklin he commanded Courtney's Battalion, Lee's Corps Artillery, Army of Tennessee. At the Battle of Nashville, while he was covering

Hood's southward retreat, Douglas lost his guns when they became stuck in the mud.

After the War he returned to Tyler, Texas, and resumed his newspaper work. He also served as a conservative state senator, and was deeply involved in fighting the North's harsh and illegal "Reconstruction" policies.

Married twice, first to Sallie Susan White (in 1864) and second to Alice Earle Smith (in 1874), he bore a total of ten children with both women.

Douglas went on to launch several railroads. Also a wealthy planter, he owned a chain of canning factories as well as East Texas' first peach farm.

Captain Douglas passed away November 27, 1901, and was buried in Tyler's Oakwood Cemetery.

DOUGLAS' TEXAS BATTERY (CSA): This Rebel battery fought at the Battle of Franklin with Courtney's Battalion, Lee's Corps Artillery, C.S. Army of Tennessee.

DOZIER, N. B.: The wife of Nathaniel B. Dozier of Company G of the Fourth Tennessee Cavalry, Mrs. Dozier (her maiden name is unknown) was a courageous and patriotic Southerner, who in the early 1900s, promoted the idea of establishing a national military park and cemetery in Franklin in honor of those who fought and died at the Battle of Franklin.

Mrs. Dozier's entreaties to the U.S. House of Representatives went unheeded, and 100 years later the Battle of Franklin has still not received the national attention it deserves.

DUCK RIVER: Nearly 300 miles in length, the Duck is the longest river in Tennessee and one of the most biologically diverse rivers in the U.S.

Where it flows through the town of Columbia, the river played an important role in the days before the Battle of Franklin.

In particular, during the Battle of Columbia (November 24-29, 1864), the Duck served as a central point, hindering and protecting both Confederate and Union forces as they passed over it on their way north.

DYER, SAMUEL M. (CSA): Confederate Colonel Dyer led the Third Mississippi Infantry at the Battle of Franklin, where he was wounded in action.

ECTOR, MATTHEW DUNCAN (CSA): Ector was born February 28, 1822, in Putnam County, Georgia. He attended college in Kentucky, became a lawyer, and served as a Georgia congressman.

After moving to Texas in 1851, he married Letitia Graham and was elected to the state legislature in 1855. His wife passed away in 1859, and in 1864 he married Sallie P. Chew. Their daughter Anne Ector, subsequently married Ruffin Pleasant, the governor of Louisiana.

With the onset of Lincoln's War, Ector sided with the South and the Constitution. After joining the Confederate army, he rose up the ranks, eventually attaining brigadier general. He fought at the Battles of Murfreesboro, Richmond, and Chickamauga. During the Atlanta Campaign his left leg was so badly injured it had to be amputated.

Ector's Brigade served with the Army of Tennessee in Samuel G. French's Division. During the Battle of Franklin, however, Ector himself was still recovering from his amputation, and his brigade, though present, was on detached duty under the command of Colonel David Coleman, and so saw no action there as a result.

After the War Ector returned to Texas where he worked in the judicial system until his death in Tyler on October 29, 1879. He was buried in Greenwood Cemetery, Marshall, Texas. A county in the Lone Star State was named after him.

ECTOR'S BRIGADE (CSA): This Rebel infantry brigade served in French's Division, Stewart's Corps, C.S. Army of Tennessee.

Led by Confederate Colonel David Coleman, the brigade was comprised of the Twenty-ninth North Carolina Infantry, Thirtieth North Carolina Infantry, Ninth Texas

Infantry, Tenth Texas Cavalry, Fourteenth Texas Cavalry, and Thirty-second Texas Cavalry.

Coleman was put in command of Ector's Brigade while its original leader Brigadier General Matthew Duncan Ector was recovering from a leg amputation. The brigade was at Franklin, Tennessee, during the Battle of Franklin. However, it was not involved in actual combat as it was on detached duty at the time.

EIGHTEENTH ALABAMA (CSA): This Rebel infantry regiment fought at the Battle of Franklin in Holtzclaw's Brigade, Clayton's Division, Lee's Corps, C.S. Army of Tennessee.

EIGHTEENTH TEXAS CAVALRY - DISMOUNTED (CSA): This Rebel unit fought at the Battle of Franklin in Granbury's Brigade, Cleburne's Division, Cheatham's Corps, C.S. Army of Tennessee.

EIGHTH ARKANSAS (CSA): This Rebel infantry regiment fought at the Battle of Franklin in Govan's Brigade, Cleburne's Division, Cheatham's Corps, C.S. Army of Tennessee.

EIGHTH IOWA (USA): This Yankee cavalry regiment fought at the Battle of Franklin in Croxton's First Brigade, McCook's First Division, Wilson's Cavalry Corps.

EIGHTH KANSAS (USA): This Yankee infantry regiment fought at the Battle of Franklin in Streight's First Brigade, Wood's Third Division, Fourth U.S. Army Corps.

EIGHTH KENTUCKY MOUNTED INFANTRY (CSA): This Rebel unit fought at the Battle of Franklin in Crossland's Brigade, Buford's Division, Forrest's Cavalry Corps, C.S. Army of Tennessee.

EIGHTH MICHIGAN CAVALRY (USA): This Yankee cavalry regiment fought at the Battle of Franklin in Biddle's Second Brigade, Johnson's Sixth Division, Wilson's Cavalry Corps.

EIGHTH MISSISSIPPI (CSA): This Rebel infantry regiment fought at the Battle of Franklin in Lowrey's Brigade, Cleburne's Division, Cheatham's Corps, C.S. Army of Tennessee.

EIGHTH TENNESSEE (CSA): This Rebel infantry regiment fought at the Battle of Franklin in Maney's Brigade, Brown's Division, Cheatham's Corps, C.S. Army of Tennessee.

EIGHTH TENNESSEE (USA): This Yankee infantry regiment fought at the Battle of Franklin in Reilly's First Brigade, Cox's Third Division, Twenty-third U.S. Army Corps.

EIGHTH TENNESSEE CAVALRY (USA): This Yankee cavalry regiment fought at the Battle of Franklin in Johnson's Second Brigade, Knipe's Seventh Division, Wilson's Cavalry Corps.

EIGHTIETH ILLINOIS (USA): This Yankee infantry regiment fought at the Battle of Franklin in Grose's Third Brigade, Kimball's First Division, Fourth U.S. Army Corps.

EIGHTIETH INDIANA (USA): This Yankee infantry regiment fought at the Battle of Franklin in Moore's Second Brigade, Ruger's Second Division, Twenty-third U.S. Army Corps.

EIGHTY-EIGHTH ILLINOIS (USA): This Yankee infantry regiment fought at the Battle of Franklin in Opdycke's First Brigade, Wagner's Second Division, Fourth U.S. Army Corps.

EIGHTY-FIRST INDIANA (USA): This Yankee infantry regiment fought at the Battle of Franklin in Kirby's First Brigade, Kimball's First Division, Fourth U.S. Army Corps.

EIGHTY-FOURTH ILLINOIS (USA): This Yankee infantry regiment fought at the Battle of Franklin in Grose's Third Brigade, Kimball's First Division, Fourth U.S. Army Corps.

EIGHTY-FOURTH INDIANA (USA): This Yankee infantry regiment fought at the Battle of Franklin in Grose's Third Brigade, Kimball's First Division, Fourth U.S. Army Corps.

EIGHTY-NINTH ILLINOIS (USA): This Yankee infantry regiment fought at the Battle of Franklin in Streight's First Brigade, Wood's Third Division, Fourth U.S. Army Corps.

EIGHTY-SIXTH INDIANA (USA): This Yankee infantry regiment fought at the Battle of Franklin in Beatty's Third Brigade, Wood's Third Division, Fourth U.S. Army Corps.

ELDRIDGE'S BATTALION (CSA): This Rebel battalion fought at the Battle of Franklin in Lee's Corps Artillery, C.S. Army of Tennessee.

Led by Confederate Captain Charles E. Fenner, it was comprised of the Eufaula Alabama Battery, Fenner's Louisiana Battery, and Stanford's Mississippi Battery.

ELEVENTH INDIANA CAVALRY (USA): This Yankee cavalry regiment fought at the Battle of Franklin in Stewart's First Brigade, Hatch's Fifth Division, Wilson's Cavalry Corps.

ELEVENTH TENNESSEE (CSA): This Rebel infantry regiment fought at the Battle of Franklin in Vaughan's Brigade, Brown's Division, Cheatham's Corps, C.S. Army of Tennessee.

ELM SPRINGS: Located in Columbia, Tennessee, this two-story brick antebellum estate was built in 1837 by Nathan Vaught, a master builder from Maury County, for two Irish brothers, James and Nathaniel Dick.

During Lincoln's War Elm Springs was marked for burning by Union troops, and was only saved by the brave efforts of Confederate General Frank C. Armstrong and his men.

The historic Greek Revival home has been lived in by several different families since its construction, and is today owned by the Sons of Confederate Veterans, who use Elm Springs as their national headquarters.

EMANCIPATION PROCLAMATION: U.S. President Abraham Lincoln wrote out four versions of the Emancipation Proclamation (two of them drafts). Unfortunately, only the fourth and final version, issued January 1, 1863, is known to the general public.

What the average person does not realize is that the racist Yankee leader had to be badgered and even bullied for several years before he issued the final version. Why? Because, as he often said in his speeches, he had no interest in black civil rights, disliked abolitionists, considered abolition even more dangerous than slavery, and merely wanted to stop the spread of slavery—not slavery itself.

Thus the issuance of the Final Emancipation Proclamation was not for the benefit of blacks, but for the benefit of Lincoln and his white soldiers. In the proclamation itself Lincoln refers to it as nothing more than a "fit and necessary war measure for suppressing said rebellion."

This is why he often publicly called it, not a *civil rights* emancipation," but a *"military* emancipation," exposing the true reason he published it to begin with: by 1863 he desperately needed black soldiers to replace the thousands of white soldiers he had lost due to defection, desertion, disease, injuries, and death.

Lincoln's Preliminary Emancipation Proclamation, issued a few months earlier on September 22, 1862, is even more revealing as to Lincoln's actual feelings toward African-Americans and abolition. Included in it is the following remarkable clause:

". . . it is my purpose, upon the next meeting of Congress to again recommend the adoption of a practical measure tendering pecuniary aid to the free acceptance or rejection of all slave States, so called, the people whereof may not then be in rebellion against the United States and which States may then have voluntarily adopted, or thereafter may voluntarily adopt, immediate or gradual abolition of slavery within their respective limits; and that the effort to colonize persons of African descent, with their consent, upon this continent, or elsewhere, with the previously obtained consent of the Governments existing there, will be continued."

Lincoln here is clearly in no hurry to end the "peculiar institution." Instead, he says that the Southern states may "voluntarily adopt, immediate or gradual abolition of slavery."

Even more explicit is Lincoln's next statement, in which he declares that his campaign to deport all blacks out of the United States (known then as colonization) "will be continued." A lifelong member and Illinois chapter leader of the Yankee invented American Colonization Society, Lincoln wholly backed the organization's ultimate goal to make America "white from coast to coast." Their remedy to ridding the U.S. of its black population? As Lincoln so often phrased it in his public speeches, ship them all "back to their native land."

While pro-North writers have done their best to hide the

real Lincoln, the president's words themselves continue to betray the truth, as they did during his Second Annual Message to Congress on December 1, 1862:

"I cannot make it better known than it already is, that I strongly favor colonization."

Only four years earlier, during a speech at Springfield, Illinois, on July 17, 1858, the anti-black president had said:

"What I would most desire would be the separation of the white and black races."

His feelings concerning colonization and American apartheid never changed. Union General Benjamin F. "The Beast" Butler testified that only a few days before Lincoln's assassination, the president called him to his office at the White House to discuss his latest ideas on how to rid the nation of its African-American population. This is the same man that Lincoln worshipers and the uneducated continue to call the "Great Emancipator."

In the end, neither the Preliminary or the Final Emancipation Proclamation freed any slaves, either in the North or the South, for being a "military emancipation," it was only activated in those parts of the South that had been captured by the Union army. All other areas, which included the entire North and areas of the South still under Confederate control, were, in the proclamation's words to be "left precisely as if this proclamation were not issued."

As the leader of a country has no authority to pass laws in any other, Lincoln had no authority whatsoever to issue the Emancipation Proclamation in the Confederate States of America. Thus no slaves were freed, and life went on across the South just as it had before.

Lincoln's illegal racist decree certainly had no effect on the whites and blacks of Franklin, Tennessee: sixty-five blacks fought at the Battle of Franklin with Confederate General Nathan Bedford Forrest alone.

South Carolina diarist Mary Chesnut noted that after the proclamation came out, nothing changed. Contented black servants could still be seen working in the fields of Dixie, whistling and singing as they went—as if the proclamation had never been issued.

ENFILADE FIRE: From the French word *enfiler*, meaning "to thread," enfilade fire refers to gunfire that is raked along the length—that is, along the sides—of an enemy battle line. This method was used to great and destructive effect by both the Confederacy and the Union throughout Lincoln's War.

ENTRENCHMENT: A defensive hole dug into the ground. One of the many reasons the South lost the War was because of old-fashioned traditional generals, like John Bell Hood, who thought that shooting from trenches was "unmanly."

The preference of such officers was to march their troops in long lines directly toward the enemy, a tactic dating from ancient Roman times and which was already obsolete by the start of Lincoln's War.

This is precisely what occurred at the Battle of Franklin, and certainly accounts for much of the Confederacy's great loss of life there.

EUFAULA ALABAMA BATTERY (CSA): This Rebel battery fought at the Battle of Franklin with Eldridge's Battalion, Lee's Corps Artillery, C.S. Army of Tennessee.

EVERBRIGHT: The name of Franklin, Tennessee's Bostick House, as it is also known, the home was located near Carters Creek Pike. During Lincoln's War it was owned by Rebecca Letitia Bostick (née Cannon), the widow of Richard Whitman Hyde Bostick—the great-grandson of Bethenia Perkins of Halifax County, Virginia.

According to local legend, during the Battle of Franklin Rebecca's son Cannon was injured nearby. He managed to make his way home, where Mrs. Bostick hid him from the Yanks. Today a number of Franklin streets memorialize the family and their house: Everbright Avenue, Bostick Street, Cannon Street, and Perkins Drive.

EWING, SUSAN LEE: The daughter of Herbert Ewing and Sally Hughes, Ewing was born April 4, 1863, at Brentwood, Tennessee. On February 5, 1883, she married Winder McGavock, the grandson of Randal McGavock, founder of Franklin's famed Carnton Plantation. The couple had five children together.

After Winder's death in 1907, Susie, as she was known, inherited Carnton. Unable to maintain the huge estate, she sold it in 1911 and moved with her remaining family members to downtown Franklin.

Ewing died October 25, 1931, and was buried in the McGavock family plot at Mount Hope Cemetery, Franklin, Tennessee.

FACTORY, THE: Located in Franklin, Tennessee, this old manufacturing facility, recently transformed into a modern shopping center, was the site of Yankee fortifications as well as fighting during the Battle of Franklin III, December 17, 1864.

FARRELL, MIKE (CSA): Confederate Colonel Farrell led the Fifteenth Mississippi Infantry at the Battle of Franklin, where he was wounded in action. He later died from his injuries.

FEATHERSTON, WINFIELD SCOTT (CSA): Featherston was born August 8, 1820, in Murfreesboro, Rutherford County, Tennessee, the son of Charles Featherston and Lucy Pitts. Of English heritage (descending from the Featherstones of Yorkshire and Staffordshire), in 1836, while attending school in Georgia, he fought in the Creek War as a volunteer. In 1840 he became a lawyer, after which the Democrat (the conservatives of the day) was elected to Congress, serving from 1847 to 1851.

Featherston married Mary Holt Harris, the daughter of Thomas W. Harris Sr. and Harriet Hines Hold, on November 14, 1848, in Lowndes County, Mississippi. He married a second time to Elizabeth M. "Lizzie" McEwen in 1858 at Holly Springs, Marshall County, Mississippi. It is said that Elizabeth's father, Alexander C. McEwen, an early settler of the area, gave Holly Springs its name.

An ardent secessionist, in 1860 Featherston worked as a special commissioner traveling to various Southern states, such as Kentucky, to encourage them to join the Confederacy. He himself enlisted in the Confederate Army in 1861, becoming colonel of the Seventeenth Mississippi. With the Seventeenth he fought at the First Battle of Manassas and at Leesburg, and in March 1862 was promoted to the rank of brigadier general.

On June 30, 1862, the Tennessean was wounded at the Battle of Glendale (part of the Seven Days battles), in Henrico County, Virginia. He was later reassigned to the division of General William Wing Loring, at which time he commanded the Third Brigade at the Battle of Champion's Hill (Baker's Creek).

Featherston also fought under Confederate General James Longstreet in the Northern Army of Virginia, and was present at the Battles of Sharpsburg, Peachtree Creek, Harper's Ferry, Fredericksburg, Vicksburg, Resaca, and Franklin, where he was noted, by William Dudley Gale and others, for his bravery.

Later, in his report on the ill-fated Battle of Franklin, Featherston stated that the flag of the Thirty-third had been captured when the color-bearer was killed by the enemy, "his body falling in the trench, the colors falling in the works." Featherston's brigade was surrendered on April 26, 1865 along with Confederate General Joseph E. Johnston's army.

After the War Featherston returned to Mississippi to practice law. Here, he was appointed to the Mississippi legislature, serving from 1876 to 1878, and also from 1880 to 1882, and in 1887 he became a judge of the Second Judicial Circuit Court. In September 1878 his wife Elizabeth died, along with two of the Featherston children, during the epidemic of yellow fever that swept through Marshall County.

Featherston passed away thirteen years later, on May 28, 1891, and was buried in Hillcrest Cemetery, "the Little Arlington of the South," at Holly Springs, Marshall County, Mississippi, alongside numerous other Confederate heroes.

FEATHERSTON'S BRIGADE (CSA): This infantry brigade fought at the Battle of Franklin in Loring's Division, Stewart's Corps, C.S. Army of Tennessee.

Named after Confederate Brigadier General Winfield Scott Featherston, it was comprised of the First Mississippi, Third Mississippi, Twenty-second Mississippi, Thirty-first Mississippi, Thirty-third Mississippi, Fortieth Mississippi, and First Mississippi Battalion Sharpshooters.

FEDERAL ARCHITECTURE: The Federal architectural style is named after the Federal era, which, in America, roughly spanned the years from 1780 to 1830. This period included the founding of America's federal government, hence the name.

A few decades after Herculaneum (discovered in 1738) and Pompeii (discovered in 1748) were first being unearthed by archaeologists in Italy, a young United States of America was searching for a unifying style of architecture. Early Americans, like Europeans themselves, were fascinated by the discovery of these two ancient Roman cities, which had been destroyed by the eruption of Mount Vesuvius in the year 79 CE.

It was only natural then that 18th-Century American architects, such as President Thomas Jefferson, would draw inspiration from structures like the 2,000 year-old Roman temple in France known as the *Maison Quaree of Nismes*, which was used as a blueprint for the Capital Building in Richmond, Virginia. The stunning Romanesque visage of the new governmental building was a great success with the public, and soon the entire nation was caught up in the classical Federal rage.

The Federal style, which developed out of the English Georgian style, borrowed traditional characteristics from English architects, such as simple symmetrical lines, with an added unique American element: a plain and austere exterior. This look found great appeal in Puritanical New England where support for the Federal style government was strongest.

In embracing the Federal style, it became the architectural embodiment of late 18th- and early 19th-Century America: elegant, serious, steadfast, unpretentious, and powerful. Noted American Federal architects include: Jefferson, Charles Bullfinch, Samuel McIntire, Alexander Parris, and William Thornton, a British-American who is known for being the first architect of the U.S. capitol.

Common features of the Federal style are a fanlight window over the front door, narrow side windows, low-pitched roof, smooth facade, slender columns, large windows with numerous small panes, pediments over windows, oval rooms (an example being the White House's Oval Office), emphasis on the main entrance area, arched or circular windows, and use of the eagle, the archetypal Federal symbol. The paint colors most often used during the Federal period were red, ochre, white, and yellow.

Federal architecture, which led to the equally popular Greek Revival style, was just as revered in the South as it was in the North, and numerous Federal-style domestic and civic buildings associated with the Battle of Franklin in 1864 still survive. Among the best known is Carnton Mansion (which also incorporates Georgian and Greek Revival elements).

Though not connected to the Battle of Franklin, America's best-known example of Federal architecture (combined with Roman Neoclassicism) is Thomas Jefferson's home, Monticello, begun in 1769 and finished in 1809.

FEDERAL GOVERNMENT: A political body or community possessing a number of semi-self-governing regions, called "states," that are connected by a strong centralized national government. Together, these two entities (the states and the central government) form a federation, the laws of which are constitutionally based, creating a type of government known as federalism.

While the states of a federal government retain limited residuary powers of self-governorship, they surrender their individual sovereignty to the core central government with its strong authoritarian powers.

Today the United States operates as a federal government. This is not what the original thirty-nine framers intended, however. In 1781, with the ratification of the Articles of Confederation, they adopted a form of government called a confederate republic (also known as a confederacy or a republic for short)—a reaction against the monarchies of Old Europe. Indeed, the U.S. was called the "Confederacy" from 1781 to 1789 (hence the name of its constitution: The Articles of Confederation).

In a confederate republic supreme power resides within the body of its citizens, not in the government. Thus the Preamble of the Constitution begins with these words: "We the people . . ."

The sovereignty of the people and of the individual states is clearly described in the Tenth Amendment of the Bill of Rights:

"The powers not delegated to the United States by the Constitution, nor prohibited by it to the States, are reserved to the States respectively, or to the people."

A confederate republic is then, in every way, literally a government by the people, for the people, quite the opposite of a federation, which has more in common with a monarchy.

Why and when did the U.S. government change from a republic to a federation? Because of the election, in November 1860, of big government liberal Abraham Lincoln to the presidency—a man who held no affection for the South and its individualistic, freedom-loving citizens. Lincoln, who publicly proclaimed his distaste for the Founders' Constitution, preferred a federal style government to the confederate republican style government the Founders had put in place, and he set about to make the changeover—at whatever the cost.

Lincoln's political agenda, to completely alter the type of government the U.S. operates under, was, in large part, the root cause of the "Civil War." For the liberal North favored Lincoln's federal style government (with its strong centralized authority), while the conservative South favored the original confederate republican style of government as created by the Founding generation (which emphasized state sovereignty).

The U.S. Pledge of Allegiance, written by Francis Bellamy in 1892, hints at our country's original confederate form of government:

"I pledge allegiance to the flag of the United States of America, and to the Republic for which it stands . . ."

With Lincoln's federal government now installed, however, the following wording would be more accurate:

"I pledge allegiance to the flag of the United States of America, and to the Federation for which it stands . . ."

What is left out of our pro-North history books is the fact that the seceding Southern states were only seeking to maintain the original confederate republic of the Founding Fathers, which is why they named their new country the "Confederate States of America." Between 1861 and 1865, some 2 million Southern men, women, and children (of all races) needlessly died during a conflict that was essentially fought over the North's anti-constitutional form of government and the South's pro-constitutional form of government.

This struggle, of course, should have been settled diplomatically and legally in a court of law. But lawyer Lincoln was not interested in peace, or constitutional rights. Only power, money, prestige, and domination!

Lincoln got both his war and his new federal-style government. But at what cost? For four years Lincoln stood by while thousands died so that his liberal agenda could be fulfilled, even helping to pay the harsh tribute with his own life.

More importantly, the U.S. forfeited the very government the thirty-nine Founding Fathers created, and in doing so left a gapping wound between the traditional conservative South and the progressive liberal North, a wound that has not yet healed—and never will.

FENNER, CHARLES E. (CSA): Captain Fenner led Eldridge's Battalion, Lee's Corps Artillery, C.S. Army of Tennessee, at the Battle of Franklin.

FENNER'S LOUISIANA BATTERY (CSA): This Rebel battery fought at the Battle of Franklin with Eldridge's Battalion, Lee's Corps Artillery, C.S. Army of Tennessee.

FERGUSON HALL: Located on Highway 31 in Spring Hill, Maury County, Tennessee, Ferguson Hall was originally built by Dr. John Haddox, an early citizen of the area.

In 1854 Haddox sold the home to Martin Terrell Cheairs, of Anson, North Carolina. (Cheairs' brother, Confederate General Nathaniel Cheairs, constructed and owned the famous Rippavilla Plantation nearby, which was modeled after Ferguson Hall.)

Ferguson Hall was originally not known by this name. In 1905 William C. Branham and William Hughes bought the Martin Cheairs' House and its accompanying fifty-seven acres, turning it into a school, which they named Branham and Hughes Academy. They gave the house itself the name Ferguson, borrowed from one of Branham's relatives.

Despite its reputation as

one of America's finest educational institutions, the Great Depression forced the highly esteemed school to close, and in 1934 it was transformed into an orphanage for needy children. Later it was acquired by the Churches of Christ and today is known as the Tennessee Children's Home.

Despite its long and interesting history, Ferguson Hall—the Martin Cheairs' House, is actually best known for a dramatic incident that took place here in 1863, one closely linked to the men who fought at the Battle of Franklin.

During the War, Confederate Major General Earl "Buck" Van Dorn was using a downstairs room as a temporary military office, courtesy of the Cheairs family members, who were still living in the house at the time. Despite being married (to Caroline Godbold) with three children, Van Dorn was known—whether true or not—for his excesses, carousing, and unhealthy interest in alcohol and women. According to one (dubious) source, he fathered at least three out-of-wedlock children with an unknown woman even before the War.

Along with his reputation for being a drunk and a womanizer, some considered Van Dorn a failure on the battlefield as well. According to this school of thought, as the commander of Confederate General Braxton Bragg's cavalry, Van Dorn's miscalculations, inept attacks, and inferior communications on the field of action had led to serious Rebel losses at the Battles of Elkhorn Tavern (March 6-8, 1862) and Corinth (October 3-4, 1862).

While none question his courage or dedication to the Southern Cause, Van Dorn's reputation as a ladies' man eventually caught up with him. An individual named Dr. George Boddie Peters burst into Van Dorn's headquarters at the Cheairs' home on May 7, 1863, and shot the Rebel officer through the back of the head with a small carbine pistol. Van Dorn was discovered by one of Cheairs' horrified daughters, slumped at his office desk, bleeding profusely from his wound.

Though the general did not die instantly, for the next four and half hours he was in a coma. Not being able to speak, Van Dorn's assailant was not at first known. Meanwhile, Peters fled on horseback, and ended up living on the run for two years. (Van Dorn died later that day, May 7, and his body was transported back to his birthplace, near Port Gibson, Mississippi, where he was buried in the town's Wintergreen Cemetery.)

When Peters was finally hunted down and caught by Confederate forces in Mississippi in 1865, he was brought to trial, where the full story was revealed. "Distressing rumors" had been circulating, Peters stated, that Van Dorn had been having a torrid affair with his wife while he was out of town between March and May 1863, serving as a member of the state legislature. Local townsfolk came forward and spoke of Van Dorn's "late night visits" to the Peters' home, as well as long unchaperoned carriage rides with the lady of the house.

Determined to catch the culprit in the act, Peters pretended to leave town one night, then snuck back at 2:30 AM, catching Van Dorn in his home right "where I expected to find him." Van Dorn begged for his life, promising to exonerate Mrs. Peters and take full blame for the affair. Peters spared the general that night, but his fury overflowed later, leading to the murder of Van Dorn soon after at Martin Cheairs' home, Ferguson Hall.

Understandably, Confederate military officials did not want to publicize the matter. But Confederate Major General John R. Liddell conveyed the opinion of many shortly after Van Dorn's death when he noted that:

> "[The Confederate army is] clearly expressive of condemnation, mingled with little or no regret for a man whose willful violation of social rights led him to such an inglorious end."

The woman at the center of this emotional firestorm was the enchanting and lovely Scottish-American femme fatale, Jessie Helen McKissack, considered a "beguiling temptress," and known far and wide as one of the great beauties of the South. Enraged over reports of her late night trysts with the general, Peters sought revenge, in his mind, justifying the murder of Van Dorn for "violating the sanctity" of his home and marriage.

No court would convict Peters and he was eventually pardoned by Tennessee's Confederate Governor Isham Green Harris. Van Dorn's character, however, continued to be besmirched, this time by Southern newspapers.

In 1866 Peters and Jessie divorced over the murderous and lurid love triangle, but reconciled and remarried in 1868, had several children, and moved to Memphis, Tennessee.

Although nothing more than circumstantial evidence links Van Dorn and Jessie, town gossips later noted that on May 7 she had grimly remarked: "I have lost my husband and my lover on the same day."

Other comments seem to condemn her. At her husband's funeral in 1889, for example, Jessie noted drily: "I never cared for George, but I guess I owe him this much." In later life the vaunted Southern belle made yet another cryptic statement: "I was never a beauty, but I was darned smart." Were there hidden meanings behind these words?

Adding fuel to the Van Dorn legend is the fact that eight and a half months after he was killed by her husband, Jessie gave birth to a baby girl on January 26, 1864: Medora Wharton Peters. Jessie's husband, however, Dr. Peters, had been away, living as a fugitive from May 1863 to 1865, the exact time the infant was conceived.

Could Medora be the daughter of Van Dorn? Many think so.

The truth, whatever it is, was buried with Jessie when she died in 1921 and was interred next to her husband, Dr. Peters, in Elmwood Cemetery, Memphis, Tennessee.

FERGUSON'S SOUTH CAROLINA BATTERY (CSA): This Rebel battery fought at the Battle of Franklin in Cobb's Battalion, Cheatham's Corps Artillery, C.S. Army of Tennessee.

FIELD HOSPITAL: In the Autumn of 1864, the small farming town of Franklin, Tennessee, had no medical facilities of any kind. Thus, after the Battle of Franklin numerous temporary "field hospitals" were set up across the village to accommodate the wounded.

Some forty-four homes, schools, churches, and various other types of buildings in and around Franklin, Tennessee, were put into use as infirmaries on November 30, 1864. These field hospitals were identified by a plain red flag that was hung in a prominent position inside or outside the building.

According to Dr. Deering J. Roberts, a Confederate surgeon at the battle, nearly every available structure was used, including a carriage-and-wagon shop, an unoccupied brick store, and the Chancery Court Room. Other structures used included Saint Paul's Episcopal Church, the Williamson County Courthouse, the Masonic Hall, and the Franklin Female Institute. The wounded were so numerous, however, that more space was needed, and thousands ended up in tents or in people's yards, laying on the cold Autumn ground.

Of the forty-four Franklin field hospitals, forty-one were designated as Confederate, three as Union. The largest of either type was the Confederate field hospital at Carnton, a large Federal style mansion located on the McGavocks' plantation.

Some 300 men at a time were kept inside the 10,000 square-foot house, where they were operated on and allowed to convalesce over the following weeks and months. Another 1,500 wounded were kept in Carnton's yards and outbuildings. Carnton's blood-stained floors retain the memory of that awful period that began on November 30, 1864.

Adding to the general air of wretchedness and despair at Carnton, all of the wounded were considered prisoners-of-war. Yankee officers visited the house each day, examining the injured. Those found reasonably fit were handcuffed and taken away to a Union prison, often to distant Northern garrisons like Fort Chase in Columbia, Ohio, or Fort Warren in Boston, Massachusetts. Some of the Franklin Confederate soldiers were clearly not suitably healed for long distance traveling, and many acts of inhumanity were perpetuated by the Union troops during the removals of injured Rebel prisoners.

The McGavocks and their children remained in the house during its use as a field hospital, at times taking shelter in the master bedroom to protect themselves from the screams, moans, and cries that penetrated the walls twenty-four hours a day.

It was a ghastly moment in time: every square inch of the house was packed with the wounded and dying—even the tiny closet under the stairway. The dining room table, along with doors lifted from their hinges, were commandeered as operating tables, and amputated limbs by the thousands were tossed from the upper level windows out on to the lawn. One eyewitness reported that the pile of severed arms and legs reached up to the window sills on the second floor.

What happened to these gruesome stacks of body parts? They were hauled away in horse and carts and buried in mass graves somewhere nearby. To this day, the exact location of these burials is not known.

Despite such horrors, the McGavocks somehow managed to carry on living in the house, assisting in any way they could. Carrie McGavock, the "Good Samaritan of Williamson County," in particular is known for her unflagging courage and assistance during those dark and gloomy days. As she flitted from soldier to soldier serving them tea and changing their dressings, it is said that the noble woman's skirts became soaked with blood. Carrie wrote letters for the soldiers who had had their hands and arms blown off, or amputated by the surgeons.

No one was prepared for the appalling carnage produced by the Battle of Franklin, and so naturally there was a great shortage of medical supplies. Carrie helped compensate for this deficiency by tearing up the family's linens, their bedding, her husband's shirts, and even her own petticoats, for the doctors to use as bandages and tourniquets.

Unfortunately, these items were of limited use: doctors of the day knew almost nothing about hygiene or sanitation, for although bacteria was discovered by the Dutch naturalist Antoni van Leeuwenhoek in the late 1600s, the connection between bacteria and infection was not widely known until the late 1870s, when the French scientist Louis Pasteur made this knowledge available to the general public for the first time.

As such, Civil War doctors rarely washed their hands or sterilized their surgical instruments. Exploring wounds with bare filthy fingers and recycling old bloody bandages were considered acceptable medical practices. Little wonder that most of the wounded survived their horrid injuries and surgeries only to die from infections transmitted to them by their own doctors.

Still, while many managed to survive their surgeons, recovery was often long and arduous. At Carnton, for example, some of the men were so badly wounded that they remained sequestered at the plantation for many months. One soldier took 180 days to recuperate. By the time he was able to leave, the War had already been over for two months. The fortunate Confederate went home instead of back to the battlefield.

FIELD, HUME R. (CSA): Confederate Colonel Field took over command of Maney's Brigade after its leader Brigadier General John Carpenter Carter was killed at the Battle of Franklin.

FIELD SERVANT: African-American servants ("slaves" to Northerners) were divided into two basic categories: house servants and field servants.

As their name implies, the latter mainly worked crop fields and gardens, plowing, planting, cultivating, and harvesting. Field servants also worked with livestock, performing such duties as milking cows, gathering eggs, killing hogs, mucking out stables, cleaning and walking horses, and blacksmithing.

The field servants were lower in rank than the house servants, and thus lived in less luxurious conditions. At Carnton Plantation, for example, field servants lived in rough-hewn log cabins while the house servants lived in a brick house with tin sheet roofing.

Contrary to Northern myth, whether a field servant or a house servant, *all* Southern bondsmen and bondswomen possessed numerous rights and privileges, and, at the time of purchase, were registered in court as legal members of their owner's family.

This helps explain the often warm relations between whites and blacks in the Old South, the oft repeated observation by eyewitnesses that black servants were typically treated as members of their white families, and the fact that freed "slaves" usually chose to stay with their emancipators and continue working for them afterward as employees.

FIFTEENTH ARKANSAS (CSA): This Rebel infantry regiment fought at the Battle of

Franklin in Govan's Brigade, Cleburne's Division, Cheatham's Corps, C.S. Army of Tennessee.

FIFTEENTH MISSISSIPPI (CSA): This Rebel infantry regiment fought at the Battle of Franklin in Adams' Brigade, Loring's Division, Stewart's Corps, C.S. Army of Tennessee.

FIFTEENTH MISSOURI (USA): This Yankee infantry regiment fought at the Battle of Franklin in Bradley's Third Brigade, Wagner's Second Division, Fourth U.S. Army Corps.

FIFTEENTH OHIO (USA): This Yankee infantry regiment fought at the Battle of Franklin in Streight's First Brigade, Wood's Third Division, Fourth U.S. Army Corps.

FIFTEENTH TENNESSEE CAVALRY (CSA): This Rebel cavalry regiment fought at the Battle of Franklin in Rucker's Brigade, Chalmers' Division, Forrest's Cavalry Corps, C.S. Army of Tennessee.

FIFTEENTH TEXAS (CSA): This Rebel infantry regiment fought at the Battle of Franklin in

Granbury's Brigade, Cleburne's Division, Cheatham's Corps, C.S. Army of Tennessee.

FIFTH ARKANSAS (CSA): This Rebel infantry regiment fought at the Battle of Franklin in Govan's Brigade, Cleburne's Division, Cheatham's Corps, C.S. Army of Tennessee.

FIFTH CONFEDERATE (CSA): This Rebel infantry regiment fought at the Battle of Franklin in Granbury's Brigade, Cleburne's Division, Cheatham's Corps, C.S. Army of Tennessee.

FIFTH IOWA CAVALRY (USA): This Yankee cavalry regiment fought at the Battle of Franklin in Harrison's First Brigade, Johnson's Sixth Division, Wilson's Cavalry Corps.

FIFTH MISSISSIPPI (CSA): This Rebel infantry regiment fought at the Battle of Franklin in Lowrey's Brigade, Cleburne's Division, Cheatham's Corps, C.S. Army of Tennessee.

FIFTH MISSISSIPPI CAVALRY (CSA): This Rebel cavalry regiment fought at the Battle of Franklin in Rucker's

Brigade, Chalmers' Division, Forrest's Cavalry Corps, C.S. Army of Tennessee.

FIFTH MISSOURI (CSA): This Rebel infantry regiment fought at the Battle of Franklin in Cockrell's Brigade, French's Division, Stewart's Corps, C.S. Army of Tennessee.

FIFTH TENNESSEE (CSA): This Rebel infantry regiment fought at the Battle of Franklin in Strahl's Brigade, Brown's Division, Cheatham's Corps, C.S. Army of Tennessee.

FIFTH TENNESSEE (USA): This Yankee infantry regiment fought at the Battle of Franklin in Casement's Second Brigade, Cox's Third Division, Twenty-third U.S. Army Corps.

FIFTH TEXAS CAVALRY (CSA): This Rebel cavalry regiment fought at the Battle of Franklin in Ross' Brigade, Jackson's Division, Forrest's Cavalry Corps, C.S. Army of Tennessee.

FIFTIETH ALABAMA (CSA): This Rebel infantry regiment fought at the Battle of Franklin in Deas' Brigade, Johnson's Division, Lee's Corps, C.S. Army of Tennessee.

FIFTIETH OHIO (USA): This Yankee infantry regiment fought at the Battle of Franklin in Strickland's Third Brigade, Ruger's Second Division, Twenty-third U.S. Army Corps.

FIFTIETH TENNESSEE (CSA): This Rebel infantry regiment fought at the Battle of Franklin in Maney's Brigade, Brown's Division, Cheatham's Corps, C.S. Army of Tennessee.

FIFTY-EIGHTH ALABAMA (CSA): This Rebel infantry regiment fought at the Battle of Franklin in Holtzclaw's Brigade, Clayton's Division, Lee's Corps, C.S. Army of Tennessee.

FIFTY-FIFTH ALABAMA (CSA): This Rebel infantry regiment fought at the Battle of Franklin in Scott's Brigade, Loring's Division, Stewart's Corps, C.S. Army of Tennessee.

FIFTY-FIFTH TENNESSEE (CSA): This Rebel infantry regiment fought at the Battle of Franklin in Quarles' Brigade, Walthall's Division, Stewart's Corps, C.S. Army of Tennessee.

FIFTY-FIRST ILLINOIS (USA): This Yankee infantry regiment fought at the Battle of Franklin in Bradley's Third Brigade, Wagner's Second Division, Fourth U.S. Army Corps.

FIFTY-FIRST INDIANA (USA): This Yankee infantry regiment fought at the Battle of Franklin in Streight's First Brigade, Wood's Third Division, Fourth U.S. Army Corps.

FIFTY-FIRST OHIO (USA): This Yankee infantry regiment fought at the Battle of Franklin in Whitaker's Second Brigade, Kimball's First Division, Fourth U.S. Army Corps.

FIFTY-FIRST TENNESSEE (CSA): This Rebel infantry regiment fought at the Battle of Franklin in Vaughan's Brigade, Brown's Division, Cheatham's Corps, C.S. Army of Tennessee.

FIFTY-FOURTH GEORGIA (CSA): This Rebel infantry regiment fought at the Battle of Franklin in Smith's Brigade, Cleburne's Division, Cheatham's Corps, C.S. Army of Tennessee.

FIFTY-NINTH ILLINOIS (USA): This Yankee infantry regiment fought at the Battle of Franklin in Post's Second Brigade, Wood's Third Division, Fourth U.S. Army Corps.

FIFTY-SECOND GEORGIA (CSA): This Rebel infantry regiment fought at the Battle of Franklin in Stovall's Brigade, Clayton's Division, Lee's Corps, C.S. Army of Tennessee.

FIFTY-SECOND TENNESSEE (CSA): This Rebel infantry regiment fought at the Battle of Franklin in Vaughan's Brigade, Brown's Division, Cheatham's Corps, C.S. Army of Tennessee.

FIFTY-SEVENTH ALABAMA (CSA): This Rebel infantry regiment fought at the Battle of Franklin in Scott's Brigade, Loring's Division, Stewart's Corps, C.S. Army of Tennessee.

FIFTY-SEVENTH GEORGIA (CSA): This Rebel infantry regiment fought at the Battle of Franklin in Smith's Brigade, Cleburne's Division, Cheatham's Corps, C.S. Army of Tennessee.

FIFTY-SEVENTH INDIANA (USA): This Yankee infantry regiment fought at the Battle of Franklin in Lane's Second Brigade, Wagner's Second Division, Fourth U.S. Army Corps.

FIFTY-SIXTH GEORGIA (CSA): This Rebel infantry regiment fought at the Battle of Franklin in Cummings' Brigade, Stevenson's Division, Lee's Corps, C.S. Army of Tennessee.

FIFTY-THIRD TENNESSEE (CSA): This Rebel infantry regiment fought at the Battle of Franklin in Quarles' Brigade, Walthall's Division, Stewart's Corps, C.S. Army of Tennessee.

FIGUERS, HARDING PERKINS: Best known as Harding Figuers (and sometimes as Hardin P. Figures), he was born April 15, 1849, at Franklin, Tennessee, the son of Thomas Norfleet Figuers Sr. and Bethenia Gardin Perkins. His mother, whose grandfather constructed the first iron furnace in the South, was a descendant of the sister of Oliver Cromwell.

Figuers attended Harpeth Male Academy, read law, and set up a law practice in 1872. He worked as both a school teacher and a Sunday school teacher, and served as the editor of the weekly newspapers the *Franklin Review* and the *Columbia Herald*.

A freemason and a member of the Knights Templar, he married Lily Dale of Columbia, Tennessee, on December 4, 1875, and bore one child: Mary Dale Figuers, an accomplished musician.

Figuers, a devoted Democrat (the conservatives of the day) and a staunch temperance advocate, served as the steward of the First Methodist Church in Columbia, for forty years. He passed away in that town on August 14, 1917, at the age of 68, and was buried in the city's Rose Hill Cemetery.

Of English heritage, Figuers is best known for being an eyewitness of the Battle of Franklin, and for being one of those who cared for the wounded (his childhood home, Boxmere, was only 600 feet from the Yankee lines). His vivid recollections have helped modern Civil War scholars piece together some of the disparate events that occurred on November 30, 1864.

It was on that day that the fifteen year old sat on top of the family barn, then later in an oak tree in the front yard of his Franklin home, and observed the battle as it unfolded. One can only imagine the thoughts and feelings the young boy must have felt as he watched his town burn, the acrid smell of powder smoke filling his nostrils, the terrifying sounds of booming cannon ringing in his ears.

Concerning the following day, December 1, he would later write:

" . . . the dead and wounded were so thick that it might be said that one could walk upon the dead and never touch the ground."

Though not generally known, Figuers is a descendant of the prestigious Harding family (hence his first name: Harding), who built Belle Meade Plantation, just outside Nashville. Considered the South's finest horse farm in the 1860s, its wartime owner, General William Giles Harding, was the husband of Elizabeth Irwin McGavock, a descendant of European royalty and the daughter of Randall McGavock, eleventh Mayor of Nashville, and his wife Sarah Dougherty Rodgers. Randal finished building Carnton Plantation in 1826, and passed it down to his son (Elizabeth's brother), Colonel John W. McGavock, who offered its use as a Confederate hospital during the Battle of Franklin.

Another interesting connection: On November 7, 1872, Figuers' older brother, Thomas Norfleet Figuers Jr., married Harriet Pointer Cheairs—also a descendant of European royalty—the niece of Major Nathaniel Francis Cheairs, the Confederate officer who built Rippavilla Plantation, in Spring Hill, Maury County, Tennessee. It was at Rippavilla, the day after the lost Battle of Spring Hill, that Confederate Generals John Bell Hood and Nathan Bedford Forrest had their famous quarrel on the morning of November 30, 1864.

During the Battle of Franklin, Figuers' parents' house on Carters Creek Pike was illegally commandeered by U.S. Brigadier General William Grose, and used as his headquarters, much to the dismay of the Confederate family.

After the conflict, the house was turned into one of Franklin's numerous Confederate field hospitals, with countless wounded Rebels—now considered Yankee prisoners—quickly filling up its rooms. As no doctor could be found, young Figuers assisted in making up beds and pillows, dressing wounds, and gathering and preparing food.

As an adult years later, Figuers recalled one soldier in particular who had been recuperating at his parents' house. Confederate Colonel William L. Butler had been wounded badly, a bullet having passed through his entire body. Though in no condition to move, let alone travel, Union doctors declared him cured, and promptly sent him off to prison. Figuers cringed as Butler was dragged from the house screaming in pain, another one of the millions of victims of Yankee cruelty in an illicit and unnecessary war.

FINLEY, JESSE JOHNSON (CSA): Also known as Jesse J. Finley, Esquire, he was born on November 18, 1812, near Lebanon, Wilson County, Tennessee. Finley became interested in politics early on and was elected to the Arkansas state senate in 1841. This was followed by term as mayor of Memphis, Tennessee, from 1845 to 1846.

Moving to Florida, Finley held numerous offices, including becoming a member of the Florida state senate (1850) and a circuit judge (1853-1861). His service as a Confederate district judge from 1861 to 1862 led to a speedy rise through the ranks of the Confederate Army.

As colonel of the Florida Sixth Infantry Regiment in the C.S. Army of Tennessee, Finley fought at numerous conflicts, including the Battle of Chattanooga.

Severely wounded at the Battle of Jonesboro (August 31-September 1, 1864), he was unable to return to his troops. However, his unit, "Finley's Brigade," as it later became known, also fought bravely at Franklin, Chickamauga, Dalton, Missionary Ridge, the Atlanta Campaign, Murfreesboro, Nashville, and in the Carolinas Campaign.

Surviving the War, Finley went on to become a Republican U.S. representative of the Florida legislature, serving various terms between 1876 and 1882. On November 12, 1904, the noted Confederate died in Lake City, Columbia County, Florida, and was buried in Evergreen Cemetery, Gainesville,

Florida.

FINLEY'S BRIGADE (CSA): At first led by Confederate Brigadier General Jesse Johnson Finley, after whom the unit was named, after Finley was wounded at the Battle of Jonesboro in the late Summer of 1864, Finley's Brigade was taken over by Confederate Colonel Robert Bullock, who commanded it at the Battle of Franklin.

Finley's Brigade was comprised of the First Florida, Third Florida, Fourth Florida, Sixth Florida, Seventh Florida, and First Florida Cavalry (dismounted).

FIRST ALABAMA (CSA): This Rebel infantry regiment fought at the Battle of Franklin in Quarles' Brigade, Walthall's Division, Stewart's Corps, C.S. Army of Tennessee.

FIRST ARKANSAS (CSA): This Rebel infantry regiment fought at the Battle of Franklin in Govan's Brigade, Cleburne's Division, Cheatham's Corps, C.S. Army of Tennessee.

FIRST ARKANSAS MOUNTED RIFLES - DISMOUNTED (CSA): This Rebel unit fought at the Battle of Franklin in Reynolds' Brigade, Walthall's Division, Stewart's Corps, C.S. Army of Tennessee.

FIRST FLORIDA (CSA): This Rebel infantry regiment fought at the Battle of Franklin in Finley's Brigade, Bate's Division, Cheatham's Corps, C.S. Army of Tennessee.

FIRST FLORIDA CAVALRY - DISMOUNTED (CSA): This Rebel infantry regiment fought at the Battle of Franklin in Finley's Brigade, Bate's Division, Cheatham's Corps, C.S. Army of Tennessee.

FIRST GEORGIA BATTALION SHARPSHOOTERS (CSA): This Rebel infantry regiment fought at the Battle of Franklin in Jackson's Brigade, Bate's Division, Cheatham's Corps, C.S. Army of Tennessee.

FIRST GEORGIA CONFEDERATE (CSA): This Rebel infantry regiment fought at the Battle of Franklin in Jackson's Brigade, Bate's Division, Cheatham's Corps, C.S. Army of Tennessee.

FIRST GEORGIA VOLUNTEERS (CSA): This Rebel infantry regiment fought at the Battle of Franklin in Smith's Brigade, Cleburne's Division, Cheatham's Corps, C.S. Army of Tennessee.

FIRST ILLINOIS ARTILLERY - BATTERY I (USA): This Yankee artillery unit fought at the Battle of Franklin in Hatch's Fifth Division Artillery, Wilson's Cavalry Corps.

FIRST KENTUCKY BATTERY (USA): This Yankee artillery unit fought at the Battle of Franklin in the Fourth U.S. Army Corps Artillery.

FIRST LOUISIANA (CSA): This Rebel infantry regiment fought at the Battle of Franklin in Gibson's Brigade, Clayton's Division, Lee's Corps, C.S. Army of Tennessee.

FIRST MICHIGAN BATTERY (USA): This Yankee artillery unit fought at the Battle of Franklin in the Fourth U.S. Army Corps Artillery.

FIRST MISSISSIPPI (CSA): This Rebel infantry regiment fought at the Battle of Franklin in Featherston's Brigade, Loring's Division, Stewart's Corps, C.S. Army of Tennessee.

FIRST MISSISSIPPI BATTALION SHARPSHOOTERS (CSA): This Rebel unit fought at the Battle of Franklin in Featherston's Brigade, Loring's Division, Stewart's Corps, C.S. Army of Tennessee.

FIRST MISSISSIPPI CAVALRY (CSA): This Rebel cavalry regiment fought at the Battle of Franklin in Armstrong's Brigade, Jackson's Division, Forrest's Cavalry Corps, C.S. Army of Tennessee.

FIRST MISSOURI (CSA): This Rebel infantry regiment fought at the Battle of Franklin in Cockrell's Brigade, French's Division, Stewart's Corps, C.S. Army of Tennessee.

FIRST MISSOURI CAVALRY - DISMOUNTED (CSA): This Rebel cavalry regiment fought at the Battle of Franklin in Cockrell's Brigade, French's Division, Stewart's Corps, C.S. Army of Tennessee.

FIRST OHIO LIGHT - BATTERIES A AND G (USA): This Yankee artillery unit fought at the Battle of Franklin in the Fourth U.S. Army Corps Artillery.

FIRST OHIO LIGHT - BATTERY D (USA): This Yankee artillery unit fought at the Battle of Franklin in Cox's Third Division, Twenty-third U.S. Army Corps.

FIRST TENNESSEE (CSA): This Rebel infantry regiment fought at the Battle of Franklin in Maney's Brigade, Brown's Division, Cheatham's Corps, Army of Tennessee. The First Tennessee was organized in April 1861 in Nashville, Tennessee, and mustered into service as Company K.

Known originally as the "Williamson Grays," this famous unit fought in numerous conflicts, including the Battle of Franklin—where it was led by Confederate Brigadier General John C. Carter, and the Battle of Nashville—where it was led by Colonel Hume R. Field.

A first-hand memory of the First Tennessee has been preserved in the South's beloved classic book: *"Co. Aytch," Maury Grays, First Tennessee Regiment*, by Private Samuel Rush Watkins.

FIRST TENNESSEE CAVALRY (USA): This Yankee cavalry regiment fought at the Battle of Franklin in Croxton's First Brigade, McCook's First Division, Wilson's Cavalry Corps.

FIRST TEXAS LEGION (CSA): This Rebel unit fought at the Battle of Franklin in Ross' Brigade, Jackson's Division, Forrest's Cavalry Corps, C.S. Army of Tennessee.

FISHER, RHODES (CSA): Confederate Captain Fisher led the Sixth and Fifteenth Texas Infantries at the Battle of Franklin, where he was captured by the enemy.

FLOOR CLOTH: A type of flooring common in Victorian homes during the Civil War period.

A thin sheet of canvas was laid down on wood flooring, stretched and painted, then covered with twelve to fifteen coats of varnish. The result, a precursor to our modern-day linoleum, was a hard and durable floor covering, well suited to high traffic areas such as hallways, dining rooms, and kitchens.

The wealthy bought brand new canvas, while those less well off bought used sails from ships.

Those who lived, fought, and died in the Battle of Franklin were quite familiar with floor cloth, and modern reproductions of it can still be seen in antebellum homes around Franklin, Tennessee.

FLOURNOY, PETER C. (CSA): Cockrell's Brigade was detached prior to the Battle of Nashville after its commander Confederate Brigadier General Francis Marion Cockrell was wounded at the Battle of Franklin. The detachment took place under Colonel Flournoy.

FORREST CROSSING: Known in some early sources as Hugh's Ford, this area is located on the Harpeth River in Franklin, Tennessee, several miles southeast of the town center.

The ford was made famous by Confederate cavalryman General Nathan Bedford Forrest on November 30, 1864, when he crossed the river at this particular point in order to drive back Yankee troops during the Battle of Franklin.

In modern times, an entire area of Franklin, along with a subdivison, has been named "Forrest Crossing" in honor of the great Rebel chieftain's actions that day.

FORREST STREET: A street in Franklin, Tennessee, named in honor of local hero Confederate General Nathan Bedford Forrest.

FORREST, NATHAN BEDFORD (CSA): Forrest was born (along with a twin sister) on July 13, 1821, in Chapel Hill, Bedford (now Marshall) County, Tennessee, the son of William Forrest and Mariam Beck.

A descendant of Scottish, Irish, and English heritage, and named for the county he was born in, Forrest would later become one of America's most celebrated Civil War figures, both on and off the battlefield. His name still stirs strong emotion—among the educated, always favorable.

Born in rural poverty with no time or funds for formal education, Forrest, the embodiment of the American Dream, was a self-made multimillionaire by the time he was forty.

On April 25, 1845, at Hernando, DeSoto County, Mississippi, Forrest married high society girl Mary Ann Montgomery (a cousin of Sam Houston), and bore two children: William Montgomery Forrest and Fanny Forrest. In 1851 he moved his family to the thriving river port of Memphis, Tennessee, embarking on numerous business enterprises, including running several plantations and slave trading. In 1858 Memphis elected him an alderman.

Contrary to Northern myth, as a slave-holder Forrest was known to be respectful and kind to his African-American "servants," as they were known in the Old South, and he pledged to never sell them to cruel individuals or split up families. He was actually instrumental in reuniting several slave families, and it is said that due to his reputation for charity and forbearance, at auction African-Americans actually begged to be purchased by Forrest.

By the late 1850s his plantation was producing some 1,000 bales of cotton a year, and by 1861 Forrest was earning $50,000 a year (the equivalent of about $1,200,000 today), making him one of the largest plantation owners and one of the wealthiest men in the South.

With the start of Lincoln's War in 1861, conservative Forrest naturally sided with the South and the Constitution. After joining the Confederate army, he first served as a private in Captain J. S. White's Tennessee Mounted Rifles. Seeing the appalling lack of supplies, like many other wealthy Confederates, Forrest outfitted and equipped soldiers wherever and whenever he could (a good deed for which he was never repaid).

Despite his lack of military training, promotions came often and quickly. As a result, Forrest is the only man on either side of the War who rose from the rank of private to lieutenant general.

Forrest owned dozens of servants ("slaves" to Yankees), naturally seeing them as potential recruits in the South's fight against Northern aggression. He asked them to stay on with him and join the Confederate army, promising them their freedom—which he happily gave them in September 1863, shortly after the Battle of Chickamauga.

Forty-five of them (along with twenty other blacks) fought with their former master for the rest of the War, eight of them serving as his personal armed guard.

(It must be asked here, if Forrest was truly a "savage, racist slaveholder," as the North ignorantly teaches, why he would have trusted eight African-Americans to be his personal bodyguards, or why they themselves requested to be bought by him at the slave markets?)

Forrest fought at such famous battles as Donelson, Shiloh, Murfreesboro, Day's Gap, Vicksburg, Brice's Cross Roads, Memphis, Johnsonville, and Paducah, the latter where military reports note that the near superhuman Forrest rode his 2,500-man cavalry 100 miles in a mere fifty hours.

Union accounts at the Battle of Fort Pillow assert that Forrest's men captured, tortured, and even crucified both European-American and African-American Federal soldiers. Beyond these obvious politically motivated Yankee lies, nothing was ever proven, Forrest was never directly linked to any of the alleged atrocities, and at the end of the War a U.S. congressional committee cleared him of all charges.

General William Tecumseh Sherman confessed, with overt jealousy, that Forrest's clever maneuvers "excited my admiration." Nonetheless, he put out an order to have "that devil Forrest," as he came to be known by Yankee troops, "hunted down and killed, even if it costs 10,000 lives and bankrupts the Federal treasury!"

On November 29, 1864, the warrior-celebrity outsmarted the Yanks at the Battle of Spring Hill, and the next day, prior to the Battle of Franklin, he stood on the upper deck of Carnton Plantation, using it as an observation deck.

At Franklin, as he did elsewhere, his superior General John Bell Hood, misused Forrest, wasting his talents by sending him off to the far right to skirmish with Union soldiers on the Harpeth River.

Shortly after, as the bedraggled but still feisty Army of Tennessee marched toward Nashville for its final major showdown with the Union, Hood miscalculated once again, inexplicably detaching Forrest to Murfreesboro, while he rode on to the Tennessee capital without his most sensible and sharp-witted officer. The War's outcome would have been very different had Hood not been so shortsighted when it came to Forrest!

In early 1865, Forrest was in Selma, Alabama, driving out Federal troops with his usual ferocity when the message came: General Robert E. Lee had surrendered at Appomattox. It was all over.

In Gainesville, Alabama, on May 9, Forrest bid farewell to his men in one of the War's most beautiful speeches:

"Soldiers, By an agreement made between Lieutenant-General Taylor, commanding the Department of Alabama, Mississippi, and East Louisiana, and Major-General Canby, commanding United States forces, the troops of this department have been surrendered.

"I do not think it proper or necessary at this time to refer to causes which have reduced us to this extremity; nor is it now a matter of material consequence to us how such results were brought about. That we are beaten is a self-evident fact, and any further resistance on our part would justly be regarded as the very height of folly and rashness.

"The armies of Generals Lee and Johnson having surrendered. You are the last of all the troops of the Confederate States Army east of the Mississippi River to lay down your arms.

"The Cause for which you have so long and so manfully struggled, and for which you have braved dangers, endured privations, and sufferings, and made so many sacrifices, is today hopeless. The government which we sought to establish and perpetuate, is at an end. Reason dictates and humanity demands that no more blood be shed. Fully realizing and feeling that such is the case, it is your duty and mine to lay down our arms, submit to the "powers that be," and to aid in restoring peace and establishing law and order throughout the land.

"The terms upon which you were surrendered are favorable, and should be satisfactory and acceptable to all. They manifest a spirit of magnanimity and liberality, on the part of the Federal authorities, which should be met, on our part, by a faithful compliance with all the stipulations and conditions therein expressed. As your Commander, I sincerely hope that every officer and soldier of my command will cheerfully obey the orders given, and carry out in good faith all the terms of the cartel.

"Those who neglect the terms and refuse to be paroled, may assuredly expect, when arrested, to be sent North and imprisoned. Let those who are absent from their commands, from whatever cause, report at once to this place, or to Jackson, Mississippi; or, if too remote from either, to the nearest United States post or garrison, for parole.

"Civil war, such as you have just passed through naturally engenders feelings of animosity, hatred, and revenge. It is our duty to divest ourselves of all such feelings; and as far as it is in our power to do so, to cultivate friendly feelings towards those with whom we have so long contended, and heretofore so widely, but honestly, differed. Neighborhood feuds, personal animosities, and private differences should be blotted out; and, when you return home, a manly, straightforward course of conduct will secure the respect of your enemies. Whatever your responsibilities may be to Government, to society, or to individuals meet them like men.

"The attempt made to establish a separate and independent Confederation has failed; but the consciousness of having done your duty faithfully, and to the end, will, in some measure, repay for the hardships you have undergone.

"In bidding you farewell, rest assured that you carry with you my best wishes for your future welfare and happiness. Without, in any way, referring to the merits of the Cause in which we have been engaged, your courage and determination, as exhibited on many hard-fought fields, has elicited the respect and admiration of friend and foe. And I now cheerfully and gratefully acknowledge my indebtedness to the officers and men of my command whose zeal, fidelity and unflinching bravery have been the great source of my past success in arms.

"I have never, on the field of battle, sent you where I was unwilling to go myself; nor would I now advise you to a course which I felt myself unwilling to pursue. You have been good soldiers, you can be good citizens. Obey the laws, preserve your honor, and the Government to which you have surrendered can afford to be, and will be, magnanimous."

After the War Forrest returned to civilian life, taking up a new business partner in the process: a former Yankee officer. In Memphis, after building a new home on the Mississippi River, he became president of the Selma, Marion, and Memphis Railroad.

Though neither the founder or the leader of the Ku Klux Klan, as Northern myth claims, Forrest *was* responsible for shutting down the organization in 1869, asserting that it had served its purpose and was no longer necessary.

The General has been much maligned for his alleged "racism" toward African-Americans, and for this he has been detested by many. That this is both false and unfair is evident in not only the manner in which he treated those he procured through the slave trade (all who freed in 1859, two years before the War and five years before Lincoln issued his fake and illegal Emancipation Proclamation), but also in a speech he gave to a group of black Southerners in Memphis in 1875:

"I assure you that every man who was in the Confederate army is your friend.

We were born on same soil, breathe the same air, live in the same land, and why should we not be brothers and sisters?"

In reality, Forrest was an ardent Christian and a compassionate civil rights worker after the War, fighting for employment and voting rights for blacks. Not only had Forrest enlisted blacks to fight in his militia during the War, but while president of the Selma, Marion, and Memphis Railroad, he had hired African-Americans to work as conductors, engineers, foremen, and architects, jobs still forbidden to blacks in the North at that time. This is not surprising, for as official records, letters, and diaries show, blacks were treated much better in the South than they were in the North before, during, and after the War.

In his senior years Forrest donated much of his remaining fortune to charities for Confederate veterans and their widows and children.

White haired and frail, but still possessing his fiery Celtic spirit, on October 29, 1877, he died at Memphis, Shelby County, Tennessee, from complications due to diabetes and his war wounds. His wife Mary Ann buried him in the city's Elmwood Cemetery.

It is notable that while blacks were banned from Lincoln's funeral, they were not only allowed at Forrest's, they were openly welcomed. Indeed, of the 10,000 individuals who attended his burial to pay their respects to the famed Confederate general that day, roughly one-third, or about 3,000 of them, were African-Americans.

In 1904 his body was re-interred in the Memphis landmark that still bears his name: Nathan Bedford Forrest Park.

Nearly 140 years after his death, Forrest continues to be highly venerated by traditional Southerners. The penultimate personification of the Old South, his very name is synonymous with not only the Southern Cause (constitutionalism), but with heroism, rugged individualism, and states' rights.

Little wonder that thousands of children, schools, parks, cemeteries, libraries, office buildings, country clubs, and subdivisons across America are named after the Tennessee hero, or that author Winston Groom named the lead character in his film "Forrest Gump" after him.

FORREST'S CAVALRY CORPS (CSA): This Rebel cavalry corps, named after its commander Confederate General Nathan Bedford Forrest, was present at the Battle of Franklin. It was comprised of Chalmers' Division, Buford's Division, Jackson's Division, and Forrest's Cavalry Corps Artillery.

FORREST'S CAVALRY CORPS ARTILLERY (CSA): Named after its corps commander, Confederate Lieutenant General Nathan Bedford Forrest, this Rebel corps was comprised of a single unit: Morton's Tennessee Battery.

FORREST'S REGIMENT TENNESSEE CAVALRY (CSA): This Rebel unit fought at the Battle of Franklin in Rucker's Brigade, Chalmers' Division, Forrest's Cavalry Corps, C.S. Army of Tennessee.

FORT CASINO: Also known as Blockhouse Casino, Fort Casino was a Yankee garrison once located in Nashville between Edgehill Avenue, Wedgewood Avenue, 8th Avenue South, and Hillside Avenue. It served as a fortification for Union troops during the Battle of Nashville, two weeks after the Battle of Franklin.

FORT GILLEM: This Yankee garrison—named after Middle Tennessee Union General Alvan Cullem Gillem—was one of the many forts illegally built by the Union around the city of Nashville. During December 1864, shortly after the Battle of Franklin, it was used by Federal troops during the Battle of Nashville.

Fort Gillem was located near the present site of Fisk University, at the corner of Jefferson Street and Dr. D. B. Todd Jr. Boulevard.

FORT GRANGER: Named after Yankee General Gordon Granger, Fort Granger was an earthen Union garrison built between March and May 1863, its purpose being to monitor and protect the Nashville and Decatur Railroad, the Nashville Pike, and the Harpeth River. It is located in Franklin, Tennessee, on Figuers' Bluff on the Harpeth River, behind modern day Pinkerton Park.

The original twelve acre fort was about 346 feet wide and

781 feet long, and featured two fortified frontal ramparts on the eastern and northern sides. These walls were ten feet deep and sixteen feet wide, and were made of packed dirt supported by roughly cut timber.

Fort Granger was used by U.S. soldiers during both the Battle of Franklin I (April 10, 1863)—when it was attacked by Confederate General Nathan Bedford Forrest, and the Battle of Franklin II (November 30, 18654)—when it was used by Union General John M. Schofield as his headquarters. The fort was capable of holding about 8,500 soldiers and twenty-four pieces of artillery.

Like *all* Union forts built in the South during Lincoln's War, the construction of Fort Granger was, of course, illegal, and a gross insult to the citizens of the Confederate States of America. Its ghostly presence in Franklin remains so to this day. For the U.S. government had no lawful right to invade the towns of a foreign nation and build its own military structures in them.

The sinister motivations behind the design of Fort Granger can be seen in its powder magazine, which was constructed using bricks from nearby Harpeth Academy. Earlier, the Franklin school had been cruelly and senselessly bombed to rubble by Yankee troops, a clear violation of both civilized warfare and the Geneva Conventions.

Though today only the outline of the earthwork fort is visible, a commemorative park with interpretive signage has been set up at the site for visitors.

FORT HOUSTON: A small illegally built Yankee garrison once located at the corner of present day Music Square West and 17th Avenue South.

The fort was named after the Union sympathizer whose property was stolen to build the structure on.

FORT JOHNSON (TENNESSEE STATE CAPITOL): In late February 1862, Nashville, Tennessee, became the first major Confederate town to be captured by the Union. Federal forces quickly set about turning the city into a Yankee stronghold, beginning with the state capitol, which they named Fort Johnson after the new military governor of Tennessee, Andrew Johnson.

Designed by the noted Philadelphia architect William

Strickland, construction of the Tennessee State Capitol building was begun on July 4, 1845, using slaves and convicts. It was completed on July 21, 1855, with additional work done in 1859.

Strickland passed away in 1854, one year prior to the Capitol's completion, after which his son, Francis W. Strickland, took over supervision of the project. In honor of the elder Strickland's majestic work, the Tennessee legislature had him interred within the walls of the Capitol.

Like many 19th-Century homes and buildings, the Capitol, intentionally sited on a large hill, was built in the Greek Revival style, with Ionic features patterned on ancient Athenian temples. From ground to tower tip it is 206 feet tall, with a length of 236 feet and a width of 109 feet.

During Lincoln's War the Union Army illegally commandeered the Southern antebellum building and heavily fortified it with guns and cannon. Fortunately, it was not harmed during the ensuing battles, and the classic structure continues today to function as the seat of Tennessee's primary political bodies.

Housed here are the offices of the governor, the state senate chambers, and the House of Representatives. America's eleventh president, James K. Polk, and his wife Sarah Childress, are buried on the Capitol's grounds, only feet from an imposing statue of America's seventh president, Andrew "Old Hickory" Jackson.

FORTIETH GEORGIA (CSA): This Rebel infantry regiment fought at the Battle of Franklin in Stovall's Brigade, Clayton's Division, Lee's Corps, C.S. Army of Tennessee.

FORTIETH INDIANA (USA): This Yankee infantry regiment fought at the Battle of Franklin in Lane's Second Brigade, Wagner's Second Division, Fourth U.S. Army Corps.

FORTIETH MISSISSIPPI (CSA): This Rebel infantry regiment fought at the Battle of Franklin in Featherston's Brigade, Loring's Division, Stewart's Corps, C.S. Army of Tennessee.

FORT MORTON: Designed by Major James R. Willett, Fort Morton was another one of the numerous small Yankee garrisons unlawfully built in the city of Nashville after it was captured by the Union in February 1862.

Fort Morton was located at the present site of Rose Park, at the corners of 11th Avenue South and Edgehill Avenue.

FORT NEGLEY: Located in Nashville, Tennessee, on Saint Cloud Hill off Chesnut Street (between Greer Stadium and the Cumberland Science Museum), Fort Negley was primarily built by Southern slaves ("forced labor gangs") under the direction of U.S. forces. Construction took place between October and December 1862, after the city's capture by the U.S. in February of that year.

Constructed using railroad iron, logs, earth, and rock, it was the largest stone fort built inland during the entire War. Its eastern and western parapets were constructed in the shape of stars, a method of foiling attack while providing gunners with both optimal protection and visual range.

Named after Yankee General James Scott Negley of Pennsylvania (whose inferior command at the Battle of Chickamauga caused the fort to be renamed in 1865), Fort Negley was the southernmost of a ring of Yankee fortifications purposefully built around Nashville. Though ordnance from its artillery fired the opening rounds of the Battle of Nashville (December 15-16, 1864) two weeks after the Battle of Franklin, Confederate forces never directly attacked the fort.

Comprised of stockades, inner works, casements, parapets, bastions, tunnels, and a main gate, the four acre garrison was constructed upon the designs of European forts, and was 300 feet wide and 600 feet long. It cost $130,000 to build, the modern equivalent of about $3 million.

The fort, like all Yankee garrisons constructed in the South, was illegal, since it is against international law for one country to build military fortifications (or any other type of structure) in a foreign nation without authorization. But such laws, of course, never deterred dictator Lincoln and his officers. In fact, the site seems to have been purposefully chosen to inflict the maximum inconvenience and humiliation on the great people of Nashville: originally, the prominence it sits on, the once lovely wooded Saint

Cloud Hill, was a favorite picnic spot for Southern families and couples.

Though the fort has long been in a state of disrepair and deterioration, it is now undergoing restoration and is open to the public. Next to the remains of the fort is the Fort Negley Visitor's Center (at 1100 Fort Negley Boulevard), which features the usual pro-North exhibits, activities, and events.

FORTY-EIGHTH TENNESSEE (CSA): This Rebel infantry regiment fought at the Battle of Franklin in Quarles' Brigade, Walthall's Division, Stewart's Corps, C.S. Army of Tennessee.

FORTY-FIFTH ALABAMA (CSA): This Rebel infantry regiment fought at the Battle of Franklin in Lowrey's Brigade, Cleburne's Division, Cheatham's Corps, C.S. Army of Tennessee.

FORTY-FIFTH OHIO (USA): This Yankee infantry regiment fought at the Battle of Franklin in Whitaker's Second Brigade, Kimball's First Division, Fourth U.S. Army Corps.

FORTY-FIRST GEORGIA (CSA): This Rebel infantry regiment fought at the Battle of Franklin in Stovall's Brigade, Clayton's Division, Lee's Corps, C.S. Army of Tennessee.

FORTY-FIRST MISSISSIPPI (CSA): This Rebel infantry regiment fought at the Battle of Franklin in Sharp's Brigade, Johnson's Division, Lee's Corps, C.S. Army of Tennessee.

FORTY-FIRST OHIO (USA): This Yankee infantry regiment fought at the Battle of Franklin in Post's Second Brigade, Wood's Third Division, Fourth U.S. Army Corps.

FORTY-FIRST TENNESSEE (CSA): This Rebel infantry regiment fought at the Battle of Franklin in Strahl's Brigade, Brown's Division, Cheatham's Corps, C.S. Army of Tennessee.

FORTY-FOURTH ILLINOIS (USA): This Yankee infantry regiment fought at the Battle of Franklin in Opdycke's First Brigade, Wagner's Second Division, Fourth U.S. Army Corps.

FORTY-FOURTH MISSISSIPPI (CSA): This Rebel infantry regiment fought at the Battle of Franklin in Sharp's Brigade, Johnson's Division, Lee's Corps, C.S. Army of Tennessee.

FORTY-NINTH ALABAMA (CSA): This Rebel infantry regiment fought at the Battle of Franklin in Scott's Brigade, Loring's Division, Stewart's Corps, C.S. Army of Tennessee.

FORTY-NINTH OHIO (USA): This Yankee infantry regiment fought at the Battle of Franklin in Streight's First Brigade, Wood's Third Division, Fourth U.S. Army Corps.

FORTY-NINTH TENNESSEE (CSA): This Rebel infantry regiment fought at the Battle of Franklin in Quarles' Brigade, Walthall's Division, Stewart's Corps, C.S. Army of Tennessee.

FORTY-SECOND GEORGIA (CSA): This Rebel infantry regiment fought at the Battle of Franklin in Stovall's Brigade, Clayton's Division, Lee's Corps, C.S. Army of Tennessee.

FORTY-SECOND ILLINOIS (USA): This Yankee infantry regiment fought at the Battle of Franklin in Bradley's Third Brigade, Wagner's Second Division, Fourth U.S. Army Corps.

FORTY-SECOND TENNESSEE (CSA): This Rebel infantry regiment fought at the Battle of Franklin in Quarles' Brigade, Walthall's Division, Stewart's Corps, C.S. Army of Tennessee.

FORTY-SEVENTH TENNESSEE (CSA): This Rebel infantry regiment fought at the Battle of Franklin in Vaughan's Brigade, Brown's Division, Cheatham's Corps, C.S. Army of Tennessee.

FORTY-SIXTH ALABAMA (CSA): This Rebel infantry regiment fought at the Battle of Franklin in Pettus' Brigade, Stevenson's Division, Lee's Corps, C.S. Army of Tennessee.

FORTY-SIXTH GEORGIA (CSA): This Rebel infantry regiment fought at the Battle of Franklin in Gist's Brigade, Brown's Division, Cheatham's Corps, C.S. Army of Tennessee.

FORTY-SIXTH MISSISSIPPI (CSA): This Rebel infantry regiment fought at the Battle of Franklin in Sears' Brigade, French's Division, Stewart's Corps, C.S. Army of Tennessee.

FORTY-SIXTH TENNESSEE (CSA): This Rebel infantry regiment fought at the Battle of Franklin in Quarles' Brigade, Walthall's Division, Stewart's Corps, C.S. Army of Tennessee.

FORTY-THIRD GEORGIA (CSA): This Rebel infantry regiment fought at the Battle of Franklin in Stovall's Brigade, Clayton's Division, Lee's Corps, C.S. Army of Tennessee.

FORTY-THIRD MISSISSIPPI (CSA): This Rebel infantry regiment fought at the Battle of Franklin in Adams' Brigade, Loring's Division, Stewart's Corps, C.S. Army of Tennessee.

FOSTER, SAMUEL T. (CSA): Foster began as a Confederate private in 1861 in Texas under Captain James W. Winters, whose orders were to protect European-American settlements from Native Americans. Later, as a captain who served under General Patrick R. Cleburne, he became a member of the Twenty-fourth Texas Cavalry (known as Granbury's Texas Brigade) and fought at the Battles of Franklin, Arkansas Post, Chickamauga, Pickett's Mill, and nearly all of the Army of Tennessee's battles during the Atlanta Campaign. He survived capture and the rigors of being a prisoner of war.

Foster is best known as a Confederate writer who recorded his impressions and experiences in his diaries during the War.

FOURTEENTH ILLINOIS CAVALRY (USA): This Yankee cavalry regiment fought at the Battle of Franklin in Biddle's Second Brigade, Johnson's Sixth Division, Wilson's Cavalry Corps.

FOURTEENTH LOUISIANA BATTALION SHARPSHOOTERS (CSA): This Rebel unit fought at the Battle of Franklin in Gibson's Brigade, Clayton's Division, Lee's Corps, C.S. Army of Tennessee.

FOURTEENTH MISSISSIPPI (CSA): This Rebel infantry regiment fought at the Battle of Franklin in Adams' Brigade, Loring's Division, Stewart's

Corps, C.S. Army of Tennessee.

FOURTEENTH OHIO BATTERY (USA): This Yankee artillery unit fought at the Battle of Franklin in Knipe's Seventh Division Artillery, Knipe's Seventh Division, Wilson's Cavalry Corps.

FOURTEENTH TENNESSEE CAVALRY (CSA): This Rebel cavalry regiment fought at the Battle of Franklin in Rucker's Brigade, Chalmers' Division, Forrest's Cavalry Corps, C.S. Army of Tennessee.

FOURTEENTH TEXAS CAVALRY - DISMOUNTED (CSA): This Rebel cavalry regiment served in Ector's Brigade, French's Division, Stewart's Corps, C.S. Army of Tennessee.

Ector's Brigade was at Franklin, Tennessee, during the Battle of Franklin. However, it did not participate in the battle as it was on detached duty at the time.

FOURTH ARKANSAS (CSA): This Rebel infantry regiment fought at the Battle of Franklin in Reynolds' Brigade, Walthall's Division, Stewart's Corps, C.S. Army of Tennessee.

FOURTH ARMY CORPS (USA): This particular Fourth Corps, which served with the U.S. Army of the Cumberland in the Western Theater, was led by Yankee Major General David Sloane Stanley at the Battle of Franklin. It is not to be confused with the Fourth Corps that served with the U.S. Army of the Potomac in the Eastern Theater.

FOURTH ARMY CORPS ARTILLERY (USA): This Yankee artillery unit fought at the Battle of Franklin under the command of U.S. Captain Lyman A. Bridges.

The unit was comprised of the Twenty-fifth Indiana Light Battery, First Michigan Battery, First Kentucky Battery, First Ohio Light (Batteries A and G), Sixth Ohio Battery, Twentieth Ohio Battery, Second Pennsylvania Battery, and the Fourth U.S. Regular (Battery M).

FOURTH FLORIDA (CSA): This Rebel infantry regiment fought at the Battle of Franklin in Finley's Brigade, Bate's Division, Cheatham's Corps, C.S. Army of Tennessee.

FOURTH GEORGIA BATTALION SHARPSHOOTERS (CSA): This Rebel infantry regiment fought at the Battle of Franklin in Tyler's Brigade, Bate's Division, Cheatham's Corps, C.S. Army of Tennessee.

FOURTH KENTUCKY MOUNTED INFANTRY (USA): This Yankee cavalry regiment fought at the Battle of Franklin in Croxton's First Brigade, McCook's First Division, Wilson's Cavalry Corps.

FOURTH LOUISIANA (CSA): This Rebel infantry regiment fought at the Battle of Franklin in Gibson's Brigade, Clayton's Division, Lee's Corps, C.S. Army of Tennessee.

FOURTH LOUISIANA BATTALION (CSA): This Rebel unit fought at the Battle of Franklin in Gibson's Brigade, Clayton's Division, Lee's Corps, C.S. Army of Tennessee.

FOURTH MISSISSIPPI (CSA): This Rebel infantry regiment fought at the Battle of Franklin in Sears' Brigade, French's Division, Stewart's Corps, C.S. Army of Tennessee.

FOURTH MISSOURI (CSA): This Rebel infantry regiment fought at the Battle of Franklin in Cockrell's Brigade, French's Division, Stewart's Corps, C.S. Army of Tennessee.

FOURTH TENNESSEE (CSA): This Rebel infantry regiment fought at the Battle of Franklin in Strahl's Brigade, Brown's Division, Cheatham's Corps, C.S. Army of Tennessee.

FOURTH TENNESSEE - PROVISIONAL (CSA): This Rebel infantry regiment fought at the Battle of Franklin in Maney's Brigade, Brown's Division, Cheatham's Corps, C.S. Army of Tennessee.

FOURTH TENNESSEE CAVALRY (USA): This Yankee cavalry regiment fought at the Battle of Franklin in Hammond's First Brigade, Knipe's Seventh Division, Wilson's Cavalry Corps.

FOURTH U.S. REGULAR ARTILLERY - BATTERY I (USA): This Yankee artillery unit fought at the Battle of Franklin in Hatch's Fifth Division Artillery,

Wilson's Cavalry Corps.

FOURTH U.S. REGULAR BATTERY (USA): This Yankee artillery unit fought at the Battle of Franklin in the Fourth U.S. Army Corps Artillery.

FRANKLIN, BENJAMIN: The great American inventor, printer, diplomat, scientist, publisher, and statesmen earns a spot in this encyclopedia for not only lending his name to the city of Franklin, Tennessee, but for being related to some of the families who are associated with the Battle of Franklin.

In particular are the McGavocks of Carnton Plantation, whose spacious mansion became the largest and most important Confederate field hospital during the conflict. Franklin's great great-grandson, Dr. Dallas Bache, for example, married Alberta Pugsley McGavock, the grandniece of Randal McGavock, the eleventh mayor of Nashville and the founder of Carnton.

FRANKLIN PIKE: This was a primary thoroughfare in the 1860s that ran, and still runs, southwest from Nashville, Tennessee, all the way to historic Franklin Center, a distance of about twenty miles. The road was used December 16-17 by John Bell Hood's Confederate Army of Tennessee as an escape route after the disastrous Rebel loss at the Battle of Nashville, December 15-16, 1864.

Union General George H. Thomas' army chased the ragged fleeing Confederate troops along Franklin Pike, harassing them and skirmishing with them along the way, as they desperately fled south toward Franklin. Many Confederate soldiers deserted, or were wounded or captured, during the "shameful rout," as one Rebel officer called it.

Today Franklin Pike, which merges with Highway 31, is a busy avenue also known as Franklin Road. Few of the speeding motorists who now hurtle along its scenic curves take notice of the small historical markers along its roadsides with the tragic caption: "Hood's Retreat."

FRANKLIN RAILROAD DEPOT: Located at Franklin, Tennessee, this plain brick railroad storage facility was constructed in 1858 by the Tennessee and Alabama Railroad

Company for the sole purpose of shipping and receiving freight. It is one of only two antebellum railroad buildings left standing in the state of Tennessee.

In 1862 U.S. troops illegally seized both the depot and the surrounding rail lines, using them to transfer troops and military supplies in and out of the area. Before and during the Battle of Franklin II (November 30, 1864) the depot housed Union arms and ammunition.

During the Battle of Franklin III (December 17, 1864), Confederate troops under General Stephen Dill Lee tried to burn the depot down in an attempt to prevent the Yanks from acquiring seven wagon loads of ammunition being stored there at the time. Fortunately for history, a local citizen doused out the fire, averting a major explosion and saving the building for posterity.

After the Battle of Franklin III, damaged railroad track was repaired and wounded Yankee soldiers were evacuated to Nashville for further convalescence.

After Lincoln's War, in 1866, the line was reorganized as the Nashville and Decatur Railroad. The "road," as it was known to Victorians, has changed hands numerous times since the War, and is still in use to this day.

While the Franklin Railroad Depot is certainly one of America's most important historical treasures, it has been largely ignored over the years, probably due to its cheerless appearance and out of the way location. And though it is eligible for the National Register of Historic Places, as of this writing it has not yet been included. It is hoped that this oversight will be soon corrected.

FRANKLIN, TENNESSEE: Established in 1799—three years after Tennessee became a state, and named after celebrated American statesman and Founding Father Benjamin Franklin, the town of Franklin is located in Williamson County, in Middle Tennessee, and is the site of the topic of this book.

The county seat of Williamson County, Franklin has tripled in population since 1980. This is due, in large part, to its scenic beauty, booming economy, easy access to interstate highways, quality educational system, temperate weather, and eighteen-mile proximity to Music City: Nashville, world headquarters of country music.

The fifteen-block historic downtown area of Franklin is on the National Register of Historic Places, and indeed history breathes from literally every brick and blade of grass in the region. Despite the fact that the city is developing at an ever increasingly rapid rate, for the time being it remains a visually stunning city, surrounded by rolling green hills, sweeping horse farms, and vast crop lands.

To those interested in the War for Southern Independence, Franklin is most famous for the Battle of Franklin II, one of the nation's bloodiest and most senseless conflicts, fought here on November 30, 1864. Under the catastrophic orders of Confederate General John Bell Hood, the day was lost. The Confederacy, along with some 1,750 Rebel boys and men, was mortally wounded that day on the Plain of Franklin in a conflict that should never have been fought.

Forty-four Franklin homes, churches, and various buildings were used as field hospitals during and after the battle, many which still stand to this day. Numerous Civil War sites are available for touring, the most poignant being the McGavock Confederate Cemetery, where 1,480 Rebel soldiers from the conflict rest in America's largest privately owned Confederate graveyard.

General stats: Franklin is thirty square miles, situated at 648 feet above sea level, and had a population of about 48,000 in 2005. It is in America's Central Time Zone and GPS coordinates locate it at latitude 35.9 north by longitude 86.9 west.

It possesses fifteen colleges and professional schools, eight technical schools, and fifteen students per teacher. Median household income in 2005 was $74,691, while the median price for a home in Franklin in 2005 was $244,221. Sales tax in 2005 was 9.25%.

Franklin has an annual rainfall of 54.33 inches, with the average low temperature in January being 25 degrees and the average high temperature in July being 88 degrees. Though in the past, Franklin winters were harsh and long (similar to Northern winters today), 21st-Century Franklin sees little snow. During the winter of 2004 the town had less than one inch.

Franklin was voted, by at least one organization, the number one best American city to retire in. Nearby Brentwood was voted number one best town in which to raise children.

An important note: the Confederate Flag is never seen displayed in any official capacity in the town of Franklin. Tragically, one will not even see a Confederate Flag at the site of the Confederate Memorial in Franklin Center, the one place where it should be openly and proudly exhibited.

Presumably the city's ban on the South's most sacred banner is because it "represents slavery and bigotry."

There are several problems with this view, however, starting with Franklin itself: the town's namesake, Benjamin Franklin, was an ardent slave owner and racist, who believed in the concept of "white racial purity," and felt that the presence of blacks in America sullied the "pure nature" of whites.

As for the Confederate Flag being a symbol of slavery and bigotry, nothing could be further from the truth.

To begin with, the South did not fight over slavery, as President Jefferson Davis himself repeatedly asserted. She fought to preserve the Constitution of the Founding Fathers, the Confederate Republic they created, and the idea of states' rights—as tacitly promised in the Ninth and Tenth Amendments. Lincoln had pledged to alter all of these important facets of American tradition, which is the very reason the Southern states began seceding immediately after he was elected on November 8, 1860 (the first Southern state to secede, South Carolina, left the Union only a few weeks later, on December 20).

If the South fought over slavery, as the uneducated continue to insist, the Southern states would have seceded decades earlier, perhaps as early as the 1830s, when New England busybody William Lloyd Garrison began criticizing the South for practicing slavery at a time when slavery was still legal under the Constitution in every state, including those in the North. The hypocrisy of Garrison's attacks were even more absurd when we consider that both the American slave trade and American slavery got their start in his home state: Massachusetts.

In any event, if the "Civil War" had been over slavery, then the conflict would have ended on January 1, 1863, when Lincoln issued his fraudulent and unlawful Final Emancipation Proclamation. Instead, the War continued for another two years.

On August 15, 1864, Lincoln himself stated:

"My enemies pretend I am now carrying on this war for the sole purpose of abolition. So long as I am president, it shall be carried on for the sole purpose of restoring the Union."

Concerning the Confederate Flag, it could not be a symbol of racial hatred, and never has been, because by some estimates as many as 1 million African-Americans—along with 70,000 Native-Americans, 60,000 Latin-Americans, 50,000 foreigners, 12,000 Jewish-Americans, and 10,000 Asian-Americans—fought for the Confederacy. And the Confederate armies were not segregated like the Union armies. They were racially integrated, with every color fighting side by side on the battlefield from the first day of the War to the last.

It is the opinion of traditional Southerners then that if the town of Franklin is truly concerned with racism (and all decent people, whatever their color, are), the only reasonable decision would be to change the name of the city and start prominently displaying the Confederate Flag.

FRANKLIN TURNPIKE BRIDGE: No longer standing, this river crossing played a significant role during the Battles of Franklin I, II, and III.

Constructed in the Summer of 1819, at the time of the Battle of Franklin II, the two-lane covered bridge (with windows cut out on the sides) had earlier been burned by Confederate soldiers. Afterward, the remaining timbers were washed away by flooding, hampering both Confederate and Union troop movements.

The bridge was burned and rebuilt many more times over the following years. Falling into disrepair, it finally disappeared completely in 1927, replaced by the present day modern highway bridge over the Harpeth.

The Battle of Franklin III (December 17, 1864) took place around the bridge, and some of the original cut stone abutments can still be seen. As of this writing, this important Civil War location has not been preserved, and what little remains of the fragile site is slowly vanishing under brambles and refuse.

FRENCH, SAMUEL GIBBS (CSA): Of Norman and English heritage, French was born at Mullica Hill, Gloucester, New Jersey, November 22, 1818, the son of Yankee Quaker parents, Samuel French Sr. and Rebecca Clark.

French graduated fourteenth in his class from West Point in 1843, and on July 1 was assigned as lieutenant to the Third U.S. Artillery. For his gallantry at the Battles of Monterey, Palo Alta, Resaca de la Palma, and Buena Vista (Mexican-American War, 1846-1848), he was awarded twice for meritorious conduct.

On April 26, 1853, French married Eliza Matilda Roberts, from Philadelphia, Pennsylvania, with whom he had one child: Matilda Roberts French, born 1854 in Natchez, Mississippi.

When Lincoln's War came in 1861, French sided with the South and the Constitution. After leaving the U.S. army he joined the Confederacy, fighting at the Battle of Vicksburg and also throughout the Atlanta Campaign.

As a major general of one of the Confederate divisions under Lieutenant General Alexander P. Stewart, he was present at the Battle of Franklin. At the height of conflict French joined forces with Generals Patrick R. Cleburne and John C. Brown near the Carter House, where they engaged in violent hand-to-hand combat with U.S. General Emerson Opdycke and his men.

When the thirty-minute skirmish was over, the Union was still in control of its position, while Cleburne, one of the South's most brilliant officers, lay dead amidst the smoking carnage. Within hours the Confederacy itself would nearly perish at Franklin.

Suffering from a serious eye infection, French was not present at the Battle of Nashville.

Four months before the War ended, and eight years after his first wife Eliza passed away, French married Mary Fontaine Abercrombie, from Russell County, Alabama, on January 12, 1865. He had three children with Mary: Samuel Gibbs Jr., Ada Mary, and Robert Abercrombie.

By all accounts French lived a full and rich life. He died on April 20, 1901, in Florida (some say at Florala, Alabama)—one of the last remaining Confederate officers.

He was buried in Saint John's Cemetery, Pensacola, Florida. The French family home (built about 1766) can still be seen at 136 South Broad Street, Woodbury, New Jersey.

The story of how French, a Yankee-born Quaker, ended up a Confederate military man, is a fascinating one, which he chronicled in a detailed 1901-book with a lengthy title: *Two Wars: An Autobiography of General Samuel G. French, an Officer in the Armies of the United States and the Confederate States, a Graduate From the U.S. Military Academy, West Point, 1843 (Mexican War; War Between the States; A Diary; Reconstruction Period, His Experience; Incidents, Reminiscences, etc.).*

FRENCH'S DIVISION (CSA): This Rebel division, named after Confederate General Samuel Gibbs French, was present at the Battle of Franklin.

It was comprised of Ector's Brigade, Cockrell's Brigade, and Sears' Brigade.

FRENCH, THEODOSIA: Born on June 16, 1801 in Kentucky, Theodosia was the mother of Confederate Major General John Bell Hood, commander of the C.S. Army of Tennessee. Hood led the Confederacy at the Battle of Franklin, November 30, 1864.

Theodosia had three sons with her husband, Hood's father, John W. Hood. She died on January 12, 1866, in Montgomery County, Kentucky, and was buried in the French Graveyard, Montgomery County, Kentucky.

FULLERTON, JOSEPH SCOTT (USA): Fullerton was born on December 3, 1835, at Chillicothe, Ross County, Ohio, and graduated from the Miami University in 1855. He graduated from the Cincinnati Law School in 1858, then moved to Missouri.

With the onset of Lincoln's War, Fullerton sided with the North and against the Constitution. After joining the U.S. army, he became a lieutenant in the Second Missouri Infantry and an aide-de-camp of Union Major General Gordon Granger (after whom Franklin's Fort Granger was named).

After the Battle of Chickamauga, Fullerton rose to the rank of lieutenant colonel and was appointed an assistant adjutant general. Now serving with the Union's Army of the

Tennessee, he fought at such battles as Lovejoy Station, Kenesaw Mountain, Shelbyville, Dalton, New Hope Church, Pine-Top Mountain, Peach-Tree Creek, Atlanta, Jonesboro, Resaca, Buzzard Roost Gap, Columbia, Missionary Ridge, Spring Hill, and Nashville.

At the Battle of Franklin Fullerton served as the chief of staff of U.S. General David S. Stanley. Here he maintained a detailed diary of the events as they unfolded, important records that are of great use to historians to this day. For his service at Franklin he was brevetted brigadier general.

After the War he served under President Andrew Johnson as military secretary. During his tenure in this position, in a report known as *The Freedmen's Bureau: Reports of Generals [James B.] Steedman and Fullerton on the Condition of the Freedmen's Bureau in the Southern States*, he revealed the truth about the North's corrupt and racist Freedmen's Bureau, whose foul deeds he reported in great detail—much to the chagrin of liberal Northern politicians. The *New York Tribune* reported that Fullerton's investigations of the Bureau have "pricked some pretty bubbles. . . . [He has] exposed the hollowness of much maudlin [Yankee] sympathy for the Negro, etc."

Subsequently Fullerton was made postmaster at Saint Louis, Missouri, then afterward returned to his law practice, "disgusted with political life."

In 1890 he accepted the chairmanship of the Chickamauga and Chattanooga National Military Park Commission. On March 19, 1897, while returning to Washington, D.C. from a visit to the Chattanooga battlefield, he died in an accident on the Baltimore and Ohio Railroad near Oakland, Maryland. He was buried in Grandview Cemetery, Chillicothe, Ohio.

GALE, WILLIAM DUDLEY (CSA): Born in 1834 at Ashwood, Maury County, Tennessee, the son of Dr. Thomas Gale and Ann M. Greene, he is best known as "W. D. Gale."

Early on Fate connected this Tennessean of English descent with one of America's most famous families. On December 14, 1858, in Nashville, Davidson County, Tennessee, he married (his second wife) Katherine Polk, a second cousin once removed of U.S. President James K. Polk.

An enthusiastic supporter of the Confederate Cause, at the onset of Lincoln's War Gale sided with the South and the Constitution. Eagerly joining the militia, he served as a staff officer for his father-in-law, General (Philemon) Leonidas Polk. When Polk died in 1864 at the Battle of Pine Mountain, Georgia, Gale was appointed assistant adjutant general to Confederate General Alexander P. Stewart, under whom he served at the Battle of Franklin.

A talented writer and a keen observer of detail, Gale's vivid writings and letters have often been quoted by Civil War researchers and historians.

Gale and Polk had six known children: Frances, William Dudley Jr., Katherine, Leonidas Polk, Josephine, and Ethel. Gale passed away at Nashville, Tennessee, on January 30, 1888. Katherine followed him to the grave twenty-eight years later, on February 8, 1916.

GARDNER, A. V. (CSA): Confederate Captain Gardner led the Twenty-ninth Alabama Infantry at the Battle of Franklin, where he was wounded in action.

GARLAND, HUGH ALFRED, JR. (CSA): The son of Hugh Alfred Garland Sr. and Ann Powell Burwell, Garland was born in Saint Louis, Missouri, in 1835.

With the onset of

Lincoln's War, he sided with the South and the Constitution. After joining the Confederate army he served as a captain (of Company F, Second Regiment, Missouri Volunteer Militia), a major, and finally as a lieutenant colonel.

He fought at numerous battles, including Shiloh and Corinth. It was on November 30, 1864, at the Battle of Franklin, while leading the First Missouri Infantry, that Colonel Garland lost his life. He was temporarily buried on the battlefield. His remains were later reinterred in Bellefontaine Cemetery, Saint Louis, Missouri.

GARRETT, M. P. (CSA): Confederate Captain Garrett led the First and Fifteenth Arkansas Infantries at the Battle of Franklin, where he was killed in action.

GARRITY'S ALABAMA BATTERY (CSA): This Rebel battery fought at the Battle of Franklin with Courtney's Battalion, Lee's Corps Artillery, C.S. Army of Tennessee.

GARVIN, JOHN S. (CSA): Confederate Colonel Garvin led the Twenty-sixth Alabama Infantry at the Battle of Franklin, where he was wounded in action.

GATES, ELIJAH (CSA): Confederate Colonel Gates led the First and Third Missouri Cavalries (dismounted) at the Battle of Franklin, where he was wounded in action.

GEORGIAN STYLE: In Great Britain, Georgian was the predominant architectural style from 1714 to 1837. It was named for three English kings named George who reigned during this period. It is commonly divided into three time frames: Early, Palladian, and Late.

Considered a response to the earlier more staid Baroque style of the 1600s, some important British Georgian architects and designers were Inigo Jones, Thomas Chippendale, Robert Adams, and George Hepplewhite

The Georgian style emphasizes a square symmetry, light and balance, spaciousness and comfort, pastel colors, and soft elegant furnishings, and conveys an image of distinction and prosperity. Georgian floors are bare wood, marble, or stone, covered with tasteful rugs, while front doors have fanlight and sidelight windows. Typical Georgian colors are pale, sometimes dusky, and include greys, blues, pinks, burgundys, and greens.

In Europe the Georgian period is called Neoclassical, while in America it was referred to as the Colonial style until about 1775. After the American Revolution it was called the Federal style, the style most popular among Victorians during the time of the Battle of Franklin.

American Georgian Colonial houses feature a rectangular shape, a centered front door, paired chimneys, five windows across the front upper part of the house, nine to twelve panes in each window, and columns on either side of the front door—which are often enclosed in a type of portico influenced by Italian, and even ancient Roman and Greek architectural designs.

Georgian-style houses that survived the Battle of Franklin into the present day can be seen along the "Tennessee Antebellum Trail."

GETTYSBURG OF THE WEST: Another name for the Battle of Franklin, alluding to the devastating carnage and high casualty rate of this very short but extremely bloody conflict.

GHOSTS: In the city of Franklin, Tennessee, the passing of a century and a half has not yet dimmed the memories of November 30, 1864. The suffering, violence, and carnage of the Battle of Franklin has left its imprint in the very buildings, homes, and forlorn bluegrass fields of surrounding Williamson County.

Indeed, despite its stunning outward beauty and charm, to this day Franklin retains a melancholy ambiance, a somber heaviness that is felt by young and old alike. Little wonder. Nearly 2,000 Confederates perished, and many thousands more were wounded on the Plain of Franklin on that mild Indian Summer afternoon.

For believers, the dark side of the Battle of Franklin manifests in hundreds of legends, tales, and stories of ghosts, goblins, and demonic apparitions, said to thoroughly haunt the area. Though all of Franklin is considered haunted by some, perhaps no single place so epitomizes the ghostly aspect of the Battle of Franklin as Carnton

Plantation. Indeed, there is good reason to believe that it well deserves its moniker: "Tennessee's most haunted Civil War house"!

For one thing, the family who built it and lived there for eighty-five years, the McGavocks, are thought to have been cursed. After nearly nine decades of family misfortunes, the incredible suffering experienced here left behind powerful psychic imprints of family tragedies, including everything from intimidation and theft by Yankee troops, to murder, a beheading, and the premature deaths of numerous infants, adolescents, and teens. Many adults passed away at Carnton as well, most presumably from "natural causes."

It is Carnton's role in the Battle of Franklin, however, that most powerfully connects it to the world of the supernatural.

For six months, thousands of soldiers were operated on, convalesced, and died in Carnton's spacious rooms, in her outbuildings, and in her surrounding yards. Thousands of limbs were amputated and piled outside the windows, while the wailing of the wounded and dying echoed through Carnton's walls for 180 days, outlasting even than the War itself (which ended two months earlier, in April 1865).

Add to this the McGavock Confederate Cemetery, the largest privately owned Confederate cemetery in the U.S. Within its cheerless black iron fences rest nearly 1,500 soldiers, many whose graves are still visited by relations and strangers alike. The cemetery even has its own resident ghostly "guide," a solemn looking soldier dressed in full Confederate regalia, who leads people through the grounds, then vanishes into thin air at the far end.

Every manner of supernatural being has been witnessed around Carnton. Among them: floating heads, shapeless masses, headless torsos, odd balls of light, Victorian perfumes, colored mists, and moving objects; and of course, the specters of Confederate generals, Victorian ladies, and mischievous 19th-Century children. Screams, cries, and moans have been heard around Carnton, as well, as have been the sounds of battle and galloping horses. I myself have captured ghostly images on camera at

Carnton.

Even the most hard-nosed skeptic might become a believer during a visit to Franklin, Tennessee, the once bloody site upon which the Confederacy was mortally wounded.

GIBSON, RANDALL LEE (CSA): Gibson was born September 10, 1832, on a plantation at Versailles, Kentucky. He graduated from Yale University in 1853, received a law degree from the University of Louisiana (later renamed Tulane University), then removed to Madrid, Spain, where he worked for the American embassy.

With the onset of Lincoln's War, Gibson sided with the South and the Constitution. After Louisiana seceded from the Union, he became an aide-de-camp to Louisiana Governor Thomas Moore. He then joined the Confederate army, becoming colonel of the Thirteenth Louisiana Infantry—which fought at the battles of Chickamauga and Shiloh.

In early 1864 Gibson attained the rank of brigadier general, fighting in the Atlanta Campaign and, under General John Bell Hood, at the battles of Franklin and Nashville.

After the War he served as a board member of various institutions, including stints as regent of the Smithsonian Institution and president of Tulane University's board of administration. (The school's Gibson Hall was named after him.)

Gibson served as a democratic (then a conservative) Louisiana congressman and later as a senator. He passed away at Hot Springs, Arkansas, on December 15, 1892, before his senatorial term ended, however. The general was buried in Lexington Cemetery, Lexington, Kentucky.

GIBSON'S BRIGADE (CSA): This Rebel infantry brigade fought at the Battle of Franklin in Clayton's Division, Lee's Corps, C.S. Army of Tennessee.

Named after Confederate Brigadier General Randall Lee Gibson, it was comprised of the First Louisiana, Fourth Louisiana, Thirteenth Louisiana, Sixteenth Louisiana, Nineteenth Louisiana, Twentieth Louisiana, Twenty-fifth Louisiana, Thirtieth Louisiana, Fourth Louisiana Battalion, and Fourteenth Louisiana Battalion

Sharpshooters.

GIST STREET: A Franklin, Tennessee, street named in honor of Confederate Brigadier General States Rights Gist, who died at the Battle of Franklin fighting for constitutional freedom.

GIST, STATES RIGHTS (CSA): Of English and Irish descent, and born in Union County, South Carolina, on September 3, 1831, Gist was the son of Nathaniel Gist and Elizabeth Lewis McDaniel, and a first cousin of South Carolina Governor William Henry Gist.

After graduating from South Carolina College, he attended Harvard Law School, then returned to his home state where he became a successful attorney.

The late 1850s saw an explosive resistance in the South toward the North's dictatorial tendencies and flagrant violations of the Constitution regarding states' rights. Gist, from a strong Confederate family, eagerly joined the South Carolina militia in 1859, where upon, acting as inspector general, he was sent to obtain weaponry for the looming and fateful Battle of Fort Sumter.

In July 1861, as an aide to Brigadier General Barnard E. Bee, Gist fought at the Battle of First Manassas, taking over temporary command of the brigade when Bee was killed shortly thereafter.

Impressed with his valor and mastery of military tactics, his superiors promoted Gist to the rank of brigadier general on March 20, 1862, whereupon he began serving under Confederate General John Clifford Pemberton in South Carolina.

On May 6, 1863, Gist found time to travel back to South Carolina and marry Jane Margaret Adams, the daughter of South Carolina Governor James Hopkins Adams, both descendants of the royal Dudley family of England. The couple's marriage, and happiness, were to be short-lived, however.

After fighting with Confederate General Joseph E. Johnston at Vicksburg, Mississippi, in July 1863, Gist was reassigned to the Army of Tennessee, which unbeknownst to him, would seal his doom. With the Tennesseans, Gist fought courageously at Atlanta, Chattanooga, and Chickamauga.

In the fall of 1864 Gist found himself on the Plain of Franklin commanding a brigade under General John C. Brown. It was here, on November 30, that Gist gave his life for the Southern Cause. Leading his men, the Twenty-fourth South Carolina, into the smoke-laden battlefield, his horse was shot out from under him. As he was continuing his fearless assault on foot toward the enemy, a single bullet pierced him through the heart, and he went into shock.

According to local Franklin tradition, Gist died on the field, after which his body was taken to Carnton Plantation. Here, so it is said, his body was laid out on the lower porch, along with the corpses of generals Cleburne, Strahl, and Adams, so the soldiers could pay their final respects.

Objective research has revealed, however, that Gist did not die on the battlefield, nor was he taken to Carnton. According to Gist's African-American servant, Wiley Howard, the general, still clinging to life, was taken to a field hospital (house) two miles west of the Carter House, where he perished on the night of November 30. His body was then taken to the home of William White on Boyd Mill Road, where it was buried under a cedar tree. Gist was later reinterred in the Trinity Episcopal Church Cemetery at Columbia, Richland County, South Carolina.

Besides his impressive military record and valiant death at the Battle of Franklin, it is Gist's first and middle names that inspire the most awe (from Southerners) and curiosity (from Northerners). In 1831, his parents, being enthusiastic Confederates, hopefully named (or nicknamed) the boy, one of eight sons, for the cause for which the South would later enter into Lincoln's tragic and senseless nightmare: the War for Southern Independence. To this day, both the man and the name States Rights Gist, live on in the hearts of freedom lovers everywhere.

GIST'S BRIGADE (CSA): This Rebel infantry brigade fought at the Battle of Franklin in Brown's Division, Cheatham's Corps, C.S. Army of Tennessee.

The brigade, named after Confederate Brigadier General States Rights Gist, was comprised of the Forty-sixth Georgia, Sixty-fifth Georgia, Sixteenth South Carolina, Twenty-fourth South Carolina, and Second Battalion Georgia Sharpshooters.

After General Gist was killed at Franklin, command of the brigade was taken over by Lieutenant Colonel Zachariah L. Watters.

GOLDTHWAITE'S ALABAMA BATTERY (CSA): This Rebel battery fought at the Battle of Franklin in Hotchkiss' Battalion, Cheatham's Corps Artillery, C.S. Army of Tennessee.

GORDON, GEORGE WASHINGTON (CSA): Best known as George W. Gordon, and of Scottish and Irish descent, he has the unique distinction of being called "the last Confederate general," living into the second decade of the 20th Century.

Gordon was born on October 5, 1836, at Pulaski, Giles County, Tennessee. He was the son of Andrew Gordon and Elizabeth Kennedy Goff. He attended the University of Nashville, where it is believed he was a classmate of the famous "boy hero of the Confederacy," Sam Davis, who at age twenty-one was hanged by Yankee troops for refusing to reveal military information. An accomplished violinist, when war came, Gordon, along with his entire class, volunteered their lives for the Confederate Cause: self-determination.

Described as 5'8", with brown hair to his shoulders and a face "without a trace of effeminacy," the twenty-nine year old began military life as a regimental drill master, quickly becoming captain, lieutenant, lieutenant-colonel, and colonel. He was finally promoted to brigadier general, remaining the youngest of that rank until the end of the War.

Gordon fought in countless battles, including Chattanooga, Missionary Ridge, Chickamauga, Resaca, Kennesaw Mountain, Dead Angle, Peach Tree Creek, Jonesboro, and Murfreesboro. Through this he survived two serious injuries, two captures, and two imprisonments, all while serving under Confederate Generals Felix Zollicoffer, Kirby Smith, and Braxton Bragg.

Finally, Gordon, known for his long warrior-like hair, marched with the Army of Tennessee to Franklin, November 30, 1864, into the doomed Battle of Franklin. It was here, while leading Vaughan's Brigade, Cheatham's Corps, that every commander in

Brown's Division was killed except Gordon, who was wounded and captured and taken to Fort Warren, George's Island, Boston, Massachusetts, where he remained a prisoner until his release on July 24, 1865.

Gordon returned to Tennessee just as so-called "Reconstruction" was beginning, another humiliation to an already defeated and oppressed South. He was appalled to find bands of scallywags and carpetbaggers—along with gangs of freed blacks—looting, pillaging, raping, and burning their way across his beloved land. Hundreds of innocent men, women, and children were suffering, and even dying, because of nothing more than their former support of the Confederacy.

In response, Gordon joined in the operation of the newly found "Order of the White Rose," a movement whose stated goals were the enforcement of civil law and the protection of all Southern people, whatever their race, color, or creed.

Later renamed the Ku Klux Klan, Gordon became the first Grand Dragon of the Tennessee chapter, and also the author of the Klan's first handbook describing its purposes (i.e., the protection of Confederate families from the general lawlessness that was then spreading in the postwar years).

By 1869, in reaction to violent and racist black gangs (indoctrinated by Yankee anti-South groups), certain elements of the KKK began to take on racist overtones. As this was not what the founders had intended, staunch supporter General Nathan Bedford Forrest disbanded the group.

Gordon became attorney-general of Shelby County, Tennessee, and on September 5, 1876, in the town of Bartlett, he married Ora Susan Paine, becoming an uncle by marriage of the future mayor of Memphis, Rowlett Paine. Tragically, within weeks of their honeymoon at Niagra Falls, Ora passed away of disease while in a "weakened state of body," and a sorrowful Gordon lived alone for the next twenty-three years.

At Pulaski, Tennessee, he practiced law and served as a state railroad commissioner (in 1883). A lover of Nature, solitude, and the great outdoors, in 1885 the U.S. Department of the Interior assigned him to head an Indian Agency in Nevada and Arizona, a position which he must have eagerly embraced. When his term expired he returned to Memphis and was appointed superintendent of schools in 1892.

In 1899 he married a second time, on this occasion to Mary Harbor "Minnie" Hannah of Memphis, and in 1906 he was elected Tennessee's Representative in Congress (Democrat, Tenth District), and was reelected in 1908 and 1910.

While still in office in Memphis, and also serving as the commander-in-chief of the United Confederate Veterans, the aging commander died on August 9, 1911. Gordon, the last living Confederate general, was buried at Elmwood Cemetery, Memphis, Shelby County, Tennessee. A 1912-memorial address honoring Gordon noted that his funeral cortege was "a weeping city."

"George Washington" is a fitting name for a Confederate general like Gordon. America's first president is a hero to Southerners for his work in ratifying the new republic's Constitution, which empowered each state with its own individual rights (later completely ignored by big government, Constitution-hating liberals like Abraham Lincoln and Barack Obama). To this day, President Washington appears on horseback on the Great Confederate Seal.

GORDON'S BRIGADE (CSA): See Vaughan's Brigade.

GOVAN, DANIEL CHEVILLETTE (CSA): Of Scottish descent, and best known as Daniel C. Govan, he was born on July 3, 1827, in Northampton County, North Carolina, and raised in Mississippi. After attending South Carolina College, Govan, like thousands of other 19th-Century Americans, "headed for the hills" of California during the Gold Rush (1848-1858), in search of fame and fortune.

In 1852 he returned, empty-handed, to Mississippi, and there, in December of 1853, he married a Tennessee girl, Mary Otey. In 1861 the couple moved to Helena, Arkansas, where he became a farmer.

When Lincoln's War broke out, Govan, like most of his Confederate brethren, was quick to join, thinking they would "whip the Yanks" in a month or two. But such was not to be. Over the next four years he would fight at such battles as

Chickamauga, Shiloh, Missionary Ridge, Perryville, Pickett's Mill, and the Atlanta Campaign. At the Battle of Jonesboro he was captured, but later exchanged for a Union soldier.

As a brigadier general in the Army of Tennessee, he gallantly led Govan's Brigade at the Battle of Franklin in Cleburne's Division.

After the War he returned to his home in Helena, and was elected to the Arkansas Legislature. He served a brief stint as an Indian agent in Washington state at the request of President Grover Cleveland.

Govan spent his remaining years traveling between the homes of his fourteen children, finally passing away at Memphis, Tennessee, on March 12, 1911. He was buried in Hill Crest Cemetery, "the Little Arlington of the South," at Holly Springs, Marshall County, Mississippi.

GOVAN'S BRIGADE (CSA): This Rebel infantry brigade fought at the Battle of Franklin in Cleburne's Division, Cheatham's Corps, C.S. Army of Tennessee.

Named after Confederate Brigadier General Daniel Chevillette Govan it was comprised of the First Arkansas, Second Arkansas, Fifth Arkansas, Sixth Arkansas, Seventh Arkansas, Eighth Arkansas, Thirteenth Arkansas, Fifteenth Arkansas, Nineteenth Arkansas, and Twenty-fourth Arkansas.

GRANBURY STREET: A Franklin, Tennessee, street named in honor of Confederate Brigadier General Hiram Bronson Granbury, who fought for constitutional government at the Battle of Franklin.

GRANBURY, HIRAM BRONSON (CSA): Of Scandinavian and Irish descent, and the son of Baptist preacher Norvil R. Granberry and his wife Nancy McLaurin, Granbury was born March 1, 1831, in Copiah County, Mississippi. (Confusion over the spelling of Granbury's surname has continued into the present day. His family spelled it Granberry, but in later years the general preferred the spelling Granbury, for reasons unknown.)

After graduating from the Presbyterian school Oakland College, at Rodney, the lanky 6' 2" Mississippian moved to Sequin, Texas, around 1851, to practice law.

In 1858, while living in

Waco, he met and married Fannie Sims of Tuscaloosa, Alabama. He served as the chief justice of McLennan County, Texas, from 1856 to 1858, and on March 4, 1861, joined the Confederate Army to fight Lincoln and his illegal invasion of the South.

It was not long before Granbury achieved the rank of captain and was placed in charge of the Waco Guards, a group later combined with the Seventh Texas Infantry.

In February 1862, now a major, Granbury was captured at Fort Donelson, spending one month as a prisoner of war at Fort Chase in Columbia, Ohio, then an additional six months in the Union prison at Fort Warren, George's Island, Boston, Massachusetts.

A side note: The famed Confederate lieutenant-colonel, Randal McGavock, was captured with Granbury at Fort Donelson. After their release, they would fight alongside each other once more at the Battle of Raymond (Mississippi), on May 12, 1863. Granbury survived, but McGavock would lose his life at Raymond to Yankee steel. In a strange twist of fate, unbeknownst to Granbury at the time, Randal's first cousin, Confederate Colonel John W. McGavock, owned Carnton Plantation, on whose lower back porch Granbury's corpse would be laid in less than two years.

Not allowed on George's Island, Fannie took up residence at the house of a Confederate friend in Hagerstown, Maryland. While he was in prison she wanted to be as near to her beloved husband as possible—a fatal error motivated by all the right reasons. Exposure to the harsh northern elements soon took their toll, and that, along with an unusual abdominal malady, forced Fannie to return to the South. Sadly, she was so ill by then that a full recovery was now impossible.

After his release from prison on August 27, 1862 (he had been exchanged for two Yankee lieutenants), Granbury took Fannie to several doctors, then traveled with her from Hagerstown back to her father's home in Tuscaloosa.

As her death approached, Granbury took her to Providence Hospital in Mobile, where she passed away on March 20, 1863, only a few days shy of their fifth wedding anniversary. He could not afford a gravestone, let alone a grave plot, and Fannie was buried in an unmarked location in Magnolia Cemetery, Mobile, where she remains to this day.

Returning to the battlefield, the thirty-one year old widower fought at Vicksburg, Chattanooga, Jackson, (as mentioned) Raymond, Chickamauga, and Ringgold Gap, where, for his valor, he was promoted to brigadier general. Serving under the famed Irish cavalryman General Patrick R. Cleburne, Granbury soon won both his commander's admiration and friendship.

But, like his childless marriage, this friendship too would last but a brief time.

On November 30, 1864, Granbury marched out on to the Plain of Franklin to meet his destiny in General John Bell Hood's senseless attack against the Union forces under Hood's former West Point roommate, General John McAllister Schofield.

Charging through the chaos of smoke, artillery bursts, and mangled corpses, Granbury received a Yankee bullet below his right eye. According to eyewitnesses, the top of his head was blown off, and he sank to his knees with his face in his hands. He remained in this gruesome death pose until his corpse could be safely removed from the field the next day.

It was on this day, December 1, that Granbury's body was taken to Colonel John McGavock's house, Carnton Mansion, in Franklin, Tennessee, and laid upon its lower deck, along with three other Confederate generals who were killed at the Battle of Franklin: Patrick R. Cleburne, Otho F. Strahl, and John C. Adams. Hundreds of teary-eyed soldiers marched by with their hats in their hands, paying their last respects to the commanders they adored.

Granbury was first buried in Ashland Cemetery near Columbia, Tennessee. In 1893, however, Confederate veterans living in Hood County, Texas, funded the general's reinterment in the town named for him.

On November 30, 1893, twenty-nine years to the day of Granbury's death, 5,000 people, including both Confederate and Union veterans, gathered at Granbury Cemetery, Granbury, Texas, for his ceremonial reburial.

It is worth noting that on that day over 100 years ago, one

of the speakers, Colonel M. D. Herring, reminded the mourners that the Confederate soldiers did not fight for slavery, but for the principal of states' rights as embodied in the Ninth and Tenth Amendments.

A final epitaph: Granbury's courageous and battle-hardened infantry, the Seventh Texas, finally surrendered a mere five months later, in April 1865 in Durham, North Carolina, with only sixty-seven out of the 1,005 men it had started with just a few years earlier. Granbury's name and legend lives on.

GRANBURY'S BRIGADE (CSA): This Rebel infantry brigade fought at the Battle of Franklin in Cleburne's Division, Cheatham's Corps, C.S. Army of Tennessee.

This brigade, named after Confederate Brigadier General Hiram Bronson Granbury, was comprised of the Fifth Confederate, Thirty-fifth Tennessee, Sixth Texas, Seventh Texas, Tenth Texas, Fifteenth Texas, Seventeenth Texas Cavalry (dismounted), Eighteenth Texas Cavalry (dismounted), Twenty-fourth Texas Cavalry (dismounted), Twenty-fifth Texas Cavalry (dismounted), and Nutt's Louisiana Cavalry (dismounted).

After General Granbury was killed in action at Franklin, the brigade was taken over by Captain Edward Thomas Broughton Jr.

GRANNY WHITE PIKE: This Tennessee road, which today runs from Woodmont Boulevard in Nashville south to Murray Lane in Franklin, was the principle line followed by Confederate General John Bell Hood and his troops following the disaster at the Battle of Nashville, December 15-16, 1864.

Chased by Union forces from Nashville, the route is today known as "Hood's Retreat." Arriving back in Franklin on the seventeenth, Hood's forces skirmished with the Yanks again, culminating in the Battle of Franklin III.

GRANT, ULYSSES S. (USA): The son of Jesse Root Grant and Hannah Simpson, he was born on April 27, 1822 in a cabin at Point Pleasant, Ohio. Of English descent, his birth name was Hiram Ulysses Grant.

In 1839 he attended West Point, where his name was

mistakenly written Ulysses S. Grant (the "S" indicating Simpson, his mother's maiden name) on his application. The patriotic name, "U. S. Grant," stuck, to the delight of his classmates. But there must have been some disappointment when he graduated four years later, in 1843, with below average grades.

An unenthusiastic soldier, over the next few years he served posts in Detroit, Michigan, Sackets Harbor, New York, Fort Vancouver, Oregon, and Fort Humboldt, California. In Texas he served under the soon-to-be twelfth president of the U.S., General Zachary Taylor, and also fought in the Mexican War (1846-1848).

While serving in Missouri in 1847, he met Julia Boggs Dent, who he married on August 22, 1848 in Saint Louis, Missouri. They had four children: Ellen, Jesse, Ulysses Jr., and Frederick.

Trying his hand at countless occupations, Grant's early life was typified by numerous failures. Woodcutting, real estate, farming, rent collecting, selling ice, customs, leather work, all neglected to turn a profit, nearly forcing him into bankruptcy. By 1857 Grant's financial bottom had fallen out, and the depressed thirty-five year old pawned his watch to purchase Christmas presents for his family.

When the Southern states seceded from the U.S., Grant sided with the North and against the Constitution. After joining the Federal army in Illinois, he rose rapidly up the ranks from colonel to brigadier general. In February 1862 he captured Fort Donelson and Fort Henry, stunning victories that won him promotion to major general.

At the Battle of Shiloh in April 1862, Grant lost time, ground, and men in an ill-planned attack, when Confederate forces overran him. Charges of "drunkenness and gross negligence" were filed against him, and Lincoln was asked to remove him from his command.

Refusing on the grounds that Grant was a true fighter, Lincoln made him commander of both the U.S. Army of the Tennessee and the U.S. Army of the Ohio, an appointment that would later prove to be—from a Federal point of view—an incredibly shrewd move.

Victories at Jackson, Mississippi, Vicksburg, Mississippi, and Gettysburg, Pennsylvania, soon followed, making Grant a household name. Promoted to supreme commander in the West, he went on to yet another victory in November 1863, this time at the Battle of Chattanooga.

Another promotion, now to lieutenant general, finally led to the highest rank the U.S. military could bestow: in February 1864 Lincoln appointed Grant "supreme commander of all Union forces."

With 500,000 men now under his auspices, Grant set about the job of putting an end to the War as quickly as possible. This he did by seeking the destruction of Confederate armies rather than the mere capture of cities and regions. It was in this way that he earned the nickname "Unconditional Surrender" Grant.

In addition, he planned to coordinate the Union Army and the Union River Fleet in an effort to cut off supplies to the South. At the same time he kept shipping routes open from the North, which allowed a constant stream of fresh men, horses, artillery, ammunition, food, and clothing to continue pouring in. His strategy was brilliant and would prove to be the lynchpin that would ultimately undo the South.

But much Yankee blood would be spilled before Grant's final conquest.

In May and June 1864, for example, he lost nearly 60,000 men against Confederate General Robert E. Lee at the Battle of Cold Harbor, in Virginia. Some 7,000 Yankees were lost in one day alone. The appalling Union bloodbath earned him a new nickname, "the butcher," and Grant himself later wrote regretfully of the entire incident. This was only a temporary setback in his career, however.

In November 1864, Grant's commander, U.S. General John McAllister Schofield, scored a major victory at the bloody Battle of Franklin, against the old-fashioned Confederate General John Bell Hood, while another of Grant's commanders, U.S. General George Henry Thomas, captured Nashville just two weeks later.

With the loss of thousands of men and dozens of commanding officers, not to mention the loss of the cities of Franklin and Nashville, the South's Army of Tennessee—the Confederacy's last great hope—was crushed. A humiliated Hood and the tattered remains of his once great army were chased all the way back to Tupelo, Mississippi. Hood resigned in Alabama and his command was taken over by Confederate General Richard Taylor—though the post had little meaning by then.

As Franklin and Nashville were falling, Union war criminal General Philip H. Sheridan took over the Shenandoah Valley, while another Yankee war criminal, General William T. Sherman, burned and pillaged his way across South Carolina and Georgia.

On April 9, 1865, Lee surrendered to Grant at Appomattox Court House, Virginia. After four long bloody, and many would say, useless, years, the Union had militarily—though not emotionally or psychologically, defeated its Confederate neighbors to the South.

It was not a happy day for anyone. Grant, to his credit, did not gloat over his hard-won victory. Instead he felt

"sad and depressed . . . rather than rejoicing at the downfall of a foe who had fought so long and valiantly, and had suffered so much for a cause."

Three years later, in 1868, still riding high on his military successes, the Republican (then liberal) Grant was easily elected eighteenth President of the U.S., the youngest man to take the office up to that time. But though commanding armies had come quite naturally to him, Grant was quick to discover that commanding a nation was something else entirely. Trying to run the government as if he were still a military officer was one problem. Choosing a series of unsuitable men, mainly friends, for his cabinet was another.

Not surprisingly, Grant's two-term presidency was filled with scandal, fraud, abuses, swindling, irregularities, charges of cronyism, and general improprieties, and to this day it is considered by many historians to be the second most corrupt administration in U.S. history after Lincoln's.

When his second term ended in 1877, Grant decided to travel, sailing with his family to Liverpool, England, where they excitedly began a two year trip around the world.

Years earlier, when he left the army to enter politics, he had forfeited a lifelong military income. Thus upon his return, financial problems continued to haunt the former president, despite his worldwide status as a famous military hero.

In early 1885 Congress finally agreed to put Grant back on a military salary, but by then it was too late: he was terminally ill with throat cancer (probably due to his lifelong cigar smoking habit).

Grant died on July 23, 1885, at Mount McGregor, New York, one week after he finished a book about his life in the army: *Personal Memoirs of U. S. Grant (1885-1886).* He was buried with full military honors in the famous "Grant's Tomb," located on the Hudson River in New York City.

By most accounts, the noted Union general and shy Yankee celebrity lived a double life, one in which he was a slovenly, indolent, and quarrelsome drunk, and the other in which he was a hardworking, moral and devoted husband and father. Which was he? It would be safe to say that he was something of both.

Close friends attest to his penchant for alcohol, and though he was not an overt daily drinker, their descriptions reveal a man with all the symptoms of alcoholism. Fortunately, though all admitted that he had an "inordinate love for liquors," Grant was able to keep his disease under control for the most part, even recruiting the help of clergy when his discipline weakened.

A more interesting question, and one directly pertaining to the nature of this encyclopedia, is Grant's position on slavery. Grant said it best himself:

"The North do not want, nor will they want, to interfere with the institution [of slavery]. . . . I [myself] never was an abolitionist, not even what could be called anti-slavery . . ."

Despite these sentiments, Grant felt strongly that the Union could not survive while slavery remained legal. It is strange then, in a little known fact of history, that Grant and his wife Julia who owned slaves.

Though his own father was an abolitionist, Grant had married a Southern girl whose parents, Frederick "Colonel" Dent and Ellen Bray Wrenshall, owned eighteen slaves. These African-American "servants," as they were more properly called, helped the Dents run their plantation, known as "White

Haven," at Saint Louis, Missouri.

Julia herself brought four personal slaves into her marriage with Grant, servants who, according to her memoirs, lived and worked with the couple until December 1865, well after the War had ended, and long after the passage of the Emancipation Proclamation in 1863.

Before the War, in the late 1850s, Grant too had been a slave owner. Grant's personal correspondences reveal that he owned three or four "Negro men," slaves who probably worked as field servants for the up-and-coming Union general and U.S. president. Contrary to most portrayals, Grant, like most other average Northern and Southern slave owners, was respectful and humane toward his African-American servants, and all were freed several years before the passage of the Emancipation Proclamation in 1863.

What is most disturbing is that Grant, at one time a non-abolitionist slaveholder, eventually accepted Lincoln's politically motivated fabrication that "slavery was the cause of the Civil War." In his 1885 memoir, even while openly admitting that *he gave little thought to slavery prior to the War*, Grant writes:

"The cause of the great War of the Rebellion against the United States will have to be attributed to slavery."

As history has shown, Grant could not have been more wrong. This statement still raises the hackles of traditional Southerners, and for good reason.

Unbeknownst to the unenlightened Yankee hero, as his men were firing at the enemy at Vicksburg in July of 1863, on the opposing side of the battlefield there rode a brave Confederate calvary officer whose name was States Rights Gist. His name was no accident. It was the very embodiment of the Southern Cause, one for which thousands of Southerners fought and died: constitutional freedom and self-government.

If Grant had been right, however, Gist's first name would have been "Slavery" (not States Rights), a laughable idea. For no Southerner would have left his home and family, or risked his life on the battlefield, to preserve a then legal institution which few Confederate families engaged in and which was already waning by the beginning of Lincoln's War.

However, the North chooses to view Grant, and despite his gentlemanly manner at the Confederacy's surrender, in the traditional South he will always be known as a flagrant war criminal, one who not only sanctioned numerous outrages against the Southern people, but who himself participated in the illegal, unconstitutional, un-Christian, and immoral destruction of Dixie—both during the War and afterward during so-called "Reconstruction."

GREAT SEAL OF THE CONFEDERATE STATES:

Little known to non-Southerners, the Confederacy had her own great seal, just as the U.S. had hers.

Known officially as the Great Seal of the Confederate States of America, it was engraved in 1864 by Joseph S. Wyon, of London, England. The original was made of silver and was about four inches in diameter.

According to the *Southern Historical Society Papers*, Vol. 16, Richmond, Virginia, January-December 1888:

"At the evacuation [of the Confederate Capital at Richmond, Virginia, in April 1865], [the seal] . . . was overlooked by the Confederate authorities, and subsequently fell into the possession of the late genial and accomplished [Confederate] Colonel John T. Pickett, of Washington, D.C., who, after having a number of electrotype copies in copper, silver and gold plating made from it, presented the original to Colonel William E. Earle, of Washington, D.C. This last gentleman, on December 27th, 1888, formally presented it to the State of South Carolina."

The center of the seal features an equestrian statue of Southern hero George Washington. Around him is a wreath of farm crops symbolizing the all important agrarian nature of the South.

Around the outer margin are the words: "The Confederate States of America: 22 February 1862." This is both the date of the start of the official Confederate government and the date of Washington's birthday.

Below the date are the words: "*Deo Vindice*," Latin for "God Will Vindicate Us," or "Under God, Our Vindicator."

To this day, exact replicas of the Great Seal of the Confederate States of America hang in the homes and offices of thousands of proud Southerners across Dixie. Educated non-Southerners also display the magnificent symbol of self-determination and states' rights.

GREEK REVIVAL ARCHITECTURE:

The American Greek Revival period began with the onset of the War of 1812 (against England) and ended in the 1850s. America's democratic roots in ancient Greece, along with a growing antipathy toward Anglo-style architecture (which was based on ancient Roman architecture and known in the U.S. as Federal), lent a particularly romantic appeal to Greek architectural styling.

Greek Revival features include: large doors and windows, low-pitched gabled roof, a porch (portico) with Corinthian, Doric, or Ionic square or rounded columns, rectangular lines around the front (arch-less) door (e.g., narrow sidelights and transom), and a cornice trim around the roof and porch.

In the early 1800s the Greek Revival swept across America in a momentous wave, and by the 1840s it was "all the rage" among architects and the public alike. The trend was so popular nationwide it came to be called the "National" style, and entire towns, such as Smyrna, Ithaca, Utica, Sparta, Troy, and Athens, were given Greek names.

Nineteenth-Century Tennesseans too were caught up in the Greek Revival craze, and many surviving Battle of Franklin houses and buildings are famous for their Greek Revival features.

The most important example is Rattle and Snap, the 18th-Century home of George Polk, a close of relation of U.S. President James K. Polk. Known as "the finest existing example of Greek Revival architecture in the South," the lovely plantation house was nearly burned to the ground by Yankee troops in 1862. Other 19th-Century War homes possessing Greek Revival features are Rippavilla, Elm Springs, Ferguson Hall, and Rally Hill.

The best known examples in Franklin are the porticos at Carnton Plantation. These were added to the house in the 1840s by Confederate Colonel John W. McGavock, and have their own unique legends and intriguing history. Confederate General Nathan Bedford Forrest, for instance, stood upon the upper deck and surveyed the Plain of Franklin prior to the battle, while the bodies of four Confederate generals (Cleburne, Carter, Strahl, Adams) were laid out upon the lower deck on December 1, 1864, so their men could pay their final respects. Carnton's Greek Revival porches even have their own ghosts, demons, and specters.

GROSE, WILLIAM (USA): The grandson of two Revolutionary War veterans, Grose was born on December 16, 1812, at Dayton, Ohio, after which his father moved the family to Henry County, Indiana. After studying law, Grose went on to serve as a state legislator and a judge.

With the opening of Lincoln's War he sided with the North and against the Constitution. As a U.S. colonel, he recruited the Thirty-sixth Indiana Infantry. Grose fought at such battles as Shiloh, Vicksburg, Chickamauga, and Chattanooga.

Appointed brigadier general in the Summer of 1864, he commanded the Third Brigade at the Battles of Franklin and Nashville in Kimball's First Division, Fourth U.S. Army Corps. During Franklin General Grose illegally used the home of the Figuers family on Carters Creek Pike as his headquarters.

After the War he served variously as collector of internal revenue, a builder of psychiatric hospitals, and an Indian senator. In 1891 he published a chronicle of the Thirty-sixth Indiana.

Grose passed away at his home in New Castle, Henry County, Indiana, on July 30, 1900, and was buried in the city's South Mound Cemetery.

GROSE'S THIRD BRIGADE (USA): This Yankee infantry brigade fought at the Battle of Franklin in Kimball's First Division, Fourth U.S. Army Corps. Named after U.S. Brigadier General William Grose, it was comprised of the Seventy-fifth Illinois, Eightieth Illinois, Eighty-fourth Illinois, Ninth Indiana, Thirtieth Indiana, Thirty-sixth Indiana, Eighty-fourth Indiana, and Seventy-seventh Pennsylvania.

GUIBOR'S MISSOURI BATTERY (CSA): This Rebel battery fought at the Battle of Franklin in Storrs' Battalion, Stewart's Corps Artillery, C.S. Army of Tennessee.

HAMILTON, A. S. (CSA): Confederate Lieutenant Colonel Hamilton led the Sixty-sixth Georgia Infantry at the Battle of Franklin, where he was wounded in action.

HAMMOND JOHN H. (USA): As a brevet brigadier general, Hammond commanded his own Yankee unit at the Battle of Franklin: Hammond's First Brigade, Knipe's Seventh Division, Wilson's Cavalry Corps.

HAMMOND, JOHN W. (USA): Hammond was born August 31, 1840. He commanded the Sixty-fifth Indiana Infantry in Colonel John S. Casement's Second Brigade at the Battle of Franklin. Hammond died April 11, 1904, and was buried in Forest Cemetery, Oskaloosa, Mahaska County, Iowa.

HAMMOND'S FIRST BRIGADE (USA): This Yankee brigade fought at the Battle of Franklin in Knipe's Seventh Division, Wilson's Cavalry Corps.

Named after U.S. brevet Brigadier General John H. Hammond, it was comprised of the Ninth Indiana Cavalry, Tenth Indiana Cavalry, Nineteenth Pennsylvania Cavalry, Second Tennessee Cavalry, and Fourth Tennessee Cavalry.

HARDING, SELENE: The daughter of Tennessee General William Giles Harding (son of John Harding, founder of Belle Meade Plantation in Nashville) and Elizabeth Irwin McGavock (daughter of Randal McGavock, founder of Carnton Plantation in Franklin), she was born April 5, 1846, and married Confederate General William Hicks "Red" Jackson on December 15, 1868.

Four years earlier, on December 15, 1864, shortly after the Battle of Franklin, Selene stood on the stone arm of the front steps of Belle Meade Mansion during a skirmish between the Confederates and the Yanks. To encourage the Rebels, she waved her handkerchief in the air as their cavalry came roaring through her yard. Despite the entreaties of the troops to get back in the house (as bullets were flying in every direction), she refused to move, standing firm until every last cavalryman had ridden past. Later, eyewitnesses called her "the bravest person on the scene."

Harding died on December 13, 1892, and was first buried at Belle Meade Plantation. In 1906, however, her remains were reinterred in Mount Olivet Cemetery, Nashville, Tennessee.

HARDING, WILLIAM GILES: The son of John Harding of Virginia (founder of Belle Meade Plantation) and Susannah Shute, Harding was born September 15, 1808, at Nashville, Tennessee. In 1853 Harding completed construction of his father's famous horse breeding farm, Belle Meade.

He served as a brigadier general in the Tennessee State Militia prior to Lincoln's War. During Lincoln's War he headed Tennessee's Military and Financial Board—until his illegal arrest by Yankees in 1862. He spent the next six months in prison while his wife Elizabeth Irwin McGavock, the daughter of Carnton Plantation founder Randal McGavock (eleventh mayor of Nashville), maintained Belle Meade in his absence.

General Harding passed away on December 15, 1886, and was buried at Belle Meade. In 1906 he was reinterred in Mount Olivet Cemetery, Nashville, Tennessee.

HARLINSDALE FARM: This once enormous horse-breeding farm in Franklin, Tennessee, is famous for being the home of the noted Tennessee Walking Horse, "Midnight Sun."

On December 17, 1864, the farm became the site of severe fighting during the Battle of Franklin III, when Confederate troops were cornered by Yankee cavalry during the Rebels' hasty southward retreat from the disastrous Battle of Nashville, December 15-16. One day later, during Franklin III, the largest gathering of cavalry on American soil took place on what is now Harlinsdale property.

HARPETH RIVER: One of the primary waterways in Tennessee, the Harpeth runs for some 115 miles through the north-central section of Middle Tennessee. It is one of the Cumberland River's main tributaries and forms part of the Mississippi River watershed.

The etymology of the word harpeth is not known with any certainty. One theory holds that it derives from the names of two early Tennessee highwaymen, Big Harp and Little Harp. Or it may be either a lost Indian word or a corruption of the more probable original river name, Fairpath.

The Harpeth played a major role in the Battle of Franklin, both hindering and facilitating each side. Indeed, it could be said that this small river was the veritable cause of the conflict, for Union General John M. Schofield never planned on stopping in Franklin after the Battle of Spring Hill on November 29, 1864. His original intention had been to move directly on to Nashville, where he was to meet up with Union General George H. Thomas.

The only reason Schofield halted his troops in Franklin was because he could not get them across the ice cold Harpeth: the swollen river had knocked out the two main bridges in town. The Battle of Franklin took place when Confederate General John Bell Hood caught up with Schofield, who was still in the process of repairing the bridges.

HARRISON HOUSE: This antebellum home in Franklin, Tennessee, played an important role in the Battle of Franklin. Confederate General John Bell Hood planned his doomed attack here, used the house as his headquarters during the conflict, and held his last staff meeting here before deploying his troops—a conference that ended in a bitter quarrel between Hood and his officers.

After the battle, Confederate Brigadier General John C. Carter was taken to the home to recover from his wounds. He passed away there on December 10 and was buried in Rose Hill Cemetery, Columbia, Tennessee.

Just prior to the Battle of Franklin, Confederate Brigadier General John H. Kelly suffered a mortal wound during a skirmish with Union troops operating under Brigadier General James D. Brownlow. Kelly was buried in the garden, but in 1866 was reinterred at Mobile, Alabama.

Located just south of Winstead and Breezy Hills on modern Columbia Pike, the Harrison House is today privately owned and is not open to the public.

HARRISON, THOMAS JEFFERSON (USA): Born June 8, 1824, in Shelby County, Kentucky, Harrison grew up in Indiana, where he attended law school, became an attorney, and served as a state representative in 1859.

With the start of Lincoln's War, he sided with the North and against the Constitution. Joining the U.S. army, he was made captain of the Sixth Indiana Infantry. As a colonel, he fought at the Battles of Liberty Gap, Middleton, Lovejoy Station, Murfreesboro, and Chickamauga. At the Battle of Franklin, Harrison commanded the Union's First Brigade, Johnson's Sixth Division, Wilson's Cavalry Corps.

After the War he moved to Tennessee, where he served as a U.S. marshal. He passed away at Nashville on September 28, 1871, and was buried in Crown Point Cemetery, Kokomo, Howard County, Indiana.

HARRISON'S FIRST BRIGADE (USA): This Yankee cavalry brigade fought at the Battle of Franklin in Johnson's Sixth Division, Wilson's Cavalry Corps.

Named after U.S. Colonel Thomas Jefferson Harrison, it was comprised of the Sixteenth Illinois Cavalry, Fifth Iowa Cavalry, and Seventh Ohio Cavalry.

HATCH, EDWARD (USA): Hatch was born at Bangor, Maine, on December 22, 1832. A relative of U.S. Republican Senator Orrin Hatch, he was schooled at Vermont's Norwich University, after which he moved to Iowa and became a lumber dealer.

With the start of Lincoln's War, Hatch sided with the North and against the Constitution. After joining the U.S. army, he was commissioned a captain of the Second Iowa Cavalry, after which a rapid series of promotions followed. In April 1864 he was made brigadier general, leading the Fifth Division, Wilson's Cavalry Corps, at the Battle of Franklin that November. Between 1861 and 1865 he was responsible for a number of atrocities against the

Southern people, and is still considered a war criminal in Dixie.

After the War Hatch was commissioned colonel of the Ninth U.S. Cavalry and led the Department of the Southwest. In recognition of his military service, he was brevetted a major general. He passed away on April 11, 1889, at Fort Robinson, Nebraska, and was buried in Fort Leavenworth National Cemetery, Fort Leavenworth, Kansas.

HATCH'S FIFTH DIVISION (USA): This Yankee cavalry division, named after U.S. Brigadier General Edward Hatch, served in Wilson's Cavalry Corps at the Battle of Franklin. The Second Division was comprised of Stewart's First Brigade, Coon's Second Brigade, and Hatch's Fifth Division Artillery.

HATCH'S FIFTH DIVISION ARTILLERY (USA): This Yankee artillery unit fought at the Battle of Franklin in Hatch's Fifth Division, Wilson's Cavalry Corps. It was comprised of the First Illinois Artillery, Battery I.

HAUNTED HOUSES: (see Ghosts).

HENPECK LANE: A long straight road in Franklin, Tennessee, which runs about two miles, from Columbia Pike at its western point to Lewisburg Pike at its eastern point.

During the Battle of Franklin, Henpeck Lane was used by Confederate General Alexander P. Stewart, who marched his men down it toward Lewisburg Pike, flanking the waiting Union soldiers on Columbia Pike.

HICKS, J. M. (CSA): Confederate Colonel Hicks led the Forty-first Mississippi Infantry at the Battle of Franklin, where he was wounded in action.

HIRAM MASONIC LODGE: This beautiful Masonic temple was constructed in 1823, making it the first three story building in Tennessee, and the tallest building west of the Appalachian Mountain Range at the time.

Built specifically for Hiram Lodge Number 7, the group still occupies the temple, which also served as the site of U.S. President Andrew Jackson's 1830 treaty with the Chickasaw.

Before and during the Battle of Franklin in 1864, Confederate troops used the temple as an observation post. After the conflict it was used as one of Franklin's three Yankee field hospitals.

HOLTZCLAW, JAMES THADEUS (CSA): Holtzclaw was born December 17, 1833, at McDonough, Georgia, and was raised in Chambers County, Alabama. After studying law at Montgomery, Alabama, in 1855 he began a lifelong career as an attorney.

With the onset of Lincoln's War, Holtzclaw sided with the South and the Constitution. Joining the Confederacy, he rose rapidly up the ranks. After recovering from a near mortal wound at the Battle of Shiloh, he went on to fight at Chickamauga and Chattanooga.

Promoted to brigadier general in the Summer of 1864, at the Battle of Franklin he led Holtzclaw's Brigade, Clayton's Division, Lee's Corps, C.S. Army of Tennessee. After the equally disastrous Battle of Nashville two weeks later, he and his men served as rear guard.

A Democrat (then a conservative), after the War he returned to his law practice and served on the Alabama Railroad Commission. He died on July 19, 1893, at Montgomery, Alabama, and was buried in the city's Oakwood Cemetery.

HOLTZCLAW'S BRIGADE (CSA): This Rebel infantry brigade fought at the Battle of Franklin in Clayton's Division, Lee's Corps, C.S. Army of Tennessee.

Named after Confederate Brigadier General James Thadeus Holtzclaw, it was comprised of the Eighteenth Alabama, Thirty-second Alabama, Thirty-sixth Alabama, Thirty-eighth Alabama, and Fifty-eighth Alabama.

HOOD, JOHN BELL (CSA): Nicknamed "Sam," Hood was born June 29, 1831, at Owingsville, Bath County, Kentucky. Against the wishes of his parents, he entered West Point Military Academy in 1849, graduating forty-fourth out of a class of fifty-two in 1853. He then served as a cavalry officer in the U.S. army in Texas and California.

With the start of Lincoln's War, Hood sided with the South and the Constitution. Resigning his U.S. commission on April 17, 1861, he joined the Confederate army. After serving as a division commander in the

Northern Army of Virginia, in March 1862 he was made brigadier general. In October 1862 he was made a division commander under Confederate General James Longstreet.

Hood fought bravely at numerous battles, including Second Manassas, Sharpsburg, and Fredericksburg. At Gettysburg he lost the use of his arm and at Chickamauga he lost a severely wounded leg to amputation, after which he had to be strapped into his saddle.

In July 1864 Confederate President Jefferson Davis made the fateful decision to replace General Joseph E. Johnston with his friend Hood, now a full general in command of the Army of Tennessee. Hood immediately lost the Battle of Atlanta, then ignored Davis' plan (to follow Sherman) by moving his army northwest into Tennessee.

There followed in rapid succession the Battles of Columbia, Spring Hill, Franklin, and Nashville, all which were poorly commanded and which culminated in the near demise of the Army of Tennessee.

In late December 1864, Hood and his remaining battered troops retreated to Mississippi where, in January 1865, he asked to be relieved. The request was granted, and the Army of Tennessee was turned over to Confederate General Richard Taylor (son of U.S. President Zachary Taylor, and brother of President Davis' first wife, Sarah Knox Taylor).

After the War Hood moved to New Orleans, Louisiana, where he penned his memoirs (*Advance and Retreat*), took up cotton brokering, and married Anna Marie Hennen in 1868. The couple bore eleven children, among whom were three sets of twins.

Tragically, during the yellow fever epidemic that ravaged the city in the late 1870s, the town's cotton industry was destroyed and Hood, his wife, and one of their children (Lydia), all perished. The ten remaining Hood orphans were later fostered out to various families across the South.

Hood's death came on August 30, 1879. He was buried in the city's Metairie Cemetery.

Much ink has been spilled by historians trying to come to terms with Hood's military career. There is no question that he was a gallant soldier and fearless officer. On the other hand, his stubborn adherence to outmoded military tactics and strategies—such as forbidding the use of trenches and earthworks, and his rule of advancing on the enemy in long frontal lines—proved utterly disastrous, and certainly contributed to the downfall of the Confederacy in the Western Theater, if not the Confederacy itself.

Of Hood's mad plan at the Battle of Franklin, for example, Confederate Captain Samuel T. Foster of Granbury's Texas Brigade, wrote:

"General Hood has betrayed us. This is not the kind of fighting he promised us at Tuscumbia and Florence, Alabama when we started into Tennessee. This was not a 'fight with equal numbers and choice of the ground' by no means. And the wails and cries of widows and orphans made at Franklin, Tennessee, November 30, 1864, will heat up the fires of the bottomless pit to burn the soul of General J. B. Hood for murdering their husbands and fathers at that place that day. It can't be called anything else but cold blooded murder."

Debate over Hood's true role in the War for Southern Independence—with reasoned arguments on both sides—will continue for as long as the human race.

HOSKIN'S MISSISSIPPI BATTERY (CSA): This Rebel battery fought at the Battle of Franklin in Storrs' Battalion, Stewart's Corps Artillery, C.S. Army of Tennessee.

HOTCHKISS' BATTALION (CSA): This Rebel battalion fought at the Battle of Franklin in Cheatham's Corps Artillery, C.S. Army of Tennessee. It was comprised of Bledsoe's Missouri Battery, Goldthwaite's Alabama Battery, and Key's Arkansas Battery.

HOUSE SERVANT: House servants ("slaves" to Northerners) made up the second half of the American servant system, the other half being field servants.

The chief occupations of the house servant were cleaning, washing clothes, preparing, cooking, and serving meals, along with various miscellaneous tasks given them by the master and mistress of the house.

The head house servant was the Mammy, whose primary job was to manage the other house servants and mind, tutor, feed, entertain, and clothe the owners' children. Often the Mammy would even suckle the white infants if necessary.

(White Southern mistresses were known to do the same in return for their black female servants.)

House servants were much loved by their young white charges, who, by tradition, respectfully referred to the older family slaves as "uncle" and "aunty." As all servants were registered in court as members of their white families at the time of purchase, they were literally all members of one big family—and, contrary to Northern myth, in nearly every case they were viewed as such.

The black house servants who lived and worked in Franklin, Tennessee, were known to have been well treated, and, as was common on most plantations throughout the South, were allowed to marry, have families, and purchase their freedom (all rights that separated them from true slaves).

Confederate Colonel John W. McGavock of Carnton Plantation, for example, taught his children that their African-American servants were "part of the family." One of Carnton's servants, Mariah Reddick, voluntarily returned after Lincoln's War and continued working for the McGavocks until the early 1900s. In 1905 she gave the eulogy at the funeral of her former mistress, Carrie McGavock.

HOWARD, WILEY: Howard was the loyal body servant of Confederate General States Rights Gist, who died the night of the Battle of Franklin, November 30, 1864.

After the conflict, Gist was buried under a cedar tree at the home of William White on Boyd Mill Road, just to the west of Franklin, Tennessee. On December 2, "Uncle Wiley," as Howard was known, lovingly dug up Gist's body and transported it back to the Gist family plantation in South Carolina, where it was reinterred in the Trinity Episcopal Churchyard at Columbia.

HOXTON'S BATTALION (CSA): This Rebel battalion fought at the Battle of Franklin in Cheatham's Corps Artillery, C.S. Army of Tennessee. It was comprised of Perry's Florida Battery, Phelan's Alabama Battery, and Turner's Mississippi Battery.

HUEY'S KENTUCKY BATTALION (CSA): This Rebel unit fought at the Battle of

Franklin in Crossland's Brigade, Buford's Division, Forrest's Cavalry Corps, C.S. Army of Tennessee.

HUGHES' FORD: A crossing on the Harpeth River used by Confederate forces at the Battle of Franklin. According to one 19th-Century eyewitness, it is located between two and three miles "above Franklin, and about as far from the Columbia Turnpike where that road passes the Winstead Hill."

At least one known skirmish was fought here between General Nathan Bedford Forrest and Union troops. The area is today called "Forrest Crossing."

HUME, ISAAC N. (CSA): Confederate Colonel Hume led the Forty-second Tennessee Infantry at the Battle of Franklin, where he was wounded in action.

ISOLA BELLA: This historic home in Brentwood, Tennessee, whose name is Italian for "beautiful island," was built around 1840 by James Johnston and his wife Narcissa Merritt, on land that was originally part of Nashville.

Confederate General John Bell Hood stopped here after the Battle of Franklin in December 1864, where he met with his staff and drew up plans for what would be the Battle of Nashville on December 15.

Both Confederate and Union soldiers marched their wagons and artillery across the house's yards, and after Nashville Isola Bella served as a field hospital.

The 10,000 square foot mansion and surrounding land (worth an estimated $3.5 million), is as impressive today as it was in the Victorian Era. The mantle in the house's parlor is believed to come from Victor Hugo's home in Paris, France.

Like Franklin's Carnton Plantation, Isola Bella went through a period of neglect and vacancy, at which time it was used to store crops such as tobacco and hay.

Since the 1940s the landmark home has been owned and restored by several different families dedicated to preserving this important piece of William County history.

IVES, SAMUEL SPENCER (CSA): Confederate Colonel Ives was born August 5, 1832. He led the Twenty-seventh, Thirty-fifth, and Forty-ninth Alabama Infantries at the Battle of Franklin, where he was wounded in action. He passed away March 23, 1917, and was buried in Florence Cemetery, Florence, Alabama.

JACKSON, HENRY ROOTES (CSA): Born June 24, 1820 at Athens, Georgia, Jackson graduated with honors from Yale University in 1839, and entered the law profession. Also a newspaperman, he served as a U.S. district attorney, a colonel in the Mexican-American War, a judge, a U.S. ambassador to Austria, and a democratic elector (then a conservative) who supported the secession of Georgia.

With the opening of Lincoln's War, Jackson sided with the South and the Constitution. He entered Confederate service as a brigadier general, first serving under General Robert E. Lee. He led his own unit, Jackson's Brigade, Bate's Division, Cheatham's Corps, C.S. Army of Tennessee, at the Battle of Franklin.

Two weeks later, at the Battle of Nashville, he was captured and sent to Fort Warren at Boston, Massachusetts, where he was not paroled until four months after the War, on July 8, 1865.

Jackson then returned to his law practice, and in 1885 he was appointed by U.S. President Grover Cleveland to act as minister to Mexico. Also a poet, a railroad executive, and the president of the Georgia Historical Society, Jackson died on May 23, 1898, at Savannah, Georgia. He was buried in the city's Bonaventure Cemetery.

JACKSON'S BRIGADE (CSA): This Rebel infantry brigade fought at the Battle of Franklin in Bate's Division, Cheatham's Corps, C.S. Army of Tennessee.

Named after Confederate Brigadier General Henry Rootes Jackson, it was comprised of the Twenty-fifth Georgia, Twenty-ninth Georgia, Thirtieth Georgia, First Georgia Confederate, and First Georgia Battalion Sharpshooters.

JACKSON, WILLIAM HICKS (CSA): The son of Dr. Alexander Jackson and Mary Hurt of Virginia, he was born October 1, 1835, at Paris, Tennessee. After his schooling at West Tennessee College (now part of Union University), Jackson attended West Point Military Academy, graduating in 1856.

He then entered the U.S. army as a brevetted second lieutenant, serving at Fort Bliss, Texas, in 1857, fighting Native-Americans until 1860.

With the start of Lincoln's War, Jackson sided with the South and the Constitution. He entered the Confederate army as a captain of artillery. After being severely wounded at the Battle of Belmont, he received numerous promotions, serving as chief of cavalry under various Rebel officers.

As brigadier general he fought at the Battle of Vicksburg, then commanded Confederate General Leonidas Polk's cavalry at Meridian, Mississippi. At Atlanta he led the cavalry division of the Army of Mississippi.

In the Fall of 1864 Jackson was made commander of all Tennessee cavalry under Confederate General Nathan Bedford Forrest, leading Jackson's Division, at the Battle of Franklin on November 30, 1864.

After the War, "Red," as he was nicknamed, resumed his life in Tennessee, working on his father's cotton plantation. On December 15, 1868, he married Selene Harding, the daughter of General William Giles Harding of Belle Meade Plantation, Nashville, Tennessee, and began co-managing the estate. Under Jackson's tutelage, Belle Meade maintained its reputation as one of the nation's finest thoroughbred horse breeding farms.

Jackson was a strong supporter of the Grange Movement (a pro-farm, pro-agricultural group), today known as the National Grange, and served as president of such organizations as the Tennessee Bureau of Agriculture and the National Agricultural Congress.

On March 30, 1903, Jackson passed into the Better World, and was buried at Belle Meade. In 1906 his remains were reinterred in Mount Olivet Cemetery, Nashville.

JACKSON'S DIVISION (CSA): This Rebel division fought at the Battle of Franklin in Forrest's Cavalry Corps, C.S. Army of Tennessee. Named after its commander Confederate Brigadier William Hicks Jackson, it was comprised of Armstrong's Brigade and Ross' Brigade.

JOHNSON, EDWARD (CSA): Johnson was born April 16, 1816, at Salisbury, Chesterfield County, Virginia, after which his family moved to Kentucky.

He graduated from West Point in 1838, and went on to fight in the Seminole Wars in Florida and the Mexican-American War, receiving rapid promotion along the way.

With the start of Lincoln's War, Johnson sided with the South and the Constitution. He resigned his commission in the U.S. army and entered Confederate service as colonel of the Twelfth Georgia Infantry.

In western Virginia Johnson fought at Rich Mountain, Greenbrier River, and Cheat Mountain. At the Battles of Gettysburg, the Wilderness, and Spotsylvania, now major general, he commanded Stonewall Jackson's division after that general's tragic death by friendly fire on May 10, 1863.

As a brigadier general, Johnson received the nickname "Allegheny Johnson" while leading the Army of the Northwest on Allegheny Mountain.

At Spotsylvania on May 12, 1864, he was captured and imprisoned at Morris Island. After his exchange in late Summer 1864, he was placed under the command of Confederate General John Bell Hood, leading a division in Confederate General Stephen Dill Lee's Corps at the Battle of Franklin.

At the Battle of Nashville two weeks later, Johnson was captured once again, and was this time imprisoned at Johnson's Island and later at the Old Capitol Prison at Washington, D.C. Falsely and cruelly accused of participating in the assassination of President Abraham Lincoln, he was eventually exonerated and released July 22, 1865.

Johnson then returned to farming in Virginia and worked diligently to help Confederate veterans and their families. He passed away at Richmond on March 2, 1873, and was buried in the city's Hollywood Cemetery.

JOHNSON, GEORGE D. (CSA): Confederate Brigadier General Johnson took over command of Quarles' Brigade after its leader Brigadier General William Andrew Quarles was injured at the Battle of Franklin II, November 30, 1864, and captured at the Battle of Franklin III, December 17, 1864.

JOHNSON, GILBERT MARQUIS LAFAYETTE (USA): Born November 4, 1837, in Indiana, at the start of Lincoln's War Johnson sided with the North and against the Constitution. After joining the U.S. army, he fought at the Battle of Franklin, where the colonel led his own unit: Johnson's Second Brigade, Knipe's Seventh Division, Wilson's Cavalry Corps.

After the War Johnson married Southern belle Susan Clarke Bradley and bore one child, Isabelle Bradley Johnson. He then served as postmaster of Huntsville, Alabama.

On January 9, 1871, he passed away at age thirty-three from complications related to his wartime injuries and was buried in Huntsville's Maple Hill Cemetery.

JOHNSON, J. M. (CSA): Confederate Lieutenant Colonel Johnson led the Thirtieth Mississippi Infantry at the Battle of Franklin, where he was wounded in action.

JOHNSON, RICHARD W. (USA): He was born of Virginia parents on February 27, 1827, near the town of Smithland, Kentucky. He was schooled at West Point Military Academy, graduating in 1849.

In the early 1850s he married Rachel Elizabeth Steele and bore several children. He went on to serve with the U.S. army in the Western Territories, continuing his service with the North after the start of Lincoln's War in April 1861.

In the Summer of 1862 Johnson was captured by Confederate Colonel John Hunt Morgan, but was exchanged in December. He went on to fight in such battles as Murfreesboro, Chattanooga, Chickamauga, and New Hope Church, where he was seriously injured. He led the Union's Sixth Division, Wilson's Cavalry Corps, at the Battle of Franklin, and was also present at the Battle of Nashville.

After the War Johnson continued his U.S. military

service until 1867, when he retired as a major general. He authored numerous military works (such as *A Soldier's Reminiscences in Peace and War*) and, as a professor, taught at several universities.

He died on April 21, 1897, at Saint Paul, Minnesota, and was buried in the city's Oakland Cemetery.

JOHNSON'S BATTALION (CSA): This Rebel battalion fought at the Battle of Franklin in Lee's Corps Artillery, C.S. Army of Tennessee.

Led by Confederate Captain John B. Rowan, it was comprised of Corput's Georgia Battery, Marshall's Tennessee Battery, and Stephen's Light Artillery.

JOHNSON'S DIVISION (CSA): This Rebel division, named after Confederate General Edward Johnson, was present at the Battle of Franklin. It was comprised of Deas' Brigade, Manigault's Brigade, Sharp's Brigade, and Brantley's Brigade.

JOHNSON'S SECOND BRIGADE (USA): This Yankee brigade fought at the Battle of Franklin in Knipe's Seventh Division, Wilson's Cavalry Corps.

Named after U.S. Colonel Gilbert Marquis Lafayette Johnson, it was comprised of the Twelfth Indian Cavalry, Thirteenth Indiana Cavalry, and Eighth Tennessee Cavalry.

JOHNSON'S SIXTH DIVISION (USA): This Yankee division, named after U.S. Brigadier General Richard W. Johnson, served in Wilson's Cavalry Corps at the Battle of Franklin. The Second Division was comprised of Harrison's First Brigade, Biddle's Second Brigade, and Johnson's Sixth Division Artillery.

JOHNSON'S SIXTH DIVISION ARTILLERY (USA): This Yankee artillery unit fought at the Battle of Franklin in Johnson's Sixth Division, Wilson's Cavalry Corps. It was comprised of the Fourth U.S. Regular Artillery, Battery I.

JOHNSTON, JOHN W. (CSA): Major Johnston, a twenty-five year old lawyer from Virginia, led Lee's Corps Artillery at the Battle of Franklin after its former commander

Colonel Robert Franklin Beckham was mortally wounded on November 29, 1864 (Beckham passed away a few days later on December 5).

KELLAR, ANDREW J. (CSA): As a Confederate colonel, Kellar was a member of the Fourth Tennessee Infantry. He led Strahl's Brigade at the Battles of Franklin and Nashville after the death of its original commander, Otho F. Strahl, at the former conflict. After the War Kellar worked for the Memphis newspaper, the *Avalanche*, and was a board member of the Western Associated Press.

KELLEY, DAVID CAMPBELL (CSA): The son of Reverend John Kelley and Margaret Lavinia Campbell, Kelley was born in a log cabin on December 25, 1833, at Leeville, Wilson County, Tennessee.

After graduating from Lebanon, Tennessee's Cumberland University in 1851, he became a preacher under the auspices of the Tennessee Methodist Conference, then spent time in China working as a missionary. Upon returning to the U.S. he moved to Huntsville, Alabama, serving as a pastor in 1860.

With the onset of Lincoln's War, Kelley sided with the South and the Constitution. Joining the Confederate army, he organized "Kelley's Rangers," a cavalry unit that was attached to Confederate General Nathan Bedford Forrest's battalion at Memphis.

The "fightin' preacher," as Kelley soon became known, rose rapidly up the ranks, fighting at such battles as Donelson, Fallen Timbers, Shiloh, Brice's Cross Roads, Tupelo, Oxford, Spring Hill, Franklin, and Nashville. Lieutenant Colonel Kelley served with Forrest until the end of the War, surrendering with the celebrated Rebel chieftain in May 1865. A site in Nashville, known as "Kelley's Point Battlefield," memorializes the colonel and his soldiers.

After the War Kelley moved to Tennessee, leading churches in Lebanon and Nashville. On January 14, 1869, he married children's author Mary Owen Campbell, with whom he bore several children.

As a member of the first Board of Trustees of Vanderbilt University in 1872, he helped organize the institution, in 1888 he was made president of the Tennessee Society of the Friends of the American Revolution, and in 1890 he lost his run for Tennessee governor as a Prohibition candidate.

A member of the Scotch-Irish Society of America, and a proud supporter of the Confederate Veterans movement, in the Spring of 1901 he headed the dedication ceremony for the memorial statue of his good friend General Forrest at Memphis' Forrest Park.

On May 19, 1909, at Nashville, after uttering the words "my work is done," Kelley passed into the Better World. He was buried in the city's Mount Olivet Cemetery.

KEY'S ARKANSAS BATTERY (CSA): This Rebel battery fought at the Battle of Franklin in Hotchkiss' Battalion, Cheatham's Corps Artillery, C.S. Army of Tennessee.

KIMBALL, NATHAN (USA): Kimball was born November 22, 1822, at Fredericksburg, Indiana. From 1839 to 1841 he attended Indiana Asbury College (now DePauw University), and in 1844 he attended the University of Louisville Medical School, after which he took up the occupation of doctor in his home state.

On September 22, 1845, he married Martha A. McPhetters, and bore one child. He fought in the Mexican-American War the following year, after which he resumed his medical practice in Indiana. With the premature death of his wife, he married a second time in August 1850.

With the start of Lincoln's War Kimball sided with the North and against the Constitution, serving as colonel of the Union's Fourteenth Indiana Infantry. After his first major combat at the Battle of Cheat Mountain, he went on to fight at the Battles of Kernstown, Second Manassas, Sharpsburg, and Fredericksburg.

After recovering from a wound received at Fredericksburg, he served briefly under Yankee General William T. Sherman. Indiana Governor Oliver P. Morton sent Kimball to

Indiana to illegally suppress the Knights of the Golden Circle, after which he led the Union's First Division, Fourth Army Corps, at the Battles of Franklin and Nashville.

After the War Kimball returned to Indiana where he was elected state commander of the Grand Army of the Republic. In 1867 he became state treasurer, in 1869 he joined the Freemasons, and in 1873 he was elected an Indiana state representative.

Later that year, when President Ulysses S. Grant made him surveyor general of the Utah Territory, Kimball moved to the Beehive State. In 1879 President Rutherford B. Hayes appointed him postmaster of Ogden, Weber County, Utah, where Kimball lived until his death on January 21, 1898. He was buried in Ogden's Aultorest Memorial Park—also known as Mountain View Cemetery.

KIMBALL'S FIRST DIVISION (USA): This Yankee division, named after U.S. Brigadier General Nathan Kimball, served in the Fourth U.S. Army Corps at the Battle of Franklin. It was comprised of Kirby's First Brigade, Whitaker's Second Brigade, and Grose's Third Brigade.

KIRBY, ISAAC MINOR (USA): Kirby was born February 10, 1835, in Ohio. As a Yankee colonel he led the First Brigade, First Division, Fourth Army Corps at the Battle of Franklin, November 30, 1864.

Kirby passed away at Upper Sandusky, Wyandot County, Ohio, on May 30, 1917, and was buried in the town's Oak Hill Cemetery.

KIRBY'S FIRST BRIGADE (USA): This Yankee infantry brigade fought at the Battle of Franklin in Kimball's First Division, Fourth U.S. Army Corps.

Named after U.S. Colonel Isaac M. Kirby, it was comprised of the Twenty-first Illinois, Thirty-eighth Illinois, Thirty-first Indiana, Eighty-first Indiana, Ninetieth Ohio, and One hundred first Ohio.

KNEFLER, FREDERICK (USA): Knefler, a Hungarian Jew, was born April 12, 1824. According to some sources, while Union General Samuel Beatty was ill, Colonel Knefler led the Union's Third Brigade, Wood's

Third Division, Fourth U.S. Army Corps, at the Battle of Franklin. He passed away at Indianapolis, Indiana, in 1901 and was buried in the city's Crown Hill Cemetery.

KNIPE, JOSEPH FARMER (USA): German-American Knipe was born November 30, 1823, at Mount Joy, Pennsylvania. As a young man he worked as a cobbler in Philadelphia, then enlisted in the U.S. army in 1842. As a sergeant he fought in the Mexican-American War, after which he worked in the railroad industry at Harrisburg in 1847.

With the outbreak of Lincoln's War, Colonel Knipe raised the Forty-Sixth Pennsylvania Volunteer Infantry, and went on to fight at such battles as First Winchester, Cedar Mountain, and Chancellorsville.

At the Battle of Franklin Brigadier General Knipe led the U.S. Seventh Division, Wilson's Cavalry Corps. At the Battle of Nashville two weeks later he is accredited with capturing some 6,000 Confederates and eight flags.

After the War President Andrew Johnson appointed him postmaster of Harrisburg. Knipe passed away in the city on August 18, 1901, and was buried next to his wife Elizabeth in Harrisburg Cemetery.

KNIPE'S SEVENTH DIVISION (USA): This Yankee division, named after U.S. Brigadier General Joseph Farmer Knipe, served in Wilson's Cavalry Corps at the Battle of Franklin.

The Seventh Division was comprised of Hammond's First Brigade, Johnson's Second Brigade, and Knipe's Seventh Division Artillery.

KNIPE'S SEVENTH DIVISION ARTILLERY (USA): This Yankee artillery unit fought at the Battle of Franklin in Knipe's Seventh Division, Wilson's Cavalry Corps. It was comprised of the Fourteenth Ohio Battery.

KNOX, SAMUEL L. (CSA): Confederate Major Knox led the First Alabama Infantry at the Battle of Franklin, where he was wounded in action. He later died of his injuries.

KOLB'S ALABAMA BATTERY (CSA): This Rebel battery fought at the Battle of Franklin in Storrs' Battalion, Stewart's Corps Artillery, C.S. Army of Tennessee.

LANE, JOHN QUINCY (USA): Colonel Lane led the Union's Second Brigade, Second Division, Fourth U.S. Army Corps, at the Battle of Franklin.

LANE'S SECOND BRIGADE (USA): This Yankee infantry brigade fought at the Battle of Franklin in Wagner's Second Division, Fourth U.S. Army Corps.

Named after U.S. Colonel John Q. Lane, it was comprised of the One hundredth Illinois, Fortieth Indiana, Fifty-seventh Indiana, Twenty-eighth Kentucky, Twenty-sixth Ohio, and Ninety-seventh Ohio.

LAUREL HILL: This elegant antebellum home was built in Franklin, Tennessee, in the early 1800s on what is now Columbia Pike. It was named after the laurel that grew profusely on the property.

The house is known for its walnut, poplar, and ash floors, its hand-carved mantels, and its grand staircase. Confederate General John Bell Hood and his staff made a quick stop here on their way to meet their destiny at the Battle of Franklin on November 30, 1864.

Laurel Hill is today privately owned and is not open to the public.

LAWTON, HENRY WARE (USA): The son of George W. Lawton and Catherine Daley, Lawton was born in Maumee, Ohio, March 17, 1843, but spent much of his childhood in Indiana. At the start of Lincoln's War he was attending the Methodist Episcopal College at Fort Wayne.

Only days after the Battle of Fort Sumter—where Lincoln devilishly tricked the South into firing the first shot—Lawton enlisted in the U.S. army, soon becoming first lieutenant of the Thirtieth Indiana Infantry.

He fought in nearly two dozen major battles, including the Battle of Franklin, where, as captain, he led the Thirtieth

Indiana, Grose's Third Brigade, Kimball's First Division, Fourth U.S. Army Corps.

After the War ended he graduated from Harvard Law School in 1866, after which he rejoined the U.S. army. In 1881 he married Mary Craig of Louisville, Kentucky, with whom he bore four children.

As a captain he was stationed in the southwest, where he was in charge of suppressing Indian uprisings. An advocate for Native-American rights, in late Summer 1886 he and his men were responsible for bringing in famed Bedonkohe Apache leader Geronimo.

Lawton went on to fight in the Spanish-American War, where, as major general, he led the Second Division in Cuba in 1898. During this period he became friends with both U.S. Presidents William McKinley and Theodore Roosevelt.

In late 1898 he was sent to the Philippines to take part in the Philippine-American War. On December 19, 1899, during the Battle of Paye, Lawton was killed by a Filipino sharpshooter.

His body was returned to the U.S., where he was buried in Arlington National Cemetery, Arlington, Virginia.

LEE, STEPHEN DILL (CSA): The son of Dr. Thomas Miles Lee and Caroline Alison, Lee was born on September 22, 1833, at Charleston, South Carolina. He attended West Point Military Academy in 1850, graduating seventeenth in his class in 1854.

That year he entered the service of the U.S. army, serving in Florida in 1857, and in the Western Territories from 1858 to 1861.

With the onset of Lincoln's War, Lee sided with the South and the Constitution. After resigning his U.S. commission, he began his service with the Confederate army as a captain in the South Carolina Militia. As the aide-de-camp of Confederate General Pierre G. T. Beauregard, he was present at the Battle of Sumter, where Lincoln deceived the South into firing the first shot.

Lee rose rapidly up the ranks and, as an artillerist, fought at numerous battles, including Fair Oaks, Savage's Station, Malvern Hill, Second Manassas, Sharpsburg, Chickasaw Bayou, and Champion Hill.

On June 23, 1864, Lee was made lieutenant general, the youngest in the Confederate army, after which he was placed under the command of Confederate General John Bell Hood and the Army of Tennessee.

After the Battle of Atlanta, he led Lee's Corps at the disastrous Battles of Spring Hill, Franklin, and Nashville. In early 1865 Lee was placed under Confederate General Joseph Eggleston Johnston, surrendering with his commander in April 1865 in North Carolina.

On February 9, 1865, Lee, a cousin of Rebel Generals Robert E. Lee and Fitzhugh Lee, married Regina Lilly Harrison and bore one child: Blewett Harrison Lee.

After the War Lee and his family settled at Columbus, Mississippi, where he worked his plantation, served as a senator, and became the first president of the Agricultural and Mechanical College of Mississippi (now Mississippi State University).

In 1899 he oversaw the Vicksburg National Park Association, and beginning in 1904 he was elected commander-in-chief of the United Confederate Veterans (today the Sons of Confederate Veterans).

Throughout the early 1900s Lee wrote and gave speeches, vigorously defending the Confederate Cause (limited government and states' rights). During an April 25, 1906, speech at New Orleans, Louisiana, he made the now following famous statement to his fellow former Confederates:

"To you, Sons of Confederate Veterans, we will commit the vindication of the cause for which we fought. To your strength will be given the defense of the Confederate soldier's good name, the guardianship of his history, the emulation of his virtues, the perpetuation of those principles which he loved and which you love also, and those ideals which made him glorious and which you also cherish. Remember: It is your duty to see that the true history of the South is presented to future generations."

On May 28, 1908, at Vicksburg, General Lee fell ill and died. He was buried in Friendship Cemetery, Columbus, Mississippi.

LEE'S CORPS (CSA): This Rebel corps, named after Confederate Lieutenant General Stephen Dill Lee, was present at the Battle of Franklin, where it was led by Confederate Major John W. Johnston. It was comprised of Johnson's Division, Stevenson's Division, and Clayton's Division.

LEE'S CORPS ARTILLERY (CSA): This Rebel artillery corps, named after Confederate Lieutenant General Stephen Dill Lee, was present at the Battle of Franklin. Led by Confederate Major John W. Johnston, it was comprised of Courtney's Battalion, Eldridge's Battalion, and Johnson's Battalion.

LEWISBURG PIKE: This road, which stretches for thirty-five miles from Franklin to Lewisburg, Tennessee, played a major role in the Battle of Franklin. It was used by Confederate and Union troops as both a roadway and a defensive line.

Where it runs along the Harpeth River, it funneled the Rebels into tight formations as they approached Franklin Center, making them easy targets for the waiting Yankees. The results were devastating for the Confederacy.

LINCOLN, ABRAHAM (USA): Our sixteenth U.S. president had no direct connection to the Battle of Franklin. Yet if not for him, the Battle of Franklin would never have taken place, earning him an entry in this encyclopedia.

Among traditional Southerners, Lincoln's name, image, and reputation will always be associated with utter revulsion, disrespect, and dishonor. Why?

If one reads Lincoln's own words rather than those of his idolatrous and misguided followers, it will quickly become apparent that he was nothing close to what our pro-North history books have taught us. In fact, he was the opposite.

Lincoln's own writings and speeches prove him to be a white racist and separatist who fought his entire life for American apartheid; a power hungry dictator who would stop at nothing to achieve his goals (including rigging the 1860 and 1864 elections, shutting down some 300 Yankee newspapers, committing a mass execution of Native-Americans, and torturing and even murdering white Northerners who promoted peace with the South); an overt hypocrite and demagogue who said one thing to his Northern audiences and the reverse to his Southern ones; a socialistic politician whose intention was to launch big government in Washington; a violent madman who used the concept of total war to force the Southern states back into what the Founding Fathers intended to be a "voluntary union of friendly states"; a tyrant who committed so many crimes against humanity that they have never been fully counted; and a liberal extremist who detested the Constitution and purposefully set out to alter it. Little wonder that in the traditional South he is still known as one of the world's greatest war criminals.

Indeed, it was Lincoln's many violations of the Constitution which not only led to the "Civil War" *and* the Battle of Franklin, but which greatly aided the U.S. in eventually subduing the South.

For those interested in a complete discussion of these topics, as well as an in-depth examination of "Honest Abe" from the Southern perspective, see my books:

- *Abraham Lincoln: The Southern View*
- *Lincolnology: The Real Lincoln Revealed in His Own Words*
- *The Unquotable Lincoln: The President's Quotes They Don't Want You To Know!*
- *Honest Jeff and Dishonest Abe: A Southern Children's Guide to the Civil War*

LORING, WILLIAM WING (CSA): The descendant of a Massachusetts family, he was the son of Reuben and Hannah Loring of North Carolina, where he was born at Wilmington on December 4, 1818.

Raised in Florida, at age fourteen he fought the Seminoles, then went on to study law and win election as a state legislator. In the Mexican-American War, he was wounded at the Battle of Churubusco and lost an arm at the Battle of Chapultepec.

With the outbreak of Lincoln's War, Loring sided with the South and the Constitution, entering Confederate military service as a brigadier general in May 1861.

Appointed major general in February 1862, he went on to serve under a number of generals, many with whom he had rancorous relationships. Among them were Stonewall Jackson, Leonidas Polk, Robert E. Lee, John Bell Hood, and Joseph E. Johnston, the latter with whom he surrendered in April 1865.

At the Battle of Franklin he led Loring's Division, Stewart's Corps, C.S. Army of Tennessee. He came to be nicknamed "Old Blizzards" for his war cry: "Give 'em blizzards boys!"

After the War he served as a general in the army of the Khedive of Egypt in 1869. Returning to the U.S. in 1879, he was thenceforth known as "Loring Pacha," *pacha* (or *pasha*) being a Turkish word meaning a military officer. In 1884 he published a book about his experiences entitled, *A Confederate Soldier in Egypt*.

He passed away on December 30, 1886, at New York City, and was buried in Loring Park at Saint Augustine, Florida.

LORING'S DIVISION (CSA): This Rebel division, named after Confederate General William Wing Loring, was present at the Battle of Franklin.

It was comprised of Featherston's Brigade, Adams' Brigade, and Scott's Brigade.

LOTZ HOUSE: This fine antebellum home was built in 1858 by German immigrant, piano maker, and master carpenter Johann Albert Lotz.

During the Battle of Franklin, Johann, his wife Margaretha, and their three children (Augustus, Matilda, and Paul), fled to the cellar of the Carter House across the street for safety.

Damage from the conflict can still be seen in the Lotz House, which was used as a field hospital afterward. Johann moved his family to California not long after Lincoln's War ended.

The home, located in Franklin, Tennessee, on Columbia Avenue, is open for public touring.

LOWREY, MARK PERRIN (CSA): The son of Adam Lowrey and Margaret Doss, he was one of eleven children. He was born on December 29, 1828, in McNairy County, Tennessee. In 1845, after his father died unexpectedly, the young boy and the rest of the Lowrey family moved to Farmington, Mississippi.

In 1846 he volunteered to fight in the Mexican-American War, but saw no combat. Denied a formal education, he then took up the occupation of masonry, specializing in brick laying.

In the late 1840s Lowrey married Sarah Raleigh Holmes and bore several children, and in the early 1850s he became a Baptist minister at Kossuth,

Alcorn County, Mississippi.

With the start of Lincoln's War, he sided with the South and the Constitution. After joining the Confederate army he rose quickly to the rank of brigadier general. He fought at numerous conflicts, including the Kentucky Campaign, Chickamauga, Atlanta, and Nashville.

Nicknamed the "Preacher General" for the numerous baptisms he performed each week, at the Battle of Franklin he led Lowrey's Brigade, Cleburne's Division, Cheatham's Corps, C.S. Army of Tennessee.

After the War Lowrey resumed his work as a minister, serving as president of the Mississippi Baptist State Convention. In September 1873 he founded the Blue Mountain Female Institute (now Blue Mountain College), serving there as both president and a history professor.

Lowrey died suddenly at a railway station on February 27, 1887, while on a trip with his students at Middleton, Tennessee. He was buried in Blue Mountain Cemetery, Blue Mountain, Tippah County, Mississippi.

LOWREY'S BRIGADE (CSA): This Rebel infantry brigade fought at the Battle of Franklin in Cleburne's Division, Cheatham's Corps, C.S. Army of Tennessee.

Named after Confederate Brigadier General Mark Perrin Lowrey, it was comprised of the Sixteenth Alabama, Thirty-third Alabama, Forty-fifth Alabama, Fifth Mississippi, Eighth Mississippi, Thirty-second Mississippi, and Third Mississippi Battalion.

LOWRY, ROBERT GADDEN HAYNES (CSA): He was born March 10, 1829, in the Chesterfield District of South Carolina, but was raised in Tennessee and Mississippi.

Lowry was schooled to be a lawyer, a profession he followed until Lincoln's War erupted in April 1861. Siding with the South and the Constitution, he joined the Confederate army and rapidly ascended the ranks, fighting in such battles as Port Gibson, Bayou Pierre, Champion Hill, Second Corinth, Port Hudson, Shiloh, Vicksburg, and Atlanta.

At the Battle of Franklin he took over command of Adams' Brigade after its original leader Brigadier General John Adams was killed.

Appointed brigadier general, Lowry fought at the Battles of Nashville and Bentonville, then surrendered with his troops, officially leaving service in May 1865.

After the War he resumed his law practice at Brandon, Mississippi, served as a state senator, and fought against the illegalities of the North's corrupt and violent carpetbag-scallywag government. He was elected to two consecutive terms as governor of Mississippi, penned a history of the state, and served as president of the United Confederate Veterans.

Battling rheumatism, Lowry passed away at Jackson, Mississippi, on January 19, 1910, at the home of his granddaughter on State Street. He was buried in Brandon Cemetery, Brandon, Rankin County, Mississippi.

LUMSDEN, CHARLES L. (CSA): Born in 1834, Captain Lumsden was a graduate of the Virginia Military Institute, and commandant of Cadets at the University of Alabama. At the Battle of Franklin he led Lumsden's Alabama Battery, Stewart's Corps Artillery, Walthall's Division. He died in 1867.

LUMSDEN'S ALABAMA BATTERY (CSA): This battery fought at the Battle of Franklin with Truehart's Battalion, Stewart's Corps Artillery, C.S. Army of Tennessee. Commanded by Confederate Captain Charles L. Lumsden, it was organized November 4, 1861, and surrendered May 4, 1865.

MACARTHUR, ARTHUR, JR. (USA): The son of Arthur MacArthur and Aurelia Belcher, he was born June 2, 1845, at Chicopee Falls (formerly part of what is now Springfield), Massachusetts.

With the outbreak of Lincoln's War, MacArthur, then a resident of Wisconsin, sided with the North and against the Constitution, promptly enlisting with the Twenty-fourth Wisconsin Volunteer Infantry. The eighteen year old fought at such battles as Chickamauga, Murfreesboro, Chattanooga, Atlanta, and Franklin. For his gallantry at the Battle of Missionary Ridge he was later awarded the Medal of Honor.

He was brevetted colonel in 1864, and was from thence forward known as the "Boy Colonel."

After the War he was recommissioned with the U.S. army, serving as a lieutenant general against the Indians. In 1875 he married Mary Pinkney Hardy of Norfolk, Virginia, with whom he bore three sons—two who would later become famous World War II heros: U.S. army General Douglas MacArthur and U.S. navy Captain Arthur MacArthur III.

MacArthur went on to serve as a brigadier general in the Spanish-American War, then led the U.S. Second Division, Eighth Corps, in the Philippine-American War. In 1900 he was appointed military governor of the Philippines, and was promoted to major general in 1902.

In the years that followed, MacArthur, now a lieutenant general, served in a wide variety of governmental positions, including military attaché to the U.S. Embassy at Tokyo, Japan.

In 1909, on his sixty-fourth birthday, he retired from the U.S. army. On September 5, 1912, while giving a speech on the "Civil War" at Milwaukee, Wisconsin, he died of a heart attack. He was first buried in Milwaukee, but his body was later reinterred in Arlington National Cemetery.

MAGEE, T. D. (CSA): Confederate Major Magee led the Forty-sixth Mississippi Infantry at the Battle of Franklin, where he was wounded in action.

MAGEVNEY, MICHAEL (CSA): Confederate Colonel Magevney led the One hundred fifty-fourth Tennessee Infantry at the Battle of Franklin, where he was wounded in action.

MANEY, GEORGE EARL (CSA): Maney was born August 24, 1826, at Nashville (some sources say Franklin), Tennessee. He attended Nashville Seminary and the University of Nashville, graduating in 1845.

He fought in the Mexican-American War, then studied law and was admitted to the bar in 1850. He ran a successful law practice in Nashville until the start of Lincoln's War, when he sided with the South and the Constitution.

Joining the Confederate army he first served as an officer in the Eleventh Tennessee, then in the First Tennessee. He fought at numerous battles, including Shiloh, Murfreesboro, Chattanooga, Perryville, Atlanta, and Chickamauga, eventually rising to the rank of brigadier general.

He is most famous for his unit Maney's Brigade, which fought at the Battle of Franklin. Maney himself, however, was not present at that conflict. His location during this period is a mystery, for after he was given a medical leave of absence on August 31, 1864, he disappears from the official records, then reappears May 1, 1865, when he was paroled in Greensboro, North Carolina.

Postbellum, Maney resumed his work as an attorney, served as president of the Tennessee and Pacific Railroad, went into politics, and served as a U.S. ambassador to various South American nations. He died February 9, 1901, at Washington, D.C., and was buried in Mount Olivet Cemetery, Nashville, Tennessee.

MANEY'S BRIGADE (CSA): This Rebel infantry brigade fought at the Battle of Franklin in Brown's Division, Cheatham's Corps, C.S. Army of Tennessee.

Named after Confederate Colonel George Earl Maney of Franklin, Tennessee, it was commanded by Brigadier General John Carpenter Carter at the Battle of Franklin after Maney was given a leave of absence (on August 31, 1864) due to a physical disability.

Carter himself was severely wounded in the conflict and died a little over a week later on December 10, 1864. The brigade was then taken over by Confederate Colonel Hume R. Field.

Maney's Brigade, known in some sources as Carter's Brigade, was comprised of the First Tennessee, Fourth Tennessee, Sixth Tennessee, Eighth Tennessee, Ninth Tennessee, Sixteenth Tennessee, Twenty-seventh Tennessee, Twenty-eighth Tennessee, and Fiftieth Tennessee.

MANIGAULT, ARTHUR MIDDLETON (CSA): The son of Joseph Manigault and Charlotte Drayton, this descendant of Huguenots from France was born October 26, 1824, at Charleston, South Carolina.

Manigault was schooled at the College of Charleston, which he left early to pursue his interest in the export business. In 1846 he served as a U.S. lieutenant in the Mexican-American War. Afterward he resumed his job as an export merchant, and in 1850 he married Mary Procter Huger.

With the outbreak of Lincoln's War, he sided with the South and the Constitution, fighting at the opening battle at Fort Sumter—where Lincoln cunningly maneuvered the Confederacy into firing the first shot. A few weeks later he was made colonel of the Tenth South Carolina Infantry, which was attached to the Army of Tennessee in the Spring of 1862.

Manigault fought at such battles as Shiloh, Corinth, Murfreesboro, Missionary Ridge, Chickamauga, and Atlanta. At the Battle of Franklin, where he led his own unit, Manigault's Brigade, he was seriously wounded, forcing him from active service.

After the War he returned to his rice plantation in South Carolina, and, from 1880 to 1886, served as the inspector general of his state. He died August 17, 1886, at South Island, South Carolina, due to complications from his war wounds. He was buried in Magnolia Cemetery, Charleston, South Carolina.

MANIGAULT'S BRIGADE (CSA): This Rebel infantry brigade fought at the Battle of Franklin in Johnson's Division, Lee's Corps, C.S. Army of Tennessee.

Named after Confederate Brigadier General Arthur Middleton Manigault, it was comprised of the Twenty-fourth Alabama, Twenty-eighth Alabama, Thirty-fourth Alabama, Tenth South Carolina, and Nineteenth South Carolina.

MAPLELAWN: See Owen-Cox House.

MARSHALL, ALEXANDER (USA): Yankee Captain Marshall led the Union's First Ohio Battery "G", Fourth Corps Artillery, Wood's Third Division, Fourth U.S. Army Corps, at the Battle of Franklin.

MARSHALL'S TENNESSEE BATTERY (CSA): This Rebel battery fought at the Battle of Franklin with Johnson's Battalion, Lee's Corps Artillery, C.S. Army of Tennessee.

MARTIN CHEAIRS HOUSE: See Ferguson Hall.

MCCOOK, EDWARD MOODY (USA): He was born June 15, 1833, at Steubenville, Ohio. After his early schooling the sixteen year old moved to Colorado (at the time part of Kansas Territory). One of the first European-American settlers in the Pike's Peak area, he served as a Kansas legislator and started up a successful law practice.

With the start of Lincoln's War, McCook sided with the North and against the Constitution, serving as one of Lincoln's many notorious secret agents—gathering intelligence which the president would later use to illegally arrest, imprison, torture, and even murder innocent people (mainly Northerners).

In May 1861 McCook began a rapid ascension through the ranks, eventually attaining brigadier general. Like thousands of other Yankee officers, McCook is known as a war criminal in the South for his numerous crimes against humanity, such as the wanton, cruel, unnecessary, and illegal destruction of civilian homes, particularly in Georgia.

He fought at such battles

as Perryville, Brown's Mill, Chickamauga, and Selma. At the Battle of Franklin McCook led the Union's First Division, Wilson's Cavalry Corps.

After the War President Andrew Johnson appointed him U.S. minister to Hawaii, after which he served as territorial governor of Colorado. His interests in mining, real estate, and the newly invented telephone made him a wealthy man.

He passed away on September 9, 1909, at Chicago, Illinois, and was buried in Union Cemetery, Steubenville, Ohio.

MCCOOK'S FIRST DIVISION (USA): This Yankee cavalry division, named after U.S. Brigadier General Edward Moody McCook, served with Wilson's Cavalry Corps at the Battle of Franklin. It was comprised of Croxton's First Brigade and McCook's First Division Artillery.

MCCOOK'S FIRST DIVISION ARTILLERY (USA): This Yankee artillery unit fought at the Battle of Franklin in McCook's First Division, Wilson's Cavalry Corps. Named after U.S. Brigadier General Edward Moody McCook, it was comprised of the Chicago Board of Trade Battery.

MCDONALD, JOSEPH E. (CSA): Confederate Major McDonald led the Fifty-fifth Tennessee Infantry at the Battle of Franklin, where he was killed in action. He was buried in the McGavock Confederate Cemetery, Franklin, Tennessee.

MCEWEN HOUSE: This beautiful antebellum house in Franklin, Tennessee, built in 1849, was used as a field hospital during and after the Battle of Franklin. The home, also known as the Harris-McEwen House, is today privately owned.

MCGAVOCK CONFEDERATE CEMETERY: Set on the current northwest corner of Carnton Plantation, Franklin, Tennessee, the McGavock Confederate Cemetery is the final resting place of some 1,500 Southern soldiers, nearly all who perished at the Battle of Franklin, November 30, 1864.

The two acre plot was kindly donated in 1866 by Confederate Colonel John W. McGavock, at the time the owner of Carnton Plantation. The graves were positioned by state, representing most of the states of the Confederacy. A separate area has been set aside for "unknowns."

This beautiful graveyard is the largest privately owned Confederate cemetery in the U.S. A complete list of the dead (and the location of their remains) is included in this book.

MCGAVOCK CREEK: This small waterway runs along the east side of the present day property of Carnton Plantation. It was used for a variety of purposes by Native-Americans, and later by the McGavocks, for such things as fishing, washing clothes, and "refrigerating" perishable food.

MCGAVOCK, CARRIE: See Caroline Elizabeth Winder.

MCGAVOCK, ELIZABETH IRWIN: The wife of General William Giles Harding, the owner of Belle Meade Plantation during Lincoln's War, she was born May 17, 1819, at Nashville, Tennessee.

McGavock and Harding had six known children, one of whom was Selene Harding, wife of Confederate General William Hicks "Red" Jackson, who led a division at the Battle of Franklin.

McGavock was the daughter of Randal McGavock, founder of Franklin's Carnton Plantation. She died August 9, 1867, and was originally buried in the Harding-Jackson Mausoleum at Belle Meade. In 1906 her remains were moved to Mount Olivet Cemetery, Nashville, Tennessee.

MCGAVOCK, HARRIET YOUNG: The daughter of Confederate Colonel John W. McGavock and Caroline Elizabeth Winder, she was born at Carnton Plantation, Franklin, Tennessee, July 2, 1855.

Known as "Hattie," in 1884 she married Confederate Lieutenant George Limerick Cowan of General Nathan Bedford Forrest's fearsome Escort. The couple, who lived at the foot of Carnton's driveway in a house called "Windermere," bore five known children.

As a nine year old, McGavock was an eyewitness to the Battle of Franklin, later relating her memories of the terrifying event that changed the little town of Franklin forever.

She passed away July 19, 1932, and was buried in the Cowan Family Plot at Mount Hope Cemetery, Franklin,

Tennessee.

MCGAVOCK, JAMES RANDAL: The brother of Elizabeth Irwin McGavock and the son of Carnton Plantation founder Randal McGavock, he was born January 9, 1812, at Nashville, Tennessee.

In 1832 he married Louisa C. Chenault of Kentucky and bore ten known children. Around this same time McGavock began construction of Riverside Plantation, located across the Harpeth River—not far from Carnton Plantation, his brother Colonel John W. McGavock's home.

McGavock died February 12, 1862, and so was spared the horror of the second and third Battles of Franklin. However, his family watched the latter conflict from the hilltop at Riverside Mansion several miles to the southeast of the core fight.

MCGAVOCK, JOHN W. (CSA): The son of Carnton Plantation founder Randal McGavock and his wife Sarah Dougherty Rodgers, he was born April 2, 1815, at Nashville, Tennessee.

In 1848 he married Caroline Elizabeth Winder of Louisiana, with whom he bore five children. One of them, Harriet Young "Hattie" McGavock, married Confederate Lieutenant George Limerick Cowan of County Derry, Ireland—a noted member of General Nathan Bedford Forrest's famous Escort.

After the death of his mother Sarah in 1854, McGavock inherited Carnton Plantation and set about remodeling it. He was the owner at the time of the Battle of Franklin. At the start of the War, according to local Franklin lore, Confederate President Jefferson Davis had asked McGavock if his home could be used as a Confederate field hospital if needed. McGavock agreed and was made a colonel in return for his generosity (he never saw combat however).

A traditional conservative Southerner and a staunch member of the United Confederate Veterans (the forerunner of today's Sons of Confederate Veterans), McGavock passed away June 7, 1893, and was buried in the McGavock Family Cemetery at Carnton Plantation.

MCGAVOCK, RANDAL: The son of Captain James McGavock Sr. (of Country Antrim, Northern Ireland) and Mary "Sally" Cloyd, he was born June 20, 1766, in Rockbridge County, Virginia.

In 1811 McGavock married Sarah Dougherty Rodgers, with whom he bore seven known children. Among them were: Elizabeth Irwin McGavock (of Belle Meade Plantation), James Randal McGavock (of Riverside Plantation), and Colonel John W. McGavock (of Carnton Plantation).

Sometime in the early 1800s, perhaps around 1815, McGavock began work on Carnton Plantation, named after his family's ancestral Irish home, Cairnton. He moved his family into the home in 1826 upon its completion.

After the Battle of Franklin Carnton was used as a Confederate field hospital over the next six months. The plantation itself was located on the southeast corner of the battle, but suffered no permanent damage as the main fighting was several miles away to the northwest.

McGavock served as the eleventh mayor of Nashville, Tennessee. His brother David, a surveyor, laid out the lines of Davidson County, Tennessee. McGavock passed away September 27, 1843, and was buried in the McGavock Family Cemetery at Carnton Plantation.

MCGAVOCK'S FORD: A crossing on the Harpeth River in Franklin, Tennessee, it was used by Union forces at the Battle of Franklin. According to 19th-Century sources, it is located about one mile "below Hughes' Ford."

MCGAVOCK'S GROVE: No longer in existence, this once elegant stand of trees was located near the mansion of Franklin's Carnton Plantation. The owners, the McGavock family, held numerous family picnics and political rallies here beneath the shade of cedar and boxwood trees.

Famous guests who frequented, and probably gave rousing speeches, at the Grove included Andrew Jackson, Sam Houston, James Knox Polk, and Felix Grundy.

MCGAVOCK, WINDER: The son of Colonel John W. McGavock and Caroline Elizabeth Winder, he was born July 13, 1857, at Carnton Plantation, founded in the early 1800s by his grandfather Randal McGavock.

In 1864 the seven year old witnessed the Battle of Franklin firsthand when his family home was turned into one of Franklin's forty-four field hospitals. In 1883 he married Susan Lee "Susie" Ewing, with whom he bore five children.

After his mother Caroline died in 1905, McGavock inherited Carnton. He died himself only two years later, on June 3, 1907, after which the famous home passed to his wife Susie. He was buried in the McGavock Family Plot at Mount Hope Cemetery, Franklin, Tennessee.

MCKISSACK, JESSIE HELEN: Born on January 3, 1838, in Spring Hill, Maury County, Tennessee, Jessie was held to be an uncommon beauty, one known as the "beguiling temptress" of Middle Tennessee.

Her charms led to tragedy, however, when her husband Dr. George B. Peters murdered Confederate Major General Earl Van Dorn at Ferguson Hall on May 7, 1863, for allegedly carrying on an affair with Jessie.

To this day much intrigue and mystery continues to surround this star-crossed Victorian trio. Confederate General Nathan Bedford Forrest took over Van Dorn's command after his death.

MCLEMORE HOUSE: Built in 1880 at Franklin, Tennessee, this postbellum home was of course not connected to the Battle of Franklin. However, it is indirectly connected as it was constructed by former black servants who lived through the conflict.

The McLemore House, one of the last remaining freedmen's homes in Franklin, is located in an area of town called "Hard Bargain." It was kept in the same African-American family for 117 years, and is listed on the National Register of Historic Places.

MCNEILLY, JAMES H. (CSA): Dr. McNeilly was a chaplain in Confederate General William A. Quarles' brigade. According to Franklin legend, before the Battle of Franklin,

Rebel soldiers asked the clergyman if he would keep their watches, photos, and letters, and send them home to their families if they perished in the fight. Unfortunately, he himself was fighting that day and had to refuse them.

McNeilly, whose name is also sometimes spelled M'Neilly, survived the conflict but his brother did not. The brave soldier's body was discovered on the evening of November 30, 1864. The chaplain went in search of him the next morning, commenting: "The dead were piled up in the trenches almost to the top of the earthworks. . . . I could have trodden on a dead man at every step." His brother was discovered near the Carter family cotton gin, not far from where Confederate Generals Patrick R. Cleburne and John Adams were also killed.

Dr. McNeilly conducted the funeral service of Carnton Plantation owner Caroline Elizabeth Winder (Carrie McGavock) in 1905.

MCPHAIL OFFICE: See Visitors Center.

MCQUAIDE, JOHN (CSA): A soldier with Confederate General Alexander P. Stewart's artillery, he was one of the first on the Franklin battlefield December 1, 1864, the morning after the conflict. It was McQuaide who discovered the body of Confederate General Patrick R. Cleburne about fifty-five yards from the Carter family cotton gin.

Cleburne, who had been shot in the chest, had had his hat (kepi) and boots stolen by Yankees during the night. McQuaide helped load Cleburne's body into a nearby ambulance, after which it was transported to Carnton Plantation, where it was laid on the back porch so his troops could pay their final respects.

MEEK, ALEXANDER T. (CSA): Confederate Major Meek led the Second and Twenty-fourth Arkansas Infantries at the Battle of Franklin, where he was killed in action.

MERRILL HILL: See Privet Knob.

MIDDLE, TENNESSEE: Traditionally, Tennessee has long been separated into three "Grand

Divisions": East, Middle, and West Tennessee. The Battle of Franklin was fought in Middle Tennessee, an area composed of 17,000 square miles and forty counties, with the state's capital city Nashville at its center.

MIDWAY PLANTATION: This once enormous farm was named for its location in Brentwood, Tennessee, "midway" between Nashville and Franklin. The fourteen-room mansion was constructed around 1829 on what was originally a prehistoric Native-American site, by Lysander McGavock and his wife Elizabeth Crockett (third cousin of famed frontiersman Davy Crockett). Lysander was the son of David McGavock and Elizabeth McDowell, both of Rockbridge County, Virginia.

A number of the Indian artifacts discovered here are today stored at the Smithsonian Institution. Most of the 1,000 acres Midway once sat on was inherited by Elizabeth Crockett from her family. These included her parents James Crockett and Mary Drake, who migrated to Williamson County, Tennessee, from Wythe County, Virginia, settling in Brentwood about 1799 on land James received from a Revolutionary War grant.

A number of "Civil War" skirmishes were fought around Midway, which served as both a field hospital and an officer's command post. Some of the breastworks, swales, and trenches from Lincoln's War could still be seen up until quite recently when Midway's land was divided up and developed into modern subdivisions.

The plantation, or what is left of it, is today owned and maintained by the Brentwood Country Club, which has transformed the original spacious crop fields into a golf course, with Midway mansion now serving as the clubhouse. Many of the members of the McGavock family who founded Midway are buried in the McGavock-Hayes Cemetery located across the street.

MITCHELL, GEORGE H. (USA): A lieutenant of artillery, Mitchell commanded a Yankee battery serving as rearguard during the Battle of Franklin.

MOORE, ORLANDO HURLEY (USA): Colonel Moore was born July 13, 1827. He commanded the Union's Second Brigade, Ruger's Second

Division, Twenty-third U.S. Army Corps at the Battle of Franklin. He died October 31, 1890, at Detroit, Michigan, and was buried in Tulare Cemetery, Tulare, California.

MOORE'S SECOND BRIGADE (USA): This Yankee infantry brigade fought at the Battle of Franklin in Ruger's Second Division, Twenty-third U.S. Army Corps.

Named after U.S. Colonel Orlando Hurley Moore, it was comprised of the One hundred seventh Illinois, Eightieth Indiana, One hundred twenty-ninth Indiana, Twenty-third Michigan, One hundred eleventh Ohio, and One hundred eighteenth Ohio.

MORTON, JOHN WATSON, JR. (CSA): Morton was born September 19, 1842, in Williamson County, Tennessee, and was schooled at Nashville's Western Military Institute. With the outbreak of Lincoln's War he sided with the South and the Constitution, and enlisted in the Confederate army.

After learning of Confederate General Nathan Bedford Forrest's "brave and masterful escape" from Fort Donelson, the enamored twenty year old artillerist requested a transfer to Forrest's cavalry, fighting with the distinguished Rebel commander until the close of the War.

The pair served together in such battles as Brice's Cross Roads, Johnsonville, Thompson's Station, Chickamauga, and Parker's Cross Roads—the last site where a monument was erected to Morton and his battery in 2007.

At the Battle of Franklin Captain Morton headed his artillery unit, Morton's Tennessee Battery, on the far right near the Harpeth River. He surrendered with Forrest at Gainesville, Alabama, May 10, 1865.

After the War he studied medicine at the University of Tennessee, and took up farming and journalism. In the 1880s he served as assistant commissioner of agriculture, and in the early 1900s he served as Tennessee's secretary of state.

The first president of the Tennessee Division of the United Confederate Veterans (now known as the Sons of Confederate Veterans), he published his memoirs, *The Artillery of Nathan Bedford Forrest's Cavalry*, in 1909.

While living with his daughter in Memphis, Tennessee, Morton passed away on November 21, 1914. He was buried in Nashville's Mount Olivet Cemetery.

MORTON'S TENNESSEE BATTERY (CSA): Named for Confederate Captain John Watson Morton Jr., this Rebel unit fought at the Battle of Franklin in Forrest's Cavalry Corps Artillery, Forrest's Cavalry Corps, C.S. Army of Tennessee.

MOTHERSPAW, THOMAS W. (USA): He was born in 1828 in Ohio. After marrying Sarah Jane Rush in 1852, the couple moved to Illinois and began farming.

Major Motherspaw commanded the Seventy-third Illinois Infantry, Opdycke's First Brigade, Wagner's Second Division, Fourth U.S. Army Corps, at the Battle of Franklin.

He died December 18, 1864, from wounds received at that conflict. His grave site is not known, but may be in Piatt County, Illinois (where his wife is buried).

MURPHEY, VIRGIL S. (CSA): Confederate Colonel Murphey commanded the Seventeenth Alabama Infantry, Shelley's Brigade, Walthall's Division, Stewart's Corps, C.S. Army of Tennessee, at the Battle of Franklin. Colonel Murphey was wounded at that conflict and taken prisoner by the enemy.

MUSIC CITY: A popular modern nickname for Nashville, Tennessee, the world's capital of country music.

December 15-16, 1864, two weeks after the Battle of Franklin, the Battle of Nashville ended all hopes of a Confederate resurgence in the Western Theater. It was here that, for all practical purposes, the Army of Tennessee met an inglorious end under the command of Confederate General John Bell Hood.

MYRICK'S BATTALION (CSA): This Rebel battalion fought at the Battle of Franklin in Stewart's Corps Artillery, C.S. Army of Tennessee. It was comprised of Bouanchaud's Louisiana Battery, Cowan's Mississippi Battery, and Darden's Mississippi Battery.

NASHVILLE AND DECATUR RAILROAD: The postwar name (1866) of the railroad tracks that run through Franklin, and which were followed by Confederate General Alexander P. Stewart's men on the right flank during the Battle of Franklin.

During the Battle of Franklin the "road" was known as the Tennessee and Alabama Railroad, due to the fact that it was built and owned (at the time) by the Tennessee and Alabama Railroad Company.

NASHVILLE AND DECATUR RAILROAD UNDERPASS: This underpass, located near downtown Franklin, Tennessee, was once part of Yankee occupied Fort Granger, which played a major role in the Battle of Franklin.

The underpass area contained Union campsites, horse stables, corrals, warehouses, guard posts, and march and drill fields. Nearby were Yankee earthworks and gun emplacements. The area was also the site of severe fighting during the Battle of Franklin III, December 17, 1864.

NASHVILLE, TENNESSEE: Founded in 1779 and originally called Fort Nashborough, Nashville is located on the Cumberland River in Middle Tennessee, and serves as the state's capital city.

The second largest city in Tennessee (after Memphis) and the fourth largest in the southeastern U.S., "Music City" was the site of the Battle of Nashville (December 15-16, 1864), which took place two weeks after the Battle of Franklin. It was here that Confederate power in the Western Theater was finally lost, helping lead to Lee's surrender and the end of Lincoln's War April 9, 1865.

NEGROES: See African-Americans and Black Confederates.

NELSON, NOEL LIGDON (CSA): Confederate Colonel Nelson led the Twelfth Louisiana Infantry at the Battle of Franklin, where he was wounded in action. He later died from his injuries.

NINETEENTH ALABAMA (CSA): This Rebel infantry regiment fought at the Battle of Franklin in Deas' Brigade, Johnson's Division, Lee's Corps, C.S. Army of Tennessee.

NINETEENTH ARKANSAS (CSA): This Rebel infantry regiment fought at the Battle of Franklin in Govan's Brigade, Cleburne's Division, Cheatham's Corps, C.S. Army of Tennessee.

NINETEENTH LOUISIANA (CSA): This Rebel infantry regiment fought at the Battle of Franklin in Gibson's Brigade, Clayton's Division, Lee's Corps, C.S. Army of Tennessee.

NINETEENTH OHIO (USA): This Yankee infantry regiment fought at the Battle of Franklin in Beatty's Third Brigade, Wood's Third Division, Fourth U.S. Army Corps.

NINETEENTH OHIO BATTERY (USA): This Yankee artillery unit fought at the Battle of Franklin in Ruger's Second Division, Twenty-third U.S. Army Corps.

NINETEENTH PENNSYLVANIA CAVALRY (USA): This Yankee cavalry regiment fought at the Battle of Franklin in Hammond's First Brigade, Knipe's Seventh Division, Wilson's Cavalry Corps.

NINETEENTH SOUTH CAROLINA (CSA): This Rebel infantry regiment fought at the Battle of Franklin in Manigault's Brigade, Johnson's Division, Lee's Corps, C.S. Army of Tennessee.

NINETEENTH TENNESSEE (CSA): This Rebel infantry regiment fought at the Battle of Franklin in Strahl's Brigade, Brown's Division, Cheatham's Corps, C.S. Army of Tennessee.

NINETEENTH TENNESSEE CAVALRY (CSA): This Rebel cavalry regiment fought at the Battle of Franklin in Bell's Brigade, Buford's Division, Forrest's Cavalry Corps, C.S.

Army of Tennessee.

NINETIETH OHIO (USA): This Yankee infantry regiment fought at the Battle of Franklin in Kirby's First Brigade, Kimball's First Division, Fourth U.S. Army Corps.

NINETY-FIRST INDIANA (USA): This Yankee infantry regiment fought at the Battle of Franklin in Strickland's Third Brigade, Ruger's Second Division, Twenty-third U.S. Army Corps.

NINETY-NINTH OHIO (USA): This Yankee infantry regiment, though attached to Ruger's Second Division, Twenty-third U.S. Army Corps, was with Cooper's Brigade—which was on detached duty at the time of the Battle of Franklin. It was thus not present or involved in the fighting.

NINETY-SEVENTH OHIO (USA): This Yankee infantry regiment fought at the Battle of Franklin in Lane's Second Brigade, Wagner's Second Division, Fourth U.S. Army Corps.

NINETY-SIXTH ILLINOIS (USA): This Yankee infantry regiment fought at the Battle of Franklin in Whitaker's Second Brigade, Kimball's First Division, Fourth U.S. Army Corps.

NINETY-THIRD OHIO (USA): This Yankee infantry regiment fought at the Battle of Franklin in Post's Second Brigade, Wood's Third Division, Fourth U.S. Army Corps.

NINTH ARKANSAS (CSA): This Rebel infantry regiment fought at the Battle of Franklin in Reynolds' Brigade, Walthall's Division, Stewart's Corps, C.S. Army of Tennessee.

NINTH ILLINOIS CAVALRY (USA): This Yankee cavalry regiment fought at the Battle of Franklin in Coon's Second Brigade, Hatch's Fifth Division, Wilson's Cavalry Corps.

NINTH INDIANA (USA): This Yankee infantry regiment fought at the Battle of Franklin in Grose's Third Brigade, Kimball's First Division, Fourth U.S. Army Corps.

NINTH INDIANA CAVALRY (USA): This Yankee cavalry regiment fought at the Battle of Franklin in Hammond's First Brigade, Knipe's Seventh Division, Wilson's Cavalry Corps.

NINTH MISSISSIPPI (CSA): This Rebel infantry regiment fought at the Battle of Franklin in Sharp's Brigade, Johnson's Division, Lee's Corps, C.S. Army of Tennessee.

NINTH MISSISSIPPI BATTALION SHARPSHOOTERS (CSA): This Rebel regiment fought at the Battle of Franklin in Sharp's Brigade, Johnson's Division, Lee's Corps, C.S. Army of Tennessee.

NINTH TENNESSEE (CSA): This Rebel infantry regiment fought at the Battle of Franklin in Maney's Brigade, Brown's Division, Cheatham's Corps, C.S. Army of Tennessee.

NINTH TENNESSEE CAVALRY (CSA): According to some sources this Rebel cavalry regiment fought at the Battle of Franklin in Biffle's Brigade, Chalmers' Division, Forrest's Cavalry Corps, C.S. Army of Tennessee.

NINTH TEXAS (CSA): This Rebel infantry regiment served in Ector's Brigade, French's Division, Stewart's Corps, C.S. Army of Tennessee.

Ector's Brigade was at Franklin, Tennessee, during the Battle of Franklin. However, it did not participate in the battle as it was on detached duty at the time.

NINTH TEXAS CAVALRY (CSA): This Rebel cavalry regiment fought at the Battle of Franklin in Ross' Brigade, Jackson's Division, Forrest's Cavalry Corps, C.S. Army of Tennessee.

NIXON'S TENNESSEE CAVALRY REGIMENT (CSA): This Rebel cavalry regiment fought at the Battle of Franklin in Bell's Brigade, Buford's Division, Forrest's Cavalry Corps, C.S. Army of Tennessee.

NUTT'S LOUISIANA CAVALRY - DISMOUNTED (CSA): This Rebel unit fought at the Battle of Franklin in Granbury's Brigade, Cleburne's

Division, Cheatham's Corps, C..S. Army of Tennessee.

OAKLAWN PLANTATION: This fine estate, located in Spring Hill, Tennessee, served as the headquarters of Confederate General John Bell Hood during the Battle of Spring Hill, November 29, 1864—one day prior to the Battle of Franklin.

Oaklawn was built in 1835 by Absalom Thompson, and so is sometimes called the Absalom Thompson House. It is also known as Hood's Haven.

The home holds many secrets from the Civil War period, as well as many memories from the modern era: Country artists George Jones and Tammy Wynette once lived here; the film *Daltry Calhoun* was shot here; and a recent episode of HGTV's "Design Star" took place at Oaklawn.

OLD FACTORY STORE: This historic building, located on East Main Street, Franklin, Tennessee, is famous for being used as a field hospital during and after the Battle of Franklin.

The property it sits on was sold in 1799 to Joseph McBride by Franklin founder Abram Maury. The Greek Revival brick store, along with a nearby steam-powered cotton and grist mill, was constructed sometime in the early 1820s.

It is fortunate that the building still stands today. Like so many other structures in Franklin, it was marked for burning by heartless Yankee troops.

On December 12, 1862, for example, U.S. General David S. Stanley had the cotton factory destroyed and the stones of the grist mill torn down. He only spared the Old Factory Store because it contained valuable food supplies (including whiskey), which he stole from the owner at his leisure.

Stanley would go on to lead the Fourth U.S. Army Corps at the Battle of Franklin on November 30, 1864. He was responsible for the wounding and deaths of hundreds of innocent

Confederate soldiers, many of them from the Franklin area.

After the War the Old Factory Store changed owners numerous times, serving variously as a grocery store, an antiques store, a furniture repair store, a restaurant, and a bank. Today it is the home of a bookstore. In 1972 the building was placed on the National Register of Historic Places.

ONE HUNDRED EIGHTEENTH OHIO (USA): This Yankee infantry regiment fought at the Battle of Franklin in Moore's Second Brigade, Ruger's Second Division, Twenty-third U.S. Army Corps.

ONE HUNDRED EIGHTY-THIRD OHIO (USA): This Yankee infantry regiment fought at the Battle of Franklin in Strickland's Third Brigade, Ruger's Second Division, Twenty-third U.S. Army Corps.

ONE HUNDRED ELEVENTH OHIO (USA): This Yankee infantry regiment fought at the Battle of Franklin in Moore's Second Brigade, Ruger's Second Division, Twenty-third U.S. Army Corps.

ONE HUNDRED FIFTEENTH ILLINOIS (USA): This Yankee infantry regiment fought at the Battle of Franklin in Whitaker's Second Brigade, Kimball's First Division, Fourth U.S. Army Corps.

ONE HUNDRED FIFTY-FOURTH TENNESSEE (CSA): This Rebel infantry regiment fought at the Battle of Franklin in Vaughan's Brigade, Brown's Division, Cheatham's Corps, C.S. Army of Tennessee.

ONE HUNDRED FIRST OHIO (USA): This Yankee infantry regiment fought at the Battle of Franklin in Kirby's First Brigade, Kimball's First Division, Fourth U.S. Army Corps.

ONE HUNDRED FOURTH OHIO (USA): This Yankee infantry regiment fought at the Battle of Franklin in Reilly's First Brigade, Cox's Third Division, Twenty-third U.S. Army Corps.

ONE HUNDRED SEVENTH ILLINOIS (USA): This Yankee infantry regiment fought at the Battle of Franklin in Moore's Second Brigade, Ruger's Second Division, Twenty-third U.S. Army Corps.

ONE HUNDRED SEVENTY-FIFTH OHIO (USA): This Yankee infantry regiment fought at the Battle of Franklin in Reilly's First Brigade, Cox's Third Division, Twenty-third U.S. Army Corps.

ONE HUNDRED THIRD OHIO (USA): This Yankee infantry regiment fought at the Battle of Franklin in Casement's Second Brigade, Cox's Third Division, Twenty-third U.S. Army Corps.

ONE HUNDRED THIRTIETH INDIANA (USA): This Yankee infantry regiment, though attached to Ruger's Second Division, Twenty-third U.S. Army Corps, was with Cooper's Brigade—which was on detached duty at the time of the Battle of Franklin. It was thus not present or involved in the fighting.

ONE HUNDRED TWELFTH ILLINOIS (USA): This Yankee infantry regiment fought at the Battle of Franklin in Stiles' Third Brigade, Cox's Third Division, Twenty-third U.S. Army Corps.

ONE HUNDRED TWENTIETH INDIANA (USA): This Yankee infantry regiment fought at the Battle of Franklin in Stiles' Third Brigade, Cox's Third Division, Twenty-third U.S. Army Corps.

ONE HUNDRED TWENTY-EIGHTH INDIANA (USA): This Yankee infantry regiment fought at the Battle of Franklin in Stiles' Third Brigade, Cox's Third Division, Twenty-third U.S. Army Corps.

ONE HUNDRED TWENTY-FIFTH OHIO (USA): This Yankee infantry regiment fought at the Battle of Franklin in Opdycke's First Brigade, Wagner's Second Division, Fourth U.S. Army Corps.

ONE HUNDRED TWENTY-FOURTH INDIANA (USA): This Yankee infantry regiment fought at the Battle of Franklin in Casement's Second Brigade, Cox's Third Division, Twenty-third U.S. Army Corps.

ONE HUNDRED TWENTY-FOURTH OHIO (USA): This Yankee infantry regiment fought at the Battle of Franklin in Post's Second Brigade, Wood's Third Division, Fourth U.S. Army Corps.

ONE HUNDRED TWENTY-NINTH INDIANA (USA): This Yankee infantry regiment fought at the Battle of Franklin in Moore's Second Brigade, Ruger's Second Division, Twenty-third U.S. Army Corps.

ONE HUNDRED TWENTY-THIRD INDIANA (USA): This Yankee infantry regiment fought at the Battle of Franklin in Strickland's Third Brigade, Ruger's Second Division, Twenty-third U.S. Army Corps.

ONE HUNDREDTH ILLINOIS (USA): This Yankee infantry regiment fought at the Battle of Franklin in Lane's Second Brigade, Wagner's Second Division, Fourth U.S. Army Corps.

ONE HUNDREDTH OHIO (USA): This Yankee infantry regiment fought at the Battle of Franklin in Reilly's First Brigade, Cox's Third Division, Twenty-third U.S. Army Corps.

OPDYCKE, EMERSON (USA): Born Samuel Emerson Opdycke on January 7, 1830, at Hubbard, Trumbull County, Ohio, he took part in the California gold rush, eventually settling in Warren, Ohio.

With the outbreak of Lincoln's War, he sided with the North and against the Constitution, and joined the U.S. army. He proved to have a naturally militaristic mind and soon rose up the ranks, fighting at such battles as Shiloh, Chattanooga, Chickamauga, Missionary Ridge, and Atlanta. As a colonel, he led the Union's First Brigade, Wagner's Second Division, Fourth U.S. Army Corps, at the Battle of Franklin.

After the War, at which time he received the rank of brigadier general, he moved to New York City and worked in the dry goods industry.

On April 22, 1884, while cleaning a handgun, he accidently shot himself in the stomach. The injury proved fatal, and he passed away on April 25. His body was returned to Warren, Ohio, where he was buried in the town's Oakwood Cemetery.

OPDYCKE'S FIRST BRIGADE (USA): This Yankee infantry brigade fought at the Battle of Franklin in Wagner's Second Division, Fourth U.S. Army Corps.

Named after U.S. Colonel Emerson Opdycke, it

was comprised of the Thirty-sixth Illinois, Forty-fourth Illinois, Seventy-third Illinois, Seventy-fourth Illinois, Eighty-eighth Illinois, One hundred twenty-fifth Ohio, and Twenty-fourth Wisconsin.

OSAGE ORANGE TREE: Named for a Native-American people, the Osage Nation of Kentucky, the Osage orange is a member of the mulberry family, and was extremely popular among farmers before the invention of barbed wire.

For being tough, limber, strong, and extremely resistant to decay, rot, termites, disease, and ice, it proved to be ideal as a windbreak and shelterbelt, and more especially as a living fence (called a hedge fence) for enclosing livestock.

Even after the advent of barbed wire the Osage orange continued to be used by Western farmers, this time as fence posts for attaching the wire.

Native-Americans also found its wood perfect for making war clubs and bows, hence another one of its nicknames, the bodark tree, from the French words *bois d'arc*, meaning "bow wood." Osage orange wood is still used by archers to this day.

Still another nickname, the hedge apple tree, derives from its large yellowish fruits, known as hedge apples, which give off an orange-like aroma, hence its most common name, Osage orange.

During Lincoln's War soldiers found a more nefarious use for the Osage orange trees they discovered growing around Franklin. Using techniques dating back to ancient times, they felled the trees and carved their branches into sharp dagger-like points.

These obstacles, known as abatis, from the Old French word *abateis* (meaning "a pile of things thrown down"), were laid in front of the approaching enemy with the sharp ends pointing forward. The idea was to slow him down long enough to make him an easy target; or to give one time to flee.

Many a Rebel soldier was cut to pieces by Yankee abatis at the Battle of Franklin, while many more, pausing to figure out a way around it, were shot and died on the treacherous spear-like branches.

OVERTON HILL: Known as Peach Orchard Hill during Lincoln's War, Overton Hill is located in Nashville, Tennessee. It was the site of a Confederate stronghold during the Battle of Nashville, December 15-16, 1864, which was overrun by Union forces.

Though the prominence—and the conflict that took place here (known as the Battle of Peach Orchard Hill)—is today hailed by scallywags and pro-North historians as a memorial to several hundred black Union soldiers fighting in the Thirteenth U.S. Colored Infantry, no mention is ever made of the 1 million blacks who fought for the Confederacy. This was far more than the mere 190,000 that fought for the Union.

There is also no discussion of the name "Thirteenth U.S. Colored Infantry." Why was it called a "colored" infantry? It is because white racist, white supremacist, and white separatist Abraham Lincoln intentionally segregated the U.S. army into all white and all black units. He would not even allow blacks to become commissioned officers. Instead, his "colored troops" could only be commanded by white men—most who did not want the job to begin with because it was considered "demeaning" by white Northerners.

Lincoln, the man behind all of this overt racism, is the same one who not only fought for the deportation of African-Americans throughout his entire adult life and who was a lifelong member of the Yankee founded American Colonization Society (whose stated goal was to make America "white from coast to coast"), this is also the same man who, during a public speech at Springfield, Illinois, on July 17, 1858, said: "What I would most desire would be the separation of the white and black races."

Contrast this with the Confederate army. Under President Jefferson Davis, who adopted a black orphaned boy named Jim Limber during the "Civil War," Southern troops were fully integrated, with white, black, brown, red, and yellow soldiers fighting side by side.

Rebel officers, like General Nathan Bedford Forrest, routinely enlisted Southern blacks into their commands. Forrest alone had sixty-five blacks fighting with him (eight who served as his personal armed guard), while Stonewall Jackson had some 3,000 black Confederate soldiers in his army.

The sight of thousands of armed black Confederate soldiers on the opposite side of the battlefield stunned those Union troops who witnessed them, for this type of racial tolerance was almost completely unheard of in the far more prejudiced North—a fact often testified to by early non-Southern observers, such as Alexis de Tocqueville, Edward Dicey, James Silk Buckingham, and Frederick Law Olmsted.

Finally it should be noted that most of the Union fortifications in Nashville, such as Fort Negley, were built almost entirely by "forced" black labor battalions. None of these Southern "slaves" went to work for the Union voluntarily. All were arrested by armed U.S. military police, given the derogatory name "contraband" (meaning "illegal goods"), then physically coerced into doing the same type of labor they had done as "slaves." This was Lincoln and the North's idea of racial equality and abolition!

Under orders of Union officers at Fort Negley, black men, for example, were forced to dig trenches and cut timbers, while black women were required to wash clothes and haul debris away from the site.

When Confederate troops attempted to take back the city of Nashville in November 1862, Lincoln's black laborers at Fort Negley asked for weapons so they could join in the fight. As per Lincoln's racist personal order, however, they were refused, for at the time he would still not allow African-Americans or Native-Americans (both whom he referred to as "inferior races") to enlist in the U.S. army.

This only finally changed when, on January 1, 1863, Lincoln realized he was running out of white soldiers. It was on this day that he issued what he called his "military emancipation": the Final Emancipation Proclamation. In the document itself Lincoln refers to it, not as a "fit and necessary *black civil rights* measure," but as a "fit and necessary *war* measure."

OVERTON, JOHN, SR.: The son of Captain James Overton and Mary Waller, he was born April 9, 1766, in Louisa County, Virginia. In 1799 he established the plantation Travellers Rest at Nashville, Tennessee.

He married Mary McConnell White, the daughter of General James White, the founder of Knoxville, Tennessee. Their son Colonel John Overton Jr. married Harriet Virginia Maxwell, and named an inn he built in Nashville after her: the Maxwell House Hotel (Maxwell House Coffee was named after the fine coffee served there).

John Jr. and Harriet's daughter Martha Overton married Jacob McGavock Dickinson Sr. The first cousin of Colonel John W. McGavock of Carnton Plantation, Franklin, Tennessee, Jacob served as U.S. secretary of war (under President William Howard Taft) and U.S. assistant attorney general (under President Grover Cleveland).

Between the Battle of Franklin and the Battle of Nashville, Confederate General John Bell Hood used the plantation house at Travellers Rest as his Army of Tennessee headquarters.

John Overton Sr. was a good friend of Andrew "Old Hickory" Jackson. The two, along with General James Winchester (the grandfather of Colonel Edmund Winchester Rucker, who led Rucker's Brigade at the Battle of Franklin) cofounded the city of Memphis, Tennessee, in 1819.

Overton died April 12, 1833, and was buried in Mount Olivet Cemetery, Nashville, Tennessee.

OWEN-COX HOUSE: This home, also known as Maplelawn, is located on Moore's Lane, Brentwood, Tennessee. It was built around 1830 by Nathan Owen on 300 acres he purchased in 1809.

After Owen's death in 1865, the property was sold to Nicholas N. Cox, a colonel in the Tenth Tennessee Cavalry under General Nathan Bedford Forrest.

In the 1870s Cox updated the residence in an Italianate style. Neo-Classical elements were added in the early 1900s. The house is today privately owned.

PERRY'S FLORIDA BATTERY (CSA): This Rebel battery fought at the Battle of Franklin in Hoxton's Battalion, Cheatham's Corps Artillery, C.S. Army of Tennessee.

PETTUS, EDMUND WINSTON (CSA): The son of John Pettus and Alice Taylor Winston, he was born July 6, 1821, in Limestone County, Alabama. He graduated from Clinton College, New Middleton, Tennessee.

At Tuscumbia, Alabama, he studied law and was admitted to the bar in 1842. At Gainesville, Alabama, he began his law practice and served as both a district solicitor and a judge.

In 1844 Pettus married Mary L. Chapman, with whom he bore three children. In 1846 he fought in the Mexican-American War, after which he returned to Alabama to continue his law practice.

With the onset of Lincoln's War, he sided with the South and the Constitution, and was appointed major, then lieutenant general, of the Twentieth Alabama Infantry—which he helped organize.

Pettus fought at numerous battles, including Vicksburg (where he was captured and exchanged), Chattanooga, Bentonville, and Atlanta. Now brigadier general, at the Battle of Franklin he led Pettus' Brigade, Stevenson's Division, Lee's Corps, C.S. Army of Tennessee.

After the War he returned to life as an attorney in Alabama. A traditional Southern conservative (known as a Democrat in the 1860s), he was elected state senator in 1896, and reelected in 1902, serving until his death at Hot Springs, North Carolina, July 27, 1907. He was buried in Live Oak Cemetery, Selma, Alabama. The Edmund Pettus Bridge at Selma was named after him.

PETTUS' BRIGADE (CSA): This Rebel infantry brigade fought at the Battle of Franklin in Stevenson's Division, Lee's Corps, C.S. Army of Tennessee.

Named after Confederate Brigadier General Edmund Winston Pettus, it was comprised of the Twentieth Alabama, Twenty-third Alabama, Thirtieth Alabama, Thirty-first Alabama, and Forty-sixth Alabama.

PHELAN'S ALABAMA BATTERY (CSA): This Rebel battery fought at the Battle of Franklin in Hoxton's Battalion, Cheatham's Corps Artillery, C.S. Army of Tennessee.

PHILLIP'S TENNESSEE BATTERY (CSA): This Rebel battery fought at the Battle of Franklin in Cobb's Battalion, Cheatham's Corps Artillery, C.S. Army of Tennessee.

PLAIN OF FRANKLIN: An essentially flat, two square mile parcel of land upon which the town of Franklin was built.

Bound by undulating crop lands and gently rolling hills on nearly every side, the Franklin Plain was the site of much of the fighting during the Battle of Franklin, and was one of the primary causes of both the stunning Confederate casualty rate and the defeat of Confederate General John Bell Hood and the Army of Tennessee.

POST, PHILIP SIDNEY (USA): He was born March 19, 1833, at Florida, Orange County, New York. With the outbreak of Lincoln's War he sided with the North and against the Constitution.

As a colonel in the Union army, he led the Second Brigade, Wood's Third Division, Fourth U.S. Army Corps at the Battle of Franklin. He was also present at the Battle of Nashville. For his service he was awarded the Medal of Honor.

He died January 6, 1895, at Washington, D.C., and was buried in Hope Cemetery, Galesburg, Illinois.

POST'S SECOND BRIGADE (USA): This Yankee infantry brigade fought at the Battle of Franklin in Wood's Third Division, Fourth U.S. Army Corps.

Named after U.S. Colonel Philip Sidney Post, it was comprised of the Fifty-ninth Illinois, Forty-first Ohio,

Seventy-first Ohio, Ninety-third Ohio, and One hundred twenty-fourth Ohio.

PRESSTMAN, STEPHEN W. (CSA): A Confederate colonel of artillery, Presstman commanded a Rebel six-gun battery at the Battle of Franklin. His unit was first positioned near Privet Knob, and later on a knoll at the Bostick House near Carters Creek Pike.

PRESTON, SARAH BUCHANAN: The daughter of Confederate General John Smith Preston (of Smithfield, Virginia) and Caroline Martha Hampton, she was born October 22, 1842, at Columbia, Richland County, South Carolina.

Preston, called "Sally" by her family and "Buck" by her friends, was known as a great Southern beauty and a beguiling flirt, who captured the hearts of many unsuspecting men. One of them was Confederate General John Bell Hood, who led the Army of Tennessee at the Battle of Franklin. The besotted Rebel officer proposed to Buchanan numerous times, but never received a definitive reply.

The captivating Southern belle went on to marry Confederate Captain Rawlins Lowndes, with whom she bore several children. Preston died December 15, 1880, at Columbia, South Carolina, and was buried in Magnolia Cemetery, Charleston, South Carolina.

PRIVET KNOB: Identical to Merrill Hill, and known as Stone Hill to early Franklinites, this small, 100 foot tall rocky prominence in Franklin, Tennessee, is located on the west side of Columbia Pike, about one mile north of Winstead and Breezy Hills. It was named for the privet (a small shrub plant) thicket which originally blanketed the area.

During the Battle of Franklin, Privet Knob was utilized at different times by both sides. Just prior to the conflict it was used by Confederate General Patrick R. Cleburne as an observation post, and also by Union troops, who set up a temporary defensive position on it. Confederate General Benjamin F. Cheatham later commandeered it as the site for his headquarters.

The site is today being heavily encroached upon by modern development.

QUARLES, WILLIAM ANDREW (CSA): The son of Garrett Minor Quarles and Mary J. Poindexter, he was born July 4, 1825, at Jamestown, Virginia, but was raised in Christian County, Kentucky, and Clarksville, Tennessee.

Like most Southern children he was homeschooled. He later attended the University of Virginia, where he studied law. Admitted to the bar in 1848, he started up a law practice in Clarksville.

An ardent Democrat (the conservatives of the day), he supported Franklin Pierce in the 1852 presidential election, and served as both a circuit court judge and the president of the Memphis, Clarksville, and Louisville Railway Company. In 1856 he became a Freemason, eventually attaining the degree of Royal Arch Mason.

With the start of Lincoln's War, Quarles sided with the South and the Constitution. Joining the Confederate army, he served as colonel of the Forty-second Tennessee Infantry. He was captured at the Battle of Fort Donelson. After his exchange he was promoted to brigadier general, fighting in both the Atlanta and the Tennessee Campaigns.

He led Quarles' Brigade, Walthall's Division, Stewart's Corps, Army of Tennessee at the Battle of Franklin, where he was wounded and captured a second time.

After the War Quarles returned to Clarksville and resumed his law practice. In 1867 he was elected a trustee of the Tennessee Orphans Society, and in 1871 he joined the Knights Templar. He supported Horace Greeley's presidential bid in 1872, and was himself elected state senator, serving from 1875 to 1889.

During so-called "Reconstruction," Quarles was one of thirteen former Confederate generals to demand that anti-South, liberal Tennessee Governor William Gannaway Brownlow remove the numerous political constraints illegally and unfairly imposed on ex-Confederates by the U.S. government.

Quarles had three marriages, the third and last to his cousin Louisa Minor Meriwether—a cousin of famed American explorer Meriwether Lewis of the Lewis and Clark Expedition.

Quarles died in Logan County, Kentucky, December 28, 1893, at the home of his daughter, and was buried in Flat Lick Baptist Cemetery, Valley Oak, Pulaski County, Kentucky.

QUARLES' BRIGADE (CSA): This Rebel infantry brigade fought at the Battle of Franklin in Walthall's Division, Stewart's Corps, C.S. Army of Tennessee.

Named after Confederate Brigadier General William Andrew Quarles, it was comprised of the First Alabama, Forty-second Tennessee, Forty-sixth Tennessee, Forty-eighth Tennessee, Forty-ninth Tennessee, Fifty-third Tennessee, and Fifty-fifth Tennessee.

After General Quarles was wounded at Franklin November 30, 1864, and captured on December 17, the brigade was taken over by Confederate Brigadier General George D. Johnson.

QUINTARD, CHARLES TODD (CSA): The son of Isaac Quintard and Clarissa Hoyt, he was born at Stamford, Connecticut, December 22, 1824. He graduated from New York University in 1847 with a medical degree, then opened up a doctor's practice in Georgia. Moving to Tennessee, he served as a professor of anatomy at Memphis Medical College.

It was in Tennessee that Quintard began an association with Bishop James Otey and the Episcopal Church, becoming an ordained priest in 1856. He was then appointed rector of Nashville's Church of the Advent, a position he held for many years thereafter.

With the outbreak of Lincoln's War, Quintard—a Yankee from New England—sided with the South and the Constitution. Joining the Confederate army, he served as chaplain of the First Tennessee Infantry for the entire duration of the War.

Before the Battle of

Franklin the clergyman had baptized many Confederates, such as General Otho F. Strahl. After that conflict he led Strahl's funeral, as well as those of many other fallen Confederates, such as Generals Patrick R. Cleburne and Hiram B. Granbury. When their bodies were at first buried too near the graves of detested Yankee soldiers, Dr. Quintard had them moved to a more South-friendly location. He also served as a surgeon during the hostilities.

After the War he returned to Nashville where he was made bishop in the Fall of 1865. He went on to oversee the reconstruction of the University of the South at Sewanee, Tennessee, which had been illegally destroyed by Yankee troops. As the first vice chancellor of the school, he raised money for building supplies and welcomed the first crop of new students in 1868.

The husband of Eliza C. Hand, he passed away February 15, 1898, at Darien, Georgia, and was buried in the University of the South Cemetery, Sewanee, Franklin County, Tennessee.

In his famed book *Company Aytch*, Confederate soldier Sam R. Watkins of the First Tennessee wrote the following about the beloved wartime minister:

"Dr. C. T. Quintard was our Chaplain for the First Tennessee Regiment during the whole war, and he stuck to us from the beginning even unto the end. During week days he ministered to us physically, and on Sundays spiritually. He was one of the purest and best men I ever knew. He would march and carry his knapsack every day the same as any soldier. He had one text he preached from which I remember now. It was 'the flying scroll.' He said there was a flying scroll continually passing over our heads, which was like the reflections in a lookingglass, and all of our deeds, both good and bad, were written upon it. He was a good Doctor of Medicine, as well as a good Doctor of Divinity, and above either of these, he was a good man per se. Every old soldier of the First Tennessee Regiment will remember Dr. C. T. Quintard with the kindest and most sincere emotions of love and respect. He would go off into the country and get up for our regiment clothing and provisions, and wrote a little prayer and song book, which he had published, and gave it to the soldiers. I learned that little prayer and song book off by heart, and have a copy of it in my possession yet, which I would not part with for any consideration. Dr. Quintard's nature was one of love. He loved the soldiers, and the soldiers loved him, and deep down in his heart of hearts was a deep and lasting love for Jesus Christ, the Redeemer of the world, implanted there by God the Father Himself."

RALLY HILL ROAD: A road that runs from present day Bear Creek Pike, Columbia, Tennessee, to Kedron Road, Spring Hill, Tennessee.

Before and during the Battle of Spring Hill, November 29, 1864, the road was used by both Confederates and Yankees during skirmishes one day prior to the Battle of Franklin, November 30.

The modern Battle of Spring Hill Memorial Site is located on nearby Kedron Road.

RATTLE AND SNAP PLANTATION: Known as "the finest existing example of Greek Revival architecture in the South," this beautiful estate in Mount Pleasant, Tennessee, was built between 1842 and 1845 by George Washington Polk (a cousin of U.S. President James K. Polk) and his wife Sallie Hilliard.

George's father, William Polk of North Carolina, won the original 5,648 acres that the estate was built on during a game of chance called "rattle and snap" (played with beans), a name that was later given to the plantation itself.

William parceled the enormous plot of land out to four of his many sons, each one who constructed a house on his own portion of the property: P. Leonidas Polk built Ashwood Hall; Rufus K. Polk built Westwood; Lucius J. Polk built Hamilton Place; and George W. Polk built Rattle and Snap.

The four brothers constructed Saint John's Episcopal Church on the property as well. Only Hamilton Place, Rattle and Snap, and the church have survived into the present day.

Like most large Southern antebellum homes, Rattle and Snap was made by highly skilled black servants specializing in home construction and wood working. The designer is not known, but evidence points to famed German-American architect Adolphus Heiman, who built Belmont Mansion in Nashville.

Celebrated for its beautiful Corinthian porch and ten magnificent Greek columns, Rattle and Snap was the last of a number of great houses built by the Polk family in the surrounding area.

Once also known as Oakwood Hall, the plantation's connection with Lincoln's War and the Confederate and Union soldiers who fought at the Battle of Franklin is not yet known with certainty. However, as many troops passed through this area on their way to the Battles of Columbia, Spring Hill, Franklin, and Nashville (and also during "Hood's Retreat" as well) in late 1864, we can be sure that it was well known among the soldiery on both sides.

We do know of one story associated with Rattle and Snap and Lincoln's War. In 1862 vicious Yankee soldiers were preparing to illegally, wantonly, and unnecessarily torch the lovely estate and burn it to the ground—just as they had done to so many other stately antebellum homes across the South, including in Franklin. Just as the fire was about to be lit, one of the Union officers paused to observe a painting of George Polk. As he was enjoying a last minute look, he noticed that there was a Masonic ring on Polk's finger. Recalling that his commander U.S. General Don Carlos Buell was also a Mason, the officer reported the finding to his superior. Buell immediately ordered that Rattle and Snap be exempted from the torch.

Whatever war crimes Buell may have committed during the North's invasion of the South (and there were many), we can be thankful that he spared Rattle and Snap Plantation that day.

REBEL YELL: A high pitched Indian-like war whoop used by Confederate soldiers to put the fear of God into Yankees.

The primitive banshee scream so terrified Union soldiers that it gave the Rebels an edge on the battlefield: in the first few moments after the fearsome shriek was let loose, as stunned Federal troops were trying to decide whether to flee or fight, Confederate troops were able to pick off dozens of the enemy.

RECONSTRUCTION: A twelve year period from the end of Lincoln's War April 9, 1865, to April 10, 1877, during which time the U.S. illegally placed the entire South under military law.

What Yankees still disingenuously refer to as "Reconstruction" should have actually been called "Deconstruction," for its sole purpose was to destroy the "rebellious" Old South and replace it with the tame "New South." This was to be accomplished by Northernizing the Southern people, their culture, their government, and their economy, and by killing off every last bit of states' rights sentiment still pulsing in the breast of every true Southerner.

To this end Northern politicians barred former Confederate officers from voting or running for political office, banned the display of the Confederate Flag and the wearing of Confederate uniforms, and allowed illiterate and often violent racist blacks to take over local governments.

Meanwhile, armed U.S. soldiers were placed on every street corner across Dixie, Southern men were routinely beaten and arrested, and Southern women were regularly harassed and even sexually assaulted. Not even children, the elderly, or blacks were spared the savagery of the North's tyrannical iron fist. Those who protested these Yankee outrages were made to "disappear," and were never heard from again.

It was this brutal suppression of the South's constitutional, civil, legal, moral, ethical, and religious rights that launched the formation of the original Ku Klux Klan, a group that served as a social welfare organization and patriotic military wing intended to protect Confederate veterans, widows, orphans, refugees, and the South's downtrodden—*whatever their race, creed, or color.* Proof of this is that there was an all-black chapter of the KKK that operated in Nashville in the late 1860s.

The savage nightmare of Reconstruction only came to an end with the inauguration of the beneficent President Rutherford B. Hayes in 1877. Hayes wisely pulled the last Yankee troops out of the South that year and allowed former Confederates to once again hold political office.

In the end not only was Reconstruction a complete failure, it did not even "reconstruct" anything. Instead, it prolonged the horrors of the "Civil War" from four years to sixteen years, and deepened the already existing animosity between South and North.

Needless to say, as far as the South has always been concerned, both the War and Reconstruction were nothing but destructive in nature. Both are still widely regarded here as barbarous illegal acts of punishment and vengeance, intentionally inflicted by the North on a freedom loving, independent minded, Constitution adoring people.

Though most Southerners long ago forgave the North for her sins against us between 1861 and 1877, we will never forget. The bitterness is still palpable across Dixie, the War—and all of the U.S. crimes committed against us—are still discussed as if they happened yesterday, scallywags and carpetbaggers are still abhorred, and the names of most Northern leaders and officers are still spoken with disdain.

REEVES, CHARLOTTE: The daughter of a Presbyterian minister and the wife of James Robertson, cofounder of the city of Nashville, Tennessee, Reeves was responsible for teaching her husband to read and write. Charlotte Avenue, which traverses much of Middle Tennessee, was named after her.

REILLY, JAMES WILLIAM (USA): He was born May 20, 1828, at Akron, Ohio. He was schooled at Maryland's Mount Saint Mary's College, where he read law. After being admitted to the bar, he went on to become an Ohio state representative.

With the onset of Lincoln's War he sided with the North and against the Constitution, first serving as colonel of the One hundred fourth Ohio Infantry, which he led at the Battles of Knoxville and Atlanta.

Appointed brigadier general in the Summer of 1864, he temporarily commanded Cox's Third Division, Twenty-third U.S. Army Corps at the Battle of Franklin. Here, according to Yankee legend, he captured a 1,000 Rebels and twenty-two Confederate flags.

After the War Reilly went back to Ohio where he returned to his law practice and served in various civil capacities, including acting as president of Wellsville, Ohio's First National Bank.

He never married. Reilly passed away in Wellsville

November 6, 1905, and was buried in the town's Saint Elizabeth Cemetery.

REILLY'S FIRST BRIGADE (USA): This Yankee infantry brigade fought at the Battle of Franklin in Cox's Third Division, Twenty-third U.S. Army Corps.

Named after U.S. Brigadier General James William Reilly, it was comprised of the Twelfth Kentucky, Sixteenth Kentucky, One hundredth Ohio, One hundred fourth Ohio, One hundred seventy-fifth Ohio, and Eighth Tennessee.

REST HAVEN CEMETERY: Begun in 1855 on property donated by celebrated Tennessee lawyer John Marshall, the graveyard is located across from the old Franklin City Cemetery, at the northwestern end of downtown Franklin, Tennessee.

The seven acre lot is the final resting place for numerous Civil War soldiers, including Confederate Captain Tod Carter and Union General James P. Brownlow.

REYNOLDS, DANIEL HARRIS (CSA): The son of Amos Reynolds and Sophia Houck, he was born December 14, 1832, at Centerburg, Ohio. After attending Ohio Wesleyan University, in 1853 he became a Freemason. At Somerville, Tennessee, he studied law, after which he was admitted to the bar and set up a law practice in Lake Village, Chicot County, Arkansas.

With the start of Lincoln's War, he sided with the South and the Constitution. After organizing the cavalry company known as the Chicot Rangers, he commanded Company A of the First Arkansas Mounted Rifles. Rising rapidly up the ranks, Reynolds fought at such battles as Wilson's Creek, Atlanta, Pea Ridge, and Bentonville, the latter where he lost his left leg.

As a brigadier general he led Reynolds' Brigade, Walthall's Division, Stewart's Corps, C.S. Army of Tennessee, at the Battle of Franklin.

After the War Reynolds resumed his law practice at Lake Village, served as a state senator, and in 1868 married Martha Jane Wallace—with whom he had five children.

He died March 14, 1902, at Lake Village, and was buried in the town's Lake Village Cemetery.

REYNOLDS, GEORGE W. (CSA): Confederate Major Reynolds led the Twenty-ninth Mississippi Infantry at the Battle of Franklin, where he was killed in action.

REYNOLDS' BRIGADE (CSA): This Rebel infantry brigade fought at the Battle of Franklin in Walthall's Division, Stewart's Corps, C.S. Army of Tennessee.

Named after Confederate Brigadier General Daniel Harris Reynolds, it was comprised of the Fourth Arkansas, Ninth Arkansas, Twenty-fifth Arkansas, First Arkansas Mounted Rifles, and Second Arkansas Mounted Rifles.

RIPPAVILLA PLANTATION: Located in Spring Hill, Tennessee, Rippavilla Plantation was constructed in 1853 by Nathaniel Frances Cheairs IV, who served as a Confederate colonel in Lincoln's War. The Greek Revival mansion was modeled on the town's equally magnificent Ferguson Hall, built by Nathaniel's brother Martin Cheairs.

Rippavilla is rich in "Civil War" history, with both Rebel and Yankee officers using it as a headquarters at different times during the conflict.

Confederate General Nathan Bedford Forrest and his men camped here at the time of the Battle of Thompson's Station, March 5, 1863.

On the night of November 29, 1864, after the Battle of Spring Hill that day, a portion of Hood's command camped at Rippavilla. The battle itself spilled over on to the grounds of the plantation.

The next morning, the day of the Battle of Franklin, Confederate General John Bell Hood and his officers had a rancorous breakfast at the plantation—where the men quarreled over their now infamous "missed opportunity" at Spring Hill. According to local lore, while they were there some of Hood's officers autographed several window panes in the mansion house.

The home and grounds, listed on the National Register of Historic Places, are today open for public tours.

RITTENBURY, JAMES J. (CSA): Confederate Captain Rittenbury led the Fifty-third Tennessee Infantry at the Battle of Franklin, where he was wounded in action and captured.

RIVERSIDE PLANTATION: Located across the Harpeth River, a stone's throw from Carnton Plantation, at Franklin, Tennessee, Riverside was built in the 1830s by James Randal McGavock—the brother of Confederate Colonel John W. McGavock of Carnton—on land owned by their father, Randal McGavock, the founder of Carnton Plantation.

Upon his death in 1843 Randal willed the Riverside property to James. While the large plantation house was being built, James and his wife Louisa C. Chenault lived in a rustic log cabin James had constructed in the backyard.

It was at this time that Randal's good friend former U.S. President Andrew Jackson stopped by and planted several young cedar trees on the property, which grow there to this day.

Sallie, the daughter of Riverside founders James and Louisa, owned the McGavock family Bible, which can still be seen on display at Carnton, as can numerous other household items from the Riverside McGavocks.

Like Carnton, Riverside was once famous for its beautiful stables and fine horses. It even had its own race track. During the Battle of Franklin horrified members of the family watched the conflict from the relative safety of their hilltop location (the center of the fighting took place several miles to the northwest). Having passed away in 1862 James was spared the terrible scene.

The home seen today is not James and Louisa's original house, which partially burned down in 1905. This new neo-classical home was constructed afterward around the solid brick remains of the first Riverside Manor house. Riverside is today privately owned.

ROBERTS, DEERING J. (CSA): Dr. Roberts was a member of the Twentieth Tennessee Infantry, Smith's Brigade, Bate's Division, Cheatham's Corps, C.S. Army of Tennessee.

After the Battle of Franklin Roberts treated Confederate Captain Tod Carter at the boy's home (the Carter House), and organized hospitals in Franklin for the wounded in his division.

RODGERS, SARAH DOUGHERTY: The daughter of American Revolutionary War veteran John Rodgers and his wife Anne Phillips, she was born April 1, 1786, probably at Max Meadows, Wythe County, Virginia.

In 1811 she married Randal McGavock, eleventh mayor of Nashville and the founder of Carnton Plantation. The couple bore seven known children together. Rodgers' sister Ann Phillips Rodgers married celebrated Tennessee statesman and senator Felix Grundy.

Sarah passed away December 28, 1854, at Carnton and was buried in the plantation's McGavock Family Cemetery.

ROPER'S KNOB: Located in Franklin, Tennessee, this massive hill played an important role in the area's Civil War history, serving primarily as a Union fortification and signal station. Confederate forces too made use of the prominence, in particular in October 1864, just prior to the Battle of Franklin.

The original fortifications, built in April and May 1863 by 5,000 U.S. troops, were intentionally placed on Roper's Knob due to the 360 degree, six mile view from its summit. The completed Union defensive structure contained a redoubt, four large guns, a blockhouse, an enormous magazine, and two 4,500 gallon cisterns.

Employed as a communications post by both Confederate and Union troops at various times during the War, flags and lights were used to send important messages to other nearby hilltop fortifications, including those at Triune to the east, those at La Vergne to the northeast, and those at Nashville to the north. Unhappily for the citizens of Franklin, Yankees occupied Roper's Knob until the end of Lincoln's War.

As of this writing, not only is Roper's Knob neither protected or open to the public, but development, both commercial and residential, is quickly advancing around the entire area. Civil War preservation groups are scrambling to save the site.

RORER, WALTER ABRAM (CSA): The son of Rudolph Rohrer and Millicent Lamb, Confederate Lieutenant Colonel Rorer (also spelled Rohrer) was born July 24, 1826.

He led the Twentieth Mississippi Infantry at the Battle of Franklin, where he was wounded in action. He died later that day from his wounds, and was buried in the McGavock Confederate Cemetery, Franklin, Tennessee.

ROSS, LAWRENCE SULLIVAN (CSA): He was born September 27, 1838, at Bentonsport, Iowa, but was raised in Texas. After graduating from Wesleyan University in 1859, he served as captain of a unit of Texas Rangers, suppressing Indian uprisings in the Western Territories.

In 1860 he married Elizabeth Dorothy Tinsley of Macon, Georgia, with whom he bore several children.

With the outbreak of Lincoln's War, he sided with the South and the Constitution, serving as colonel of the Sixth Texas Cavalry. Rising to the rank of brigadier general, he was greatly respected by other Rebel officers, particularly General Nathan Bedford Forrest, under whose cavalry corps he commanded Ross' Brigade, Jackson's Division, at the Battle of Franklin.

After the War the celebrated Southern hero returned to Texas to farm, at which time he was made sheriff of McLennan County. Shortly thereafter he was elected state senator, then governor of Texas for two terms.

At the time of his death on January 3, 1898, at College Station, Texas, "Sul Ross" as he was affectionately nicknamed, was serving as president of the Agricultural and Mechanical College of Texas. He was buried in Oakwood Cemetery, Waco, Texas.

ROSS' BRIGADE (CSA): This Rebel cavalry brigade fought at the Battle of Franklin in Jackson's Division, Forrest's Cavalry Corps, C.S. Army of Tennessee.

Named after its commander Confederate Brigadier General Lawrence Sullivan Ross, it was comprised of the Fifth Texas Cavalry, Sixth Texas Cavalry, Ninth Texas Cavalry, and First Texas Legion.

ROUSSEAU, LAWRENCE H. (USA): Yankee Lieutenant Colonel Rousseau commanded the Twelfth Kentucky Infantry, Reilly's First Brigade, Cox's Third Division, Twenty-third

U.S. Army Corps, at the Battle of Franklin.

ROWAN, JOHN B. (CSA): Rebel Captain Rowan led Johnson's Battalion, Lee's Corps Artillery, at the Battle of Franklin.

RUCKER, EDMUND WINCHESTER (CSA): The son of Dr. Edmund P. Rucker and Louisa Orville Winchester, he was born July 22, 1835, at Stones River, Rutherford County, Tennessee.

With the opening of Lincoln's War, Rucker sided with the South and the Constitution. After joining the Confederate army he rose to the rank of colonel, commanding Rucker's Brigade, Chalmers' Division, Forrest's Cavalry, Cheatham's Corps, C.S. Army of Tennessee at the Battle of Franklin. At the Battle of Nashville two weeks later he was wounded, captured, and lost his left arm.

After the War he went into the railroad business from 1869 to 1874 with his former commander General Nathan Bedford Forrest. He married Mary Woodfin in 1873.

Colonel Rucker died April 13, 1924, at his home in Birmingham, Alabama. He was buried in the city's Oak Hill Cemetery.

Rucker was the grandson of General James Winchester, a noted pioneer, an officer in the War of 1812, and cofounder of the city of Memphis, Tennessee.

RUCKER'S BRIGADE (CSA): This Rebel cavalry brigade fought at the Battle of Franklin in Chalmers' Division, Forrest's Cavalry Corps, C.S. Army of Tennessee.

Named after its commander Confederate Brigadier General Edmund Winchester Rucker, it was comprised of the Seventh Alabama Cavalry, Fifth Mississippi Cavalry, Seventh Tennessee Cavalry, Twelfth Tennessee Cavalry, Fourteenth Tennessee Cavalry, Fifteenth Tennessee Cavalry, and Forrest's Regiment Tennessee Cavalry.

RUGER, THOMAS HOWARD (USA): He was born April 2, 1833, at Lima, New York, but was raised in Janesville, Wisconsin. He graduated from West Point Military Academy in 1854, third in his class, and returned to Janesville to practice law.

At the start of Lincoln's War he sided with the North and against the Constitution, reentering the U.S. army as lieutenant colonel of the Third Wisconsin Volunteer Regiment.

Ruger fought at such battles as Second Manassas, Cedar Mountain, Sharpsburg, Chancellorsville, and Gettysburg. As a brigadier general he led the Second Division, Twenty-third U.S. Army Corps at the Battle of Franklin.

After the War he remained in the service, eventually rising to the rank of major general, then served as superintendent of West Point from 1871 to 1876. His final military years were spent in the Western Territories suppressing Indian uprisings and protecting the Western railroad system.

He died at Stamford, Connecticut, June 3, 1907, and was buried in the United States Military Academy Post Cemetery at West Point, Orange County, New York.

RUGER'S SECOND DIVISION (USA): This Yankee division, named after U.S. Brigadier General Thomas Howard Ruger, served in the Twenty-third U.S. Army Corps at the Battle of Franklin. The Second Division was comprised of Cooper's First Brigade, Moore's Second Brigade, and Strickland's Third Brigade.

RUGER'S SECOND DIVISION ARTILLERY (USA): This Yankee artillery unit fought at the Battle of Franklin in the Twenty-third U.S. Army Corps. It was comprised of the Thirteenth Indiana Battery and the Nineteenth Ohio Battery.

RUTHERFORD'S CREEK: A small waterway located, according to early sources, eight miles south of Spring Hill, Tennessee. Modern sources place it about two and a half miles southeast of Spring Hill. The creek played a role in the hours leading up to the Battle of Spring Hill, one day before the Battle of Franklin.

SAINT JOHN'S EPISCOPAL CHURCH: Located in the town of Ashwood, Tennessee (midway between Mount Pleasant and Columbia), Saint John's was built in the 1840s by the Polk brothers, all cousins of U.S. President James K. Polk: Leonidas, Rufus, Lucius, and George.

The land on which the church was constructed was given to them by their father Colonel William Polk of North Carolina. James Hervey Otey, first Episcopal Bishop of Tennessee, consecrated the building on September 4, 1842.

Saint John's cemetery is the final resting place for a number of Polk family members, their servants, and a number of Confederate soldiers, at least one who died at the Battle of Franklin.

As with so many other beautiful buildings in the South, during Lincoln's War Yankee soldiers could not resist the temptation to wreak havoc on Saint John's. As U.S. General Don Carlos Buell was marching his army past the site on their way to the upcoming Battle of Shiloh (April 6-7, 1862), for example, his troops broke into the church and stole everything that they could not destroy. After pulling the organ apart, ripping down the bell, overturning the pews, smashing the vestry, and breaking out the windows, they pilfered the clergy's sacred altar linens and used them for saddle blankets. This act was nothing more than sheer malevolence, and a violation of both universal military law and the Geneva Conventions.

The church is also notable for an occurrence that took place just prior to the Battle of Franklin, November 30, 1864. As Confederate General John Bell Hood and the Army of Tennessee were marching through Mount Pleasant on their way to the Battle of Columbia (November 24-29, 1864), one of his officers, General Patrick R. Cleburne, paused to admire the church and the little burial ground. The lovely setting reminded him of the church he attended as a boy back in Ireland. "It is almost worth dying for, to be buried in such a beautiful spot," the Celtic warrior remarked prophetically.

Only days later Cleburne would be gunned down at the Battle of Franklin, and his body would be buried temporarily at Saint John's.

SAINT PAUL'S EPISCOPAL CHURCH: This antebellum church, located in Franklin, Tennessee, was built in the early 1830s. Known as the "Mother Church of the Diocese of Tennessee," its first rector was the famed first bishop of Tennessee, James Hervey Otey.

During the Battle of Franklin, the church was used as a Yankee barracks, afterward as a military field hospital. Damage to the structure from Lincoln's War was extensive, and in 1870 it was remodeled. The church is listed on the National Register of Historic Places.

SCALLYWAG: The opposite of its Northern counterpart, the carpetbagger, the 19th-Century scallywag was a white Southerner who, after Lincoln's War, turned his back on the South and cruelly preyed upon his Confederate brothers and sisters, usually for financial gain.

Sadly, 21st-Century scallywags are alive and well, and now make up a great percentage of the Southern population. Usually historically ignorant, politically liberal, and extremely pro-North in their views, they continue to suppress the truth about the "Civil War," while extolling the "virtues" of overt war criminals such as Abraham Lincoln, Ulysses S. Grant, and William T. Sherman.

Not surprisingly, some 150 years after Lincoln's War scallywagism has become a major problem in Dixie. Many of these Southern traitors are now in positions of great power and authority, running everything from our city and state governments, newspapers, and TV stations, to our Civil War battles sites, historic homes, and museums. This allows them to control the facts about the American "Civil War" in order to prevent them from ever being seen by the public. The usual methods of suppression are to censor pro-South writers and ban pro-South books, while completely burying the truth under a mountain of pro-North mythology and anti-South propaganda.

Traditional Southerners, as well as all lovers of Truth, can fight back by promoting Southern works such as this one, which factually chronicle the War for Southern Independence.

SCHOFIELD, JOHN MCALLISTER (USA): He was born September 29, 1831, at Gerry, New York, but was raised in both Illinois and Wisconsin. He graduated from West Point in 1853, seventh in his class, where he served as an instructor. A year before the "Civil War" he became a professor of physics at Washington University, Saint Louis, Missouri.

With the opening of Lincoln's War he sided with the North and against the Constitution. By November 1861 he had risen to the rank of brigadier general. In February 1864 he was made head of the Army of the Ohio, after which he was put under the command of U.S. General George Henry Thomas in Tennessee.

As Schofield moved north to join Thomas at Nashville, Confederate General John Bell Hood went in pursuit, resulting in the Battles of Columbia, Springhill, Franklin, and Nashville.

At Franklin Schofield commanded the entire 35,000 man U.S. Armies of the Ohio and the Cumberland, comprising the Fourth Army Corps and the Twenty-third Army Corps.

Schofield, who suffered about 2,300 casualties, considered Franklin a Union victory because he was able to retreat to Nashville during the night. Hood, who suffered about 7,000 casualties, considered the conflict a Confederate victory because he drove the Yankees from the battlefield.

But it was not a Rebel win, it was a major Rebel loss, for Schofield had never intended on stopping or fighting at Franklin. The battle occurred only because Schofield had been detained at Franklin due to flooded and burned out bridges over the Harpeth River.

Schofield helped Thomas finish off Hood and the Army of Tennessee at the Battle of Nashville two weeks later.

In the final days of Lincoln's War, Schofield commanded the Department of North Carolina, working with

Yankee war criminal General William Tecumseh Sherman in what would be their last military operations against the South.

After the War he was sent to Paris, France, as a U.S. ambassador to help obtain the removal of U.S. troops from Mexico. During so-called "Reconstruction" Schofield participated in the illegal military rule of the Southern states, serving as the military governor of Virginia.

U.S. President Andrew Johnson appointed him secretary of war, after which he returned to military service. Among his numerous occupations he served as commandant of West Point from 1876 to 1881. In 1872 he organized the first U.S. naval base at Pearl Harbor. Sixty-nine years later, on December 7, 1941, Schofield's Hawaiian base would be attacked by the Japanese, drawing the U.S. into World War II.

After the death of Yankee war criminal Philip H. Sheridan in 1888, Schofield was made general-in-chief of the U.S. army, finally attaining the rank of lieutenant general in 1895. He was awarded the Congressional Medal of Honor in 1892.

General Schofield died March 4, 1906, at Saint Augustine, Florida, and was buried in Arlington National Cemetery.

By illegally occupying the town of Franklin on November 30, 1864, then unnecessarily killing nearly 2,000 of the South's finest, the U.S. officer dramatically altered the history of both Tennessee and America. His name is still spoken in Franklin with disdain by all true Southerners.

SCOFIELD, LEVI TUCKER (USA): Born November 9, 1842, Captain Scofield served as a topographical engineer under Union General Jacob D. Cox at the Battle of Franklin. His infantry, the One hundred third Ohio, was attached to Union Colonel John S. Casement's Second Brigade.

After the War Scofield published a book about the conflict entitled: *The Retreat From Pulaski to Nashville, Tenn.*

Also an architect, Scofield was responsible for designing numerous famous buildings and memorials, including the Soldiers' and Sailors' Monument in Cuyahoga County, Ohio. He passed away February 25, 1917, and was buried in Lake View Cemetery, Cleveland, Ohio.

SCOTT, THOMAS MOORE (CSA): He was born in 1829 at Athens, Georgia, and later moved to Claiborne Parish, Louisiana, where he took up farming.

With the start of Lincoln's War, he sided with the South and the Constitution, joined the Confederate army, and enlisted in the Twelfth Louisiana Infantry. He fought in numerous battles, rising to the rank of brigadier general in the Spring of 1864.

At the Battle of Franklin Scott led his own command, Scott's Brigade, Loring's Division, Stewart's Corps, C.S. Army of Tennessee. Here he was severely injured by cannon fire, after which he appears to have left military service.

After the War he returned to his Louisiana sugar plantation near Homer. He passed away April 21, 1876, at New Orleans, and was buried in the town's Greenwood Cemetery.

SCOTT'S BRIGADE (CSA): This Rebel infantry brigade fought at the Battle of Franklin in Loring's Division, Stewart's Corps, C.S. Army of Tennessee.

Named after Confederate General Thomas Moore Scott, it was comprised of the Twenty-seventh Alabama, Thirty-fifth Alabama, Forty-ninth Alabama, Fifty-fifth Alabama, Fifty-seventh Alabama, and Twelfth Louisiana.

After General Moore was wounded at Franklin, the brigade was taken over by Colonel John Snodgrass.

SCOVILLE, CHARLES W. (USA): Scoville commanded a Union battery at the Battle of Franklin. In his 1909 book *The Retreat From Pulaski to Nashville, Tenn.*, Yankee Captain Levi Tucker Scofield writes:

"During one of the [Confederate] charges that was made on this part of the [Union] line, an incident occurred at Scoville's battery which is worth relating.

"A slight [Southern] boy of not more than 15 years, with [a marching] drum on his back, belonging to one of the [Rebel] Missouri regiments, foolishly attempted to force his way through one of the embrasures and thrust a fence rail into the mouth of the cannon, thinking, by his brave act, to stop the use of that gun. It was heavily loaded at the time, and was fired, tearing the poor boy to shreds, so that nothing was ever found of him."

SEARS, CLAUDIUS WISTAR (CSA): The son of Thomas Sears and Sophia James, Sears was born November 18, 1817, at Peru, Berkshire County, Massachusetts.

He graduated from West Point in 1841, and was then appointed a second lieutenant in the Eighth U.S. Infantry, with which he fought in Florida in the Seminole Wars.

He taught school at Saint Thomas' Hall at Holly Springs, Mississippi, then moved to New Orleans, Louisiana, where he worked as a professor of mathematics at Tulane University (then known as the University of Louisiana).

On August 6, 1853, at Houston, Texas, he married Susan Alice Gray of Fredericksburg, Virginia. In 1860 he returned to Saint Thomas' Hall to serve as its president.

With the start of Lincoln's War, Sears sided with the South and the Constitution, joined the Confederate army, and was made captain of Company G of the Seventeenth Mississippi Infantry. He would go on to fight at such battles as Vicksburg, First Manassas, Ball's Bluff, Yorktown, Fair Oaks, Sharpsburg, Chickasaw Bayou, Port Gibson, and Champion Hill.

In 1864, after he was made brigadier general, he joined the Army of Tennessee, fighting in the Battle of Atlanta. At the Battle of Franklin November 30, 1864, he led his own unit, Sears' Brigade, French's Division, Stewart's Corps.

At the Battle of Nashville two weeks later he lost a leg during a cannon shelling, and was taken prisoner by the enemy at Pulaski on December 21 (cruelly and unnecessarily, he was not released until the Summer of 1865).

After the War he taught mathematics at the University of Mississippi until 1889. On February 15, 1891, Sears passed away at Oxford, Mississippi, and was buried in the city's Oxford Memorial Cemetery.

SEARS' BRIGADE (CSA): This Rebel infantry brigade fought at the Battle of Franklin in French's Division, Stewart's Corps, C.S. Army of Tennessee.

Named after Confederate Brigadier General Claudius Wistar Sears, the brigade was comprised of the Fourth Mississippi, Thirty-fifth Mississippi, Thirty-sixth Mississippi, Thirty-ninth

Mississippi, Forty-sixth Mississippi, and Seventh Mississippi Battalion.

After General Sears was wounded at the Battle of Nashville (December 15, 1864) then captured almost two weeks later (December 27), the brigade was taken over by Confederate Lieutenant Colonel Reuben H. Shotwell.

SECOND ARKANSAS (CSA): This Rebel infantry regiment fought at the Battle of Franklin in Govan's Brigade, Cleburne's Division, Cheatham's Corps, C.S. Army of Tennessee.

SECOND ARKANSAS MOUNTED RIFLES - DISMOUNTED (CSA): This Rebel unit fought at the Battle of Franklin in Reynolds' Brigade, Walthall's Division, Stewart's Corps, C.S. Army of Tennessee.

SECOND GEORGIA BATTALION SHARPSHOOTERS (CSA): This Rebel unit fought at the Battle of Franklin in Gist's Brigade, Brown's Division, Cheatham's Corps, C.S. Army of Tennessee.

SECOND IOWA CAVALRY (USA): This Yankee cavalry regiment fought at the Battle of Franklin in Coon's Second Brigade, Hatch's Fifth Division, Wilson's Cavalry Corps.

SECOND MICHIGAN CAVALRY (USA): This Yankee cavalry regiment fought at the Battle of Franklin in Croxton's First Brigade, McCook's First Division, Wilson's Cavalry Corps.

SECOND MISSISSIPPI CAVALRY (CSA): This Rebel cavalry regiment fought at the Battle of Franklin in Armstrong's Brigade, Jackson's Division, Forrest's Cavalry Corps, C.S. Army of Tennessee.

SECOND MISSOURI (CSA): This Rebel infantry regiment fought at the Battle of Franklin in Cockrell's Brigade, French's Division, Stewart's Corps, C.S. Army of Tennessee.

SECOND PENNSYLVANIA BATTERY (USA): This Yankee artillery unit fought at the Battle of Franklin in the Fourth U.S. Army Corps Artillery.

SECOND TENNESSEE (CSA): This Rebel infantry regiment fought at the Battle of Franklin in Tyler's Brigade, Bate's Division, Cheatham's Corps, C.S. Army of Tennessee.

SECOND TENNESSEE CAVALRY (CSA): This Rebel cavalry regiment fought at the Battle of Franklin in Bell's Brigade, Buford's Division, Forrest's Cavalry Corps, C.S. Army of Tennessee.

SECOND TENNESSEE CAVALRY (USA): This Yankee cavalry regiment fought at the Battle of Franklin in Hammond's First Brigade, Knipe's Seventh Division, Wilson's Cavalry Corps.

SELDEN'S ALABAMA BATTERY (CSA): This Rebel battery fought at the Battle of Franklin in Trueheart's Battalion, Stewart's Corps Artillery, C.S. Army of Tennessee.

SEVENTEENTH ALABAMA (CSA): This Rebel infantry regiment fought at the Battle of Franklin in Cantley's Brigade, Walthall's Division, Stewart's Corps, C.S. Army of Tennessee.

SEVENTEENTH TEXAS CAVALRY - DISMOUNTED (CSA): This Rebel unit fought at the Battle of Franklin in Granbury's Brigade, Cleburne's Division, Cheatham's Corps, C.S. Army of Tennessee.

SEVENTH ALABAMA CAVALRY (CSA): This Rebel cavalry regiment fought at the Battle of Franklin in Rucker's Brigade, Chalmers' Division, Forrest's Cavalry Corps, C.S. Army of Tennessee.

SEVENTH ARKANSAS (CSA): This Rebel infantry regiment fought at the Battle of Franklin in Govan's Brigade, Cleburne's Division, Cheatham's Corps, C.S. Army of Tennessee.

SEVENTH FLORIDA (CSA): This Rebel infantry regiment fought at the Battle of Franklin in Finley's Brigade, Bate's Division, Cheatham's Corps, C.S. Army of Tennessee.

SEVENTH ILLINOIS CAVALRY (USA): This Yankee cavalry regiment fought at the Battle of Franklin in Coon's Second Brigade, Hatch's Fifth Division, Wilson's Cavalry Corps.

SEVENTH KENTUCKY MOUNTED INFANTRY (CSA): This Rebel unit fought at the Battle of Franklin in Crossland's Brigade, Buford's Division, Forrest's Cavalry Corps, C.S. Army of Tennessee.

SEVENTH MISSISSIPPI (CSA): This Rebel infantry regiment fought at the Battle of Franklin in Sharp's Brigade, Johnson's Division, Lee's Corps, C.S. Army of Tennessee.

SEVENTH MISSISSIPPI BATTALION (CSA): This Rebel unit fought at the Battle of Franklin in Sears' Brigade, French's Division, Stewart's Corps, C.S. Army of Tennessee.

SEVENTH OHIO CAVALRY (USA): This Yankee cavalry regiment fought at the Battle of Franklin in Harrison's First Brigade, Johnson's Sixth Division, Wilson's Cavalry Corps.

SEVENTH TENNESSEE CAVALRY (CSA): This Rebel cavalry regiment fought at the Battle of Franklin in Rucker's Brigade, Chalmers' Division, Forrest's Cavalry Corps, C.S. Army of Tennessee.

SEVENTH TEXAS (CSA): This Rebel infantry regiment fought at the Battle of Franklin in Granbury's Brigade, Cleburne's Division, Cheatham's Corps, C.S. Army of Tennessee.

SEVENTY-FIFTH ILLINOIS (USA): This Yankee infantry regiment fought at the Battle of Franklin in Grose's Third Brigade, Kimball's First Division, Fourth U.S. Army Corps.

SEVENTY-FIRST OHIO (USA): This Yankee infantry regiment fought at the Battle of Franklin in Post's Second Brigade, Wood's Third Division, Fourth U.S. Army Corps.

SEVENTY-FOURTH ILLINOIS (USA): This Yankee infantry regiment fought at the Battle of Franklin in Opdycke's First Brigade, Wagner's Second Division, Fourth U.S. Army Corps.

SEVENTY-NINTH ILLINOIS (USA): This Yankee infantry regiment fought at the Battle of Franklin in Bradley's Third Brigade, Wagner's Second Division, Fourth U.S. Army Corps.

SEVENTY-NINTH INDIANA (USA): This Yankee infantry regiment fought at the Battle of Franklin in Beatty's Third Brigade, Wood's Third Division, Fourth U.S. Army Corps.

SEVENTY-SEVENTH PENNSYLVANIA (USA): This Yankee infantry regiment fought at the Battle of Franklin in Grose's Third Brigade, Kimball's First Division, Fourth U.S. Army Corps.

SEVENTY-THIRD ILLINOIS (USA): This Yankee infantry regiment fought at the Battle of Franklin in Opdycke's First Brigade, Wagner's Second Division, Fourth U.S. Army Corps.

SHANNON, ISAAC N. (CSA): Lieutenant Shannon was a Rebel sharpshooter who fought at the Battle of Franklin under Confederate Lieutenant John M. Ozanne. Shannon was posted with the Second Battalion Georgia Sharpshooters, Gist's Brigade, Brown's Division, Cheatham's Corps, C.S. Army of Tennessee.

SHARP, JACOB HUNTER (CSA): The son of Elisha Hunter Sharp and Sallie Carter, he was born February 6, 1833, at Pickensville, Alabama, but was raised in Lowndes County, Mississippi.

After graduating from the University of Alabama, he started a law practice in Columbus, Mississippi. In 1858 he married Sarah H. Harris.

With the start of Lincoln's War, Sharp sided with the South and the Constitution, enlisting in the First Battalion Mississippi Infantry. Rising up the ranks he fought at such battles as Chickamauga, Shiloh, Jonesboro, Bentonville, and Murfreesboro.

Now a brigadier general, at the Battle of Franklin he commanded his own unit, Sharp's Brigade, Johnson's Division, Lee's Corps, C.S. Army of Tennessee.

After the War he returned to Mississippi where he continued to practice law. Purchasing a newspaper, the Columbus *Independent*, he was appointed president of the Mississippi Press Association, and served as a state representative until 1890.

A traditional Southern

conservative, in his final days he fought for European-American rights (which were being eroded under the Northern liberal regime). Sharp passed away September 16, 1907, at Columbus, Mississippi, and was buried in the town's Friendship Cemetery.

SHARP'S BRIGADE (CSA): This Rebel infantry brigade fought at the Battle of Franklin in Johnson's Division, Lee's Corps, C.S. Army of Tennessee.

Named after Confederate Brigadier General Jacob Hunter Sharp, it was comprised of the Seventh Mississippi, Ninth Mississippi, Tenth Mississippi, Forty-first Mississippi, Forty-fourth Mississippi, and Ninth Battalion Mississippi Sharpshooters.

SHAW, THOMAS P. (CSA): Confederate Colonel Shaw led the Nineteenth South Carolina Infantry at the Battle of Franklin, where he was wounded in action.

SHELLENBERGER, JOHN K. (USA): He was born in 1843 at Sparta, Georgia. He married Amanda Rowland.

With the outbreak of Lincoln's War, he sided with the North and against the Constitution. At the Battle of Franklin Captain Shellenberger commanded a company in the Sixty-fourth Ohio Volunteer Infantry, Bradley's Third Brigade, Wagner's Second Division, Fourth U.S. Army Corps.

After the War he wrote a book on the Battle of Franklin, emphasizing both the gallantry of his men and the blunders and lies of his superiors—in particular Union Generals John M. Schofield and Jacob D. Cox, as well as Union Captain Levi T. Scofield. (Shellenberger blamed Schofield and Cox for ignoring obvious signs of a coming Confederate assault, resulting in the injury, capture, and deaths of hundreds of Yankee soldiers. He also claimed that Captain Scofield later intentionally covered up this fact in his postwar writings.)

Shellenberger passed away in Florida March 30, 1926, and was buried in Saint Augustine National Cemetery, Saint Augustine, Saint John's County, Florida.

SHELLEY, CHARLES MILLER (CSA): He was born December 28, 1833, in Sullivan County, Tennessee, but was raised at Talladega, Alabama. He trained and worked in construction, taking up the occupation of architect.

With the outbreak of Lincoln's War, Shelley sided with the South and the Constitution, at first serving as a lieutenant with the Talladega Artillery, later a part of the Fifth Alabama. Rising up the ranks, he fought at such battles as First Manassas, Port Gibson, Chattanooga, Greensboro, and Vicksburg.

Now brigadier general, at the Battle of Franklin he led his own unit, Cantey's Brigade (sometimes known as Shelley's Brigade), Walthall's Division, Stewart's Corps, C.S. Army of Tennessee. Here, under withering Yankee fire, 432 of his 1,100 man brigade were either wounded or killed. Shelley survived.

After the War he returned to Alabama, where he was made sheriff of Dallas County. In 1876 the conservative Southerner (then known as a Democrat) was elected a congressman, a position in which he served four consecutive terms. He also served as an auditor of the U.S. Treasury under President Grover Cleveland.

Shelley died January 20, 1907, at Birmingham, Alabama, and was buried in Oak Hill Cemetery, Talladega, Alabama.

SHERWOOD, ISAAC RUTH (USA): He was born August 13, 1835, at Stanford, New York. After studying law he served as the editor of Bryan, Ohio's *Williams County Gazette*, then married Kate Brownlee, with whom he bore several children.

After the onset of Lincoln's War, Sherwood sided with the North and against the Constitution, enlisting as a private in the Fourteenth Ohio Infantry. At the Battle of Franklin Lieutenant Colonel Sherwood commanded the One hundred eleventh Ohio, Moore's Second Brigade, Ruger's Second Division, Twenty-third U.S. Army Corps—after which has was brevetted brigadier general.

Postbellum, he returned to Ohio where he resumed work as a newspaperman. A liberal (then known as a Republican), he was elected state representative, serving one term.

Sherwood went on to edit several more newspapers and serve as a probate judge, eventually switching political parties. Now a Democrat, he served seven consecutive terms as a state representative, his pacifist views essentially ending his political career by 1924.

He retired to Toledo, Ohio, where he passed away October 15, 1925. He was buried in the city's Woodlawn Cemetery.

SHOTWELL, REUBEN H. (CSA): Confederate Lieutenant Colonel Shotwell took over command of Sears' Brigade after its leader Confederate General Claudius W. Sears was injured at the Battle of Nashville December 15, 1864, then captured several days later.

SHY'S HILL: Originally known as Compton's Hill, it is located in Nashville, Tennessee, near Benton Smith Road and Shy's Hill Road.

The prominence was later renamed Shy's Hill after Confederate Colonel William Mabry Shy of the famed Twentieth Tennessee Infantry, who was killed on this spot during the Battle of Nashville, December 16, 1864. (Shy, who had suffered a massive wound to the head, was found naked and unceremoniously bayoneted to a tree, no doubt the work of Yankee war criminals. He was buried in Shy Cemetery, Franklin, Tennessee)

It was at Shy's Hill—two weeks after the Battle of Franklin—that Union forces overwhelmed one of the last Confederate positions in Nashville, routing the Rebels and nearly decimating the Army of Tennessee as it fled back south toward Franklin.

SIMS, W. H. (CSA): Confederate Colonel Sims led the Tenth Mississippi Infantry at the Battle of Franklin, where he was wounded in action.

SIXTEENTH ALABAMA (CSA): This Rebel infantry regiment fought at the Battle of Franklin in Lowrey's Brigade, Cleburne's Division, Cheatham's Corps, C.S. Army of Tennessee.

SIXTEENTH ILLINOIS CAVALRY (USA): This Yankee cavalry regiment fought at the Battle of Franklin in Harrison's First Brigade, Johnson's Sixth Division, Wilson's Cavalry Corps.

SIXTEENTH KENTUCKY (USA): This Yankee infantry regiment fought at the Battle of Franklin in Reilly's First Brigade, Cox's Third Division, Twenty-third U.S. Army Corps.

SIXTEENTH LOUISIANA (CSA): This Rebel infantry regiment fought at the Battle of Franklin in Gibson's Brigade, Clayton's Division, Lee's Corps, C.S. Army of Tennessee.

SIXTEENTH SOUTH CAROLINA (CSA): This Rebel infantry regiment fought at the Battle of Franklin in Gist's Brigade, Brown's Division, Cheatham's Corps, C.S. Army of Tennessee.

SIXTEENTH TENNESSEE (CSA): This Rebel infantry regiment fought at the Battle of Franklin in Maney's Brigade, Brown's Division, Cheatham's Corps, C.S. Army of Tennessee.

SIXTH ARKANSAS (CSA): This Rebel infantry regiment fought at the Battle of Franklin in Govan's Brigade, Cleburne's Division, Cheatham's Corps, C.S. Army of Tennessee.

SIXTH FLORIDA (CSA): This Rebel infantry regiment fought at the Battle of Franklin in Finley's Brigade, Bate's Division, Cheatham's Corps, C.S. Army of Tennessee.

SIXTH ILLINOIS CAVALRY (USA): This Yankee cavalry regiment fought at the Battle of Franklin in Coon's Second Brigade, Hatch's Fifth Division, Wilson's Cavalry Corps.

SIXTH INDIANA CAVALRY (USA): This Yankee cavalry regiment fought at the Battle of Franklin in Biddle's Second Brigade, Johnson's Sixth Division, Wilson's Cavalry Corps.

SIXTH MISSISSIPPI (CSA): This Rebel infantry regiment fought at the Battle of Franklin in Adams' Brigade, Loring's Division, Stewart's Corps, C.S. Army of Tennessee.

SIXTH MISSOURI (CSA): This Rebel infantry regiment fought at the Battle of Franklin in Cockrell's Brigade, French's Division, Stewart's Corps, C.S. Army of Tennessee.

SIXTH OHIO BATTERY (USA): This Yankee artillery unit fought at the Battle of Franklin in the Fourth U.S. Army Corps Artillery.

SIXTH TENNESSEE (CSA): This Rebel infantry regiment fought at the Battle of Franklin in Maney's Brigade, Brown's Division, Cheatham's Corps, C.S. Army of Tennessee.

SIXTH TENNESSEE (USA): This Yankee infantry regiment, though attached to Ruger's Second Division, Twenty-third U.S. Army Corps, was with Cooper's Brigade—which was on detached duty at the time of the Battle of Franklin. It was thus not present or involved in the fighting.

SIXTH TEXAS (CSA): This Rebel infantry regiment fought at the Battle of Franklin in Granbury's Brigade, Cleburne's Division, Cheatham's Corps, C.S. Army of Tennessee.

SIXTH TEXAS CAVALRY (CSA): This Rebel cavalry regiment fought at the Battle of Franklin in Ross' Brigade, Jackson's Division, Forrest's Cavalry Corps, C.S. Army of Tennessee.

SIXTY-FIFTH GEORGIA (CSA): This Rebel infantry regiment fought at the Battle of Franklin in Gist's Brigade, Brown's Division, Cheatham's Corps, C.S. Army of Tennessee.

SIXTY-FIFTH ILLINOIS (USA): This Yankee infantry regiment fought at the Battle of Franklin in Casement's Second Brigade, Cox's Third Division, Twenty-third U.S. Army Corps.

SIXTY-FIFTH INDIANA (USA): This Yankee infantry regiment fought at the Battle of Franklin in Casement's Second Brigade, Cox's Third Division, Twenty-third U.S. Army Corps.

SIXTY-FIFTH OHIO (USA): This Yankee infantry regiment fought at the Battle of Franklin in Bradley's Third Brigade, Wagner's Second Division, Fourth U.S. Army Corps.

SIXTY-FOURTH OHIO (USA): This Yankee infantry regiment fought at the Battle of Franklin in Bradley's Third Brigade, Wagner's Second Division, Fourth U.S. Army Corps.

SIXTY-THIRD GEORGIA (CSA): This Rebel infantry regiment fought at the Battle of Franklin in Smith's Brigade, Cleburne's Division, Cheatham's

Corps, C.S. Army of Tennessee.

SIXTY-THIRD INDIANA (USA): This Yankee infantry regiment fought at the Battle of Franklin in Stiles' Third Brigade, Cox's Third Division, Twenty-third U.S. Army Corps.

SLAVES: See Field Servant and House Servant.

SLOCUMB'S LOUISIANA BATTERY (CSA): This Rebel battery fought at the Battle of Franklin in Cobb's Battalion, Cheatham's Corps Artillery, C.S. Army of Tennessee.

SMITH, GEORGE A. (CSA): Confederate Colonel Smith led the First Georgia Infantry at the Battle of Franklin, where he was killed in action.

SMITH, JAMES ARGYLE (CSA): Smith was born July 1, 1831, in Maury County, Tennessee. He graduated from West Point in 1853 and, as a member of the U.S. Sixth Infantry, served in the Western Territories.

With the start of Lincoln's War, Smith sided with the South and the Constitution, joined the Confederate army, and soon rose up the ranks. He fought at such battles as Perryville, Gettysburg, Murfreesboro, Atlanta, Missionary Ridge, Chickamauga, and Shiloh.

Brigadier General Smith led his own unit, Smith's Brigade, at the Battle of Franklin. He took over command of Cleburne's Division after its leader Major General Patrick R. Cleburne was killed in action at Franklin.

After the War Smith took up farming in Mississippi, then served as Mississippi State Superintendent of Education and an agent of the U.S. Indian Service. He died in Jackson, Mississippi, December 6, 1901, and was buried in the city's Greenwood Cemetery.

SMITH, MELANCTHON (CSA): Confederate Colonel Smith commanded Cheatham's Corps Artillery at the Battle of Franklin.

SMITH'S BRIGADE - 1 (CSA): This Rebel infantry brigade fought at the Battle of Franklin in Cleburne's Division, Cheatham's Corps, C.S. Army of Tennessee.

Named after Confederate Brigadier General James Argyle

Smith, it was comprised of the First Georgia Volunteers, Fifty-fourth Georgia, Fifty-seventh Georgia, and Sixty-third Georgia.

SMITH'S BRIGADE - 2 (CSA): For Confederate Brigadier General Thomas Benton Smith's Brigade, see Tyler's Brigade.

SMITH, THOMAS, BENTON (CSA): He was born February 24, 1838, at Mechanicsville, Tennessee (once a small village in Rutherford County). An inventor from a young age, he enrolled in Nashville's Western Military Institute at sixteen, and worked in the railroad business until the start of Lincoln's War.

Siding with the South and the Constitution, Smith raised a company of volunteers in the Triune, Tennessee, area that eventually became part of Company B of the famous Twentieth Tennessee Infantry.

After the Battle of Shiloh, at which time he was made colonel of Company B, he led his command through the Battles of Murfreesboro, Chickamauga, and Missionary Ridge. After the Battle of Atlanta he was appointed brigadier general, making him, at the time, the youngest officer of this rank in the Army of Tennessee.

Smith went on to fight under Confederate General John Bell Hood, leading his own unit, Smith's Brigade, Bate's Division, Cheatham's Corps, Army of Tennessee, at the Battles of Franklin and Nashville. At Franklin, Smith was the man responsible for leading the Carter family to their wounded son Confederate Captain Tod Carter, as he lay dying on the battlefield.

At the Battle of Nashville two weeks later, Smith was captured on Shy's Hill and taken prisoner. Unarmed and under heavy guard, he was needlessly and heartlessly beaten by Yankee officer Colonel William Linn McMillan. Struck three times in the head with McMillan's saber (which broke open his skull), Smith managed to survive the brutal attack, only to be sent to the filthy U.S. prison Fort Warren in Boston Harbor, Massachusetts.

After the War Smith attempted to return to his job in the Nashville railroad industry, but soon was overcome with bouts of depression brought on by his wartime head wound. Sad and forlorn, and increasingly incapable of taking care of himself, he finally ended up in the Tennessee State Asylum (now the Central State Psychiatric Hospital).

Smith passed away on May 21, 1923, and was buried in the Confederate Circle at Mount Olivet Cemetery, Nashville. He was one of the last surviving Confederate generals.

SNODGRASS, JOHN (CSA): Confederate Colonel Snodgrass took over command of Scott's Brigade after its leader General Thomas Moore Scott was wounded at the Battle of Franklin.

SONS OF CONFEDERATE VETERANS: Known as the SCV by its members, this organization evolved from out of the United Confederate Veterans (UCV), making it the oldest hereditary organization for male descendants of Confederate soldiers in the world.

Organized at Richmond, Virginia, in 1896, according to the group, "the SCV continues to serve as a historical, patriotic, and nonpolitical organization dedicated to insuring that a true history of the 1861-1865 period is preserved."

Any male twelve years of age or older is eligible for membership, as long as he is a descendant of a veteran who served honorably in the Confederate armed forces.

The primary goal of the SCV is to preserve the history and legacy of the Confederate soldier "so future generations can understand the motives that animated the Southern Cause."

SCV headquarters is located in the historic home known as Elm Springs at Columbia, Tennessee, site of the Battle of Columbia—which occurred just prior to the Battle of Franklin.

SPRING HILL CEMETERY: Begun in 1840, this graveyard (located in the center of Spring Hill, Tennessee) holds the remains of ten unknown soldiers from the Battles of Spring Hill and Franklin, as well as the body of Martin T. Cheairs, founder of Ferguson Hall.

SPRING HILL, TENNESSEE: Located in Middle Tennessee between Thompson's Station to the north and Columbia to the south, Spring Hill straddles two counties: Williamson and Maury. The seventeen square mile city is about thirty miles south of

Nashville and has a current population of around 30,000.

Once a quaint farming community, Spring Hill was founded in 1809 and was the site, on November 29, 1864, of the Battle of Spring Hill and what has become known as the "Spring Hill Debacle."

This great "missed opportunity"—in which Hood and his officers allowed Yankee troops to sneak past their encampment at Spring Hill on the night of the 29th—helped lead to the Battle of Franklin the next day.

STAFFORD, FOUNTAIN E. P. (CSA): Confederate Lieutenant Colonel Stafford led the Thirty-first Tennessee Infantry at the Battle of Franklin, where he was killed in action.

STANFORD'S MISSISSIPPI BATTERY (CSA): This Rebel battery fought at the Battle of Franklin with Eldridge's Battalion, Lee's Corps Artillery, C.S. Army of Tennessee.

STANLEY, DAVID SLOANE (USA): A descendant of New England stock, he was born June 1, 1828, at Cedar Valley, Ohio. After graduating from West Point in 1852 he was sent to the Western Territories where he battled Indians from his post at Fort Washita (now in Oklahoma). He then married Anna Maria Wright, with whom he bore several children.

With the onset of Lincoln's War, Stanley turned down an offer to side with the South and the Constitution, and instead remained with the U.S. army, rising quickly up the ranks. He fought at such battles as Wilson's Creek, Chickamauga, Iuka, Island Number Ten, Murfreesboro, Atlanta, and Second Corinth.

At the Battle of Franklin Stanley led his own Yankee command, the Fourth U.S. Army Corps. Later, in 1893, he was awarded the Congressional Medal of Honor for his service at Franklin.

After the War he returned to the Indian Territories. Appointed colonel of the Twenty-second U.S. Infantry, he went on to head the Department of Texas until 1892, when he retired from military service.

While serving as president of the Soldiers' Home at Washington, D.C., he died on March 13, 1902, and was buried in the District's U.S. Soldiers' and Airmen's Home National Cemetery.

STEPHENS, MARCUS D. L. (CSA): Confederate Colonel Stephens led the Thirty-first Mississippi Infantry at the Battle of Franklin, where he was wounded in action.

STEPHEN'S LIGHT ARTILLERY (CSA): This Rebel unit fought at the Battle of Franklin with Johnson's Battalion, Lee's Corps Artillery, C.S. Army of Tennessee.

STEVENS HILL: The name used by several Union officers (who fought at the Battle of Franklin) in their reports for what is now known as Winstead Hill, Franklin, Tennessee.

STEVENSON, CARTER LITTLEPAGE (CSA): He was born September 21, 1817, at Fredericksburg, Virginia. He graduated from West Point Military Academy in 1838, and went on to fight as a U.S. soldier in the Mexican-American War, as well as against both Indians and the non-Christian Mormons of Utah.

At the start of Lincoln's War, Stevenson resigned his U.S. commission, siding with the South and the Constitution. Appointed a colonel in the Confederate army, he ascended rapidly up the ranks, fighting in such battles as Champion's Hill, Chattanooga, Atlanta, Bentonville, and Nashville.

According to some sources, Stevenson was not present at the Battle of Franklin. Others, however, say he was, or that at least some elements of his command were: Stevenson's Division, Lee's Corps, C.S. Army of Tennessee.

After the War he worked as an engineer, specializing in mining. He passed away August 15, 1888, in Caroline County, Virginia, and was buried in the Confederate Cemetery at Fredericksburg.

STEVENSON'S DIVISION (CSA): This Rebel division (or parts of it), named after Confederate General Carter Littlepage Stevenson, was present at the Battle of Franklin. It was comprised of Cummings' Brigade and Pettus' Brigade.

STEWART, ALEXANDER PETER (CSA): He was born October 2, 1821, at Rogersville,

Hawkins County, Tennessee, then later raised in Winchester, Tennessee. Contrary to Northern myth, like nearly all Southern families his too was religious and supported abolition.

A Scottish-American redhead, he entered West Point in 1838, graduating in 1842 twelfth in his class. He served for a time as a mathematics instructor at West Point, then in 1845 he married Harriet Chase.

Resigning from the U.S. army, he accepted the chair of mathematics and natural history at Lebanon, Tennessee's Cumberland University. He later occupied the same position at Nashville University.

With the start of Lincoln's War, Stewart sided with the South and the Constitution. After volunteering for Confederate service, he soon rose up the ranks, making brigadier general by November 1861. He went on to fight at such battles as Murfreesboro, Missionary Ridge, New Madrid, Perryville, Chickamauga, and Shiloh.

In the Summer of 1864 he was promoted to lieutenant general, and was assigned to the C.S. Army of Tennessee under Confederate General John Bell Hood.

At the Battles of Franklin and Nashville Stewart led his own command: Stewart's Corps. He and his men surrendered April 26, 1865, and he returned to civilian life.

After the War he resumed his professor's chair at Cumberland University, then took on a series of odd jobs, including cotton brokering, insurance, and surveying. In 1874 he was appointed chancellor of the University of Mississippi.

In 1890 he was asked to participate in the organization of the U.S. National Battlefield Park system, working alongside his old Yankee nemesis General William S. Rosecrans.

Stewart went on to serve as commissioner of the newly created Chickamauga and Chattanooga National Military Park, a post he held until his death on August 30, 1908, at Biloxi, Mississippi. He was buried in Bellefontaine Cemetery, Saint Louis, Missouri.

Nicknamed "Old Straight," Stewart was instrumental in founding the United Confederate Veterans, today known as the Sons of Confederate Veterans.

STEWART, ROBERT R. (USA): Yankee Colonel Stewart led his own unit, Stewart's First Brigade, Hatch's Fifth Division, Wilson's Cavalry Corps, at the Battle of Franklin.

STEWART'S CORPS (CSA): This Rebel corps, named after Confederate General Alexander Peter Stewart, was present at the Battle of Franklin.

It was comprised of Loring's Division, French's Division, and Walthall's Division.

STEWART'S CORPS ARTILLERY (CSA): This Rebel artillery corps, named after Confederate General Alexander Peter Stewart, was present at the Battle of Franklin.

Led by Lieutenant Colonel Samuel C. Williams, it was comprised of Truehart's Battalion, Myrick's Battalion, and Storrs' Battalion.

STEWART'S FIRST BRIGADE (USA): This Yankee cavalry brigade fought at the Battle of Franklin in Hatch's Fifth Division, Wilson's Cavalry Corps.

Named after U.S. Colonel Robert R. Stewart, it was comprised of the Third Illinois Cavalry, Eleventh Indiana Cavalry, Twelfth Missouri Cavalry, and Tenth Tennessee Cavalry.

STILES, ISRAEL NEWTON (USA): The son of Anson Stiles and Elvira Allen, he was born July 16, 1833, at Suffield, Hartford County, Connecticut. He studied law and in 1860 he married Jennie Coney.

He was working as a prosecuting attorney at Lafayette, Indiana, when Lincoln devilishly hoodwinked the South into firing the first shot at Fort Sumter in April 1861.

Stiles sided with the North and against the Constitution, enlisting in the U.S. army as a private in the Twentieth Indiana Infantry in July 1861.

He rose rapidly up the ranks, serving in such battles as Malvern Hill (where he was captured and spent six weeks in Libby Prison), Atlanta, and Nashville. At the Battle of Franklin, Colonel Stiles commanded his own unit, Stiles' Brigade, Cox's Third Division, Twenty-third U.S. Army Corps. Brevetted brigadier general in January 1865, he was mustered out of service in June 1865.

After the War he resumed his law practice, passing away in Illinois January 17, 1895. He was buried in Pine Ridge Cemetery, Loda, Illinois.

STILES' THIRD BRIGADE (USA): This Yankee infantry brigade fought at the Battle of Franklin in Cox's Third Division, Twenty-third U.S. Army Corps.

Named after U.S. Colonel Israel Newton Stiles, the Third Brigade was comprised of the One hundred twelfth Illinois, Sixty-third Indiana, One hundred twentieth Indiana, and One hundred twenty-eighth Indiana.

STONE HILL: See Privet Knob.

STORRS' BATTALION (CSA): Named after Confederate Major George S. Storrs, this Rebel battalion fought at the Battle of Franklin in Stewart's Corps Artillery, C.S. Army of Tennessee. It was comprised of Guibor's Missouri Battery, Hoskin's Mississippi Battery, and Kolb's Alabama Battery.

STOVALL, MARCELLUS AUGUSTUS (CSA): He was born September 18, 1818, at Sparta, Georgia. He was schooled in Massachusetts, after which he enlisted in the U.S. army and fought in the Seminole Wars. He attended West Point, but left after one year due to sickness.

With the outbreak of Lincoln's War, Stovall sided with the South and the Constitution. Joining the Confederate army, by October 1861 he was serving as lieutenant colonel of the Third Georgia Infantry. He went on to fight at such battles as Chickamauga, Atlanta, and Nashville.

Now a brigadier general, at the Battle of Franklin he commanded his own unit: Stovall's Brigade, Clayton's Division, Lee's Corps, C.S. Army of Tennessee.

After the War Stovall returned to his estate in Augusta, Georgia, where he worked in the cotton and fertilizer industries. He died at Augusta on August 4, 1895, and was buried in the city's Magnolia Cemetery.

STOVALL'S BRIGADE (CSA): This Rebel infantry brigade fought at the Battle of Franklin in Clayton's Division, Lee's Corps, C.S. Army of Tennessee.

Named after Confederate Brigadier General Marcellus Augustus Stovall, it was comprised of the Fortieth Georgia, Forty-first Georgia, Forty-second Georgia, Forty-third Georgia, and Fifty-second Georgia.

STRAHL STREET: A street in Franklin, Tennessee, named in honor of Confederate General Otho French Strahl, who died during the Battle of Franklin, November 30, 1864. The street is located not far from where he fell.

STRAHL, OTHO FRENCH (CSA): The son of Phillip Strahl and Rhoda Ann French, he was born June 3, 1831, at McConnelsville, Ohio. After his schooling at Ohio Wesleyan University, he took up the study of law, was admitted to the bar in 1858, and opened up a law office in Dyersburg, Tennessee.

With the onset of Lincoln's War, Strahl (a Northerner) sided with the South and the Constitution, joining the Confederate army as a captain of the Fourth Tennessee Infantry. He quickly ascended the ranks, fighting at such battles as Chickamauga, Shiloh, and Murfreesboro.

Now a brigadier general, at the Battle of Franklin he commanded his own unit: Strahl's Brigade, Brown's Division, Cheatham's Corps, Army of Tennessee. It was here that General Strahl gave his life for the Confederate Cause (self-determination): shot three times then collapsing in a ditch just west of Columbia Pike, he was one of the six generals who would die of mortal wounds received at Franklin.

Strahl's body was taken to nearby Carnton Plantation and laid on the back lower porch for viewing by his soldiers. He was then buried at Rose Hill Cemetery, Columbia, Tennessee. Situated too close to detested Yankee soldiers, his body was then moved to Saint John's Episcopal Church, Mount Pleasant, Tennessee. Finally, his remains were reinterred in Dyersburg City Cemetery, Dyersburg, Tennessee.

STRAHL'S BRIGADE (CSA): This Rebel infantry brigade fought at the Battle of Franklin in Brown's Division, Cheatham's Corps, C.S. Army of Tennessee.

Named after Confederate Brigadier General Otho French Strahl, it was comprised of the Fourth Tennessee, Fifth Tennessee, Nineteenth

Tennessee, Twenty-fourth Tennessee, Thirty-first Tennessee, Thirty-third Tennessee, Thirty-eighth Tennessee, and Forty-first Tennessee.

After General Strahl was killed in action at Franklin, the brigade was taken over by Confederate Colonel Andrew J. Kellar.

STREIGHT, ABEL D. (USA): Streight was born June 17, 1828, at Wheeler, Steuben County, New York. By the late 1850s he was living in Indianapolis, Indiana, and was working as a publisher and a lumber manufacturer.

With the start of Lincoln's War, Streight sided with the North and against the Constitution. After joining the U.S. army, he was serving as a colonel of the U.S. Fifty-first Indiana Infantry by late 1861.

Streight's wife Lovina McCarthy often joined her husband on the battlefield, giving aid and comfort to the wounded. She was captured and exchanged three times, and was given full military honors at her funeral in June 1910.

One of the great Civil War stories is associated with Colonel Streight, and so bears telling here.

Seeing little combat during his first two years of the War, he proposed a plan to his superior Union General William S. Rosecrans: he would take a fast moving force into the Deep South and disrupt the Confederate railroad lines running from Chattanooga to Atlanta.

After his plan was approved, Streight took his 1,700 man command southeast, arriving at Sand Mountain in Alabama on April 30, 1863. Here he was met by the irresistible Confederate force known as General Nathan Bedford Forrest. Over the next few days Forrest chased, harassed, and eventually pinned down Streight and his men in Georgia. Forrest sent forward his usual demand for surrender to "avoid the further effusion of blood."

The chilling message was readily accepted, but first Streight wanted to know how many men Forrest had, for he would not give up unless their forces were equal.

Forrest met with Streight in a nearby woods, parading his artillery and troops around in circles on a hill to give the appearance of a much greater force. "Great God, how many guns have you got"? the stupefied Yankee officer finally asked. "Wall, that thar's 'bout fifteen I've counted so far," Forrest replied nonchalantly, chewing on a long piece of grass. Then for added effect: "Reckon that's all that has kept up."

Streight looked nervous, but he was not quite convinced yet. At this Forrest looked him dead in the eye and said: "Let's put it this way colonel. I've got enough to whip ya out of yer boots."

A terrified Streight could bear it no more and surrendered there and then. It was only afterward that he learned that Forrest actually only had two cannons, was almost out of ammunition, and had a mere 400 men, more than four times less than he himself had!

When Streight demanded his arms back so they could fight to the finish, Forrest laughed and said: "All is fair in love and war sir!"

Streight's humiliation was doubled when he learned that Forrest's men were calling the affair the "Jackass Raid," for many of Streight's soldiers had been riding mules when they were captured.

After the fight the grateful townspeople of Rome, Georgia, presented Forrest with a gift of appreciation: a sturdy iron-gray horse named King Philip. The Rebel warhorse became nearly as famous as Forrest himself, in part because of his habit of instantly attacking anyone wearing blue clothing—a remnant of King Philip's training under the great Confederate chieftain!

Streight was sent to the Confederates' Libby Prison, where he spent ten months, only escaping by tunneling out with 107 other Union soldiers.

Returning to duty he was placed in command of the First Brigade, Wood's Third Division, Fourth U.S. Army Corps, which fought at the Battle of Franklin November 30, 1864.

He went on to fight at Nashville as well, after which he was brevetted brigadier general, then resigned from service.

After the War he returned to Indiana where he served several terms as a state senator. He also dabbled in other pursuits: the 1880 U.S. Census lists his occupation as "lumber dealer."

Streight died May 27, 1892, at Indianapolis and was

buried in the town's Crown Hill Cemetery.

STREIGHT'S FIRST BRIGADE (USA): This Yankee infantry brigade fought at the Battle of Franklin in Wood's Third Division, Fourth U.S. Army Corps.

Named after U.S. Colonel Abel D. Streight, it was comprised of the Eighty-ninth Illinois, Fifty-first Indiana, Eighth Kansas, Fifteenth Ohio, and Forty-ninth Ohio.

STRICKLAND, SILAS ALLEN (USA): Strickland was born September 17, 1830, at Rochester, New York. He studied law and was a resident of Nebraska before 1861.

With the outbreak of Lincoln's War, he sided with the North and against the Constitution, serving in the U.S. First Nebraska Infantry. At the Battle of Franklin Brigadier General Strickland commanded the Third Brigade, Ruger's Second Division, Twenty-third U.S. Army Corps.

After the War he resumed his law practice at Omaha, Nebraska, where he died March 31, 1878. He was buried in the town's Prospect Hill Cemetery.

STRICKLAND'S THIRD BRIGADE (USA): This Yankee infantry brigade fought at the Battle of Franklin in Ruger's Second Division, Twenty-third U.S. Army Corps.

Named after U.S. Colonel Silas A. Strickland, it was comprised of the Ninety-first Indiana, One hundred twenty-third Indiana, Fiftieth Ohio, and One hundred eighty-third Ohio.

TARRANT'S ALABAMA BATTERY (CSA): This Rebel battery was present at the Battle of Franklin. It served with Stewart's Corps Artillery, Walthall's Division, Stewart's Corps, C.S. Army of Tennessee.

TAYLOR, RICHARD (CSA): The son of U.S. President Zachary Taylor and Margaret Mackall Smith, Taylor was born January 27, 1826, on the family estate Springfield near Louisville, Kentucky. He was schooled in Europe, then later graduated from Yale University in 1845.

During the Mexican-American War he served as aide-de-camp to his father. After his father's death in 1850, he inherited the family's sugar plantation Fashion, located in Saint Charles Parish, Louisiana. Successfully run, Taylor was soon one of the wealthiest men in the South.

In 1851 he married Louise Marie Myrthe Bringier, with whom he bore five children. A traditional Southerner, he entered politics and served for several years as a Democratic (then a conservative) senator.

With the outbreak of Lincoln's War, Taylor sided with the South and the Constitution, joined the Confederate army, and served as colonel of the Ninth Louisiana Infantry. He rose rapidly up the ranks, fighting at such battles as First Manassas, First Winchester, Front Royal, Fort Bisland, Irish Bend, Mansfield, and Pleasant Hill.

Taylor did not fight at the Battle of Franklin. He appears here because he took over command of the Army of Tennessee shortly after Confederate General John Bell Hood resigned in January 1865, just a few weeks after the disastrous Battle of Nashville.

The brother-in-law of C.S. President Jefferson Davis (whose first wife, Sarah Knox Taylor, was General Taylor's sister), his troops were the last to surrender east of the Mississippi

River in May 1865.

After the War Taylor continued his fight against the North, this time against so-called "Reconstruction," which was nothing more than a plan of Yankee vengeance against the independent minded South. He penned his memoirs, *Destruction and Reconstruction*, and proudly defended President Davis and the South to the end.

The well respected Taylor (he was one of the few Confederate officers genuinely liked by Rebel General Nathan Bedford Forrest) passed away April 12, 1879, at New York City, and was buried in Metairie Cemetery, New Orleans, Louisiana.

TAYLOR, WILLIAM A. (CSA): Confederate Major Taylor led the Twenty-fourth and Twenty-fifth Texas Cavalries (dismounted) at the Battle of Franklin, where he was captured by the enemy.

TENNESSEE AND ALABAMA RAILROAD: Franklin, Tennessee's railroad was constructed and originally owned by the Tennessee and Alabama Railroad Company. The line was illegally seized by Union troops before the Battle of Franklin, and was held by them until the end of Lincoln's War.

TENNESSEE STATE CAPITOL: See Fort Andrew Johnson.

TENTH INDIANA CAVALRY (USA): This Yankee cavalry regiment fought at the Battle of Franklin in Hammond's First Brigade, Knipe's Seventh Division, Wilson's Cavalry Corps.

TENTH MISSISSIPPI (CSA): This Rebel infantry regiment fought at the Battle of Franklin in Sharp's Brigade, Johnson's Division, Lee's Corps, C.S. Army of Tennessee.

TENTH SOUTH CAROLINA (CSA): This Rebel infantry regiment fought at the Battle of Franklin in Manigault's Brigade, Johnson's Division, Lee's Corps, C.S. Army of Tennessee.

TENTH TENNESSEE (CSA): This Rebel infantry regiment fought at the Battle of Franklin in Tyler's Brigade, Bate's Division, Cheatham's Corps, C.S. Army of Tennessee.

TENTH TENNESSEE CAVALRY (CSA): According to some sources this Rebel cavalry regiment fought at the Battle of Franklin in Biffle's Brigade, Chalmers' Division, Forrest's Cavalry Corps, C.S. Army of Tennessee.

TENTH TENNESSEE CAVALRY (USA): This Yankee cavalry regiment fought at the Battle of Franklin in Stewart's First Brigade, Hatch's Fifth Division, Wilson's Cavalry Corps.

TENTH TEXAS (CSA): This Rebel infantry regiment fought at the Battle of Franklin in Granbury's Brigade, Cleburne's Division, Cheatham's Corps, C.S. Army of Tennessee.

TENTH TEXAS CAVALRY - DISMOUNTED (CSA): This Rebel cavalry regiment served in Ector's Brigade, French's Division, Stewart's Corps, C.S. Army of Tennessee.

Ector's Brigade was at Franklin, Tennessee, during the Battle of Franklin. However, it did not participate in the battle as it was on detached duty at the time.

THIRD FLORIDA (CSA): This Rebel infantry regiment fought at the Battle of Franklin in Finley's Brigade, Bate's Division, Cheatham's Corps, C.S. Army of Tennessee.

THIRD ILLINOIS CAVALRY (USA): This Yankee cavalry regiment fought at the Battle of Franklin in Stewart's First Brigade, Hatch's Fifth Division, Wilson's Cavalry Corps.

THIRD KENTUCKY MOUNTED INFANTRY (CSA): This Rebel unit fought at the Battle of Franklin in Crossland's Brigade, Buford's Division, Forrest's Cavalry Corps, C.S. Army of Tennessee.

THIRD MISSISSIPPI (CSA): This Rebel infantry regiment fought at the Battle of Franklin in Featherston's Brigade, Loring's Division, Stewart's Corps, C.S. Army of Tennessee.

THIRD MISSISSIPPI BATTALION (CSA): This Rebel unit fought at the Battle of Franklin in Lowrey's Brigade, Cleburne's Division, Cheatham's Corps, C.S. Army of Tennessee.

THIRD MISSOURI (CSA): This Rebel infantry regiment fought at the Battle of Franklin in Cockrell's Brigade, French's Division, Stewart's Corps, C.S. Army of Tennessee.

THIRD MISSOURI CAVALRY BATTALION - DISMOUNTED (CSA): This Rebel cavalry regiment fought at the Battle of Franklin in Cockrell's Brigade, French's Division, Stewart's Corps, C.S. Army of Tennessee.

THIRD TENNESSEE (USA): This Yankee infantry regiment, though attached to Ruger's Second Division, Twenty-third U.S. Army Corps, was with Cooper's Brigade—which was on detached duty at the time of the Battle of Franklin. It was thus not present or involved in the fighting.

THIRD TENNESSEE VOLUNTEER INFANTRY (USA): This Yankee infantry regiment fought at the Battle of Franklin in Biddle's Second Brigade, Johnson's Sixth Division, Wilson's Cavalry Corps.

THIRTEENTH ARKANSAS (CSA): This Rebel infantry regiment fought at the Battle of Franklin in Govan's Brigade, Cleburne's Division, Cheatham's Corps, C.S. Army of Tennessee.

THIRTEENTH INDIANA BATTERY (USA): This Yankee artillery unit fought at the Battle of Franklin in Ruger's Second Division, Twenty-third U.S. Army Corps.

THIRTEENTH INDIANA CAVALRY (USA): This Yankee cavalry regiment fought at the Battle of Franklin in Johnson's Second Brigade, Knipe's Seventh Division, Wilson's Cavalry Corps.

THIRTEENTH LOUISIANA (CSA): This Rebel infantry regiment fought at the Battle of Franklin in Gibson's Brigade, Clayton's Division, Lee's Corps, C.S. Army of Tennessee.

THIRTEENTH OHIO (USA): This Yankee infantry regiment fought at the Battle of Franklin in Beatty's Third Brigade, Wood's Third Division, Fourth U.S. Army Corps.

THIRTEENTH TENNESSEE (CSA): This Rebel infantry regiment fought at the Battle of Franklin in Vaughan's Brigade, Brown's Division, Cheatham's Corps, C.S. Army of Tennessee.

THIRTIETH ALABAMA (CSA): This Rebel infantry regiment fought at the Battle of Franklin in Pettus' Brigade, Stevenson's Division, Lee's Corps, C.S. Army of Tennessee.

THIRTIETH GEORGIA (CSA): This Rebel infantry regiment fought at the Battle of Franklin in Jackson's Brigade, Bate's Division, Cheatham's Corps, C.S. Army of Tennessee.

THIRTIETH INDIANA (USA): This Yankee infantry regiment fought at the Battle of Franklin in Grose's Third Brigade, Kimball's First Division, Fourth U.S. Army Corps.

THIRTIETH LOUISIANA (CSA): This Rebel infantry regiment fought at the Battle of Franklin in Gibson's Brigade, Clayton's Division, Lee's Corps, C.S. Army of Tennessee.

THIRTIETH MISSISSIPPI (CSA): This Rebel infantry regiment fought at the Battle of Franklin in Brantley's Brigade, Johnson's Division, Lee's Corps, C.S. Army of Tennessee.

THIRTIETH NORTH CAROLINA (CSA): This Rebel infantry regiment served in Ector's Brigade, French's Division, Stewart's Corps, C.S. Army of Tennessee.

Ector's Brigade was at Franklin, Tennessee, during the Battle of Franklin. However, it did not participate in the battle as it was on detached duty at the time.

THIRTY-EIGHTH ALABAMA (CSA): This Rebel infantry regiment fought at the Battle of Franklin in Holtzclaw's Brigade, Clayton's Division, Lee's Corps, C.S. Army of Tennessee.

THIRTY-EIGHTH ILLINOIS (USA): This Yankee infantry regiment fought at the Battle of Franklin in Kirby's First Brigade, Kimball's First Division, Fourth U.S. Army Corps.

THIRTY-EIGHTH TENNESSEE (CSA): This Rebel infantry regiment fought at the Battle of Franklin in Strahl's Brigade, Brown's Division, Cheatham's Corps, C.S. Army of Tennessee.

THIRTY-FIFTH ALABAMA (CSA): This Rebel infantry regiment fought at the Battle of Franklin in Scott's Brigade, Loring's Division, Stewart's Corps, C.S. Army of Tennessee.

THIRTY-FIFTH INDIANA (USA): This Yankee infantry regiment fought at the Battle of Franklin in Whitaker's Second Brigade, Kimball's First Division, Fourth U.S. Army Corps.

THIRTY-FIFTH MISSISSIPPI (CSA): This Rebel infantry regiment fought at the Battle of Franklin in Sears' Brigade, French's Division, Stewart's Corps, C.S. Army of Tennessee.

THIRTY-FIFTH TENNESSEE (CSA): This Rebel infantry regiment fought at the Battle of Franklin in Granbury's Brigade, Cleburne's Division, Cheatham's Corps, C.S. Army of Tennessee.

THIRTY-FIRST ALABAMA (CSA): This Rebel infantry regiment fought at the Battle of Franklin in Pettus' Brigade, Stevenson's Division, Lee's Corps, C.S. Army of Tennessee.

THIRTY-FIRST INDIANA (USA): This Yankee infantry regiment fought at the Battle of Franklin in Kirby's First Brigade, Kimball's First Division, Fourth U.S. Army Corps.

THIRTY-FIRST MISSISSIPPI (CSA): This Rebel infantry regiment fought at the Battle of Franklin in Featherston's Brigade, Loring's Division, Stewart's Corps, C.S. Army of Tennessee.

THIRTY-FIRST TENNESSEE (CSA): This Rebel infantry regiment fought at the Battle of Franklin in Strahl's Brigade, Brown's Division, Cheatham's Corps, C.S. Army of Tennessee.

THIRTY-FOURTH ALABAMA (CSA): This Rebel infantry regiment fought at the Battle of Franklin in Manigault's Brigade, Johnson's Division, Lee's Corps, C.S. Army of Tennessee.

THIRTY-FOURTH MISSISSIPPI (CSA): This Rebel infantry regiment fought at the Battle of Franklin in Brantley's Brigade, Johnson's Division, Lee's Corps, C.S. Army of Tennessee.

THIRTY-NINTH ALABAMA (CSA): This Rebel infantry regiment fought at the Battle of Franklin in Deas' Brigade, Johnson's Division, Lee's Corps, C.S. Army of Tennessee.

THIRTY-NINTH GEORGIA (CSA): This Rebel infantry regiment fought at the Battle of Franklin in Cummings' Brigade, Stevenson's Division, Lee's Corps, C.S. Army of Tennessee.

THIRTY-NINTH MISSISSIPPI (CSA): This Rebel infantry regiment fought at the Battle of Franklin in Sears' Brigade, French's Division, Stewart's Corps, C.S. Army of Tennessee.

THIRTY-SECOND ALABAMA (CSA): This Rebel infantry regiment fought at the Battle of Franklin in Holtzclaw's Brigade, Clayton's Division, Lee's Corps, C.S. Army of Tennessee.

THIRTY-SECOND MISSISSIPPI (CSA): This Rebel infantry regiment fought at the Battle of Franklin in Lowrey's Brigade, Cleburne's Division, Cheatham's Corps, C.S. Army of Tennessee.

THIRTY-SECOND TEXAS CAVALRY - DISMOUNTED (CSA): This Rebel cavalry regiment served in Ector's Brigade, French's Division, Stewart's Corps, C.S. Army of Tennessee.

Ector's Brigade was at Franklin, Tennessee, during the Battle of Franklin. However, it did not participate in the battle as it was on detached duty at the time.

THIRTY-SEVENTH GEORGIA (CSA): This Rebel infantry regiment fought at the Battle of Franklin in Tyler's Brigade, Bate's Division, Cheatham's Corps, C.S. Army of Tennessee.

THIRTY-SEVENTH MISSISSIPPI (CSA): This Rebel infantry regiment fought at the Battle of Franklin in Cantley's Brigade, Walthall's Division, Stewart's Corps, C.S. Army of Tennessee.

THIRTY-SEVENTH TENNESSEE (CSA): This Rebel infantry regiment fought at the Battle of Franklin in Tyler's Brigade, Bate's Division, Cheatham's Corps, C.S. Army of Tennessee.

THIRTY-SIXTH ALABAMA (CSA): This Rebel infantry regiment fought at the Battle of Franklin in Holtzclaw's Brigade, Clayton's Division, Lee's Corps, C.S. Army of Tennessee.

THIRTY-SIXTH GEORGIA (CSA): This Rebel infantry regiment fought at the Battle of Franklin in Cummings' Brigade, Stevenson's Division, Lee's Corps, C.S. Army of Tennessee.

THIRTY-SIXTH ILLINOIS (USA): This Yankee infantry regiment fought at the Battle of Franklin in Opdycke's First Brigade, Wagner's Second Division, Fourth U.S. Army Corps.

THIRTY-SIXTH INDIANA (USA): This Yankee infantry regiment fought at the Battle of Franklin in Grose's Third Brigade, Kimball's First Division, Fourth U.S. Army Corps.

THIRTY-SIXTH MISSISSIPPI (CSA): This Rebel infantry regiment fought at the Battle of Franklin in Sears' Brigade, French's Division, Stewart's Corps, C.S. Army of Tennessee.

THIRTY-THIRD ALABAMA (CSA): This Rebel infantry regiment fought at the Battle of Franklin in Lowrey's Brigade, Cleburne's Division, Cheatham's Corps, C.S. Army of Tennessee.

THIRTY-THIRD MISSISSIPPI (CSA): This Rebel infantry regiment fought at the Battle of Franklin in Featherston's Brigade, Loring's Division, Stewart's Corps, C.S. Army of Tennessee.

THIRTY-THIRD TENNESSEE (CSA): This Rebel infantry regiment fought at the Battle of Franklin in Strahl's Brigade, Brown's Division, Cheatham's Corps, C.S. Army of Tennessee.

THOMAS, GEORGE HENRY (USA): The son of Welsh-American John Thomas and Elizabeth Rochelle, Thomas was born July 31, 1816, at Newsom's Depot, Southampton County, Virginia. His family was one of the fortunate ones who survived the diabolical murder spree of the psychotic black racist and slave rebel Nat Turner in 1831.

Thomas entered West Point in 1836, graduating twelfth in his class in 1840. He then fought in both the Seminole Wars and the Mexican-American War.

In 1851 Thomas returned to West Point where he served as an instructor, specializing in all three arms of combat: infantry, cavalry, and artillery (one of the few Civil War officers with such a background). The following year he married a Northerner, Frances Lucretia Kellogg of Troy, New York.

With the onset of Lincoln's War Thomas sided with the North and against the Constitution (a decision no doubt influenced by his Yankee wife), angering his family members and disappointing his many friends across the South.

Thomas' sisters in particular were not happy with their brother's decision: not only did they turn his pictures toward the wall and burn his letters, they shunned him for the rest of their lives, forbade him from ever returning home again, and advised him to change his name. Some Confederate officers suggested hanging him as a traitor.

Thomas' reception by his new Yankee cohorts was not much better: being a Southerner, many Union officers and soldiers treated the native Virginian with animosity and suspicion, a distrust that continued in some quarters until the end of the War.

Despite the negativity, Thomas remained with the U.S. army, rising quickly up the ranks. He fought at such battles as First Manassas, Mill Springs, Shiloh, Perryville, Murfreesboro, and Chickamauga, where he earned the nickname "Rock of Chickamauga" for his aggressive command and defensive actions.

In the Fall of 1864 Thomas left Atlanta, Georgia, for Nashville, Tennessee, where he hoped to acquire reenforcements from the already Union occupied city. Confederate General John Bell Hood gave chase, but was sidetracked by some of Thomas' troops under the command of Union General John McAllister Schofield, who was following the same route to Nashville as Hood. The results were the Battles of Columbia, Spring Hill, Franklin, and Nashville.

At the latter conflict, which took place December 15-16, 1864, Thomas smashed Hood and the Army of Tennessee, sending them into a full scale retreat back south to Franklin (resulting in the Battle of Franklin III on December 17). This earned the Yankee officer a second nickname: the "Sledge of Nashville." In January 1865 he was appointed major general and given an official thanks from the U.S. Congress.

After the War, still siding against his homeland, he continued serving with the U.S. army—a position which he used to further abuse and suppress his Southern brothers and sisters.

Eventually assigned to command the Division of the Pacific at San Francisco, California, Thomas was replying to an article critical of his military career (written by his former subordinate General John M. Schofield), when he died of a heart attack.

His body was taken back to his wife's hometown in New York where he was buried in Troy's Oakwood Cemetery. No one from his family in Virginia attended his funeral.

TISON, WILLIAM H. H. (CSA): Confederate Colonel Tison led the Thirty-second Mississippi Infantry at the Battle of Franklin, where he was wounded in action.

TOUSSAINT L'OUVERTURE CEMETERY: This African-American graveyard in Franklin, Tennessee, was named after François Dominique Toussaint, a self-educated slave who led the black Haitian Rebellion in 1791. The earliest burials at the site begin around 1869.

Many of Franklin's former black servants ("slaves" to Northerners) are buried here, including famed servant Mariah Reddick, who worked at Carnton Plantation before, during, and after Lincoln's War. In 1996 the cemetery was put on the National Register of Historic Places.

TRAVELLERS REST: Located in Nashville, Tennessee, this plantation was established in 1799 by judge John Overton of Louisa County, Virginia, a good friend of U.S. President Andrew "Old Hickory" Jackson.

Along with Jackson and General James Winchester (the grandfather of General Edmund Winchester Rucker, who led Rucker's Brigade at the Battle of Franklin), Overton was one of the cofounders of Memphis, Tennessee in 1819.

Between the Battles of Franklin and Nashville, Confederate General John Bell Hood used Travellers Rest as his Army of Tennessee headquarters. The home is today open for public tours.

TRUEHART'S BATTALION (CSA): This Rebel battalion fought at the Battle of Franklin in Stewart's Corps Artillery, C.S. Army of Tennessee. It was comprised of Lumsden's Alabama Battery and Selden's Alabama Battery.

TRUETT HOUSE: Also known as Truett Place or the Alpheus Truett Home, this beautiful residence is located in Franklin, Tennessee, and is listed on the National Register of Historic Places.

Built around 1846 by Alpheus Truett, an agriculturalist from Hickman County, Tennessee, it is most famous for being the temporary headquarters of Yankee General John M. Schofield just prior to the Battle of Franklin.

Around noon on November 30, 1864, Schofield stood on the front upper balcony of the home and peered through his field glasses south toward Winstead Hill. What he saw took him by surprise: Confederate John Bell Hood was amassing his army into battle formation in preparation for an attack.

Schofield then quickly transferred his command post to nearby Fort Granger. The Battle of Franklin was launched shortly thereafter at 4:00 PM.

The Truett House is today privately owned and is not open to the public.

TURNER'S MISSISSIPPI BATTERY (CSA): This Rebel battery fought at the Battle of Franklin in Hoxton's Battalion, Cheatham's Corps Artillery, C.S. Army of Tennessee.

TWELFTH INDIANA CAVALRY (USA): This Yankee cavalry regiment fought at the Battle of Franklin in Johnson's Second Brigade, Knipe's Seventh Division, Wilson's Cavalry Corps.

TWELFTH KENTUCKY (USA): This Yankee infantry regiment fought at the Battle of Franklin in Reilly's First Brigade, Cox's Third Division, Twenty-third U.S. Army Corps.

TWELFTH KENTUCKY CAVALRY (CSA): This Rebel cavalry regiment fought at the Battle of Franklin in Crossland's Brigade, Buford's Division, Forrest's Cavalry Corps, C.S. Army of Tennessee.

TWELFTH KENTUCKY MOUNTED INFANTRY (CSA): This Rebel unit fought at the Battle of Franklin in Crossland's Brigade, Buford's Division, Forrest's Cavalry Corps, C.S. Army of Tennessee.

TWELFTH LOUISIANA (CSA): This Rebel infantry regiment fought at the Battle of Franklin in Scott's Brigade, Loring's Division, Stewart's Corps, C.S. Army of Tennessee.

TWELFTH MISSOURI CAVALRY (USA): This Yankee cavalry regiment fought at the Battle of Franklin in Stewart's First Brigade, Hatch's Fifth Division, Wilson's Cavalry Corps.

TWELFTH TENNESSEE (CSA): This Rebel infantry regiment fought at the Battle of Franklin in Vaughan's Brigade, Brown's Division, Cheatham's Corps, C.S. Army of Tennessee.

TWELFTH TENNESSEE CAVALRY (CSA): This Rebel cavalry regiment fought at the Battle of Franklin in Rucker's Brigade, Chalmers' Division, Forrest's Cavalry Corps, C.S. Army of Tennessee.

TWELFTH TENNESSEE CAVALRY (USA): This Yankee cavalry regiment fought at the Battle of Franklin in Coon's Second Brigade, Hatch's Fifth Division, Wilson's Cavalry Corps.

TWENTIETH ALABAMA (CSA): This Rebel infantry regiment fought at the Battle of Franklin in Pettus' Brigade, Stevenson's Division, Lee's Corps, C.S. Army of Tennessee.

TWENTIETH LOUISIANA (CSA): This Rebel infantry regiment fought at the Battle of Franklin in Gibson's Brigade, Clayton's Division, Lee's Corps, C.S. Army of Tennessee.

TWENTIETH MISSISSIPPI (CSA): This Rebel infantry regiment fought at the Battle of Franklin in Adams' Brigade, Loring's Division, Stewart's Corps, C.S. Army of Tennessee.

TWENTIETH OHIO BATTERY (USA): This Yankee artillery unit fought at the Battle of Franklin in the Fourth U.S. Army Corps Artillery.

TWENTIETH TENNESSEE (CSA): This Rebel infantry regiment fought at the Battle of Franklin in Tyler's Brigade, Bate's Division, Cheatham's Corps, C.S. Army of Tennessee.

TWENTIETH TENNESSEE CAVALRY (CSA): This Rebel cavalry regiment fought at the Battle of Franklin in Bell's Brigade, Buford's Division, Forrest's Cavalry Corps, C.S. Army of Tennessee.

TWENTY-EIGHTH ALABAMA (CSA): This Rebel infantry regiment fought at the Battle of Franklin in Manigault's Brigade, Johnson's Division, Lee's Corps, C.S. Army of Tennessee.

TWENTY-EIGHTH KENTUCKY (USA): This Yankee infantry regiment fought at the Battle of Franklin in Lane's Second Brigade, Wagner's Second Division, Fourth U.S. Army Corps.

TWENTY-EIGHTH MISSISSIPPI CAVALRY (CSA): This Rebel cavalry regiment fought at the Battle of Franklin in Armstrong's Brigade, Jackson's Division, Forrest's Cavalry Corps, C.S. Army of Tennessee.

TWENTY-EIGHTH TENNESSEE (CSA): This Rebel infantry regiment fought at the Battle of Franklin in Maney's Brigade, Brown's Division, Cheatham's Corps, C.S. Army of Tennessee.

TWENTY-FIFTH ALABAMA (CSA): This Rebel infantry regiment fought at the Battle of Franklin in Deas' Brigade, Johnson's Division, Lee's Corps, C.S. Army of Tennessee.

TWENTY-FIFTH ARKANSAS (CSA): This Rebel infantry regiment fought at the Battle of Franklin in Reynolds' Brigade, Walthall's Division, Stewart's Corps, C.S. Army of Tennessee.

TWENTY-FIFTH GEORGIA (CSA): This Rebel infantry regiment fought at the Battle of Franklin in Jackson's Brigade, Bate's Division, Cheatham's Corps, C.S. Army of Tennessee.

TWENTY-FIFTH INDIANA BATTERY (USA): This Yankee artillery unit fought at the Battle of Franklin in the Fourth U.S. Army Corps Artillery.

TWENTY-FIFTH LOUISIANA (CSA): This Rebel infantry regiment fought at the Battle of Franklin in Gibson's Brigade, Clayton's Division, Lee's Corps, C.S. Army of Tennessee.

TWENTY-FIFTH MICHIGAN (USA): This Yankee infantry regiment, though attached to Ruger's Second Division, Twenty-third U.S. Army Corps, was with Cooper's Brigade—which was on detached duty at the time of the Battle of Franklin. It was thus not present or involved in the fighting.

TWENTY-FIFTH TEXAS CAVALRY - DISMOUNTED (CSA): This Rebel unit fought at the Battle of Franklin in Granbury's Brigade, Cleburne's Division, Cheatham's Corps, C.S. Army of Tennessee.

TWENTY-FIRST ILLINOIS (USA): This Yankee infantry regiment fought at the Battle of Franklin in Kirby's First Brigade, Kimball's First Division, Fourth U.S. Army Corps.

TWENTY-FIRST KENTUCKY (USA): This Yankee infantry regiment fought at the Battle of Franklin in Whitaker's Second Brigade, Kimball's First Division, Fourth U.S. Army Corps.

TWENTY-FIRST TENNESSEE CAVALRY (CSA): This Rebel cavalry regiment fought at the Battle of Franklin in Bell's Brigade, Buford's Division, Forrest's Cavalry Corps, C.S. Army of Tennessee.

TWENTY-FOURTH ALABAMA (CSA): This Rebel infantry regiment fought at the Battle of Franklin in Manigault's Brigade, Johnson's Division, Lee's Corps, C.S. Army of Tennessee.

TWENTY-FOURTH ARKANSAS (CSA): This infantry regiment fought at the Battle of Franklin in Govan's Brigade, Cleburne's Division, Cheatham's Corps, C.S. Army of Tennessee.

TWENTY-FOURTH GEORGIA (CSA): This Rebel infantry regiment fought at the Battle of Franklin in Cummings'

Brigade, Stevenson's Division, Lee's Corps, C.S. Army of Tennessee.

TWENTY-FOURTH MISSISSIPPI (CSA): This Rebel infantry regiment fought at the Battle of Franklin in Brantley's Brigade, Johnson's Division, Lee's Corps, C.S. Army of Tennessee.

TWENTY-FOURTH MISSOURI (USA): This Yankee infantry regiment fought at the Battle of Franklin in Moore's Second Brigade, Ruger's Second Division, Twenty-third U.S. Army Corps.

TWENTY-FOURTH SOUTH CAROLINA (CSA): This Rebel infantry regiment fought at the Battle of Franklin in Gist's Brigade, Brown's Division, Cheatham's Corps, C.S. Army of Tennessee.

TWENTY-FOURTH TENNESSEE (CSA): This Rebel infantry regiment fought at the Battle of Franklin in Strahl's Brigade, Brown's Division, Cheatham's Corps, C.S. Army of Tennessee.

TWENTY-FOURTH TEXAS CAVALRY - DISMOUNTED (CSA): This Rebel unit fought at the Battle of Franklin in Granbury's Brigade, Cleburne's Division, Cheatham's Corps, C.S. Army of Tennessee.

TWENTY-FOURTH WISCONSIN (USA): This Yankee infantry regiment fought at the Battle of Franklin in Opdycke's First Brigade, Wagner's Second Division, Fourth U.S. Army Corps.

TWENTY-NINTH ALABAMA (CSA): This Rebel infantry regiment fought at the Battle of Franklin in Cantley's Brigade, Walthall's Division, Stewart's Corps, C.S. Army of Tennessee.

TWENTY-NINTH GEORGIA (CSA): This Rebel infantry regiment fought at the Battle of Franklin in Jackson's Brigade, Bate's Division, Cheatham's Corps, C.S. Army of Tennessee.

TWENTY-NINTH MISSISSIPPI (CSA): This Rebel infantry regiment fought at the Battle of Franklin in Brantley's Brigade, Johnson's Division, Lee's Corps, C.S. Army of Tennessee.

TWENTY-NINTH NORTH CAROLINA (CSA): This Rebel infantry regiment served in Ector's Brigade, French's Division, Stewart's Corps, C.S. Army of Tennessee.

Ector's Brigade was at Franklin, Tennessee, during the Battle of Franklin. However, it did not participate in the battle as it was on detached duty at the time.

TWENTY-NINTH TENNESSEE (CSA): This Rebel infantry regiment fought at the Battle of Franklin in Vaughan's Brigade, Brown's Division, Cheatham's Corps, C.S. Army of Tennessee.

TWENTY-SECOND ALABAMA (CSA): This Rebel infantry regiment fought at the Battle of Franklin in Deas' Brigade, Johnson's Division, Lee's Corps, C.S. Army of Tennessee.

TWENTY-SECOND MISSISSIPPI (CSA): This Rebel infantry regiment fought at the Battle of Franklin in Featherston's Brigade, Loring's Division, Stewart's Corps, C.S. Army of Tennessee.

TWENTY-SEVENTH ALABAMA (CSA): This Rebel infantry regiment fought at the Battle of Franklin in Scott's Brigade, Loring's Division, Stewart's Corps, C.S. Army of Tennessee.

TWENTY-SEVENTH MISSISSIPPI (CSA): This Rebel infantry regiment fought at the Battle of Franklin in Brantley's Brigade, Johnson's Division, Lee's Corps, C.S. Army of Tennessee.

TWENTY-SEVENTH TENNESSEE (CSA): This Rebel infantry regiment fought at the Battle of Franklin in Maney's Brigade, Brown's Division, Cheatham's Corps, C.S. Army of Tennessee.

TWENTY-SIXTH ALABAMA (CSA): This Rebel infantry regiment fought at the Battle of Franklin in Cantley's Brigade, Walthall's Division, Stewart's Corps, C.S. Army of Tennessee.

TWENTY-SIXTH KENTUCKY (USA): This Yankee infantry regiment, though attached to Ruger's Second Division, Twenty-third U.S. Army Corps, was with Cooper's

Brigade—which was on detached duty at the time of the Battle of Franklin. It was thus not present or involved in the fighting.

TWENTY-SIXTH OHIO (USA): This Yankee infantry regiment fought at the Battle of Franklin in Lane's Second Brigade, Wagner's Second Division, Fourth U.S. Army Corps.

TWENTY-THIRD ALABAMA (CSA): This Rebel infantry regiment fought at the Battle of Franklin in Pettus' Brigade, Stevenson's Division, Lee's Corps, C.S. Army of Tennessee.

TWENTY-THIRD ARMY CORPS (USA): The Twenty-third, known at one point as the Army of the Ohio, was normally led by Yankee Major General John McAllister Schofield. At the Battle of Franklin, however, Schofield had been put in charge of both the Twenty-third U.S. Army Corps and the Fourth U.S. Army Corps. Thus, at Franklin the Twenty-third was temporarily commanded by Yankee Brigadier General Jacob Dolson Cox. It was comprised of Ruger's Second Division and Cox's Third Division.

TWENTY-THIRD INDIANA BATTERY (USA): This Yankee artillery unit fought at the Battle of Franklin in Cox's Third Division, Twenty-third U.S. Army Corps.

TWENTY-THIRD KENTUCKY (USA): This Yankee infantry regiment fought at the Battle of Franklin in Whitaker's Second Brigade, Kimball's First Division, Fourth U.S. Army Corps.

TWENTY-THIRD MICHIGAN (USA): This Yankee infantry regiment fought at the Battle of Franklin in Moore's Second Brigade, Ruger's Second Division, Twenty-third U.S. Army Corps.

TWENTY-THIRD MISSISSIPPI (CSA): This Rebel infantry regiment fought at the Battle of Franklin in Adams' Brigade, Loring's Division, Stewart's Corps, C.S. Army of Tennessee.

TYLER'S BRIGADE (CSA): This Rebel brigade was present at the Battle of Franklin, and was led by Confederate Brigadier General Thomas Benton Smith—who was wounded and captured two weeks later at the Battle of Nashville. The unit is thus sometimes called Smith's Brigade.

Tyler's Brigade was comprised of the Thirty-seventh Georgia, Fourth Georgia Battalion Sharpshooters, Second Tennessee, Tenth Tennessee, Twentieth Tennessee, and Thirty-seventh Tennessee.

UNION, THE: The Union, otherwise known as the United States of America, was created by the Founding Fathers to be what President Thomas Jefferson called a "voluntary union of friendly states." Inherent in this phrase is the guarantee of the states' rights of accession and secession, as silently promised in the Ninth and Tenth Amendments of the U.S. Constitution.

Abraham Lincoln claimed he waged war against the South to "preserve the Union." Yet his only accomplishment was to force the states into an involuntary Union at the tip of a gun barrel. Clearly this violated the Founders' intention. In short, Lincoln destroyed the Union, making his war illegal and he himself a war criminal.

UNITED DAUGHTERS OF THE CONFEDERACY: Known by its members as the UDC, it is the oldest patriotic organization in the U.S. Its roots are associated with the Daughters of the Confederacy (DOC) in Missouri and the Ladies' Auxiliary of the Confederate Soldiers Home in Tennessee, both which were organized by 1890.

Shortly thereafter, on September 10, 1894, Mrs. Caroline Meriwether Goodlett of Tennessee and Mrs. Anna Davenport Raines of Georgia founded the National Association of the Daughters of the Confederacy at Nashville, Tennessee. In 1895, at Atlanta, Georgia, the name was changed to the United Daughters of the Confederacy, and on July 18, 1919, it was incorporated under the laws of the District of Columbia.

According to the UDC, membership is open to females sixteen years of age or older, who are "blood descendants, lineal or collateral, of men and women who served honorably in the Army, Navy or Civil Service of the Confederate States of America, or gave Material Aid to the Cause."

"Objectives of the organization are Historical, Educational, Benevolent, Memorial and Patriotic:

- "To collect and preserve the material necessary for a truthful history of the War Between the States and to protect, preserve, and mark the places made historic by Confederate valor.
- "To assist descendants of worthy Confederates in securing a proper education.
- "To fulfill the sacred duty of benevolence toward the survivor of the War and those dependent upon them.
- "To honor the memory of those who served and those who fell in the service of the Confederate States of America.
- "To record the part played during the War by Southern women, including their patient endurance of hardship, their patriotic devotion during the struggle, and their untiring efforts during the post-War reconstruction of the South.
- "To cherish the ties of friendship among the members of the Organization."

The UDC's official symbol is the Confederacy's First National Flag ("Stars and Bars"). Their motto is: "Love, Live, Pray, Think, Dare."

VAUGHAN'S BRIGADE (CSA): This Rebel infantry brigade fought at the Battle of Franklin in Brown's Division, Cheatham's Corps, C.S. Army of Tennessee.

Led by Confederate Brigadier General George Washington Gordon, Vaughan's Brigade was sometimes known as Gordon's Brigade, and was comprised of the Eleventh Tennessee, Twelfth Tennessee, Thirteenth Tennessee, Twenty-ninth Tennessee, Forty-seventh Tennessee, Fifty-first Tennessee, Fifty-second Tennessee, and One hundred fifty-fourth Tennessee.

After General Gordon was captured at Franklin, the brigade was taken over by Confederate Colonel William M. Watkins.

VISITORS CENTER: This small building, located on East Main Street, Franklin, Tennessee, was constructed in 1817 by Dr. Daniel McPhail, hence it is sometimes known as "McPhail's Office."

At the time of the Battle of Franklin it was being used as a medical office by Franklin resident Dr. Daniel Cliffe, who—until he switched his allegiance to the Union—had earlier served as Confederate General Felix K. Zollicoffer's brigade surgeon.

On the morning of November 30, 1864, Yankee General John M. Schofield took over the office as his temporary headquarters (no doubt with Union supporter Cliffe's permission).

By early afternoon Schofield's couriers had informed him that Confederate General John Bell Hood was marching his army into Franklin from the south. Schofield then quickly moved his headquarters to the Truett House, located about a mile north of Cliffe's office building.

Around 4:00 PM, after learning that Hood had actually launched an attack against U.S.

troops in Franklin, Schofield's command post was transferred to nearby Fort Granger.

WAGNER, GEORGE DAY (USA): Wagner was born September 22, 1829, in Ross County, Ohio, but was raised in Warren County, Indiana. In 1856 he served as a state representative, and in 1858 he served as a state senator.

With the outbreak of Lincoln's War, Wagner sided with the North and against the Constitution, enlisting in the U.S. army, where he was commissioned colonel of the Fifteenth Indiana Infantry in the Summer of 1861. He went on to fight in numerous battles, including Shiloh, Murfreesboro, Perryville, Chickamauga, and Atlanta.

At the Battle of Franklin he commanded his own unit: the Second Division, Fourth U.S. Army Corps. It was here, on November 30, 1864, that Wagner destroyed his military career by disobeying orders: when his superior Yankee General Jacob D. Cox commanded him to withdraw his soldiers from an indefensible position, he refused. He and his men were soon overrun by Confederate troops who broke through the Union line, resulting in numerous Federal casualties.

A few days later, December 9, Wagner was relieved of duty, and was honorably mustered out of service August 24, 1865.

His wife passed away that same year, after which he opened a law office in Williamsport, Indiana. He also served (for a second time) as president of the State Agricultural Society until his sudden death February 13, 1869, at Indianapolis, Indiana. He was buried in Armstrong Chapel Cemetery, Green Hill, Warren County, Indiana.

WAGNER'S SECOND DIVISION (USA): This Yankee division, named after U.S. Brigadier General George Day Wagner, served in the Fourth U.S. Army Corps at the Battle of Franklin. It was comprised of

Opdycke's First Brigade, Lane's Second Brigade, and Bradley's Third Brigade.

WALTHALL, EDWARD CARY (CSA): The son of Barrett White Walthall and Sarah Southall, Walthall was born April 4, 1831, at Richmond, Virginia. He was raised at Holly Springs, Mississippi, studied law, and served two terms as district attorney beginning in 1856.

With the start of Lincoln's War, Walthall sided with the South and the Constitution, after which he was commissioned lieutenant colonel of the Fifteenth Mississippi Regiment. He went on to fight at such battles as Mill Springs, Chickamauga, Chattanooga, and Atlanta.

At the Battle of Franklin, now a major general, he led his own unit: Walthall's Division, Stewart's Corps, C.S. Army of Tennessee. Here he had two horses shot out from under him.

After the Battle of Nashville two weeks later, Walthall was with Hood and the Army of Tennessee from its retreat into Mississippi to its surrender in the Spring of 1865.

After the War he returned to his legal practice and joined in the fight to resist the barbaric, illegal, and unjust Northern policies known collectively by the misnomer "Reconstruction."

Walthall served out the remainder of his days as a conservative (then known as a Democrat) U.S. senator, passing away April 21, 1898, at Washington, D.C. He was buried in Hillcrest Cemetery, Holly Springs, Marshall County, Mississippi.

WALTHALL'S DIVISION (CSA): This Rebel division, named after Confederate General Edward Cary Walthall, was present at the Battle of Franklin. It was comprised of Quarles' Brigade, Cantley's Brigade, and Reynolds' Brigade.

WAR BETWEEN THE STATES: See War for Southern Independence.

WAR FOR SOUTHERN INDEPENDENCE: In the four years between April 1861 and April 1865, America inflicted upon itself not only its most bloody conflict, but certainly one of the most senseless and savage wars the world has ever known.

Southern historians

estimate that some 2 million Southerners alone (both white and black) died in America's great monument to political conniving, greed, stupidity, arrogance, lawlessness, insanity, Northern tyranny, and the romanticization of war.

It has been estimated that some 10,000 battles and skirmishes were fought and that between both armies, America suffered some 1 million military casualties overall (this includes dead, wounded captured, missing, and deserters).

On the Confederate side alone, a Rebel soldier was, on average, wounded or struck down with disease six times while serving out his term. And with no knowledge of hygiene and sanitation, army surgeons were just as likely to cripple, and even kill, as were bullets, knives, and cannon balls. Little wonder that for every soldier injured, five became ill, or that for every soldier who perished in battle, three died from disease.

Today we cringe at the news of the death of a single American soldier. Compare this with the War for Southern Independence, where soldiers alone (not counting civilians) died at a rate of nearly 500 a day for four years.

We must also consider that, in addition, as many as 1 million civilians may have died—mostly Southern women, children, and seniors, at the hands of Yankee generals like Sherman and Sheridan.

Using a total of 3 million total deaths (2 million Southerners, 1 million Northerners) as a rough estimate then, this would mean that on both sides a staggering 2,054 individuals died each day during the War. In total, more people died in the War for Southern Independence than in all of America's wars combined, from the Revolutionary War (1775-1783) to the Vietnam War (1946-1975).

Another way of understanding these deaths is to look at percentages. The 3 million Americans who died in the "Civil War" represented one tenth of the total U.S. population of 30 million at the time. One tenth of today's U.S. population of 300 million is 30 million. Thus the modern equivalent of those who died in Lincoln's War would today be 30 million Americans!

Why were so many so willing to sacrifice so much over

so little?

There is no simple answer, and indeed one can point to many causes of the War. Whatever they were, one result was the devastating Battle of Franklin, the topic of this encyclopedia. Therefore to understand Franklin, we need to look inside the greater War itself.

Thousands of books have been written on what the North has always incorrectly called the "Civil War," most brimming with falsehoods, distortions, and outright lies, in a transparent attempt to justify the conflict. They fail to convince though. Most have been penned by the descendants of the Northern victors, individuals nurtured by generations of both pro-Northern mythology and anti-Southern prejudice.

Thankfully, today more and more writers, historians, and scholars are correcting this imbalance with books that view the War from the Southern perspective. The truth is not attractive, but it must be examined.

When the original thirteen American colonies seceded from Britain in the 1770s, they were operating under principles laid down in the Declaration of Independence, which guarantee the right of self-determination. Ninety years later, the Southern states, using the same legal basis, also attempted to separate themselves from a government they considered too controlling and powerful. They were not only blocked, however, but were also militarily attacked, defeated, and humiliated by their American brothers and sisters in the North. Why?

The simplest, and therefore the most correct, answer is economics. In the mid-1800s, just as is true today, the South was the agricultural bread basket of the U.S., producing more for less than any other region of the country. It also possessed seaports that were open year round (due to the warm climate), whose ships were full of products produced by some 3.5 million servants. If the South seceded and formed its own nation, the North would lose the enormous wealth produced by the South's agrarian economy. (To this day, the South is home to one fourth of America's population, but produces one third of the nation's goods and services at lower wages, while paying higher taxes than most of the rest of America.)

But war, especially upon a fellow citizen, can never be justified over commercial interests alone. Lincoln had to fabricate a reason for taking the offensive and oppressing the South. The notion he invented was politically brilliant. Unfortunately for America, it was also morally, legally, and ethically wrong.

Lincoln's justification for going to war against his own countrymen was elementary: the United States (the Union) could not survive without the Southern states. And so on April 12, 1861, in an attempt to "preserve the Union," he ordered a fake provision ship to Fort Sumter in an overt attempt to provoke the South into firing the first shot. The conniving plot worked.

What Lincoln did not tell his constituents was that a political Union like the U.S. was not and could never be destroyed by the secession of any of its states. History has shown that individual states of nations all over the world have seceded, not only without bloodshed, but also without causing any harm to their former original parent government. The secession of states is recorded as early as ancient Greece and Rome, yet neither nation perished. Rather they continued to grow in strength and authority, each becoming world dominating superpowers in their own right, nations that lasted for centuries.

In more recent times, Norway broke away from Sweden, Portugal seceded from Spain, and Ireland separated from England. In every case, each nation, both old and new, has continued to flourish and prosper into the present day.

America itself also seceded from England, provoking the American Revolutionary War. Neither England or America was destroyed, and both remain powerful and influential Western nations, leading the world in education, medicine, and economics.

All of this was lost on most Victorian Americans, however. Lincoln's charismatic oratory about "preserving the Union" had blinded them to the truth; namely, that the secession of the South would in no way hurt let alone demolish the U.S., as he repeatedly claimed. And so the lie was promulgated and the War went on, just as the liberal Yankee president had planned it.

Over the next two years,

hundreds of thousands died and entire Southern towns and cities were wiped out. Millions of dollars were poured into weaponry, uniforms, and food, and in the process entire branches of the nation's family trees were cut off, becoming extinct.

Meanwhile, Lincoln had crowned himself king, ruling America with the iron fist of an ancient Roman Emperor. In the process he broke countless laws (e.g., suspending the right of *habeas corpus* and closing down over 300 newspapers that disagreed with him), while committing innumerable war crimes (e.g., sanctioning a scorched-earth policy across the South and imprisoning, torturing, and hanging thousands of Northern war protestors).

Though Lincoln would die at the hand of an assassin's bullet at the start of his second term, in the end the socialistic president was able to achieve his primary objectives before his death: install big government in Washington, temporarily suppress states' rights sentiment in the South, and begin the northernization process of Dixie.

The War for Southern Independence did not end April 9, 1865, with Lee's surrender at Appomattox Court House, Virginia. It continues to this day, now not only a struggle for self-government and personal freedom, but a fight to preserve the Truth about an illegal and needless war, instigated by one of the most ruthless, devilish, and autocratic dictators the world has even known: Abraham Lincoln.

And what is that Truth? It is that, despite the needless deaths of some 3 million Americans, Lincoln did not "preserve the Union." By using physical coercion to force the states into an involuntary compact, the opposite of the what the Founding Fathers intended, he actually destroyed the Union. Since 1865 the United States has indeed become, as Horace Greeley lamented, "a republic . . . whereof one section is pinned to the residue with bayonets."

WATKINS, ELIHU P. (CSA): Confederate Colonel Watkins led Cummings' Brigade at the Battle of Franklin. (Cummings' Brigade is thus sometimes referred to as Watkins' Brigade.)

WATKINS, SAMUEL RUSH (CSA): Best known as Sam R. Watkins, he was born June 26, 1839, at Mount Pleasant, Maury

County, Tennessee. After his schooling at nearby Jackson College, Columbia, Tennessee, he worked as store clerk up to the start of Lincoln's War—at which time he sided with the South and the Constitution.

Shortly after his enlistment in the Confederate army he was transferred to Company H of the First Tennessee Infantry, better known as the "Maury Grays."

He went on to fight at such battles as Chickamauga, Chattanooga, Corinth, Shelbyville, Missionary Ridge, Shiloh, Atlanta, Jonesboro, Murfreesboro, Franklin, and Nashville. He was one of only seven of the 120 original Maury Grays who survived the War.

After the conflict he married his longtime sweetheart Virginia "Jennie" Mayes, and opened a store in Columbia, Tennessee. Nearly twenty years later, in 1882, he published his wartime memoirs entitled: *"Co. Aytch," Maury Grays, First Tennessee Regiment; or, A Side Show of the Big Show*—still one of the most widely read Confederate histories ever written.

As occurred with Confederate Generals Robert E. Lee, Nathan Bedford Forrest, and so many other great Southern soldiers, the incredible stress of Lincoln's War eventually caught up with Watkins. He passed away July 20, 1901, at his home in the Ashwood community near Mount Pleasant, Tennessee. He was buried in the Zion Presbyterian Church Cemetery just outside Columbia, Tennessee.

WATKINS' BRIGADE (CSA): See Cummings' Brigade.

WATKINS, WILLIAM M. (CSA): Confederate Colonel Watkins took over command of Vaughan's Brigade after its leader Brigadier General George Washington Gordon was captured at the Battle of Franklin.

WATTERS, ZACHARIAH L. (CSA): Confederate Lieutenant Colonel Watters took over command of Gist's Brigade after its leader Brigadier General States Rights Gist was killed in action at the Battle of Franklin.

WEIR, JOHN (CSA): Confederate Colonel Weir led the Fifth Mississippi Infantry at the Battle of Franklin, where he was wounded in action.

WHITAKER, WALTER CHILES (USA): Whitaker was born August 8, 1823, at Shelbyville, Kentucky. He studied law, fought in the Mexican-American War, and served as a liberal state representative.

He was married twice: to Elizabeth Dickinson and Henrietta Ormsby, with whom he bore at least ten known children combined.

With the start of Lincoln's War, he sided with the North and against the Constitution, joining the U.S. army as a colonel of the Union's Sixth Kentucky Infantry. He went on to fight at such battles as Shiloh, Murfreesboro, Chickamauga, Chattanooga, Atlanta, and Nashville.

At the Battle of Franklin he led his own Yankee unit: the Second Brigade, Kimball's First Division, Fourth U.S. Army Corps. He left military service in August 1865, having been brevetted major general.

After the War the Freemason returned to his law practice at Louisville, Kentucky, where he operated a prosperous farm.

According to some sources, at this time he became known as a drinker with psychological problems. Indeed, Whitaker spent considerable time in an institute for the mentally insane.

He passed away July 9, 1887, at Lyndon, Kentucky, and was buried in Grove Hill Cemetery, Shelbyville, Shelby County, Kentucky.

WHITAKER'S SECOND BRIGADE (USA): This Yankee infantry brigade fought at the Battle of Franklin in Kimball's First Division, Fourth U.S. Army Corps.

Named after U.S. Brigadier General Walter Chiles Whitaker, it was comprised of the Ninety-sixth Illinois, One hundred fifteenth Illinois, Thirty-fifth Indiana, Twenty-first Kentucky, Twenty-third Kentucky, Forty-fifth Ohio, and Fifty-first Ohio.

WILLIAM MCKISSACK HOUSE: Begun about 1840 and completed in 1845 by William McKissack of North Carolina (the father of Jessie Helen McKissack), this lovely home was the first brick house in Spring Hill, Maury County, Tennessee.

Though the Battle of Franklin was a dozen miles to the

north of the McKissack home, hearing the distant booming cannon, some twenty-five residents of Spring Hill fled to the house for safety, fearing for their lives.

On November 28, 1864, one day prior to the Battle of Spring Hill and two days prior to the Battle of Franklin, Yankee General John M. Schofield stopped at the William McKissack house, which he used as his temporary headquarters. Thinking he would shortly be captured by the Confederates, he left his pistol and sword with the family, fearing they would be taken from him.

After the Battle of Nashville, Schofield returned to the McKissack House to pick up his weapons. Hood and the Army of Tennessee were by now in full retreat southward into Alabama and Mississippi.

WILLIAMS, SAMUEL C. (CSA): Confederate Lieutenant Colonel Williams commanded Stewart's Corps Artillery at the Battle of Franklin.

WILLIAMSON COUNTY COURTHOUSE: The current courthouse, located in the heart of Franklin, Tennessee, is the county's third. Construction was completed in 1858, making it one of seven of the state's antebellum courthouses. According to historical records, its four front iron columns were forged at Fernvale, Tennessee, and cast at a foundry in Franklin.

During the Battle of Franklin, Yankee troops illegally used the courthouse as one of several Union headquarters. After the conflict the building became one of the town's forty-one Confederate field hospitals.

WILLIAMSON COUNTY, TENNESSEE: This 584 square mile administrative district is located in Middle Tennessee, with the city of Franklin serving as the county seat. It was named after North Carolinian and U.S. Constitution signatory Hugh Williamson.

With a current population of about 200,000, it began as the prehistoric home for a number of Native-American peoples, including the Shawnee, Chickasaw, Creek, Choctaw, and Cherokee.

During the War for Southern Independence, Williamson County hosted numerous battles and skirmishes, including the Battles of Franklin I,

Franklin II (the subject of this book), Franklin III, Brentwood, and Thompson's Station.

With the ever increasing arrival of transplanted Yankees, as well as the takeover of the local government, media, and historic sites by scallywags and anti-South Northerners (carpetbaggers), Williamson County is slowly but surely discarding her once ardent pride in her beautiful Southern history and Confederate heritage.

It is hoped that future generations of Williamson County residents—wherever they come from—will embrace the region's Southernness rather than reject it, and that the county's *true* history will be preserved instead of suppressed, as it is at present. This book is but one small effort toward that goal.

WILLIAM WHITE HOUSE: Confederate General States Rights Gist's body was first taken to this Franklin, Tennessee, home (on present day Boyd Mill Pike) after he was killed at the Battle of Franklin. He was temporarily buried here, after which his servant "Uncle" Wiley Howard took his remains back to the Gist family plantation in South Carolina.

WILSON, JAMES HARRISON (USA): Wilson was born September 2, 1837, at Shawneetown, Illinois. Graduating from West Point in 1860 he sided with the North and against the Constitution at the start of Lincoln's War.

He spent the first few years of the conflict serving as a topographical engineer in the Department of the South. He then served as an aide-de-camp to Union General George B. McClellan, fighting at both South Mountain and Sharpsburg. He was soon appointed a staff lieutenant colonel under Union General Ulysses S. Grant.

In the early Winter of 1864 he was made chief of the cavalry bureau at Washington, D.C. At the Battle of Franklin Wilson commanded his own cavalry corps, wreaking devastation on Confederate General John Bell Hood and the Army of Tennessee.

After the Battle of Nashville, Wilson went on to defeat Confederate General Nathan Bedford Forrest at the Battle of Selma, the one and only time the magnificent Rebel chieftain was ever beaten during the entire War while leading his own command.

After the War Wilson continued with his service in the U.S. military, finally leaving in 1870 with an honorable discharge requested by himself.

In 1883 he moved to Wilmington, Delaware, where he engaged in numerous business ventures. In 1898 he fought in the Spanish-American War, then went to China where he fought in the Boxer Rebellion. At the coronation of England's King Edward VII in 1902, Wilson represented U.S. President Theodore Roosevelt.

Wilson passed away at Wilmington, Delaware, February 23, 1925, one of the longest living of the "Civil War" generals. He was buried in the city's Old Swedes Churchyard.

WILSON, JOHN A. (CSA): Confederate Colonel Wilson led the Twenty-fourth Tennessee Infantry at the Battle of Franklin, where he was wounded in action.

WILSON'S CAVALRY CORPS (USA): This Yankee cavalry corps fought at the Battle of Franklin under the Twenty-third U.S. Army Corps and the Fourth U.S. Army Corps.

Named after its commander U.S. Major General James Harrison Wilson, it was comprised of McCook's First Division, Hatch's Fifth Division, Johnson's Sixth Division, and Knipe's Seventh Division.

WINDER, CAROLINE ELIZABETH: Winder (whose surname rhymes with cinder), was born September 9, 1829, in either Mississippi or Louisiana. Known by her family and friends as "Carrie," she was the daughter of sugar plantation owner Colonel Van Perkins Winder Sr. and Martha Anne Grundy—the daughter of celebrated Tennessee statesman, senator, and lawyer Felix Grundy.

In 1848 Carrie married John W. McGavock, the son of Randal McGavock, founder of Franklin's Carnton Plantation. After their marriage at her parents' home, Ducros Plantation, Houma, Terrebonne Parish, Louisiana, the couple moved into Carnton permanently, where they bore five children—the first three dying before reaching the age of fourteen.

November 30, 1864, brought the Battle of Franklin to Carnton's front doorstep. Winder's husband John, now a Confederate colonel, had offered their plantation as a Rebel field hospital, and during and after the battle hundreds of wounded and dying men were brought into the mansion and also into the yards.

As the couple's two surviving children, Hattie and her younger brother Winder, hid in their parents' bedroom upstairs (the only room off limits to the military), Colonel John and Carrie, along with their loyal black servant Maria Reddick and her son Theopolis, helped all they could. Carrie in particular showed what Southern women are made of.

Confederate Captain William D. Gale, who was present at Carnton at the time (and who, in a few short weeks, would act as assistant adjutant general of Stewart's Corps at the Battle of Nashville), penned one of the most memorable accounts of the conditions at the plantation on Wednesday, November 30, and on Thursday, December 1. In it he included a description of Carrie's sterling humanitarianism. Mrs. McGavock's mansion, Gale wrote,

"was in the rear of our line. The house is one of the large old-fashioned houses of the better class in Tennessee, two stories high, with many rooms. . . . This was taken as a hospital, and the wounded, in their hundreds, were brought to it during the battle, and all the night after. Every room was filled, every bed had two poor, bleeding fellows, every spare space, niche, and corner under the stairs, in the hall, everywhere—but one room for her family.

"And when the noble old house could hold no more, the yard was appropriated until the wounded and the dead filled that, and all were not yet provided for.

"Our doctors were deficient in bandages, and she began by giving her old linen, then her towels and napkins, then her sheets and tablecloths, then her husband's shirts and her own undergarments.

"During all this time the surgeons plied their dreadful work amid the sighs and moans and death rattle. Yet, amid it all, this noble woman . . . was very active and constantly at work. During all the night neither she nor any of the household slept, but dispensed tea and coffee and such stimulants as she had, and that, too, with her own hands. . . . She walked from room to room, from man to man, her skirts stained in blood, the incarnation of pity and mercy. Is it strange that all who were there praise and call her blessed?"

Carrie personally nursed some of the wounded at Carnton for long periods, such as General William Andrew Quarles, who remained at the plantation for two months. Little wonder that Confederate soldiers referred to Carrie as an "Angel of Mercy."

But her strong sense of compassion and concern for the less fortunate did not begin with Lincoln's War.

Far earlier she was known to periodically take in two or three orphans from the orphanage in New Orleans to act as household servants at Carnton. She would raise them at the Mansion, educate them, and give them religious training, then later pay to find them suitable homes and employment.

For her unselfish service to the Confederacy, kind heart, Christ-like ways, loving generous nature, and lifelong faithfulness to her husband, children, and relatives, she would later be called "the Good Samaritan of Williamson County," putting to shame all of the mean-spirited attacks on her character by heartless Northerners and cruel New South scallywags that continue to this day.

Following is an early article that mentions Carrie and her many wonderful attributes:

"CHRISTMAS OF THE LONG AGO IN THE GOOD COUNTY OF WILLIAMSON, by Anna Bland [name of newspaper and date of publication unknown]:

"Mrs. McGavock, member of one of the most prominent and, at one time, wealthiest families of this section, was mistress of the beautiful and historic Carnton estate, situated near Franklin. She was particularly noted for her charity, and reared in her own home a number of orphan children. It is said that she once gave shelter at one time to seven little waifs. Mrs. McGavock was devoted to the Confederate cause, and did a great deal for its soldiers. The two acres occupied by the Confederate cemetery are on the original McGavock place, and were given by Carnton's mistress and Colonel McGavock for the purpose."

Carrie passed away February 22, 1905, at her daughter Hattie's house, "Windermere" (located across the street from Carnton), and was buried in the McGavock Family Cemetery in Carnton's backyard. Her eulogy, according to local legend, was read by Maria Reddick, one of the McGavocks' many loyal former black servants.

WINSTEAD HILL: This small prominence, located at Franklin, Tennessee's southern end, served as Confederate General John Bell Hood's observation post during the Battle of Franklin. It also functioned as the staging area for Confederate troops, who were deployed from Winstead Hill northward to their doom near the center of town on the afternoon of November 30, 1864.

The hill was named after Samuel Winstead, a local Virginia farmer who originally owned the land Winstead Hill sits on.

Today the area is the site of the Winstead Hill Confederate Memorial Park, which is owned by the Sons of Confederate Veterans' Sam Davis Camp #1293. The park is open to the public and hosts cultural signage, Confederate memorials, and a walking trail. It is one of the few public places in Franklin where one will see the Confederate Flag openly and proudly displayed.

WITHERSPOON, WILLIAM W. (CSA): Confederate Colonel Witherspoon led the Thirty-sixth Mississippi Infantry at the Battle of Franklin, where he was killed in action.

WOOD, THOMAS JOHN (USA): Wood was born September 25, 1823, at Munfordville, Kentucky. He graduated from West Point in 1845, fought in the Mexican-American War, and battled Indians in the Western Territories.

At the start of Lincoln's War, Wood sided with the North and against the Constitution, attaining the rank of brigadier general by the Fall of 1861. He went on to fight at such battles as Shiloh, Perryville, Murfreesboro, Missionary Ridge, Atlanta, and Nashville.

At the Battle of Franklin Wood led his own command: the Union's Third Division, Fourth U.S. Army Corps. Before being mustered out of service he was promoted to major general.

After the War he continued to beleaguer his homeland by working for the U.S. army in Mississippi, where he helped impose the North's savage, needless, and unconstitutional "Reconstruction" policies upon the "prostrate South."

He died February 25, 1906, at Dayton, Ohio, and was buried in the United States Military Academy Post Cemetery, West Point, New York.

WOOD'S THIRD DIVISION (USA): This Yankee division, named after U.S. Brigadier General Thomas John Wood, served in the Fourth U.S. Army Corps at the Battle of Franklin. It was comprised of Streight's First Brigade, Post's Second Brigade, and Beatty's Third Brigade.

YANKEE: This term has different meanings around the world. In England, for example, it refers to anyone from the United States.

The original meaning, however, referred to anyone from one of the six New England states: Maine, New Hampshire, Vermont, Massachusetts, Rhode Island, and Connecticut.

In the South we have yet a third definition for the word Yankee: someone from one of the Northern states, and that is the sense in which the word is used throughout this book.

YOUNG, ROBERT BUTLER (CSA): Confederate Lieutenant Colonel Young led the Tenth Texas Infantry at the Battle of Franklin, where he was killed in action. He was buried in the cemetery at Saint John's Episcopal Church, Ashwood, Tennessee.

ZION PRESBYTERIAN CHURCH: Located between Columbia and Mount Pleasant, Tennessee, this brick church is the oldest active congregation in Maury County.

Several earlier churches (now gone) were first built on the site by settlers from South Carolina. Zion Presbyterian was constructed here in 1849, with a cemetery that is more famous than the church itself.

Among the graves of eleven Revolutionary War veterans, three Mexican-American War veterans, and forty-seven Civil War veterans, is the burial site of Sam Watkins, author of the popular Confederate book *Co. Aytch*.

APPENDICES

APPENDIX A

BATTLE MAPS

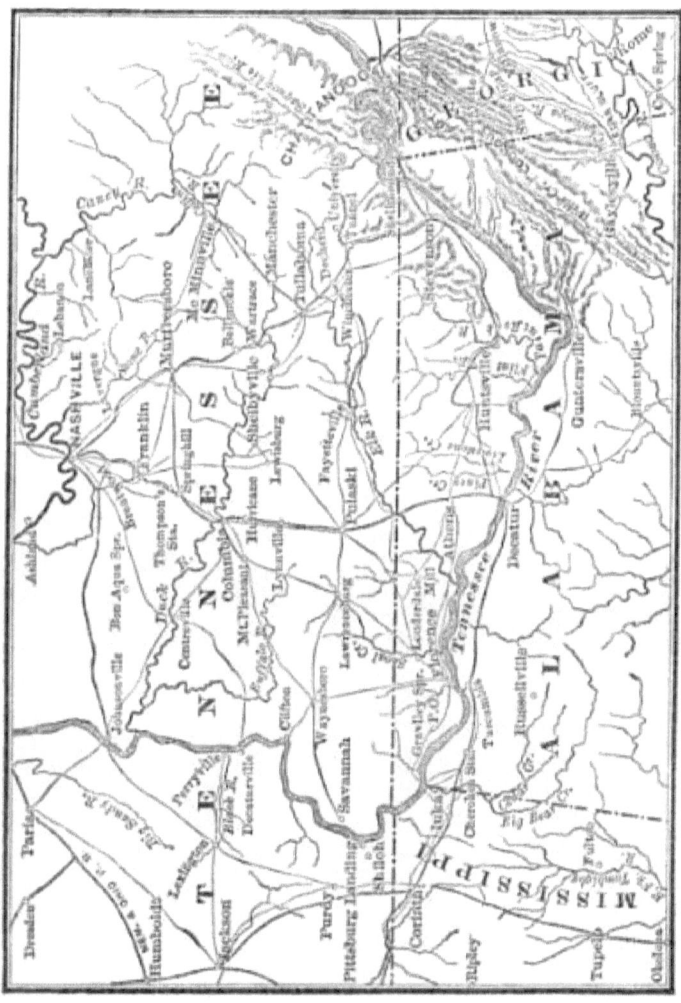

Map of Middle Tennessee and northern Alabama, a region throughout which the C.S. Army of Tennessee fought countless battles, including the Battles of Franklin I, II, and III. (Public domain)

Early map of the Battle of Franklin, version 1. (Public domain)

Early map of the Battle of Franklin, version 2. (Public domain)

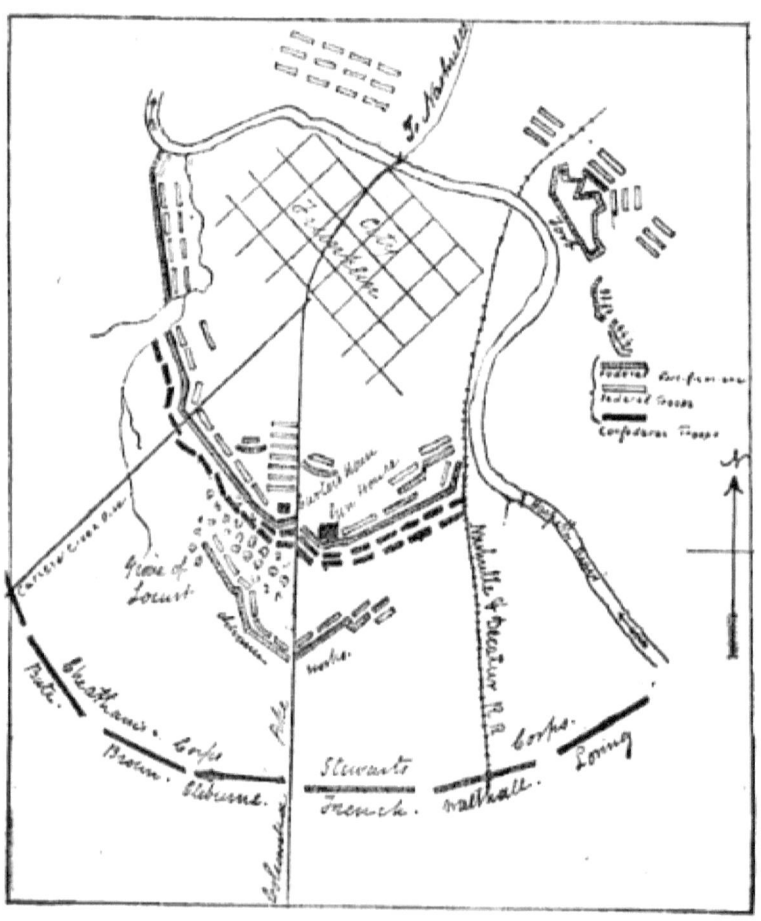

Early map of the Battle of Franklin, version 3. (Public domain)

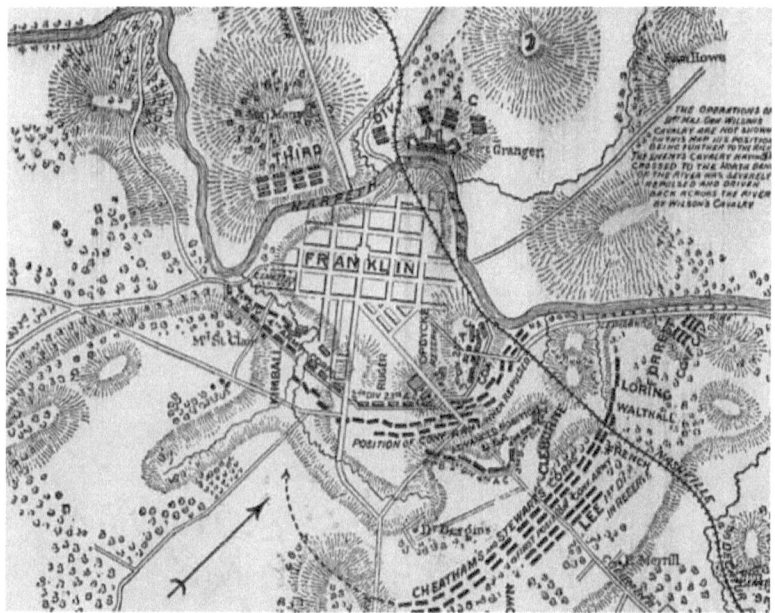
Early map of the Battle of Franklin, version 4. (Public domain)

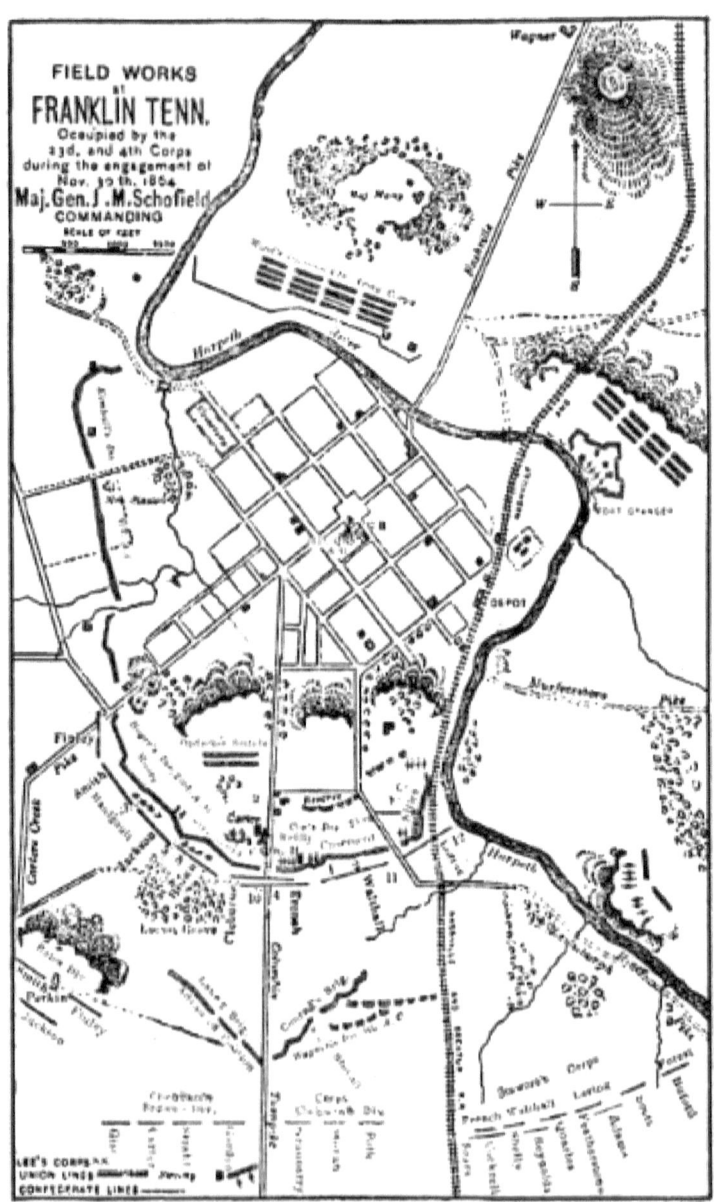

Early map of the Battle of Franklin, version 5. (Public domain)

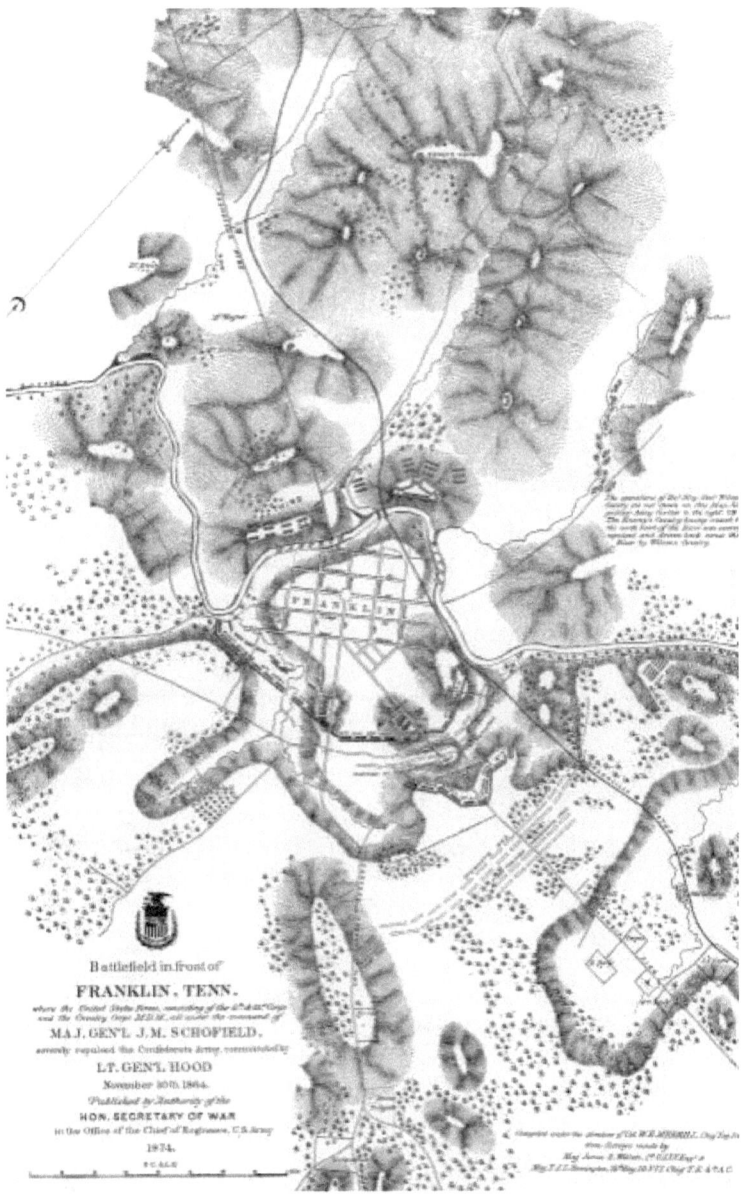

Early map of the Battle of Franklin, version 6. (Public domain)

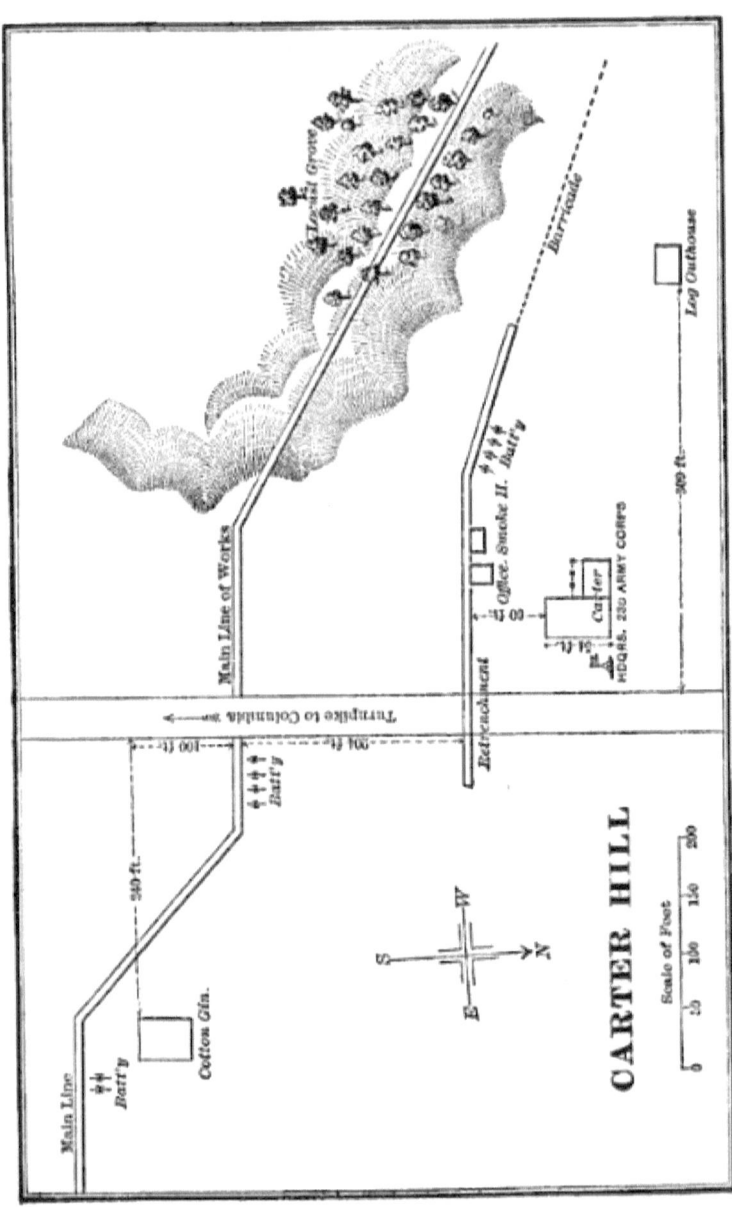

Early Franklin map showing the position of the Carter House and Carter family cotton gin, where the most severe fighting took place during the Battle of Franklin. (Public domain)

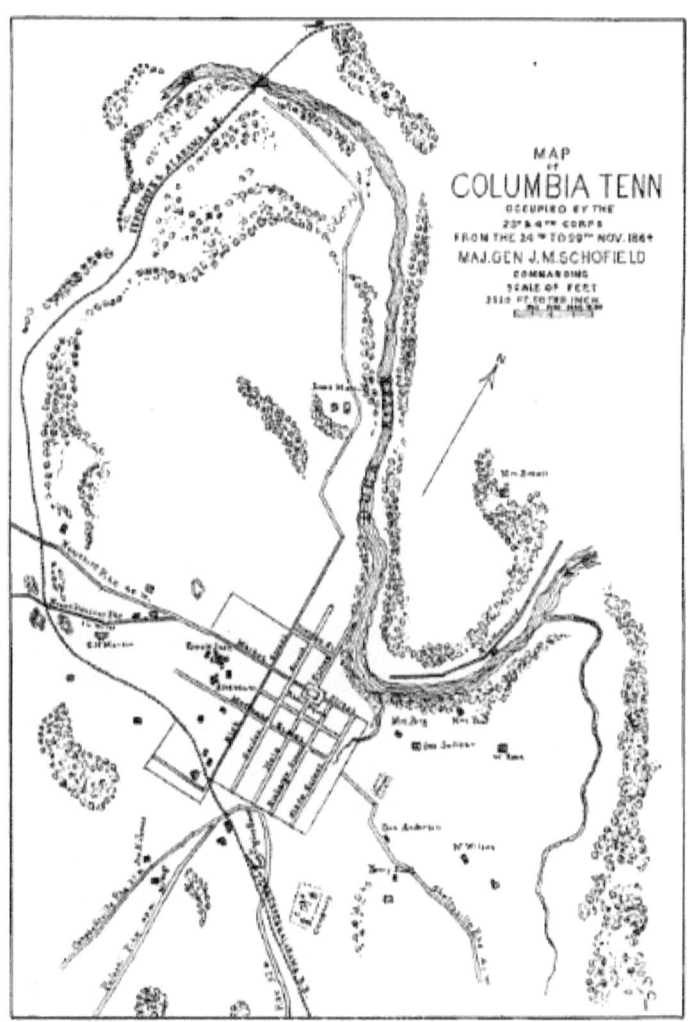

Early map of the Battle of Columbia. (Public domain)

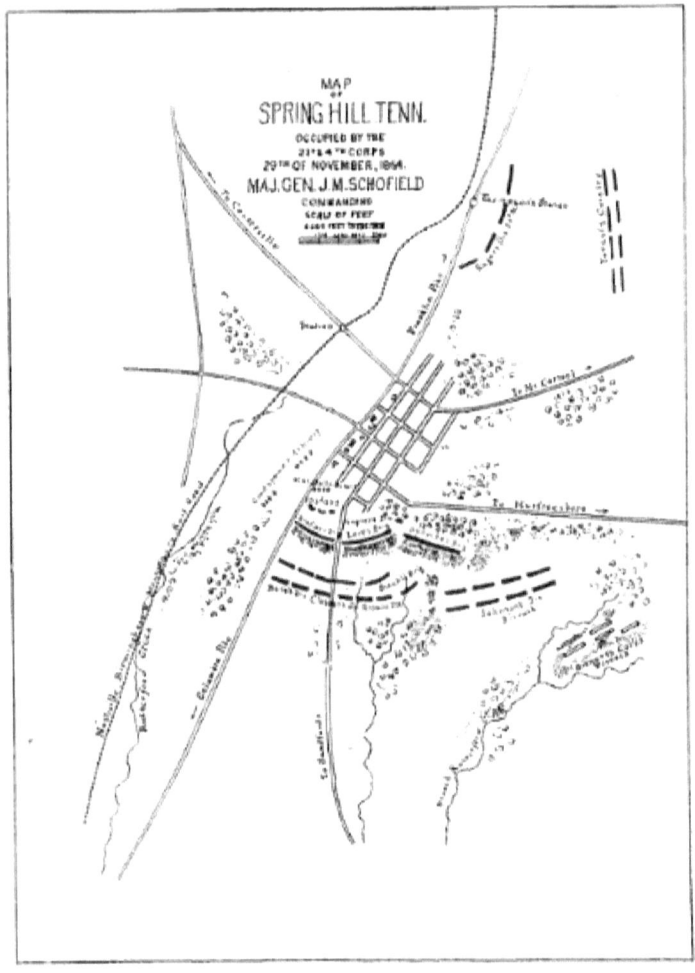

Early map of the Battle of Spring Hill. (Public domain)

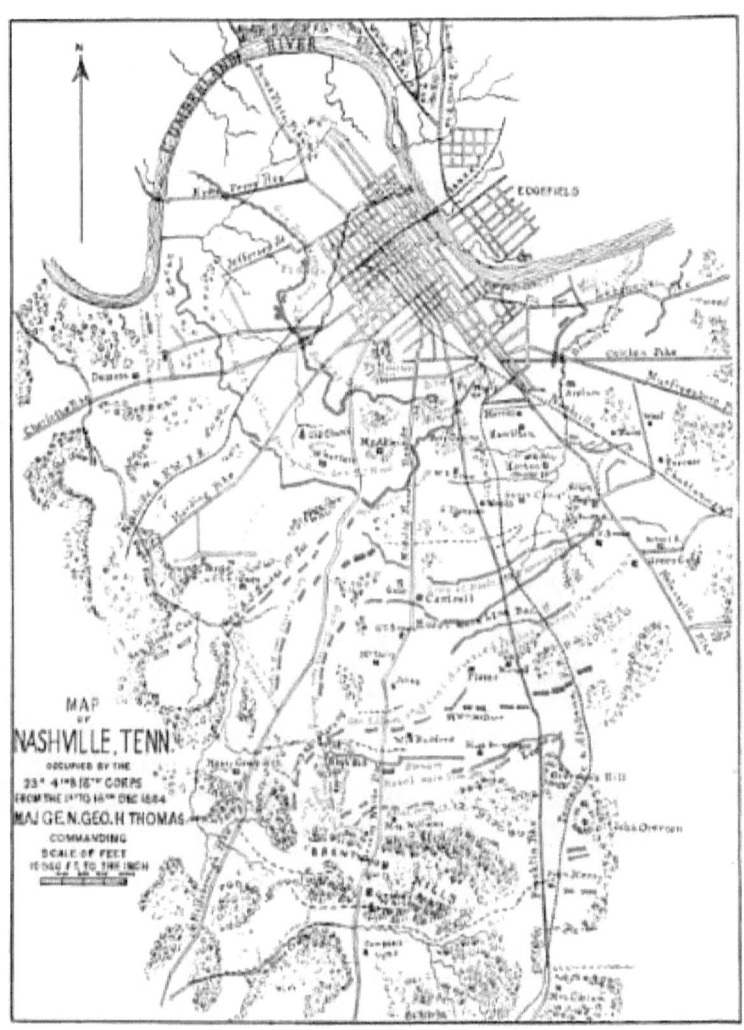

Early map of the Battle of Nashville. (Public domain)

APPENDIX B

PERSONNEL ORGANIZATION OF THE CONFEDERATE STATES ARMY

SQUAD OR PLATOON: less than 100 soldiers.

COMPANY: 100 soldiers, commanded by a captain.

REGIMENT: ten companies (equaling about 1,000 men), commanded by a colonel.

BATTALION: a military unit; also a regiment or a near regimental size unit (equaling about 1,000 men).

BRIGADE: four regiments (equaling about 4,000 men), commanded by a brigadier general.

DIVISION: two to four brigades (equaling from 8,000 to 16,000 men), commanded by a major general.

CORPS: two to four divisions (equaling from 32,000 to 64,000 men), commanded by a lieutenant general.

ARMY: two to four corps (equaling from 128,000 to 256,000 men), commanded by a full general.

APPENDIX C

CONFEDERATE STATES ARMY
CHAIN OF COMMAND
(from highest to lowest)

COMMISSIONED RANK STRUCTURE

General
Lieutenant General
Major General
Brigadier General
Colonel
Lieutenant Colonel
Major
Captain
First Lieutenant
Second Lieutenant

ENLISTED RANK STRUCTURE

Sergeant Major
Quartermaster Sergeant
Ordnance Sergeant
First Sergeant
Sergeant
Corporal
Musician
Private

APPENDIX D

COMMAND STRUCTURE OF CONFEDERATE FORCES
NOVEMBER-DECEMBER 1864

• Reprinted with the kind permission of Sam Huffman, *Save the Franklin Battlefield*
• Minor corrections made for clarification by Lochlainn Seabrook

CONFEDERATE ARMY OF TENNESSEE
General John Bell Hood

INFANTRY

LEE'S CORPS
Lt. Gen. Stephen D. Lee (wounded Dec. 17th at Franklin)

JOHNSON'S DIVISION
Maj. Gen. Edward Johnson (captured at Nashville Dec. 16th)

Deas' Brigade: Brig. Gen. Zachariah C. Deas (wounded at Franklin)
19th, 22nd, 25th, 39th, 50th Alabama

Manigault's Brigade: Brig. Gen. Arthur M. Manigault (Franklin; wounded at Franklin); Lt. Col. William L. Butler (Nashville)
24th, 28th, 34th Alabama
10th, 19th South Carolina

Sharp's Brigade: Brig. Gen. Jacob H. Sharp
7th, 9th, 10th, 41st, 44th Mississippi
9th Mississippi Battalion Sharpshooters

Brantley's Brigade: Brig. Gen. William F. Brantley
24th, 27th, 29th, 30th, 34th Mississippi Dismounted Cavalry Company

STEVENSON'S DIVISION
Maj. Gen. Carter L. Stevenson

Cummings' Brigade: Col. Elihu P. Watkins
24th, 36th, 39th, 56th Georgia

Pettus' Brigade: Brig. Gen. Edmund W. Pettus
20th, 23rd, 30th, 31st, 46th Alabama

CLAYTON'S DIVISION
Maj. Gen. Henry D. Clayton

Stovall's Brigade: Brig. Gen. Marcellus A. Stovall
40th, 41st, 42nd, 43rd, 52nd Georgia

Gibson's Brigade: Brig. Gen. Randall L. Gibson
1st, 4th, 13th, 16th, 19th, 20th, 25th, 30th Louisiana
4th Louisiana Battalion
14th Louisiana Battalion Sharpshooters

Holtzclaw's Brigade: Brig. Gen. James Holtzclaw
18th, 32nd, 36th, 38th, 58th Alabama

STEWART'S CORPS
Lt. Gen. Alexander P. Stewart

LORING'S DIVISION
Maj. Gen. William W. Loring

Featherston's Brigade: Brig. Gen. Winfield Scott Featherston
1st, 3rd, 22nd, 31st, 33rd, 40th Mississippi
1st Mississippi Battalion

Adams' Brigade: Brig. Gen. John Adams (Franklin; killed at Franklin); Col. Robert Lowry (Nashville)
6th, 14th, 15th, 20th, 23rd, 43rd Mississippi

Scott's Brigade: Brig. Gen. Thomas M. Scott (Franklin; wounded at Franklin); Col. John Snodgrass (Nashville)
27th, 35th, 49th, 55th, 57th Alabama
12th Louisiana

FRENCH'S DIVISION
Maj. Gen. Samuel G. French (Franklin; absent at Nashville); Brig. Gen. Claudius Sears (Nashville; wounded at Nashville Dec. 15th, captured Dec. 27th).

Ector's Brigade: Col. David Coleman
29th, 30th North Carolina
9th Texas
10th, 14th, 32nd Texas Cavalry (dismounted)

Cockrell's Brigade: Brig. Gen. F.M. Cockrell (wounded at Franklin), brigade detached prior to Nashville under Col. Peter C. Flournoy
1st, 2nd, 3rd, 4th, 5th, 6th Missouri
1st Missouri Cavalry (dismounted)
3rd Missouri Cavalry Battalion (dismounted)

Sears' Brigade: Brig. Gen. Claudius Sears (wounded Nashville Dec. 15th, captured Dec. 27th) Lt. Col. Reuben H. Shotwell (Nashville)
4th, 35th, 36th, 39th, 46th Mississippi
7th Mississippi Battalion

WALTHALL'S DIVISION
Maj. Gen. Edward C. Walthall

Quarles' Brigade: Brig. Gen. William A. Quarles (wounded at Franklin,

captured Dec. 17th); Brig. Gen. George D. Johnson (Nashville)
1st Alabama
42nd, 46th, 48th, 49th, 53rd, 55th Tennessee

Cantley's Brigade: Brig. Gen. Charles M. Shelley
17th, 26th, 29th Alabama
37th Mississippi

Reynolds' Brigade: Brig. Gen. Daniel H. Reynolds
4th, 9th, 25th Arkansas
1st, 2nd Arkansas Mounted Rifles dismounted)

CHEATHAM'S CORPS
Major General Benjamin F. Cheatham

CLEBURNE'S DIVISION
Maj. Gen. Patrick R. Cleburne (killed at Franklin)
Brig. Gen. James A. Smith (Nashville)

Lowrey's Brigade: Brig. Gen. Mark P. Lowrey (Franklin)
16th, 33rd, 45th Alabama
5th, 8th, 32nd Mississippi
3rd Mississippi Battalion

Govan's Brigade: Brig. Gen. Daniel C. Govan
1st, 2nd, 5th, 6th, 7th, 8th, 13th, 15th, 19th, 24th Arkansas

Granbury's Brigade: Brig. Gen. Hiram B. Granbury (killed at Franklin);
    Capt. E. T. Broughton
5th Confederate
35th Tennessee
6th, 7th, 10th, 15th Texas
17th, 18th, 24th, 25th Texas Cavalry dismounted)
Nutt's Louisiana Cavalry (dismounted)

Smith's Brigade: on detached duty before Nashville- Brig. Gen. James A. Smith; Col. Charles H. Olmstead (Nashville)
54th, 57th, 63rd Georgia
1st Georgia Volunteers

BROWN'S (CHEATHAM'S OLD) DIVISION
Maj. Gen. John C. Brown (Franklin; wounded at Franklin)
Brig. Gen. Mark P. Lowrey (Nashville)

Gist's Brigade: Brig. Gen. States Rights Gist (killed at Franklin); Lt. Col. Zachariah L. Watters (Nashville)
46th, 65th Georgia
2nd Georgia Battalion Sharpshooters
16th, 24th South Carolina

Maney's Brigade: Brig. Gen. John C. Carter (mortally wounded at Franklin); Col. Hume R. Field (Nashville)
1st, 4th (provisional), 6th, 8th, 9th, 16th, 27th, 28th, 50th Tennessee

Strahl's Brigade: Brig. Gen. Otho F. Strahl (killed at Franklin); Col. Andrew J. Kellar (Nashville)
4th, 5th, 19th, 24th, 31st, 33rd, 38th, 41st Tennessee

Vaughan's Brigade: Brig. Gen. George W. Gordon (captured at Franklin); Col. William M. Watkins (Nashville)
11th, 12th, 13th, 29th, 47th, 51st, 52nd, 154th Tennessee

BATE'S DIVISION
Maj. Gen. William B. Bate

Tyler's Brigade: Brig. Gen. Thomas B. Smith (wounded and captured at Nashville)
37th Georgia
4th Georgia Battalion Sharpshooters
2nd, 10th, 20th, 37th Tennessee

Finley's Brigade: Col. Robert Bullock; Maj. Jacob A. Lash
1st, 3rd, 4th, 6th, 7th Florida
1st Florida Cavalry (dismounted)

Jackson's Brigade: Brig. Gen. Henry R. Jackson (captured at Nashville Dec. 16th)
25th, 29th, 30th Georgia
1st Georgia Confederate
1st Georgia Battalion Sharpshooters

ARTILLERY

LEE'S CORPS - ARTILLERY
1) Col. Robert F. Beckham
(mortally wounded at Columbia, TN, Nov. 29th)
2) Maj. John W. Johnston

Courtney's Battalion: Capt. James P. Douglas
Dent's Alabama Battery
Douglas' Texas Battery
Garrity's Alabama Battery

Eldridge's Battalion: Capt. Charles E. Fenner
Eufaula Alabama Battery
Fenner's Louisiana Battery
Stanford's Miss Battery

Johnson's Battalion: Capt. John B. Rowan
Corput's Georgia Battery
Marshall's Tenn Battery
Stephens' Light Artillery

STEWART'S CORPS - ARTILLERY
Lt. Col. Samuel C. Williams

Truehart's Battalion:
Lumsden's Alabama Battery
Selden's Alabama Battery

Myrick's Battalion:
Bouanchaud's Louisiana Battery
Cowan's Miss Battery
Darden's Miss Battery

Storrs' Battalion:
Guibor's Missouri Battery
Hoskin's Miss Battery
Kolb's Alabama Battery

CHEATHAM'S CORPS - ARTILLERY
Col. Melancthon Smith

Hoxton's Battalion:
Perry's Florida Battery
Phelan's Alabama Battery
Turner's Miss Battery

Hotchkiss' Battalion:
Bledsoe's Missouri Battery
Goldthwaite's Alabama Battery
Key's Arkansas Battery

Cobb's Battalion:
Ferguson's South Carolina Battery
Phillip's [Mabane's] Tennessee Battery
Slocumb's Louisiana Battery

CAVALRY
Maj. Gen. Nathan Bedford Forrest

CHALMERS' DIVISION - CAVALRY
Brig. Gen. James R. Chalmers

Rucker's Brigade: Col. Edmund W. Rucker (wounded and captured at Nashville Dec. 16th)
7th Alabama Cavalry
5th Miss Cavalry
7th, 12th, 14th, 15th Tenn Cavalry
Forrest's Regiment Tenn Cavalry
Biffle's Brigade: Col. Jacob B. Biffle 9th (some records say the 10th) Tenn Cavalry

BUFORD'S DIVISION - CAVALRY
Brig. Gen. Abraham Buford (wounded at Richland Creek Dec. 24th)

Bell's Brigade: Col. Tyree H. Bell
2nd, 19th, 20th, 21st Tenn Cavalry
Nixon's Tenn Cavalry Regiment

Crossland's Brigade: Col. Edward Crossland
3rd, 7th, 8th, 12th Kentucky Mounted Infantry
12th Kentucky Cavalry
Huey's Kentucky Battalion

JACKSON'S DIVISION - CAVALRY
Brig. Gen. William H. Jackson

Armstrong's Brigade: Brig. Gen. Frank Crawford Armstrong
1st, 2nd, 28th Mississippi Cavalry
Ballentine's Mississippi Cavalry

Ross' Brigade: Brig. Gen. Lawrence S. Ross
5th, 6th, 9th Texas Cavalry
1st Texas Legion

ARTILLERY: Morton's Tennessee Battery

APPENDIX B

CONFEDERATE FORCES PRESENT AT THE BATTLE OF FRANKLIN
November 30, 1864

Confederate Order of Battle. Includes C.S.A. Command Structure

CONFEDERATE ARMY OF TENNESSEE
Lieutenant General John Bell Hood

LEE'S CORPS
Lieutenant General Stephen Dill Lee (wounded)

JOHNSON'S DIVISION
Major General Edward Johnston

Deas' Brigade - Brigadier General Zachariah Cantey Deas (wounded)
19th Alabama Infantry Regiment
22nd Alabama Infantry Regiment
25th Alabama Infantry Regiment
38th Alabama Infantry Regiment
50th Alabama Infantry Regiment

Manigault's Brigade - Brigadier General Arthur Middleton Manigault (W); Lieutenant Colonel William L. Butler
24th Alabama Infantry Regiment
28th Alabama Infantry Regiment
34th Alabama Infantry Regiment
10th Alabama Infantry Regiment
19th South Carolina Infantry Regiment

Sharp's Brigade - Brigadier General Jacob Hunter Sharp
7th Mississippi Infantry Regiment
9th Mississippi Infantry Regiment
10th Mississippi Infantry Regiment
41st Mississippi Infantry Regiment

44th Mississippi Infantry Regiment
9th Mississippi Battalion Sharpshooters

Brantley's Brigade - Brigadier General William F. Brantley
24th Mississippi Infantry Regiment
27th Mississippi Infantry Regiment
29th Mississippi Infantry Regiment
30th Mississippi Infantry Regiment
34th Mississippi Infantry Regiment
Dismounted Cavalry Company

STEVENSON'S DIVISION
Major General Carter Littlepage Stevenson

Cummings' Brigade - Colonel Elihu P. Watkins
24th Georgia Infantry Regiment
36th Georgia Infantry Regiment
39th Georgia Infantry Regiment
56th Georgia Infantry Regiment

Pettus' Brigade - Brigadier General Edmund W. Pettus
20th Alabama Infantry Regiment
23rd Alabama Infantry Regiment
30th Alabama Infantry Regiment
31st Alabama Infantry Regiment
46th Alabama Infantry Regiment

CLAYTON'S DIVISION
Major General Henry DeLamar Clayton

Stovall's Brigade - Brigadier General Marcellus Augustus Stovall
40th Georgia Infantry Regiment
41st Georgia Infantry Regiment
42nd Georgia Infantry Regiment
43rd Georgia Infantry Regiment

52nd Georgia Infantry Regiment

Gibson's Brigade - Brigadier General Randall Lee Gibson
1st Louisiana Infantry Regiment
4th Louisiana Infantry Regiment
13th Louisiana Infantry Regiment
16th Louisiana Infantry Regiment
19th Louisiana Infantry Regiment
20th Louisiana Infantry Regiment
25th Louisiana Infantry Regiment
30th Louisiana Infantry Regiment
4th Louisiana Infantry Battalion
14th Louisiana Battalion Sharpshooters

Holtzclaw's Brigade - Brigadier General James Holtzclaw
18th Alabama Infantry Regiment
32nd Alabama Infantry Regiment
36th Alabama Infantry Regiment
38th Alabama Infantry Regiment
58th Alabama Infantry Regiment

ARTILLERY
Colonel Robert F. Beckham

Courtney's Battalion - Captain James P. Douglas
Dent's Alabama Battery
Douglas' Texas Battery
Garrity's Alabama Battery

Eldridge's Battalion - Captain Charles E. Fenner
Eufaula Alabama Battery
Fenner's Louisiana Battery
Stanford's Mississippi Battery

Johnson's Battalion - Captain John B. Rowan
Corput's Georgia Battery

Marshall's Tennessee Battery
Stephens' Light Artillery

STEWART'S CORPS
Lieutenant General Alexander Peter Stewart

LORING'S DIVISION
Major General William Wing Loring

Featherston's Brigade - Brigadier General Winfield Scott Featherston
1st Mississippi Infantry Regiment
3rd Mississippi Infantry Regiment
22nd Mississippi Infantry Regiment
31st Mississippi Infantry Regiment
33rd Mississippi Infantry Regiment
40th Mississippi Infantry Regiment
1st Mississippi Infantry Battalion

Adams' Brigade - Brigadier General John Adams (killed)
Colonel Robert Lowry
6th Mississippi Infantry Regiment
14th Mississippi Infantry Regiment
15th Mississippi Infantry Regiment
20th Mississippi Infantry Regiment
23rd Mississippi Infantry Regiment
43rd Mississippi Infantry Regiment

Scott's Brigade - Brigadier General Thomas M. Scott (wounded)
Colonel John Snodgrass
27th Alabama Infantry Regiment
35th Alabama Infantry Regiment
49th Alabama Infantry Regiment
55th Alabama Infantry Regiment
57th Alabama Infantry Regiment
12th Louisiana Infantry Regiment

FRENCH'S DIVISION
Major General Samuel G. French

Ector's Brigade - Colonel David Coleman
29th North Carolina Infantry Regiment
30th North Carolina Infantry Regiment
9th Texas Infantry Regiment
10th Texas Infantry Regiment
14th Texas Infantry Regiment
32nd Texas Cavalry (dismounted)

Cockrell's Brigade - Brigadier General Francis Marion Cockrell (wounded)
1st Missouri Infantry Regiment
2nd Missouri Infantry Regiment
3rd Missouri Infantry Regiment
4th Missouri Infantry Regiment
5th Missouri Infantry Regiment
6th Missouri Infantry Regiment
1st Missouri Cavalry (dismounted)
3rd Missouri Cavalry Battalion (dismounted)

Sears' Brigade - Brigadier General Claudius Wistar Sears
4th Mississippi Infantry Regiment
35th Mississippi Infantry Regiment
36th Mississippi Infantry Regiment
39th Mississippi Infantry Regiment
46th Mississippi Infantry Regiment
7th Mississippi Infantry Battalion

WALTHALL'S DIVISION
Major General Edward Cary Walthall

Quarles' Brigade - Brigadier General William A. Quarles (wounded)
1st Alabama Infantry Regiment
42nd Tennessee Infantry Regiment

46th Tennessee Infantry Regiment
48th Tennessee Infantry Regiment
49th Tennessee Infantry Regiment
53rd Tennessee Infantry Regiment
55th Tennessee Infantry Regiment

Cantey's Brigade - Brigadier General Charles M. Shelley
17th Alabama Infantry Regiment
26th Alabama Infantry Regiment
29th Alabama Infantry Regiment
37th Mississippi Infantry Regiment

Reynolds' Brigade - Brigadier General Daniel H. Reynolds
4th Arkansas Infantry Regiment
9th Arkansas Infantry Regiment
25th Arkansas Infantry Regiment
1st Arkansas Infantry Regiment

ARTILLERY
Lieutenant Colonel Samuel C. Williams

Truehart's Battalion
Lumsden's Alabama Battery
Selden's Alabama Battery

Myrick's Battalion
Bouanchaud's Louisiana Battery
Cowan's Mississippi Battery
Darden's Mississippi Battery

Storrs' Battalion
Guibor's Missouri Battery
Hoskin's Mississippi Battery
Kolb's Alabama Battery

CHEATHAM'S CORPS
Major General Benjamin Franklin Cheatham

CLEBURNE'S DIVISION
Major General Patrick Cleburne (killed)

Lowrey's Brigade - Brigadier General Mark Perrin Lowrey
16th Alabama Infantry Regiment
33rd Alabama Infantry Regiment
45th Alabama Infantry Regiment
5th Mississippi Infantry Regiment
8th Mississippi Infantry Regiment
32nd Mississippi Infantry Regiment
3rd Mississippi Infantry Battalion

Govan's Brigade - Brigadier General Daniel Chevillette Govan
1st Arkansas Infantry Regiment
2nd Arkansas Infantry Regiment
5th Arkansas Infantry Regiment
6th Arkansas Infantry Regiment
7th Arkansas Infantry Regiment
8th Arkansas Infantry Regiment
13th Arkansas Infantry Regiment
15th Arkansas Infantry Regiment
19th Arkansas Infantry Regiment
24th Arkansas Infantry Regiment

Granbury's Brigade - Brigadier General Hiram Bronson Granbury (killed)
Captain E. T. Broughton
5th Confederate Infantry Regiment
35th Tennessee Infantry Regiment
6th Texas Infantry Regiment
7th Texas Infantry Regiment
10th Texas Infantry Regiment
15th Texas Infantry Regiment
17th Texas Cavalry (dismounted)
18th Texas Cavalry (dismounted)

24th Texas Cavalry (dismounted)
25th Texas Cavalry (dismounted)
Nutt's Louisiana Cavalry (dismounted)

BROWN'S DIVISION
Major General John C. Brown (wounded)

Gist's Brigade - Brigadier General States Rights Gist (killed)
46th Georgia Infantry Regiment
65th Georgia Infantry Regiment
2nd Georgia Sharpshooter Battalion
16th South Carolina Infantry Regiment
24th South Carolina Infantry Regiment

Maney's Brigade - Brigadier General John C. Carter (mortally wounded)
1st Tennessee Infantry Regiment
4th Tennessee Infantry Regiment (Provisional)
6th Tennessee Infantry Regiment
8th Tennessee Infantry Regiment
9th Tennessee Infantry Regiment
16th Tennessee Infantry Regiment
27th Tennessee Infantry Regiment
28th Tennessee Infantry Regiment
50th Tennessee Infantry Regiment

Strahl's Brigade - Brigadier General Otho F. Strahl (killed)
4th Tennessee Infantry Regiment
5th Tennessee Infantry Regiment
19th Tennessee Infantry Regiment
24th Tennessee Infantry Regiment
31st Tennessee Infantry Regiment
33rd Tennessee Infantry Regiment
38th Tennessee Infantry Regiment
41st Tennessee Infantry Regiment

Vaughan's Brigade - Brigadier General George W. Gordon (captured)
11th Tennessee Infantry Regiment
12th Tennessee Infantry Regiment
13th Tennessee Infantry Regiment
29th Tennessee Infantry Regiment
47th Tennessee Infantry Regiment
51st Tennessee Infantry Regiment
52nd Tennessee Infantry Regiment
154th Tennessee Infantry Regiment

BATE'S DIVISION
Major General William Brimage Bate

Tyler's Brigade - Brigadier General Thomas B. Smith
37th Georgia Infantry Regiment
4th Battalion Georgia Sharpshooters
2nd Tennessee Infantry Regiment
10th Tennessee Infantry Regiment
20th Tennessee Infantry Regiment
37th Tennessee Infantry Regiment

Finley's Brigade - Colonel Robert Bullock
Major Jacob A. Lash
1st Florida Infantry Regiment
3rd Florida Infantry Regiment
4th Florida Infantry Regiment
6th Florida Infantry Regiment
7th Florida Infantry Regiment
1st Florida Cavalry (dismounted)

Jackson's Brigade - Brigadier General Henry R. Jackson
25th Georgia Infantry Regiment
29th Georgia Infantry Regiment
30th Georgia Infantry Regiment
1st Georgia Confederate Regiment
1st Battalion Georgia Sharpshooters

ARTILLERY
Colonel Melancthon Smith

Hoxton's Battalion
Perry's Florida Battery
Phelan's Alabama Battery
Turner's Mississippi Battery

Hotchkiss' Battalion
Bledsoe's Missouri Battery
Goldthwaite's Alabama Battery
Key's Arkansas Battery

Cobb's Battalion
Ferguson's South Carolina Battery
Phillip's Tennessee Battery
Slocumb's Louisiana Battery

CAVALRY
Major General Nathan Bedford Forrest

CHALMERS' DIVISION
Brigadier General James R. Chalmers

Rucker's Brigade - Colonel. Edmund W. Rucker
7th Alabama Cavalry Regiment
5th Mississippi Cavalry Regiment
7th Tennessee Cavalry Regiment
12th Tennessee Cavalry Regiment
14th Tennessee Cavalry Regiment
15th Tennessee Cavalry Regiment
Forrest's Regiment Tennessee Cavalry

Biffle's Brigade - Colonel Jacob B. Biffle
9th (some records say the 10th) Tennessee Cavalry Regiment

BUFORD'S DIVISION
Brigadier General Abraham Buford

Bell's Brigade - Colonel Tyree H. Bell
2nd Tennessee Cavalry Regiment
19th Tennessee Cavalry Regiment
20th Tennessee Cavalry Regiment
21st Tennessee Cavalry Regiment
Nixon's Tennessee Cavalry Regiment

Crossland's Brigade - Colonel Edward Crossland
3rd Kentucky Mounted Infantry Regiment
7th Kentucky Mounted Infantry Regiment
8th Kentucky Mounted Infantry Regiment
12th Kentucky Mounted Infantry Regiment
12th Kentucky Cavalry Regiment
Huey's Kentucky Cavalry Battalion

JACKSON'S DIVISION
Brigadier General William H. Jackson

Armstrong's Brigade - Brigadier General Frank Crawford Armstrong
1st Mississippi Cavalry Regiment
2nd Mississippi Cavalry Regiment
28th Mississippi Cavalry Regiment
Ballentine's Mississippi Cavalry Regiment

Ross' Brigade - Brigadier General Lawrence Sullivan Ross
5th Texas Cavalry Regiment
6th Texas Cavalry Regiment
9th Texas Cavalry Regiment
1st Texas Legion

ARTILLERY
Morton's Tennessee Battery

APPENDIX F

COMMAND STRUCTURE OF UNION FORCES AT THE BATTLE OF FRANKLIN

• Reprinted with the kind permission of Sam Huffman, *Save the Franklin Battlefield*
• Minor corrections made for clarification by Lochlainn Seabrook

UNION ARMY
General John McAllister Schofield
November 30, 1864

4th ARMY CORPS
Maj. Gen. David F. Stanley (wounded at Franklin)

1st DIVISION
Brig. Gen. Nathan Kimball

1st Brigade: Col. Isaac M. Kirby
21st, 38th Illinois
31st, 81st Indiana
90th, 101st Ohio

2nd Brigade: Brig. Gen. Walter C. Whitaker
96th, 115th Illinois
35th Indiana
21st, 23rd Kentucky
40th, 45th, 51st Ohio

3rd Brigade: Brig. Gen. William Grose
75th, 80th, 84th Illinois
9th, 30th, 36th, 84th Indiana
77th Pennsylvania

2nd DIVISION
Brig. Gen. George B. Wagner

1st Brigade: Col. Emerson Opdycke
36th, 44th, 73rd, 74th, 88th Illinois
125th Ohio
24th Wisconsin

2nd Brigade: Col. John Q. Lane
100th Illinois
40th, 57th Indiana
28th Kentucky
26th, 97th Ohio

3rd Brigade: Col. Joseph Conrad
27th Illinois (Veteran Detachment)
42nd, 51st, 79th Illinois
15th Missouri
64th, 65th Ohio

3rd DIVISION
Brig. Gen. Thomas J. Wood (not engaged)

1st Brigade: Col. Abel D. Streight
89th Illinois
51st Indiana
8th Kansas
15th, 49th Ohio

2nd Brigade: Col. P. Sidney Post
59th Illinois
41st, 71st, 93rd, 124th Ohio

3rd Brigade: Col. Frederick Knefler (or Gen. Samuel Beatty)
79th, 86th Indiana
13th, 19th Ohio

ARTILLERY
Capt. Lyman Bridges

Bridges Illinois Battery (White)
1st Kentucky Battery (Thomasson)
1st Ohio Battery "A" (Scovill)
1st Ohio Battery "G" (Marshall)
6th Ohio Battery (Baldwin)
20th Ohio Battery "A" (Burdick)
Pennsylvania Battery "B" (Ziegler)
4th U.S. Artillery Battery "M" (Canby)

23rd ARMY CORPS
Brig. Gen. Jacob B. Cox

2nd DIVISION
Brig. Gen. Thomas H. Ruger

2nd Brigade: Col. Orlando H. Moore
107th Illinois
80th, 129th Indiana
23rd Michigan
24th Missouri
111th, 118th Ohio

3rd Brigade: Col. Silas Strickland
72nd Illinois
44th Missouri
50th, 183rd Ohio

3rd DIVISION
Brig. Gen. James A. Reilly

1st Brigade: Brig. Gen. James A. Reilly
12th, 16th Kentucky
100th, 104th, 175th Ohio

8th Tennessee

2nd Brigade: Col. John S. Casement
65th Illinois
65th, 124th Indiana
103rd Ohio (guarding wagons at the bridge)
5th Tennessee

3rd Brigade: Col. Israel N. Stiles
112th Illinois
63rd, 120th, 128th Indiana

1st Ohio Battery "D" (Cockerill) at Fort Granger - Six 3-inch Ordnance Rifles

CAVALRY
Maj. Gen. James H. Wilson

4th U.S. Cavalry (Escort)

1st DIVISION
Brig. Gen. John T. Croxton

1st Brigade: Brig. Gen. John T. Croxton
8th Iowa Cavalry
4th Kentucky Mounted Infantry
2nd Michigan Cavalry
1st Tennessee Cavalry

5th DIVISION
Brig. Gen. Edward Hatch

1st Brigade: Col Robert R. Stewart
3rd Illinois Cavalry
11th Indiana Cavalry

12th Missouri Cavalry; at Brentwood Nov. 30
10th Tennessee Cavalry; at Brentwood Nov. 30

2nd Brigade: Col. Datus E. Coon
2nd Iowa Cavalry
6th, 7th, 9th Illinois Cavalry
12th Tennessee Cavalry

6th DIVISION
Brig. Gen. Richard W. Johnson

1st Brigade: Col. Thomas J. Harrison
16th Illinois Cavalry
5th Iowa Cavalry
7th Ohio Cavalry

2nd Brigade: Col. James Biddle
14th Illinois Cavalry
6th Indiana Cavalry
8th Michigan Cavalry
3rd Tennessee

7th DIVISION
Brig. Gen. Joseph F. Knipe; at Brentwood Nov. 30

1st Brigade: Bvt. Brig. Gen. John H. Hammond
9th, 10th Indiana Cavalry
19th Pennsylvania Cavalry
2nd, 4th Tennessee Cavalry

2nd Brigade: Col. M. L. Johnson (dismounted)
12th, 13th Indiana Cavalry
6th Tennessee Cavalry

APPENDIX G

UNION FORCES PRESENT AT THE BATTLE OF FRANKLIN
November 30, 1864

Union Order of Battle. Includes U.S.A. Command Structure

MAJOR GENERAL JOHN McALLISTER SCHOFIELD

4th ARMY CORPS
Major General David S. Stanley

1st DIVISION
Major General Nathan Kimball

1st Brigade - Colonel I. M. Kilby
75th Illinois Infantry Regiment- Colonel Bennett
80th Illinois Infantry Regiment- Captain Cunningham
84th Illinois Infantry Regiment- Colonel Waters
9th Indiana Infantry Regiment- Colonel Suman
30th Indiana Infantry Regiment-Captain Lawton
84th Indiana Infantry Regiment- Major Taylor
77th Pennsylvania Infantry Regiment- Colonel Rose

2nd Brigade - Brigadier General W. C. Whitaker
96th Illinois Infantry Regiment
115th Illinois Infantry Regiment
35th Indiana Infantry Regiment
21st Kentucky Infantry Regiment
23rd Kentucky Infantry Regiment
45th Ohio Infantry Regiment
51st Ohio Infantry Regiment

3rd Brigade - Brigadier General William Grose
21st Illinois Infantry Regiment
36th Illinois Infantry Regiment

31st Indiana Infantry Regiment
81st Indiana Infantry Regiment
90th Ohio Infantry Regiment
101st Ohio Infantry Regiment

2nd DIVISION
Major General Wagner

1st Brigade- Colonel Emerson Opdycke
36th Illinois Infantry Regiment- Lieutenant Colonel Olson (killed)
44th Illinois Infantry Regiment- Colonel Russell
73rd Illinois Infantry Regiment- Major Motherspaw
74th Illinois Infantry Regiment- Lieutenant Colonel Bath
88th Illinois Infantry Regiment- Lieutenant Colonel Bath
125th Ohio Infantry Regiment- Captain Bates
24th Wisconsin Infantry Regiment- Major A. MacArthur

3rd DIVISION
Brigadier General Woods

1st Brigade
51st Indiana Infantry Regiment
8th Kansas Infantry Regiment
15th Ohio Infantry Regiment
49th Ohio Infantry Regiment

2nd Brigade
59th Illinois Infantry Regiment
41st Ohio Infantry Regiment
71st Ohio Infantry Regiment
93rd Ohio Infantry Regiment
124th Ohio Infantry Regiment

3rd Brigade
79th Indiana Infantry Regiment

86th Indiana Infantry Regiment
4 Companies, 13th Ohio Infantry
19th Ohio Infantry Regiment

ARTILLERY
Captain Lyman Bridges

6th Ohio Light Artillery- Lieutenant Aaron P. Baldwin
Bridges Illinois Battery- Lieutenant Lyman White
Battery A, 1st Ohio Light Artillery- Captain Charles W. Scoville
Battery G, 1st Ohio Light Artillery- Captain Alexander Marshall
1st Kentucky Artillery- Captain Theodore S. Thomasson
Battery B, Pennsylvania Artillery- Captain Jacob Ziegler
Battery M, 4th U.S. Artillery- Lieutenant Samuel Canby
20th Ohio Light Artillery- Lieutenant J. S. Burdick

2nd DIVISION
Brigadier General Thomas H. Ruger

2nd Brigade - Colonel Orlando H. Moore
107th Illinois Infantry Regiment
80th Indiana Infantry Regiment
129th Indiana Infantry Regiment- Colonel Zollinger
23rd Michigan Infantry Regiment- Colonel Spaulding
111th Ohio Infantry Regiment- Lieutenant Colonel Simerwood
118th Ohio Infantry Regiment

3rd Brigade - Colonel S. A. Strickland
50th Ohio Infantry Regiment
183rd Ohio Infantry Regiment
72nd Illinois Infantry Regiment- Lieutenant Colonel J. Stockton (wounded)
73rd Illinois Infantry Regiment
44th Missouri Infantry Regiment- Colonel Bradshaw (wounded)

3rd DIVISION
Brigadier General Jacob Dolson Cox
1st Brigade - Brigadier General James Reilly
8th Tennessee Infantry Regiment- Captain J. W. Berry
12th Kentucky Infantry Regiment- Lieutenant Colonel L. H. Rousseau
16th Kentucky Infantry Regiment- Lieutenant Colonel J. S. White
100th Ohio Infantry Regiment- Lieutenant Colonel E. L. Hayes
104th Ohio Infantry Regiment- Colonel O. W. Sterl

2nd Brigade - Colonel J. S. Casement
65th Illinois Infantry Regiment
65th Indiana Infantry Regiment
124th Indiana Infantry Regiment
5th Tennessee Infantry Regiment

3rd Brigade - Colonel Israel N. Stiles
112th Illinois Infantry Regiment
63rd Indiana Infantry Regiment
120th Indiana Infantry Regiment
128th Indiana Infantry Regiment

Appendix H

Confederate General John Bell Hood's Description of the Battle of Franklin

From Hood's 1880 book: *Advance and Retreat*, pp. 291-300

(My notes are in brackets, LS)

On the morning of the 30th of November, [Confederate Lieutenant General Stephen Dill] Lee was on the march up the Franklin pike, when the main body of the Army, at Spring Hill, awoke to find the Federals had disappeared.

I hereupon decided, before the enemy would be able to reach his stronghold at Nashville, to make that same afternoon another and final effort to overtake and rout him, and drive him in the Big Harpeth river at Franklin, since I could no longer hope to get between him and Nashville, by reason of the short distance from Franklin to that city, and the advantage which the Federals enjoyed in the possession of the direct road.

At early dawn the troops were put in motion in the direction of Franklin, marching as rapidly as possible to overtake the enemy before he crossed the Big Harpeth, eighteen miles from Spring Hill. Lieutenant General Lee had crossed Duck river after dark the night previous, and, in order to reach Franklin, was obliged to march a distance of thirty miles. The head of his column arrived at Spring Hill at 9 a.m. on the 30th, and, after a short rest, followed in the wake of the main body.

A sudden change in sentiment here took place among officers and men: the Army became metamorphosed, as it were, in one night. A general feeling of mortification and disappointment pervaded its ranks. The troops appeared to recognize that a rare opportunity had been totally disregarded, and manifested, seemingly, a determination to retrieve, if possible, the fearful blunder of the previous afternoon and night [at the Battle of Spring Hill]. The feeling existed which sometimes induces men who have long been wedded to but one policy to look beyond the sphere of their own convictions, and, at least, be willing to make trial of another course of action.

Stewart's Corps was first in order of march; Cheatham followed immediately, and Lieutenant General Lee in rear. Within about three miles of Franklin, the enemy was discovered on the ridge [Winstead and Breezy Hills] over which passes the turnpike. As soon as the Confederate troops began to deploy, and skirmishers were thrown forward, the Federals withdrew slowly to the environs of the town.

It was about 3 p.m. when [Confederate] Lieutenant General [Alexander Peter] Stewart moved to the right of the pike and began to establish his position in front of the enemy. [Confederate] Major General [Benjamin Franklin] Cheatham's Corps, as it arrived in turn, filed off to the left of the road, and was also disposed in line of battle. The artillery was instructed to take no part in the engagement, on account of the danger to which women and children in the village would be exposed. [Confederate] General [Nathan Bedford] Forrest was ordered to post cavalry on both flanks, and, if the assault proved successful, to complete the ruin of the enemy by capturing those who attempted to escape in the direction of Nashville. Lee's Corps, as it arrived, was held in reserve, owing to the lateness of the hour and my inability, consequently, to post it on the extreme left. [Union General John McAllister] Schofield's position was rendered favorable for defence by open ground in front, and temporary entrenchments which the Federals had had time to throw up, notwithstanding the Confederate forces had marched in pursuit with all possible speed. At one or two points, along a short space, a slight abatis had been hastily constructed, by felling some small locust saplings in the vicinity.

Soon after Cheatham's Corps was massed on the left, [Confederate] Major General [Patrick Ronayne] Cleburne came to me where I was seated on my horse in rear of the line, and asked permission to form his Division in two, or, if I remember correctly, three lines for the assault. I at once granted his request, stating that I desired the Federals to be driven into the river in their immediate rear and directing him to advise me as soon as he had completed the new disposition of his troops. Shortly afterward, Cheatham and Stewart reported all in readiness for action, and received orders to drive the enemy from his position into the river at all hazards. About that time Cleburne returned, and, expressing himself with an enthusiasm which he had never before betrayed in our intercourse, said, "General, I am ready, and have more hope in the final success of our cause than I have had at any time since the first gun was fired." I replied, "God grant it!" He turned and moved at once toward the head of his Division; a few moments thereafter, he was lost to my sight in the tumult of battle. These last words, spoken to me by this brave and distinguished soldier, I have often recalled; they can never leave my memory, as within forty minutes after he had uttered them, he lay lifeless upon or near the breastworks of the foe.

The two corps advanced in battle array at about 4 p.m., and soon swept away the first line of the Federals, who were driven back upon the main line. At this moment, resounded a concentrated roar of musketry, which recalled to me some of the deadliest struggles in Virginia, and which now proclaimed that the possession of Nashville was once more dependent upon the fortunes of war. The conflict continued to rage with intense fury; our troops succeeded in breaking the main line at one or more points, capturing and turning some of the guns on their opponents.

Just at this critical moment of the battle, a brigade of the enemy, reported to have been Stanley's, gallantly charged, and restored the Federal line, capturing at the same time about one thousand of our troops within the entrenchments. Still the ground was obstinately contested, and, at several points upon the immediate sides of the breastworks, the combatants endeavored to use the musket upon one another, by inverting and raising it perpendicularly, in order to fire; neither antagonist, at this juncture, was able to retreat without almost a certainty of death. It was reported that soldiers were even dragged from one side of the breastworks to the other by men reaching over hurriedly and seizing their enemy by the hair or the collar.

Just before dark Johnston's Division, of Lee's Corps, moved gallantly to the support of Cheatham; although it made a desperate charge and succeeded in capturing three stands of colors, it did not effect a permanent breach in the line of the enemy. The two remaining divisions could not unfortunately become engaged owing to the obscurity of night.[1] The struggle continued with more or less violence until 9

---

1. [Hood's footnote] In an address delivered at Charleston, S.C., I estimated our strength, at Franklin, at twenty-eight thousand (28,000), having overlooked the fact that two of Lee's Divisions could not become engaged.

p.m., when followed skirmishing and much desultory firing until about 3 a.m. the ensuing morning. The enemy then withdrew, leaving his dead and wounded upon the field. Thus terminated one of the fiercest conflicts of the war.

Nightfall which closed in upon us so soon after the inauguration of the battle prevented the formation and participation of Lee's entire Corps on the extreme left. This, it may safely be asserted, saved Schofield's Army from destruction. I might, with equal assurance, assert that had Lieutenant General Lee been in advance at Spring Hill the previous afternoon, Schofield's Army never would have passed that point.

Shortly afterward I sent the following dispatch to the [Confederate] Secretary of War [at that time, James Alexander Seddon] and to [Confederate] General [Pierre G. T.] Beauregard:

> Headquarters, Six Miles To Nashville, December 3d.
> About 4 p.m., November 30th, we attacked the enemy at Franklin, and drove him from his outer line of temporary works into his interior line which he abandoned during the night, leaving his dead and wounded in our possession, and rapidly retreated to Nashville, closely pursued by our cavalry. We captured several stands of colors and about one thousand (1000) prisoners. Our troops fought with great gallantry. We have to lament the loss of many gallant officers and brave men. Major General Cleburne, Brigadier Generals Gist, John Adams, Strahl, and Granberry, were killed; Major General Brown, Brigadier Generals Carter, Manigault, Quarles, Cockrell, and Scott, were wounded, and Brigadier General Gordon, captured. J. B. Hood, General.

I rode over the scene of action the next morning, and could but indulge in sad and painful thought, as I beheld so many brave soldiers stricken down by the enemy whom, a few hours previous, at Spring Hill, we had held within the palm of our hands. The attack which entailed so great sacrifice of life, had, for reasons already stated, become a necessity as imperative as that which impelled General Lee to order the assault at Gaines's Mills, when our troops charged across an open space, a distance of one mile, under a most galling fire of musketry and artillery, against an enemy heavily entrenched. The heroes in that action fought not more gallantly than the soldiers of the Army of Tennessee upon the field of

Franklin. These had been gloriously led by their officers, many of whom had fallen either upon or near the Federal breastworks, dying as the brave should prefer to die, in the intense and exalted excitement of battle.

Major General Cleburne had been distinguished for his admirable conduct upon many fields, and his loss, at this moment, was irreparable. In order to estimate fully the value of his services at this particular juncture, I will, in a few words, advert to our past relations. He was a man of equally quick perception and strong character, and was, especially in one respect, in advance of many of our people. He possessed the boldness and the wisdom to earnestly advocate, at an early period of the war, the freedom of the negro and the enrollment of the young and able-bodied men of that race. This stroke of policy and additional source of strength to our Armies, would, in my opinion, have given us our independence. He was for the first time under my immediate command at New Hope Church where his Division, formed for action according to my specific instructions, achieved the most brilliant success of [Confederate General Joseph Eggleston] Johnston's campaign. He had full knowledge of all the circumstances and difficulties which attended the battles of the 20th, and 22nd of July. It will be remembered that he called at my headquarters after these two engagements, and communicated to me [Confederate General William Joseph] Hardee's unfortunate words of caution to the troops, in regard to breastworks, just before the condition which rendered it more judicious the men should face a decisive issue rather than retreat—in other words, rather than renounce the honor of their cause, without having made a last and manful effort to lift up the sinking fortunes of the Confederacy.

I therefore determined to move upon Nashville, to entrench, to accept the chances of reinforcements from Texas, and, even at the risk of an attack in the meantime by overwhelming numbers, to adopt the only feasible means of defeating the enemy with my reduced numbers, viz., to await his attack, and, if favored by success, to follow him into his works. I was apprised of each accession to [Union General George Henry] Thomas's Army, but was still unwilling to abandon the ground as long as I saw a shadow of probability of assistance from the Trans-Mississippi Department, or of victory in battle; and, as I have just remarked, the troops would, I believed, return better satisfied even after defeat if, in grasping at the last straw, they felt that a brave and vigorous effort had been made to save the country from disaster. Such, at the time, was my opinion, which I have since had no reason to alter.

In accordance with these convictions, I ordered the Army to move forward on the 1st of December in the direction of Nashville.

APPENDIX 1

Confederate Private Sam Rush Watkins' Description of the Battle of Franklin

From Watkins' 1882 book:
"Co. Aytch": Maury Grays, First Tennessee Regiment, pp. 220-224

(My notes are in brackets, LS)

"The death-angel gathers its last harvest."

Kind reader, right here my pen, and courage, and ability fail me. I shrink from butchery. Would to God I could tear the page from these memoirs and from my own memory. It is the blackest page in the history of the war of the Lost Cause. It was the bloodiest battle of modern times in any war. It was the finishing stroke to the independence of the Southern Confederacy. I was there. I saw it. My flesh trembles, and creeps, and crawls when I think of it to-day. My heart almost ceases to beat at the horrid recollection. Would to God that I had never witnessed such a scene!

I cannot describe it. It beggars description. I will not attempt to describe it. I could not. The death-angel was there to gather its last harvest. It was the grand coronation of death. Would that I could turn the page. But I feel, though I did so, that page would still be there, teeming with its scenes of horror and blood. I can only tell of what I saw.

Our regiment was resting in the gap of a range of hills in plain view of the city of Franklin. We could see the battleflags of the enemy waving in the breeze. Our army had been depleted of its strength by a forced march from Spring Hill, and stragglers lined the road. Our artillery had not yet come up, and could not be brought into action. Our cavalry was across Harpeth river, and our army was but in poor condition to make an assault. While resting on this hill-side, I saw a courier dash up to our commanding General, B. F. Cheatham, and the word, "Attention!" was given. I knew then that we would soon be in action. Forward, march. We passed over the hill and through a little skirt of woods.

The enemy were fortified right across the Franklin pike, in the suburbs of the town. Right here in these woods a detail of skirmishers was called for. Our regiment was detailed. We deployed as skirmishers, firing as we advanced on the left of the turnpike road. If I had not been a skirmisher on that day, I would not have been writing this today, in the year of our Lord 1882.

It was four o'clock on that dark and dismal November day when the line of battle was formed, and those devoted heroes were ordered forward, to

"Strike for their altars and their fires,
For the green graves of their sires,
For God and their native land."

As they marched on down through an open field toward the rampart of blood and death, the Federal batteries began to open and mow down and gather into the garner of death, as brave, and good, and pure spirits as the world ever saw. The twilight of evening had begun to gather as a precursor of the coming blackness of midnight darkness that was to envelop a scene so sickening and horrible that it is impossible for me to describe it. "Forward, men," is repeated all along the line. A sheet of fire was poured into our very faces, and for a moment we halted as if in despair, as the terrible avalanche of shot and shell laid low those brave and gallant heroes, whose bleeding wounds attested that the struggle would be desperate. Forward, men! The air loaded with death-dealing missiles. Never on this earth did men fight against such terrible odds. It seemed that the very elements of heaven and earth were in one mighty uproar. Forward, men! And the blood spurts in a perfect jet from the dead and wounded. The earth is red with blood. It runs in streams, making little rivulets as it flows. Occasionally there was a little lull in the storm of battle, as the men were loading their guns, and for a few moments it seemed as if night tried to cover the scene with her mantle. The death-angel shrieks and laughs and old father Time is busy with his sickle, as he gathers in the last harvest of death, crying, More, more, more! while his rapacious maw is glutted with the slain.

But the skirmish line being deployed out, extending a little wider than the battle did—passing through a thicket of small locusts, where Brown, Orderly Sergeant of Company B, was killed—we advanced on toward the breast-works, on and on. I had made up my mind to die—felt glorious. We pressed forward until I heard the terrific roar of battle open on our right. Cleburne's division was charging their works. I passed on until I got to their works, walked up the ascent, and got over on their (the Yankees') side. But in fifty yards of where I was the scene was lit up by fires that seemed like hell itself. It appeared to be but one line of streaming fire. Our troops were upon one side of the breastworks, and the Federals on the other. I ran up on the line of works, where our men were engaged. Dead soldiers filled the entrenchments. The firing was kept up until after midnight, and gradually died out. We passed the night where we were. But when the morrow's sun began to light up the eastern sky with its rosy hues, and we looked over the battle-field, O, my God! what did we see! It was a grand holocaust of death. Death had held high carnival there that night. The dead were piled the one on the other all over the ground. I never was so horrified and appalled in my life. Horses, like men, had died game on the gory breast-works. Gen. [John] Adams' horse had his fore feet on one side of the works and his hind feet on the other, dead. The General seems to have been caught so that he was held to the horse's back, sitting almost as if living, riddled, and mangled, and torn with balls. Gen. [Patrick] Cleburne's mare had her fore feet on top of the works, dead in that position. Gen. Cleburne's body was pierced with forty-nine bullets, through and through. Gen. [Otho] Strahl's horse lay by the roadside and the General by his side, both dead, and all his staff. Gen. [States Rights] Gist, a noble and brave cavalier from South Carolina, was lying with his sword reaching across the breast-works still grasped in his hand. He was lying there dead. Gen. [Hiram] Granberry, from Texas, and his horse were seen, horse and rider, right on top of the breastworks, dead. All dead! They sleep in the graveyard yonder at Ashwood [Tennessee], almost in sight of my home, where I am writing to-day. They sleep the sleep of the brave. We love and cherish their memory. They sleep beneath the ivy-mantled walls of St. John's church, where they expressed a wish to be buried. The private soldier sleeps where he fell, piled in one mighty heap. Four thousand five hundred privates! all lying side by side in death! Thirteen Generals were killed and wounded. Four thousand five hundred men slain, all piled and heaped together at one place. I cannot tell the number of others killed and wounded. God alone knows that. We'll all find out on the morning of the final resurrection.

 Kind friends, I have attempted in my poor and feeble way to tell you of this (I can hardly call it) battle. It should be called by some other name. But like all other battles, it, too, has gone into history. I leave it with you. I do not know who was to blame. It lives in the memory of the poor old Rebel soldier who went through that trying and terrible ordeal. We shed a tear for the dead. They are buried and forgotten. We meet no more on earth. But up yonder, beyond the sunset and the night, away beyond the clouds and tempest, away beyond the stars that ever twinkle and shine in the blue vault above us, away yonder by the great white throne, and by the river of life, where the Almighty and Eternal God sits, surrounded by the angels and archangels and the redeemed of earth, we will meet again and see those noble and brave spirits who gave up their lives for their country's cause that night at Franklin, Tennessee. A life given for one's country is never lost. It blooms again beyond the grave in a land of beauty and of love. Hanging around the throne of sapphire and gold, a rich garland awaits the coming of him who died for his country, and when the horologe of time has struck its last note upon his dying brow, Justice hands the record of life to Mercy, and Mercy pleads with Jesus, and God, for his sake, receives him in his eternal home beyond the skies at last and forever.

Confederate Chaplain Charles Todd Quintard's Description of the Battle of Franklin

From Quintard's 1905 book:
Doctor Quintard: Chaplain C.S.A. and Second Bishop of Tennessee, pp. 112-124

(My notes are in brackets, LS)

The Battle of Franklin was fought on the 30th of November, 1864, and was one of the bloodiest of the war. On that dismal November day, our line of battle was formed at 4 o'clock in the afternoon and marched directly down through an open field toward the outer breastworks of the enemy. A sheet of fire was pouring into the very faces of our men. The command was: "Forward! Forward men!" Never on earth did men fight against greater odds, but they advanced towards the breastworks,—on and on,—and met death without flinching. The roar of battle was kept up until after midnight and then gradually died away, as the enemy abandoned their interior line of defences and rapidly retreated to Nashville.

We had about 23,000 men engaged. They fought with great gallantry, drove the enemy from their outer line of temporary works into their interior line, captured several stands of colors and about one thousand prisoners. But our losses were about 4,500 brave men, and among them Major-General Pat Cleburne, Brigadier-General John Adams, Brigadier-General O. F. Strahl, Brigadier-General Gist, Brigadier-General Granberry and Brigadier-General John C. Carter was mortally wounded. Among the wounded were Major General John C. Brown, Brigadier-Generals Manigault, Quarles, Cockrell, Scott and George Gordon.

General John Adams, on reaching the vicinity of Franklin, had immediately formed his line of battle near the residence [Carnton Plantation] of Colonel John McGavock and led his troops into the fight. A more gallant set of officers and men never faced a foe. General Adams was calm, cool and self-possessed and vigilantly watched and directed the movements of his men and led them on for victory or for death. He was severely wounded early in the action and was urged to leave the field.

He calmly replied: "No, I will not! I will see my men through!" and at the same time gave an order to Captain Thomas Gibson, his aid-de-camp and Brigade Inspector. When he fell he was in the act of leaping his horse, "Old Charlie," over the outer works. Both horse and his rider were instantly killed,— the General falling within our lines, while old Charlie lay astride the works. The General received two wounds in the right leg, four balls entered his body, one ball passed through his breast and one entered his right shoulder-blade. These wounds were all received simultaneously and his death was instantaneous.

Major-General Cleburne's mare was dead on the works and the General himself was pierced with no less than forty-nine bullets. The bodies of these two brave Generals were brought from the battlefield in an ambulance and taken to the residence of Colonel McGavock, whose house and grounds were literally filled with the Confederate dead and wounded. Mrs. McGavock [Caroline E. Winder] rendered every assistance possible and her name deserves to be handed down to future generations as that of a woman of lofty principle, exalted character and untiring devotion.

Captain Gibson, General Adams' aid and Brigade Inspector, although badly wounded, accompanied by Captain Blackwell, conveyed the body of his commander to the residence of the General's brother, Major Nathan Adams, in Pulaski. I officiated at the funeral and his mortal remains were placed in the cemetery by the side of those of his father and mother.

As a soldier, General Adams was active, calm and self-possessed, brave without rashness, quick to perceive and ever ready to seize the favorable moment. He enjoyed the confidence of his superiors and the love and respect of his soldiers and officers. In camp and on the march he looked closely to the comfort of his soldiers, and often shared his horse on long marches with his sick and broken-down men.

He was a member of the Episcopal Church and a sincere and humble Christian. For a year or more before his death he engaged, morning, noon and night in devotional exercises. He invariably fasted on Friday and other days of abstinence appointed by the Book of Common Prayer. He was guided in all his actions by a thoughtful and strict regard for truth, right and duty. In all the relations of life he was upright, just and pure. There is no shadow on his memory and he left to his children the heritage of an unblemished name and to coming generations the sublime heroism of a Southern Soldier.

After the battle General Strahl's horse lay by the road-side and the General by his side,— both dead. All his staff were killed. General Strahl was a native of Ohio, but he had come to Tennessee in his youth, and was as thoroughly identified with the latter state as any of her sons. He gave to the Fourth Tennessee Regiment its drill and discipline and made it a noted regiment before he succeeded General A. P. Stewart in command of a brigade. He was just recovering from a dangerous wound received at Atlanta the previous July when he entered upon the Tennessee campaign, which ended for him fatally.

General Gist, of South Carolina, was lying dead with his sword still grasped in his hand and reaching across the fatal breastworks. General Granberry of Texas, and his horse were seen on the top of the breastworks,—horse and rider,— dead! I went back to Columbia, hired a negro to make some plain coffins, helped him to put them into a wagon, drove with him about sixteen miles, and buried these brave men,— Strahl, Gist, and Granberry,—under the shadow of the ivy-mantled tower of St. John's Church, Ashwood,— with the services of the Church. Then I returned to the field.

Major-General John C. Brown, General George Gordon, and General Carter were seriously wounded,— the last named, mortally. After ministering to these and many another, I returned to Columbia [Tennessee] to the hospital in the Columbia Institute. Here I found Captain William Flournoy and Adjutant McKinney of the First Tennessee Regiment, both severely wounded. There were hundreds of wounded in the Institute.

I buried Major-General Cleburne [a short distance from?] from the residence of Mrs. William Polk. A military escort was furnished by Captain Long and every token of respect was shown to the memory of the glorious dead. After the funeral, I rode out to Hamilton Place with General Lucius Polk. There I found General Manigault wounded in the head and Major Prince, of Mobile, wounded in the foot.

Returning to Columbia, I met Captain Stepleton and through him paid the burial expenses of my dear friend, John Marsh,— three hundred dollars. The dear fellow had given me a farewell kiss as he entered the battle. I also gave the Rev. Dr. Pise one hundred dollars and left myself without funds. While in Columbia I sent wagons down to the Webster settlement to procure supplies for our wounded at Franklin.

Having visited the sick and wounded in the hospitals at Columbia, I went with Captain Stepleton towards Franklin. I reached the house of Mr. Harrison, about three miles from Franklin, at dark, and stopped to see my friends, General Carter, General Quarles, Captain Tom Henry, and Captain Matt Pilcher. Captain Pilcher was shot in the side. Captain Henry was wounded slightly in the head. Both were doing well. General Quarles had his left arm shattered. General Carter was shot through the body and his wound was mortal. I knelt by the side of the wounded and commended them to God. I had prayers with the family before retiring. All that night we could hear the guns around Nashville very distinctly, but all I could learn in the morning was that our lines were within a mile and a half of the city.

The following day was the Second Sunday in Advent, December 4th. I rode to Franklin to see Dr. Buist, the Post Surgeon. All along the way were abundant marks of the terrific battle,—dead horses and burnt wagons,— but at the line of the breastworks near Mr. Carter's house, where the heaviest fighting was done, there was a great number of horses piled almost one upon another. Mr. Carter's son was shot within a few yards of his home. Returning to Mr. Harrison's house with Dr. Buist, who went down to attend to the wounded, I visited them all and had prayers with them. The Doctor and myself returned to Franklin in the evening and William Clouston called and took me to his house for the night.

There I found General Cockrell of Missouri, wounded in the legs and in the right arm but full of life and very cheerful. Lieutenant Anderson, one of his staff, who had lost a part of one foot at Vicksburg, was now wounded in the other. Captain John M. Hickey, in command of a company in a Missouri regiment, while charging the main lines of the works just in front of the cotton gin, was desperately wounded, his leg being shattered. He fell into the mud and while in this deplorable condition, his left arm was badly broken by a minnie ball and soon afterwards he was shot in the shoulder. With thousands of dead and wounded lying about him, he lay upon the field of battle for fifteen hours, without food, water or shelter, in the freezing cold, and half of that time exposed to the plunging shot and shell of both friend and foe.

I devoted my time while in Franklin, to visiting the hospitals. In one room of Brown's Division hospital, in the Court House, I dressed a goodly number of wounds, after which I went to visit General Cockrell and thence to army headquarters at the residence [Travellers Rest] of John Overton. I met with a most cordial welcome, not only from General Hood, but also from Mr. Overton's family and several ladies from Nashville.

On Wednesday, I rode with Governor Harris to Franklin and thence to Mr. Harrison's, to be with General John C. Carter who was nearing his end. I found General Quarles and Captain Pilcher both doing well. Major Dunlap was also improving. Lieutenant-Colonel Jones of the Twenty-fourth South Carolina, however, was not doing so well, having had a profuse hemorrhage. On visiting General Carter, I read a short passage of Holy Scripture and had prayers with him for which he thanked me in the most earnest manner. In his lucid moments my conversation with him was exceedingly interesting. But his paroxysms of pain were frequent and intense and he craved for chloroform and it was freely administered to him.

He could not be convinced that he was going to die. "But," I said, "General, if you should die, what do you wish me to say to your wife?"

"Tell her," he replied, "that I have always loved her devotedly and regret leaving her more than I can express."

I had prayers with all the wounded and with the family of Mr. Harrison, and sat up with General Carter until half past twelve o'clock. Lieutenant-Colonel Jones died some time in the night. General Carter died the following Saturday [December 10, 1864]. I wrote to the Rev. Dr. Pise at Columbia to attend his funeral as his body was to be taken there for temporary burial. It was bitterly cold and the roads were very slippery.

General Carter was a native of Georgia but a citizen of Tennessee. He had been advanced for merit from a lieutenant at the beginning of the war to the command of a brigade. He had a wonderful gentleness of manner coupled with dauntless courage. Every field officer of his brigade but one, was killed, wounded or captured on the enemy's works at the dreadful battle of Franklin.

The following Sunday, (Third Sunday in Advent,) I celebrated the Holy Communion at army headquarters. That night General Forrest shared my bed with me. One of the men remarked: "It was the lion and the lamb lying down together."

The following day, in the Methodist Church at Brentwood, I united in the holy bonds of matrimony, Major William Clare and Miss Mary Hadley, of Nashville. The Major's attendants were Dr. Foard, Medical Director, and Major Moore, Chief Commissary. A large number of officers were present. After the marriage, the party returned to the residence of Mr. Overton where a sumptuous dinner was provided. My empty purse was replenished by a fee of two hundred dollars, besides which a friend sent me, the following morning, fifty dollars in greenbacks.

I left headquarters the following day in Dr. Foard's ambulance for Franklin and on the way picked up a couple of wounded men and carried them to the hospital. We met Governor Harris and Colonel Ray, Secretary of State. I spent the evening at Mrs. Carter's with my friends, Colonel Rice and Captain Tom Henry. The next day I made efforts to purchase shoes for my family. The merchants had hidden their goods and were unwilling to dispose of them for Confederate money. But by offering to pay in greenbacks, I not only secured shoes but all sorts of goods.

Meeting Captain Kelly, of the Rock City Guard, then off duty in consequence of wounds received in the recent battle, I proposed to him to go to Georgia for clothing for the soldiers. To this he agreed and we left for Columbia. While there I attended a meeting of the ladies, the object of which was to organize a Relief Association.

Distressing reports began to come in of a reverse to our arms at Nashville. At first I did not credit them, but later I met Colonel Harvie, the Inspector General, who not only confirmed the very worst of the reports, but expressed both indignation and disgust at the conduct of our troops.

General Lucius Polk sent a buggy for me and I drove out to Hamilton Place and spent the night. The next day, (Fourth Sunday in Advent,) I celebrated the Holy Communion in the parlor at Hamilton Place, and after administering to the company assembled there, carried the consecrated elements to the rooms of General Manigault and Major Prince, that they might also receive the Comfortable Sacrament. In the afternoon I drove back to Columbia and assisted the Rev. Dr. Pise at the marriage of Miss Hages to Major William E. Moore, Chief Commissary of the Army. After this I rode to the residence of Mr. Vaught, where I found General Hood and his staff.

I was glad to find the General bearing up well under the disaster to our arms. It was now a very serious question whether General Hood should hold the line of Duck River, (even if it were possible for him to do so,) or fall back across the Tennessee. One officer remarked to the General in my presence, that while God was on our side so manifestly that no man could question it, it was still very apparent that our people had not yet passed through all their sufferings.

The General replied that the remark was a just one. He had been impressed with the fact at Spring Hill, where the enemy was completely within our grasp, and notwithstanding all his efforts to strike a decisive blow, he had failed. And now again at Nashville, after the day's fighting was well nigh over, when all had gone successfully until the evening, our troops had broken in confusion and fled.

Early the following morning, General Forrest reached headquarters and advised strongly that General Hood withdraw without delay south of the Tennessee. "If we are unable to hold the state, we should at once evacuate it," were the words of General Forrest. At nine o'clock in the morning, cannonading began at Rutherford Hill. After a couple of hours, word came from General Cheatham that he had repulsed the enemy, and the firing ceased. General Hood finally decided to fall back south of the Tennessee; and Governor Harris, in whose judgment I had great confidence, thought it the best we could do. Still it was a dark day to me, and the thought of leaving the state of Tennessee once more, greatly depressed me.

Tuesday, the 20th of December, was a day of gloominess. I felt in bidding farewell to Columbia, that I was parting with my dearest and most cherished hopes. I recalled the days of our march into Tennessee, so full of delightful intercourse with Strahl, and Marsh and other friends. After saying "goodbye," I rode on to Pulaski, thirty miles, where I was cordially received at the home of Mrs. Ballentine. The next day I baptized six persons there, and later at the headquarters of General Hood, in the residence of the Honorable Thomas Jones, four of Mr. Jones' children. After this baptism Mr. Jones joined us at prayers in

General Hood's room. The General said, "I am afraid that I have been more wicked since I began this retreat than for a long time past. I had so set my heart upon success,—had prayed so earnestly for it,—had such a firm trust that I should succeed, that my heart has been very rebellious. But," he added, "let us go out of Tennessee, singing hymns of praise."

The weather was exceeding inclement. So many of our poor boys were barefooted that there was very great suffering. The citizens of Pulaski did all they could to provide shoes. I dined on Wednesday with Governor Harris, at Major Nathan Adams' and spent the night with Colonel Rice. The General informed me the next day that the enemy effected a crossing of Duck River at Columbia at noon, and began shelling the town. But Forrest told them by flag, that if the shelling were not stopped, he would put their wounded directly under the fire. The firing consequently ceased.

Our forces all moved on towards Bainbridge. General Hood left the following morning. I joined Governor Harris as he was not to be detained en route. We rode thirty miles to a little town called Lexington, where Colonel Rice, Captain Ballentine and myself obtained rough accommodations for the night. The next day, we started for Lamb's Ferry, thinking to find a boat there, but learned that General Roddy had ordered it to Elk River to cross his command. I therefore had another journey of eighteen miles to make. Just at the close of the day I found my friend, Major-General Clayton, camped by the roadside, and not knowing General Hood's location, I decided to accept General Clayton's very cordial invitation to spend the night with him. It was Christmas eve. After supper the General called up all his staff and couriers and we had prayers.

The next day, Christmas day and Sunday, was very sad and gloomy. I had prayers at General Clayton's headquarters, after which I rode down to the river and watched the work of putting down the pontoons. Some one brought me a Christmas gift of two five dollar gold pieces from Mrs. Thomas Jones of Pulaski.

The following day I crossed the river at nine o'clock. On crossing the river on our forward march, I had sung "Jubilate." Now I was chanting "De Profundis." I joined General Hood at Tuscumbia on the 27th and found the General feeling the disaster more since he reached Tuscumbia than at any time since the retreat began. And after various adventures, I reached Aberdeen on Saturday, the last day of 1864. Though an entire stranger in Aberdeen, I received a most cordial welcome at the home of Mr. Needham Whitfield, whose family were church people. And thus ended the year 1864.

APPENDIX K

Confederate Captain Joseph Boyce's Description of the Battle of Franklin

From *Confederate Veteran*
Vol. 24, No. 1, January 1916, Nashville, TN, pp. 101-103, 138

(My notes are in brackets, LS)

MISSOURIANS IN BATTLE OF FRANKLIN
BY CAPTAIN JOSEPH BOYCE, IN ST. LOUIS REPUBLIC

y command, the 1st Missouri Confederate Brigade, Gen. F. M. Cockrell commanding, was a part of Gen. A. P. Stewart's corps, Gen. Samuel G. French's division, and after the Georgia campaign fought Sherman's advance from Kingston until the fall of Atlanta and the subsequent battles of Jonesboro, Allatoona, and Tilton. General Hood decided to move his army toward Nashville, Tenn., about two hundred miles distant.

We left Lovejoy Station about the last week of September, and during October the nights were cold and frosts very heavy. It was a dismal journey. Our clothing was not suitable for the severe weather; we were without overcoats, and shoes were scarce. We were obliged to leave behind at Tuscumbia and Florence many men who were so badly shod and clothed that they could not make the march toward Nashville.

We were bivouacked at Tuscumbia from November 1 until the 20th, awaiting the arrival of pontoon boats and supplies so that we could cross the Tennessee River, which was out of banks owing to the heavy and almost incessant rains. Despite the dreary march through cold and rainy weather, exhausting and depressing on troops not prepared for such trials and not enthused by past victories in Georgia, they were anxious to push on to the end to accomplish the defeat of the enemy at all hazards.

On the 20th of November we crossed the Tennessee River on pontoons and marched through Florence on a cold, rainy day. The mud was thinned by the rain and snow to the consistency of gruel. The roadbed was macadam and our footing sure, but we waded through this awful mess for several miles before reaching the point where we were to bivouac. It took the best part of the night to clean up and make ourselves comfortable. We were much cheered at this place by meeting Forrest and his cavalry. They had just returned from Johnsonville and other points on the Tennessee River after a grand and victorious campaign. Among his troopers we saw our old friends of the famous 2d Missouri Cavalry, Col. Bob McCollough, and King's 2d Missouri Battery. This was a superb company of flying artillery, well equipped and drilled to perfection, commanded by Captain Faris and J. Russell Dougherty. Most of its members were from St. Charles, Mo. These two commands represented Missouri with Forrest's Cavalry during most of the war and always bore Missouri's banner in the front of the conflict with the enemy.

After a few days at Florence we started north with the army for Middle Tennessee. The morning we moved out on the road was gloomy and cloudy. Presently a snowstorm set in, the first heavy snow of the season. The men set up a shout and hurrahed for Missouri. "This is the kind of weather we want, regular old Missouri weather. This is none of your Southern rains; this is something decent. Hurrah for old Missouri! We are on our way home." After several hours the sun came out. We had by this time reached the pike road, and from that time on we had delightful weather and most excellent roads—very little rain, the nights cool and slightly frosty, the days warm and pleasant. This march was kept up for several days. We were received everywhere with great enthusiasm and kindness by the people along our route. We passed through the finest farming country we ever saw, and, to the enemy's credit, there were no signs of destruction to private property such as we saw in Georgia and Alabama.

We had several brushes with the enemy during our advance, but they were only skirmishes and did not give us any concern until the morning of the 30th of November, when a heavy skirmish line was thrown out from our brigade on the left of us. We marched in parallel lines and with the main body mostly on the road or pike passing through Spring Hill. I believe we were the advance infantry of Hood's army that day. Forrest was in our front with his cavalry, and he crowded the enemy fiercely at every point. This was very evident to us by the abandoned wagons of commissary stores. The enemy was too hotly pressed to have time to unhitch the mules. We found the poor creatures dead in their harness, having been shot through the head by the drivers or rear guard. Their bodies were still warm and smoking from the great exertion made to escape our advance. Forrest was certainly the "Wizard of the Saddle," and he must have traveled like the wind, for on the road near Franklin we saw two locomotives which he had captured steam up and blow off seemingly with indignation at their bad luck.

The citizens, nearly all old people or boys too young for military service, and any number of enthusiastic young ladies lined the fences, cheering us and crying out: "Push on, boys; you will capture all of the Yanks soon. They have just passed here on the dead run." We received the news with joyous cheers and kept our double-quick step along the road for several hours. About noon we reached a point near Franklin, a range of hills, and after passing over them came out in full view of the Federal position.

The ground appeared to us as level as a floor. The main [Confederate] army came on the field, and the divisions of Loring and Walthall, of our corps (Stewart's), took positions for the battle. In the rear of Cheatham's and Cleburne's Divisions our division (French's) was the reserve. It consisted of Cockrell's and Sears's Brigades. Our other brigade (Ector's Texans) was not with us that day, having been left behind at Florence on guard duty. After considerable delay the Army of Tennessee was in position. It was a beautiful sight. As far as the eye could see it beheld troops moving into line for the attack. The troops were placed in echelon, and while moving to other places, except for the shells rushing over us, we might have been thought to be getting ready for inspection.

While we were in line of battle some one in the company, impressed with the scene, quoted [Lord] Nelson's famous order at Trafalgar: "England expects every man to do his duty." Sergt. Denny Callahan took it up at once, saying: "It's damned little duty England would get out of this Irish crowd." Nearly all the company and regiment were composed of Irishmen or their descendants. The laugh Denny raised on this was long and hearty. They were noble fellows, indeed, laughing in the face of death. Four years of war hardens men, and yet there were few in the command over twenty-two years of age.

About four o'clock the corps of [Confederate Generals S. D.]

Lee and [B. F.] Cheatham were ready for the grand assault. The sun was going down behind a bank of dark clouds, as if to hide from sight the impending slaughter. His slanting rays threw a crimson light over the field and intrenchments in front, prophetic of our fate. Our brigade was in the rear, formed in the same order as at Allatoona's bloody field, recollections of which were so many thrilling reminders that it was no boy's play to charge this veteran Western infantry when well intrenched. General Cockrell gave orders to march straight for the position in quick time and not to fire a shot until we gained the top of the works; then when the decisive moment arrived, in clear, ringing tones came the final commands: "Shoulder arms! Right shoulder shift arms! Brigade forward! Guide center! Music! Quick time! March!" And this array of hardened veterans, every eye straight to the front, in actual perfection of drill and discipline, moved forward to our last and bloodiest charge. Our brass band, one of the finest in the army, went up with us, starting with "The Bonnie Blue Flag," changing to "Dixie" as we reached the deadly point.

The enemy instantly opened heavily with musketry and artillery in front and an enfilading fire from a battery on our right, on the far side of the Harpeth River, which was deliberate and deadly as we fired not a shot in return. Men commenced dropping fast from the start. The distance we marched from our position where we first formed line of battle to the enemy's works was, I remember, about nine hundred yards. In that space our flag fell three times. Joseph T. Donavan, ensign, of St. Louis, was the first to fall, badly hurt by a fragment of shell. Two other members of the regiment, John S. Harris and Robert Bently, were killed a few moments later while carrying it. Sergt. Denny Callahan was the last bearer, and this brave Irish boy carried it successfully to the works, where he planted it, and was wounded and captured, the flag falling into the hands of the Federals when we were forced from the position.

Advancing in echelon (stair step) order, our long, swinging step soon brought us abreast of Cleburne's Division, just to the right of the Franklin Pike, and with that superb command we crossed the enemy's advance line of rifle pits, raised the glorious old [Rebel] yell, and rushed upon the main works a frantic, maddened body with overpowering impulse to reach the enemy and kill, murder, destroy. On and on we went right up to the murderous parapet, delivered one smashing volley as General Cockrell had directed, and the line rolled over the works with empty guns, the bayonet now their only trust. I should have said what was left of the line, for the ground in the rear was all too thickly covered with the bodies of our comrades. Our colonel, Garland, of St. Louis was killed soon after we started, and as senior captain the command of the regiment devolved upon me.

As we crossed the rifle pits our line was delayed a moment, when, finding myself alone, I cried out: "Who is going to stay with me?" Lieut. A. B. Barnett, Dick Saulsbery, Robert Bonner, and Denny Callahan dashed up, flag in hand, and we led the regiment up on the Federal works, where we all went down together. I made a stroke at a bluecoat [Yankee soldier], felt my leg give way, and fell on top of the works. He was too quick for me, my sword flying from my hand. In another second our men were on top of the parapet. The enemy's fire ceased abruptly, and I crawled forward and picked up my sword; then, finding that I could walk a little, I started back to hunt for a surgeon; but my wound was too severe, and I fell. Two slightly wounded men of the 5th Missouri assisted me off the field and placed me in an ambulance of General Quarles.

The enemy gave way, and we made another successful assault. It may sound boastful, but it is true, that never during the entire war did our Missouri command fail to carry a line we were ordered to take, and never did the enemy succeed in breaking our line. This can be said of very few commands in all the history of war, but the official reports of both sides agree in confirming the statement.

But our triumph was very short. With empty guns, without officers, out of breath, our thin line rested a few seconds, when it was assailed by the enemy's second line. The scene inside the fatal fortifications of Corinth was repeated. A solid wall of blue infantry advanced at the double quick and poured in a volley. It was too much. Our brave fellows came out of the works as quickly as they had entered them and sought refuge behind the rifle pits a short distance back.

As we moved forward to the charge two guns of Guibor's St. Louis Battery, under command of Lieuts. A. W. Harris and Sam Kennard, advanced with us and opened fire at close range. As I limped back I saw the cannoneers pushing their guns by hand to the front, right up to the rifle pits, where the infantry rallied upon them, and all opened fire. Night put a stop to the slaughter. During this last firing nearly all our wounded lying in front were killed by the enemy's fire. Poor fellows! Their cries for help and for water could occasionally be heard; but no one could reach them, and they were gradually silenced by the fire from that awful parapet. After midnight the enemy withdrew, leaving his dead and severely wounded in our possession. Following the custom of Federal authorities in similar battles, this might be claimed as a Confederate victory. I can safely say that just two such victories will wipe out any army the power of man can organize. "Surely the path of glory leads but to the grave."

Our appalling loss was not generally realized until next morning, when a ghastly sight was revealed to those still living. Among the dead of our regiment were Col. Hugh A. Garland, brave and daring in battle, in camp as gentle as a child, and always in a good humor. Capt Cadmus Bray, Lieuts. A. B. Barnett and _____ Cannon, and Sergt. William Hopkins. Of the wounded, I remember Lieut. Harry Thompson and Sergeant Jones.

The heroic bravery and thorough discipline of our brigade on the field of Franklin almost lost them their organization as Missourians. Those remaining did not make a good-sized regiment, while the regiments looked like companies. Our regiment had but three officers left for duty, Capt. James Wickersham and Lieuts. James Kennerly and Patrick Collins. This loss was proportionate throughout the brigade.

As it was rather an unusual thing for the "tooters" [musicians] to go up in a charge with the "shooters," I think it but justice to give the names of the veterans composing our band. Every member had carried his musket in the ranks for two years and through many battles, and I believe all of them would have exchanged their instruments for muskets if ordered to remain in the rear. They were Prof. John O'Neil (leader), John and Chris O'Neil, James and Thad Doyle, Charles Ketchum, Sam Lyon, James Young, Shelby Jones, James Robinet, and Simeon Phillips.

Our army was a wreck. Our comrades were lying in the embrace of death. So many young hearts were stilled forever which a few hours ago beat high in the prospect of soon being at home in Missouri! The sad news quickly reached our people, and many, many families of Missouri friends bowed their heads in sorrow for the poor boys laid low on the ill-fated field of Franklin.

Gen. F. M. Cockrell was badly wounded in two places, but despite this he led his brigade to the works. Col. Elijah Gates was severely wounded in both arms, losing one by amputation. Maj. James M. Loughborough, of St. Louis, rode to the front and dashed his horse upon the works, waving his hat and cheering us on. Strange that those who appear to be in the most danger escape without injury. Such was Loughborough's case. I think he was the only one of General Cockrell's staff unhurt.

It is a well known fact that one man behind a well-intrenched line is equal to five men in front. Thus we were confronted at Franklin. The "War Records" state that [Union General J. M.] Schofield had 25,400 and Hood had 21,874 men, without artillery, except two guns brought with him, Guibor's Battery.

The task of burying the dead was commenced and continued through the day until finished. The wounded were sent into Franklin and made as comfortable as possible. Among the killed was General Cleburne, the model soldier. We felt his loss as deeply as the men of his own division. Men would say to one another, "Why, Cleburne is killed!" and appeared to doubt it, as if such a calamity could not befall the army. Then the death of Capt. Patrick Canniff, commanding the 5th Missouri, caused us great grief. He was also a model soldier. After passing through so many battles, he was killed when needed most. He was wounded near the works and was too badly hurt to crawl away to a place of safety and received his death wound later on. Also among the killed were Lieut. William A. Crow, Patrick Marnell, and Thomas Hogan, all from St. Louis.

The day after burying the dead the command took up the line of march toward Nashville, passing to the right of the town of Franklin. After arriving at Nashville, the brigade, under command of Col. Peter F. Flournoy, of Linneus, Mo., was sent to the mouth of Duck River on outpost duty, passing through Franklin on its way. It did not remain long at this point, as news of the overwhelming disaster to our army at Nashville was brought by couriers to the brigade, and it was hurried off to join the retreating forces of Hood near Columbia.

On that dreadful retreat in the midst of winter, the weather turning suddenly and intensely cold, we were followed by a victorious foe, who showed no signs of fatigue or desire to let us rest. Our rear guard was engaged all the time and met him with the same unflinching courage shown in attacking him at Franklin. The men were distressed by hunger and exhaustion. Bloody foot tracks in the frozen snow and upon the icy roads were to be seen in many places. Yet, like Napoleon's Old Guard on the retreat from Moscow, they presented a front for fight at all times. The weather was not as severe as a Russian winter, it is true, but the hardships our poor fellows had to endure were similar, because they were so poorly clad and fed. The patriotism of the Confederate soldier can never be doubted by any one familiar with the horrors of that retreat. All his troubles would end if he were to fall out of the ranks and allow himself to be taken [prisoner]. The Federals would clothe him, feed him, administer the oath of loyalty (or royalty, as we used to call it), and send him to his home. In fact, many a man marched wearily along within sight of his home. No; he would rather die of exposure than desert his flag. Those who were taken fell overcome by fatigue and hunger. After many days of hardships and nights of suffering, the command reached Bainbridge and recrossed the Tennessee River. At this point the enemy abandoned the pursuit, and Hood and his suffering men proceeded on their way unmolested.

The Missouri troops took a prominent part in the rear guard under Generals Forrest and Walthall. Col. Bob McCollough and his 2d Missouri Cavalry were always on the alert, while Bledsoe and his noble battery thundered defiance at the enemy almost continuously during the retreat. All the attempts of the enemy to break the line of the rear guard were in vain. The most remarkable fact in connection with the veterans composing this heroic body of men was that when the retreat ended they had as trophies more Federal prisoners than their entire number and about twelve more pieces of artillery than when they began to fall back from Nashville.

Gen. S. G. French, our division commander, says in his account of Franklin: "It was a terrible battle. One of my brigades the 1st Missouri (Gen. F. M. Cockrell) made the assault with six hundred and ninety-six officers and men, and when it was over he had two hundred and seventy-seven men in his brigade. His loss was: Killed, nineteen officers and seventy-nine men; wounded, thirty-one officers and one-hundred and ninety-eight men; missing, thirteen officers and seventy-nine men; total, four hundred and nineteen, which was over sixty per cent. The missing were captured inside the works, as stated by some who escaped. The battle raged furiously at intervals till near midnight, especially on the west side of the pike, mainly between our troops in the ditch and on the captured parapet, with the enemy on inside lines; and the bright glare of musketry, with the flashes of artillery, lit up the surroundings with seeming fitful volcanic fires, presenting a night scene frightfully wild and weird."

APPENDIX L

Southern Journalist Edward Alfred Pollard's Description of "Hood's Tennessee Campaign"

From Pollard's 1866 book: *The Lost Cause*, pp. 584-588

(My notes are in brackets, LS)

On the 20th November, Gen. Hood commenced to move his army from Northern Alabama to Tennessee. He pushed forward as if to cut off Schofield's retreat from Pulaski; this Federal commander having taken position there, with the greater part of two army corps, and an aggregation of fort-garrisons from the surrounding country, while Thomas remained at Nashville. Schofield fearing that his position was about to be flanked, abandoned Pulaski, and attempted by a forced march to reach Columbia.

The want of a good map of the country, and the deep mud through which the army marched, prevented Hood overtaking the enemy before he reached Columbia; but on the evening of the 27th of November the Confederate army was placed in position in front of his works at that place. During the night, however, the enemy evacuated the town, taking position on the opposite side of the river, about a mile and a half from the town, which was considered quite strong in front. Late in the evening of the 23th November, Gen. Forrest, with most of his command, crossed Duck River, a few miles above Columbia, and Hood followed early on the morning of the 20th, with Stewart's and Cheatham's corps, and Johnson's division of Lee's corps, leaving the other divisions of Lee's corps in the enemy's front at Columbia. The troops moved in light marching order, the object being to turn the enemy's flank by marching rapidly on roads parallel to the Columbia and Franklin pike, at or near Spring Hill, and to cut off that portion of the enemy at or near Columbia.

BATTLE OF SPRING HILL

The enemy, discovering the intentions of the Confederates, began to retreat on the pike towards Spring Hill. About 4 P.M., Hood's infantry forces, Cheatham in the advance, commenced to come in contact with the enemy, about two miles from Spring Hill, through which place the Columbia and Franklin pike runs. The enemy was at this time moving rapidly along the pike, with some of his troops on the flank of his column to protect it. Cheatham was ordered to attack the enemy at once, vigorously, and get possession of this pike. He made only a feeble and partial attack, failing to reach the point indicated. The great object of Gen. Hood was to possess himself of the road to Franklin, and thus cut off the enemy's retreat. Though owing to delays the signal opportunity to do this had passed at daylight, there was yet a chance of dealing the enemy a heavy blow. Stewart's corps and Johnson's division were arriving upon the field to support the attack. Stewart was ordered to move his corps beyond Cheatham's, and place it across the road beyond Spring Hill. He did not succeed in getting the position he desired, owing to some misunderstanding of orders, and, night falling, he went into bivouac. About midnight, ascertaining that the enemy was moving in great confusion—artillery wagons and troops intermixed—Gen. Hood sent instructions to Cheatham to advance a heavy line of skirmishers against him, and still further impede and confuse his march. This was not accomplished. The enemy continued to move along the road in hurry and confusion, within hearing, nearly all the night. Thus was lost a great opportunity of striking the enemy, and his line of retreat secured in the face of the Confederates without a battle.

 Much of the disaster that was now to ensue in his campaign Gen. Hood attributed to the fact that "some of his Generals had failed him at Spring Hill." There was nothing left now but to pursue the enemy. At daylight Hood's army followed as fast as possible towards Franklin, Stewart in the advance, Cheatham following, and Lee with the trains, moving from Columbia on the same road. The Confederates pursued the enemy rapidly, and compelled him to burn a number of his wagons. He made a feint as if to give battle on the hills about four miles south of Franklin, but as soon as Hood's forces began to deploy for the attack, and to flank him on his left, he retired slowly to Franklin. Gen. Hood had learned from despatches captured at Spring Hill, from Thomas to Schofield, that the latter was instructed to hold that place till the position at Franklin could be made secure, indicating the intention of Thomas to hold Franklin and his strong works at Murfreesboro. Thus Hood knew that it was all-important to attack Schofield before he could make himself strong, and that if he should escape at Franklin, he would gain his works about Nashville. The nature of the position was such as to render it inexpedient to attempt any further flank movement, and he therefore determined to attack the enemy in front, and without delay.

BATTLE OF FRANKLIN
On the 30th November Stewart's corps was placed in position on the right, Cheatham's on the left, and the cavalry on either flank, the main body on the right under Forrest. Johnson's division of Lee's corps also became engaged on the left during the action. The line advanced at 4 P.M., with orders to drive the enemy, at the point of the bayonet, into or across the Big Harpeth River, while Gen. Forrest, if successful, was to cross the river and attack and destroy his trains and broken columns. The troops moved forward most gallantly to the attack. They carried the enemy's line of hastily-constructed works handsomely. They then advanced against his interiour line, and succeeded in carrying it also, in some places. Here the engagement was of the fiercest possible character. The Confederates came on with a desperation and disregard of death, such as had been shown on few battle-fields of the war. A Northern writer says: "More heroic valour was never exhibited by any troops than was shown here by the rebels." The devoted troops were mowed down by grape and canister. Many of them were killed entirely inside of the works. The brave men captured were taken inside the enemy's works on the edge of the town. The struggle lasted till near midnight, when the enemy abandoned his works and crossed the river, leaving his dead and wounded.

It is remarkable that in this hard-fought battle the Confederates used no artillery whatever; Gen. Hood's explanation being that he was restrained from using that terrible arm "on account of the women and children remaining in the town." Victory had been purchased at the price of a terrible slaughter. Hood's total loss in killed, wounded, and prisoners was 4,500. Among the killed was Maj.-Gen. P. R. Cleburne, Brig. Gens. John Adams, Strahl and Granbury; while Maj.-Gen. Brown, Brig.-Gens. Carter, Manigault, Quarles, Cockrell, and Scott were wounded, and Brig.-Gen. Gordon captured.

BATTLE OF NASHVILLE

The next morning Gen. Hood advanced upon Nashville, where Schofield had retreated, and where Thomas lay with his main force. He laid siege to the town on the 2d December, closely investing it for a fortnight. The opinion long prevailed in the Confederacy that in this pause and the operations of siege, Hood made the cardinal mistake of his campaign; and that if he had taken another course, and struck boldly across the Cumberland, and settled himself in the enemy's communications, he would have forced Thomas to evacuate Nashville, and fall back towards Kentucky. This was the great fear of Gen. Grant. That high Federal officer, in his report of the operations of 1864, has written: "Before the battle of Nashville I grew very impatient over, as it appeared to me, the unnecessary delay. This impatience was increased upon learning that the enemy had sent a force of cavalry across the Cumberland into Kentucky. I feared Hood would cross his whole army and give us great trouble here. After urging upon Gen. Thomas the necessity of immediately assuming the offensive, I started west to superintend matters there in person. Reaching Washington city, I received Gen. Thomas's despatch announcing his attack upon the enemy, and the result as far as the battle had progressed. I was delighted. All fears and apprehensions were dispelled."

On the night of the 14th December, Thomas decided upon a plan of battle, which was to make a feint on Hood's right flank, while he massed his main force to crush in Hood's left, which rested on the Cumberland, and where the cover of the Federal gunboats might be made available. The brunt of the action did not fall until evening, when the enemy drove in the Confederate infantry outposts on the left flank. Hood, however, quickly ordered up troops from his right to stay the reversed tide of battle; and the remainder of the day was occupied by the enemy in sweeping the Confederate entrenchments with artillery fire, while here and there his infantry attempted, in vain, to find a weak spot in their lines.

Under cover of the night Hood re-formed his line, and in the morning was found in position along the Overton Hills, some two miles or so to the rear of his original line. The new position was a strong one, running along the wooded crests of closely-connecting hills; while the two keys to it were the Granny White and Franklin pikes, leading to

Franklin, Columbia, Pulaski, and so down the country to the Tennessee River. Thomas' overwhelming numbers enabled him to throw heavy columns against Hood's left and centre. But every attack of the enemy was repulsed. It was four o'clock in the evening, and the day was thought to be decided for the Confederates, when there occurred one of the most extraordinary incidents of the war. It is said that Gen. Hood was about to publish a victory along his line, when Finney's Florida brigade in Bates' division, which was to the left of the Confederate centre, gave way before the skirmish line of the enemy! Instantly Bates' whole division took the panic, and broke in disorder. The moment a small breach was thus made in the Confederate lines, the whole of two corps unaccountably and instantly fled from their ditches, almost without firing a gun. It was a disgraceful panic; muskets were abandoned where they rested between the logs of the breastworks; and everything that could impede flight was thrown away as the fugitives passed down the Granny White and Franklin pikes, or fled wildly from the battle-field. Such an instance of sudden, unlooked-for, wild retreat, the abandonment of a victory almost won, could only have happened in an army where thorough demoralization, the consequence of long, heavy, weary work, and of tremendous efforts without result—in short, the reaction of great endeavours where success is not decided, already lurked in the minds of troops, and was likely to be developed at any time by the slightest and most unimportant circumstance.

 Fifty pieces of artillery and nearly all of Hood's ordnance wagons were left to the enemy. His loss in killed and wounded was disgracefully small; and it was only through want of vigour in Thomas' pursuit that Hood's shattered and demoralized army effected its retreat. Forrest's command, and Walthall, with seven picked brigades, covered the retreat. The situation on the Tennessee River was desperate; Hood had no pontoon train, and if he had been pressed, would have been compelled to surrender; but as it was, Thomas' great error in resting upon his victory at Nashville enabled a defeated Confederate army to construct bridges of timber over the Tennessee River, while the Federal gunboats in the stream were actually kept at bay by batteries of 82-pounders.

 Hood succeeded in escaping across the Tennessee, but only with a remnant of the brilliant force he had conducted across the river a few weeks before, having lost from various causes more than ten thousand men, half of his Generals, and nearly all of his artillery. Such was the disastrous issue of the Tennessee campaign, which put out of existence, as it were, the splendid army that Johnston had given up at Atlanta, and terminated forever the whole scheme of Confederate defence west of the Alleghanies.

Confederate Colonel William Dudley Gale's Description of the Battles of Franklin & Nashville

From Ridley's 1906 book: *Battles and Sketches of the Army of Tennessee*, pp. 409-415
(from a letter to Gale's wife Katherine Polk, daughter of Confederate General Leonidas Polk)

(My notes are in brackets, LS)

Headquarters Stewart's Corps, near Tupelo, Jan. 14th, 1865.

I wrote you a short account of our battles in Middle Tennessee and our flight from the State. I now give you some of the particulars in detail. After three weeks' preparation at Florence, we finally crossed the Tennessee on the 20th of November and moved forward toward Mt. Pleasant. [Union] General Thomas at that time had his army at Pulaski. When we got to Mt. Pleasant he had fallen back to Columbia. We got to Columbia on the 26th, and invested it. On the night of the 27th it was evacuated. On the 28th, this and Cheatham's corps began one of the finest moves of the war—in conception worthy of Stonewall Jackson, and in execution feeble and disgraceful—to cross Duck river above Columbia, and by a forced march over bad roads and through the woods and fields to strike the pike at Spring Hill, and cut [Union General] Schofield off from Nashville or strike him in the flank. The move was made and all was a success up to the time of striking the enemy. We struck the pike at Spring Hill just as the retreating enemy were moving by, completely surprising them. But strange to say, we remained all night in sound of the voices of the men as they retreated in the greatest haste, and not a blow was struck, though orders were sent by General Hood several times to attack at once. One time Governor Harris himself carried the order to General John B. Hood. General Lee was left in Columbia to cross and attack in the rear. He failed to come up also, and thus Tennessee was lost. General Stewart was ready and anxious to lead his corps to the attack, but was not ordered, as the other was in front. The next morning we pushed forward in pursuit of the flying column, the road strewn everywhere with the wreck of a flying army. Wagons, just set on fire and abandoned, were saved from destruction. When we got near Franklin we found the enemy in line across the road two miles from town. Preparations were made to turn the position by a flank movement, when the force fell back to their entrenchments near the town. Preparations were made at once to assault the town. Franklin is in a bend of the Harpeth [River], and the enemy's line was a circle, each wing resting upon the river. It was one of the strongest places in the world to defend. Our men went boldly up in the face of 20,000 muskets and at least 70 pieces of artillery, many of the bands playing our favorite pieces. The enemy was easily driven from the front line and sought safety behind the inner line, where his artillery was. Our line moved forward and closed around the enemy —Loring on the right, French next, then Walthall, then Cleburne, then Brown, then Bate, Johnston's division the only one of Lee's corps that was up—was held in reserve, and afterward was put in where Bate and Brown were. The fight was furious, and the carnage awful beyond anything I ever saw. Our men were mowed down by what we called an enfilade and reverse fire, i.e. in the side and rear, in addition to that in front. The enemy fought with great desperation. Our men were flushed with hope, pride and ambition as they fought for Tennessee. They felt that the eyes of our men and women all over our country, as well as Tennessee, were upon them, and the Yankee Army which they had followed so long was before them.

> "Wave, Munich! all thy banners wave,
> And charge with all thy chivalry!"

The chivalry of the South did charge as bravely as they charged Agincourt or Cressy, and Marathon and Thermopylae were not more grandly fought than Franklin. Charge after charge was made. As fast as one division was shattered and recoiled, another bravely went forward into the very jaws of death, and came back broken and bloody, again rallying quickly with their heroic officers, and again went forward to do what seemed impossible—or die. Such men as Loring, Walthall, Adams, Cockrell, Gates, Featherston, Shelby, Reynolds, Cleburne, Strahl, Gist, and others, should live in prose and poetry as long as the story of the war is written or read. No pen can do justice to the gallantry of the men. Walthall had two horses shot dead under him. The field was covered with the wounded and the dead. The enemy's line had been crossed in one or two places, but no man who went over was ever known to return. Many hundreds lay all night in the ditch separated from the enemy by the thickness of the embankment.

While the officers were collecting the scattered and broken ranks I went with General Stewart to General Hood's headquarters. He had determined to renew the attack in the morning. The plan was that all our artillery—100 pieces—which had been brought up, was to open on them at daylight, and at 9 the whole army was to assault the works. You may well think it was a bitter prospect for our poor fellows. We rode up to a part of the enemy's line which was still held, to place Strahl's brigade in position, when I was struck by the stillness in the enemy's works, and asked the officer nearest me if the enemy had not gone. He said they had, as some of his men had been down and found no one there. Further examination convinced me of the fact, and I rode back to our camp fire, and just as day was dawning [December 1, 1864] I dismounted, wet, weary, hungry and disheartened, telling General Stewart that Schofield was gone. A half hour's rest, not sleep, on the wet ground and I got up, drank a cup of coffee and went to my daily work. I rode over the field early in the day, before the details which I had ordered, had began to bury the dead. It was awful! The ditch at the enemy's line—on the right and left of the pike—was literally filled with dead bodies, lying across each other, in all unseemly deformity of violent death. General Adams rode his horse upon the breast-works and both horse and rider fell there. Cleburne was thirty yards in front of his division when he fell, shot through the heart. But I am tired of the sickening details and you all must be, too. You can see our dreadful loss from published accounts.

I have now one more scene to paint, one more story to tell you, and I am done. I wish I had a pen to do justice to the subject, for in all the annals of the war, filled as it is with the great and noble deeds of great and noble men and women, none exceed and few equal in true merit, the noble sympathy of Mrs. John McGavock [Caroline "Carrie" Elizabeth Winder, of Carnton Plantation]. When day dawned we found ourselves near her house—in her lawn—which was in the rear of our line. The house is one of the large old fashioned country houses of the better class in Tennessee, two stories high, with many rooms and every arrangement for comfort. This was taken as a hospital, and the wounded in hundreds were brought to it during the battle, and all the night after. Every room was filled, every bed had two poor bleeding fellows, every spare space niche and comer under the stairs, in the hall, everywhere—but one room [the parents' bedroom] for her own family. And when the noble old house could hold no more, the yard was appropriated until the wounded and dead filled that, and all were not yet provided for. Our doctors were deficient in bandages, and she began by giving her old linen, then her towels and napkins, then her sheets and table cloths, then her husband's shirts and her own under-garments. During all this time the surgeons plied their dreadful work amid the sighs and moans and death-rattle. Yet amid it all, this noble woman, the very impersonation of Divine sympathy and tender pity, was active and constantly at work. During all the night neither she nor any one of her household slept, but dispensed tea and coffee and such stimulants as she had, and that too, with her own hands. Unaffrighted by the sight of blood, unawed by horrid wounds, unblanched by ghastly death she walked from room to room, from man to man, her very skirts stained in blood, the incarnation of pity and mercy. Is it strange that all who were there praise her and call her blessed? About nine in the morning she sent for us—General and Staff—and gave us a nice, warm breakfast, and a warmer welcome. The brother of one of my clerks (McReady) was very badly wounded, and then in her house. I bespoke her kind attention, which she gave till he died.

  Many years ago I was in the same house [Carnton Mansion] and in the same room, on a visit. On one side of the fire sat the father of Mrs. McGavock [Colonel Van Perkins Winder], then an old man. He seemed particularly glad to see me, and told me he was a soldier in the war of 1812, and was at the battle of New Orleans. When on his way back the troops marched by the plantation of my grandfather Green, below Natchez, and his regiment was entertained by him and furnished with milk in great quantities. He spoke of the gratitude of the men. There were beeves [beef cows] killed also, and a great treat given them. Is it not strange that after fifty years a descendant of that generous man should receive hospitality on a bloody field of battle from a descendant of the tired and hungry soldier?

Not a drum was heard, not a funeral note,
As his corpse to the ramparts we hurried;
Not a soldier fired a farewell shot
O'er the graves of the heroes we buried.

The generals were buried at Ashwood cemetery.

CONFEDERATE DISASTER AT NASHVILLE
Headquarters Stewart's Corps, Tupelo, Miss., January 19, 1865

I now resume my story and will give you some account of our doings in front of Nashville. We left Franklin on the second day after the fight and move on toward Nashville, our army in mourning. When we got to John Overton's place [Travellers Rest in Nashville] I saw some ladies by the roadside in high excitement, and on riding up found them to be Mary Bradford, Miss Maxwell, Miss May, Misses Becky Allison, Mary Hadley and Buck Correy. Mary Hadley was married to Major Clare, of the Staff of General Hood, and was left behind after her three days' honeymoon. Our corps then moved across to the Granny White Pike, through Mr. Lea's place, and went to John's house and established headquarters there. Our first line was from the Franklin Pike, near Mr. Vaulx's, along the ridge in front of father's by Montgomery's house (burned some time ago), across to the Hillsboro Pike, near Mr. Rains.' This corps on the left, Lee in center, and Cheatham on the right, extending over toward and near to the Murfreesboro Pike. We remained thus for two days, intrenching and building redoubts on our left. The Yanks were in line, plain in view along the high ridge just back of Mr. Lawrence's and in front of Mr. Acklin's.

There was a force under Rousseau holding Murfreesboro which General Hood was anxious to capture. He detached most of [Confederate Nathan Bedford] Forrest's cavalry and Bate's division to that work, but they failed. Bate was then ordered back, leaving Forrest. Here we remained watching each other and intrenched as hard as we could until the morning of the 15th of December. On that morning about 9 o'clock it was reported to me that the enemy were advancing in heavy force on the Hillsboro Pike and in front of General Loring. Generals French and Walthall had their troops in bivouac along the east side of the Hillsboro Pike ready to move. I informed General Stewart, who mounted and rode to that point, leaving me to keep my office open and send dispatches. I had a signal station and sent dispatches to Generals Hood, Lee and Cheatham, and received others. In a short time the firing began and grew heavier as the enemy advanced. It was soon perceived that his main attack would be here, as his whole army appeared to be in our front.

They then stormed and took redoubt 5, our forces being entirely too small to keep them back. The re-inforcements sent to us did not arrive in time. Walthall's troops stationed along the pike in front of these works, were then driven in and the enemy were in the rear of General Loring, which, of course, compelled him to fall back, as did the whole of our line, until dark. I remained in my office until the Yankees advanced to within three hundred yards. I then mounted and made my escape through the back yard, with my clerks, and joined General Stewart in front of Mr. Planter's, where General Sears lost his life very near me.

As our men fell back before the advancing Yankees, Mary Bradford ran out under heavy fire and did all she could to induce the men to stop and fight, appealing to them and begging them, but in vain—Deas' brigade was here. General Hood told me yesterday that he intended to mention her courageous conduct in his report, which will immortalize her. The men seemed utterly lethargic and without interest in the battle. I never witnessed such want of enthusiasm and began to fear for to-morrow, hoping that General Hood would retreat during the night, cross Duck river, and then stop and fight, but he would not give it up. However, he sent all his wagons to Franklin, which prepared the men still more for the stampede of the next day.

The enemy adapted their line to ours, and about 9 a.m. began the attack on Cheatham, trying all day to turn him and get in his rear. They succeeded about 2 or 3 p.m. in gaining the pike behind the gap, and in crossing, got in the rear of General Stewart's headquarters, which were on the side of the Knob looking toward Nashville. We could see the whole line in our front —every move, advance, attack and retreat. It was magnificent. What a grand sight it was! I could see the [Tennessee State] Capitol [in Nashville] all day, and the churches. The Yanks had three lines of battle everywhere I could see, and the parks of artillery playing upon us and raining shot and shell for eight hours. I could see nearly every piece in our front, even the gunners at work. They made several heavy assaults upon General Lee's line near John Thompson's, and one in front of Mrs. Mullins'. At length having gained our rear, about 4 p.m. they made a vigorous assault upon the whole line right and left. Bate gave way, and they poured over in clouds behind Walthall, which of course, forced him to give way, and then by brigades the whole line from left to right. Lee held on bravely awhile longer than the center and left.

Here was a scene which I shall not attempt to describe, for it is impossible to give you any idea of an army frightened and routed. Some brave effort was made to rally the men and make a stand, but all control over them was gone, and they flatly refused to stop, throwing down their guns and, indeed, everything that impeded their flight, and every man fled for himself.

Reynolds' brigade was ordered to go to the right just before the rout began, and got to where I was when I halted it and got the General to form it in line across the point of the knob just in the path of the flying mass, hoping to rally some men on this and save the rest by gaining time for all to come out of the valley. Not a man would stop! The First Tennessee came by, and its Colonel, House, was the only man who could stop with us, and finding none of his men willing to stand, he, too, went on his way. As soon as I found all was lost, and the enemy closing in around us, I sent a courier to General Stewart, who had gone to General Hood's headquarters in the rear of Lea's house, to inform him of the fact that he might save himself. This courier, was mortally wounded, and left at Franklin. Finding the enemy closing in around us, and all indeed gone, I ordered the couriers and clerks who were there to follow me, and we rode as we could to where I thought General Stewart and General Hood were. They were gone and in their places the Yankees. I turned my horse's head toward the steep knobs and spurred away. It was the only chance of escape left. The first place I struck the hill was too steep for my horse to climb, and I skirted along the hills hoping to find some place easier of ascent, but none seemed to exist. Finally I reached a place not too steep, and in the midst of a thousand retreating soldiers I turned my horse's head for the ascent, resolved to try it. The bullets began to come thick and fast. Now, I found my saddle nearly off, and was forced to get down, but on I went on foot. All alone, the poor, frightened fellows were crying out to me, "Let me hold on to your stirrup, for God's sake." "Give me your hand and help me, if you please." Some were wounded and many exhausted from anxiety and over-exertion. On I struggled until I, too, became exhausted and unable to move. By this time the enemy had gotten to the foot of the hill and were firing at us freely. What was I to do? I twisted my hands in my horse's mane and was borne to the top of the hill by the noble animal, more dead than alive. I was safe, though, and so were my men. We descended the southern slope and entered the deep valley, whose shades were darkened by approaching night. The woods were filled with our retreating men. I joined the crowd and finally made my way to the Franklin Pike, where I found General Stewart, who was much relieved, for I had been reported as certainly killed or captured. All night long we fled [back south through Franklin]. The Harpeth [River] was crossed and a few hours of rest allowed, when we started on for Columbia, then Pulaski, and then Bainbridge, four miles above Florence [Alabama]. Every mind was haunted by the apprehension that we did not have boats enough to make a bridge. On we marched through ice and rain and snow, sleeping on the wet ground at night. Many thousands were bare-footed, actually leaving the prints of blood upon the ground, as the enemy pressed us in the rear. When we left the pike at Pulaski [Tennessee] we had an awful road, strewn with dead horses and mules, broken wagons, and worse than all, broken pontoons. We counted as we passed them, one, two, three to fifteen.

 Thus we toiled on till Christmas day, cold drizzly and muddy. We camped on the bank of Shoal creek, and our corps formed line of battle to protect the rear and let all cross, if the bridge could be made. Roddy had captured the enemy's pontoons at Decatur, and they were floated down over the shoals. The bridge was made and the crossing began. Then began the fight with the gun-boats, which tried to destroy our bridge. They were driven back and we crossed. 'All is well that ends well.' Every wagon, every cannon, every horse, every mule, the hogs, beeves, cavalry, infantry, and finally every scout crossed over. The retreat continued to this place, and here we are, daily expecting orders. There were many things in this memorable campaign never to be forgotten. I shall never forget the passage of Duck river—Washington crossing the Delaware was insignificant.

I wish I could send you something, but you know I have no means. I do not despair, but hope to send you and the little fellows a few things some of these days.

General Hood has been relieved and [Confederate General Richard] Taylor is in command. What next?

Union General John McAllister Schofield's Official Report on the Battles of Columbia, Spring Hill, Franklin, & Nashville

From the U.S. government's 1880 work, *Official Records* Ser. 1, Vol. 45, Pt. 1, pp. 339-347

(My notes are in brackets, LS)

Report of Maj. Gen. John M. Schofield, U.S. Army, commanding Army of the Ohio. Headquarters Army of the Ohio, Columbia, Tenn., December 31, 1864:

General [George H. Thomas]: In accordance with the desire of the major-general commanding, I have the honor to report the operations of the troops under my command from the time of the separation of the Twenty-third Army Corps from the main army, under General Sherman, to the present time.

On the 30th of October, 1864, at Rome, Ga., I received the order of [U.S.] Major General [William T.] Sherman, directing me to march with the Twenty-third Corps to Resaca, Ga., and report by telegraph to [U.S.] Major-General [George Henry] Thomas, then at Nashville, for further orders. I marched on the following day and arrived at Resaca on the 1st of November, reporting by telegraph to Major-General Thomas from Calhoun on the afternoon of the 31st of October.

At Calhoun, on the 1st of November, I received orders from Major-General Thomas directing me to move via Tullahoma to Pulaski, Tenn., which was subsequently changed, and I was ordered to move by way of Nashville and to send my wagon trains forward to Chattanooga. Accordingly the troops commenced to move as soon as the first railroad trains arrived, which was the 3d of November, but owing to delays in the railroads the last of the troops did not reach Nashville until the 9th of November. I arrived at Nashville in person on the 5th of November, and received the orders of the commanding general to go to Johnsonville instead of Pulaski, to repel an attack then being made on that place by a rebel force under [Confederate General Nathan Bedford] Forrest. My advance (Colonel Gallup's brigade of the Second Division) reached Johnsonville on the night of the 5th of November, and found the enemy had already retreated. Upon reporting this fact to the commanding general I was ordered to leave at Johnsonville such portion of my command as was necessary for a strong defense of that place, and to repair with the remainder of my troops to Pulaski and assume command of all the troops in that vicinity. I left two brigades (General Cooper's and Colonel Gallup's) at Johnsonville, with instructions to strongly fortify the place according to plans furnished by the chief engineer of the Department of the Cumberland; placed Colonel Strickland's brigade, Second Division, at Columbia, and the Third Division (General Cox's) about three miles north of Pulaski, the latter place being then occupied by the Fourth Army Corps, Major-General Stanley commanding.

My instructions from the major-general commanding were embraced in the accompanying telegram to Major-General Stanley, a copy of which was furnished with the order to assume command at Pulaski, and subsequent dispatches, explaining that the object was to hold the enemy in check, should he advance, long enough to enable General A. J. Smith's corps, then expected from Missouri, to reach Nashville, other troops in the Department of the Cumberland to be concentrated, and General Wilson's cavalry to be remounted and fitted for the field. The re-enforcements thus expected were about equal to the force we then had in the field, and would make our entire force, when concentrated, equal or somewhat superior to that of the enemy. To effect this concentration was, therefore, of vital importance—a consideration to which all others were secondary. This required that the enemy's advance should be delayed as much as possible, and, at the same time, a decisive battle avoided unless it could be fought on favorable terms.

I reached Pulaski on the night of the 13th, and assumed command on the 14th of November.

The following is my report of operations [dated December 7] from November 14 to December 1, 1864, when the troops under my command reached Nashville, which is made part of this report:

I assumed command at Pulaski on the 14th of November 1864. The forces at and near that place were the Fourth Army Corps, Major-General Stanley commanding, and General Cox's (Third) division, Twenty-third Army Corps; General Hatch's division and General Croxton's brigade of cavalry were in front of Pulaski, along Shoal Creek, and Colonel Capron's brigade was near Pulaski. My effective force was 18,000 infantry and four brigades of cavalry. The enemy, under General hood, was lying about Florence, preparing for an aggressive movement. His force consisted of the old army of Northern Georgia, which had opposed General Sherman during the latter part of his operations, increased by such fragments as could be collected in Alabama and Mississippi, together with all of Forrest's cavalry. The enemy's force was variously estimated at from 30,000 to 40,000 infantry, and from 10,000 to 20,000 cavalry; the largest estimate for the infantry and the smallest for the cavalry are most probably nearly accurate.

November 19, Hood commenced his advance via Lawrenceburg and Waynesborough toward Columbia [Tennessee]. His advance reached Lawrenceburg and drove our cavalry from that place on the 22d. I sent all the public property from Pulaski to Columbia, and fell back to Lynnville, and then to Columbia. My advance (General Cox's division) reached that place on the morning of the 24th, just in time to beat back a large rebel force which was driving in General Capron's cavalry from Mount Pleasant [Tennessee]. At Columbia I was re-enforced by one brigade and two regiments of General Ruger's division, Twenty-third Corps, the other half of that division having been sent, by order of the major-general commanding, to guard Centerville and other crossings of Duck River below Columbia.

The troops were put in position covering the pontoon bridge on the pike at Columbia and the railroad bridge two miles below. The position was much too extended for the troops I then had, but re-enforcements were expected daily, and it was essential to have that position from which to take the offensive when our force should become sufficiently large. Therefore I determined to hold it as long as possible. I also intrenched an interior line covering the railroad bridge, and short enough to be held by the Fourth Corps.

On the night of the 25th, finding that the enemy had his entire army in my front, and that he might without difficulty effect a crossing of Duck River above Columbia, I sent General Cox, with two brigades of his division, to the north bank to check any such movement, and General Ruger's troops to the railroad bridge to construct and occupy a small bridge-head at that point, and withdrew two divisions of General Stanley's corps to the interior line. General Wood's division and a brigade of General Cox's were left on the exterior line, and our picket line was maintained in its original position. At daylight in the morning the pontoon bridge was floated flown the river and laid near the railroad bridge. In this way I hoped still to hold the south bank of the river until re-enforcements should arrive.

We succeeded in holding the outer line during the 26th and 27th against a heavy pressure. But the enemy did not assault, and it became evident that he intended to turn the position by crossing the river above. To hold the south bank longer would have hazarded the loss of the army. I therefore withdrew the whole force to the north bank during the night of the 27th, left General Ruger to hold the crossing at the railroad bridge, General Cox in front of Columbia, and placed General Stanley in reserve on the Franklin pike, ready to meet the enemy should he attempt to force a crossing at any point near Columbia. The crossings below Columbia were guarded by General Ruger's infantry, and General Wilson had all his cavalry, save one brigade, to guard the river above. The troops rested in this position during the 28th, and I had strong hopes of being able to hold the line of Duck River until re-enforcements should arrive. But I learned from General Wilson, about 2 a.m. on the 29th, that the enemy's cavalry had forced a crossing near the Lewisburg pike; and about daylight in the morning that his infantry was also crossing at Huey's Mill, five miles above Columbia, from which a road leads into the Franklin pike at Spring Hill. The enemy might endeavor to reach the latter place in advance of me, and thus cut off my retreat or strike me in flank near Duck River, or both. He had already forced a column of cavalry between General Wilson and me, and cut off all communication between us. I therefore sent General Stanley, with a division of infantry, to Spring Hill to hold that point and cover the trains. General Cox was left in his position to hold the crossing at Columbia. Generals Wood and Kimball were put in line facing Huey's Mill, with a brigade thrown forward to reconnoiter, and General Ruger was ordered to move on to the pike in rear of Rutherford's Creek, leaving one regiment to hold the ford near the railroad bridge, the bridges having been destroyed.

General Stanley reached Spring Hill with General Wagner's division just in time to drive off a body of rebel cavalry and save our trains, which were assembling at that place. Late in the afternoon a division of rebel infantry arrived and attacked. A severe engagement ensued, lasting until dark. General Stanley held his position, except that his right was pressed back so as to nearly uncover the Columbia road, and the enemy's cavalry got possession of the pike, both north and south of Spring Hill. The enemy worked steadily and persistently all day to force a crossing and lay a pontoon bridge at Columbia. This was essential to him, since his artillery could not be crossed at Huey's Mill. But General Cox firmly held his ground, although it was in the concave bend of the river and commanded from the opposite bank. The enemy was repeatedly repulsed with heavy loss. About 3 p.m. I became satisfied the enemy would not attack my position on Duck River, but was pushing two corps direct for Spring Hill. I then gave the necessary orders for the withdrawal of the troops after dark, and took General Ruger's troops and pushed to Spring Hill to reopen communication with General Stanley, and was followed at a short distance by the head of the main column. I struck the enemy's cavalry at dark about three miles from Spring Hill, but we brushed them away without difficulty and reached Spring Hill about 7 o'clock.

General Whitaker's brigade, which followed General Ruger, was put in position parallel to the pike, and confronting the enemy's left, within 800 yards of the road, to cover the column as it passed, and I pushed on with General Ruger's division to clear the road at Thompson's Station, which had been occupied by a large body of the enemy's cavalry at dark that evening. On our arrival at Thompson's the enemy had disappeared, his camp-fires still burning, and General Ruger took possession of the cross-roads without opposition. I then returned to Spring Hill and met there the head of General Cox's column about midnight, he having withdrawn from in front of Columbia after dark. General Cox now took the advance and pushed rapidly for Franklin, the trains following under immediate guard of General Ruger, the men marching by the side of the wagons and General Stanley marching in rear of the trains. General Wagner's division held on at Spring Hill until near daylight, and then quietly withdrew and followed the column as rear guard. A small body of rebel cavalry made a dash upon the train a short distance north of Thompson's, and succeeded in destroying a few wagons and stampeding a few cattle; with this exception the whole column and trains arrived at Franklin without loss.

I arrived at Franklin with the head of column a little before daylight on the 30th, and found no wagon bridge for crossing the river and the fords in very bad condition. I caused the railroad bridge to be prepared for crossing wagons, and had a foot bridge built for infantry, which fortunately also proved available for wagons, and used the fords as much as possible. I hoped, in spite of the difficulties, to get all my material, including the public property, and a large wagon train at Franklin, across the river, and move the army over before the enemy could get up force enough to attack me. But I put the troops in position as they arrived on the south side, the Twenty-third Corps on the left and center, covering the Columbia and Lewisburg pikes, and General Kimball's division of the Fourth Corps on the right, both flanks resting on the river. Two brigades of General Wagner's division were left in front to retard the enemy's advance, and General Wood's division, with some artillery, was moved to the north bank of the river to cover time flanks should the enemy attempt to cross above or below.

The enemy followed close after our rear guard, brought up and deployed two full corps with astonishing celerity, and moved rapidly forward to the attack. Our outposts, imprudently brave, held their ground too long and hence were compelled to come in at a run. In passing over the parapet they carried with them the troops of the line for a short space and thus permitted a few hundred of the enemy to get in. But the reserves near by instantly sprang forward, regaining the parapet, and captured those of the enemy who had passed it. The enemy assaulted persistently and continuously with his whole force from about 3.30 p.m. until after dark, and made numerous intermittent attacks at a few points until about 10 p.m. He was splendidly repulsed along the whole line of attack. The enemy attacked on a front of about two miles, extending from our left to our right center, General Kimball's left brigade. Our two right brigades were only slightly engaged. I believe the enemy's loss in killed and wounded cannot have been less than 5,000, and may have been much greater. We captured 702 prisoners and 33 stand of colors.

Our [total] loss, as officially reported, [is 2,236.] . . . I am not able at this time to give fully the names of the killed and wounded officers. Among the latter is Major-General Stanley, commanding the Fourth Corps, who was severely wounded in the neck while gallantly urging forward his troops to regain the portion of our line which had been lost. General Stanley is deserving of special commendation, and has my hearty thanks for his cordial support and wise counsel throughout the short but eventful campaign. Brig. Gens. J. D. Cox, commanding temporarily the Twenty-third Corps, deserves a very large share of credit for the brilliant victory at Franklin. The troops were placed in position and intrenched under his immediate direction, and the greater portion of the line engaged was under his command during the battle. I recommend General Cox to the special consideration of the Government. Brigadier-General Ruger, commanding Second Division, Twenty-third Corps, held the weakest portion of our line, and that upon which the enemy's assaults were most persistent. He is entitled to very great credit. Brigadier-General Reilly, commanding (temporarily) the Third Division, Twenty-third Corps, maintained his lines with perfect firmness, and captured twenty [Confederate] battle-flags along his parapet. I am also under great obligations to the division commanders of the Fourth Army Corps, Brigadier-Generals Wood, Wagner, and Kimball, for the admirable in manner in which they discharged every duty, and cannot refrain from expressing my high commendation, though in advance of the official report of their immediate commander. Col. Emerson Opdycke, commanding First Brigade, Second Division, Fourth Army Corps, the reserve which recaptured the lost portion of our line, is spoken of by Generals Stanley and Cox as having displayed on that occasion the highest qualities of a commander. I cordially indorse their recommendation. For other special instances of gallantry and good conduct I must refer to subordinate reports.

On my arrival at Franklin I gained the first information from General Wilson since the enemy commenced his advance from Duck River. I learned that he had been driven back and had crossed the Harpeth above Franklin on the preceding day, leaving my left and rear entirely open to the enemy's cavalry. By my direction he sent General Hatch's division forward again, on the Lewisburg pike, to hold Forrest in check until my trains and troops could reach Franklin. This was successfully done, and General Hatch then retired before a superior force, and recrossed the river, connecting with my infantry pickets on the north bank, early in the afternoon. A short time before the infantry attack commenced the enemy's cavalry forced a crossing about three miles above Franklin, and drove back our cavalry, for a time seriously threatening our trains, which were accumulating on the north bank, and moving toward Nashville. I sent General Wilson orders, which he had, however, anticipated, to drive the enemy back at all hazards, and moved a brigade of General Wood's division to support him, if necessary. At the moment of the first decisive repulse of the enemy's infantry I received the most gratifying intelligence that General Wilson had driven the rebel cavalry back across the river. This rendered my immediate left and rear secure for the time being. Previous to the battle of the 30th I had ordered all trains except ammunition and hospital wagons to Nashville, preparatory to falling back from Franklin when it should become necessary, which I expected on the following day. The enemy having nearly double my force of infantry and quite double my cavalry, could easily turn any position I might take and seriously endanger my rear.

    Only one division of the enemy's cavalry had been engaged with General Wilson during the 30th. The remaining three divisions were free to strike my line of communications, which they could easily do about Brentwood by daylight time next morning. My experience on the 29th had shown how utterly inferior in force my cavalry was to that of the enemy, and that even my immediate flank and rear were insecure, while my communications with Nashville was entirely without protection. I could not even rely upon getting up the ammunition necessary for another battle. To remain longer at Franklin was to seriously hazard the loss of my army, by giving the enemy another chance to cut me off from re-enforcements, which he had made three desperate though futile attempts to accomplish. I had detained the enemy long enough to enable you to concentrate your scattered troops at Nashville, and had succeeded in inflicting upon him very heavy losses, which was the primary object. I had found it impossible to detain him long enough to get re-enforcements at Franklin. Only a small portion of the infantry and none of the cavalry could reach me in time to be of any use in the battle, which must have been fought on the 1st of December. For these reasons, after consulting with the corps and division commanders, and obtaining your approval, I determined to retire during the night of the 30th toward Nashville. The artillery was withdrawn to the north bank during the early part of the night, and at 12 o'clock the army withdrew from its trenches and crossed the river without loss. During the next day, December 1, the whole army was placed in position in front of Nashville.

Information obtained since the above report was written, and principally since the reoccupation of Franklin by our troops, makes the enemy's loss 1,750 buried upon the field, 3,800 disabled and placed in hospitals in Franklin, and 702 prisoners, making 6,252 of the enemy placed hors de combat [i.e., unable to fight], besides the slightly wounded. The enemy's loss in general officers was very great, being 6 killed, 6 wounded, and 1 captured. It is to be observed that more than half of our loss occurred in General Wagner's division of the Fourth Corps, which did not form part of the main line of defense. This loss arose in two brigades of that division from their remaining in front of the line after their proper duty as outposts had been accomplished, and after they should have taken their positions in reserve, and in the other brigade (Colonel Opdycke's) in its hand-to-hand encounter with the enemy over the portion of the parapet which had been temporarily lost by the precipitate retreat of the other two brigades. When it became apparent that we should have to fall back from Columbia, orders to rejoin the army were sent to General Cooper, commanding the troops guarding the crossings of Duck River below Columbia at Centerville, both by myself and the major-general commanding, which were obeyed as soon as received, and General Cooper marched for Franklin. Owing to delays in receiving his orders and the time necessary to concentrate his troops, General Cooper could not reach Franklin before its occupation by the enemy, and turned his column direct for Nashville. Arrived at the Brentwood Hills by the Charlotte pike on the night of December 2, and again found the enemy between him and the army. He then marched to Clarksville, where he arrived in safety on the 5th and rejoined my command on the 8th of December. General Cooper deserves great credit for the skill and judgment displayed in conducting his retreat.

BATTLES OF THE 15TH AND 16TH OF DECEMBER IN FRONT OF NASHVILLE

My command consisted of the Second and Third Divisions of the Twenty-third Army Corps, commanded, respectively, by Maj. Gen. D. N. Couch and Brig. Gen. J. D. Cox. The effective strength of each division was about 5,500 men. Previous to the battle the corps occupied the line of defense from Block House Casino to the Nolensville pike, including Fort Negley.

According to the plan of battle, as modified on the evening of the 14th, my troops were to be relieved by Major-General Steedman's at dawn of day in the morning, pass in rear of General Wood's corps, and take position in reserve near the right to support the attack on the enemy's left. The movement commenced at daylight as ordered. General Couch's division debouched from our works on the Hardin pike and formed in rear of General Smith's left, and General Cox's, save one brigade, by the Hillsborough pike, in rear of General Wood's right. General Cox's third brigade was left temporarily in his old works to support, if necessary, General Steedman, who was making a demonstration upon the enemy's right. As General Smith advanced against the enemy's position General Couch moved forward, keeping within supporting distance, while the proper position of General Cox, as reserve to the center, remained essentially unchanged. About 1 p.m. the major-general commanding, remarking that General Smith had borne more to our left than had been expected and had not reached the enemy's flank, ordered me to move my corps to the right of General Smith, attack the enemy's flank, and gain, if practicable before dark, possession of a group of fortified hills near the Hillsborough pike, which formed the left of the enemy's position. I at once put my troops in motion, moving rapidly by the flank in rear of General Smith's line, rode forward and found General Smith near the right of his line, and informed him of the movement I was taking. General Smith then put in his reserve, extending his line about half a mile to the right, and assisted General Hatch's cavalry (dismounted) in assaulting and carrying a high hill, covered by a redoubt, which proved to be a detached work commanding the Hillsborough pike and constituting the extreme flank of the enemy's infantry position, but not connected with his main line of defense.

General Couch, whose head of column had by this time arrived opposite the right of General Smith's line, at once moved forward, deploying as he advanced, passed immediately by the right of the hill just carried and across the Hillsborough pike, crossed an open valley about half a mile in breadth, and swept by the enemy's artillery and carried the left of a series of hills parallel to and overlooking the Granny White pike, one of the enemy's only two lines of retreat. This assault was made by General Cooper's brigade, led by its brave commander, and was most gallantly executed. The enemy now moved a considerable force toward our right, with the evident design of turning our flank and recovering the position just lost. General Couch sent Colonel Mehringer's brigade, the only one he had disengaged, to meet this movement. Colonel Mehringer met the enemy, much superior to him in numbers, in the valley which General Conch had just passed, and held him in check until General Cox, who had just come up, sent two brigades, Colonel Doolittle's and Colonel Casement's, to his support, when the enemy was repulsed and driven back. The engagement here was sharp, attended with considerable loss on both sides, and lasted until dark. Immediately south of the hill carried by General Couch was a still higher one held by the enemy, without the possession of which his position north of Brentwood was untenable. I had ordered this hill to be carried immediately after the success of General Cooper's assault, but the counter attack made by the enemy occupied our whole available force until dark, and compelled us to rest with the success already gained. After dark the troops intrenched their position and bivouacked for the night.

BATTLE OF THE 16TH

In the night of the 15th I waited upon the major-general commanding at his headquarters, and received his orders for the pursuit of the enemy on the following day. Our operations during the 15th had swung the right and right center forward so that the general direction of the line was nearly perpendicular to that before the attack. Only the right was in contact with the enemy, and was therefore much exposed. Apprehensive that the enemy, instead of retreating during the night, would mass and attack our right in the morning, I requested that a division of infantry be sent to re-enforce the right, which was ordered accordingly from Major-General Smith's command. In response to this order General Smith sent five regiments and a battery (about 1,600 men), which were put in reserve near the right. In the morning it was found that the enemy still held his position in our front, of which the hill in front of General Couch was the key, and had thrown up considerable breast-works during the night. He had also increased the force on his left during the night, and continued to mass troops there during the early part of the day. During the morning, therefore, our operations were limited to preparations or defense and co-operation with the cavalry, which was operating to strike the Granny White pike in rear of the enemy. About noon the troops on my left (Generals Smith and Wood) having advanced and come in contact with the enemy in his new position, the enemy again withdrew from his left a considerable force to strengthen his right and center, when I ordered General Cox to advance in conjunction with the cavalry, and endeavor to carry a high wooded hill beyond the flank of the enemy's intrenched line, and overlooking the Granny White pike. The hill was occupied by the enemy in considerable force, but was not intrenched. My order was not executed with the promptness or energy which I had expected, yet, probably, with as much as I had reason to expect, considering the attenuated character of General Cox's line and the great distance and rough ground over which the attacking force had to move. The hill was, however, carried by General

Wilson's cavalry (dismounted) whose gallantry and energy on that and other occasions, which came under my observation, cannot be too greatly praised.

Almost simultaneously with this attack on the extreme right the salient hill in front of General Couch was attacked and carried by General Smith's troops, supported by a brigade of General Couch's division, and the fortified hill in front of General Cox, which constituted the extreme flank of the enemy's intrenched line, was attacked and carried by Colonel Doolittle's brigade of General Cox's division, the latter capturing 8 pieces of artillery and 200 to 300 prisoners. These several successes, gained almost simultaneously, resulted in a complete rout of the enemy. The cavalry had cut off his line of retreat by the Granny White pike, and such of his troops as were not captured on the line could only escape by climbing the Brentwood Hills. It is believed all of the artillery along the left and center of the enemy's line fell into our hands. Our troops continued the pursuit across the valley and into the Brentwood Hills, when darkness compelled them to desist, and they bivouacked for the night.

During the operations of the 15th and 16th our troops behaved with their accustomed gallantry and even more than their ordinary enthusiasm, attacking almost inaccessible heights, crowned by breast-works and covered by numerous artillery, with a confidence which presented a most striking contrast to the feeble and spiritless resistance offered by the already demoralized enemy.

The losses of the Twenty-third Corps during the 15th and 16th amounted to only 9 killed, 154 wounded, and none missing.

The division and brigade commanders displayed their usual high qualities of gallantry and skill. Brig. Gen J. A. Cooper, commanding First Brigade, Second Division, is specially worthy of mention for gallantry in leading the assault on the 15th.

The officers of my staff were then, as always, active and efficient, discharging every duty with honor and credit. The commanding general's orders for the pursuit of the enemy placed my corps in rear of the entire army and the main portion of its trains. I was, therefore, able to do no more than follow slowly in rear from the 17th until the 26th, when I was ordered to halt at Columbia, my troops not being needed in advance. On the 30th I received the order of the commanding general, announcing that the rebel army had been driven entirely across the Tennessee River, and ordering the pursuit to cease.

I inclose herewith report of Brig. Gen. J. D. Cox, commanding temporarily Twenty-third Army Corps, of the operations during the retreat from Pulaski, including the battle of Franklin, and the reports of his subordinate commanders also the reports of Generals Couch and Cox of the operations of their divisions during the battles of December 15 and 16, including lists of killed and wounded.

No report has yet been received from Major-General Stanley (he being absent wounded) of the operations of the Fourth Corps while the troops in the field were under my command. The numbers of killed, wounded, and missing furnished by the division commanders are embraced in my report of the battle of Franklin.

I also append hereto copies of orders and correspondence relative to operations of the troops under my command, which are made part of this report.

I have the honor to be, general, very respectfully, your obedient servant, J. M. Schofield, Major-General.

Union Captain John K. Shellenberger's Description of the Battle of Franklin

From Shellenberger's 1916 book: *The Battle of Franklin, Tennessee*, pp. 11-42

(My notes are in brackets, LS)

Any facts or information concerning the Battle of Franklin coming my way has always been devoured with a greedy interest, and because of this interest, I have given far more research to this battle than to any other in which I was engaged. On account of the open character of the battle-field, the limited area, where the fighting raged, and my presence in the midst of that area, the leading features of the battle came under my personal observation, but wherever that observation was wanting for giving a clear account I have supplied the deficiency with information gathered from other reliable sources.

I was commanding Company B, Sixty-fourth Ohio regiment, Conrad's brigade, Wagner's division, Fourth [U.S. army] corps. Wagner's division was the rear guard on the retreat to Franklin, and about mid-forenoon of November 30, 1864, arrived on top of the Winsted Hills, two miles south of Franklin. Halting there long enough to snatch a hasty breakfast, the division then hurried into battle line to delay the columns of the enemy, in close pursuit, by compelling them to deploy. The position was held as long as possible without bringing on a battle and then Wagner began to retire slowly towards Franklin. The town lies nestled in a little valley in a bend of [the] Harpeth River. A stand was made to get the artillery and the long wagon train over the river and while our commanding general, Schofield, was giving his personal attention to the facilities for crossing, the main body of the army, under the supervision of General Cox, was engaged in establishing our defensive line, which stretched across the river bend, in the arc of a circle, inclosing the town. As fast as the troops arrived and were placed in position they hurried to cover themselves with breastworks, and by the time the enemy was ready to attack, Cox's line was well intrenched. The train got over the river in time for the troops to have crossed before the enemy appeared, but the opportunity thus offered for securing a much stronger defensive position, with the river in front instead of in rear, was not improved.

  By one o'clock Wagner had fallen back so close to Cox's line that he began a movement to withdraw his division behind that line. Conrad's brigade had been called in from the left flank and was marching in column of fours along the Columbia Pike, with the head of the column approaching the breastworks, when Wagner received an order from Schofield to take up a position in front of Cox's line. In obedience to this order Conrad counter-marched his brigade a short distance and then deployed it in a single line of battle, having a general direction nearly parallel with Cox's line. Five of the six regiments composing the brigade were posted on the east side and one on the west side of the pike, four hundred and seventy yards in advance of Cox's line, as measured along the pike. Lane's brigade, following Conrad's, was posted on Conrad's right, Lane's line trending backward on the right in general conformation with Cox's line. When General Hood assaulted, Conrad's five regiments east of the pike proved to be in the direct pathway of his assault and they were overwhelmed before the line west of the pike, which was greatly refused as to that pathway, became fully engaged.

  When Opdycke's brigade, the last to withdraw, came up to the position occupied by Conrad and Lane, Wagner rode forward and ordered Opdycke into line with them. Colonel Opdycke strenuously objected to this order. He declared that troops out in front of the breastworks were in a good position to aid the enemy and nobody else. He also pleaded that his brigade was worn out, having been marching for several hours during the morning in line of battle in sight of the enemy, climbing over fences and passing through woods, thickets, and muddy cornfields, while covering the rear of our retreating column, and was entitled to a relief. While they were discussing the matter they rode along the pike together, the brigade marching in column behind them, until they entered the gap in the breastworks left for the pike and finding the ground in that vicinity fully occupied by other troops, they kept along till they came to the first clear space which was about two hundred yards inside the breastworks. There Wagner turned away with the final remark, "Well, Opdycke, fight when and where you damn please; we all know you'll fight." Colonel Opdycke then had his brigade stack arms on the clear space, and his persistence in thus marching his brigade inside the breastworks proved about two hours later to be the salvation of our army.

When Conrad's brigade took up its advanced position we all supposed it would be only temporary, but soon an orderly came along the line with instructions for the company commanders and he told me that the orders were to hold the position to the last man, and to have my sergeants fix bayonets and to instruct my company that any man, not wounded, who should attempt to leave the line without orders, would be shot or bayonetted by the sergeants.

Four of Conrad's regiments, including the Sixty-fourth Ohio, had each received a large assignment of drafted men so recently that none of these men had been with their regiments more than a month and many had joined within a week. The old soldiers all believed that the harsh orders were given for effect upon these drafted men, as we never before had received any such orders on going into battle.

We then began to fortify. On the retreat that morning we had passed an abandoned wagon loaded with intrenching tools, and by order each company had taken two spades from the wagon, the men relieving each other in carrying them. These spades were the only tools we had to work with. The ground we occupied was a large old cottonfield not under cultivation that year, and had been frequently camped on by other troops who had destroyed all the fences and other materials ordinarily found so handy in building hasty breastworks, so that on this occasion our only resource was the earth thrown with the few spades we had.

Under the stimulus afforded by the sight of the enemy in our front preparing for attack, the men eagerly relieved each other in handling the spades. As soon as a man working showed the least sign of fatigue, a comrade would snatch the spade out of his hands and ply it with desperate energy. Yet in spite of our utmost exertions when the attack came we had only succeeded in throwing up a slight embankment, which was high enough to give good protection against musket balls to the man squatting down in the ditch from which the earth had been thrown; but on the outside, where there was no ditch, it was so low that a battle line could march over it without halting. The ground ascended with an easy grade from our position back to Cox's line, and all the intervening space, as well as a wide expanse to our left, was as bare as a floor of any obstruction. In our front was a wide valley extending to the Winsted Hills. This valley was dotted with a few farm-buildings, and there were also some small areas of woodland, but much the greater portion of it consisted of cleared fields. As our line was first established the Sixty-fifth Ohio was on the left of the brigade, but it was afterwards withdrawn, leaving the Sixty-fourth Ohio on the left and three companies, H, K, and B, were partially refused to cover the left flank. My position was at the refused angle.

About the time that we began to fortify, my attention was called to a group of mounted officers in a field on the side of the Winsted Hills, to the east of the Columbia Pike, and about a mile and a half in our front. This group undoubtedly consisted of General Hood and his staff. An officer who was present with Hood has stated that from their position they had a good view of Cox's line and that after giving this line a hasty survey through his field-glass, General Hood slapped the glass shut with an emphatic gesture and decisively exclaimed, "We will attack!" Staff officers then began to gallop forth from the group with orders for the troops to form for assault.

At the angle where I was, the view of the valley directly in our front and to our right was shut off by a piece of woodland a short distance in advance of our position, so that we did not see anything of the movements of Cheatham's corps, which formed astride the Columbia Pike. Looking up the valley to our left front was a wide expanse of cleared fields and in these fields we plainly saw the movements of a large part of Stewart's corps. They first came into view from behind a body of timber over towards the river, deploying from column on the right by file into line on double quick. As fast as the troops could be marched up from the rear Stewart extended his lines over towards the pike. We could see all their movements so plainly, while they were adjusting their lines, that there was not a particle of doubt in the mind of any man in my vicinity as to what was coming. Moreover the opinion was just as universal that a big blunder was being committed [by the Yankee officers in command] in compelling us to fight with our flank fully exposed in the midst of a wide field, while in plain sight in our rear was a good line of breastworks with its flank protected by the river. The indignation of the men grew almost into a mutiny and the swearing of those gifted in profanity exceeded all their previous efforts in that line. Even the green drafted men could see the folly of our position, for one of them said to me, "What can our generals be thinking about in keeping us out here! We can do no good here. We are only in the way. Why don't they take us back to the breastworks?"

    The regiment contained a number of men who had not reenlisted when the regiment had veteranized and whose time had already expired. They were to be mustered out as soon as we got back to Nashville and, with home so nearly in sight after more than three years of hard service, these men were especially rebellious. First Sergeant Libey of Company H, was a non-veteran, and was also a fine specimen, mentally and physically, of the best type of our volunteer soldiers. When the enemy was approaching he twice got up from the line and started for the breastworks, vehemently declaring that he would not submit to having his life thrown away, after his time was out, by such a stupid blunder. The little squad of non-veterans belonging to the company both times got up and started to go with him and both times they all returned to the line on the profane order of their captain, "God damn you, come back here." A few minutes later the sergeant was killed while we were retreating to the breastworks.

    It took two hours, from two till four o'clock, for the corps of Cheatham and Stewart to come up and get into position and then they advanced to the assault in heavy lines of battle. We kept the spades flying until they had approached within range of our skirmish line, which fired a few shots and then began to retreat rapidly. Then the spades were dropped and the men taking their muskets squatted down behind the low streak of earth they had thrown out to receive the coming onset. A little later Company E, from the skirmish line, came scurrying back, the men, with very serious looks on their faces, settling down with the line like a covey of flushed birds dropping into cover.

    All that has been related concerning Conrad's brigade took place in full view of that part of Cox's line extending from the river on our left to the Columbia Pike, and if there had been any previous doubt in the minds of any of these on-looking thousands as to Hood's intention, his determination to assault was as plainly advertised as it possibly could be during the intense minutes that it took his army to march in battle line from the place of its formation to our advanced position. General Cox has claimed that Wagner's division was ordered to report to him and that he was in immediate command of all the troops engaged in the battle. By his own statement he was on a knoll in the rear of Stiles' brigade, on the left of his line, where he had the best view of the whole field. From this knoll he had been watching the preparations for attack, and all the time directly under his eyes was Conrad's brigade busily engaged in fortifying to resist that attack. If Wagner was disobeying his orders by remaining in front too long, as was given out a few days later when he was made a scapegoat for the blunder of his position, Cox was watching him do it and took no measures to prevent it. If it was Cox's expectation that Wagner would withdraw the two brigades at the last moment, he must have known better when he saw Conrad's brigade squat down behind their half-built breastwork preparatory to giving battle. There was even then time, if prompt action had been taken, for a staff officer to gallop to the front, before the firing began, with a peremptory order for Conrad and Lane to get out of the way; but Cox, fresh from a personal conference with Schofield, to whom he had reported the situation and whose orders he had received with reference to holding the position, looked quietly on and thereby approved of Wagner's action.

It was a pleasant, hazy, Indian summer day, and so warm that I was carrying my overcoat on my arm. When the line squatted down I folded the coat into a compact bundle and placed it on the edge of the bank in rear of my company and sat on it, with my feet in the shallow ditch. By craning my neck, I could look over our low parapet. The battle was opened by a rebel cannon, which, unnoticed by us, had taken position on a wooded knoll off our left front over towards the river. The first shot from this cannon flew a little high, directly over the angle where I was sitting. The second shot dropped short, and I was thinking with a good deal of discomfort that the third shot would get the exact range and would probably lift some of us out of that angle; but before it came our line had opened fire on the approaching rebel line and I became so much interested in that fire that I never knew whether there was a third shot from the cannon.

Our fire checked them in front, for they halted and began to return it, but for a minute only, for, urged on by their officers they again came forward. Their advance was so rapid that my company had fired only five or six rounds to the man when the break came. The salient of our line was near the pike and there the opposing lines met in a hand-to-hand encounter in which clubbed muskets were used, but our line quickly gave way. I had been glancing uneasily along our line, watching for a break as a pretext for getting out of there, and was looking towards the pike when the break first started. It ran along the line so rapidly that it reminded me of a train of powder burning. I instantly sprang to my feet and looked to the front. They were coming on the run, emitting the shrill rebel charging yell, and so close that my first impulse was to throw myself flat on the ground and let them charge over us. But the rear was open and a sense of duty, as well as a thought of the horrors endured in rebel prisons, constrained me to take what I believed to be the very dangerous risk of trying to escape. I shouted to my company, "Fall back! Fall back!" and gave an example of how to do it by turning and running for the breastworks.

    As the men were rising to go, the rebels fired, but so hastily and with such poor aim that their fire did not prove nearly so destructive as I had feared. Probably most of their guns were empty, although I did not think so just then. The range was so close that it seemed bullets had never before hissed with such a diabolical venom, and every one that passed made a noise seemingly loud enough to tear one in two. I had forgotten my overcoat, but had run only a rod or two when I thought of it and stopped and looked back with the intention of returning to get it; but the rebels then appeared to be as close to the coat as I was and very reluctantly, for it was a new one, I let them have it. After running a few rods farther I again looked back. They were standing on the low embankment we had left, loading and firing at will, but just as I looked some of their officers waved their swords and sprang forward. The fire slackened as they started in hot pursuit to get to the breastworks with us.

    Our men were all running with their guns in their hands, which was good evidence that there was no panic among them. While knapsacks or blanket rolls were frequently thrown away, I did not see a single man drop his gun unless hit. The cry of some of our wounded who went down in that wild race, knowing they would have to lie there exposed to all the fire of our own line, had a pathetic note of despair in it, I had never heard before. A rebel account has stated that the next morning they found some of the dead with their thumbs chewed to a pulp. They had fallen with disabling wounds and the agony of their helpless exposure to the murderous fire from our breastworks, which swept the bare ground, where they were lying, had been so great that they had stuck their thumbs in their mouths and bit on them to keep from bleating like calves. Many of the bodies thus exposed were hit so frequently that they were literally riddled with bullet holes.

  Our men were nearly all directed towards the pike as if with the intention of entering the breastworks through the gap there. I reasoned, however, that the hottest fire would be directed where the crowd was densest, and I veered off in an effort to get away from there. While running rapidly with body bent over and head down, after the involuntary manner of men retreating under fire, I came into collision with a man running in a similar attitude, but headed towards the gap. The shock was so great that it knocked him down and pretty well knocked the wind out of me. Just as we met, a rebel shell exploded close over our heads and as his body was rolling over on the ground, I caught a glimpse of his upturned face and, in its horrified look, read his belief that it was the shell that had hit him. The idea was so comical that I laughed, but my laugh was of very brief duration when I found myself so much disabled that I was rapidly falling behind. With panting lungs and trembling legs I toiled along, straining every nerve to reach the breastwork, but when it was yet only a few steps away, even with life itself at stake, I could go no farther, and thought my time had come. My brave mother, the daughter of a soldier of 1812 and the granddaughter of a Revolutionary soldier had said, when I had appealed to the pride in her military ancestry so successfully that she had consented to my enlistment, "Well, if you must go, don't get shot in the back." I thought of her and of that saying and faced about to take it in front. While I was slowly turning, my eyes swept the plain in the direction of the pike. There were comparatively few of our men in my immediate vicinity, but over towards the pike the ground was thickly covered with them, extending from the breastworks nearly a hundred yards along the pike, and in some places so densely massed as to interfere with each other's movements. The fleetest footed had already crossed the breastwork and all those outside were so thoroughly winded that none of them could go any faster than a slow, labored trot. The rear was brought up by a ragged fringe of tired stragglers who were walking doggedly along, apparently with as much unconcern as if no rebels were in sight. The rebel ranks were almost as badly demoralized by pursuit as ours by retreat. Their foremost men had already overtaken our rearmost stragglers and were grabbing hold of them to detain them.

Suddenly my attention was riveted so intently on the nearest rebel to myself that in watching him I became oblivious to all other surroundings, for I thought I was looking at the man who would shoot me. He was coming directly towards me, on a dog trot, less than fifty yards away, and was in the act of withdrawing the ramrod from the barrel of his gun. When this action was completed, while holding the gun and ramrod together in one hand, he stopped to prime and then, much to my relief, aimed and fired at a little squad of our men close on my right. I heard the bullet strike and an exclamation from the man who was hit. The rebel then started to trot forward again, at the same time reaching back with one hand to draw a fresh cartridge. By this time having rested a little, I looked back over my shoulder towards the breastwork. I noticed that there was a ditch on the outside and the sight of this ditch brought renewed hope. With the fervent prayer, into which was poured all the intense longing for more life, natural to my vigorous young manhood, "O, God, give me strength to reach that ditch," I turned and staggered forward. I fell headlong into the ditch just as our line there opened fire. The roar of their guns was sweeter than music and I chuckled with satisfaction as I thought, "Now, Rebs, your turn has come and you must take your medicine." I lay as I fell, panting for breath, until I had caught a little fresh wind and then began to crawl around to take a peep and see how the rebels were getting along.

When my body was lengthwise of the ditch I happened to raise my head and was astounded by the sight of the rebels coming into the ditch between me and the pike, the nearest of them only a few yards away. They were so tired that they seemed scarcely able to put one foot before the other and many of them stopped at the ditch utterly unable to go a step farther until they had rested. It was only the strongest among them who were still capable of the exertion of climbing over the breastwork. If the men behind that work had stood fast, not one of those tired rebels would ever have crossed that parapet alive. Transfixed with amazement, I watched them until the thought flashed into my mind that in an instant some of their comrades would come in on top of me and I would be pinned down with a bayonet. The thought of a bayonet thrust was so terrifying, that it spurred me into a last effort, and with the mental ejaculation, "I never will die in that way," I sprang on top of the breastwork. Crouching there an instant with both hands resting on the headlog, I gave one startled look over my shoulder. The impression received was that if I fell backward they would catch me on their bayonets. Then followed a brief period of oblivion for which I can not account. With returning consciousness I found myself lying in the ditch on the inside of the breastwork, trampled under the feet of the men, and with no knowledge whatever of how I got there. It is possible that I was taken for a rebel when I sprang up so suddenly on top of the breastwork and that I was knocked there by a blow from one of our own men. I was lying across the body of a wounded man who had been hit by a bullet which, entering at his cheek, had passed out the back of his head. He was unconscious, but still breathing. The breast of my coat was smeared with the blood from his wound. The press was so great that I could not get on my feet, but in a desperate effort to avoid being trampled to death managed in some way to crawl out between the legs of the men to the bank of the ditch, where I lay utterly helpless with burning lungs still panting for breath. My first thought was of the rebels I had seen crossing the breastwork, and I looked toward the pike. I had crossed our line close to a cotton-gin [belonging to the Carter family] that stood just inside our works and the building obstructed my view except directly along the ditch and for a short distance in rear of it.

Our men were all gone from the ditch to within a few feet of where I was lying. A little beyond the other end of the building stood two cannon pointing towards me with a group of rebels at the breech of each one of them trying to discharge it. They were two of our own guns that had been captured before they had been fired by our gunners and were still loaded with the double charges of canister intended for the rebels. Fortunately the gunners had withdrawn the primers from the vents and had taken them along when they ran away and the rebels were having difficulty in firing the guns. As I looked they were priming them with powder from their musket cartridges, and no doubt intended to fire a musket into this priming. Just then I was too feeble to make any effort to roll my body over behind the cover of the building, but shut my eyes and set my jaws to await the outcome where I was lying. After waiting for some time and not hearing the cannon, I opened my eyes to see what was the matter. The rebels were all gone and the ditch was filled with our men as far as I could see. If the rebels had succeeded in firing those two cannon they would have widened the breach in our line so much farther to our left that it might have proved fatal, since the two brigades holding our line, from the vicinity of the cotton-gin to the river, had each but a single regiment of reserves. The men in the ditch at my side, when I first saw the cannon, were so busily engaged in keeping out the rebels who filled the ditch on the other side of the parapet, that I do not believe they ever saw the two cannon posted to rake the ditch. Their conduct was most gallant.

For a brief period the rebels held possession of the inside of our breastworks along the entire front of Strickland's brigade on the west side, and of Reilly's brigade down to the cotton-gin on the east side of the pike; and the ground in their possession was the key to Cox's entire position. This break in our line was identical in extent with the front covered by the great body of Wagner's men in falling back, and it was occasioned by the panic and confusion created by Wagner's men in crossing the breastworks. Cox's men, along this part of our line, seem to have lost their nerve at the sight of the rebel army coming and on account of their own helpless condition. They could not fire a single shot while Wagner's men were between themselves and the rebels. The first rebels crossed the breastworks side by side with the last of Wagner's men.

At some point a break started and then it spread rapidly until it reached the men who were too busily occupied in firing on the rebels to become affected by the panic. Opdycke's brigade was directly in the rear of where this break occurred. At the sound of the firing in front, Opdycke had deployed his brigade astride the pike, ready for instant action, and as soon as he saw that a stampede was coming from the breastworks, without waiting for any order, he instantly led his brigade forward. His brigade restored the break in our line, charging straight through the rout, after a desperate hand-to-hand encounter in which Opdycke himself, first firing all the shots in his revolver and then breaking it over the head of a rebel, snatched up a musket and fought with that for a club. It is true that hundreds of brave men from the four broken brigades of Conrad, Lane, Reilly, and Strickland, who were falling back, when they met Opdycke's advancing line, saw that the position would not be given up without a desperate struggle and faced about and fought as gallantly as any of Opdycke's men in recovering and afterwards in holding our line; but if Opdycke's brigade had not been where it was, the day undoubtedly would have closed with the utter rout and ruin of our four divisions of infantry south of the river. When General Cox met Opdycke on the field immediately after the break was restored, he took him by the hand and fervently exclaimed, "Opdycke, that charge saved the day."

The front line of Strickland's brigade extended along the foot of the garden of Mr. [Fountain Branch] Carter, the owner of the plantation on which the battle was fought. The reserve line was posted behind the fence at the other end of the garden, close to the Carter residence [today known as the Carter House], where the ground was a little higher, and sixty-five yards in rear of the main line. This reserve line, with the fence for a basis, had constructed a rude barricade as a protection against bullets which might come over the front line. When Opdycke's demi-brigade, charging on the west side of the pike, came to this barricade, it halted there, probably mistaking it for our main line. The rebels in the garden fell back behind the cover of Strickland's breastwork and during the remainder of the battle, on this part of the field, the opposing lines maintained these relative positions. Every attempt, made by either side to cross the garden, met with a bloody repulse. The body of one dead rebel was lying between the barricade and the Carter house and this body no doubt indicated the high water mark reached by Hood's assault. It is only fair to the gallant rebels, who penetrated our line, to state that Opdycke's charge was made too promptly to give them any time to recover their wind, and that therefore in the hand-to-hand struggle, they were laboring under the great disadvantage of the physical fatigue already described.

Returning to my personal experiences: when I had rested enough to be able to sit up, I found at my feet a can of coffee standing on the smouldering embers of a small camp fire, and beside it a tin plate filled with hard tack and fried bacon. Some soldier was evidently ready to eat his supper, when he was hastily called into line by the opening of the battle in front. I first took a delicious drink out of the coffee can and then helped myself to a liberal portion of the hard tack and bacon, and while sitting there eating and drinking, incidentally watched the progress of the fighting. By the time I had finished I was so fully rested and refreshed that thereafter I was able to shout encouragement to the men fighting in my vicinity as loud as any other company commander.

Along that part of the line only the breastwork separated the combatants. On our side we had five or six ranks deep, composed of the original line, the reserves, and Conrad's men, all mixed up together without any regard to their separate organizations. The front rank did nothing but fire. The empty guns were passed back to those in rear who reloaded them. The rear rank was kneeling with guns at a ready. If a rebel raised his head above the breastwork, down it would instantly go with one or more bullets through it, fired by these rear rank men.

In this close fighting the advantage was all on our side, for our front rank men, standing up close against the perpendicular face of the breastwork on our side, could poke the muzzle of a gun over the headlog and by elevating the breech could send a plunging shot among the rebels who filled the outside ditch and expose for an instant only the hand and a part of the arm that discharged the gun. But on account of the convex face of the work on their side the rebels could not reach us with their fire without exposing themselves above the breastwork. They kept up the vain struggle until long after dark, but finally elevated their hats on the ends of their muskets above the breastwork, as a signal to us, and called over that if we would stop shooting they would surrender. When our firing ceased, many of them came over and surrendered, but many more took advantage of the darkness and of the confusion created by their comrades in getting over the breastwork to slip back to their own lines. Soon after the firing had ceased the Sixty-fourth Ohio reformed its broken ranks a few steps in rear of the breastwork and just east of the [Carter] cotton-gin. I did not learn all the facts that night, but when they came out later, it transpired that every man in my company, save one, who had escaped the casualties of the battle, fell into line. A thousand-dollar substitute had fled to the town where he hid in a cellar. He went to sleep there and awoke the next morning inside the rebel lines. He was sent south to a prison and when returning north after the close of the war lost his life in the explosion of the Steamer Sultana.

I had lost my overcoat, but had never let go the grip on my sword. Some of my men had dropped their knapsacks or blanket rolls, but every one of them had his gun and cartridge box. They were all in high spirits over their own escape and over the part they had played in the final repulse of the rebels, and were talking and laughing over their various adventures in the greatest good humor. The condition of my company was typical of the condition of all the other companies in the regiment as I saw, while passing along the line inquiring into the fate of brother officers and other friends. I also learned in a conversation the next day with Major Coulter, who had been my old captain, and who was acting that night as assistant adjutant-general of the brigade, that every other regiment of the brigade had reformed in rear of the breastwork in the same way as the Sixty-fourth Ohio, and that the brigade as an organization, had marched from the vicinity of the cotton-gin when the order to retreat was executed that night.

I never heard from any source any intimation contrary to the truth as I have stated it until I read in 1882, with the most indignant surprise, in Cox's book on this campaign, then recently published, his statement that the brigades of Lane and Conrad rallied at the river but were not again carried into action.

When Cox made that statement he was more concerned in patching up that fatal gap in the battle line of his own command without any outside assistance, than he was in ascertaining the truth, and he took that way to dispose of two entire brigades. In his first official report, for he made two reports, Cox went to the other extreme for he then stated that on the approach of the enemy the two brigades in front had retired in a leisurely manner inside his line. "Leisurely" is so good in that connection that it always brings a smile whenever I recall the "leisurely" manner in which Conrad's brigade made its way back to Cox's line. Moreover in a letter to General Wagner, written two days after the battle, and inclosing a copy of a letter to General [George H.] Thomas, urging the promotion of Colonel Opdycke, Cox took occasion to express the opinion he then held, based on his personal observation, of the conduct of Wagner's entire division:

> I desire also to express my admiration of the gallantry of your whole command. Indeed an excess of bravery kept the two brigades a little too long in front, so that the troops at the main line could not get to firing upon the advancing enemy till they were uncomfortably near.

Soon after the regiment had reformed one of the drafted men of my company was brought in from the ditch outside mortally wounded. No doubt he had reached the ditch in too exhausted a condition to climb over the breastwork and had lain out among the rebels where he had been repeatedly hit by our own fire. The pain of his wounds had made him crazy, for he would not talk, but kept crawling about on all fours moaning in agony. There were a few men missing from the company of whom their comrades could give no account. Moved by the fate of the drafted man, I crossed the breastwork to search outside, if perchance I might find one or more of the missing ones lying there wounded and bring them aid. I went to a gun of the Sixth Ohio battery, posted a short distance east of the cotton-gin, to get over; and as I stepped up into the embrasure, the sight that met my eyes was most horrible even in the dim starlight. The mangled bodies of the dead rebels were piled up as high as the mouth of the embrasure, and the gunners said that repeatedly when the lanyard was pulled the embrasure was filled with men, crowding forward to get in, who were literally blown from the mouth of the cannon. Only one rebel got past the muzzle of that gun and one of the gunners snatched up a pick leaning against the breastwork and killed him with that. Captain Baldwin of this battery has stated that as he stood by one of his guns, watching the effect of its fire, he could hear the smashing of the bones when the missiles tore their way through the dense ranks of the approaching rebels.

While I was cautiously making my way around one side of that heap of mangled humanity, a wounded man lying at the bottom, with head and shoulders protruding, begged me for the love of Christ to pull the dead bodies off him. The ditch was piled promiscuously with the dead and badly wounded and heads, arms, and legs were sticking out in almost every conceivable manner. The ground near the ditch was so thickly covered with bodies that I had to pick my steps carefully to avoid treading on some of them. The air was filled with the moans of the wounded; and the pleadings for water and for help of some of those who saw me were heartrending. While walking along towards the pike to get in the pathway in which my company had come back, I passed two rebel flags lying on the ground close together. It did not occur to me that I would be entitled to any credit for picking up the flags under such circumstances, but I thought that if I did not find what I was looking for I would return that way and take the flags in with me. I had passed on a few steps when I heard a man behind me exclaim, "Look out, there!" Thinking he meant me, I turned hastily and saw him pitch the two flags over the breastwork. I presume that the men inside the work who got possession of the flags were afterwards sent to Washington with them and possibly may have received medals for their capture. I felt so uneasy while outside, lest the rebels should make some movement that would start our line to firing again that I kept close to the breastwork, and as it was soon manifest that the chance in the darkness of finding a friend, where the bodies were so many, was too remote to justify the risk I was taking, I returned within our line.

From what I saw while outside I have always believed that General Hood never stated his losses fully. Those losses were in some respects without precedent in either army on any other battle-field of the war. He had five generals killed, six wounded and one captured on our breastworks, and the slaughter of field and company officers, as well as of the rank and file, was correspondingly frightful. It was officially reported of Quarles's brigade that the ranking officer in the entire brigade at the close of the battle was a captain. Of the nine divisions of infantry composing Hood's army, seven divisions got up in time to take part in the assault and at least six of these seven divisions were as badly wrecked as was Pickett's division in its famous charge at Gettysburg.

Our loss was officially stated as two thousand, three hundred, twenty-six men and almost the whole of it was due to the presence of the two brigades in front of the main line. Casement's brigade, to the left of Reilly's, sustained a very determined assault which was repulsed with a loss of only three killed and sixteen wounded. But the action of Casement's men was not hampered by the presence of any of Wagner's men in their front and they could open fire as soon as the rebels came within range. If the brigades of Reilly and Strickland could have opened fire under the same conditions they would have done just as well as Casement's brigade. A critical investigation of our losses will conclusively demonstrate that at Franklin the violation of the military axiom never to post a small body of troops in a way to hamper the action of the main body was directly responsible for the unnecessary loss of more than two thousand of our soldiers. That was the frightful butchers' bill our army had to pay for a bit of incompetent generalship.

How was it possible for veteran generals of the Atlanta campaign to make such a gross blunder?

In his official report Cox states that at two o'clock the enemy came into full view and he reported that fact and the position of the two brigades in front of his breastworks to Schofield and received his orders with reference to holding the position; but he does not state what those orders were. Cox made that report and received those orders in a personal conference with Schofield when they must have fully discussed the situation, and Cox's peculiar statement in this connection seems to carry a covert threat, as if he had said to Schofield, "If you attempt to hold me responsible for the blunder I will tell what those orders of yours were."

In a written account furnished me by Captain Whitesides, Wagner's assistant adjutant-general, he states that about half past two o'clock Wagner ordered him to see Colonel Lane and find out what was going on in his front. From his position on the pike at the gap in the breastworks Wagner could see for himself Stewart's corps forming in Conrad's front, as already described, but his view of Lane's front was obstructed by the large number of trees and by the inequalities of the ground on the west side of the pike. Colonel Lane told Whitesides that Hood was forming his army in battle order and that without any doubt it was his intention to attack in force; that the position occupied by the two brigades was faulty, being without any support on either flank, and unless they were withdrawn they would be run over by the enemy or compelled to fall back to the breastworks under fire. On reporting Lane's statement to Wagner, Whitesides was directed to find General Stanley, the corps commander, and tell him what Lane had said. He found Stanley with Schofield at the house of Doctor [Daniel] Cliffe in the central part of the town, where they could see nothing of what was going on in front, and reported to them as stated above. He then returned to Wagner who, so far as he knew, received no further orders.

The report of Cox and the statement of Whitesides indicate that both Cox and Wagner believed that Hood intended to attack but that neither of them would take the responsibility, with Schofield in easy communication, of withdrawing the two brigades without his sanction from the position to which they had been assigned by his order. They reported to him the situation and then waited, and waited in vain, for him to take action.

In a personal interview Doctor Cliffe told me that Schofield came to his house about nine o'clock for breakfast and afterwards kept his headquarters there until the battle began; that after breakfast he retired to a bedroom where he slept until noon or shortly after; that a short time before the battle began Cox was there in conference with Schofield and staff officers kept coming and going until the fighting began; that Stanley was there with Schofield and they were waiting for their dinner; that they told him there would be no battle that day because Hood would not attack breastworks but that after dinner they would ride on to Nashville together and the army would follow after dark.

Stanley and Cliffe had been schoolboys together in Wayne County, Ohio, and as Cliffe was a well known Union man, it was supposed to be unsafe for him to remain in Franklin and he was invited to accompany Schofield and Stanley on their ride to Nashville. General Schofield has claimed that he scored a great success in his campaign against Hood and that this success was largely due to his intimate knowledge of Hood's character, gained while they were classmates at West Point, which enabled him to foresee what Hood would do and then make the proper dispositions to defeat him. At Franklin he relied so confidently on his ability to foretell what Hood's action would be that he not only wholly neglected to give any personal attention to the preparations for assault which Hood was making in plain sight of our front but he would not give any heed to the reports brought him by those who had seen these preparations. It was his belief, based on his intimate knowledge of Hood's character, that Hood was making an ostentatious feint to mask his real intention of executing a flank movement, for in a telegram to General Thomas, dated at three o'clock, Schofield informed Thomas that Hood was in his front with about two corps and seemed prepared to cross the river above and below.

He [Schofield] has tried to escape all personal responsibility for the blunder by the weak statement that he was across the river when the battle began. Even if that statement were true, and it is directly contradicted by the disinterested statement of Doctor Cliffe as well as by an abundance of other reliable evidence, both direct and circumstantial, there is no possible escape for Schofield from the inexorable logic of the situation. For two hours Hood was engaged in preparations for assault in plain sight of thousands of our soldiers. What was Schofield doing those two hours? If he saw anything of Hood's preparations he showed incompetence by his failure to promptly withdraw the two brigades from the blundering position to which he had assigned them. If he saw nothing of Hood's preparations, it was only because of a criminal neglect of his duty at a time when the perilous position of his army, with a greatly superior rebel army in its front and a river at its back, demanded his utmost vigilance.

It was said that General Stanley was sick but he spent the day with Schofield and he also, having had West Point experience of Hood's character, concurred fully in Schofield's belief that Hood would not assault. So great was their delusion in this respect that it could not be shaken by the reports made by their subordinates, and nothing short of the loud roar of the opening battle was able to arouse them into giving any personal attention to the situation. Then at last, when it was too late to do anything to remedy a blunder which already had gone so far that it must go on to its full culmination, Schofield and Stanley left the house of Doctor Cliffe. Stanley hurried to the front which he reached just as Opdycke's brigade was starting forward. Spurring his horse to the front of this brigade, he personally led it in its famous charge. A little later his horse was shot under him and he got a bullet through the back of his neck as he was rising to his feet. It was a flesh wound that bled freely, but Stanley declined to leave the front until after the fighting was all over. He then went to the rear to have his wound dressed and after his departure Cox was the senior general on the battle-field.

When Stanley started for the front Schofield started for the rear, and the most charitable construction that can be placed upon his action is that he interpreted the sound of the firing to mean that the expected flank movement had begun and that his duty called him across the river to provide against that flank movement. His disturbed mental condition at that time is disclosed by the fact that he abandoned in the room of Cliffe's house, where he had slept, his overcoat, gloves, and a package containing the official dispatches he had received from General Thomas. These articles were not reclaimed until our army returned to Franklin after the victory at Nashville and in the meantime Mrs. Cliffe saved the coat from being taken by some needy rebel by wearing it herself and she also safely kept the gloves and dispatches.

After crossing the river Schofield rode to the fort [Fort Granger] that had been built the year before on the high bluff which formed the north bank. From this elevated position he had a good view of a large part of the battle-field and the heavy guns in the fort were engaged in firing on the nearest flank of the enemy; but he was not only well beyond the range of every rebel bullet that was fired, but he was also so far away by the road which a staff officer must take to communicate with the firing line, that he was wholly out of touch with the troops that were fighting the battle. His presence in the fort had no more to do with the repulse of Hood's assault than if he had been the man-in-the-moon looking down upon the battle-field. The only order that he sent from the fort was the order to retreat after the army had won a great victory. When this order reached Cox he made a manly protest against it. He explained the wrecked condition of the rebel army to the staff officer, who brought the order, and giving his opinion that retreat was wholly unnecessary, he urged the officer to return to Schofield and persuade him to countermand the order. He also sent his brother, Captain Cox, of his own staff, to remonstrate with Schofield, and to say that General Cox would be responsible with his head for holding the position. When Captain Cox reached the fort he found that Schofield already had started for Nashville. The Captain hurried in pursuit and, overtaking Schofield on the pike and delivering his message, was told that the order to retreat would not be recalled and must be executed. In Wagner's division we had been marching, or fortifying, or fighting for more than forty hours continuously, and believed that we had reached the limit of human endurance, but we still had to plod the eighteen weary miles to Nashville before getting any rest.

  In January, 1865, Schofield, with the corps that he was then commanding, was transferred from Tennessee to North Carolina. When he passed through Washington en route he had the opportunity of giving to President Lincoln a personal account of his campaign in Tennessee. The president must have known in a general way, that at Franklin the rebel army had made a very desperate assault which had been most disastrously repulsed, but he certainly was ignorant of the details of the battle, and in the absence of any information to the contrary, his natural inference would be that Schofield, as our commanding general, was entitled to great credit for that repulse. At that time the truth concerning Schofield's connection with the battle was known to a few men only and those who would have exposed his pretensions, if they had had any knowledge of what he was claiming, were all far away in Tennessee. The claim for distinguished services which Schofield succeeded in impressing upon "Honest Old Abe" may be fairly inferred from the very extraordinary promotion given him over the heads of many able and deserving officers-namely, from captain to brigadier-general in the regular army, to date November 30, 1864, with a brevet as major-general "for gallant and meritorious services in the battle of Franklin, Tennessee."

IN FRONT OF THE FEDERAL WORKS AT FRANKLIN.

APPENDIX P

Tribute to Confederate General John Adams
By Confederate General Alexander Peter Stewart

From Ridley's 1906 book: *Battles and Sketches of the Army of Tennessee*, pp. 415-420

(My notes are in brackets, LS)

It is well understood that General Hood should not have fought the battle of Franklin, but should have crossed the Harpeth river above Franklin, and interposed his army between the enemy and Nashville. It has been charged that he gave the order to attack at Franklin because of chagrin at his failure at Spring Hill. This supposition does Hood great injustice. A Federal courier had been captured bearing dispatches between [Generals] Thomas and Schofield of the Federal army. The tenor of the dispatches led Hood to believe that Franklin was not in a defensible position, and that therefore, as he expressed it, he thought his "time to fight had come."

The battle was one of the bloodiest of the war, and developed a vast amount of the loftiest heroism in the Confederate army. When all the acts of real genuine heroism performed on the Confederate side during the war, and the names of the men who performed them, shall have been gathered up by the historian, it will be found that the grand old "Volunteer State" of Tennessee furnished her full quota.

At Franklin there was not a more natural or sublimer display of true heroism than was made by Brigadier-General John Adams, a Tennessean, commanding a brigade in Loring's division, Stewart's corps. It was natural because it emanated spontaneously from one whose very nature was heroic and who, consequently, could not act otherwise than heroically.

The following descriptions are by Federal officers who witnessed his death at Franklin. They need no comment. Notice that [U.S.] General Cox's official report says: "The officers showed the most heroic example and self sacrifice," and what was true of the officers was true of the men.

General Cox's report, made directly after the battle also says:

"On reaching the osage hedge in front of Stile's left, they [the Confederates] first endeavored to force their way through it. The tough and thorny shrub foiled them, and they attempted to file around the hedge by flank and under terrible withering fire from Stile's and Casement's brigades and the batteries on the flank.

"In front of Stile's right and Casement's left, the obstructions being fewer, the enemy advanced rapidly and in fine order up to the breast-works and made desperate efforts to carry them. Their officers showed the most heroic example and self sacrifice, riding up to our lines in advance of their men, cheering them on. One [Confederate] general officer (Adams) was shot down upon the parapet itself, his horse falling dead across the breast-works."

General Adams' tragic death at Franklin is described in the interesting letters of two Federal officers, written some years ago. He survived only a few minutes, his horse being killed instantly while astride the works, making it one of the most striking pictures of heroism ever seen.

The brigade entered the fight about 4 o'clock [PM] from the rear and east of Colonel McGavock's house [Carnton Mansion]. General Adams was self-possessed, vigilantly watching and directing the movements of about ten paces in front of his line of battle, and thus led his troops for about half a mile. Captain Thomas Gibson, his cousin and a member of his staff, who was with him, says that he was calm and self-possessed, vigilantly directing and watching the movements of his men. When about fifty yards from the enemy's works he rode rapidly from near the right of his brigade to near the left, then directed his course toward the enemy, and fell on their works pierced with nine bullets. He was wounded severely in his right arm near the shoulder early in the fight, and was urged to leave the field, but said: "No; I am going to see my men through." The brigade suffered terribly, having over four hundred and fifty killed and wounded, many field and line officers being of the number. After Adams' death General Robert Lowry commanded the brigade—afterward governor of Mississippi.

[U.S.] Lieutenant-Colonel Edward Adams Baker, of the Sixty-fifth Indiana infantry, in the great battle of Franklin, Tennessee, had an experience with General John Adams, of the Confederate Army, which induced him, years after the war, to publish a desire for knowledge of his family. Having secured the address of Mrs. Adams in St. Louis, he wrote from Webb City, Missouri, October 25th, 1891:

"Mrs. General Adams, St. Louis.

"Dear Madam: I am in receipt of your very kind letter of the 21st instant, and hasten to reply. I have often since the great battle of Franklin asked myself the question, who was General Adams? Has he a wife and children? And if so, how much would they give to know just how he died and all the facts as I know them?

"The battle of Franklin was one of the most desperate contests of the war. I was in command of the [Union] skirmish line of Cox's division. General Adams' and General Brown's brigades, of the Confederate Army, were massed in front of our division. We had during the forenoon thrown up breast-works of earth some ten feet thick and five feet high, behind which our men stood protected; while the enemy came up in an open field and charged upon us. They had no protection, and were mowed down like grass before the scythe. This will explain to you how desperate was the undertaking to dislodge our army from behind this impenetrable breastwork and the sublime heroism of the men who undertook the perilous task and almost succeeded.

"The Confederates came on with bayonets fixed and moving at a steady walk. My skirmishers, who were stationed some hundred yards in front of our breast-works, were brushed out of the way and rapidly fell back to the main line. By this time the enemy was within a few paces and received a terrific volley from our guns. They fell by thousands, and their decimated ranks tell back to reform, and come again. In this way nine separate and distinct charges were made, each time men falling in every direction and each time being repulsed. I doubt that if in the history of the world a single instance of such desperate and undaunted valor can be produced.

"In one of these charges, more desperate than any that followed, General Adams rode up to our works and cheering his men, made an attempt to leap his horse over them. The horse fell dead upon the top of the embankment and the General was caught under him, pierced with bullets. As soon as the charge was repulsed our men sprang upon the works and lifted the horse, while others dragged the General from under him. He was perfectly conscious, and knew his fate. He asked for water, as all dying men do in battle, as the life blood drips from the body. One of my men gave him a canteen of water, while another brought, an arm load of cotton from an old gin near by and made him a pillow. The General gallantly thanked them, and, in answer to our expressions of sorrow at his sad fate, he said: 'It is the fate of a soldier to die for his country,' and expired.

"Robert Baker, one of my men, took the saddle from the dead horse and threw it in [Union] General Casement's ambulance, who expressed it to his home in Ohio. Some three years ago I received a letter from General Casement, in which he wrote me that he had the saddle labeled and carefully laid away as a trophy of war. I write a letter to-day to the General, asking him to send the saddle to me, that I may forward it to you.

"I am also glad to know that you recovered the General's watch, chain and ring, and will say that if your sons—who, you inform me, are connected with the Missouri Pacific Railway—should have business on this branch of the road, I would be glad to have them call at my office. Mr. Wilder, the agent here, knows me, and would no doubt bring them. I hope that my imperfect description may be of some interest to you."

U.S. GENERAL JOHN S. CASEMENT'S LETTER TO THE WIFE OF CONFEDERATE GENERAL JOHN ADAMS

"Painesville, O., November 23, 1891.
"Mrs. Georgia McD. Adams.

"Dear Madam: [U.S.] Major Baker, of Webb City, Mo., informs me that you have expressed a desire to obtain the saddle used by General Adams at Franklin, Tennessee, in his last and fatal ride on the unhappy day that caused so many hearts to bleed on both sides of the line. It was my fortune to stand in our line within a foot of where the General succeeded in getting his horse's forelegs over the line. The poor beast died there, and was in that position when we returned over the same field more than a month after the battle. The saddle was taken off the horse and presented to me before the charge was fairly repulsed; that is why I have kept it all these years. It is the only trophy I have of the great war, and I am only too happy to return it to you. It has never been used since the General used it. It has hung in our attic. The stirrups were of wood, and I fear that my boys in their pony days must have taken them, for I cannot find them. I am very sorry for it.

"General Adams fell from his horse from the position in which the horse died, just over the line of the works, which were part breast-works and part ditch. As soon as the charge was repulsed I had him brought on our side of the works, and did what we could to make him comfortable. He was perfectly calm and uncomplaining. He begged me to send him to the Confederate line, assuring me that the men that would take him there would return safe. I told him that we were going to fall back as soon as we could do it safely, and that he would soon be in possession of his friends.

It was a busy time with me. Our line was broken from near its center up to where I stood in it, and in restoring it and repulsing other charges I was too busy to again see the General until after his gallant life had passed away. I had his ring and watch taken care of; his pistol I gave to one of the Colonels of my brigade, and do not know what became of it.

"These are briefly the facts connected with the death of General Adams. The ring and watch were sent to you through a flag of truce and a receipt taken for them.

"The saddle will be expressed to you to-morrow. Would that I had the power to return the gallant rider! There was not a man in my command that witnessed the gallant ride that did not express his admiration of the rider and wish that he might have lived long to wear the honors that he so gallantly won. Wishing you and his children much happiness, I am yours truly, J. S. Casement."

 APPENDIX Q

Tribute to Confederate General Otho French Strahl
By Sumner Archibald Cunningham
Editor of *Confederate Veteran*

From Ridley's 1906 book: *Battles and Sketches of the Army of Tennessee*, pp. 421-425

(My notes are in brackets, LS)

Otho French Strahl, a native of Ohio, had removed to the South and was practicing law at Dyersburg, Tenn., when the war of '61-'65 began. He enlisted promptly in the Confederate Army, was soon promoted to the command of his regiment, the Fourth Tennessee infantry, and then to Brigadier-General, holding that position when killed at Franklin, Nov. 30, 1864.

General Strahl was a model character, and it was said of him that in all the war he was never known to use language unsuited to the presence of ladies.

The editor of the Veteran [i.e., Cunningham] was a boy soldier in his brigade—Forty-first Tennessee—and was so thrilled with his noble record on that last eventful day and night, when his gallant commander gave his life for the Confederate cause, that he went on the sacred pilgrimage, a few years ago, to a Kansas ranch to see a sister, Mrs. Sigler, and tell her of his last hours.

There he procured the photograph herein engraved, and he saw a memorandum and letters from the General's trunk. Mr. Sigler, although a Northwesterner, manifested much interest, and with pride produced the General's beautiful gray uniform coat, with its collar decorated in wreathed stars.

In reply to a remark of surprise that General Strahl should have been so zealous to his death for the Confederacy, his sister said that both of his grandmothers were Southern women.

The correspondence and further comment will be read with interest, especially by all who were familiar with the awful carnage at Franklin.

Bishop Chas. Todd Quintard, who was Chaplain to the First

Tennessee infantry, and has ever been zealous in behalf of Southern people, writes:

> "I am glad to know that you have a photograph of General Strahl, and pictures of the cotton gin and the Carter House. I have a table made from the wood of the cotton gin.
>
> "The day on which the battle of Franklin was fought General Strahl presented me a beautiful mare, named Lady Polk. His inspector, Lieutenant John Marsh, as he bade me adieu, threw his arms about me and gave me a farewell kiss. My intercourse with these two men was of a most sacred character. Marsh had been fearfully wounded at the battle of Chickamauga. I had watched over him on the field and in the hospital. On the 22nd of February I had baptized him in Gilmer Hospital near Marietta; and he was confirmed by Bishop Elliott, of Georgia, on the day following. To both I had broken that bread which came down from heaven. John Marsh was knit to me by the tenderest ties of friendship. There was in him what Shaftesbury calls the 'most natural beauty in the world.' Honesty and moral truth—honesty that was firm and upright.
>
> ". . . General Strahl I baptized on the 20th of April, and I presented him for confirmation to the Right Rev. Stephen Elliott. The following is from the report of Bishop Elliott, to his convention in 1864:"
>
>> 'On Wednesday, April 20th, services were held in the Methodist Church, Dalton, upon which occasion service was read by Dr. Quintard, and baptism administered to General Strahl, of Tennessee. After service a class was presented by Dr. Quintard, among whom were four Generals of the Army of the Confederate States

These officers were Lieutenant-General Hardee, Brigadier-Generals Strahl, Shoup and Govan.

'The day of Strahl's death was to me a most pathetic one. He evidently felt that the approaching battle was to be his last—with many tender words he bade me farewell I kept the mare he gave me through the war. Afterwards I sold her and with the proceeds of the sale I erected a memorial window in St. James Church, Bolivar, to his dear memory and that of his inspector, John Marsh. I need not say how sacred these memories are.'

The editor of the Veteran read the above with moistened eyes. It is a coincidence like special providence that these two faces, Strahl and Marsh, were indelibly impressed upon him in that awful charge at Franklin—his position being right guide to the brigade, he was near Strahl in the fatal advance; and was pained at the extreme sadness in Strahl's face. He was surprised, too, that his General went in the battle on foot. Lieutenant Marsh, who formerly belonged to the artillery, and with a stiff arm from the battle of Chickamauga—he always wore an artillery jacket—was on his white horse in advance of the line of battle up to within about three hundred yards of the breast-works. There was in his face an indescribable expression—while animated and rather playful, there was mingled in its heroic action evidence that he felt he was on the brink of eternity. But he wavered not and rode on and on until rider and horse lay dead before us, terribly mangled with bullets. How strange that these reminiscences come to the writer to be recorded for the entire Southland so many years after the event!

An account of personal experience, in the Battle of Franklin went the rounds of the Southern press a few years ago, in which the following occurred:

"I was near General Strahl, who stood in the ditch and handed up guns to those posted to fire them. I had passed to him my short Enfield (noted in the regiment) about the sixth time. The man who had been firing, cocked it and was taking deliberate aim, when he was shot and tumbled down dead into the ditch upon those killed before him. When the men so exposed were shot down ,their places were supplied by volunteers until these were exhausted, and it was necessary for General Strahl to call for others. He turned to me, and though I was several feet back from the ditch, I rose up immediately ,and walking over the wounded and dead, took position with one foot upon the pile of bodies of my dead fellows, and the other upon the embankment, and fired guns which the General himself handed up to me until he, too, was shot down. One other man had position on my right, and assisted in the firing. The battle lasted until not an efficient man was left between us and the Columbia Pike, some fifty yards to our right, and hardly any behind us to hand up guns. Indeed but few of us were then left alive. It seemed as if we had no choice but to surrender or try to get away; and when I asked General Strahl for counsel, he simply answered, 'Keep firing.' But just as the man to my right was shot, and fell against me with terrible groans, he, too, was shot. He threw up his hands, falling on his face, and I thought him dead, but in asking the dying man, who still lay against my shoulders as he sank forever, how he was wounded, the General, who had not been killed, thinking my question was to him, raised up saying that he was shot in the neck, and called for Colonel Stafford to turn over his command. He crawled over the dead, the ditch being three deep, about twenty feet to where Colonel Stafford was. Staff officers and others started to carry him to the rear, but he received another shot, and directly the third, which killed him instantly. Colonel Stafford was dead in the pile, as the morning light disclosed, with his feet wedged in at the bottom, other dead across and under him after he fell, leaving his body half standing as if ready to give command to the dead!

"By that time but a handful of us were left on that part of the line, and as I was sure that our condition was not known, I ran to the rear to report to General John C. Brown, commanding the division. I met Major Hampton of his staff, who told me that General Brown was wounded, and that General Strahl was in command. This assured me that those in command did not know the real situation, so I went on the hunt for General Cheatham. Ah, the loyalty of faithful comrades in such a struggle!

"These personal recollections are all that I can give, as the greater part of the battle was fought after nightfall, and once in the midst of it, with but the light of the flashing guns, I could only see what passed directly under my sight. True, the moon was shining; but the dense smoke and dust so filled the air as to weaken its benefits, like a heavy fog before the rising sun, only there was no promise of the fog disappearing. Our spirits were crushed. It was indeed the Valley of Death."

APPENDIX R

Official Reports on the Battles of Franklin & Nashville By Confederate General Alexander Peter Stewart November 29, 1864, to January 20, 1865

From Ridley's 1906 book: Battles and Sketches of the Army of Tennessee, pp. 426-436

(My notes are in brackets, LS)

Headquarters Stewart's Corps, Army of Tenn., near Tupelo, Miss., Jan. 20, 1865.

Sir: The following brief outlines of the operations of this corps from November 29, 1864, to the close of the campaign is respectfully submitted. It is necessarily an imperfect report, being made at the request of the commanding general, without the aid of the report of subordinate commanders.

On Tuesday, November 29, following Cheatham's corps, we crossed Duck river near Columbia and arrived near sunset at Rutherford creek. Crossing it I moved to the right of Cheatham's corps, then in line near the pike from Columbia to Franklin, and about 11 p.m. bivouacked in rear of his right.

The next morning (30th) we moved at daylight, taking the advance in pursuit of the retreating enemy. About midday we came in sight of his line formed on a commanding ridge some two miles from Franklin. In compliance with the instructions of the commanding general, I moved to the right toward Harpeth river and formed to attack the enemy who fell back to an entrenched line around the town. Loring's division was to the right, Walthall's in the center, French's on the left. Ector's brigade, of the last named division, marched from Florence as guard to the pontoon train and had not rejoined. Buford's division of cavalry covered the space between Loring's right and the river, while another was thrown across to the other bank. In the meantime Cheatham's corps was formed for attack, and the two corps were to move forward simultaneously. I had one battery only, the pieces of which were distributed to the three divisions. About 4 p.m. a staff officer from the commanding general brought me the order to advance, and the word forward was given. A body of the enemy's cavalry in front of Loring and the division on his right was soon routed, and the cavalry division (Buford's) ceased to operate with us. The line moved forward in fine order, the men in high spirits drove the enemy from his outer line and fiercely assailed the second. The ground over which Loring's division advanced was obstructed by a deep railroad cut and an abatis and hedge of osage orange. With these exceptions the space in front of the enemy's position on our side was perfectly open and swept by a terrible and destructive cross-fire of artillery from the works and from the opposite bank of the narrow stream—the Harpeth. The men, however, pressed forward again and again with dauntless courage, to the ditch around the inner line of the work; which they failed to carry, but where many of them remained, separated from the enemy only by the parapet until the Federal Army withdrew.

A return of casualties has heretofore been made, the number reported amounting to something over 2,000 in killed, wounded, and missing. Among them were many of our best officers and bravest men. Brigadier-General John Adams was killed, his horse being found across the inner line of the enemy's works. Brigadier General Scott was paralyzed by the explosion near him of a shell. Brigadier-Generals Quarles and Cockrell were wounded severely, the former subsequently becoming a prisoner. Major General Walthall had two horses killed and was himself severely bruised. Many field and staff and company officers were either killed or severely wounded; they deserve special mention; but not yet having received reports from divisions, brigades, and regiments, it is not in my power to give all their names or to do justice to their heroic conduct.

On Friday, December 2, we moved to the vicinity of Nashville, finally taking a position on the left of the army extending across the Granny White (or middle Franklin) pike to a hill near the Hillsborough pike. This line was entrenched, was just a mile in length, and occupied by Loring's division alone. To protect our left flank, works were commenced on four other hills lying along near to and on either side of the Hillsborough pike, the one fartherest in rear being some mile and a half distant from the left of the front line. This latter line, to the left of the Hillsborough pike, was prolonged toward Cumberland river by the cavalry, though toward the last of our stay there Ector's brigade, under

Colonel Coleman, was placed on picket on the Harding pike, having Chalmers' cavalry on his right and left.

On the morning of December 15th information was received that the enemy was advancing west of the Hillsboro pike. General Walthall, whose troops were in bivouac, excepting the working parties engaged on the flank redoubts, was directed to place his men under arms and man the redoubts. General French having received leave of absence, his division which was small, was attached to General Walthall's. Finding the enemy were advancing in force, and that Ector's brigade and the cavalry were forced to retire, all of Walthall's command not required for the redoubts was placed behind the stone fence along the Hillsborough pike between redoubt numbered 3 and 4 on the accompanying map. This map exhibits the position of Loring's division in the front line of the five hills crowned with unfinished works, and of Walthall's command, including his own and French's divisions. Each redoubt contained a section or battery of artillery, and from 100 to 150 infantry. The enemy appeared in force along the entire line extending around redoubts 1, 2, and 3, and as far as or beyond 4 and 5. My own line was stretched to its utmost tension, but could not reach far enough toward 4 and 5 without leaving the way open to the enemy between Loring's left and Walthall's right. The commanding general who was notified as soon as practicable of the approach of the enemy, sent me as re-enforcements, first, Manigault's and soon after Deas' brigades of Johnson's division, Lee's corps, and later the two remaining brigades of that division, and I was informed that one or more divisions from Cheatham's corps (the extreme right) had been ordered to the left. As the object of the enemy seemed to be to turn our left flank by carrying the redoubts 4 and 5, Manigault's brigade on coming up was moved in line about parallel to the Hillsborough Pike and opposite redoubt 4. Major General Johnson arriving soon afterwards was directed to place Deas' brigade on Manigault's right, so as to connect with Walthall's line. By this time the enemy had carried redoubts 4 and 5 and had captured many of the men and all the artillery in them, besides killing and wounding many, and were making for the pike. The two brigades named, making but feeble resistance, fled, and the enemy crossed the pike, passing Walthall's left. Loring's line being not yet passed, a battery had been ordered from it, which, arriving just at this moment, was placed on a commanding hill, and these same brigades rallied to its support. They again fled, however, on the approach of the enemy abandoning the battery which was captured. By this time the other brigades of Johnson's division had come up, but were unable to check the progress of the enemy who had passed the Hillsborough Pike a full half mile, completely turning our flank and gaining the rear of both Walthall and Loring, whose situation was becoming perilous in the extreme. Their positions were maintained to the last possible moment, in the hope that the expected succor would arrive and restore the flight on the left. Deeming it absolutely necessary for them to fall back, orders were dispatched to that effect, when it was found that Walthall had already ordered his line to retire not a moment too soon, and this of itself made it necessary for Loring to withdraw. The latter was directed also to form along the Granny White Pike (which would place him nearly at right angles to his former position) to check the anticipated rush of the enemy from his and Walthall's fronts. This was gallantly and successfully done by this fine division, the corps retiring to a position between Granny White and Franklin pikes when night put an end to the conflict.

Brigadier-General Sears late in the day lost a leg, and subsequently fell into the enemy's hands. All the artillery in the redoubts, the battery above mentioned and another on Loring's line, the horses of which were killed or wounded, were captured by the enemy.

In the meantime one or two divisions from Cheatham's corps had come up on the left where the commanding general was in person, but being separated from that part of the field I am unable to state what occurred. Also Ector's brigade, commanded by Colonel Coleman, in falling back from its position on the Harding Pike, was thrown over on the left and beyond my personal observation. The report of Colonel Coleman is, therefore, referred to for account of its operations, which I have been told were characterized by the usual intrepidity of this small but firm and reliable body of men.

During the night of the 15th, the army was placed in position to receive the attack expected at an early hour next morning. The map shows the position of this corps, it being in the center, Lee's corps on the right, Cheatham's on the left, extending from the hill occupied by Bate's division, Cheatham's, corps, along the range of hills on the west side of the Granny White pike. The line of this corps extended from the side of the hill occupied by Bate across the pike, along a stone fence on the east side of the pike. In rear of the line and some half mile or more distant a high ridge lies in a general east and west direction, through the gaps of which run the Franklin, Granny White, and other pikes. It was the order of the commanding general that in case of disaster Lee's corps should hold the Franklin pike, this corps retiring by that pike and taking up position at or beyond Brentwood, so as to permit Lee to withdraw, while Cheatham was to move out on the Granny White pike. Instructions accordingly were given to subordinate commanders.

At an early hour in the morning the enemy approached, placing artillery in position and opening a heavy fire, which continued almost incessantly through the day. They confronted us everywhere with a force double or treble our own. Occasional attacks were made on various parts of our lines and repulsed, through their chief efforts seemed to be directed against our flanks for the purpose of gaining the roads in our rear. Every attack made on the lines occupied by this corps to the last was repulsed with severe loss to the enemy.

In the course of the morning, the commanding general calling on me for a brigade to go to the right flank, Ector's, being in reserve was dispatched. It was finally sent to the hills in our rear and on the east side of the Granny White pike to drive back the enemy who had passed our left, crossed to the east side of the pike, and held this portion of the ridge. Later in the day Reynold's (Arkansas) brigade was withdrawn from Walthall's line and sent to the assistance of Ector's. They were strong enough to check the enemy, but not sufficiently so to drive him back and regain the pass by which this pike crosses the ridge, so that retreat was cut off in that direction and greatly endangered even by the Franklin pike, the only route now left open for the entire army. At one time the enemy gained the spurs on the west side of the Granny White pike and occupied by Cheatham's men, some of whom, falling back, formed parallel to Bate's line, on the south side of the hill occupied by his division, but a few hundred yards from his line and fronting in the opposite direction.

The situation then, briefly, was this: The left flank completely turned, the enemy crossing to the east side of the Granny White pike in our rear, and holding the ridge on that side and the pass through which this road runs. The ridge was high and steep and extended beyond the

Franklin pike to the east, and was but a short distance in rear of our line. It seemed as though in case of disaster escape was impossible. There was no reserve force that could be brought up to restore any break that might occur.

About two or three o'clock in the afternoon, the commanding general sent for me, and while in conversation with him an officer of his staff announced that the line had given way. Not being present at the moment this took place, at least where I could witness it, and not yet being in possession of the official reports of subordinate commanders, I do not deem it proper to decide where the line first yielded. It would seem, however, that when once broken it very soon gave way everywhere, and the whole army made for the Franklin pike. In accordance with the orders of the commanding general before alluded to, I had dispatched Major Foster of the engineers, to find a suitable position beyond Brentwood for holding this road.

On reaching Brentwood, however, about dark I received orders to move on to Franklin, and the next morning to move toward Spring Hill and Columbia. Arriving at the latter place on the morning of the 18th, this corps took position on the north bank of Duck river, covering the passage of the entire army, and crossing about daylight of the 20th; so the following week at Tennessee river, Bainbridge, this corps covered the operations, and was the last to cross, which it did on the meaning of December 28th. At Columbia [Tennessee], a rear guard composed of several brigades from this and other corps was organized and placed under the command of Major General Walthall. This force, in connection with the cavalry, covered the retreat from Columbia to Tennessee river.

It is due to the officers and men of this corps that I should bear testimony of their patient endurance of fatigue and privation, their cheerfulness and alacrity in obeying orders, and above all, their heroic valor as displayed on many occasions since I have had the honor to command them, but pre-eminently at Franklin.

My thanks are due to Major Generals Loring, Walthall, and French for their cordial co-operation and skillful management of their respective divisions and to the several members of my staff who have uniformly shown themselves competent, faithful, and zealous in the discharge of their duties.

I have omitted to state in its proper place that a short time after our advance to the vicinity of Nashville, Cockrell's brigade of Missourians, French's division, was ordered by the commanding general to the mouth of Duck river. It rejoined at Bainbridge where we re-crossed the Tennessee river.

Accompanying this report are maps of the fields of Franklin and Nashville, as accurate as it is possible to make them.

I deem it proper to say that after the fall of Atlanta the condition of the army and other considerations rendered it necessary, in my judgment, that an offensive campaign should be made in the enemy's rear and on his line of communications. It is not my purpose, nor does it pertain to me, to explain the reasons which prompted the campaign, but simply to express my concurrence in the views which determined the operations of the army.

I am, Colonel, very respectfully, your obedient servant, Alex. P. Stewart.

[What follows is a letter from Confederate General Alexander P. Stewart to Confederate Lieutenant General Colonel A. P. Mason.]

Assistant Adjutant-General. Headquarters Army of Tennessee, near Smithfield Depot, N.C., April 3, 1865.

Sir: In my report of the operations of my corps during the campaign made by General Hood in Tennessee, I omitted the details of what transpired near Spring Hill during the afternoon and night of the 29th of November, 1864. I respectfully submit the following statement and ask that it be filed as a part of my report.

On the morning of November 29th General Hood moved with Cheatham's corps, and mine and Johnson's division of Lee's corps, (the latter reported to me) Cheatham's corps in advance. We made a forced march to get in rear of the enemy. In the course of the afternoon about 3 o'clock, I reached Rutherford's creek as Cheatham's rear division was crossing. I received orders to halt and form on the south side of the creek, my right to rest on or near the creek so as to move down the creek if necessary. Subsequently I received an order to send a division across the creek, and finally, between sunset and dark, an order was received to cross the creek, leaving a division on the south side. Johnson's division being in rear, was designated: to remain. Riding in advance of the column, about dusk, I found General Hood some half mile from the creek and about as far west of the road on which we were marching and which led to Spring Hill. The commanding general gave me a young man of the neighborhood as a guide and told me to move on and place my right across the pike beyond Spring Hill, "your left," he added, "extending down this way." This would have placed my line in rear of Cheatham's, except that my right would have extended beyond his. The guide informed me that at a certain point the road made a sudden turn to the left, going into Spring Hill; that from this bend there used to be a road leading across the pike meeting it at the toll-gate some mile and a half beyond Spring Hill, toward Franklin. I told him if he could find it, that was the right road. Arriving at the bend of the road we passed through a large gateway, taking what appeared in the darkness to be an indistinct path. Within a short distance I found General Forrest's headquarters and stopped to ascertain the position of his pickets covering Cheatham's right and of the enemy. He informed me that his scouts reported the enemy leaving the direct pike—leading from Spring Hill to Franklin and Nashville—and taking the one down Carter's creek. While in conversation with him I was informed that a staff officer from General Hood had come up and halted the column. It turned out to be a staff (engineer) officer of General Cheatham's, who informed me that General Hood had sent him to place me in position. It striking me as strange that the commanding general should send an officer not of his own staff on this errand, or indeed any one, as he had given directions to me in person, I inquired of the officer if he had seen General Hood since I had. He replied that he had just come from General Hood and that the reason why he was sent was that I was to go in position on General Brown's right (the right of Cheatham's corps) and he and General Brown had been over the ground by daylight. Thinking it possible the commanding general had changed his mind as to what he wished me to do, I concluded it was proper to be governed by the directions of this staff officer, and therefore returned to the road and moved on toward Spring Hill. Arriving near the line of Brown's division, General Brown explained his position, which was oblique to the pike, his right being farther from it than his left. It was evident that if my command were marched up and formed on his right, it being now a late hour, it would require all night to accomplish it, and the line, instead of extending across the pike, would bear away from it. Feeling satisfied there was a mistake, I directed the troops to be bivouacked, while I rode back to find the commanding general to explain my situation, and get further instructions. On arriving at his quarters I inquired of him if he had sent this officer of General Cheatham's staff to place me in position. He replied that he had. I next inquired if he had changed his mind as to what he wished me to do. He replied that he had, "But," said he, "the fact is, General Cheatham has been here and represented that there ought to be somebody on Brown's right." I explained to him that in the uncertainty I was in, I had directed the troops, who had been marching rapidly since daylight, and it was now 11p.m. to be placed in bivouac, and had come to report. He remarked, in substance, that it was not material; to let the men rest; and directed me to move before daylight in the morning, taking the advance toward Franklin. Subsequently General Hood made to me the statement:

> "I wish you and your people to understand that I attach no blame to you for the failure at Spring Hill; on the contrary I know if I had had you there the attack would have been made."

Very respectfully, general, your obedient servant, Alex. P. Stewart, Lieutenant-General.

APPENDIX S

Complete List of the Dead at the Mcgavock Confederate Cemetery Franklin, Tennessee

Reprinted with the kind permission of Betty Jane Carl, who sorted and typed the list of deceased below

(Photo copyright © Lochlainn Seabrook)

The original list information derives from the *McGavock Confederate Cemetery Book*, and is reprinted with written permission from Frances Hall, President of the Franklin #14 United Daughters of the Confederacy.

Notes by Ms. Carl regarding some of those buried at the McGavock Cemetery:

1) On page 38 of the booklet MCGAVOCK CONFEDERATE CEMETERY, FRANKLIN, TENNESSEE by Franklin Chapter #14, United Daughters of the Confederacy, copyrighted in 1989, the total number of soldiers buried at the cemetery was said to be 1481. A note follows saying: "in the handwriting of Mrs. McGavock is the following: 'Gen. Duncan of LA removed here from E. Tenn. and his grave marked by his family who reside in New Orleans, LA.' (General Johnson Kelly Duncan)"

> A sign at the cemetery says: "Following the Battle of Franklin, Nov. 30, 1864, John McGavock, owner of "Carnton," collected and buried here the bodies of 1496 Confederates. The five general officers killed there were interred elsewhere after being brought to the house. Other Confederates were later buried here, including Brig. Gen. Johnson K. Duncan."

2) N. H. B., #66, is actually Col. William H. Bishop, according to Tim Burgess, who for the last twenty years has been researching and collecting information about the soldiers who are buried at the McGavock Confederate Cemetery, preparing to write a book about them. One of his goals is to correct the many mistakes in past records, including the very ones I used from the afore-mentioned booklet.

3) The remains of Col. G. A. Smith of Georgia, #895, were removed to the Rosehilt Cemetery in Macon, Georgia.

4) Captain J. L. Riggs of Tennessee, #804, was erroneously buried in Missouri Section 9.

5) J. C. Wells of Georgia, #1029, was erroneously buried in Tennessee Section 79.

6) In the list I used from the afore-mentioned booklet, a soldier's name was followed not by the state he served, as in my list, but by his company letter. It is not clear to which the question mark refers or if it refers to both.

7) Tim Burgess, Ibid, wrote that 565 soldiers, a "full one third of the total killed," are unknowns.

8) On page 16 of the aforementioned booklet is a picture of a tombstone for the only non-Confederate buried here:

> "An ex-slave of the McGavock family, he died while assisting in the re-interring of the soldiers. The marker reads:
>
> Marcellus Cuppert
> Born Jan. 16, 1841
> Died April 26, 1866
> Whilst assisting in re-interring of the confederate dead."

Those veterans with asterisks (*) following their names did not die on the battlefield, but died at Carnton Plantation, which served as a Confederate field hospital for six months following the BOF on November 30, 1864.

List of Confederate Dead

Name	State	Company	Regiment	Section	Grave
	MO	K	1	8	22
	MO		2	11	75
	MS		15	29	106
	MO		1	8	22
	MO		2	11	75
	MS		15	29	106
	MS		15	29	110
	MS		14	29	116
	MS		14	29	117
	MS		14	30	121
In cedar case	MS			44	337
	TN		41	51	5
	TN	B	12	58	100
	GA		4	79	40
	TX	H	25	5	69
	TX		25	5	71
, Barney	MO	B	3	7	11
, B. F.	MO			10	52
, Capt. Elmer	MS			42	311
H. H.	MS	E	4	45	353
, James	MS			42	312
, John	MS			42	304

, John	MS			48	401
, Lieut. C.	MO				102
, N. B.	MO			9	37
, R. W.	MO	K	1 & 3	10	60
, Sgt.	KY		8th KY Cav.	103	5
, Sgt. R. J.	AL			69	24
, T.	MS	B		25	54
, Thos. S.	MO		1	13	95
A., J. W.	AL	E	29	68	7
Ables, L. C.	TN	E	12	54	44
Adams, E. P.	TN	D	46	65	209
Adams, J.	GA	H	29	77	11
Adams, Sgt. D. M.	MS	D	39	23	26
Adcock, T. P.	MS	A	20	33	178
Adcock, Wm.	TN	H	50	61	141
Allen, Capt. J. B.	AL		29	76	127
Allen, Sgt. J. G.	MS	B	40	40	283
Allen, S. D.	TN	A	42	51	3
Allen, Lt. T. W.	MS	E	15	29	112
Allen, W.	AL	F	4	70	31
Allison, Wm. M.	AR	G	1st	20	76

Allman, Sgt. P. F.	TN	A	49	65	203
Allon, Wm. M.*	AR	G	1st		
Anders, D. F.	MS	C	7	33	180
Anderson, A.	MS		41	34	187
Anthan, G. W.	MS	K	20	33	177
Anthony, J. L.	TN	B	47	58	96
Armistead, Col.*					
Armistead, Wm.*					
Armstrong, St. J. A.	MS	D	40	22	7
Arner, A. C.	TN	B	8	63	177
Arnet, T. M.	MS	G	14	29	120
Arnett, Jas. F.	AR	F	8	21	86
Arnold, Ensign J. C.	SC		16	85	38
Arnold, J. C.*					
Arnold, R. P.	AR	H	5	18	42
Arnst, T. H.*	MS	G	14		
Atkins, G. L.	KY	E	2nd KY Cav.	103	2
Atkinson, D. G.	AL		29	75	116
Atkinson, D. G.*	AL		29		

Atkinson, Capt. B.	MO	G	3	8	18
Ault, Thomas H.	MS		14	48	396
Avrit, Sgt. M.	TN	A	49	65	202
B., G. W.	TN	G	42	64	192
B., J. H.	LA		12	87	17
B., J. W.	MS	A	35	27	78
B., N. H.	MS		7	34	182
B., W. M.	MS	I	4	33	167
Bagwell, J. C.	MS	D	31	28	99
Bailey, Ely	MS		32	45	360
Bailu, John	AL	E	15	73	76
Baker, J. L.	AR	I	7	17	30
Balden, J. C.	MS	G	10	34	191
Barnes, J. H.	TN	F	11	59	116
Barnes, J. W.	MS	C	8	32	163
Barnett, J. R.	AR	A	1st	67	95
Barnett, W. D.	TN		4	60	126
Barnett, Lt. W. H.	AL	F	4	73	79
Barron, Sgt. E. V.	MS	F	6	47	381
Bartlett, Bob	MO	H	3	13	100
Bass, J. M.	TX		3rd CA.	2	19
Bass, W. W.	MS	A	35	28	104
Bathvue, J. L.	GA	I	46	77	15

Batson, N. Y.	SC	G	16	84	19
Battelle, S. A.	TX	G	24	5	68
Battols, C. L.	TN	K	154	60	127
Battols, C. L.*	TN	K	154		
Baugh, W. A.	MS	C	8	31	148
Bawrey, Wm. A.	TN	G	19	66	225
Bayne, Capt. Griffin	MO		3 & 5	14	112
Beard,	MS		14	29	114
Beavers, R.	TN	A	29	55	57
Bell, J. M.	AR				
Bell, J. S.	MS	A	24	35	205
Bell, M.	TN	A	49	65	201
Bell, W. O.	TN		4	63	172
Bennett, A. B.	MO	A	1st	12	86
Bentley, R.	MO	G	1st	12	87
Berry, S. S.	TN	A	55	66	229
Bevins, D. R.	MO	C	3 & 5	14	119
Billerny, W. H.	AR	H	15	20	78
Bird, N. R.	TN			51	11
Black, W. G.	MO	H	3 & 5	14	110
Blankenboker, D. W.*					
Blankinship, Geo.	TN	G	42	64	194

Bleeker, J.	TX	F	24	5	72
Boalk, J. A.	AR	A	17	15	3
Boid, J. L.	SC	H	24	84	29
Boid, Lt. J.	MS	F	31	28	103
Bolger, A. A.	AR	C	6	16	13
Bolin, J.	AL	H	1st	76	123
Bond, M.	MS		3	22	11
Booker, Lt. G. R.	GA	E	39	77	7
Booker, J. A.	MS	D	31	28	100
Bookman, J. T.	TX	A	10	6	81
Bost, G. W.	AR	B	M. P. 2	19	59
Bostick, Lt. T. J.	SC	I	10	86	47
Bowlin, J.	AR	K	9	19	55
Bowman, J. N.	TN	C	8	62	163
Boyd, Jno. O.	AR	G	7	21	84
Boyd, Jno. O.*					
Boyd, John Coleman	TN	E	154	51	20
Braddock, Stephen	MS	E	32	30	131
Bradford, W. H.	MS	A	10	35	197
Braibu, Capt. A. D.	TN			59	112

Bramy, J.	TN	E	42	64	199
Brantley, J. A.	MS	F	4	45	349
Brantley, J. K.	MS	K	5	25	47
Braugher, J. T.	MS	C	29	39	263
Brewer, W. T.	MS	D	10	42	314
Brewer, *					
Brim, W. A. J.	MO		2 & 5	15	124
Brinson, M. C.	GA	K	25	79	45
Brister, Lt. S.	MS	D	40	22	6
Brogen, Pri.	MS	C	14	30	122
Brooks, S. H.	AL	E	1st	72	66
Brooks, Lt. W. G.	MS	K	4	42	308
Brown, G. M.	MO	H	1	10	50
Brown, H. T.	TN	A	2	57	82
Brown, H. T.*	TN	A	2		
Brown, J. R.	TN	H	50	61	144
Brown, J. T.	GA		29	81	66
Brown, M. E.	AL	A	29	75	111
Brown, W. A.	TN	B	4	56	79
Brown, W. C.	AL	K	1st	72	61
Brown, Sgt. W. H.	KY	A	8th KY Cav.	103	3
Brown, William	MS	K	30	37	235
Brown, Wilson S.	SC	A	16	84	17

Bruder, Herman (Farmersville)	LA			87	6
Brummer, Herman*					
Bryan, J. E.	MS	G	Cav. 28	45	346
Bryan, J. H.	MS	D	8	31	146
Bryant, H.	MS	C	8	32	159
Bryant, Marcus*					
Bryant, M. L.	TN	F	28	53	22
Bullots, C. L.	TN	H	15	59	122
Burchett, Capt. J. W.	TN	G	29	57	81
Burdine, Lt. W. C.	SC	C	16	85	43
Burdine, Lt. W. C.	SC	C	16	85	45
Burgit, Henry	AL	D	33	76	124
Burnaws, Thos. B.*	AL	A	27		
Burnes, J.	MO	C	3	7	13
Burris, Geo.	TN	G	8	62	164
Burris, Jake	TN	G	8	62	162
Burrow, Thos. P.	AL	A	27	75	117
Byan, B. S.	AL	H	27	74	103
Byers, A. F.	MS	H	1st	34	184
Byrd, W. C.	AR	F	8	17	26

Byrd, W. C.	AL	I			71	48
C., J. C.	AL	A	39		68	14
C., T. A.	MS	E	5		25	59
Caddy, W.	MO				15	122
Cadenline, M. M.	MS	K	5		25	49
Cagie, Sgt. James	TN	E	42		64	187
Caldwell, W. J.	MS	G	45		26	64
Cambril, A. J.	MS	E	32		30	132
Campbell, F. J. P.	MS	H	15		46	370
Campbell, Nolvin	AL			1st	76	129
Canbery, Lt. Jas.	AR	K	9		18	45
Cane, Marion	GA			1st	80	49
Cannon, Lt.	MO				15	123
Canton, John*						
Cantrell, H.	TN	A	15		61	150
Cape, Jacob S.	TN	F	8		62	168
Capels, R. S.	MS		33		46	374
Capie, Lt. C.	MO	H	2 & 5		12	77
Cargile, C. H.	AL	G		1st	72	63
Cargile, W. H.	MS	Katt's Battery			46	375

Carpenter, G. C.	GA	C	8 GA Battery	78	22
Carpenter, O.	MS	G	29	47	385
Carr, Lt. S. F.	MS	E	7th BTT	41	295
Carrington, C.	TN	K	51	59	118
Carrington, James*					
Carson, H.	SC	D	16	84	22
Carson, Capt. J. P.	AL	K	45	70	39
Carson, W.	SC	D	16	84	23
Carter, C. B.	TN		3	51	18
Carter, Capt. F. M.	TN	A	13	57	88
Carter, Henry*					
Carter, J. M.*					
Carter, J. M.*					
Cather, J. A.*					
Cather, J. A.*					
Catlin, Capt. A. D.	MS	L	41	48	393
Cavenaugh, Jno. W.	AL	A	1st	75	108
Cavendon, John*					
Cawthon, Lt. J. J.	LA	B	19	87	15

Cawthon, T. W.	GA	I	65	80	46
Cecill	TX	D	2	1	2
Cecill*	TX	D	5		
Chaisty, Sgt.	MO		2	13	98
Chamberlin, E.	MO	C	1 & 3	14	118
Chamberlin, E.*					
Chamberlin, W. W.	TN		57	54	42
Chambers, M. A.	TN	K	20	53	31
Chambliss, J.	AL		45	70	40
Chandanan, W.*					
Chandler, J. W.	MS	B	30	35	209
Chane, John	AR	B	M. P. 31	19	61
Chapman, E.	SC	E	16	83	2
Chappel, S. P.	AL	G	1st	72	62
Chase, Sgt. Ben	MO		1 & 3	9	44
Childress, R.	MO	D	2	11	67
Church, E. J.*					
Clark, L.	AR	B	M. P. 2	19	58
Clark, Sgt. R. L.	GA	B	1st Confed.	78	17
Claymore, Henry*					

Clayton, Henry*					
Clayton, John*					
Cochran, Capt. W. T.	GA	F	37	81	62
Cocington, Thos. J.	TN	G	49	53	27
Cole, W. C.	TN	D	29	55	59
Coleman, J. L.	MO	F	2	13	92
Coleman, Sgt. J. W.	MS	D	22	47	390
Comce, P. B.	AR	K	1	20	67
Con, Chas.	TX	K	24	5	66
Conley, Ensign O. L.	MS		33	47	386
Conn, M. A.	MS	D	32	30	127
Connell, J. H.	TN	A	15	61	148
Cook, W. H.	MS	B	8	32	165
Cooper, Robt.	AL	H	15	74	94
Copeland, W. T.	TX	I	7	3	38
Corbitt, Sgt. D. J.	TN	A	55	66	228
Cotton,	GA	A	37	81	63
Courtney, D. H.	MO	F	1 & 3	10	46
Covington, J. T.	MO		1	8	30

Covington, Wm. R.	MS		37	42	305
Cowley, Maj. S. A.	TN	AAA-I. G. Quarles Staff	51	6	
Cox,	MS			46	373
Cox, John*					
Crandey, J. M.	GA			79	44
Cremer, W. H.	SC	E	16	83	3
Crocker, John	AR	F	8	21	88
Crocker, John	AL	F	8	68	4
Crocker, John*		F	8		
Cronan, P.	TN	A	11	54	50
Cross, J. D.	AR	E	6	67	102
Crother, Lt. A. W.	MS			22	4
Croxton, R. A.	AL	F	17	69	26
Crumpton, Maj. W. F.	MS		14	30	123
Crymes,	AL		1st	73	83
D., G. W.	TN	K	4	60	131
Darby, Wm.	GA	H	1st Confed.	78	16
Dougherty, J. K.	MO		3 & 5	14	120
Davidson, J.	MO	H	1	10	57

Davidson, J. C.	TN	A	41	58	109	
Davis, Lt. Ed.	MO	E	3	7	15	
Davis, I.	AL			73	80	
Davis, Sgt. L.	MS	C	32	30	134	
Davis, R. B.	MO	E	3	7	12	
Davis, Capt. W. A.	GA	I	46	77	13	
Davis, W. R.	SC	E	16	83	14	
Davis, W. R.*	SC	E	16			
Dawson, J. M.	AR	K	7	15	4	
Dean, Lt. J. D.	MS	A	10	35	196	
Deborah,	MS	E	41	34	188	
Denbow, Dave	MO	C	2	9	36	
Dennis, John	MS	B	22	41	299	
Depu, J.	AL	E	1st	75	107	
Devall, C. M.	MS	K	8	32	160	
Devon, R.	SC		24	83	10	
Dias, J. J.	MS	D	8	31	139	
Dickey, Rev. D. L.	TN	H	47	57	93	
Dil, W. H.	AL		13	75	113	
Dill, L. C.	SC	D	16	84	24	
Dillehey, W. H.	AR		13			
Dixon, E.	MO	E	3 & 5	7	4	
Dixon, J. P.	AR	H	7	17	34	

Dorman, C.	MS	E	1	46	364	
Dreux, P. E.	TN	G	29	66	218	
Driscoll, W. B.	TX	A	10	6	82	
Dubose, J. T.	AL	G	13	75	118	
Dubose, J. T.	LA	G	13	87	14	
Dubose, J. T.*	LA		13			
Duffatther, L. C.	MS	D	1st	44	344	
Duke, J. C.	MS	L	41	47	389	
Dunaway, Pinknew	MS	E	33	46	368	
Duncan, C. H.	SC	K	16	85	35	
Duncan, C. M.*	SC	K	16			
Duncan, J. W.	MO	C	3	8	16	
Dunn, A. J.	MS	E	3	26	63	
Dunn, J. A.	MS		33	24	45	
Dunn, L.	MS			24	38	
Dunn, R. B.	MS		10	34	193	
E., J. S.	MS			34	186	
Eake, "Bud"	MS	I	40	23	25	
Easterling, J. F.	SC			83	5	
Eddins, F. M.	AL	H	17	69	28	
Edgar, W. J.	TN	H	5	60	132	
Edge, E. D.	MS	A	32	31	138	

Edwards, J. W.	MS	D	14	29		118
Edwards, W. C.	TN		55	65		214
Eiland, W. F.	MS	H	5	25		50
Ellis, Sgt. A. J.	MS	F	15	25		58
Ellis, Sgt. J. R.	MS	I	43	42		303
Ellison, L.	MS	H	3	8		20
Embry, H. W.	TX	C	10	4		48
English, J. P.	MS	E	32	30		130
Enix, J.	AL	C	33	69		19
Eubank, J. M.	MS			28		93
Eubanks, R. C.	TN	E	11	55		53
Evans, A. H.	MS	D	41	34		181
Evans, A. O.	SC	C	16	85		34
Ewing, W. H.*				42		
Exum, W. W.	TN	51	5 Confed.	63		184
FL., Lt. A.	AL		1st	73		82
F., A. W.	MS			41		298
F., J. W.	TN	C	50	60		136
F., M. E.	AR	I		21		87
F., W. L.	TN	K	4	60		129
Falwell, C. H.	TN	B	13	54		36
Fanage, Hiram	NC			103		2
Farmer, S. A.	MS	A	3	24		31

Farr, J. E.	MS	C	4	45	354
Farrell, Col. Michael	MS		15	22	1
Farris, E. N.	AL	C	55	74	96
Ferguson, J. D.	MS	E	5	43	325
Ferguson, John	TN			59	113
Ferguson, John*					
Ferrer, Lt. J. H.	GA	B	1st Confed.	78	20
Fink, F. M.	MO		2	15	125
Finkerton, H.	MS	C	31	27	81
Finley, Lt. Geo. W.	TN	F	8	62	169
Finton, W. W.	MO		1 & 3	11	64
Fisher, Lt. L. C.	AL		57	69	27
Fisher, Lt. W. W.	GA	R	27	81	64
Fitts, W. C.	TN	L	1st	60	134
Fivas, Alfred D.	TN		Armstrong's Escort	51	8
Fleming, Berton	TN		10	56	80
Flowers, G. W.	AR	E	6	21	82
Foote, G. A.	MO	K	1	13	99
Foote, G. A.*	MO	K	1		

Foriester, Asa	SC	I	16	85	42
Fowler, L. B.	MS	A	5	25	53
Fowler, Stephen	TN	Bates' Escort		56	66
Fowles, Stephen*					
Fox, Lt. W.	MS	D	3	39	268
Frazier, Lt. J.	TN	K	49	65	206
French, C. E.	TN	I	11	55	51
French, Lt. L. C.	AR	G	M. P. 2	19	57
Frisby, James*					
Fuller, B. F.	MS	D	31	28	101
Fuller, S.	MO			9	41
Furlough, Stephen	AL			68	8
Furlough, Stephen*	AL				
Furr, F. E.	MS	K	20	33	176
Fusser, J. C.	FL	E		103	3
G., Lt. J. D.	MS	F		39	261
G., N. B.	MO		2	11	74
Gable, J. J.	MS		Stanford's Battery	40	272
Gailey, Lt. A.	SC	F	24	85	31
Gailey, L.*					
Gailey, Lewis*					

Gailey, W. A.	MS	G	22	26	73	
Gant, Oliver	AL	G	45	75	119	
Gar, T. E. S. D.	TX	C	10	4	46	
Garrett, Wm. L.	AR	K	6	16	7	
Garrie, C.	SC	E	24	84	30	
Gatlin, Capt. A. D.*						
Gattlebrun, J. D.*						
Gauch,	TN		1st	51	10	
Gee, J. A.	TN	G	12	57	92	
Gentry, W. P.	TX	C	10	4	47	
Gibson, B.	MS	B	10	43	322	
Gilbert, S. R.	MS	D	3	22	12	
Gill, P. H.	MO	B	3 & 5	8	23	
Gillespie, J. J.	TX	I	7	3	39	
Gillis,	TX	B	7	2	26	
Gilmer, A. A.	MS	B	30	35	207	
Glass, G. W.	MO		2	12	82	
Glen, J. R.	MO	D	5 Cav.	11	63	
Glenn, Peter	TN	I	4	56	68	
Goff, Pat	TN	G	11	55	52	
Gooch, Sgt. John	TN	A	42	64	191	

Goodwin, T. M.	MS	I	1	46	365
Grace, George	MO	C	3	8	26
Grace, Sgt. W. A.	AR		M. P.	19	62
Graves, D. Y.	MS	C	3	22	15
Gray, Frank	AR	C	6	16	12
Gray, J. A.	MS	I	1st	40	285
Gray, J. F.	TN	A	11	54	49
Green, J. H.	AL		33	74	93
Green, J. M.*	AL		35		
Green, Lt. J. P.	TN	E	15	61	146
Green, J. W.	SC	C	16	85	44
Green, M.	AR	A	6	20	77
Green, Lt. T. B.	MO	H	1	10	48
Greenhow, Lt. J.	MS	G	15	29	111
Gregory, R. C.	MS	I	15	47	378
Griffin, J.	GA			81	67
Grisset, Wm. G.	AL	C	57	76	126
Grogan, Henry	SC			84	21
Gross, Adam	MS	I	40	23	16
Grubbs, D. F.	MS	F	39	23	27
Gunel, W. M.	SC	E	16	83	1

Gunn, N. R.	MS	H	40	40	284
H., W. J.	AL	E	33	71	49
Haipan, J. N.	MS	G	35	27	76
Haiton, J. R.	MS	E	30	39	226
Hale, Lt. Franklin	TN	H	19	56	78
Hale, H. M.	AR	A	7	17	33
Hale, J. B.	MS	C	27	39	264
Hale, S. G.	MO	F	3	7	5
Hall, Ellis	SC	G	16	84	20
Hall, Capt. J. S.	TN		46	66	230
Hall, John	GA	G	1st Confed.	79	33
Hall, Wesley	MS	I	40	22	10
Hamdon, J. A.	MS	H	41	34	185
Hamilton, D. R.	MS	H	31	28	96
Hamlet, J. N.	AR			17	28
Hamlit, Jo.	TN		8	62	167
Hammock, G. W.	GA	K	46	78	28
Hamous, J. W.	TN	B	29	55	61
Hampton,	MS			49	414
Handcock, J.	FL	E		103	2
Hanrick, N. B.	TN	I	16	59	123
Hardin, W. J.	MO	G	3	8	19
Hardy, D. G.	MS	C	3	23	19

Hargroves, T. W.	MS	I	1	46	363
Harper, K.	MS	G	15	29	109
Harper, S. H.	TN	G	42	64	193
Harper, Thos.	TN			51	17
Harris, Lt. B. I.	MS	G	6	47	382
Harris, C. B.	TN	K	38	55	54
Harris, Capt. F. A.	TN	F	9	59	111
Harris, Jno. S.	MO	F	1 & 4	15	130
Harrison, Lt. J. L.	AR	F	7	17	20
Hart, J. S.	TN	D	57	54	39
Hartley, Lt. H. C.	AL		17	75	112
Hastett, M. V.	TN	K	4	56	76
Hatchet, W. S.	GA	A	8 GA. Bat.	79	42
Hawkins, Calvin	MS	G	43	44	336
Hawkins, H.	TN	A	8	63	178
Hawkins, P. S.	TN			59	119
Hawkins, P. S.*					
Hawkins, P. S.*					
Haynie, Lt. E. R.	TN	H	51	63	180
Hays, J. P.	AR	C	7	16	9

Hemphill, C. H.	MS			28	105
Henderson, D. W.*					
Henderson, S. E.	SC	E	16	83	4
Henry, J.	MS	B	8	31	142
Herring, J. L.	MS	I	Cav. 28	45	347
Herrod, D.	MS	D	40	22	8
Higdon, Sgt. D.	LA	A	12	87	7
Higginbotham, Jno. L.	GA	H	37	80	56
Hightower, W. G.	MS	C	31	27	85
Hill, Albert	MS		1st Cavalry	50	424
Hill, J. P.	AL	B	16	69	20
Hill, John	MS	K	24	35	203
Hilton, E. G.	AL			70	45
Hindman, J.	MS	E	5	25	52
Hing, W.	AL			70	37
Hinkle, A. L.	MS	E	27	43	318
Hinson, Wesley	MS	I	40	23	24
Hiviey, J. H.	AR			17	29
Hodge, H. C.	MO	B	3 & 5	15	129
Hodges, E. P.*	MO	B	3 & 5		
Hodges, H. C.	MO	B	3	13	101

Hodges, J. P.	MS	I	40	23	28	
Hodges, J. T.	MS	I	40	23	29	
Hogan, E. P.	AR	K	19	21	85	
Hogan, E. P.*	AR	K	19			
Holcomb, J. C.	AL	B	1st	73	87	
Holey, J. B.	MS	K	31	27	87	
Holinshead, Wm. K.	MS		35	48	395	
Hollock, J. R.	MS			49	420	
Holmes, J. G.	MS	E	4	30	124	
Holt, W. J.	MO		1	10	51	
Hooker,	MS	K	45	26	68	
Hooks, D.	TX	A	7	3	30	
Hope, Capt. P. M.	TN	D	46	53	33	
Hope, Lt. W. L.	TN		46	51	14	
Hopkins, John	TN	F	5	64	200	
Hopkins, M.	MO	C	1 & 4	13	105	
Hopkins, W. C.	MO	I	2	12	76	
Hopkins, W. C. (St. Charles)*	MO		76			
Horn, J.	AL	H	45	70	38	
Horne, J. W.	AR	C	M. P. 1st	19	63	
Hostedler,	MO		3 & 6	14	113	

Howard, H. D.	TN	A	28	63	174
Hucke, C.	MO	C	2	11	72
Hughes, W.	MS	A	32	31	136
Hunnicut,	MO	C	2	9	35
Hunt, J. F.	SC	C	16	84	16
Hunt, John*					
Hunt, Adjt. R. B.	TN		33	51	2
Hunt, Thomas*					
Hunt, W.	TX			2	18
Hunter, Henry*					
Hutchinson, J. H.	MS	A	10	35	198
Hutton, A. J.	TN	G	29	55	64
Ingols, Capt.*					
Ingraham, J. H.	MS	D	3	26	71
Irvine, Lt.	MO	G	1	7	1
Irving, John*					
Jackson, J. A.	TN	D	28	63	173
Jackson, Lt. J. W.	AR	K	1	20	66
Jackson, Capt. S. B.	MS	C	10	33	179
Jacobs, J. J.	TN			59	125

Jacobs, J. J.*					
James, John*					
James, Stephen*					
Jameson, Adgt. Jno.	MS		20	33	172
Jarrell, Corp. J. S.	TN	A	49	65	204
Jay, Lt. Wm.	SC	H	19	86	51
Jetton, Tom J. N.	MO	C	2	9	34
Johnson, Jemmie	AL			74	105
Johnson, W. E.	AR		M. P. 2	19	56
Jones, Sgt. A. P.	MS	F	8	27	80
Jones, Isaac	MS	A	8	32	156
Jones, J. A.	SC	B	24	85	33
Jones, J. B.	TN	E	12	56	75
Jones, J. C.	TN	G	31	66	221
Jones, J. D.	MS	I	40	23	30
Jones, J. M.	GA	D	46	78	27
Jones, J. R.	MS	I	40	22	9
Jones, Lt. Col. Jessie	SC		24	86	46
Jones, John	LA	A	18	87	5
Jones, W. H.	MO	A	1st		

Jones, W. H.	AR	F	9	21	92	
Jones, Wm.*	MO	A	1 & 4	14	109	
Jones, Wm.	AR	G	9	19	51	
Jordan, C. M.	TN	G	15	61	155	
Kavina, P. S.	MS	D	33	24	39	
Keelow, J. C.	TN	I	24	66	216	
Keen, W. H.	MS	E	3	39	269	
Keeton, E. P.	MS	R	15	29	107	
Keith, A. R.*						
Kemp, S. D.	MO		1 & 4	8	29	
Kendoll, B. F.*						
Kennedy, J.	MO	G	2 & 6	13	97	
Kennedy, J. A.	AL	H	1st	73	81	
Kennel, S. C.	MS	D	5	25	55	
Kenney, James	MS	A	10	34	195	
Kersey, A. J.	TN	A	18	53	28	
King, G.	MS	A	31	28	92	
King, Lt. J. P.	TN	G	29	55	65	
King, T. J.	AL	D	1st	75	106	
King, Wm.	MO		3 & 5	15	126	
Kirk, H. P.	MS	D	28	45	359	
Kirkpatrick, W. H.	MS	K	24	35	204	
Kizer, Lt. E. J.	MS	G	20	41	288	

Knight, William	SC	I	16	85	40
Knowles, B.	TN	K	8	53	23
Knowles, B.*					
Knox, G. W.	TN	D	19	66	223
Kruey, J.	MS	D	8	31	147
Kuhlenthal, W.	TX	H	2	1	4
Kuhn, M. R.	MO	C	2 & 5	14	106
Kuhn, M. R.*	MO	C	2 & 5		
L., C. M.	AR	B	6	17	31
L., J. B.	AR			67	98
L., R. J.	AL	E	29	68	6
Lafayette, James Venable	MS			43	327
Laney, A. M.	MS	F	5	25	51
Laney, J.	MS	D	5	26	62
Langino, Lt. T. J.	MS	A	22	41	293
Lanier, Lt. J.	GA	I	29	77	10
Lankford, T. M.	TN	D	46	65	208
Laster, S.	TN	D	50	60	138
Lauderdale, J. S.	AL	D	17	76	128
Lawhon, S.	AL			71	59
Lawrence, Lt. J. P.	AR		4	67	100

Laws, Thos.	TX	A	7	3	32	
Ledbetter, A. J.*						
Leach, Alex	GA	B	1st Confed.	77	4	
Lee, W. T.	TX	E	10	1	3	
Lemons, A. B.	TX			6	84	
Leonard, J.	MS	B	3	23	17	
Lepseits, Lt. Jos.	TN	G	8	62	165	
Lessell, J. M.*						
Lester, C. C.	AR	E	6	16	15	
Lester, J. C.	TN	K	4	59	114	
Lester, J. C.*						
Lewis, J. C.*						
Lewis, John	SC	M	10	85	36	
Lewis, John*	SC	M	10			
Lewis, P. H.	MS	E	8	32	158	
Lewis, W. A.	TN	E	5	62	157	
Lockhart, E.*	TN	C	5			
Lockhart, E. C.	TN	C	5	59	121	
Lockwood, W. L.	AL	B	11	68	15	
Lott, W.	MS	B	7	39	267	
Lott, W. M.	MS	E	15	41	300	
Low, A. G.	TN		42	64	189	
Lowe, Ogle	TX	K	24	6	77	

Lusk, John D.	MS			34	48	405
Lusk, John D.*	MS			34		
Lusk, Sgt. S. C.	TN	D		15	61	145
Lynn,	LA				87	12
M., C. P.	TN	G		42	64	195
M., H.	AR				19	50
M., H. M.	MS			22	27	79
M., J.	MS				44	341
M., J.	MS	L		41	47	388
M., J. B.	MS	E			28	91
M., S. B.	MS				27	90
M., W. L.	MS	E		4	47	380
Mabry, W. D.	MS	G		40	22	2
Mackey, Wm.	TX	C		6	1	6
Maddox,	KY			2nd KY Cav.	103	1
Malaney, Martin	MS			20	41	290
Mallory, G. S.	TN	E		50	60	139
Maloney, Martin*						
Manhorn, Robert*	MO	I		1 & C		
Martan, Capt.	MS	A		8	32	162
Martin, J. A.	TX				3	42
Martin, L. W.	AL	B		1st	73	86

Martin, R. M.	TN	A	15	61	149
Martin, W. A., Ensign	GA			80	53
Marton,	AL			74	104
Marton, B. F.	AR	K	7	16	8
Mason, A. O.	MO	E	3 & 5	13	93
Massy, C.	TX	I	25	5	70
Mathes, R.	MO		1 & 3	13	94
Mathis, Z.	GA	G	29	77	12
Matthers, Lt. C. D. (in pencil)	MS		3	50	
Matthews, Capt. C. D.	MS	G	1	46	362
Matthews, J. R.	TN	B	12	58	99
Matthews, Z. D.*					
May, Sgt. Ed.	MS	K	33	46	367
Mc., J. T.	MS	H	3	42	310
McBeath, A. C.	MS	K	5	25	48
McBride, W. H.	MS	H	31	28	98
McCammon, J.	MS	D	5	43	323
McClany, J. A.	AL	G	1st	72	64
McCloud, A. R.	MS	A	24	38	241

McCollister, J. T.*						
McCone, W. I.	AR	G	9	20	65	
McCoy, Matt	TN	L	1st	60	135	
McCright, J. R.	TN	C	9	62	160	
McCue, Lt. J. F.	TN		8	62	166	
McDermit, J. H.	TN			65	211	
McDill, W. J.	TN	C	9	62	159	
McDonald, Maj. J. E.	TN		33	51	1	
McDonaugh, Capt. Jas.	MS	E	14	29	115	
McGehee, Capt. E. A.	TN	F	16	66	226	
McGill, D. O.	MS	B	10	34	190	
McGraw, Lt. J. P.	MO	H	1	10	53	
McGuire, E. N.	MS	E	15	29	108	
McKinney, W. A.	TN	H	29	57	83	
McLarty, Lt. W. H.	MS	B	31	27	89	
McMillan, D. P.	MO		2 & 5	14	115	
McMillen, Lt. B. F.	AL	H	7	68	2	

McMillen, John*					
McMullen, Thos.*					
McMullen, Wm.	MS	R	3	23	18
McNelly, T. L.	TN	D	47	51	12
McNulty, H.	MS			42	309
McQueen, W.	MS	A	14	48	400
McQuinter, Jos. S.	TX	A	5	1	12
McQuister, James S.*	TX	A	6		
McQuiston, Hugh S.	TN		9	53	21
Meadows, J. A.	GA	G	4	79	37
Meek, Maj. A. T.	AR		2	21	80
Mickey, Lt.	MS	G	5	25	56
Miller, J. B.	TN	F	55	51	15
Miller, J. W.	TX	E	6	1	14
Mingles, J. M.	TN	B	50	53	26
Mise, F. B.*					
Mitchel, P. Y.	TN	K	8	59	116
Mitchell, P. Y.*					
Mobley, T. J.	MS	A	3	26	70

Moncrief, Lt. Thos.	AR			21	81
Monercif, Lt. T. B.*	AR	H	2		
Monk, J. S.	AL	D	17	69	22
Monoref, Lt. T. B.	AR			20	75
Montgomery, F. M.	AR	K	1	20	68
Montgomery, J. M.	MS	I	1	46	361
Montgomery, R. S.	TX	I	7	3	37
Montgomery, S. R.	MS		10	45	358
Montgomery, S. R.*	MS		10		
Montgomery, T. W.	AL	F	33	75	109
Moon, J.	MO	G	3	8	21
Moore, Jordan	MS	G	6	46	371
Moore, R. E.	AR	E	M. P. 25	19	60
Moore, W. F.	MS	I	4	33	168
Moran, M. A.	TX	C	7	4	45
Moreman, H. A.	MS	F	20	48	403
Morgan, E.	MS	G	3	26	69
Morgan, J. C.*					
Morgan, J. H.	TN	G	19	66	224

Morris, J. T.	MS	C	8	31	149
Morris, S. W.*					
Mullenax, M.	AL	G	55	74	98
Murf, J. D.	AR	I	6	67	104
Murff, W. W. M.	TN	A	49	65	205
Murph, F. L.	AR	K	6	16	5
Murphy, T. J.	TN	D	50	60	137
Murrell, Thos. L.	TN		6	51	7
Myers, G. W.	MS	B	8	31	144
Myers, J. M.	MS	B	8	31	143
N., J. W.	MS			24	35
N., S. W.	MS	A	4	42	313
Napier, Thos. L.	AR	H	15		
Napier, Thos. L.	AR	H	15	21	90
Neason, W.	MO	K	1 & 3	11	69
Neil, W. H.	TX	B	7	4	51
Nelson,	AR			21	89
Nelson, Col. N. L.	LA		12	87	1
Newberry, M. A.	TX	K	24	6	76
Nichol, S. W.	MO		3 & 5	14	111
Nicholson, ADGT. J. H.	FL			103	1

Nokes, Capt. W. H.	MS	E	31	28	102
Norris, S.	MO	E	2 & 6	14	116
Nuckols, Alfred M.	MO	C	3	8	25
Obrey, E. I. G.	MO		1 & 4	14	114
Oliver, B.	TN	H	29	55	62
Ottie, W.	TX	F	24	5	74
Owen, Sgt. F. H.	MO	C	2 & 6	11	71
Owen, James*					
Owens, Sgt. A. L.	AL	A	15	74	95
P. (supposed to be Potts), H.	TN	B		60	130
P., D. C.	AR		7	16	16
P., J. R. W.	TN	C	47	58	97
P., J. T.	AL	E	29	68	5
P., J. W.	TN		42	64	190
P., L. F.	GA			77	2
P., Lt. W. A.	TN		53	63	185
Padgitt, Lt. J. D.	SC	I	24	83	6
Page, J. J.	SC	D	16	85	39
Pangle, D. N.	TN		28	63	171
Papers, O.	TX	K	24	6	78

Paris, Capt. L. O.	MS	D	4	33	171	
Parker, W. L.	MS	A	32	30	135	
Parkes, Maj. W. C.	MO		1 & 3	15	128	
Pasley, C. W.	AR	B		20	69	
Patton, W. H.	MS	D	4	33	170	
Payne, P. F.	GA		46	78	18	
Peacock, J. W.	AR	F	9	67	97	
Peazel, J. D.	LA	I	12	87	13	
Peck, W. A.	GA	B	30	81	65	
Pepper, A.	TN	C	15	61	151	
Perry, Lt. P. A.	TX	F	10	6	83	
Petit, Lt. L. M.	TN	G	15	61	154	
Pitman, M. H.	GA	D	37	80	47	
Pitman, M. H.*	GA		37			
Pitts, Moses	MS			41	296	
Pitts, T. O.	MO		2	12	78	
Pogue, J.	MO	H	3	8	24	
Pool, W. H.*						
Poole, Sgt. W. H.	AL		45	75	114	
Pope, W. W.	MS	E	5	25	57	
Porter, Ed	MO	K	3	8	27	

Posey, G. H.	AL	C	17	69	23
Potts, James*						
Powell, C. W.	TN	H	13	54	38
Powell, Hobson	MS	Walthall's Staff		47	376
Prescott, William	MS		34	48	402
Presley, E.	TN	H	50	61	142
Price, J. P.	MS	A	22	26	75
Price, J. S.	TN	H	47	57	94
Price, R. L.	NC		39	103	1
Pritchet, J.	AL	B	1st	76	121
Proffit, C.	MO	D	2	11	66
Prost, P. H.	SC	F	24	84	28
Pruit, A. C.	GA			80	52
Purcel, John	MO	A	1st	12	85
Quinnie, L.	MO	G	3	7	14
R., A.	AL	F	45	70	36
R., J. D.	MS	I	20	33	174
R., S. H.	AR	I	1	21	94
Rad, Charles*						
Ramsey, Sgt. D. M.	MS	A	3	47	387
Read, T. A.*						
Rear, Lt. E. O.	AL	A	29	68	12
Reddick, N. L.	AR	K	6	16	6

Reece, J. H.	MS	F	15	41	291	
Reed, C. L.	GA		1st Confed.	78	19	
Reeves, R.	MS	B	8	31	145	
Reid,	AR			17	27	
Reid, A.*						
Reid, C.*						
Renfro, J. M.	MO	D	2	11	68	
Reynolds, Maj. C. W.	MS		29	48	392	
Rhodes, T. J.	MS	B	8	31	141	
Rich, J. B.	MS	G	8	31	140	
Rich, W.	MS	G	8	32	154	
Richards, Sgt. J. R.	AL	F	1st	73	84	
Richards, R. M.	MS	I	31	27	86	
Richardson, John	TN	K	13	57	86	
Richardson, R. C.	TX			3	43	
Riggs, Capt. J. L. (TN)	MO	E	154	9	39	
Riggway, W. N.	TN	E	5	60	133	
Rion, John*						
Rion, Robt.	TN			59	120	
Rion, Robt.*						
Roach, Oliver	AL	G	45	68	1	

Roads, J. W.	MS	C	31	27	83
Roberts, J. J.	MO	C	3 & 5	14	108
Roberts, J. J.	MO	C	3	15	127
Roberts, J. J.*	MO	C	3 & 5		
Roberts, Lt. J. L.	MS	L	41	47	384
Roberts, W. E.	SC	C	16	85	32
Roberston, C. F.	MS	I	33	24	44
Robertson, J. M.	TX	B	3	1	1
Robertson, J. W.	MS	G	22	26	74
Robinson, B. F.	TX	B	7	3	34
Robinson, David*					
Robinson, J. M.	MS	C	8	32	151
Robinson, Jack	TN	E	42	64	198
Robuck, Tom H.	MO	C	2 & 6	9	33
Rochelle, J. A.	SC	I	24	83	7
Roden, A.	AL	H	55	74	97
Rogers,	MS			41	292
Rogers, Sgt. E. B.	TX	B	7	2	15
Rogers, Wm.	MS	E	8	41	297

Roland, B.	TN	F	53	51	16	
Rose, Lt.	SC		16	84	18	
Ross, Lt. M. J.	MS	G	33	46	369	
Rouck, Oliver*						
Rover, Lt. Col. W. A.	MS		20	41	286	
Ruber, Lt. T.	TN	H	154	57	85	
Rucker, H.	TN	Cheatham's	M's Escort	56	77	
Ruff, N. B.	MS	E	5	25	60	
Russell, Lt. A. J.	MS	I	3	23	22	
Russell, J. L.	AR	C	6	16	11	
Russell, R. J.	TN	H	9	63	179	
Russell, R. J.	TN	H	19	66	222	
Ryan, John*						
S., Dr. J. F.	MS		30	39	265	
S., J. G.	MS		14	48	399	
S., H. H.	GA		8 GA Batt.	78	23	
S., N. P.	MS			40	282	
S., S. G.	AL			75	110	
S., Sgt. T. M.	TX	G	16	6	85	
Sadler, W. A.	AL	B	1st	73	88	
Sanders, C.	TX	B	25	6	79	
Sanders, I.	AL	B	1st	76	122	
Sandlin, J. W.	AL	C	35	74	101	

Santon, Thos. B.	AL	G	45	74	91	
Sappington, H. C.	MO	A	2	13	104	
Sartain, W. H.	MS	G	4	33	169	
Satterfield, Wm. O.	SC			84	26	
Savage, J.	TN	G	38	56	71	
Schmidt, Geo.	GA	G	1st Confed.	79	34	
Scott, J. W.	TX		7	4	49	
Scott, Jno.	TN	C	57	54	41	
Scruggs, Lt. M. L.	MO	G	1 & 3	12	89	
Scruggs, Lt. W. J.	MS	G	20	41	289	
Searcy, J. D.	GA	I	46	77	14	
Seed, Lt. J. P.	TN		49	65	207	
Segman, J. W.	MO	E	1	9	31	
Sela,	TN			53	25	
Sela, T. W.*						
Senders, C.	MO	C	2	11	73	
Senn, D. C.	AL	E	1st	72	73	
Sentre, W. H.	MS	F	24	35	201	
Shabley, M. A. E.	AR		15	20	70	
Shafer,	AR			21	91	
Shafter, H. C.	TN	D	31	66	220	

Name	State	Co.	Unit		
Shain, W. H.*					
Sharp, J. S.	MO		1 & 4	13	96
Sharp, W. F.	MS	I	43	44	338
Shaw, E.	SC		10	83	15
Shaw, J. N.	MS			36	214
Shaw, John*					
Shaw, T. E.	MS	C	30	35	208
Shaw, Lt. W. C.	MS	K	33	25	46
Shelton, G. W.	TN	B	29	55	60
Shillinger, Theodore	MS		14	39	270
Shirkill, G. W.	AR	K	2	20	79
Shrinskie, S.	MS		Cav. 28	44	345
Shulax, Sgt. W.	SC	G	24	83	12
Shuler, Lt. J. G.	MS		15	50	421
Simmons, J. C.	GA		8 GA. Batt.	78	21
Sims, Capt. W. M.	TN		31	53	34
Skelton, S. J. A.	TN			53	29
Slaughter, G. T.	TX		7	4	50
Small, Lt. E. P.	MS	D	8	32	153
Smith, A. J.*					

Smith, E. J.	AR	G	2	21	83	
Smith, E. J.*	AR	G	2			
Smith, Col. G. A.	GA		1st	77	1	
Smith, Adgt. H. N.	TX	B	25	6	80	
Smith, J. B.*						
Smith, J. C.	TX	B	7	3	36	
Smith, J. E.	TX		7	1	11	
Smith, J. E.*	TX					
Smith, J. J.	AR	K	9	67	96	
Smith, Capt. J. M.	SC	E	16	86	48	
Smith, John*						
Smith, Laacy	MS	C	14	47	379	
Smith, Lee	MS			42	301	
Smith, Capt. S. T.	MS	E	15	29	113	
Smith, W.*						
Smith, W. B.	AR	C	6	16	14	
Smith, W. J.	TN	C	11	54	47	
Smith, W. N.	MO	D	1 & 4	14	107	
Smith, W. N.*	MO	D	1 & 4			
Smith, W. S.	SC	F	16	86	49	
Smith, Wm.	TN	D	4	56	67	
Smith, Wm.*						

Smithard, Abner	MS			23	21
Snelling, Lt.*					
Snodgrass, Lt. J. V.	TN	K	50	59	117
Spence, J. H.	MS	C	31	28	97
Spencer, C.	MO	H	1	10	49
Spencer, Capt. W. W.	GA	E	29	80	48
Spivey, J. G.	MS	E	4	30	126
Spratt, A.	MO	I	1 & 5	10	56
Stabler, W. R.	MS	E	8	32	157
Stafford, Lt. Col. F. E. P.	TN			53	35
Stanley,	TN			53	24
Statum, W.	TN	I	41	58	110
Sterling, Capt. E. R.	MS	F	20	41	287
Stevens, W. B.	TX	A	18	2	16
Stewart, Sgt. E. P.	GA	D	8 GA. Batt.	78	24
Stewart, J. R.	AL	G	45	68	10
Stewart, J. R.*	AL	G	45		
Stewart, O. R.	AL	C	45	68	9
Stewart, O. R.*	AL	C	45		
Stewart, Capt. S. D.	AL	B	35	76	125

Still, Lt. A.	MO		1 & 3	9	40
Stokes, Lt. J. T.	TX	I	10	4	59
Stokey, W. A.	TX	C	11	54	48
Stomant, E. M.	MS	H	32	30	129
Store, W. D.	SC	I	19	86	50
Stout, A. L. R.	MO		1 & 3	13	103
Stovall, W. P.	MS	E	4	30	125
Street, Sgt. Maj. C. N. B.	MS		33	48	397
Stricklin, J. C.	GA	A	29	77	9
Sumter, J. L.	MS	D	14	48	398
Swain, James	AR			67	101
Swiney, Capt. J. W.	MS	C	32	30	128
T., J. P.	TN			57	90
T., J. W.	MS	C	20	33	173
T., M.	AR		M.P. 1st	19	64
Tabb, W. T.	MS	C	31	27	82
Tankson, J. C.	MS	D	5	26	61
Tanson,	LA	Bragg's Escort		87	16
Tanton, Thos. B.	AL	G	45	68	3
Tanton, Thos. B.*	AL	G	45		
Tayey, W.*					

Taylor, Adolph	TX	A	5	1	13
Taylor, Adolphus*	TX	A	6		
Taylor, G. W.*					
Taylor, J.	TN	C	29	55	63
Taylor, James	SC	G	24	83	11
Taylor, S. S.	GA	E	48	77	5
Taylor, T.	SC	F	24	84	27
Teamer, Capt. B. F.	MS	F	24	35	202
Tedder, A. F.	GA			77	3
Templeton, A. A.	TN	C	9	62	158
Terril, S. M.	MO	E	3	12	90
Thaxton, M.	TN	D	28	63	175
Thomas, Capt. A. D.	TN	B	54	57	87
Thomas, Barry	MS	A	32	31	137
Thomas, W. A.	TN	K	31	66	219
Thompson, A. W.	MS			43	324
Thompson, Lt. E.	TX	E	8	5	63
Thompson, H. M.	TN	H	47	57	95
Thompson, J.	AL	C	39	68	13

Thompson, J. R.	MS	K	30	37	234	
Thompson, Capt. W. J.	TN	H	50	60	140	
Thompson, W. T.	TN	C	15	61	152	
Thornton, J.	MS	B	8	32	164	
Thornton, Capt. S. M.	MS	B	31	27	88	
Thoxton, Meredith	TN			62	170	
Thurmond, P. M.	SC	I	24	83	9	
Tilas, W. R.	TN	G	28	63	176	
Time, F. M.*						
Townes, C. H.	TN	I	12	57	91	
Townsend, Capt. L. R.	MS	C	4	45	355	
Townsend, Capt. M.	MO	E	3 & 5	7	3	
Trammel, Henry	GA	E	1st Confed.	79	31	
Trammel, Lt.	AL	D	29	68	11	
Tranton,	AR			18	36	
Trenor, N. B.	MS	D	3	22	14	
Trull, E. E.	MS	C	31	28	95	
Tullos, C. W.	MS	C	8	32	152	
Turner, Sgt. B. H.	AL	C	17	69	25	

Name	State	Co.			
V., H. L.	AR	I	1	21	93
Vaughn, J.	MS	D	3	22	13
Vauhorn, R.	MO		1 & 3	15	121
Venable, W. H.*					
Vick, J. A.	MS	A	14	48	404
Vick, N. P.	TN	A	49	51	13
Vickery, L. J.	MS			22	5
W	MS	L	41	34	183
W., E. H.	TN		42	64	188
W., J. C.	MS		15	47	377
W., J. T.	MS	C	8	31	150
W., W. T.	TN	C	47	58	98
Wade, Ben	MS	H	10	34	192
Wade, John	KY		8th KY Cav.	103	4
Waggoner, J. O.	AR		4	67	103
Wakefield, J. J.	TX	E	8	5	64
Walker, Danl.	SC	I	24	83	8
Walker, L. B.	GA	A		81	69
Walker, S. H.	AL	B	7	69	30
Walker, W. C.	TN	H	50	61	143
Walters, B. L.	AL	D	33	71	51
Walters, L. B.	GA	D	37	80	54
Walton, Ben	MS		30	39	262

Ward, Capt. J. W.	MS	L	24	48	394
Watkins, J. M.	GA	C	46	80	50
Watkins, Jos.	MO	E	1 & 3	11	62
Watts, W. J.	MS	E	23	44	333
We . . . . Lt. T. J.	AR	F	5	18	46
Weakley, J. K. P.	TN	G	42	64	197
Weakley, Rufus	TN	G	42	64	196
Weatherall, A. S.	MS	B	41	34	189
Weatherly, Jas.	TN	D	57	54	40
Weaver, D. J.*					
Week, C. A.	MS	C	31	27	84
Wells, J. C.	GA	D	1st Confed.	79	32
Wells, J. C. (GA)	TN			59	124
Wells, Jno. C.*	GA		32		
Wells, R. J.	MS	G	3	26	65
West, J. S.	TN		4	60	128
Westfall, Lt.	TX	K	24	5	67
Whatley, V. D. (S S)	GA	C	4	80	57
Wheeler, J. W.	MS	D	32	30	133

White, G. M.	SC	I	16	85	41
White, I	MO	K	2	12	81
Whiteville, T. B.	TN			51	9
Wiley, J. W.	MS	B	30	35	210
Wilhite, D.	TN		29	55	56
Wilhite, W.	TN	K	15	61	153
Wilkins, John	TN	F	42	64	186
Willerford, Lt.	TN			63	181
Williams,	MO	H	2	14	117
Williams,	MS		35	27	77
Williams, Capt.	TN		15	53	32
Williams, A. G.	TN	D	5	62	156
Williams, C.*					
Williams, D.	TN	D	29	55	58
Williams, E. H.	TN	A	55	65	215
Williams, Lt. E. H.	MS	G	40	22	3
Williams, F. W.	MS			42	302
Williams, G. W.	TX	A	7	3	31
Williams, Sgt. J. L.	SC	A	16	84	25
Williams, R.	TX	G	25	6	89

Williams, R.	MO	F	5	7	2
Williams, R. C.	AL	H	27	74	102
Williams, S. G.	MS	K	3	43	326
Williams, Sgt. S. M.	AR	H	2	15	2
Williams, S. P.	MO	H	1	10	54
Williams, T. J.	TN			54	37
Williams, W. A.	MO	E	1 & 3	11	61
Williford, Lt. J. J. H.	TN	C	51	56	69
Willis, J.	TN	C	42	51	4
Willis, Lt. S. J.	MS	H	8	32	161
Willog, Sgt. F. R.	MS	R	8	32	155
Wilmuth, Capt.	MS	C	10	34	194
Wilson, H.	MS	F	27	38	245
Wilson, H. A.	MS	E	44	40	271
Wilson, Lt. Jno. W.	MS	D	4	47	383
Wilson, T. K.	TX	H	6	6	88
Winn, J.	GA	H	25	80	58
Wisdom, M. T.	GA	E	46	77	8
Wise, B. F.	AL		34	74	92

Witherspoon, Col. W. W.	MS		35	48	391
Womack, J. B.	TN	E	15	61	147
Wood,	MS			46	366
Wood, W. A.	AL	E	1st	73	85
Woodard, Capt. A. A.	MO	D	2 & 6	11	65
Woodruff, C.	AL		45	70	41
Woodruff, W. B.	TN	F	11	54	46
Wray, D. J.*					
Wray, Lt. W. L. Max	MS	E	4	45	352
Wright, A. J.	TN	F	38	66	217
Wright, J. P. S.	TN	H	42	56	70
Wynn, G. F.	AL	D	45	75	115
Wynne, R. M.*					
Young, Lt. L. T.	MS	R	3	23	20
Young, N.	MS	G	31	28	94
Young, T. D.	MO	F	3	8	17
Zube, J. B.	GA	D	65	80	51

ILLUSTRATIONS

Notes for the Illustrations

- Generally, illustrations are arranged in alphabetical order, to correspond with the encyclopedia entries.
- Not all entries have corresponding illustrations.
- Not all illustrations have corresponding entries.
- Military men are usually listed as the rank they were at the time of the Battle of Franklin.

A type of Civil War abatis known as chevaux-de-frise. (Public domain)

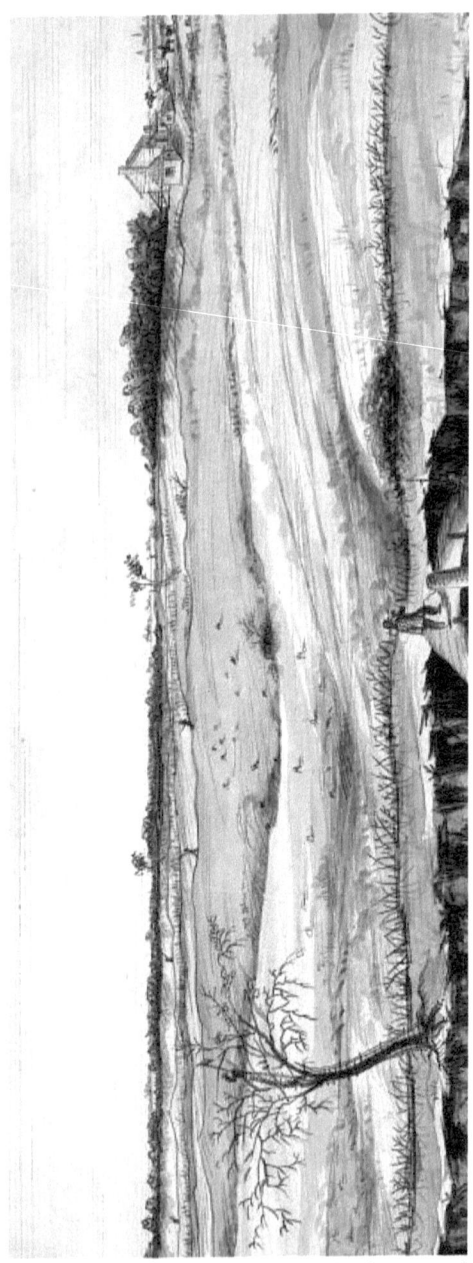

Abatis, made of tree branches, in the foreground during the War for Southern Independence. (Public domain)

Confederate General John Adams at the Battle of Franklin. (Public domain)

Street sign, Franklin, Tennessee, commemorating Confederate General John Adams, who died at the Battle of Franklin fighting for the Ninth and Tenth Amendments. (Photo copyright © Lochlainn Seabrook)

Wood marker, Franklin, Tennessee, showing approximately where General John Adams fell during the Battle of Franklin. (Photo copyright © Lochlainn Seabrook)

Confederate General Frank Crawford Armstrong, with signature. (Public domain)

Athenaeum Rectory, Columbia, Tennessee. (Photo copyright © Lochlainn Seabrook)

Bald Hill, Nashville, Tennessee. (Photo copyright © Lochlainn Seabrook)

Confederate General William Brimage Bate. (Public domain)

Battle of Franklin signage, Franklin, Tennessee. (Photo copyright © Lochlainn Seabrook)

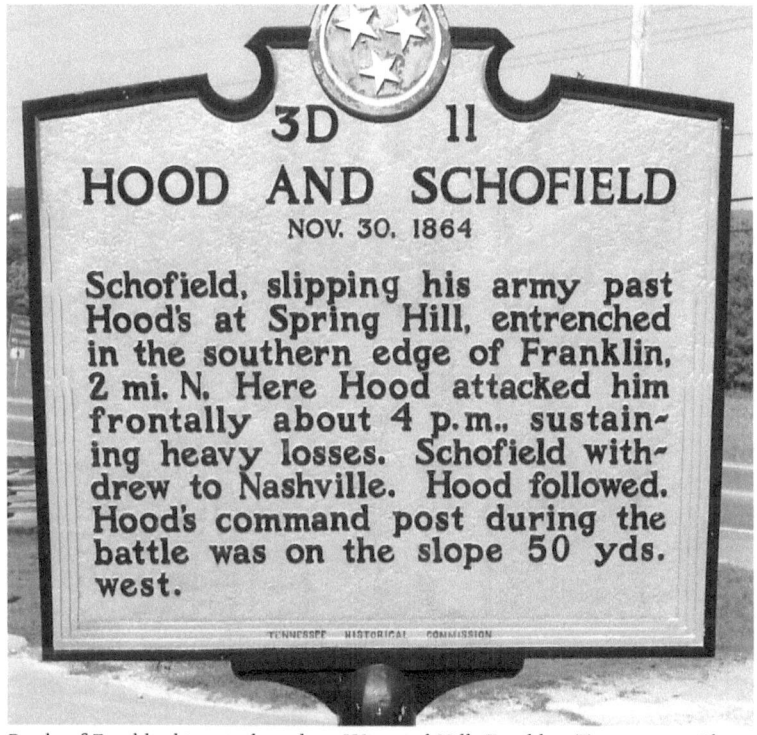

Battle of Franklin historical marker, Winstead Hill, Franklin, Tennessee. (Photo copyright © Lochlainn Seabrook)

Battle of Franklin memorial plaque, Franklin, Tennessee. (Photo copyright © Lochlainn Seabrook)

Battle of Franklin historical marker, Franklin, Tennessee. (Photo copyright © Lochlainn Seabrook)

Remnants of the Franklin Turnpike Bridge, a covered bridge that once crossed over the Harpeth River near the center of Franklin, Tennessee, and which played an important role in the Battles of Franklin I, II, and III. (Photo copyright © Lochlainn Seabrook)

Yankee earthworks and accompanying swale, Franklin, Tennessee. One of the last remaining physical signs of the Battle of Franklin, this Union breastworks, located on private property, is still visible after a century and a half. The earthen fortification was illegally occupied by U.S. General William Grose's Brigade, which was repeatedly but unsuccessfully attacked by Confederate troops from Finley's Brigade and Chalmers' Division. The area has never been officially studied or archaeologically explored. (Photo copyright © Lochlainn Seabrook)

Battle of Franklin stone marker, Franklin, Tennessee. (Photo copyright © Lochlainn Seabrook)

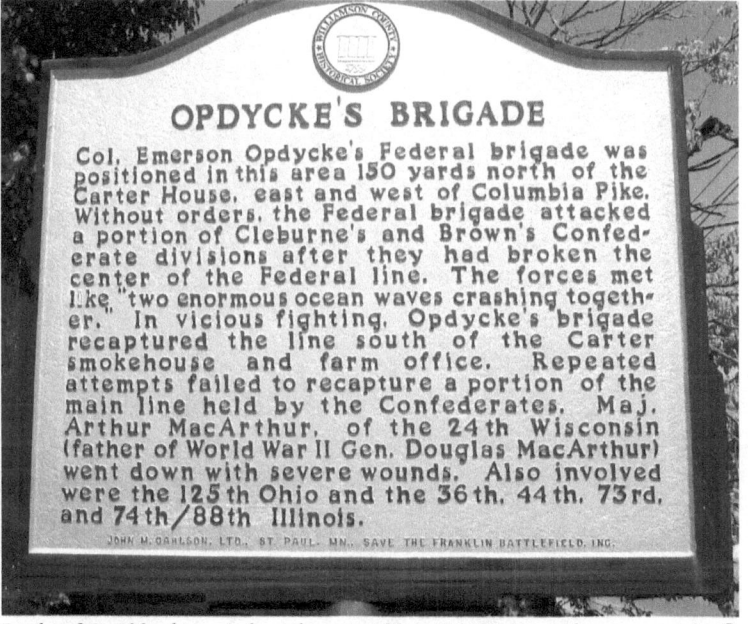

Battle of Franklin historical marker, Franklin, Tennessee. (Photo copyright © Lochlainn Seabrook)

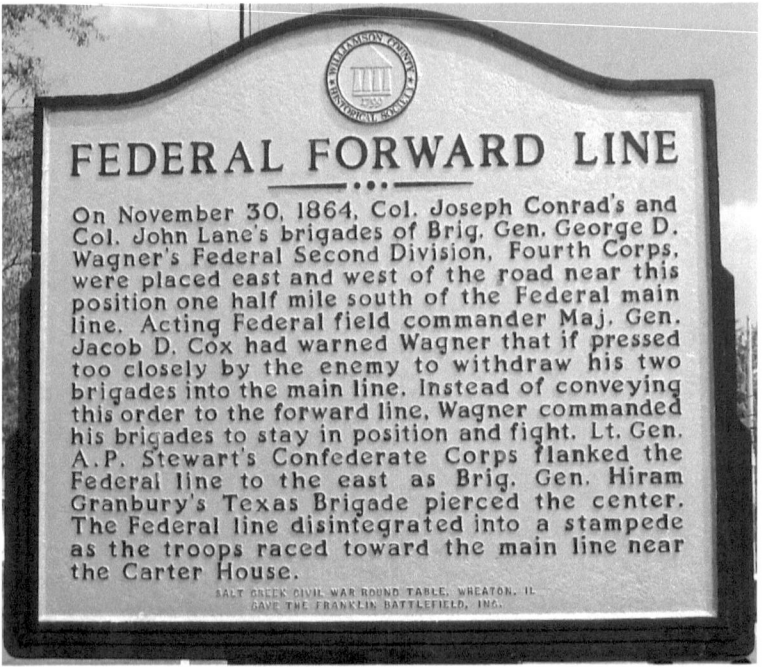

Another Yankee-oriented Battle of Franklin historical marker, Franklin, Tennessee. (Photo copyright © Lochlainn Seabrook)

The Factory, Franklin, Tennessee. The Battle of Franklin III, fought December 17, 1864—as Confederate General John Bell Hood and the Army of Tennessee were retreating south back through Franklin—spilled over into this area from what is now Harlinsdale Farm across the street, Franklin Road (known to Victorians as Franklin Pike). During Franklin III Yankees used fortifications from both the Battle of Franklin I (April 10, 1863) and the Battle of Franklin II (the subject of this book), along with Federal gun emplacements that were located here. The Factory, now a retail shopping mall, is located on what were empty fields and farmland at the time. (Photo copyright © Lochlainn Seabrook)

The core combat area, the location where the heaviest fighting took place during the Battle of Franklin—at the corner of present day Cleburne Street and Columbia Avenue—is now one of Franklin, Tennessee's busiest and most commercialized intersections. Few motorists or pedestrians passing through this area are aware of the bloodshed, inhumanity, horror, and carnage that occurred on this very spot 150 years ago. According to eyewitnesses, the morning after the battle (December 1, 1864), it was piled high with dead bodies (in some places several corpses deep) and red rain water, stained with the blood of the dead and the dying, was pouring off the fields. From the wounded came screams, sobs, and moans, as terrified mothers, sisters, and wives desperately combed the smouldering battlefield for their loved ones. More men died here, in a shorter amount of time, than at any other battle during Lincoln's War, including Gettysburg. Little wonder that the Battle of Franklin is still widely referred to as "five tragic hours." (Photo copyright © Lochlainn Seabrook)

Battle of Nashville Monument Park, Nashville, Tennessee. (Photo copyright © Lochlainn Seabrook)

Battle of Nashville historical marker, Brentwood, Tennessee. Confederate Colonel Rucker, who fought at the Battle of Franklin, is mentioned. (Photo copyright © Lochlainn Seabrook)

Battle of Nashville historical marker, Brentwood, Tennessee. (Photo copyright © Lochlainn Seabrook)

Battle of Nashville historical marker, Thompson's Station, Tennessee. (Photo copyright © Lochlainn Seabrook)

Battle of Spring Hill site, Spring Hill, Tennessee. (Photo copyright © Lochlainn Seabrook)

Battle of Spring Hill historical marker, Battle of Spring Hill site, Spring Hill, Tennessee. (Photo copyright © Lochlainn Seabrook)

Union General Samuel Beatty. (Public domain)

Confederate Colonel Tyree Harris Bell. (Public domain)

Confederate General Pierre Gustave Toutant Beauregard. (Public domain)

Beechlawn, Columbia, Tennessee. (Photo copyright © Lochlainn Seabrook)

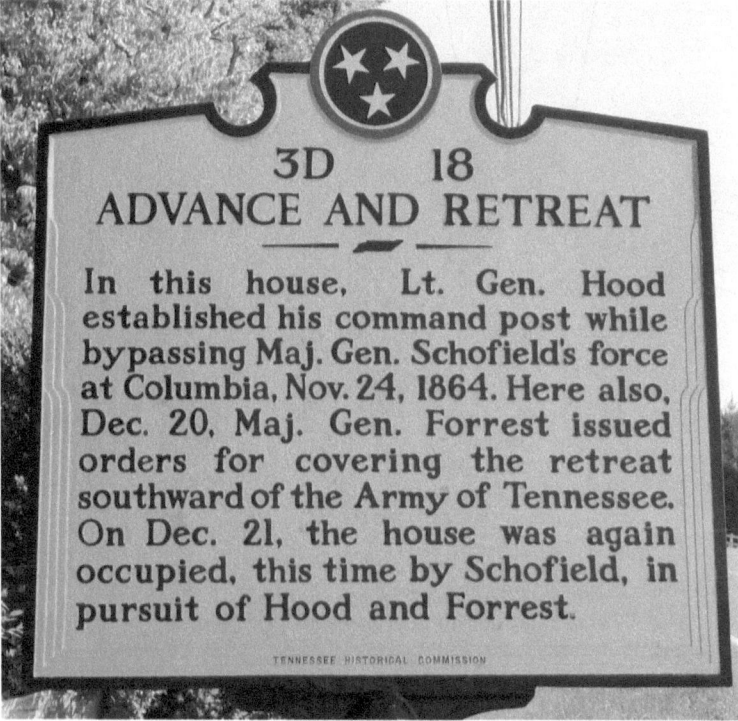

Historical marker, Beechlawn, Columbia, Tennessee. (Photo copyright © Lochlainn Seabrook)

Belle Meade Plantation, Nashville, Tennessee. (Photo copyright © Lochlainn Seabrook)

Belmont Mansion, Nashville, Tennessee. (Photo copyright © Lochlainn Seabrook)

Historical marker, Belmont Mansion, Nashville, Tennessee. (Photo copyright © Lochlainn Seabrook)

An African-American Confederate soldier, one of the 1 million blacks who fought for the Southern Cause: states' rights. (Public domain)

Street sign, Franklin, Tennessee, memorializing the famous Bostick family. (Photo copyright © Lochlainn Seabrook)

Boxmere, Franklin, Tennessee. (Photo copyright © Lochlainn Seabrook)

Union General Luther Prentice Bradley. (Public domain)

Confederate General Braxton Bragg. (Public domain)

Breezy Hill, Franklin, Tennessee. (Photo copyright © Lochlainn Seabrook)

Confederate General John Calvin Brown. (Public domain)

Union General Don Carlos Buell. (Public domain)

Confederate General Abraham Buford. (Public domain)

Street sign, Franklin, Tennessee, commemorating Confederate General Abraham Buford, who fought for self government at the Battle of Franklin. (Photo copyright © Lochlainn Seabrook)

Caldwell House, Spring Hill, Tennessee. (Photo copyright © Lochlainn Seabrook)

Gravestone of St. Claire Caldwell, Caldwell Family Cemetery, Spring Hill, Tennessee. (Photo copyright © Lochlainn Seabrook)

Carnton Plantation (front view), Franklin, Tennessee. (Photo copyright © Lochlainn Seabrook)

Carnton Plantation (rear view), Franklin, Tennessee. (Photo copyright © Lochlainn Seabrook)

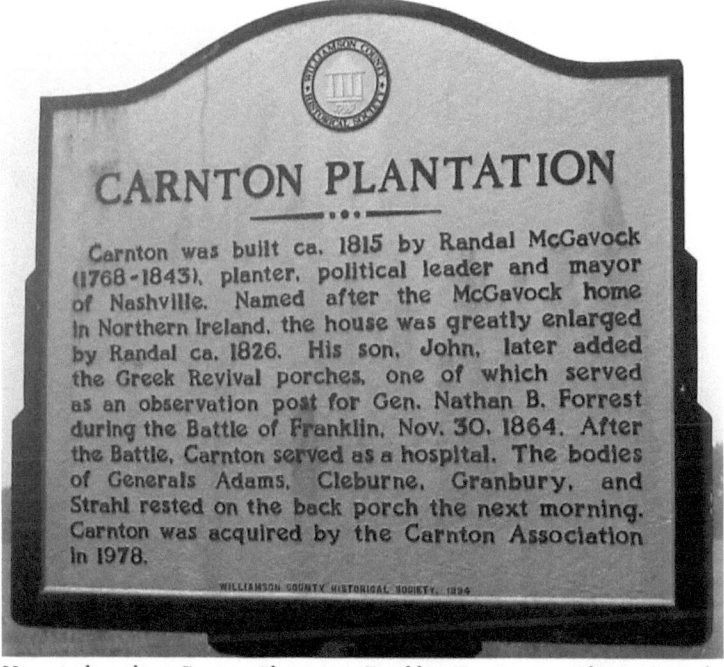

Historical marker, Carnton Plantation, Franklin, Tennessee. (Photo copyright © Lochlainn Seabrook)

Cultural signage, Franklin, Tennessee. (Photo copyright © Lochlainn Seabrook)

Back lower porch, Carnton Plantation, Franklin, Tennessee. It was here that the bodies of the four Confederate generals (Adams, Cleburne, Strahl, and Granbury) who died at the Battle of Franklin were laid out for viewing on December 1, 1864. (Photo copyright © Lochlainn Seabrook)

Another view of Carnton Plantation, Franklin, Tennessee. (Photo copyright © Lochlainn Seabrook)

Carter family cotton gin house, Franklin, Tennessee. (Public domain)

Carter House, Franklin, Tennessee. (Photo copyright © Lochlainn Seabrook)

Historical marker, Carter House, Franklin, Tennessee. Confederate Captain Theodrick Carter's first name is misspelled. (Photo copyright © Lochlainn Seabrook)

Confederate General John Carpenter Carter. (Public domain)

Street sign, Franklin, Tennessee, commemorating Confederate General John C. Carter, who died from wounds received at the Battle of Franklin, fighting for the Constitution. (Photo copyright © Lochlainn Seabrook)

Gravestone of Confederate Captain Theodrick "Tod" Carter, Rest Haven Cemetery, Franklin, Tennessee. (Photo copyright © Lochlainn Seabrook)

Union General John Stephen Casement. (Public domain)

Confederate General James Ronald Chalmers. (Public domain)

Stone memorial at grave site of Martin Terrell Cheairs (founder of Ferguson Hall), Spring Hill Cemetery, Spring Hill, Tennessee. (Photo copyright © Lochlainn Seabrook)

Gravestone of Martha Ann Bond, wife of Martin T. Cheairs, Spring Hill Cemetery, Spring Hill, Tennessee. (Photo copyright © Lochlainn Seabrook)

Confederate General Benjamin Franklin Cheatham. (Public domain)

A typical "Civil War" illustration from the 1800s. (Public domain)

Confederate General Henry DeLamar Clayton Sr. (Public domain)

Confederate General Patrick Ronayne Cleburne. (Public domain)

Street sign, Franklin, Tennessee, commemorating Confederate General Patrick R. Cleburne, who died at the Battle of Franklin fighting for personal freedom. (Photo copyright © Lochlainn Seabrook)

Wood marker, Franklin, Tennessee, indicating the area where Confederate General Patrick R. Cleburne fell during the Battle of Franklin. (Photo copyright © Lochlainn Seabrook)

Dr. Daniel Bonaparte Cliffe. (Public domain)

Confederate General Francis Marion Cockrell. (Public domain)

Street sign, Franklin, Tennessee, commemorating Confederate Colonel David Coleman, who led Ector's Brigade at the Battle of Franklin. (The unit's original commander, General Matthew D. Ector, was recovering from a leg amputation at the time.) (Photo copyright © Lochlainn Seabrook)

Collins' Farm, Franklin, Tennessee. (Photo copyright © Lochlainn Seabrook)

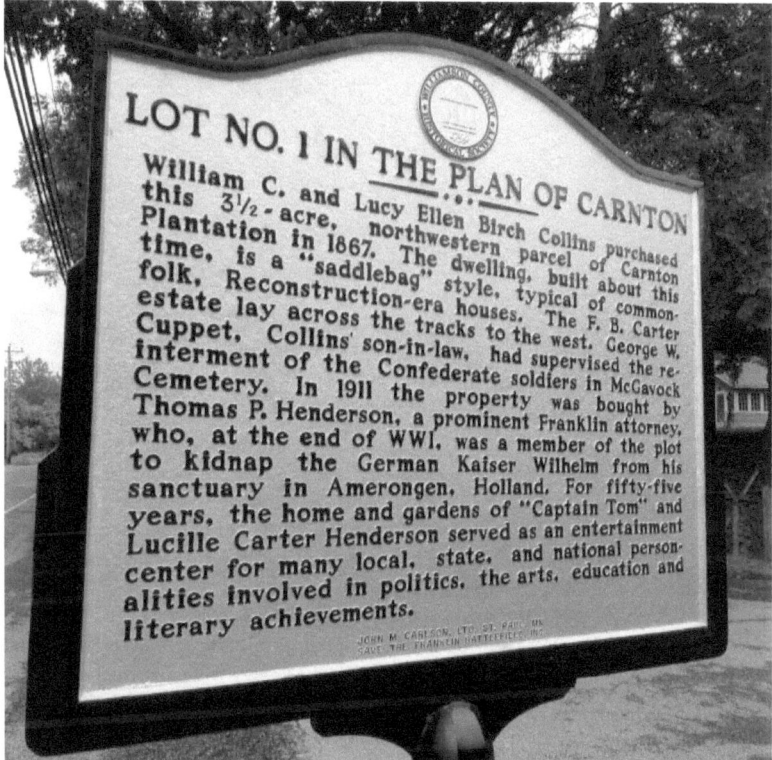

Historical marker, Collins' Farm, Franklin, Tennessee. (Photo copyright © Lochlainn Seabrook)

Columbia Avenue, looking north toward Franklin Center from between Winstead and Breezy Hills. Known as Columbia Turnpike in the 1800s, Confederate troops marched north along this road toward the waiting Yankees, entrenched in a horseshoe shape around the town. At the time of the battle, November 30, 1864, Columbia Pike was a country dirt road. (Photo copyright © Lochlainn Seabrook)

Confederate Flag, known as the First National or "Stars and Bars." (Public domain)

The beautiful Confederate Battle Flag, also known as the "Soldier's Flag," was codesigned and created by Confederate General Pierre Beauregard of Louisiana. (Public domain)

The much abused and misunderstood Confederate Monument at Franklin Tennessee. (Photo copyright Lochlainn Seabrook)

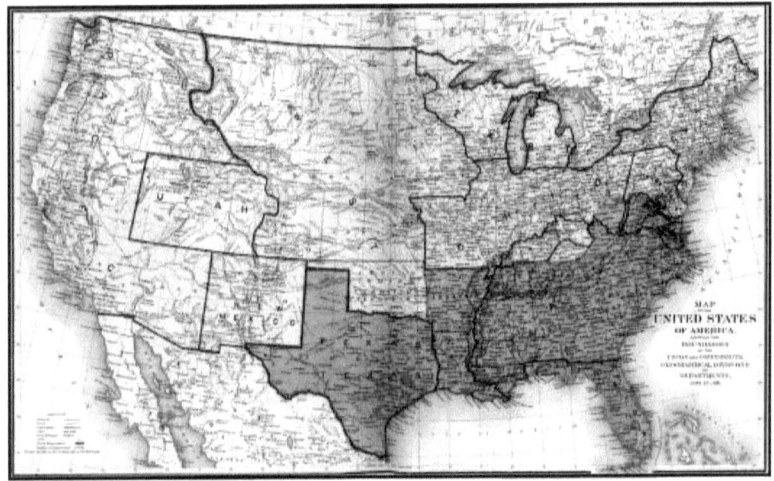
Confederate States in 1861 (shaded area at bottom). (Public domain)

Union General Joseph Conrad. (Public domain)

Union Colonel Datus Ensign Coon. (Public domain)

Union General Joseph Alexander Cooper. (Public domain)

Confederate Lieutenant George Limerick Cowan. (Public domain)

Gravestone of Confederate Lieutenant George Limerick Cowan, Cowan Family Plot, Mount Hope Cemetery, Franklin, Tennessee. (Photo copyright © Lochlainn Seabrook)

Union General Jacob Dolson Cox. (Public domain)

Confederate Sergeant Sumner Archibald Cunningham. (Public domain)

Confederate President Jefferson Davis. (Public domain)

Confederate General Zachariah Cantey Deas. (Public domain)

Confederate General George Gibbs Dibrell. (Public domain)

Sign, Columbia, Tennessee, marking the famous Duck River. (Photo copyright © Lochlainn Seabrook)

Confederate General Matthew Duncan Ector. (Public domain)

Elm Springs, Columbia, Tennessee. (Photo copyright © Lochlainn Seabrook)

U.S. President Abraham Lincoln reading his fake, illegal, and cynical political ploy, the Emancipation Proclamation, to members of his cabinet. Lincoln referred to the document, not as a "civil rights emancipation," but as a "military emancipation," revealing the true purpose behind it. His Preliminary Emancipation Proclamation, issued on September 22, 1862, contained the racist president's personal order to continue his efforts to deport all African-Americans out of the country. The clause was only removed from the Final Emancipation Proclamation (the version best known by the public, issued January 1, 1863) because his cabinet persuaded him that it might lose him the abolitionist vote, which he needed in his upcoming bid for reelection. (Public domain)

Street sign, Franklin, Tennessee, memorializing the Bostick House, also known as Everbright. (Photo copyright © Lochlainn Seabrook)

Our massive overly powerful federal style government is based in the U.S. Capitol Building at Washington, D.C. The Founding Fathers, most who were conservatives, never intended the national government to assume the powers and proportions it has today. Instead, as noted tacitly in the Ninth and Tenth Amendments, they designed a small federal government that was to be supported by strong independent states, a type of government known as a confederacy. In 1861 the Southern states rightly viewed big government liberal Abraham Lincoln as a threat to the Founders' form of government, and so they seceded from the Union. They called their new country the Confederate States of America, or "the Confederacy" for short, the original name of the United States (from 1781 to 1789). The secession of the Southern states then was merely an attempt to preserve the government and Constitution of the Founding generation, not protect slavery, as pro-North historians disingenuously continue to claim. (Public domain)

Ferguson Hall (also known as the Martin Cheairs House), Spring Hill, Tennessee. (Photo copyright © Lochlainn Seabrook)

Confederate General Winfield Scott Featherston. (Public domain)

A typical Civil War field hospital. This one, from the Summer of 1862, is located at Savage Station, Virginia. (Public domain)

Southern field servants, 1860s. (Public domain)

Confederate Colonel Hume R. Field. (Public domain)

Confederate General Jesse Johnson Finley. (Public domain)

Confederate General Nathan Bedford Forrest. (Public domain)

General Nathan Bedford Forrest (center) and his staff. From upper right to upper left, clockwise: George Dashiell, William M. Forrest (General Forrest's son), James B. Cowan, Charles W. Anderson, John W. Morton, and Samuel Donelson. (Public domain)

An area in Franklin, Tennessee, known as Forrest Crossing, memorializes the location where General Forrest and his cavalry forded the Harpeth River on the right flank during the Battle of Franklin. (Photo copyright © Lochlainn Seabrook)

Street sign, Franklin, Tennessee, honoring local hero General Nathan Bedford Forrest and his actions at the Battle of Franklin. (Photo copyright © Lochlainn Seabrook)

Another one of the many street signs in Franklin, Tennessee, honoring General Forrest. (Photo copyright © Lochlainn Seabrook)

Fort Johnson (the Tennessee State Capitol), Nashville, Tennessee. (Photo copyright © Lochlainn Seabrook)

Fort Granger, Franklin, Tennessee. (Photo copyright © Lochlainn Seabrook)

Historical marker, Fort Granger, Franklin, Tennessee. (Photo copyright © Lochlainn Seabrook)

Historical marker, Fort Negley, Nashville, Tennessee. (Photo copyright © Lochlainn Seabrook)

This historical marker near Fort Negley in Nashville, Tennessee, reveals the overt anti-South bias, Northernized scallywag prejudice, and generally uneducated views regarding Southern blacks that are so prevalent across Dixie today. For example, no mention is made here that the Southern blacks who "built" Fort Negley did so involuntarily, under extreme physical force, and that severe punishment, from whipping and beating, to imprisonment and even death, awaited those who resisted. In other words, these were "emancipated" slaves, laboring with Yankee guns pointed at their heads. Thus the idea that they "helped" and "assisted" in the building of Fort Negley is wholly inaccurate and misleading. Also not mentioned are the well documented facts that not only did far more blacks fight for the Confederacy than the Union, but hundreds if not thousands of blacks were with Confederate General John Bell Hood and the Army of Tennessee at the Battle of Nashville. (Photo copyright © Lochlainn Seabrook)

Franklin Railroad Depot, Franklin, Tennessee. (Photo copyright © Lochlainn Seabrook)

Historical marker, Franklin Railroad Depot, Franklin, Tennessee. (Photo copyright © Lochlainn Seabrook)

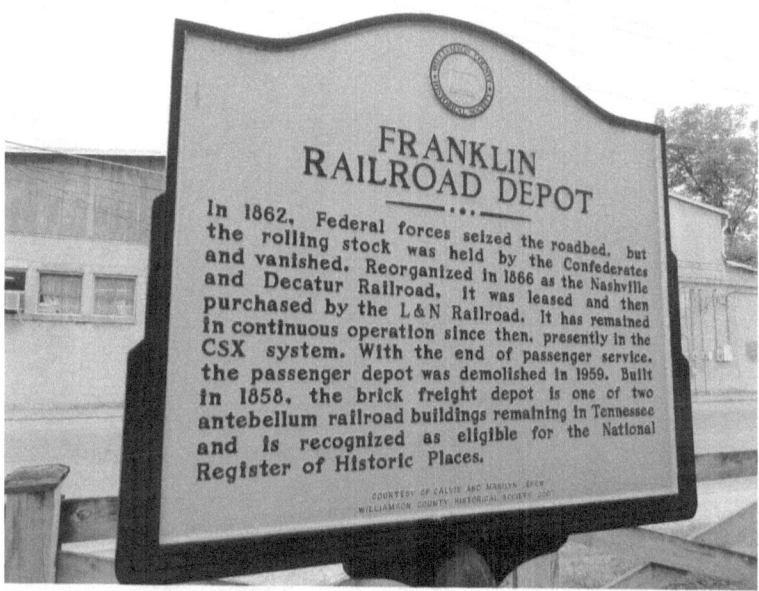

Historical marker, Franklin Railroad Depot, Franklin, Tennessee. (Photo copyright © Lochlainn Seabrook)

American statesman, inventor, Yankee Founding Father, and the man after whom Franklin, Tennessee, was named. (Public domain)

Franklin, Tennessee, with the town's beleaguered Confederate Monument in the background. (Photo copyright © Lochlainn Seabrook)

Cannon, Franklin, Tennessee. (Photo copyright © Lochlainn Seabrook)

Stone marker, Franklin, Tennessee. (Photo copyright © Lochlainn Seabrook)

Cultural signage, Franklin, Tennessee. (Photo copyright © Lochlainn Seabrook)

Cultural signage, Franklin, Tennessee. (Photo copyright © Lochlainn Seabrook)

Historical marker, Franklin, Tennessee, concerning Ewen Cameron, the first European-American to construct a house in the town in 1798. (Photo copyright © Lochlainn Seabrook)

Emblem of Franklin, Tennessee. (Photo copyright © Lochlainn Seabrook)

Signage, Franklin, Tennessee. (Photo copyright © Lochlainn Seabrook)

Cultural sign, Franklin, Tennessee. (Photo copyright © Lochlainn Seabrook)

Signage, Franklin, Tennessee. (Photo copyright © Lochlainn Seabrook)

Cultural signage, Franklin, Tennessee. (Photo copyright © Lochlainn Seabrook)

Confederate General Samuel Gibbs French. (Public domain)

Union Colonel Joseph Scott Fullerton, with signature. (Public domain)

Confederate General Randall Lee Gibson. (Public domain)

Confederate General States Rights Gist. (Public domain)

Street sign, Franklin, Tennessee, memorializing Confederate General States Rights Gist, who died at the Battle of Franklin fighting for the Southern Cause—embodied in his own name. (Photo copyright © Lochlainn Seabrook)

Confederate General George Washington Gordon. (Public domain)

Confederate General Daniel Chevilette Govan. (Public domain)

Confederate General Hiram Bronson Granbury. (Public domain)

Street sign, Franklin, Tennessee, memorializing Confederate General Hiram B. Granbury, who died at the Battle of Franklin fighting for independence from Northern liberalism and Yankee tyranny. (Photo copyright © Lochlainn Seabrook)

Union General Gordon Granger, after whom Fort Granger in Franklin, Tennessee, was named. (Public domain)

Union General Ulysses S. Grant. (Public domain)

Great Seal of the Confederate States. (Public domain)

Union General William Grose. (Public domain)

General William Giles Harding, with signature. (Public domain)

Harlinsdale Farm, Franklin, Tennessee. (Photo copyright © Lochlainn Seabrook)

Harpeth River, Franklin, Tennessee. (Photo copyright © Lochlainn Seabrook)

Signage, Harpeth River, Franklin, Tennessee. (Photo copyright © Lochlainn Seabrook)

Historical marker, Franklin, Tennessee, concerning Harpeth Academy, one of the many buildings in the town that was ruthlessly, unnecessarily, and illegally pillaged and burned down by U.S. troops during Lincoln's War. (Photo copyright © Lochlainn Seabrook)

Harrison House, Franklin, Tennessee. (Photo copyright © Lochlainn Seabrook)

Historical marker, Harrison House, Franklin, Tennessee. (Photo copyright © Lochlainn Seabrook)

Union Colonel Thomas Jefferson Harrison. (Public domain)

Union General Edward Hatch. (Public domain)

Street sign, Franklin, Tennessee. On November 30, 1864, Confederate General Alexander P. Stewart marched his men east down Henpeck Lane to Lewisburg Pike, on their way to the Battle of Franklin. (Photo copyright © Lochlainn Seabrook)

Henpeck Lane, Franklin, Tennessee. (Photo copyright © Lochlainn Seabrook)

Hiram Masonic Lodge, Franklin, Tennessee. (Photo copyright © Lochlainn Seabrook)

Historical marker, Hiram Masonic Lodge, Franklin, Tennessee. (Photo copyright © Lochlainn Seabrook)

Confederate General James Thadeus Holtzclaw. (Public domain)

Confederate General John Bell Hood. (Public domain)

Black house servant (back right rear), serving U.S. President George Washington and his family. (Public domain)

Isola Bella, Brentwood, Tennessee. (Photo copyright © Lochlainn Seabrook)

ISOLA BELLA

This house was built about 1840 by James and Narcissa Merritt Johnston on land that had belonged to David Johnston, pioneer to Middle Tennessee and grandfather of the builder. During the Civil War the Johnston home was passed by Confederate and Federal Armies after the battles of Franklin and Nashville. It served briefly as headquarters of Gen. John B. Hood and his staff before the conflict at Nashville and as a hospital after that ill-fated battle on Dec. 15-16, 1864.

ERECTED BY DAVE A. ALEXANDER 1996
WILLIAMSON COUNTY HISTORICAL SOCIETY

Historical marker, Isola Bella, Brentwood, Tennessee. (Photo copyright © Lochlainn Seabrook)

Confederate General William Hicks Jackson. (Public domain)

Confederate General Edward Johnson. (Public domain)

Union General Richard W. Johnson. (Public domain)

Confederate Lieutenant Colonel David Campbell Kelley (left) with his superior Lieutenant General Nathan Bedford Forrest, preparing to launch another successful attack on the invading Yanks. (Public domain)

Union General Nathan Kimball. (Public domain)

Union Colonel Isaac Minor Kirby. (Public domain)

Union Colonel Frederick Knefler. (Public domain)

Union General Joseph Farmer Knipe. (Public domain)

Union Colonel John Quincy Lane. (Public domain)

Laurel Hill, Franklin, Tennessee. (Photo copyright © Lochlainn Seabrook)

Union Captain Henry Ware Lawton. (Public domain)

Confederate General Stephen Dill Lee. (Public domain)

Lewisburg Pike, Franklin, Tennessee, the site of much fighting and bloodshed during the Battle of Franklin. (Photo copyright © Lochlainn Seabrook)

U.S. President, war criminal, big government tyrant, and socialistic liberal, Abraham Lincoln. (Public domain)

Confederate General William Wing Loring. (Public Domain)

Lotz House, Franklin, Tennessee. (Photo copyright © Lochlainn Seabrook)

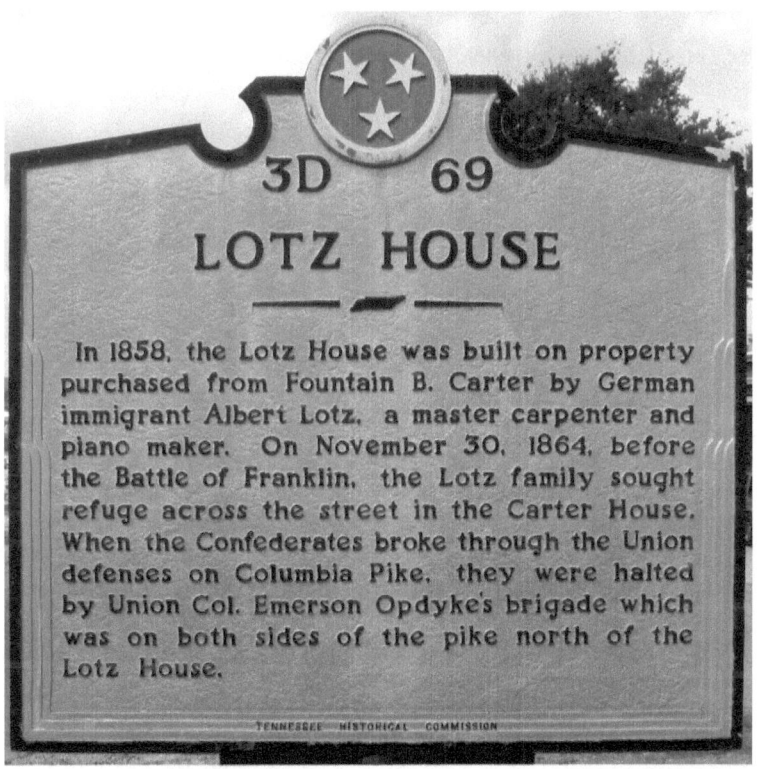

Historical marker, Lotz House, Franklin, Tennessee. (Photo copyright © Lochlainn Seabrook)

Confederate General Mark Perrin Lowrey. (Public domain)

Confederate General Robert Gadden Haynes Lowry. (Public domain)

Union Colonel Arthur MacArthur Jr. (Public domain)

Confederate General George Earl Maney. (Public domain)

Confederate General Arthur Middleton Manigault. (Public domain)

Union General Edward Moody McCook. (Public domain)

McEwen House, Franklin, Tennessee. (Photo copyright © Lochlainn Seabrook)

McGavock Confederate Cemetery, Franklin, Tennessee. (Photo copyright © Lochlainn Seabrook)

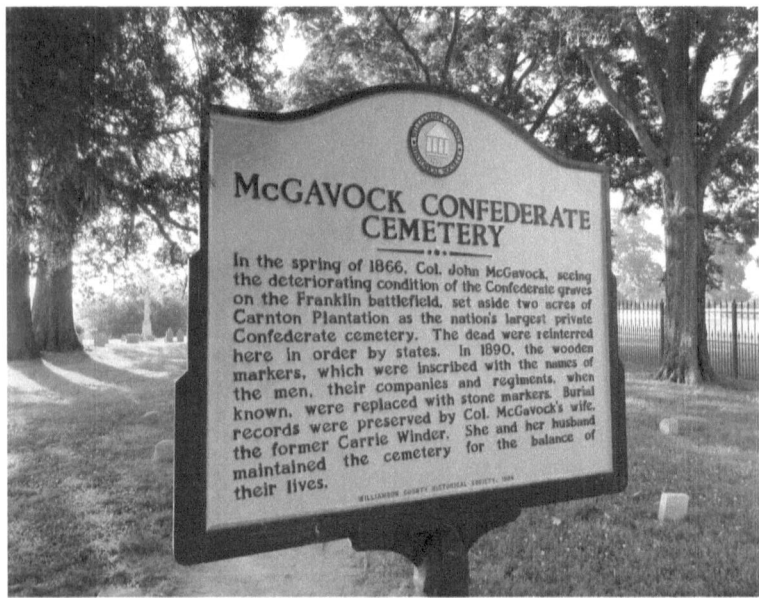

Historical marker, McGavock Confederate Cemetery, Franklin, Tennessee. (Photo copyright © Lochlainn Seabrook)

Stone monument, McGavock Confederate Cemetery, Franklin, Tennessee, commemorating the 230 soldiers from Tennessee who perished at the Battle of Franklin. (Photo copyright © Lochlainn Seabrook)

Another historical marker, McGavock Confederate Cemetery, Franklin, Tennessee. (Photo copyright © Lochlainn Seabrook)

Stone marker indicating the burial spot of fifty-three unknown Confederate soldiers whose remains were unidentifiable. McGavock Confederate Cemetery, Franklin, Tennessee. (Photo copyright © Lochlainn Seabrook)

Stone marker memorializing 225 unknown soldiers who died at the Battle of Franklin fighting Northern liberalism and tyranny. McGavock Confederate Cemetery, Franklin, Tennessee. (Photo copyright © Lochlainn Seabrook)

Historical marker, McGavock Confederate Cemetery, Franklin, Tennessee. (Photo copyright © Lochlainn Seabrook)

Historical marker (reverse side of previous marker), McGavock Confederate Cemetery, Franklin, Tennessee. (Photo copyright © Lochlainn Seabrook)

This plain Confederate stone marker, with Carnton Plantation in the background, tells the poignant story of the deaths of 424 men in four short words. McGavock Confederate Cemetery, Franklin, Tennessee. (Photo copyright © Lochlainn Seabrook)

Another view of the McGavock Confederate Cemetery, Franklin, Tennessee, the final resting place for some 1,500 Southern boys and men. (Photo copyright © Lochlainn Seabrook)

Confederate Colonel John W. McGavock. (Public domain)

Confederate Colonel John W. McGavock's gravestone, McGavock Family Cemetery, Carnton Plantation, Franklin Tennessee. (Photo copyright © Lochlainn Seabrook)

McLemore House, Franklin, Tennessee. (Photo copyright © Lochlainn Seabrook)

Historical marker, McLemore House, Franklin, Tennessee. (Photo copyright © Lochlainn Seabrook)

Midway Plantation, Brentwood, Tennessee. (Photo copyright © Lochlainn Seabrook)

MIDWAY

Midway, which takes its name from being half way between Nashville and Franklin, was built in 1846 to replace an earlier home destroyed by fire. It was built by Lysander McGavock, who married Elizabeth Crockett, daughter of the original owner of the land. Once the home to pre-historic Indians, Midway served as headquarters to generals from both sides during the Civil War, and its grounds were the scene of several skirmishes. Water was piped from its spring to the construction site when the railroad cut was dug in Brentwood. The house is home today of the Brentwood Country Club.

WILLIAMSON COUNTY HISTORICAL SOCIETY, 1931

Historical marker, Midway Plantation, Brentwood, Tennessee. (Photo copyright © Lochlainn Seabrook.)

Confederate Captain John Watson Morton, with signature. (Public domain)

Nashville and Decatur Railroad Underpass, Franklin, Tennessee. (Photo copyright © Lochlainn Seabrook)

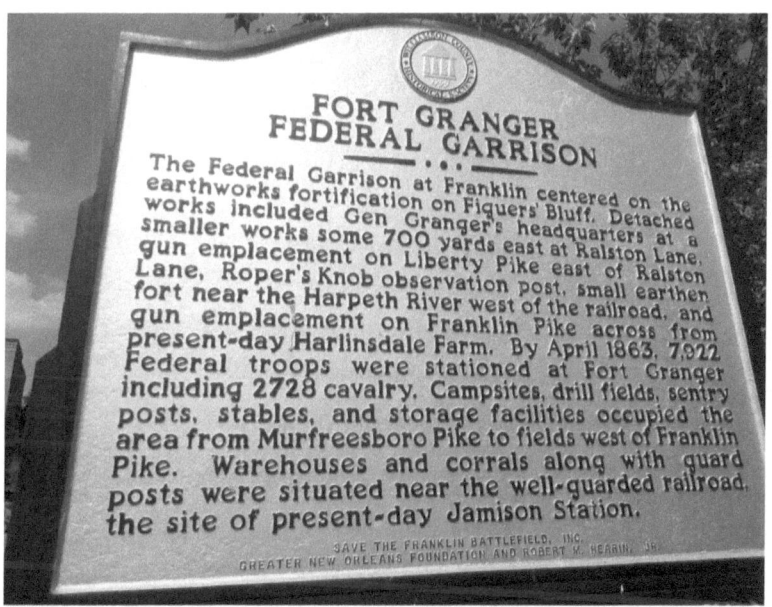

Historical marker, Nashville and Decatur Railroad Underpass, Franklin, Tennessee. (Photo copyright © Lochlainn Seabrook)

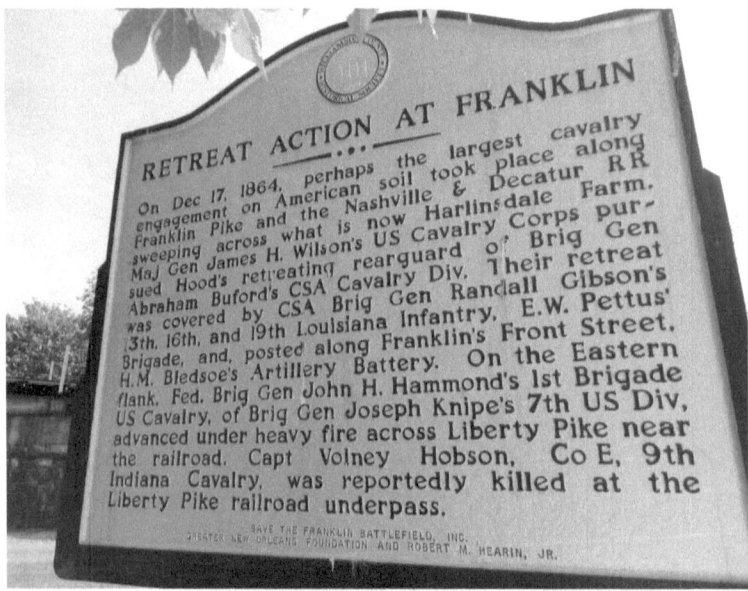

Historical marker, Nashville and Decatur Railroad Underpass, Franklin, Tennessee. (Photo copyright © Lochlainn Seabrook)

Nashville, Tennessee. (Photo copyright © Lochlainn Seabrook)

Union General James Scott Negley, after whom Nashville's Fort Negley was named. (Public domain)

Oaklawn Mansion (also known as the Absalom Thompson House), Spring Hill, Tennessee. (Photo copyright © Lochlainn Seabrook)

Interpretive wayside sign, Oaklawn Mansion, Spring Hill, Tennessee. (Photo copyright © Lochlainn Seabrook)

Old Factory Store, Franklin, Tennessee. (Photo copyright © Lochlainn Seabrook)

Union General Emerson Opdycke. (Public domain)

Fruit and leaves of the Osage orange tree. (Public domain)

Confederate General Edmund Winston Pettus. (Public domain)

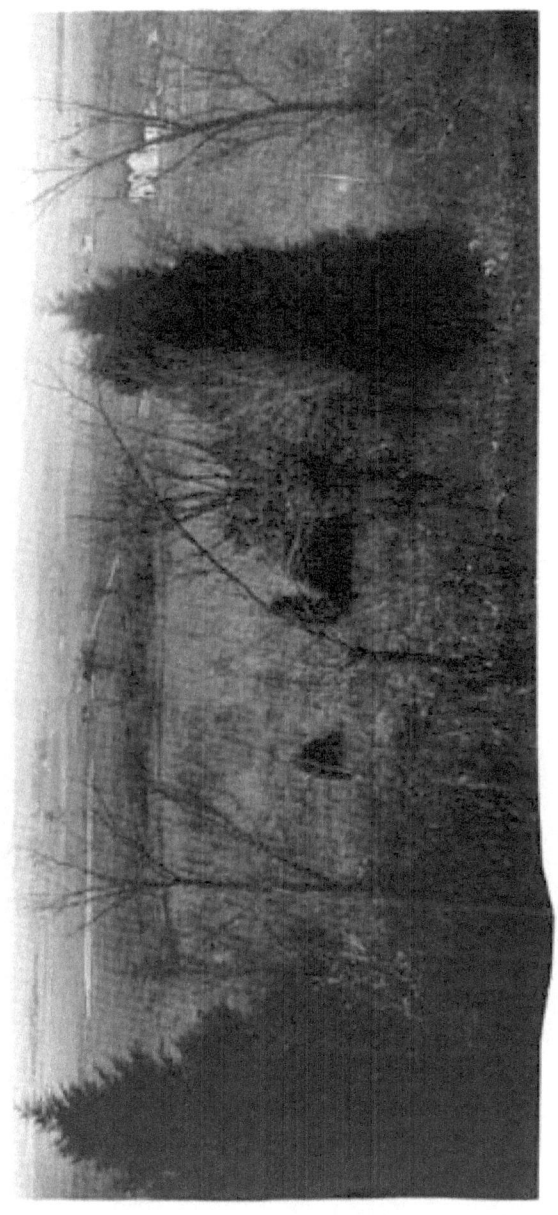

The Plain of Franklin, looking north from Winstead Hill, as it would have looked to General John Bell Hood and the Army of Tennessee as they approached the town of Franklin on November 30, 1864, from Spring Hill. (Public domain)

Union Colonel Philip Sidney Post. (Public domain)

Privet Knob area, Franklin, Tennessee. (Photo copyright © Lochlainn Seabrook)

Confederate General William Andrew Quarles. (Public domain)

Confederate Chaplain Charles Todd Quintard. (Public domain)

Rattle and Snap, Mount Pleasant, Tennessee. (Photo copyright © Lochlainn Seabrook)

Historical marker, Rattle and Snap, Mount Pleasant, Tennessee. (Photo copyright © Lochlainn Seabrook)

Union General James William Reilly. (Public domain)

Rest Haven Cemetery, Franklin, Tennessee. (Photo copyright © Lochlainn Seabrook)

Historical marker, Rest Haven Cemetery, Franklin, Tennessee. (Photo copyright © Lochlainn Seabrook)

Confederate General Daniel Harris Reynolds. (Public domain)

Rippavilla Plantation, Spring Hill, Tennessee. (Photo copyright © Lochlainn Seabrook)

Riverside Plantation, Franklin, Tennessee. (Photo copyright © Lochlainn Seabrook)

Confederate doctor Deering J. Roberts. (Public domain)

Roper's Knob, Franklin, Tennessee. (Photo copyright © Lochlainn Seabrook)

Confederate General Lawrence Sullivan Ross. (Public domain)

Confederate General Edmund Winchester Rucker. (Public domain)

Union General Thomas Howard Ruger. (Public domain)

Saint John's Episcopal Church, Mount Pleasant, Tennessee. (Photo copyright © Lochlainn Seabrook)

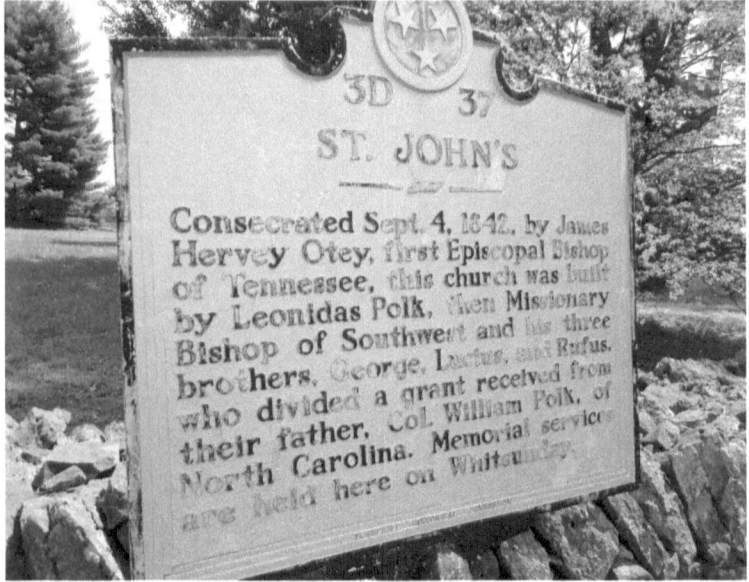

Historical marker, Saint John's Episcopal Church, Mount Pleasant, Tennessee. (Photo copyright © Lochlainn Seabrook)

Wall plaque, Saint John's Episcopal Church, Mount Pleasant, Tennessee. (Photo copyright © Lochlainn Seabrook)

Cemetery, Saint John's Episcopal Church, Mount Pleasant, Tennessee. (Photo copyright © Lochlainn Seabrook)

Saint Paul's Episcopal Church, Franklin, Tennessee. (Photo copyright © Lochlainn Seabrook)

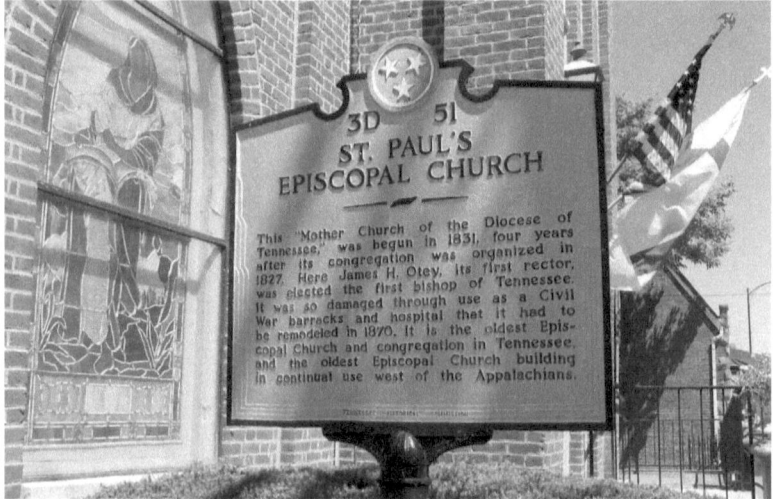

Historical marker, Saint Paul's Episcopal Church, Franklin, Tennessee. (Photo copyright © Lochlainn Seabrook)

Union General John McAllister Schofield. (Public domain)

Union Captain Levi Tucker Scofield. (Public domain)

Confederate General Thomas Moore Scott. (Public domain)

Confederate General Claudius Wistar Sears. (Public domain)

Confederate General Jacob Hunter Sharp. (Public domain)

Confederate General Charles Miller Shelley. (Public domain)

Union Colonel Isaac Ruth Sherwood. (Public domain)

Both the American slave trade and American slavery got their start in the North, in Massachusetts to be exact, not in the South. Except for the fact that they were in bondage, the Virginia servants above had a quality of life that was identical to, and in many cases superior to, most Southern whites—95 percent who were from poor farming families. Otherwise, black servants had nearly all of the same rights and privileges that free blacks and whites had. They could even purchase their own freedom, something completely unknown in true slavery. This is why they were correctly called "servants" in the South, not "slaves." Registered as members of their white owners' families at the time of purchase, Southern servants married, bore children, owned their own businesses, hired themselves out, lived in sturdy comfortable homes, received wages, worked their own gardens, had holidays and Sundays off, hunted, fished, held parties, visited friends on other plantations, and sold their products at market value, saving up the profits for the future. Additionally, by law all of the Southern servant's needs were taken care of. From birth to death he was provided with free food, housing, clothing, and medical care. After Lincoln's War, most servants stayed on with their original owners, now working as "free" laborers (though the difference in their status was seldom obvious). The bond between owner and servant was often so loving and powerful that at death they were buried near or even next to one another. (Public domain)

Confederate General James Argyle Smith. (Public domain)

Confederate General Thomas Benton Smith. (Public domain)

Logo of the Sons of Confederate Veterans. (Copyright SCV)

Spring Hill Cemetery, Spring Hill, Tennessee. (Photo copyright © Lochlainn Seabrook)

Stone memorial, Spring Hill Cemetery, Spring Hill, Tennessee. Dedicated to several unknown Confederate soldiers buried here, who died during the Battle of Franklin. Erected in 1971 by the Sparkman Chapter, United Daughters of the Confederacy. (Photo copyright © Lochlainn Seabrook)

Grave of George Blaine, Spring Hill Cemetery, Spring Hill, Tennessee. Blaine perished at the Battle of Franklin fighting for constitutional freedom against the liberal, socialistic, big government policies of authoritarian and racist Abraham Lincoln and his intolerant, Constitution loathing followers. (Photo copyright © Lochlainn Seabrook)

Spring Hill, Tennessee. (Photo copyright © Lochlainn Seabrook)

Union General David Sloane Stanley. (Public domain)

Confederate General Carter Littlepage Stevenson. (Public domain)

Confederate General Alexander Peter Stewart. (Public domain)

Union Colonel Israel Newton Stiles. (Public domain)

Confederate General Marcellus Augustus Stovall. (Public domain)

Confederate General Otho French Strahl. (Public domain)

Street sign, Franklin, Tennessee, commemorating Confederate General Otho F. Strahl, who died at the Battle of Franklin fighting for the Constitution of the Founding Fathers. (Photo copyright © Lochlainn Seabrook)

Union Colonel Abel D. Streight. (Public domain)

Union Colonel Silas Allen Strickland. (Public domain)

Confederate General Richard Taylor. (Public domain)

The Nashville and Decatur Railroad, Franklin, Tennessee, was known as the Tennessee and Alabama Railroad at the time of the Battle of Franklin. The entire road through Middle Tennessee was illegally seized and occupied by the U.S. during Lincoln's War. (Photo copyright © Lochlainn Seabrook)

Union General George Henry Thomas. (Public domain)

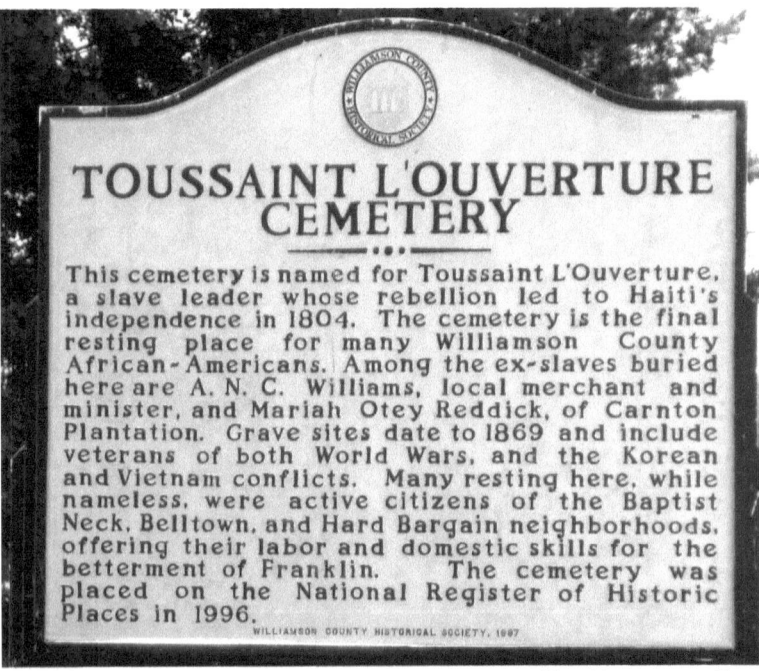

Historical marker, Toussaint L'Ouverture Cemetery, Franklin, Tennessee. (Photo copyright © Lochlainn Seabrook)

Travellers Rest, Nashville, Tennessee. (Photo copyright © Lochlainn Seabrook)

Historical marker, Travellers Rest, Nashville, Tennessee. (Photo copyright © Lochlainn Seabrook)

Truett House, Franklin, Tennessee. (Photo copyright © Lochlainn Seabrook)

Logo of the United Daughters of the Confederacy. (Copyright UDC)

Confederate General Earl Van Dorn. Had he not been murdered (by a jealous husband) May 7, 1863, at his headquarters at Ferguson Hall, Spring Hill, Tennessee, he would have been at the Battle of Franklin II, November 30, 1864. After his death, General Nathan Bedford Forrest was given Van Dorn's cavalry command, which he led on the right flank at the conflict. (Public domain)

Visitors Center (McPhail Office), Franklin, Tennessee. (Photo copyright © Lochlainn Seabrook)

Signage, Visitors Center, Franklin, Tennessee. (Photo copyright © Lochlainn Seabrook)

Union General George Day Wagner. (Public domain)

Confederate General Edward Cary Walthall. (Public domain)

Confederate Private Samuel Rush Watkins. (Public domain)

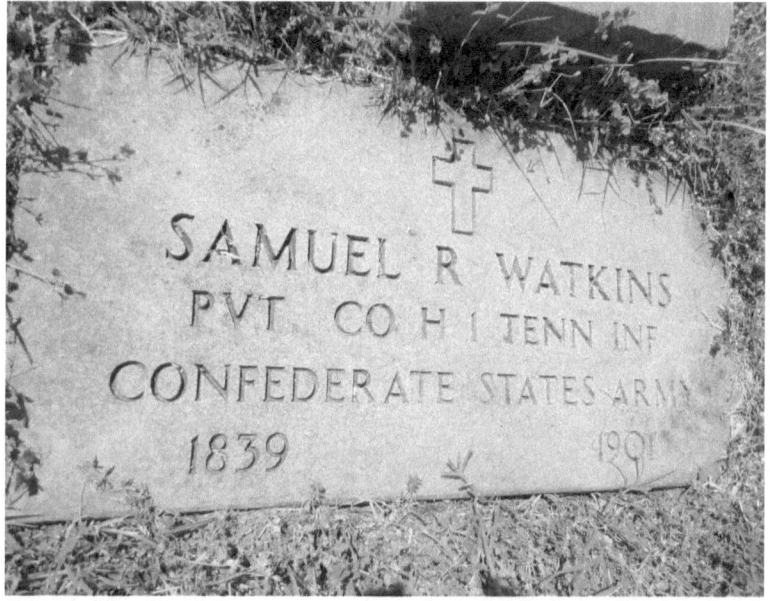
Grave marker of Confederate Private Sam Rush Watkins, Zion Presbyterian Church Cemetery, Mount Pleasant, Tennessee. (Photo copyright © Lochlainn Seabrook)

Memorial stone of Confederate Private Sam Rush Watkins and his wife Virginia Mayes, Zion Presbyterian Church Cemetery, Mount Pleasant, Tennessee. (Photo copyright © Lochlainn Seabrook)

Union General Walter Chiles Whitaker. (Public domain)

William McKissack House, Spring Hill, Tennessee. (Photo copyright © Lochlainn Seabrook)

Signage, William McKissack House, Spring Hill, Tennessee. (Photo copyright © Lochlainn Seabrook)

Gravestone of William McKissack, Spring Hill Cemetery, Spring Hill, Tennessee. (Photo copyright © Lochlainn Seabrook)

Gravestone of Jeannette Thompson, wife of William McKissack, Spring Hill Cemetery, Spring Hill, Tennessee. (Photo copyright © Lochlainn Seabrook)

Williamson County Courthouse, Franklin, Tennessee. (Photo copyright © Lochlainn Seabrook)

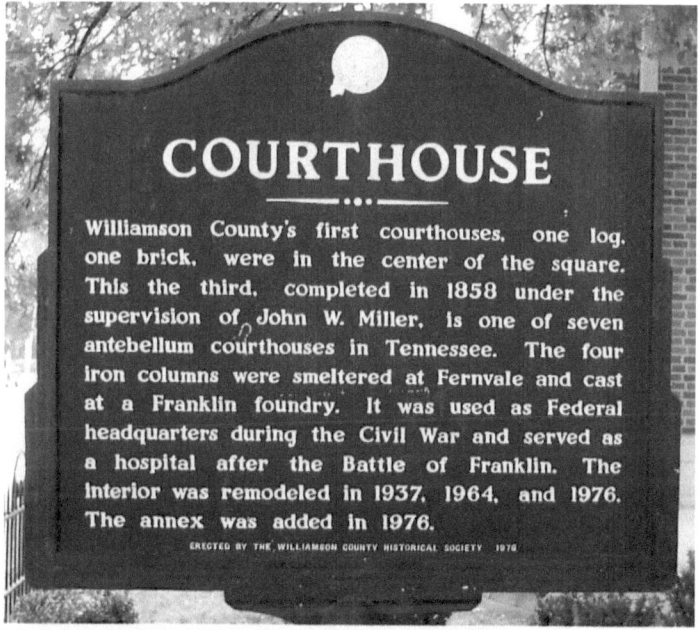

Historical marker, Williamson County Courthouse, Franklin, Tennessee. (Photo copyright © Lochlainn Seabrook)

Union General James Harrison Wilson. (Public domain)

Caroline Elizabeth Winder, better known as Carrie McGavock. (Public domain)

Carrie McGavock's gravestone, McGavock Family Cemetery, Carnton Plantation, Franklin, Tennessee. (Photo copyright © Lochlainn Seabrook)

Winstead Hill, Franklin, Tennessee. (Photo copyright © Lochlainn Seabrook)

Signage, Winstead Hill, Franklin, Tennessee. (Photo copyright © Lochlainn Seabrook)

Signage, Winstead Hill, Franklin, Tennessee. (Photo copyright © Lochlainn Seabrook)

Plaque, Winstead Hill, Franklin, Tennessee. (Photo copyright © Lochlainn Seabrook)

View from Winstead Hill looking north toward Franklin center. (Photo copyright © Lochlainn Seabrook)

Cannon, Winstead Hill, Franklin, Tennessee. (Photo copyright © Lochlainn Seabrook)

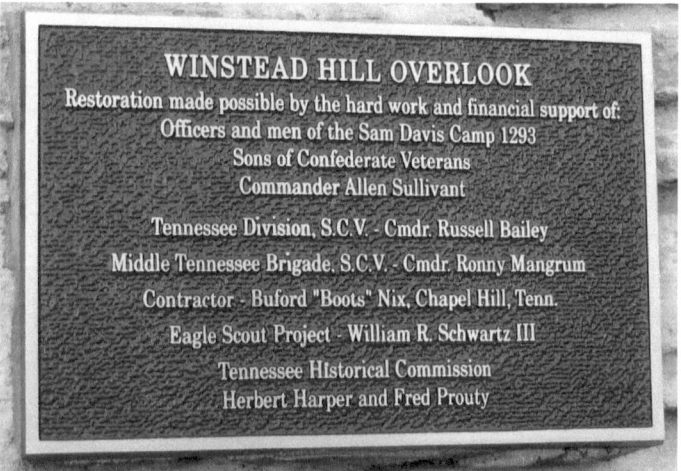

Plaque, Winstead Hill, Franklin, Tennessee. (Photo copyright © Lochlainn Seabrook)

BRIGADIER'S WALK

The sense of pride, honor and integrity of the everyday fighting man of the Army of Tennessee made the brilliant careers of these five Brigadier Generals possible. Largely non-slave owning, these brave men of the Army of Tennessee followed Adams, Carter, Strahl, Gist and Granbury across the fields to your right into certain death that November afternoon. Please pause for a moment of respect to their memory!

Plaque, Brigadier's Walk, Winstead Hill, Franklin, Tennessee. (Photo copyright © Lochlainn Seabrook)

Stone memorials to the Confederate generals who perished at the Battle of Franklin, Winstead Hill, Franklin, Tennessee. (Photo copyright © Lochlainn Seabrook)

Stone memorial to Confederate General States Rights Gist, Brigadier's Walk, Winstead Hill, Franklin, Tennessee. (Photo copyright © Lochlainn Seabrook)

Stone memorial to Cockrell's Brigade, which fought at the Battle of Franklin, Winstead Hill, Franklin, Tennessee. (Photo copyright © Lochlainn Seabrook)

WINSTEAD HILL & THE BATTLE OF FRANKLIN

Winstead Hill is historically rooted to the City of Franklin due to a significant confrontation during the Civil War. The crest of Winstead Hill rises approximately 200 feet above downtown Franklin and is located two miles to the south. Because of its exceptional location and vantage from the south, the hill served as a command and observation post for the Confederate Armies during the Battle of Franklin in 1864.

It was after General William T. Sherman sacked Atlanta in September of 1864 that Confederate General John Bell Hood led the Army of Tennessee towards the middle Tennessee area with intentions to join Gen. Robert E. Lee in Richmond, Virginia. While Hood was camped near this site south of Franklin, Maj. General John M. Schofield slipped Union troops past Confederate forces during the night, joining a well supplied Fort Granger on the north banks of the Harpeth River.

In a ▓ of ▓▓▓ and against the advice of his subordinate generals, Gen. Hood gathered the Army of Tennessee's 20,000 soldiers for an attack upon the Union camp beginning in mid afternoon. Observing from the vantage point atop Winstead Hill, Gen. Hood witnessed 13 assaults beginning at 4:00 pm and finally ending near 1:00 am in the morning. Union troops withdrew across the Harpeth River and retreated towards Nashville. Hood found his revenge in victory, but at an extreme price.

Although the Union troops retreated in defeat at this battle, the results of this confrontation were anything but a victory for the Confederacy. The Army of Tennessee lost nearly a third of its forces as Gen. Hood ▓▓▓▓▓ 6,261 wounded and killed soldiers. Gen. Schofield's troops sustained only 2,326 fatalities out of 22,000 soldiers. Hood also lost 15 allied generals in the Battle of Franklin including 8 wounded, 6 killed, and 1 taken captive. The battle signaled the end of hope for the Confederate Armies to halt Sherman's march through Georgia. The Battle of Franklin was a turning point in the Civil War, as a substantial threat to the security Washington D.C. vanished in this loss of Confederate manpower. The Battle of Nashville two weeks later culminated the loss of hope for the South.

THE BATTLE FIELD, FRANKLIN TENNESSEE, C.1883

Signage (defaced), Winstead Hill, Franklin, Tennessee. (Photo copyright © Lochlainn Seabrook)

Signage, Winstead Hill, Franklin, Tennessee. (Photo copyright © Lochlainn Seabrook)

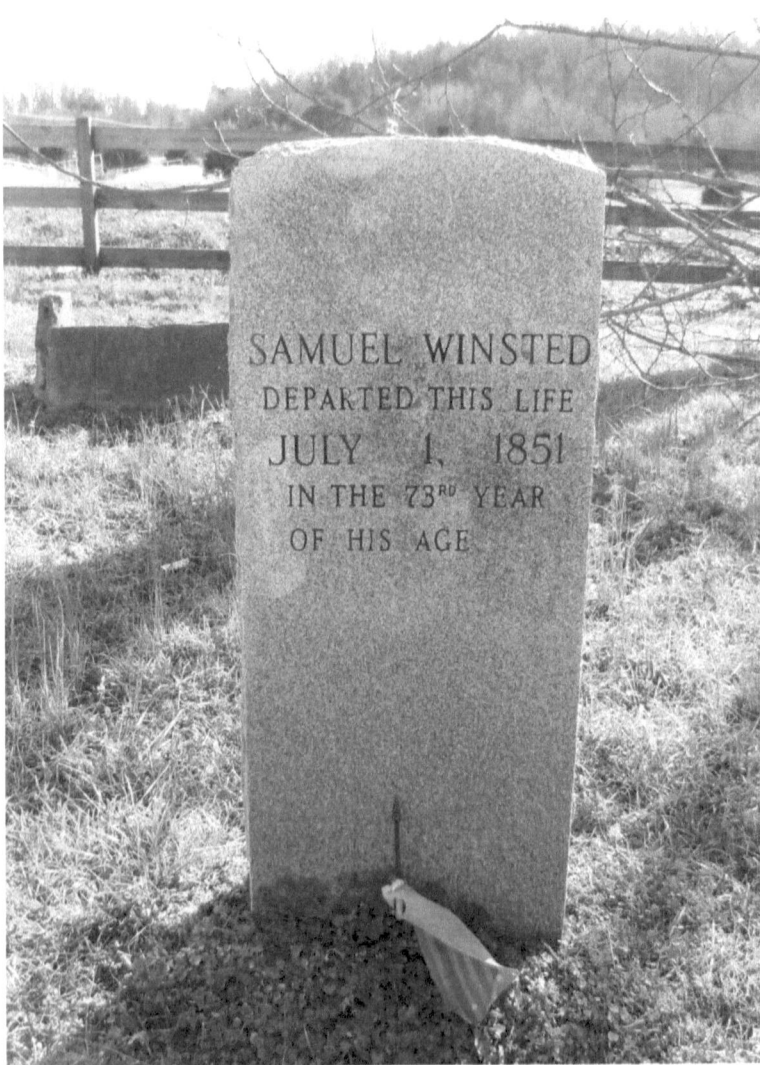

Grave site of Samuel Winstead, after whom Winstead Hill (seen in the background) was named. Winstead-McKinney Cemetery, Franklin, Tennessee. (Photo copyright © Lochlainn Seabrook)

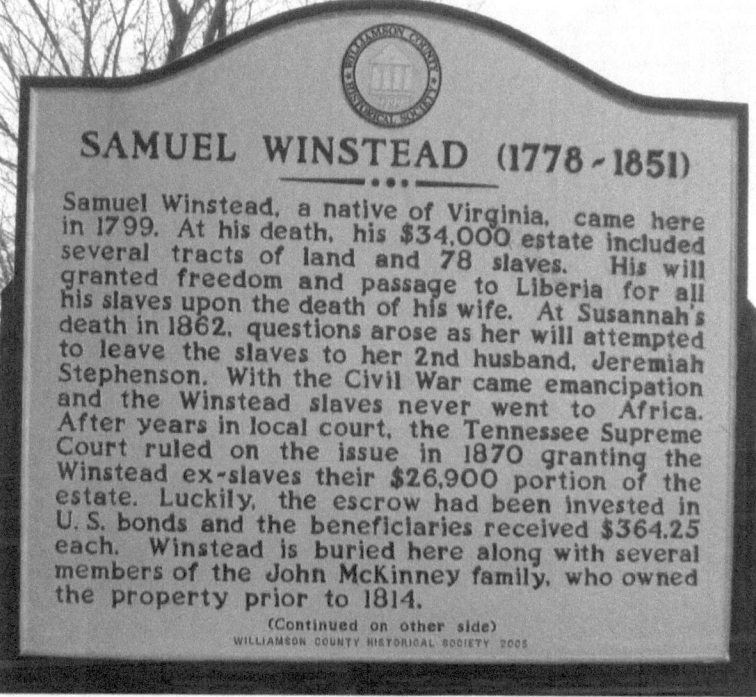

Anti-South historical marker, Winstead-McKinney Cemetery, Franklin, Tennessee. (Photo copyright © Lochlainn Seabrook.)

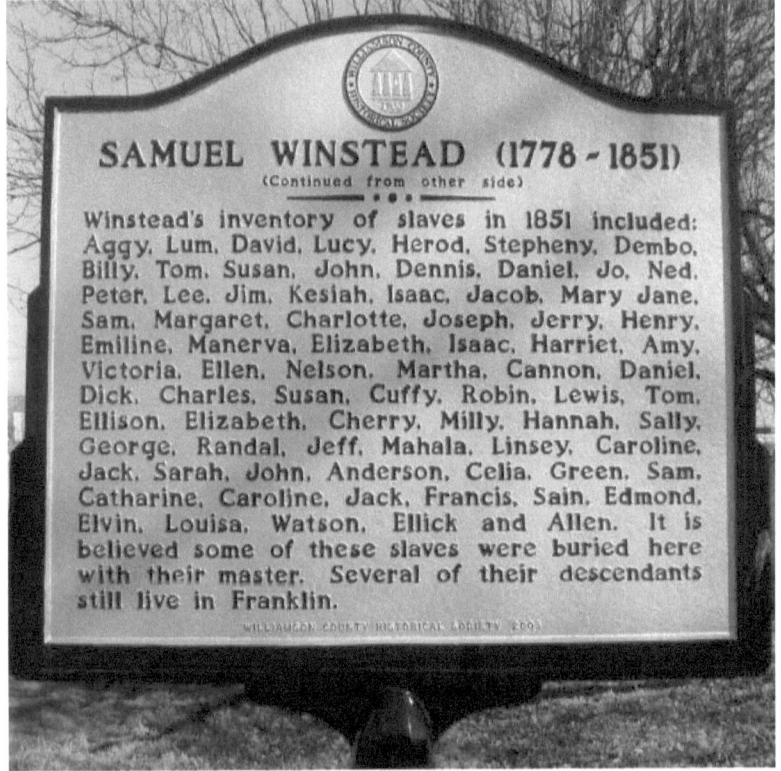

Reverse side of anti-South historical marker, Winstead-McKinney Cemetery, Franklin, Tennessee. (Photo copyright © Lochlainn Seabrook)

Union General Thomas John Wood. (Public domain)

Modern grave marker of Confederate Lieutenant Colonel Robert Butler Young, who died at the Battle of Franklin fighting for the Constitution. Saint John's Episcopal Church Cemetery, Mount Pleasant, Tennessee. (Photo copyright © Lochlainn Seabrook)

Original gravestone of Confederate Lieutenant Colonel Robert Butler Young, Saint John's Episcopal Church Cemetery, Mount Pleasant, Tennessee. (Photo copyright © Lochlainn Seabrook)

Zion Presbyterian Church Cemetery, Mount Pleasant, Tennessee. (Photo copyright © Lochlainn Seabrook)

BIBLIOGRAPHY

Abbott, John Stevens Cabot. *The Life of General Ulysses S. Grant*. Boston, MA: B. B. Russell, 1868.

Adams, Charles. *When in the Course of Human Events: Arguing the Case for Southern Secession*. Lanham, MD: Rowman and Littlefield, 2000.

Adams, Francis D., and Barry Sanders. *Alienable Rights: The Exclusion of African Americans in a White Man's Land, 1619-2000*. 2003. New York, NY: Perennial, 2004 ed.

Adams, Henry (ed.). *Documents Relating to New-England Federalism, 1800-1815*. Boston, MA: Little, Brown, and Co., 1877.

Adams, Nehemiah, Rev. *A South-side View of Slavery: Three Months at the South, in 1854*. Boston, MA: T. R. Marvin, 1855.

Alexander, William T. *History of the Colored Race in America*. Kansas City, MO: Palmetto Publishing, 1887.

Alotta, Robert I. *Civil War Justice: Union Army Executions Under Lincoln*. Shippensburg, PA: White Mane, 1989.

An Appeal From the Colored Men of Philadelphia to the President of the United States. Philadelphia, PA, 1862.

Anastaplo, George. *Abraham Lincoln: A Constitutional Biography*. Lanham, MD: Rowman and Littlefield, 1999.

Anderson, John Q. (ed.). *Brokenburn: The Journal of Kate Stone, 1861-1868*. 1955. Baton Rouge, LA: Louisiana State University Press, 1995 ed.

Anderson, John Richardson. *Richardson's Defense of the South*. Atlanta, GA: A. B. Caldwell, 1914.

Andrews, Elisha Benjamin. *The United States in Our Own Time: A History From Reconstruction to Expansion*. 1895. New York, NY: Charles Scribner's Sons, 1903 ed.

Andrews, Sidney. *The South Since the War: As Shown by Fourteen Weeks of Travel and Observation*. Boston, MA: Ticknor and Fields, 1866.

Angle, Paul M. (ed.). *The Complete Lincoln-Douglas Debates of 1858*. Chicago, IL: University of Chicago Press, 1991.

Annunzio, Frank (chairman). *The Capitol: A Pictorial History of the Capitol and of the Congress*. Washington, D.C.: U.S. Joint Committee on Printing, 1983.

Anonymous. *Life of John C. Calhoun: Presenting a Condensed History of Political Events, From 1811 to 1843*. New York, NY: Harper and Brothers, 1843.

Appleman, Roy Edgar (ed.). *Abraham Lincoln: From His Own Words and Contemporary Accounts*. Washington, D.C.: U.S. Department of the Interior, National Park Service, 1942.

Arnett, Benjamin William (ed.). *Duplicate Copy of the Souvenir From the Afro-American League of Tennessee to Honorable James M. Ashley of Ohio*. Philadelphia, PA: A. M. E. Church, 1894.

Arnold, Isaac Newton. *The History of Abraham Lincoln, and the Overthrow of Slavery*. Chicago, IL: Clarke and Co., 1866.

Aron, Stephen. *American Confluence: The Missouri Frontier from Borderland to Border State*.

Bloomington, IN: Indiana University Press, 2009.
Ashdown Paul, and Edward Caudill. *The Myth of Nathan Bedford Forrest*. 2005. Lanham, MD: Rowman and Littlefield, 2006 ed.
Ashe, Captain Samuel A'Court. *A Southern View of the Invasion of the Southern States and War of 1861-1865*. 1935. Crawfordville, GA: Ruffin Flag Co., 1938 ed.
Ashworth, John. *Slavery, Capitalism, and Politics in the Antebellum Republic*. 2 vols. New York, NY: Cambridge University Press, 2007.
Astor, Gerald. *The Right to Fight: A History of African Americans in the Military*. Cambridge, MA: Da Capo, 2001.
Baepler, Paul (ed.). *White Slaves, African Masters: An Anthology of American Barbary Captivity Narratives*. Chicago, IL: University of Chicago Press, 1999.
Bailey, Anne C. *African Voices of the Atlantic Slave Trade: Beyond the Silence and the Shame*. Boston, MA: Beacon Press, 2005.
Bailey, Hugh C. *Hinton Rowan Helper: Abolitionist-Racist*. Tuscaloosa, AL: University of Alabama Press, 1965.
Bailyn, Bernard, Robert Dallek, David Brion Davis, David Herbert Donald, John L. Thomas, and Gordon S. Wood. *The Great Republic: A History of the American People*. 1977. Lexington, MA: D. C. Heath and Co., 1992 ed.
Baker, George E. (ed.). *The Works of William H. Seward*. 5 vols. 1861. Boston, MA: Houghton, Mifflin and Co., 1888 ed.
Baker, Jean H. *Mary Todd Lincoln: A Biography*. New York, NY: W. W. Norton and Co., 1989.
Ballagh, James Curtis. *White Servitude in the Colony of Virginia: A Study of the System of Indentured Servitude in the American Colonies*. Whitefish, MT: Kessinger Publishing, 2004.
Bancroft, Frederic. *The Life of William H. Seward*. 2 vols. New York, NY: Harper and Brothers, 1900.
———. *Slave-Trading in the Old South*. Baltimore, MD: J. H. Furst, 1931.
Bancroft, Frederic, and William A. Dunning (eds.). *The Reminiscences of Carl Schurz*. 3 vols. New York, NY: McClure Co., 1909.
Barnes, Gilbert H., and Dwight L. Dumond (eds.). *Letters of Theodore Dwight Weld, Angelina Grimké Weld and Sarah Grimké, 1822-1844*. 2 vols. New York, NY: D. Appleton-Century Co., 1934.
Barney, William L. *Flawed Victory: A New Perspective on the Civil War*. New York, NY: Praeger Publishers, 1975.
Barrow, Charles Kelly, J. H. Segars, and R. B. Rosenburg (eds.). *Black Confederates*. 1995. Gretna, LA: Pelican Publishing Co., 2001 ed.
———. *Forgotten Confederates: An Anthology About Black Southerners*. Saint Petersburg, FL: Southern Heritage Press, 1997.
Bartlett, Irving H. *John C. Calhoun: A Biography*. New York, NY: W. W. Norton, 1994.
———. *Wendell Phillips: Brahmin Radical*. Boston, MA: Beacon Press, 1961.
Barton, William E. *The Soul of Abraham Lincoln*. New York, NY: George H. Doran, 1920.

Basler, Roy Prentice (ed.). *Abraham Lincoln: His Speeches and Writings*. 1946. New York, NY: Da Capo Press, 2001 ed.
—— (ed.). *The Collected Works of Abraham Lincoln*. 9 vols. New Brunswick, NJ: Rutgers University Press, 1953.
Bateman, William O. *Political and Constitutional Law of the United States of America*. St. Louis, MO: G. I. Jones and Co., 1876.
Baxter, Maurice G. *Henry Clay and the American System*. Lexington, KY: University Press of Kentucky, 2004.
Beard, Charles A., and Birl E. Schultz. *Documents on the State-Wide Initiative, Referendum and Recall*. New York, NY: Macmillan, 1912.
Beard, Charles A., and Mary R. Beard. *The Rise of American Civilization*. 1927. New York, NY: MacMillan, 1930 ed.
Beck, Glenn. *Glenn Beck's Common Sense: The Case Against an Out-of-Control Government, Inspired by Thomas Paine*. New York, NY: Threshold, 2009.
Belz, Herman. *Abraham Lincoln, Constitutionalism, and Equal Rights in the Civil War Era*. Bronx, NY: Fordham University Press, 1997.
Bennett, Lerone. *Forced into Glory: Abraham Lincoln's White Dream*. Chicago, IL: Johnson Publishing Co., 2000.
Benton, Thomas Hart. *Thirty Years View; or A History of the Working of the American Government for Thirty Years, From 1820 to 1850*. 2 vols. New York, NY: D. Appleton and Co., 1854.
Bergeron, Paul H., Stephen V. Ash, and Jeanette Keith. *Tennesseans and Their History*. Knoxville, TN: University of Tennessee Press, 1999.
Bergh, Albert Ellery (ed.). *The Writings of Thomas Jefferson*. 20 vols. Washington, D.C.: Thomas Jefferson Memorial Association of the U.S., 1905.
Bernhard, Winfred E. A. (ed.). *Political Parties in American History* (Vol. 1, 1789-1828). New York, NY: G. P. Putnams' Sons, 1973.
Berry, Stephen William. *House of Abraham: Lincoln and the Todds, A Family Divided by War*. New York, NY: Houghton Mifflin, 2007.
Berry, Wendell. *The Unsettling of America: Culture and Agriculture*. San Francisco, CA: Sierra Club Books, 1996.
Berwanger, Eugene H. *The Frontier Against Slavery: Western Anti-Negro Prejudice and the Slavery Extension Controversy*. 1967. Urbana, IL: University of Illinois Press, 1971 ed.
Beschloss, Michael R. *Presidential Courage: Brave Leaders and How They Changed America, 1789-1989*. New York, NY: Simon and Schuster, 2007.
Beveridge, Albert Jeremiah. *Abraham Lincoln: 1809-1858*. 2 vols. Boston, MA: Houghton Mifflin, 1928.
Black, Chauncey F. *Essays and Speeches of Jeremiah S. Black*. New York, NY: D. Appleton and Co., 1886.
Black, Robert W., Col. *Cavalry Raids of the Civil War*. Mechanicsburg, PA: Stackpole, 2004.
Blackerby, Hubert R. *Blacks in Blue and Gray*. New Orleans, LA: Portals Press, 1979.
Blair, William A., and Karen Fisher Younger (eds.). *Lincoln's Proclamation: Emancipation*

Reconsidered. Chapel Hill, NC: University of North Carolina Press, 2009.
Blassingame, John W. *The Slave Community: Plantation Life in the Antebellum South.* 1972. New York, NY: Oxford University Press, 1974 ed.
Bledsoe, Albert Taylor. *An Essay on Liberty and Slavery.* Philadelphia, PA: J. B. Lippincott and Co., 1856.
——. *A Theodicy; or a Vindication of the Divine Glory, as Manifested in the Constitution and Government of the Moral World.* New York, NY: Carlton and Porter, 1856.
——. *Is Davis a Traitor; or Was Secession a Constitutional Right Previous to the War of 1861?* Richmond, VA: Hermitage Press, 1907.
Blee, Kathleen M. *Women of the Klan: Racism and Gender in the 1920s.* 1991. Berkeley, CA: University of California Press, 1992 ed.
Blight, David W. *Frederick Douglass' Civil War: Keeping Faith in Jubilee.* 1989. Baton Rouge, LA: Louisiana State University Press, 1991 ed.
Bliss, William Dwight Porter (ed.). *The Encyclopedia of Social Reform.* New York, NY: Funk and Wagnalls, 1897.
Boatner, Mark Mayo. *The Civil War Dictionary.* 1959. New York, NY: David McKay Co., 1988 ed.
Bode, Carl, and Malcolm Cowley (eds.). *The Portable Emerson.* 1941. Harmondsworth, UK: Penguin, 1981 ed.
Boorstin, Daniel J. *The Discoverers: A History of Man's Search to Know His World and Himself.* 1983. New York, NY: Vintage, 1985 ed.
Boritt, Gabor S. *Lincoln and the Economics of the America Dream.* Urbana, IL: University of Illinois Press, 1994.
——. (ed.) *Lincoln's Generals.* New York, NY: Oxford University Press, 1995.
——. *The Gettysburg Gospel: The Lincoln Speech That Nobody Knows.* New York, NY: Simon and Schuster, 2006.
Bowen, Catherine Drinker. *John Adams and the American Revolution.* 1949. New York, NY: Grosset and Dunlap, 1977 ed.
Bowers, John. *Chickamauga and Chattanooga: The Battles that Doomed the Confederacy.* New York, NY: HarperCollins, 1994.
Bowman, John S. (ed.). *The Civil War Day by Day: An Illustrated Almanac of America's Bloodiest War.* 1989. New York, NY: Dorset Press, 1990 ed.
——. *Encyclopedia of the Civil War* (ed.). 1992. North Dighton, MA: JG Press, 2001 ed.
Bowman, Virginia McDaniel. *Historic Williamson County: Old Homes and Sites.* 1971. Franklin, TN: Territorial Press, 1989 ed.
Bradford, James C. (ed.). *Atlas of American Military History.* New York, NY: Oxford University Press, 2003.
Bradford, Ned (ed.). *Battles and Leaders of the Civil War.* 1-vol. ed. New York, NY: Appleton-Century-Crofts, 1956.
Bradley, Michael R. *Nathan Bedford Forrest's Escort and Staff.* Gretna, LA: Pelican Publishing Co., 2006.
——. *Forrest's Fighting Preacher: David Campbell Kelley of Tennessee.* Charleston, SC: The History Press, 2011.
Brady, Cyrus Townsend. *Three Daughters of the Confederacy.* New York, NY: G. W.

Dillingham, 1905.
Brady, James S. (ed.). *Ronald Reagan: A Man True to His Word - A Portrait of the 40th President of the United States In His Own Words*. Washington D.C.: National Federation of Republican Women, 1984.
Brandt, Robert S. *Touring the Middle Tennessee Backroads*. 1995. Winston-Salem, NC: John F. Blair, 2005 ed.
Brent, Linda. *The Deeper Wrong; or Incidents in the Life of a Slave Girl, Written by Herself*. London, UK: W. Tweedie, 1862.
Brinkley, Alan. *The Unfinished Nation: A Concise History of the American People*. 1993. Boston, MA: McGraw-Hill, 2000 ed.
Brockett, Linus Pierpont. *The Life and Times of Abraham Lincoln, Sixteenth President of the United States*. Philadelphia, PA: Bradley and Co., 1865.
Brooks, Gertrude Zeth. *First Ladies of the White House*. Chicago, IL: Charles Hallberg and Co., 1969.
Brooksher, William R., and David K. Snider. *Glory at a Gallop: Tales of the Confederate Cavalry*. 1993. Gretna, LA: Pelican Publishing Co., 2002 ed.
Brown, Dee. *Bury My Heart at Wounded Knee: An Indian History of the American West*. 1970. New York, NY: Owl Books, 1991 ed.
Brown, Rita Mae. *High Hearts*. New York, NY: Bantam, 1987.
Brown, William Wells. *The Black Man: His Antecedents, His Genius, and His Achievements*. New York, NY: Thomas Hamilton, 1863.
Browne, Ray B., and Lawrence A. Kreiser, Jr. *The Civil War and Reconstruction*. Westport, CT: Greenwood Publishing, 2003.
Bruce, Philip Alexander. *The Plantation Negro As a Freeman*. New York, NY: G. P. Putnam's Sons, 1889.
Brunner, Borgna (ed.). *The Time Almanac* (1999 ed.). Boston, MA: Information Please, 1998.
Bryan, William Jennings. *The Commoner Condensed*. New York, NY: Abbey Press, 1902.
Buchanan, James. *The Works of James Buchanan*. 12 vols. Philadelphia, PA: J. B. Lippincott Co., 1911.
Buchanan, Patrick J. *A Republic, Not an Empire: Reclaiming America's Destiny*. Washington, D.C.: Regenry, 1999.
Buckingham, James Silk. *The Slave States of America*. 2 vols. London, UK: Fisher, Son, and Co., 1842.
Buckley, Gail. *American Patriots: The Story of Blacks in the Military From the Revolution to Desert Storm*. New York, NY: Random House, 2001.
Bultman, Bethany. *Redneck Heaven: Portrait of a Vanishing Culture*. New York, NY: Bantam, 1996.
Burkhimer, Michael. *Lincoln's Christianity*. Yardley, PA: Westholme, 2007.
Burlingame, Michael. *The Inner World of Abraham Lincoln*. Champaign, IL: University of Illinois Press, 1997.
Burns, James MacGregor, and Jack Walter Peltason. *Government by the People: The Dynamics of American National, State, and Local Government*. 1952. Englewood Cliffs, NJ: Prentice-Hall, 1964 ed.

Burns, James MacGregor, Jack Walter Peltason, Thomas E. Cronin, David B. Magleby, and David M. O'Brien. *Government by the People* (National Version). 1952. Upper Saddle River, NJ: Prentice Hall, 2001-2002 ed.

Burton, Orville Vernon. *The Age of Lincoln*. New York, NY: Hill and Wang, 2007.

Burton, Robert. *The Anatomy of Melancholy*. 3 vols. 1621. London, UK: George Bell and Sons, 1896 ed.

Bushnell, Horace. *The Census and Slavery, Thanksgiving Discourse, Delivered in the Chapel at Clifton Springs, New York, November 29, 1860*. Hartford, CT: L. E. Hunt, 1860.

Butler, Benjamin Franklin. *Butler's Book (Autobiography and Personal Reminiscences of Major-General Benjamin F. Butler: A Review of His Legal, Political, and Military Career)*. Boston, MA: A. M. Thayer and Co., 1892.

Butler, Lindley S., and Alan D. Watson (eds.). *The North Carolina Experience: An Interpretive and Documentary History*. Chapel Hill, NC: University of North Carolina Press, 1984.

Butler, Trent C. (ed.). *Holman Bible Dictionary*. Nashville, TN: Holman Bible Publishers, 1991.

Calvert, Thomas H. *The Federal Statutes Annotated*. 10 vols. Northport, NY: Edward Thompson, 1905.

Cannon, Devereaux D., Jr. *The Flags of the Confederacy: An Illustrated History*. Memphis, TN: St. Luke's Press, 1988.

Carey, Matthew, Jr. (ed.). *The Democratic Speaker's Hand-Book*. Cincinnati, OH: Miami Print and Publishing Co., 1868.

Carlton, Frank Tracy. *Organized Labor in America*. New York, NY: D. Appleton and Co., 1920.

Carnahan, Burrus M. *Lincoln on Trial: Southern Civilians and the Law of War*. Lexington, KY: University Press of Kentucky, 2010.

Carpenter, Stephen D. *Logic of History: Five Hundred Political Texts, Being Concentrated Extracts of Abolitionism*. Madison, WI: published by author, 1864.

Carter, Arthur B. *The Tarnished Cavalier: Major General Earl Van Dorn, CSA*. Knoxville, TN: University of Tennessee Press, 1999.

Cartmell, Donald. *Civil War 101*. New York, NY: Gramercy, 2001.

Carwardine, Richard. *Lincoln: A Life of Purpose and Power*. New York, NY: Vintage, 2006.

Cash, W. J. *The Mind of the South*. 1941. New York, NY: Vintage, 1969 ed.

Catton, Bruce. *The Coming Fury* (Vol. 1). 1961. New York, NY: Washington Square Press, 1967 ed.

———. *Terrible Swift Sword* (Vol. 2). 1963. New York, NY: Pocket Books, 1967 ed.

———. *A Stillness at Appomattox* (Vol. 3). 1953. New York, NY: Pocket Books, 1966 ed.

Celeste, Sister Mary. *The Old World's Gifts to the New*. 1932. Long Prairie, MN: Neumann Press, 1999 ed.

Chadwick, Bruce. *The Two American Presidents: A Dual Biography of Abraham Lincoln and Jefferson Davis*. New York, NY: Citadel, 1999.

Chambers, Robert (ed.). *The Book of Days: A Miscellany of Popular Antiquities in Connection*

    with the Calender. 2 vols. London, UK: W. & R. Chambers, 1883.
Channing, Steven A. *Confederate Ordeal: The Southern Home Front.* 1984. Morristown, NJ: Time-Life Books, 1989 ed.
Chernow, Ron. *Alexander Hamilton.* New York, NY: Penguin, 2004.
Chesnut, Mary. *A Diary From Dixie: As Written by Mary Boykin Chesnut, Wife of James Chesnut, Jr., United States Senator from South Carolina, 1859-1861, and afterward an Aide to Jefferson Davis and a Brigadier-General in the Confederate Army.* (Isabella D. Martin and Myrta Lockett Avary, eds.). New York, NY: D. Appleton and Co., 1905 ed.
———. *Mary Chesnut's Civil War.* 1860-1865 (Woodward, Comer Vann, ed.). New Haven, CT: Yale University Press, 1981 ed.
Chodes, John. *Destroying the Republic: Jabez Curry and the Re-Education of the Old South.* New York, NY: Algora, 2005.
Christian, George L. *Abraham Lincoln: An Address Delivered Before R. E. Lee Camp, No. 1 Confederate Veterans at Richmond, VA, October 29, 1909.* Richmond, VA: L. H. Jenkins, 1909.
Cimprich, John. *Fort Pillow, a Civil War Massacre, and Public Memory.* Baton Rouge, LA: Louisiana State University Press, 2005.
Cisco, Walter Brian. *States Rights Gist: A South Carolina General of the Civil War.* Shippensburg, PA, White Mane Publishing Co., 1991.
———. *War Crimes Against Southern Civilians.* Gretna, LA: Pelican Publishing Co., 2007.
Civil War Book of Lists. 1993. Edison, NJ: Castle Books, 2004 ed.
Civil War Society, The. *Civil War Battles: An Illustrated Encyclopedia.* 1997. New York, NY: Gramercy, 1999 ed.
———. *The Civil War Society's Encyclopedia of the Civil War.* New York, NY: Wings Books, 1997.
Clark, L. Pierce. *Lincoln: A Psycho-Biography.* New York, NY: Charles Scribner's Sons, 1933.
Clarke, James W. *The Lineaments of Wrath: Race, Violent Crime, and American Culture.* 1998. New Brunswick, NJ: Transaction, 2001 ed.
Cluskey, Michael W. (ed.). *The Political Text-Book, or Encyclopedia.* Philadelphia, PA: Jas. B. Smith, 1859 ed.
Cmiel, Kenneth. *Democratic Eloquence: The Fight Over Popular Speech in Nineteenth-Century America.* Berkeley, CA: University of California Press, 1990.
Coe, Joseph. *The True American.* Concord, NH: I. S. Boyd, 1840.
Coffin, Charles Carleton. *Abraham Lincoln.* New York, NY: Harper and Brothers, 1893.
Coit, Margaret L. *John C. Calhoun: American Portrait.* Boston, MA: Sentry, 1950.
Collier, Christopher, and James Lincoln Collier. *Decision in Philadelphia: The Constitutional Convention of 1787.* 1986. New York, NY: Ballantine, 1987 ed.
Collins, Elizabeth. *Memories of the Southern States.* Taunton, UK: J. Barnicott, 1865.
Collins, John A. (ed.). *The Anti-Slavery Picknick: A Collection of Speeches, Poems, Dialogues and Songs Intended for Use in Schools and Anti-Slavery Meetings.* Boston, MA: H. W. Williams, 1842.

Commager, Henry Steele, and Erik Bruun (eds.). *The Civil War Archive: The History of the Civil War in Documents.* 1950. New York, NY: Black Dog and Leventhal, 1973 ed.

Connelly, Donald B. *John M. Schofield and the Politics of Generalship.* Chapel Hill, NC: University of North Carolina Press, 2006.

Conner, Frank. *The South Under Siege, 1830-2000: A History of the Relations Between the North and the South.* Newnan, GA: Collards Publishing Co., 2002.

Conway, Moncure Daniel. *Testimonies Concerning Slavery.* London, UK: Chapman and Hall, 1865.

Cooke, Alistair. *Alistair Cooke's America.* 1973. New York, NY: Alfred A. Knopf, 1984 ed.

Cooke, John Esten. *A Life of General Robert E. Lee.* New York, NY: D. Appleton and Co., 1871.

Cooley, Henry S. *A Study of Slavery in New Jersey.* Baltimore, MD: Johns Hopkins University Press, 1896.

Cooper, William J., Jr. *Jefferson Davis, American.* New York, NY: Vintage, 2000.

———. (ed.). *Jefferson Davis: The Essential Writings.* New York, NY: Random House, 2003.

Copley, John M. *A Sketch of the Battle of Franklin, Tenn.; with Reminiscences of Camp Douglas.* Austin, TX: self-published, 1893.

Cornish, Dudley Taylor. *The Sable Arm: Black Troops in the Union Army, 1861-1865.* 1956. Lawrence, KS: University Press of Kansas, 1987 ed.

Coulter, Ann. *Guilty: Liberal "Victims" and Their Assault on America.* New York, NY: Three Rivers Press, 2009.

Cox, Hank H. *Lincoln and the Sioux Uprising of 1862.* Nashville, TN: Cumberland House, 2005.

Cox, Jacob Dolson. *The Battle of Franklin, Tennessee, November 30, 1864.* New York, NY: Charles Scribner's Sons, 1897.

Cox, LaWanda. *Lincoln and Black Freedom: A Study in Presidential Leadership.* Columbia, SC: University of South Carolina Press, 1994.

Crallé, Richard Kenner. (ed.). *The Works of John C. Calhoun.* 6 vols. New York: NY: D. Appleton and Co., 1853-1888.

Craven, John J. *Prison Life of Jefferson Davis.* New York: NY: Carelton, 1866.

Crawford, Samuel Wylie. *The Genesis of the Civil War: The Story of Sumter, 1860-1861.* New York, NY: Charles L. Webster and Co., 1887.

Crocker, H. W., III. *The Politically Incorrect Guide to the Civil War.* Washington, D.C.: Regnery, 2008.

Cromie, Alice Hamilton. *A Tour Guide to the Civil War: The Complete State-by-State Guide to Battlegrounds, Landmarks, Museums, Relics, and Sites.* 1964. Nashville, TN: Rutledge Hill Press, 1990 ed.

Cromwell, John Wesley. *The Negro in American History: Men and Women Eminent in the Evolution of the American of African Descent.* Washington, D.C.: American Negro Academy, 1914.

Cross, F. L., and F. A. Livingston (eds.). *The Oxford Dictionary of the Christian Church.*

1957. London, UK: Oxford University Press, 1974 ed.
Cross, Harold A. *They Sleep Beneath the Mockingbird: Mississippi Burial Sites and Biographies of Confederate Generals*. Saint Petersburg, FL: Southern Heritage Press, 1997.
Crutchfield, James A. *Franklin: A Photographic Recollection*. 2 vols. Franklin, TN: Canaday Enterprises, 1996.
——. *Timeless Tennesseans*. Huntsville, AL: Strode, 1984.
Crutchfield, James A., and Robert Holladay. *Franklin: Tennessee's Handsomest Town*. Franklin, TN: Hillsboro Press, 1999.
Cummins, Joseph. *Anything For a Vote: Dirty Tricks, Cheap Shots, and October Surprises in U.S. Presidential Campaigns*. Philadelphia, PA: Quirk, 2007.
Current, Richard N. *The Lincoln Nobody Knows*. 1958. New York, NY: Hill and Wang, 1963 ed.
——. (ed.) *The Confederacy (Information Now Encyclopedia)*. 1993. New York, NY: Macmillan, 1998 ed.
Curry, Leonard P. *Blueprint for Modern America: Nonmilitary Legislation of the First Civil War Congress*. Nashville, TN: Vanderbilt University Press, 1968.
Curti, Merle, Willard Thorpe, and Carlos Baker (eds.). *American Issues: The Social Record*. 1941. Chicago, IL: J. B. Lippincott, 1960 ed.
Curtin, Philip D. *The Atlantic Slave Trade: A Census*. Madison, WI: The University of Wisconsin Press, 1969.
——. *The Rise and Fall of the Plantation Complex: Essays in Atlantic History*. 1990. Cambridge, UK: Cambridge University Press, 1999 ed.
Curtis, George Ticknor. *Life of James Buchanan: Fifteenth President of the United States*. 2 vols. New York, NY: Harper and Brothers, 1883.
Curtis, William Eleroy. *Abraham Lincoln*. Philadelphia, PA: J. B. Lippincott Co., 1902.
Cushman, Horatio Bardwell. *History of the Choctaw, Chickasaw and Natchez Indians*. Greenville, TX: Headlight Printing House, 1899.
Custer, George Armstrong. *Wild Life on the Plains and Horrors of Indian Warfare*. St. Louis, MO: Excelsior Publishing, 1891.
Dabney, Robert Lewis. *A Defense of Virginia and the South*. Dahlonega, GA: Confederate Reprint Co., 1999.
Daniel, John M. *The Richmond Examiner During the War*. New York, NY: John M. Daniel, 1868.
Daniel, John W. *Life and Reminiscences of Jefferson Davis by Distinguished Men of His Time*. Baltimore, MD: R. H. Woodward, and Co., 1890.
Daniel, Larry J. *Cannoneers in Gray: The Field Artillery of the Army of Tennessee*. Tuscaloosa, AL: University of Alabama Press, 2005.
Darwin, Charles. *On the Origin of Species By Means of Natural Selection*. London, UK: John Murray, 1866.
Daugherty, James. *Abraham Lincoln*. 1943. New York, NY: Scholastic Book Services, 1966 ed.
Davidson, Basil. *The African Slave Trade*. 1961. Boston, MA: Back Bay Books, 1980 ed.
Davis, Jefferson. *The Rise and Fall of the Confederate Government*. 2 vols. New York, NY: D. Appleton and Co., 1881.

———. *A Short History of the Confederate States of America*. New York, NY: Belford, 1890.
Davis, Kenneth C. *Don't Know Much About the Civil War: Everything You Need to Know About America's Greatest Conflict But Never Learned*. 1996. New York, NY: HarperCollins, 1997 ed.
Davis, Michael. *The Image of Lincoln in the South*. Knoxville, TN: University of Tennessee Press, 1971.
Davis, Varina. *Jefferson Davis: Ex-President of the Confederate States of America - A Memoir by His Wife*. 2 vols. New York, NY: Belford Co., 1890.
Davis, William C. *Jefferson Davis: The Man and His Hour*. New York, NY: HarperCollins, 1991.
———. *An Honorable Defeat: The Last Days of the Confederate Government*. New York, NY: Harcourt, 2001.
———. *Look Away: A History of the Confederate States of America*. 2002. New York, NY: Free Press, 2003 ed.
Davenport, Robert R. *Roots of the Rich and Famous: Real Cases of Unlikely Lineage*. Dallas, TX: Taylor Publishing Co., 1998.
Dawson, Sarah Morgan. *A Confederate Girl's Diary*. London, UK: William Heinemann, 1913.
Dean, Henry Clay. *Crimes of the Civil War, and Curse of the Funding System*. Baltimore, MD: William T. Smithson, 1869.
De Angelis, Gina. *It Happened in Washington, D.C.* Guilford, CT: Globe Pequot Press, 2004.
DeCaro, Louis A., Jr. *Fire From the Midst of You: A Religious Life of John Brown*. New York, NY: New York University Press, 2002.
Deems, Edward Mark. *Holy-Days and Holidays: A Treasury of Historical Material, Sermons in Full and Brief, Suggestive Thoughts, and Poetry*. New York, NY: Funk and Wagnalls, 1902.
De Forest, John William. *A Volunteer's Adventures: A Union Captain's Record of the Civil War*. 1946. North Haven, CT: Archon, 1970 ed.
DeGregorio, William A. *The Complete Book of U.S. Presidents*. 1984. New York, NY: Barricade, 1993 ed.
Delbanco, Andrew. *The Portable Abraham Lincoln*. New York, NY: Penguin, 1992.
Deloria, Vine, Jr. *Custer Died for Your Sins: An Indian Manifesto*. 1969. New York, NY: Avon, 1973 ed.
Denney, Robert E. *The Civil War Years: A Day-by-Day Chronicle of the Life of a Nation*. 1992. New York, NY: Sterling Publishing, 1994 ed.
Denson, John V. (ed.). *Reassessing the Presidency: The Rise of the Executive State and the Decline of Freedom*. Auburn, AL: Mises Institute, 2001.
Derosa, Marshall L. *The Confederate Constitution of 1861: An Inquiry into American Constitutionalism*. Columbia, MO: University of Missouri Press, 1991.
Derry, Joseph T. *Story of the Confederate States, or, History of the War for Southern Independence*. Richmond, VA: B. F. Johnson, 1898.
Desty, Robert. *The Constitution of the United States*. San Francisco, CA: Sumner Whitney and Co., 1881.

Diamond, Jared. *Guns, Germs, and Steel: The Fate of Human Societies*. 1997. New York, NY: W. W. Norton, 1999 ed.

Dicey, Edward. *Six Months in the Federal States*. 2 vols. London, UK: Macmillan and Co., 1863.

DiLorenzo, Thomas J. "The Great Centralizer: Abraham Lincoln and the War Between the States." *The Independent Review*, Vol. 3, No. 2, Fall 1998, pp. 243-271.

———. *The Real Lincoln: A New Look at Abraham Lincoln, His Agenda, and an Unnecessary War*. Three Rivers, MI: Three Rivers Press, 2003.

———. *Lincoln Unmasked: What You're Not Supposed to Know About Dishonest Abe*. New York, NY: Crown Forum, 2006.

———. *Hamilton's Curse: How Jefferson's Archenemy Betrayed the American Revolution—and What It Means for America Today*. New York, NY: Crown Forum, 2008.

DiLorenzo, Thomas J., and Joseph A. Morris. *Abraham Lincoln: Friend or Foe of Freedom?* Chicago, IL: Heartland Institute, 2008.

Dinkins, James. *1861 to 1865: Personal Recollections and Experiences in the Confederate Army, by an "Old Johnnie"*. Cincinnati, OH: Robert Clarke, 1897.

Doddridge, Joseph. *Notes on the Settlement and Indian Wars of the Western Parts of Virginia and Pennsylvania, From 1763 to 1783, Inclusive*. Albany, NY: Joel Munsell, 1876.

Dodge, Daniel Kilham. *Abraham Lincoln: Master of Words*. New York, NY: D. Appleton and Co., 1924.

Donald, David Herbert. *Lincoln Reconsidered: Essays on the Civil War Era*. 1947. New York, NY: Vintage Press, 1989 ed.

———. (ed.). *Why the North Won the Civil War*. 1960. New York, NY: Collier, 1962 ed.

———. *Lincoln*. New York, NY: Simon and Schuster, 1995.

Douglas, Henry Kyd. *I Rode With Stonewall: The War Experiences of the Youngest Member of Jackson's Staff*. 1940. Chapel Hill, NC: University of North Carolina Press, 1968 ed.

Douglass, Frederick. *Narrative of the Life of Frederick Douglass: An American Slave*. 1845. New York, NY: Signet, 1997 ed.

———. *The Life and Times of Frederick Douglass, From 1817 to 1882*. London, UK: Christian Age Office, 1882.

Drake, Edwin L. (ed.). *The Annals of the Army of Tennessee and Early Western History, Including a Chronological Summary of Battles and Engagements in the Western Armies of the Confederacy*. Nashville, TN: A. D. Haynes (printer), 1878.

Drescher, Seymour, and Stanley L. Engerman (eds.). *A Historical Guide to World Slavery*. New York, NY: Oxford University Press, 1998.

Du Bois, William Edward Burghardt. *Darkwater: Voices From Within the Veil*. New York, NY: Harcourt, Brace and Howe, 1920.

DuBose, John Witherspoon. *General Joseph Wheeler and the Army of Tennessee*. New York, NY: Neale Publishing Co., 1912.

Duff, Mountstuart E. Grant. *Notes From a Diary, 1851-1872*. 2 vols. London, UK: John Murray, 1897.

Duke, Basil W. *Reminiscences of General Basil W. Duke, C.S.A.* New York, NY:

Doubleday, Page and Co., 1911.
Dunbar, Rowland (ed.). *Jefferson Davis, Constitutionalist: His Letters, Papers, and Speeches.* 10 vols. Jackson, MS: Mississippi Department of Archives and History, 1923.
Durden, Robert F. *The Gray and the Black: The Confederate Debate on Emancipation.* Baton Rouge, LA: Louisiana State University Press, 1972.
Early, Jubal A. *A Memoir of the Last Year of the War for Independence in the Confederate States of America.* Lynchburg, VA: Charles W. Button, 1867.
Eaton, Clement. *A History of the Southern Confederacy.* 1945. New York, NY: Free Press, 1966 ed.
——. *Jefferson Davis.* New York, NY: Free Press, 1977.
Eaton, John, and Ethel Osgood Mason. *Grant, Lincoln and the Freedmen: Reminiscences of the Civil War, With Special Reference to the Work of the Contrabands and Freedmen of the Mississippi Valley.* New York, NY: Longmans, Green, and Co., 1907.
Edmonds, Franklin Spencer. *Ulysses S. Grant.* Philadelphia, PA: George W. Jacobs and Co., 1915.
Egerton, Douglas R. *Year of Meteors: Stephen Douglas, Abraham Lincoln, and the Election that Brought on the Civil War.* New York, NY: Bloomsbury Press, 2010.
Eicher, John, and David Eicher. *Civil War High Commands.* Stanford, CA: Stanford University Press, 2001.
Elliot, Jonathan. *The Debates in the Several State Conventions on the Adoption of the Federal Constitution, As Recommended by the General Convention at Philadelphia in 1787.* 5 vols. Philadelphia, PA: J. B. Lippincott, 1891.
Elliott, E. N. *Cotton is King, and Pro-Slavery Arguments: Comprising the Writings of Hammond, Harper, Christy, Stringfellow, Hodge, Bledsoe, and Cartwright, on this Important Subject.* Augusta, GA: Pritchard, Abbott and Loomis, 1860.
Ellis, Joseph J. *American Sphinx: The Character of Thomas Jefferson.* 1996. New York, NY: Vintage, 1998 ed.
——. *Founding Brothers: The Revolutionary Generation.* 2000. New York, NY: Vintage, 2002 ed.
Eltis, David. *The Rise of African Slavery in the Americas.* Cambridge, UK: Cambridge University Press, 2000.
Emerson, Bettie Alder Calhoun. *Historic Southern Monuments: Representative Memorials of the Heroic Dead of the Southern Confederacy.* New York, NY: Neale Publishing Co., 1911.
Emerson, Ralph Waldo. *The Complete Works of Ralph Waldo Emerson.* 12 vols. 1878. Boston, MA: Houghton, Mifflin and Co., 1904 ed.
——. *Journals of Ralph Waldo Emerson.* 10 vols. Edward Waldo Emerson and Waldo Emerson Forbes, eds. Boston, MA: Houghton, Mifflin and Co., 1910.
——. *The Journals and Miscellaneous Notebooks of Ralph Waldo Emerson.* 16 vols. Cambridge, MA: Belknap Press, 1975.
Emison, John Avery. *Lincoln Über Alles: Dictatorship Comes to America.* Gretna, LA: Pelican Publishing Co., 2009.
Encyclopedia Britannica: A New Survey of Universal Knowledge. 1768. Chicago, IL/London, UK: Encyclopedia Britannica, 1955 ed.

Epstein, Daniel Mark. *The Lincolns: Portrait of a Marriage*. New York, NY: Ballantine, 2008.

———. *Lincoln's Men: The President and His Private Secretaries*. New York, NY: HarperCollins, 2009.

Escott, Paul D. (ed.). *North Carolinians in the Era of the Civil War and Reconstruction*. Chapel Hill, NC: University of North Carolina Press, 2008.

———. *"What Shall We Do with the Negro?": Lincoln, White Racism, and Civil War America*. Charlottesville, VA: University of Virginia Press, 2009.

Essah, Patience. *A House Divided: Slavery and Emancipation in Delaware, 1638-1865*. Charlottesville, VA: University Press of Virginia, 1996.

Etulain, Richard W. (Ed.). *Lincoln Looks West: From the Mississippi to the Pacific*. Carbondale, IL: Southern Illinois University Press, 2010.

Evans, Clement Anselm (ed.). *Confederate Military History: A Library of Confederate States History, in Twelve Volumes, Written By Distinguished Men of the South*. 12 vols. Atlanta, GA: Confederate Publishing Co., 1899.

Evans, Eli N. *Judah P. Benjamin: The Jewish Confederate*. 1988. New York, NY: Free Press, 1989 ed.

Evans, Lawrence B. (ed.). *Writings of George Washington*. New York, NY: G. P. Putnam's Sons, 1908.

Faragher, John Mack. *Sugar Creek: Life on the Illinois Prairie*. New Haven, CT: Yale University Press, 1986.

Farrar, Victor John. *The Annexation of Russian America to the United States*. Washington D.C.: W. F. Roberts, 1937.

Farrow, Anne, Joel Lang, and Jennifer Frank. *Complicity: How the North Promoted, Prolonged, and Profited From Slavery*. New York, NY: Ballantine, 2005.

Faulkner, William. *The Unvanquished*. 1934. New York, NY: Vintage, 1966 ed.

Faust, Patricia L. (ed.). *Historical Times Illustrated Encyclopedia of the Civil War*. New York, NY: Harper and Row, 1986.

Fay, Edwin Hedge. *This Infernal War: The Confederate Letters of Edwin H. Fay*. Austin, TX: University of Texas Press, 1958.

Fehrenbacher, Don E. (ed.). *Abraham Lincoln: A Documentary Portrait Through His Speeches and Writings*. New York, NY: Signet, 1964.

———. *Lincoln in Text and Context: Collected Essays*. Stanford, CA: Stanford University press, 1987.

———. (ed.) *Abraham Lincoln: Speeches and Writings, 1859-1865*. New York, NY: Library of America, 1989.

———. *The Slaveholding Republic: An Account of the United States Government's Relations to Slavery*. New York, NY: Oxford University Press, 2002.

Fehrenbacher, Don E., and Virginia Fehrenbacher (eds). *Recollected Works of Abraham Lincoln*. Stanford, CA: Stanford University Press, 1996.

Ferris, Marcie Cohen, and Mark I. Greenberg (eds.). *Jewish Roots in Southern Soil: A New History*. Waltham, MA: Brandeis University Press, 2006.

Fields, Annie (ed.) *Life and Letters of Harriet Beecher Stowe*. Cambridge, MA: Riverside Press, 1897.

Findlay, Bruce, and Esther Findlay. *Your Rugged Constitution: How America's House of Freedom is Planned and Built.* 1950. Stanford, CA: Stanford University Press, 1951 ed.
Finkelman, Paul. *Dred Scott v. Sanford: A Brief History With Documents.* Boston, MA: Bedford Books, 1997.
Fite, Emerson David. *Social and Industrial Conditions in the North During the Civil War.* New York, NY: Macmillan, 1910.
——. *The Presidential Election of 1860.* New York, NY: MacMillan, 1911.
Fleming, Walter Lynwood. *Civil War and Reconstruction in Alabama.* New York, NY: Macmillan, 1905.
Flood, Charles Bracelen. *1864: Lincoln At the Gates of History.* New York, NY: Simon and Schuster, 2009.
Fogel, Robert William. *Without Consent or Contract: The Rise and Fall of American Slavery.* New York, NY: W. W. Norton, 1989.
Fogel, Robert William, and Stanley L. Engerman. *Time On the Cross: The Economics of American Negro Slavery.* Boston, MA: Little, Brown, and Co., 1974.
Foley, John P. (ed.). *The Jeffersonian Cyclopedia.* New York, NY: Funk and Wagnalls, 1900.
Foner, Eric. *Free Soil, Free Labor, Free Men: The Ideology of the Republican Party Before the Civil War.* New York, NY: Oxford University Press, 1970.
——. *Reconstruction: America's Unfinished Revolution, 1863-1877.* 1988. New York, NY: Harper and Row, 1989 ed.
Foote, Shelby. *The Civil War: A Narrative, Fort Sumter to Perryville, Vol. 1.* 1958. New York, NY: Vintage, 1986 ed.
——. *The Civil War: A Narrative, Fredericksburg to Meridian, Vol. 2.* 1963. New York, NY: Vintage, 1986 ed.
——. *The Civil War: A Narrative, Red River to Appomattox, Vol. 3.* 1974. New York, NY: Vintage, 1986 ed.
Ford, Paul Leicester (ed.). *The Works of Thomas Jefferson.* 12 vols. New York, NY: G. P. Putnam's Sons, 1904.
Ford, Worthington Chauncey (ed.). *A Cycle of Adams Letters.* 2 vols. Boston, MA: Houghton Mifflin, 1920.
Forman, S. E. *The Life and Writings of Thomas Jefferson.* Indianapolis, IN: Bowen-Merrill, 1900.
Fornieri, Joseph (ed.). *The Language of Liberty: The Political Speeches and Writings of Abraham Lincoln.* Washington, D.C.: Regnery, 2009.
Förster, Stig, and Jörg Nagler (eds.). *On the Road to Total War: The American Civil War and the German Wars of Unification, 1861-1871.* 1997. Cambridge, UK: Cambridge University Press, 2002 ed.
Foster, John W. *A Century of American Diplomacy.* Boston, MA: Houghton, Mifflin and Co., 1901.
Fowler, John D. *The Confederate Experience Reader: Selected Documents and Essays.* New York, NY: Routledge, 2007.
Fowler, William Chauncey. *The Sectional Controversy; or Passages in the Political History of*

the United States, Including the Causes of the War Between the Sections. New York, NY: Charles Scribner, 1864.
Fox, Gustavus Vasa. Confidential Correspondence of Gustavus Vasa Fox, Assistant Secretary of the Navy, 1861-1865. 2 vols. 1918. New York, NY: Naval History Society, 1920 ed.
Fox-Genovese, Elizabeth. Within the Plantation Household: Black and White Women of the Old South (Gender and American Culture). Chapel Hill, NC: University of North Carolina Press, 1988.
Franklin, Benjamin. The Complete Works of Benjamin Franklin. 10 vols. New York, NY: G. P. Putnam's Sons, 1887.
Franklin, John Hope. Reconstruction After the Civil War. Chicago, IL: University of Chicago Press, 1961.
Fredrickson, George M. The Black Image in the White Mind: The Debate on Afro-American Character and Destiny, 1817-1914. New York, NY: Harper and Row, 1971.
——. Big Enough to Be Inconsistent: Abraham Lincoln Confronts Slavery and Race. Cambridge, MA: Harvard University Press, 2008.
Freiling, Thomas. Walking With Lincoln: Spiritual Strength From America's Favorite President. Grand Rapids, MI: Revell, 2009.
Fremantle, Arthur James. Three Months in the Southern States, April-June, 1863. New York, NY: John Bradburn, 1864.
French, Samuel Gibbs. Two Wars: An Autobiography of General Samuel G. French, an Officer in the Armies of the United States and the Confederate States, a Graduate From the U.S. Military Academy, West Point, 1843 (Mexican War; War Between the States; A Diary; Reconstruction Period, His Experience; Incidents, Reminiscences, etc.). Nashville, TN: Confederate Veteran, 1901.
Friedman, Saul S. Jews and the American Slave Trade. New Brunswick, NJ: Transaction, 2000.
Furguson, Ernest B. Freedom Rising: Washington in the Civil War. 2004. New York, NY: Vintage, 2005 ed.
Furnas, J. C. The Americans: A Social History of the United States, 1587-1914. New York, NY: G. P. Putnam's Sons, 1969.
Galenson, David W. White Servitude in Colonial America. New York, NY: Cambridge University Press, 1981.
Garland, Hugh A. The Life of John Randolph of Roanoke. New York, NY: D. Appleton and Co., 1874.
Garraty, John A. (ed.). Historical Viewpoints: Notable Articles From American Heritage, Vol. One to 1877. 1970. New York, NY: Harper and Row, 1979 ed.
Garraty, John A., and Robert A. McCaughey. A Short History of the American Nation. 1966. New York, NY: HarperCollins, 1989 ed.
Garrison, Webb B. Civil War Trivia and Fact Book. Nashville, TN: Rutledge Hill Press, 1992.
——. The Lincoln No One Knows: The Mysterious Man Who Ran the Civil War. Nashville, TN: Rutledge Hill Press, 1993.
——. Civil War Curiosities: Strange Stories, Oddities, Events, and Coincidences. Nashville, TN:

Rutledge Hill Press, 1994.
——. *The Amazing Civil War*. Nashville, TN: Rutledge Hill Press, 1998.
Garrison, Wendell Phillips, and Francis Jackson Garrison. *William Lloyd Garrison, 1805-1879*. 4 vols. New York, NY: Century Co., 1889.
Garrison, William Lloyd. *Thoughts on African Colonization*. Boston, MA: Garrison and Knapp, 1832.
Gates, Henry Louis, Jr. (ed.) *The Classic Slave Narratives*. New York, NY: Mentor, 1987.
Gates, Henry Louis, Jr., and Donald Yacovone (eds). *Lincoln on Race and Slavery*. Princeton, NJ: Princeton University Press, 2009.
Genovese, Eugene D. *Roll, Jordan, Roll: The World the Slaves Made*. New York, NY: Pantheon, 1974.
Gerster, Patrick, and Nicholas Cords (eds.). *Myth and Southern History*. 2 vols. 1974. Champaign, IL: University of Illinois Press, 1989 ed.
Gienapp, William E. *Abraham Lincoln and Civil War America: A Biography*. Oxford, UK: Oxford University Press, 2002.
Gilmore, James Roberts. *Personal Recollections of Abraham Lincoln and the Civil War*. Boston, MA: L. C. Page and Co., 1898.
Golay, Michael. *A Ruined Land: The End of the Civil War*. New York, NY: John Wiley and Sons, 1999.
Gordon, Armistead Churchill. *Figures From American History: Jefferson Davis*. New York, NY: Charles Scribner's Sons, 1918.
Gower, Herschel, and Jack Allen (eds.). *Pen and Sword: The Life and Journals of Randal W. McGavock*. Nashville, TN: Tennessee Historical Commission, 1959.
Gragg, Rod. *The Illustrated Confederate Reader: Extraordinary Eyewitness Accounts by the Civil War's Southern Soldiers and Civilians*. New York, NY: Gramercy Books, 1989.
Graham, John Remington. *A Constitutional History of Secession*. Gretna, LA: Pelican Publishing Co., 2003.
——. *Blood Money: The Civil War and the Federal Reserve*. Gretna, LA: Pelican Publishing Co., 2006.
Grant, Arthur James. *Greece in the Age of Pericles*. London, UK: John Murray, 1893.
Grant, Ulysses Simpson. *Personal Memoirs of U. S. Grant*. 2 vols. 1885-1886. New York, NY: Charles L. Webster and Co., 1886.
Gray, Robert, Rev. (compiler). *The McGavock Family: A Genealogical History of James McGavock and His Descendants, from 1760 to 1903*. Richmond, VA: W. E. Jones, 1903.
Gray, Thomas R. *The Confessions of Nat Turner: The Leader of the Late Insurrection in Southampton, Virginia*. Richmond, VA: Thomas R. Gray, 1831.
Greeley, Horace (ed.). *The Writings of Cassius Marcellus Clay*. New York, NY: Harper and Brothers, 1848.
——. *A History of the Struggle for Slavery Extension or Restriction in the United States From the Declaration of Independence to the Present Day*. New York, NY: Dix, Edwards and Co., 1856.
——. *The American Conflict: A History of the Great Rebellion in the United States, 1861-1865*.

2 vols. Hartford, CT: O. D. Case and Co., 1867.
Green, Constance McLaughlin. *Eli Whitney and the Birth of American Technology.* Boston, MA: Little, Brown, and Co., 1956.
——. *Washington: A History of the Capital, 1800-1950.* 1962. Princeton, NJ: Princeton University Press, 1976 ed.
Greenberg, Martin H., and Charles G. Waugh (eds.). *The Price of Freedom: Slavery and the Civil War—Vol. 1, The Demise of Slavery.* Nashville, TN: Cumberland House, 2000.
Greene, Lorenzo Johnston. *The Negro in Colonial New England, 1620-1776.* New York, NY: Columbia University Press, 1942.
Greenhow, Rose O'Neal. *My Imprisonment and the First Year of Abolition Rule at Washington.* London, UK: Richard Bentley, 1863.
Grimsley, Mark. *The Hard Hand of War: Union Military Policy Toward Southern Civilians, 1861-1865.* 1995. Cambridge, UK: Cambridge University Press, 1997 ed.
Grissom, Michael Andrew. *Southern By the Grace of God.* 1988. Gretna, LA: Pelican Publishing Co., 1995 ed.
Groom, Winston. *Shrouds of Glory - From Atlanta to Nashville: The Last Great Campaign of the Civil War.* New York, NY: Grove Press, 1995.
Guelzo, Allen C. *Abraham Lincoln: Redeemer President.* Cambridge, UK: William B. Eerdmans, 1999.
——. *Abraham Lincoln As a Man of Ideas.* Carbondale, IL: Southern Illinois University Press, 2009.
Gwatkin, H. M., and J. P. Whitney (eds.). *The Cambridge Medieval History, Vol. 2: The Rise of the Saracens and the Foundation of the Western Empire.* New York, NY: Macmillan, 1913.
Hacker, Louis Morton. *The Shaping of the American Tradition.* New York, NY: Columbia University Press, 1947.
Haggard, Dixie Ray (ed.). *African Americans in the Nineteenth Century: People and Perspectives.* Santa Barbara, CA: ABC-Clio, 2010.
Hall, B. C., and C. T. Wood. *The South: A Two-step Odyssey on the Backroads of the Enchanted Land.* New York, NY: Touchstone, 1996.
Hall, Kermit L. (ed). *The Oxford Companion to the Supreme Court of the United States.* New York, NY: Oxford University Press, 1992.
Hamblin, Ken. *Pick a Better Country: An Unassuming Colored Guy Speaks His Mind About America.* New York, NY: Touchstone, 1997.
Hamilton, Alexander, James Madison, and John Jay. *The Federalist Papers.* New York, NY: Signet Classics, 2003.
Hamilton, Neil A. *Rebels and Renegades: A Chronology of Social and Political Dissent in the United States.* New York, NY: Routledge, 2002.
Hanchett, William. *Out of the Wilderness: The Life of Abraham Lincoln.* Urbana, IL: University of Illinois Press, 1994.
Hannity, Sean. *Let Freedom Ring: Winning the War of Liberty Over Liberalism.* New York, NY: HarperCollins, 2002.
Hansen, Harry. *The Civil War: A History.* 1961. Harmondsworth, UK: Mentor, 1991

ed.

Harding, Samuel Bannister. *The Contest Over the Ratification of the Federal Constitution in the State of Massachusetts*. New York, NY: Longmans, Green, and Co., 1896.

Harper, William, James Henry Hammond, William Gilmore Simms, and Thomas Roderick Dew. *The Pro-Slavery Argument, As Maintained by the Most Distinguished Writers of the Southern States*. Charleston, SC: Walker, Richards and Co., 1852.

Harrell, David Edwin, Jr., Edwin S. Gaustad, John B. Boles, Sally Foreman Griffith, Randall M. Miller, and Randall B. Woods. *Unto a Good Land: A History of the American People*. Grand Rapids, MI: William B. Eerdmans, 2005.

Harris, Joel Chandler. *Stories of Georgia*. New York, NY: American Book Co., 1896.

Harris, Norman Dwight. *The History of Negro Servitude in Illinois*. Chicago, IL: A. C. McClurg and Co., 1904.

Harris, William C. *Lincoln's Rise to the Presidency*. Lawrence, KS: University Press of Kansas, 2007.

Harrison, Peleg D. *The Stars and Stripes and Other American Flags*. 1906. Boston, MA: Little, Brown, and Co., 1908 ed.

Hartzell, Josiah. *The Genesis of the Republican Party*. Canton, OH: n.p., 1890.

Harwell, Richard B. (ed.). *The Confederate Reader: How the South Saw the War*. 1957. Mineola, NY: Dover, 1989 ed.

Hattaway, Herman, and Archer Jones. *How the North Won: A Military History of the Civil War*. 1983. Champaign, IL: University of Illinois Press, 1991 ed.

Hawthorne, Julian (ed.). *Orations of American Orators*. 2 vols. New York, NY: Colonial Press, 1900.

Hawthorne, Julian, James Schouler, and Elisha Benjamin Andrews. *United States, From the Discovery of the North American Continent Up to the Present Time*. 9 vols. New York, NY: Co-operative Publication Society, 1894.

Hay, Thomas Robson. *Hood's Tennessee Campaign*. 1929. Dayton, OH: Morningside Bookshop, 2003 ed.

Hayden, Horace Edwin. *Virginia Genealogies: A Genealogy of the Glassell Family of Scotland and Virginia*. 1885. Wilkes-Barre, PA: N.P., 1891 ed.

Haygood, Atticus G. *Our Brother in Black: His Freedom and His Future*. Nashville, TN: M. E. Church, 1896.

Hedrick, Joan D. (ed.). *The Oxford Harriet Beecher Stowe Reader*. New York, NY: Oxford University Press, 1999.

Heidler, David S., and Jeanne T. Heidler. *Henry Clay: The Essential American*. New York, NY: Random House, 2010.

Helper, Hinton Rowan. *The Impending Crisis of the South: How to Meet It*. New York, NY: A. B. Burdick, 1860.

———. *Compendium of the Impending Crisis of the South*. New York, NY: A. B. Burdick, 1860.

———. *Nojoque: A Question for a Continent*. New York, NY: George W. Carleton, 1867.

———. *The Negroes in Negroland: The Negroes in America; and Negroes Generally*. New York, NY: George W. Carlton, 1868.

——. *Oddments of Andean Diplomacy and Other Oddments*. St. Louis, MO: W. S. Bryan, 1879.
Henderson, George Francis Robert. *Stonewall Jackson and the American Civil War*. 2 vols. London, UK: Longmans, Green, and Co., 1919.
Henry, Robert Selph (ed.). *The Story of the Confederacy*. 1931. New York, NY: Konecky and Konecky, 1999 ed.
——. *As They Saw Forrest: Some Recollections and Comments of Contemporaries*. 1956. Wilmington, NC: Broadfoot Publishing Co., 1991 ed.
——. *First with the Most: Forrest*. New York, NY: Konecky and Konecky, 1992.
Henson, Josiah. *Father Henson's Story of His Own Life*. Boston, MA: John P. Jewett and Co., 1858.
Herndon, William H., and Jesse W. Weik. *Abraham Lincoln: The True Story of a Great Life*. 2 vols. New York, NY: D. Appleton and Co., 1892.
Hertz, Emanuel. *Abraham Lincoln: A New Portrait*. 2 Vols. New York, NY: H. Liveright, 1931.
——. *The Hidden Lincoln*. New York, NY: Blue Ribbon Works, 1940.
Hervey, Anthony. *Why I Wave the Confederate Flag, Written By a Black Man: The End of Niggerism and the Welfare State*. Oxford, UK: Trafford Publishing, 2006.
Hesseltine, William B. *Lincoln and the War Governors*. New York, NY: Alfred A. Knopf, 1948.
Hey, David. *The Oxford Guide to Family History*. Oxford, UK: Oxford University Press, 1993.
Hickey, William. *The Constitution of the United States*. Philadelphia, PA: T. K. and P. G. Collins, 1853.
Highsmith, Carol M. and Ted Landphair. *Civil War Battlefields and Landmarks: A Photographic Tour*. New York, NY: Random House, 2003.
Hildreth, Richard. *The White Slave: Another Picture of Slave Life in America*. Boston, MA: Adamant Media Corp., 2001.
Hinkle, Don. *Embattled Banner: A Reasonable Defense of the Confederate Battle Flag*. Paducah, KY: Turner Publishing Co., 1997.
Hitler, Adolf. *Mein Kampf*. 2 vols. 1925, 1926. New York: NY: Reynal and Hitchcock, 1941 English translation ed.
Hoffman, Michael A., II. *They Were White and They Were Slaves: The Untold History of the Enslavement of Whites in Early America*. Dresden, NY: Wiswell Ruffin House, 1993.
Hofstadter, Richard. *The American Political Tradition, and the Men Who Made It*. New York, NY: Alfred A. Knopf, 1948.
Holland, Jesse J. *Black Men Built the Capitol: Discovering African-American History in and Around Washington, D.C.* Guilford, CT: The Globe Pequot Press, 2007.
Holland, Josiah Gilbert. *The Life of Abraham Lincoln*. Springfield, MA: Gurdon Bill, 1866.
Holland, Rupert Sargent (ed.). *Letters and Diary of Laura M. Towne: Written From the Sea Islands of South Carolina, 1862-1884*. Cambridge, MA: Riverside Press, 1912.
Holzer, Harold (ed.). *The Lincoln-Douglas Debates: The First Complete, Unexpurgated Text*.

1993. Bronx, NY: Fordham University Press, 2004 ed.

Hoobler, James A. *A Guide to Historic Nashville, Tennessee.* Charleston, SC: The History Press, 2008.

Hood, John Bell. *Advance and Retreat: Personal Experiences in the United States and Confederate States Armies.* New Orleans, LA: G. T. Beauregard, 1880.

Hopkins, Luther W. *From Bull Run to Appomattox: A Boy's View.* Baltimore, MD: Fleet-McGinley Co., 1914.

Horn, Stanley F. *Invisible Empire: The Story of the Ku Klux Klan, 1866-1871.* 1939. Montclair, NJ: Patterson Smith, 1969 ed.

——. *The Decisive Battle of Nashville.* 1956. Baton Rouge, LA: Louisiana State University Press, 1991 ed.

Horwitz, Tony. *Confederates in the Attic: Dispatches From the Unfinished Civil War.* 1998. New York, NY: Vintage, 1999 ed.

House Documents, 64th Congress, 1st Session, December 6, 1915, to September 8, 1916, Vol. 145. Washington, D.C.: Government Printing Office, 1916.

Howe, Daniel Wait. *Political History of Secession.* New York, NY: G. P. Putnam's Sons, 1914.

Howe, Henry. *Historical Collections of Virginia.* Charleston, SC: William R. Babcock, 1852.

Howe, M. A. DeWolfe (ed.). *Home Letters of General Sherman.* New York, NY: Charles Scribner's Sons, 1909.

Hubbard, John Milton. *Notes of a Private.* St. Louis, MO: Nixon-Jones, 1911.

Hunt, John Gabriel (ed.). *The Essential Abraham Lincoln.* Avenel, NJ: Portland House, 1993.

Hurmence, Belinda (ed.). *Before Freedom, When I Can Just Remember: Twenty-seven Oral Histories of Former South Carolina Slaves.* 1989. Winston-Salem, NC: John F. Blair, 2002 ed.

Hurst, Jack. *Nathan Bedford Forrest: A Biography.* 1993. New York, NY: Vintage, 1994 ed.

Ingersoll, Thomas G., and Robert E. O'Connor. *Politics and Structure: Essential of American National Government.* North Scituate, MA: Duxbury Press, 1979.

Isaacson, Walter (ed.). *Profiles in Leadership: Historians on the Elusive Quality of Greatness.* New York, NY: W. W. Norton and Co., 2010.

Jaffa, Harry V. *Crisis of the House Divided: An Interpretation of the Issues in the Lincoln-Douglas Debates.* 1959. Chicago, IL: University of Chicago Press, 2009 ed.

Jahoda, Gloria. *The Trail of Tears: The Story of the American Indian Removals, 1813-1855.* 1975. New York, NY: Wings Book, 1995 ed.

Jaquette, Henrietta Stratton (ed.). *South After Gettysburg: Letters of Cornelia Hancock, 1863-1868.* Philadelphia, PA: University of Pennsylvania Press, 1937.

Jefferson, Thomas. *Notes on the State of Virginia.* Boston, MA: H. Sprague, 1802.

——. *Thomas Jefferson's Farm Book.* (Edwin Morris Betts, ed.). Charlottesville, VA: Thomas Jefferson Memorial Foundation, 1999.

Jenkins, John S. *The Life of James Knox Polk, Late President of the United States.* Auburn,

NY: James M. Alden, 1850.
Jensen, Merrill. *The New Nation: A History of the United States During the Confederation, 1781-1789*. New York, NY: Vintage, 1950.
———. *The Articles of Confederation: An Interpretation of the Social-Constitutional History of the American Revolution, 1774-1781*. Madison, WI: University of Wisconsin Press, 1959.
Jimerson, Randall C. *The Private Civil War: Popular Thought During the Sectional Conflict*. Baton Rouge, LA: Louisiana State University Press, 1988.
Johannsen, Robert Walter. *Lincoln, the South, and Slavery: The Political Dimension*. Baton Rouge, LA: Louisiana State University Press, 1991.
Johnson, Adam Rankin. *The Partisan Rangers of the Confederate States Army*. Louisville, KY: George G. Fetter, 1904.
Johnson, Benjamin Heber. *Making of the American West: People and Perspectives*. Santa Barbara, CA: ABC-Clio, 2007.
Johnson, Clint. *The Politically Incorrect Guide to the South (and Why It Will Rise Again)*. Washington, D.C.: Regnery, 2006.
Johnson, Ludwell H. *North Against South: The American Iliad, 1848-1877*. 1978. Columbia, SC: Foundation for American Education, 1993 ed.
Johnson, Michael, and James L. Roark. *Black Masters: A Free Family of Color in the Old South*. New York, NY: W.W. Norton, 1984.
Johnson, Oliver. *William Lloyd Garrison and His Times*. 1879. Boston, MA: Houghton Mifflin and Co., 1881 ed.
Johnson, Richard W. *A Soldier's Reminiscences in Peace and War*. Philadelphia, PA: J. B. Lippincott Co., 1886.
Johnson, Robert Underwood (ed.). *Battles and Leaders of the Civil War*. 4 vols. New York, NY: The Century Co., 1884-1888.
Johnson, Thomas Cary. *The Life and Letters of Robert Lewis Dabney*. Richmond, VA: Presbyterian Committee of Publication, 1903.
Jones, Howard. *Abraham Lincoln and a New Birth of Freedom: The Union and Slavery in the Diplomacy of the Civil War*. Lincoln, NE: University of Nebraska Press, 1999.
Jones, John Beauchamp. *A Rebel War Clerk's Diary at the Confederate States Capital*. 2 vols. in 1. Philadelphia, PA: J. B. Lippincott and Co., 1866.
Jones, John William. *Personal Reminiscences, Anecdotes, and Letters of Gen. Robert E. Lee*. New York, NY: D. Appleton and Co., 1874.
Jones, Wilmer L. *Generals in Blue and Gray*. 2 vols. Westport, CT: Praeger, 2004.
Jordan, Don, and Michael Walsh. *White Cargo: The Forgotten History of Britain's White Slaves in America*. New York, NY: New York University Press, 2008.
Jordan, Ervin L. *Black Confederates and Afro-Yankees in Civil War Virginia*. Charlottesville, VA: University Press of Virginia, 1995.
Jordan, Thomas, and John P. Pryor. *The Campaigns of General Nathan Bedford Forrest and of Forrest's Cavalry*. New Orleans, LA: Blelock and Co., 1868.
Joslyn, Mauriel Phillips (ed.). *A Meteor Shining Brightly: Essays on Major General Patrick R. Cleburne*. Macon GA: Mercer University Press, 2000.
Julian, George Washington. *Speeches on Political Questions*. New York, NY: Hurd and

Houghton, 1872.
Kane, Joseph Nathan. *Facts About the Presidents: A Compilation of Biographical and Historical Data.* 1959. New York, NY: Ace, 1976 ed.
Katcher, Philip. *The Civil War Source Book.* 1992. New York, NY: Facts on File, 1995 ed.
——. *Brassey's Almanac: The American Civil War.* London, UK: Brassey's, 2003.
Kautz, August Valentine. *Customs of Service for Non-Commissioned Officers and Soldiers (as Derived from Law and Regulations and Practised in the Army of the United States).* Philadelphia, PA: J. B. Lippincott and Co., 1864.
Keckley, Elizabeth. *Behind the Scenes, or Thirty Years a Slave, and Four Years in the White House.* New York, NY: G. W. Carlton and Co., 1868.
Kelly, Alfred H., Winfred A. Harbison, and Herman Belz. *The American Constitution: Its Origins and Development* (Vol. 2). 1965. New York, NY: W.W. Norton, 1991 ed.
Keneally, Thomas. *Abraham Lincoln.* New York, NY: Viking, 2003.
Kennedy, James Ronald, and Walter Donald Kennedy. *The South Was Right!* Gretna, LA: Pelican Publishing Co., 1994.
——. *Why Not Freedom!: America's Revolt Against Big Government.* Gretna, LA: Pelican Publishing Co., 2005.
——. *Nullifying Tyranny: Creating Moral Communities in an Immoral Society.* Gretna, LA: Pelican Publishing Co., 2010.
Kennedy, Walter Donald. *Myths of American Slavery.* Gretna, LA: Pelican Publishing Co., 2003.
Kennett, Lee B. *Sherman: A Soldier's Life.* 2001. New York, NY: HarperCollins, 2002 ed.
Kettell, Thomas Prentice. *History of the Great Rebellion.* Hartford, CT: L. Stebbins, 1865.
Kinder, Hermann, and Werner Hilgemann. *The Anchor Atlas of World History: From the French Revolution to the American Bicentennial.* 2 vols. Garden City, NY: Anchor, 1978.
King, Charles R. (ed.). *The Life and Correspondence of Rufus King.* 6 vols. New York, NY: G. P. Putnam's Sons, 1897.
King, Edward. *The Great South: A Record of Journeys.* Hartford, CT: American Publishing Co., 1875.
Kinshasa, Kwando Mbiassi. *Black Resistance to the Ku Klux Klan in the Wake of the Civil War.* Jefferson, NC: McFarland and Co., 2006.
Kirkland, Edward Chase. *The Peacemakers of 1864.* New York, NY: Macmillan, 1927.
Klingaman, William K. *Abraham Lincoln and the Road to Emancipation, 1861-1865.* 2001. New York, NY: Penguin, 2002 ed.
Knox, Thomas Wallace. *Camp-Fire and Cotton-Field: Southern Adventure in Time of War - Life With the Union Armies, and Residence on a Louisiana Plantation.* New York, NY: Blelock and Co., 1865.
Koger, Larry. *Black Slaveowners: Free Black Slave Masters in South Carolina, 1790-1860.* Columbia, SC: University of South Carolina Press, 1995.

Kunhardt, Philip B., Peter W. Kunhardt, and Peter W. Kunhardt, Jr. *Looking for Lincoln: The Making of an American Icon*. New York, NY: Borzoi, 2008.
Lamb, Brian, and Susan Swain (eds.). *Abraham Lincoln: Great American Historians on Our Sixteenth President*. New York, NY: PublicAffairs, 2010.
Lamon, Ward Hill. *The Life of Abraham Lincoln: From His Birth to His Inauguration as President*. Boston, MA: James R. Osgood and Co., 1872.
——. *Recollections of Abraham Lincoln: 1847-1865*. Chicago, IL: A. C. McClurg and Co., 1895.
Lang, J. Stephen. *The Complete Book of Confederate Trivia*. Shippensburg, PA: Burd Street Press, 1996.
Lanier, Robert S. (ed.). *The Photographic History of the Civil War*. 10 vols. New York, NY: Review of Reviews Co., 1911.
Lanning, Michael Lee. *The African-American Soldier: From Crispus Attucks to Colin Powell*. 1997. New York, NY: Citadel Press, 2004 ed.
Lapsley, Arthur Brooks (ed.). *The Writings of Abraham Lincoln*. 8 vols. New York, NY: The Lamb Publishing Co., 1906.
Lawrence, William. *Life of Amos A. Lawrence*. Boston, MA: Houghton, Mifflin, and Co., 1899.
Leech, Margaret. *Reveille in Washington, 1860-1865*. 1941. Alexandria, VA: Time-Life Books, 1980 ed.
Lee, Robert E., Jr. *Recollections and Letters of General Robert E. Lee*. New York, NY: Doubleday, Page and Co., 1904.
Lehrman, Lewis E. *Lincoln at Peoria: The Turning Point*. Mechanicsburg, PA: Stackpole, 2008.
Lemay, J. A. Leo, and P. M. Zall (eds.). *Benjamin Franklin's Autobiography: An Authoritative Text, Backgrounds, Criticism*. 1791. New York, NY: W. W. Norton and Co., 1986 ed.
Lemire, Elise. *Black Walden: Slavery and Its Aftermath in Concord, Massachusetts*. Philadelphia, PA: University of Pennsylvania Press, 2009.
Lester, Charles Edwards. *Life and Public Services of Charles Sumner*. New York, NY: U.S. Publishing Co., 1874.
Lester, John C., and D. L. Wilson. *Ku Klux Klan: Its Origin, Growth, and Disbandment*. 1884. New York, NY: Neale Publishing, 1905 ed.
Lewis, Lloyd. *Myths After Lincoln*. 1929. New York, NY: The Press of the Reader's Club, 1941 ed.
LeVert, Suzanne (ed.). *The Civil War Society's Encyclopedia of the Civil War*. New York, NY: Wings Books, 1997.
Levin, Mark R. *Liberty and Tyranny: A Conservative Manifesto*. New York, NY: Threshold, 2009.
Lincoln, Abraham. *The Autobiography of Abraham Lincoln* (selected from the *Complete Works of Abraham Lincoln*, 1894, by John G. Nicolay and John Hay). New York, NY: Francis D. Tandy Co., 1905.
Lincoln, Abraham, and Stephen A. Douglas. *Political Debates Between Abraham Lincoln and Stephen A. Douglas*. Cleveland, OH: Burrows Brothers Co., 1894.

Lind, Michael (ed.). *Hamilton's Republic: Readings in the American Democratic Nationalist Tradition*. New York, NY: Free Press, 1997.

Littell, Eliakim (ed.). *The Living Age*. Seventh Series, Vol. 30. Boston, MA: The Living Age Co., 1906.

Litwack, Leon F. *North of Slavery: The Negro in the Free States, 1790-1860*. Chicago, IL: University of Chicago Press, 1961.

———. *Been in the Storm So Long: The Aftermath of Slavery*. New York, NY: Vintage, 1980.

Livermore, Thomas L. *Numbers and Losses in the Civil War in America, 1861-65*. 1900. Carlisle, PA: John Kallmann, 1996 ed.

Livingstone, William. *Livingstone's History of the Republican Party*. 2 vols. Detroit, MI: William Livingstone, 1900.

Locke, John. *Two Treatises of Government* (Mark Goldie, ed.). 1924. London, UK: Everyman, 1998 ed.

Lodge, Henry Cabot (ed.). *The Works of Alexander Hamilton*. 12 vols. New York, NY: G. P. Putnam's Sons, 1904.

Logan, John Alexander. *The Great Conspiracy: Its Origin and History*. New York, NY: A. R. Hart, 1886.

Logsdon, David R. (ed.). *Eyewitnesses at the Battle of Franklin*. 1988. Nashville, TN: Kettle Mills Press, 2000 ed.

———. *Tennessee Antebellum Trail Guidebook*. Nashville, TN: Kettle Mills Press, 1995.

Long, David E. *The Jewel of Liberty: Abraham Lincoln's Re-election and the End of Slavery*. Mechanicsburg, PA: Stackpole, 2008.

Long, Everette Beach, and Barbara Long. *The Civil War Day by Day: An Almanac, 1861-1865*. 1971. New York, NY: Da Capo Press, 1985 ed.

Lonn, Ella. *Foreigners in the Confederacy*. 1940. Chapel Hill, NC: University of North Carolina Press, 2002 ed.

Loring, William Wing. *A Confederate Soldier in Egypt*. New York, NY: Dodd, Meade and Co., 1884.

Lott, Stanley K. *The Truth About American Slavery*. 2004. Clearwater, SC: Eastern Digital Resources, 2005 ed.

Lowry, Don. *Dark and Cruel War: The Decisive Months of the Civil War, September-December 1864*. New York, NY: Hippocrene, 1993.

Lubbock, Francis Richard. *Six Decades in Texas, or Memoirs of Francis Richard Lubbock, Governor of Texas in War-Time, 1861-1863*. 1899. Austin, TX: Ben C. Jones, 1900 ed.

Ludlow, Daniel H. (ed.). *Encyclopedia of Mormonism: The History, Scripture, Doctrine, and Procedure of the Church of Jesus Christ of Latter-Day Saints*. New York, NY: Macmillan, 1992.

Lytle, Andrew Nelson. *Bedford Forrest and His Critter Company*. New York, NY: G. P. Putnam's Sons, 1931.

MacDonald, William. *Select Documents Illustrative of the History of the United States 1776-1861*. New York, NY: Macmillan, 1897.

Mackay, Charles. *Life and Liberty in America, or Sketches of a Tour in the United States and Canada in 1857-58*. New York, NY: Harper and Brothers, 1859.

Madison, James. *Letters and Other Writings of James Madison, Fourth President of the United States*. 4 vols. Philadelphia, PA: J. B. Lippincott and Co., 1865.
Maihafer, Harry J. *War of Words: Abraham Lincoln and the Civil War Press*. Dulles, VA: Brassey's, 2001.
Main, Jackson Turner. *The Anti-Federalists: Critics of the Constitution, 1781-1788*. 1961. New York, NY: W. W. Norton and Co., 1974 ed.
Malone, Laurence J. *Opening the West: Federal Internal Improvements Before 1860*. Westport, CT: Greenwood Press, 1998.
Mandel, Bernard. *Labor, Free and Slave: Workingmen and the Anti-Slavery Movement in the United States*. New York, NY: Associated Authors, 1955.
Manegold, Catherine S. *The Forgotten History of Slavery in the North*. Princeton, NJ: Princeton University Press, 2010.
Manning, Timothy D., Sr. (ed.) *Lincoln Reconsidered: Conference Reader*. High Point, NC: Heritage Foundation Press, 2006.
Marshall, Jessie Ames. *Private and Official Correspondence of General Benjamin F. Butler During the Period of the Civil War*. 5 vols. Norwood, MA: The Plimpton Press, 1917.
Marten, James. *The Children's Civil War*. Chapel Hill, NC: University of North Carolina Press, 1998.
Martin, Iain C. *The Quotable American Civil War*. Guilford, CT: Lyons Press, 2008.
Martineau, Harriet. *Retrospect of Western Travel*. 3 vols. London, UK: Saunders and Otley, 1838.
Martinez, James Michael. *Carpetbaggers, Cavalry, and the Ku Klux Klan: Exposing the Invisible Empire During Reconstruction*. Lanham, MD: Rowman and Littlefield, 2007.
Martinez, Susan B. *The Psychic Life of Abraham Lincoln*. Franklin Lakes, NJ: New Page Books, 2009.
Masur, Louis P. *The Real War Will Never Get In the Books: Selections From Writers During the Civil War*. New York, NY: Oxford University Press, 1993.
Mathes, Capt. J. Harvey. *General Forrest*. New York, NY: D. Appleton and Co., 1902.
Maury, Dabney Herndon. *Recollections of a Virginian in the Mexican, Indian, and Civil Wars*. New York, NY: Charles Scribner's Sons, 1894.
Mayer, David N. *The Constitutional Thought of Thomas Jefferson*. Charlottesville, VA: University of Virginia Press, 1995.
Mayer, Henry. *All on Fire: William Lloyd Garrison and the Abolition of Slavery*. New York, NY: St. Martin's Press, 1998.
McAfee, Ward M. *Citizen Lincoln*. Hauppauge, NY: Nova History Publications, 2004.
McCabe, James Dabney. *Our Martyred President: The Life and Public Services of Gen. James A. Garfield, Twentieth President of the United States*. Philadelphia, PA: National Publishing Co., 1881.
McClintock, Russell. *Lincoln and the Decision for War: The Northern Response to Secession*. Chapel Hill, NC: University of North Carolina Press, 2008.
McClure, Alexander Kelly. *Abraham Lincoln and Men of War-Times: Some Personal Recollections of War and Politics During the Lincoln Administration*. Philadelphia,

PA: Times Publishing Co., 1892.
——. *Our Presidents and How We Make Them.* New York, NY: Harper and Brothers, 1900.
McCullough, David. *John Adams.* New York, NY: Touchstone, 2001.
McDonald, Forrest. *States' Rights and the Union: Imperium in Imperio, 1776-1876.* Lawrence, KS: University Press of Kansas, 2000.
McDonough, James Lee. *Nashville: The Western Confederacy's Final Gamble.* Knoxville, TN: University of Tennessee Press, 2004.
McDonough, James Lee, and Thomas L. Connelly. *Five Tragic Hours: The Battle of Franklin.* 1983. Knoxville, TN: University of Tennessee Press, 2001 ed.
McElroy, Robert. *Jefferson Davis: The Unreal and the Real.* 1937. New York, NY: Smithmark, 1995 ed.
McFeely, William S. *Yankee Stepfather: General O. O. Howard and the Freedmen - The Story of a Civil War Promise to Former Slaves Made—and Broken.* 1968. New York, NY: W. W. Norton, 1994.
McGehee, Jacob Owen. *Causes That Led to the War Between the States.* Atlanta, GA: A. B. Caldwell, 1915.
McGuire, Hunter, and George L. Christian. *The Confederate Cause and Conduct in the War Between the States.* Richmond, VA: L. H. Jenkins, 1907.
McHenry, George. *The Cotton Trade: Its Bearing Upon the Prosperity of Great Britain and Commerce of the American Republics, Considered in Connection with the System of Negro Slavery in the Confederate States.* London, UK: Saunders, Otley, and Co., 1863.
McIlwaine, Shields. *Memphis Down in Dixie.* New York, NY: E. P. Dutton, 1848.
McKissack, Patricia C., and Frederick McKissack. *Sojourner Truth: Ain't I a Woman?* New York: NY: Scholastic, 1992.
McManus, Edgar J. *A History of Negro Slavery in New York.* Syracuse, NY: Syracuse University Press, 1966.
——. *Black Bondage in the North.* Syracuse, NY: Syracuse University Press, 1973.
McMaster, John Bach. *Our House Divided: A History of the People of the United States During Lincoln's Administration.* 1927. New York, NY: Premier, 1961 ed.
McPherson, Edward. *The Political History of the United States of America, During the Great Rebellion (From November 6, 1860, to July 4, 1864).* Washington, D.C.: Philp and Solomons, 1864.
——. *The Political History of the United States of America, During the Period of Reconstruction, (From April 15, 1865, to July 15, 1870,) Including a Classified Summary of the Legislation of the Thirty-ninth, Fortieth, and Forty-first Congresses.* Washington, D.C.: Solomons and Chapman, 1875.
McPherson, James M. *The Struggle for Equality: Abolitionists and the Negro in the Civil War and Reconstruction.* 1964. Princeton, NJ: Princeton University Press, 1992 ed.
——. *The Negro's Civil War: How American Negroes Felt and Acted During the War for the Union.* 1965. Chicago, IL: University of Illinois Press, 1982 ed.
——. *Battle Cry of Freedom: The Civil War Era.* Oxford, UK: Oxford University Press, 2003.

———. *The Atlas of the Civil War*. Philadelphia, PA: Courage Books, 2005.
McPherson, James M., and the staff of the *New York Times*. *The Most Fearful Ordeal: Original Coverage of the Civil War by Writers and Reporters of the New York Times*. New York, NY: St. Martin's Press, 2004.
McWhiney, Grady, and Judith Lee Hallock. *Braxton Bragg and Confederate Defeat*. 2 vols. Tuscaloosa, AL: University of Alabama Press, 1991.
McWhiney, Grady, and Perry D. Jamieson. *Attack and Die: Civil War Military Tactics and the Southern Heritage*. Tuscaloosa, AL: University of Alabama Press, 1982.
Melish, Joanne Pope. *Disowning Slavery: Gradual Emancipation and 'Race' in New England 1780-1860*. Ithaca, NY: Cornell University Press, 1998.
Meltzer, Milton. *Slavery: A World History*. 2 vols. in 1. 1971. New York, NY: Da Capo Press, 1993 ed.
Meriwether, Elizabeth Avery. *Facts and Falsehoods Concerning the War on the South, 1861-1865*. (Originally written under the pseudonym "George Edmonds.") Memphis, TN: A. R. Taylor, 1904.
Merry, Robert W. *A Country of Vast Designs: James K. Polk, the Mexican War and the Conquest of the American Continent*. New York, NY: Simon and Schuster, 2009.
Message of the President of the United States and Accompanying Documents to the Two Houses of Congress at the Commencement of the Third Session of the 40th Congress. Washington, D.C.: Government Printing Office, 1868.
Metzger, Bruce M., and Michael D. Coogan (eds.). *The Oxford Companion to the Bible*. New York, NY: Oxford University Press, 1993.
Miller, Francis Trevelyan. *Portrait Life of Lincoln*. Springfield, MA: Patriot Publishing Co., 1910.
Miller, John Chester. *The Wolf By the Ears: Thomas Jefferson and Slavery*. 1977. Charlottesville, VA: University Press of Virginia, 1994 ed.
Miller, Marion Mills (ed.). *Great Debates in American History*. 14 vols. New York, NY: Current Literature, 1913.
Miller, Nathan. *Star-Spangled Men: America's Ten Worst Presidents*. New York, NY: Touchstone, 1998.
Miller, William Lee. *Lincoln's Virtues: An Ethical Biography*. New York, NY: Vintage, 2003.
Mills, A. D. Oxford Dictionary of English Place-names. 1991. Oxford, England: Oxford University Press, 1998 ed.
Min, Pyong Gap (ed.). *Encyclopedia of Racism in the United States*. 3 vols. Westport, CT: Greenwood Press, 2005.
Minor, Charles Landon Carter. *The Real Lincoln: From the Testimony of His Contemporaries*. Richmond, VA: Everett Waddey Co., 1904.
Mirabello, Mark. *Handbook for Rebels and Outlaws*. Oxford, UK: Mandrake of Oxford, 2009.
Mish, Frederick C. (ed.). *Webster's Ninth New Collegiate Dictionary*. Springfield, MA: Merriam-Webster, 1984.
Mitchell, Margaret. *Gone With the Wind*. 1936. New York, NY: Avon, 1973 ed.
Mitgang, Herbert (ed.). *Lincoln As They Saw Him*. 1956. New York, NY: Collier, 1962

ed.
Mode, Peter George. *Source Book and Bibliographical Guide for American Church History*. Menasha, WI: Collegiate Press, 1921.
Mode, Robert L. (ed.). *Nashville: Its Character in a Changing America*. Nashville, TN: Vanderbilt University, 1981.
Montgomery, David Henry. *The Student's American History*. 1897. Boston, MA: Ginn and Co., 1905 ed.
Moore, Frank (ed.). *The Rebellion Record: A Diary of American Events*. 12 vols. New York, NY: G. P. Putnam, 1861.
Moore, George Henry. *Notes on the History of Slavery in Massachusetts*. New York, NY: D. Appleton and Co., 1866.
Moorhead, James H. *American Apocalypse: Yankee Protestants and the Civil War, 1860-1869*. New Haven, CT: Yale University Press, 1971.
Morel, Lucas E. *Lincoln's Sacred Effort: Defining Religion's Role in American Self-Government*. Lanham, MD: Lexington Books, 2000.
Morris, Benjamin Franklin (ed.). *The Life of Thomas Morris: Pioneer and Long a Legislator of Ohio, and U.S. Senator from 1833 to 1839*. Cincinnati, OH: Moore, Wilstach, Keys and Overend, 1856.
Morris, Roy, Jr. *The Long Pursuit: Abraham Lincoln's Thirty-Year Struggle with Stephen Douglas for the Heart and Soul of America*. New York, NY: HarperCollins, 2008.
Morris, Thomas D. *Free Men All: The Personal Liberty Laws of the North, 1780-1861*. Baltimore, MD: John Hopkins University Press, 1974.
Morton, John Watson. *The Artillery of Nathan Bedford Forrest's Cavalry*. Nashville, TN: The M. E. Church, 1909.
Moses, John. *Illinois: Historical and Statistical, Comprising the Essential Facts of Its Planting and Growth as a Province, County, Territory, and State* (Vol. 2). Chicago, IL: Fergus Printing Co., 1892.
Mullen, Robert W. *Blacks in America's Wars: The Shift in Attitudes From the Revolutionary War to Vietnam*. 1973. New York, NY: Pathfinder, 1991 ed.
Munford, Beverly Bland. *Virginia's Attitude Toward Slavery and Secession*. 1909. Richmond, VA: L. H. Jenkins, 1914 ed.
Murphy, Jim. *A Savage Thunder: Antietam and the Bloody Road to Freedom*. New York, NY: Margaret K. McElderry, 2009.
Napolitano, Andrew P. *The Constitution in Exile: How the Federal Government has Seized Power by Rewriting the Supreme Law of the Land*. Nashville, TN: Nelson Current, 2006.
Neely, Mark E., Jr. *The Fate of Liberty: Abraham Lincoln and Civil Liberties*. New York, NY: Oxford University Press, 1991.
Neilson, William Allan (ed.). *Webster's Biographical Dictionary*. Springfield, MA: G. and C. Merriam Co., 1943.
Neufeldt, Victoria (ed.). *Webster's New World Dictionary of American English* (3rd college ed.). 1970. New York, NY: Prentice Hall, 1994 ed.
Nevins, Allan. *The Evening Post: A Century of Journalism*. New York, NY: Boni and

Liveright, 1922.
Nicolay, John G., and John Hay (eds.). *Abraham Lincoln: A History*. 10 vols. New York, NY: The Century Co., 1890.
——. *Complete Works of Abraham Lincoln*. 12 vols. 1894. New York, NY: Francis D. Tandy Co., 1905 ed.
——. *Abraham Lincoln: Complete Works*. 12 vols. 1894. New York, NY: The Century Co., 1907 ed.
Nivola, Pietro S., and David H. Rosenbloom (eds.). *Classic Readings in American Politics*. New York, NY: St. Martin's Press, 1986.
Norris, Mary Harriot (ed.). *Sir Walter Scott's Marmion*. Boston, MA: Leach, Shewell, and Sanborn, 1891.
Norwood, Thomas Manson. *A True Vindication of the South*. Savannah, GA: Citizens and Southern Bank, 1917.
Nye, Russel B. *William Lloyd Garrison and the Humanitarian Reformers*. Boston, MA: Little, Brown and Co., 1955.
Oakes, James. *The Radical and the Republican: Frederick Douglass, Abraham Lincoln, and the Triumph of Antislavery Politics*. New York, NY: W. W. Norton, 2008.
Oates, Stephen B. *Abraham Lincoln: The Man Behind the Myths*. New York, NY: Meridian, 1984.
——. *The Approaching Fury: Voices of the Storm, 1820-1861*. New York, NY: Harper Perennial, 1998.
O'Brien, Cormac. *Secret Lives of the U.S. Presidents: What Your Teachers Never Told You About the Men of the White House*. Philadelphia, PA: Quirk, 2004.
——. *Secret Lives of the Civil War: What Your teachers Never Told You About the War Between the States*. Philadelphia, PA: Quirk, 2007.
Oglesby, Thaddeus K. *Some Truths of History: A Vindication of the South Against the Encyclopedia Britannica and Other Maligners*. Atlanta, GA: Byrd Printing, 1903.
Olmsted, Frederick Law. *A Journey in the Seaboard Slave States, With Remarks on Their Economy*. New York, NY: Dix and Edwards, 1856.
——. *A Journey Through Texas; or a Saddle-Trip on the Western Frontier*. New York, NY: Dix and Edwards, 1857.
——. *A Journey in the Back Country*. New York, NY: Mason Brothers, 1860.
——. *The Cotton Kingdom: A Traveler's Observations on Cotton and Slavery in the American Slave States*. 2 vols. London, UK: Sampson Low, Son, and Co., 1862.
Olson, Ted (ed.). *CrossRoads: A Southern Culture Annual*. Macon, GA: Mercer University Press, 2004.
ORA (full title: *The War of the Rebellion: A Compilation of the Official Records of the Union and Confederate Armies*. (Multiple volumes.) Washington, D.C.: Government Printing Office, 1880.
ORN (full title: *Official Records of the Union and Confederate Navies in the War of the Rebellion*). (Multiple volumes.) Washington, D.C.: Government Printing Office, 1894.
Ostergard, Philip L. *The Inspired Wisdom of Abraham Lincoln: How Faith Shaped an American President and Changed the Course of a Nation*. Carol Stream, IL: Tyndale House,

2008.
Owsley, Frank Lawrence. *King Cotton Diplomacy: Foreign Relations of the Confederate States of America*. 1931. Chicago, IL: University of Chicago Press, 1959 ed.
Page, Thomas Nelson. *Robert E. Lee, Man and Soldier*. New York, NY: Charles Scribner's Sons, 1911.
Palin, Sarah. *Going Rogue: An American Life*. New York, NY: HarperCollins, 2009.
Paludan, Phillip Shaw. *The Presidency of Abraham Lincoln*. Lawrence, KS: University Press of Kansas, 1994.
Parker, Bowdoin S. (ed.). *What One Grand Army Post Has Accomplished: History of Edward W. Kinsley Post, No. 113*. Norwood, MA: Norwood Press, 1913.
Parry, Melanie (ed.). *Chambers Biographical Dictionary*. 1897. Edinburgh, Scotland: Chambers Harrap, 1998 ed.
Patrick, Rembert W. *Jefferson Davis and His Cabinet*. Baton Rouge, LA: Louisiana State University Press, 1944.
Paul, Ron. *The Revolution: A Manifesto*. New York, NY: Grand Central Publishing, 2008.
Pearson, Henry Greenleaf. *The Life of John A. Andrew, Governor of Massachusetts, 1861-1865*. 2 vols. Boston, MA: Houghton, Mifflin and Co., 1904.
Perkins, Henry C. *Northern Editorials on Secession*. 2 vols. D. Appleton and Co., 1942.
Perry, James M. *Touched With Fire: Five Presidents and the Civil War Battles That Made Them*. New York, NY: Public Affairs, 2003.
Perry, John C. *Myths and Realities of American Slavery: The True History of Slavery in America*. Shippenburg, PA: Burd Street Press, 2002.
Perry, Mark. *Lift Up Thy Voice: The Grimké Family's Journey From Slaveholders to Civil Rights Leaders*. New York, NY: Penguin, 2001.
Peter, Laurence J., and Raymond Hull *The Peter Principle: Why Things Always Go Wrong*. New York, NY: William Morrow and Co., 1969.
Peterson, Merrill D. (ed.). *James Madison, A Biography in His Own Words*. (First published posthumously in 1840.) New York, NY: Harper and Row, 1974 ed.
——. (ed.). *Thomas Jefferson: Writings, Autobiography, A Summary View of the Rights of British America, Notes on the State of Virginia, Public Papers, Addresses, Messages and Replies, Miscellany, Letters*. New York, NY: Literary Classics, 1984.
——. *Lincoln in American Memory*. New York, NY: Oxford University Press, 1994.
Peterson, Paul R. *Quantrill of Missouri: The Making of a Guerilla Warrior, The Man, the Myth, the Soldier*. Nashville, TN: Cumberland House, 2003.
Phillips, Michael. *White Metropolis: Race, Ethnicity, and Religion in Dallas, 1841-2001*. Austin, TX: University of Texas Press, 2006.
Phillips, Robert S. (ed.). *Funk and Wagnalls New Encyclopedia*. 1971. New York, NY: Funk and Wagnalls, 1979 ed.
Phillips, Ulrich Bonnell. *American Negro Slavery: A Survey of the Supply, Employment and Control of Negro Labor as Determined by the Plantation Régime*. New York, NY: D. Appleton and Co., 1929.
Phillips, Wendell. *Speeches, Letters, and Lectures*. Boston, MA: Lee and Shepard, 1894.
Piatt, Donn. *Memories of the Men Who Saved the Union*. New York, NY: Belford, Clarke,

and Co., 1887.
Piatt, Donn, and Henry V. Boynton. *General George H. Thomas: A Critical Biography*. Cincinnati, OH: Robert Clarke and Co., 1893.
Pickett, George E. *The Heart of a Soldier: As Revealed in the Intimate Letters of General George E. Pickett, CSA*. 1908. New York, NY: Seth Moyle, 1913 ed.
Pickett, William Passmore. *The Negro Problem: Abraham Lincoln's Solution*. New York, NY: G. P. Putnam's Sons, 1909.
Pike, James Shepherd. *The Prostrate State: South Carolina Under Negro Government*. New York, NY: D. Appleton and Co., 1874.
Pinsker, Matthew. *Lincoln's Sanctuary: Abraham Lincoln and the Soldiers' Home*. Oxford, UK: Oxford University Press, 2003.
Pollard, Edward A. *Southern History of the War*. 2 vols. in 1. New York, NY: Charles B. Richardson, 1866.
———. *The Lost Cause*. 1867. Chicago, IL: E. B. Treat, 1890 ed.
———. *The Lost Cause Regained*. New York, NY: G. W. Carlton and Co., 1868.
———. *Life of Jefferson Davis, With a Secret History of the Southern Confederacy, Gathered "Behind the Scenes in Richmond."* Philadelphia, PA: National Publishing Co., 1869.
Post, Lydia Minturn (ed.). *Soldiers' Letters, From Camp, Battlefield and Prison*. New York, NY: Bunce and Huntington, 1865.
Potter, David M. *The Impending Crisis: 1848-1861*. New York, NY: Harper and Row, 1976.
Powell, Edward Payson. *Nullification and Secession in the United States: A History of the Six Attempts During the First Century of the Republic*. New York, NY: G. P. Putnam's Sons, 1897.
Powell, William S. *North Carolina: A History*. 1977. Chapel Hill, NC: University of North Carolina Press, 1988 ed.
Pratt, Harry E. *Concerning Mr. Lincoln: As He Appeared to Letter Writers of His Time*. Springfield, IL: The Abraham Lincoln Association, 1944.
Pritchard, Russ A., Jr. *Civil War Weapons and Equipment*. Guilford, CT: Lyons Press, 2003.
Putnam, Samuel Porter. *400 Years of Free Thought*. New York, NY: Truth Seeker Co., 1894.
Quarles, Benjamin. *The Negro in the Civil War*. 1953. Cambridge, MA: Da Capo Press, 1988 ed.
———. *Lincoln and the Negro*. 1962. Cambridge, MA: Da Capo Press, 1990 ed.
Quintard, Charles Todd. *Dr. Quintard: Chaplain C.S.A. and Second Bishop of Tennessee, Being His Story of the War (1861-1865)*. Sewanee, TN: University Press, 1905.
Quintero, José Agustín, Ambrosio José Gonzales, and Loreta Janeta Velazquez (Phillip Thomas Tucker, ed.). *Cubans in the Confederacy*. Jefferson, NC: McFarland and Co., 2002.
Rable, George C. *The Confederate Republic: A Revolution Against Politics*. Chapel Hill, NC: University of North Carolina Press, 1994.
Ramage, James A. *Rebel Raider: The Life of General John Hunt Morgan*. Lexington, KY:

University Press of Kentucky, 1986.
Randall, James Garfield. *Lincoln: The Liberal Statesman*. New York, NY: Dodd, Mead and Co., 1947.
Randall, James Garfield, and Richard N. Current. *Lincoln the President: Last Full Measure*. 1955. Urbana, IL: University of Illinois Press, 2000 ed.
Randolph, Thomas Jefferson (ed.). *Memoir, Correspondence, and Miscellanies, from the Papers of Thomas Jefferson*. 4 vols. Charlottesville, VA: F. Carr and Co., 1829.
Ransom, Roger L. *Conflict and Compromise: The Political Economy of Slavery, Emancipation, and the American Civil War*. Cambridge, UK: Cambridge University Press, 1989.
Rawle, William. *A View of the Constitution of the United States of America*. Philadelphia, PA: Philip H. Nicklin, 1829.
Rayner, B. L. *Sketches of the Life, Writings, and Opinions of Thomas Jefferson*. New York, NY: Alfred Francis and William Boardman, 1832.
Reaney, P. H., and R. M. Wilson. *A Dictionary of English Surnames*. 1958. Oxford, UK: Oxford University Press, 1997 ed.
Reid, Richard M. *Freedom for Themselves: North Carolina's Black Soldiers in the Era of the Civil War*. Chapel Hill, NC: University of North Carolina Press, 2008.
Remsburg, John B. *Abraham Lincoln: Was He a Christian?* New York, NY: The Truth Seeker Co., 1893.
Reports of Committees of the Senate of the United States (for the Thirty-eighth Congress). Washington, D.C.: Government Printing Office, 1864.
Report of the Joint Committee on Reconstruction (at the First Session, Thirty-ninth Congress). Washington, D.C.: Government Printing Office, 1866.
Reports of Committees of the Senate of the United States (for the Second Session of the Forty-second Congress). Washington, D.C.: Government Printing Office, 1872.
Report of the Joint Select Committee to Inquire into the Condition of Affairs in the Late Insurrectionary States. Washington, D.C.: Government Printing Office, 1872.
Report of the Twenty-first Annual Meeting of the American Bar Association, Held at Saratoga Springs, New York, August 17-19, 1898. Philadelphia, PA: Dando Printing and Publishing Co., 1898.
Reuter, Edward Byron. *The Mulatto in the United States*. Boston, MA: Gorham Press, 1918.
Rhodes, James Ford. *History of the United States from the Compromise of 1850 to the Final Restoration of Home Rule at the South in 1877*. 7 vols. 1895. New York, NY: Macmillan Co., 1907 ed.
Rice, Allen Thorndike (ed.). *The North American Review*, Vol. 227. New York, NY: D. Appleton and Co., 1879.
———. *Reminiscences of Abraham Lincoln, by Distinguished Men of His Time*. New York, NY: North American Review, 1888.
Rich, Burdett A., and Henry P. Farnham (eds.). *Lawyers' Reports, Annotated* (Book 22). Rochester, NY: The Lawyers' Co-Operative Publishing, Co., 1894.
Richardson, James Daniel (ed.). *A Compilation of the Messages and Papers of the Confederacy*. 2 vols. Nashville, TN: United States Publishing Co., 1905.

Ridley, Bromfield Lewis. *Battles and Sketches of the Army of Tennessee.* Mexico, MO: Missouri Printing and Publishing Co., 1906.

Riley, Franklin Lafayette (ed.). *Publications of the Mississippi Historical Society.* Oxford, MS: The Mississippi Historical Society, 1902.

———. *General Robert E. Lee After Appomattox.* New York, NY: MacMillan Co., 1922.

Riley, Russell Lowell. *The Presidency and the Politics of Racial Inequality.* New York, NY: Columbia University Press, 1999.

Rives, John (ed.). *Abridgement of the Debates of Congress: From 1789 to 1856* (Vol. 13). New York, NY: D. Appleton and Co., 1860.

Roberts, Paul M. *United States History: Review Text.* 1966. New York, NY: Amsco School Publications, 1970 ed.

Roberts, R. Philip. *Mormonism Unmasked: Confronting the Contradictions Between Mormon Beliefs and True Christianity.* Nashville, TN: Broadman and Holman, 1998.

Robertson, James I., Jr. *Soldiers Blue and Gray.* 1988. Columbia, SC: University of South Carolina Press, 1998 ed.

Rockwell, Llewellyn H., Jr. "Genesis of the Civil War." Website: www.lewrockwell.com/rockwell/civilwar.html.

Rogers, Joel Augustus. *Africa's Gift to America: The Afro-American in the Making and Saving of the United States.* St. Petersburg, FL: Helga M. Rogers, 1961.

———. *The Ku Klux Spirit.* 1923. Baltimore, MD: Black Classic Press, 1980 ed.

Rosen, Robert N. *The Jewish Confederates.* Columbia, SC: University of South Carolina Press, 2000.

Rosenbaum, Robert A. (ed). *The New American Desk Encyclopedia.* 1977. New York, NY: Signet, 1989 ed.

Rosenbaum, Robert A., and Douglas Brinkley (eds.). *The Penguin Encyclopedia of American History.* New York, NY: Viking, 2003.

Rothschild, Alonzo. *"Honest Abe": A Study in Integrity Based on the Early Life of Abraham Lincoln.* Boston, MA: Houghton Mifflin Co., 1917.

Rouse, Adelaide Louise (ed.). *National Documents: State Papers So Arranged as to Illustrate the Growth of Our Country From 1606 to the Present Day.* New York, NY: Unit Book Publishing Co., 1906.

Rowland, Dunbar (ed.). *Jefferson Davis, Constitutionalist: His Letters, Papers, and Speeches.* 10 vols. Jackson, MS: Mississippi Department of Archives and History, 1923.

Rozwenc, Edwin Charles (ed.). *The Causes of the American Civil War.* 1961. Lexington, MA: D. C. Heath and Co., 1972 ed.

Rubenzer, Steven J., and Thomas R. Faschingbauer. *Personality, Character, and Leadership in the White House: Psychologists Assess the Presidents.* Dulles, VA: Brassey's, 2004.

Ruffin, Edmund. *The Diary of Edmund Ruffin: Toward Independence: October 1856-April 1861.* Baton Rouge, LA: Louisiana State University Press, 1972.

Rutherford, Mildred Lewis. *Four Addresses.* Birmingham, AL: The Mildred Rutherford Historical Circle, 1916.

———. *A True Estimate of Abraham Lincoln and Vindication of the South.* N.p., n.d.

———. *Truths of History: A Historical Perspective of the Civil War From the Southern Viewpoint.*

Confederate Reprint Co., 1920.
———. *The South Must Have Her Rightful Place In History*. Athens, GA, 1923.
Rutland, Robert Allen. *The Birth of the Bill of Rights, 1776-1791*. 1955. Boston, MA: Northeastern University Press, 1991 ed.
Sachsman, David B., S. Kittrell Rushing, and Roy Morris, Jr. (eds.). *Words at War: The Civil War and American Journalism*. West Lafayette, IN: Purdue University Press, 2008.
Salley, Alexander Samuel, Jr. *South Carolina Troops in Confederate Service*. 2 vols. Columbia, SC: R. L. Bryan, 1913 and 1914.
Salzberger, Ronald P., and Mary C. Turck (eds.). *Reparations For Slavery: A Reader*. Lanham, MD: Rowman and Littlefield, 2004.
Samuel, Bunford. *Secession and Constitutional Liberty*. 2 vols. New York, NY: Neale Publishing, 1920.
Sancho, Ignatius. *Letters of the Late Ignatius Sancho, an African*. 1782. New York, NY: Cosimo Classics, 2005 ed.
Sandburg, Carl. *Abraham Lincoln: The War Years*. 4 vols. New York, NY: Harcourt, Brace and World, 1939.
———. *Storm Over the Land: A Profile of the Civil War*. 1939. Old Saybrook, CT: Konecky and Konecky, 1942 ed.
Sargent, F. W. *England, the United States, and the Southern Confederacy*. London, UK: Sampson Low, Son, and Co., 1863.
Scharf, John Thomas. *History of the Confederate Navy, From Its Organization to the Surrender of Its Last Vessel*. Albany, NY: Joseph McDonough, 1894.
Schauffler, Robert Haven. *Our American Holidays: Lincoln's Birthday - A Comprehensive View of Lincoln as Given in the Most Noteworthy Essays, Orations and Poems, in Fiction and in Lincoln's Own Writings*. 1909. New York, NY: Moffat, Yard and Co., 1916 ed.
Schlüter, Herman. *Lincoln, Labor and Slavery: A Chapter from the Social History of America*. New York, NY: Socialist Literature Co., 1913.
Schofield, John McAllister. *Forty-six Years in the Army*. New York, NY: Century Company, 1897.
Schurz, Carl. *Life of Henry Clay*. 2 vols. 1887. Boston, MA: Houghton, Mifflin and Co., 1899 ed.
Schwartz, Barry. *Abraham Lincoln and the Forge of National Memory*. Chicago, IL: University of Chicago Press, 2000.
Scofield, Levi Tucker. *The Retreat From Pulaski to Nashville, Tenn.: Battle of Franklin, Tennessee, November 30th, 1864*. Cleveland, OH: Press of the Caxton Co., 1909.
Scott, Emmett J., and Lyman Beecher Stowe. *Booker T. Washington: Builder of a Civilization*. Garden City, NY: Doubleday, Page, and Co., 1916.
Scott, James Brown. *James Madison's Notes of Debates in the Federal Convention of 1787, and Their Relation to a More Perfect Society of Nations*. New York, NY: Oxford University Press, 1918.
Scruggs, *The Un-Civil War: Truths Your Teacher Never Told You*. Hendersonville, NC:

Tribune Papers, 2007.

Seabrook, Lochlainn. *Britannia Rules: Goddess-Worship in Ancient Anglo-Celtic Society - An Academic Look at the United Kingdom's Matricentric Spiritual Past.* 1999. Franklin, TN: Sea Raven Press, 2007 ed.

———. *The Caudills: An Etymological, Ethnological, and Genealogical Study - Exploring the Name and National Origins of a European-American Family.* 2003. Franklin, TN: Sea Raven Press, 2010 ed.

———. *Carnton Plantation Ghost Stories: True Tales of the Unexplained From Tennessee's Most Haunted Civil War House!* 2005. Franklin, TN: Sea Raven Press, 2010 ed.

———. *Nathan Bedford Forrest: Southern Hero, American Patriot: Honoring a Confederate Hero and the Old South.* 2007. Franklin, TN: Sea Raven Press, 2010 ed.

———. *Abraham Lincoln: The Southern View.* 2007. Franklin, TN: Sea Raven Press, 2010 ed.

———. *The McGavocks of Carnton Plantation: A Southern History - Celebrating One of Dixie's Most Noble Confederate Families and Their Tennessee Home.* 2008. Franklin, TN: Sea Raven Press, 2011 ed.

———. *A Rebel Born: A Defense of Nathan Bedford Forrest, Confederate General, American Legend.* Franklin, TN: Sea Raven Press, 2010.

———. *Everything You Were Taught About the Civil War is Wrong, Ask a Southerner!* Franklin, TN: Sea Raven Press, 2010.

———. *Lincolnology: The Real Abraham Lincoln Revealed In His Own Words.* Franklin, TN: Sea Raven Press, 2011.

———. *The Unquotable Abraham Lincoln: The President's Quotes They Don't Want You To Know!* Franklin, TN: Sea Raven Press, 2011.

———. *The Quotable Jefferson Davis: Selections From the Writings and Speeches of the Confederacy's First President.* Franklin, TN: Sea Raven Press, 2012.

———. *The Quotable Robert E. Lee: Selections From the Writings and Speeches of the South's Most Beloved Civil War General.* Franklin, TN: Sea Raven Press, 2011.

———. *The Old Rebel: Robert E. Lee As He Was Seen By His Contemporaries.* Franklin, TN: Sea Raven Press, 2012.

———. *The Quotable Nathan Bedford Forrest: Selections From the Writings and Speeches of the Confederacy's Most Brilliant Cavalryman.* Franklin, TN: Sea Raven Press, 2012.

———. *Give 'Em Hell Boys! The Complete Military Correspondence of Nathan Bedford Forrest.* Franklin, TN: Sea Raven Press, 2012.

———. *Honest Jeff and Dishonest Abe: A Southern Children's Guide to the Civil War.* Franklin, TN: Sea Raven Press, 2012.

Segal, Charles M. (ed.). *Conversations with Lincoln.* 1961. New Brunswick, NJ: Transaction, 2002 ed.

Segars, J. H., and Charles Kelly Barrow. *Black Southerners in Confederate Armies: A Collection of Historical Accounts.* Atlanta, GA: Southern Lion Books, 2001.

Seligmann, Herbert J. *The Negro Faces America.* New York, NY: Harper and Brothers, 1920.

Semmes, Admiral Ralph. *Service Afloat, or the Remarkable Career of the Confederate Cruisers Sumter and Alabama During the War Between the States.* London, UK: Sampson

Low, Marston, Searle, and Rivington, 1887.
Sewall, Samuel. *Diary of Samuel Sewall*. 3 vols. Boston, MA: The Society, 1879.
Sewell, Richard H. *John P. Hale and the Politics of Abolition*. Cambridge, MA: Harvard University Press, 1965.
Shellenberger, Captain John K. *The Battle of Franklin, Tennessee, 1864: A Statement of the Erroneous Claims Made By General Schofield, and An Exposition of the Blunder Which Opened the Battle*. Cleveland, OH: Self published, 1916.
———. *The Battle of Spring Hill, Tennessee*. Military Order of the Loyal Legion of the United States, Commandery of the State of Missouri, 1907.
Shenk, Joshua Wolf. *Lincoln's Melancholy: How Depression Challenged a President and Fueled His Greatness*. New York, NY: Houghton Mifflin, 2005.
Shenkman, Richard, and Kurt Edward Reiger. *One-Night Stands with American History: Odd, Amusing, and Little-Known Incidents*. 1980. New York, NY: Perennial, 2003 ed.
Sherman, William Tecumseh. *Memoirs of General William T. Sherman*. 2 vols. 1875. New York, NY: D. Appleton and Co., 1891 ed.
———. *Memoirs of Gen. W. T. Sherman*. 2 vols. 1875. New York, NY: Charles L. Webster and Co., 1892 ed.
Shillington, Kevin. *History of Africa*. 1989. New York, NY: St. Martin's Press, 1994 ed.
Shorto, Russell. *Thomas Jefferson and the American Ideal*. Hauppauge, NY: Barron's, 1987.
Shotwell, Walter G. *Life of Charles Sumner*. New York, NY: Thomas Y. Crowell and Co., 1910.
Sieburg, Evelyn, & James E. Hansen, II (eds.). *Memoirs of a Confederate Staff Officer: From Bethel to Bentonville* (James Ratchford, 1840-1910). Shippensburg, PA: White Mane Books, 1998.
Siepel, Kevin H. *Rebel: The Life and Times of John Singleton Mosby*. New York, NY: St. Martin's Press, 1983.
Sifakis, Stewart. *Who Was Who in the Union* (Vol. 1). New York, NY: Facts on File, 1989.
———. *Who Was Who in the Confederacy* (Vol. 2). New York, NY: Facts on File, 1989.
Simkins, Francis Butler. *A History of the South*. New York, NY: Random House, 1972.
Simmons, Henry E. *A Concise Encyclopedia of the Civil War*. New York, NY: Bonanza Books, 1965.
Simon, James F. *Lincoln and Chief Justice Taney: Slavery, Secession, and the President's War Powers*. New York, NY: Simon and Schuster, 2006.
Simon, Paul. *Lincoln's Preparation for Greatness: The Illinois Legislative Years*. 1965. Chicago, IL: University of Illinois Press, 1971 ed.
Simpson, Lewis P. (ed.). *I'll Take My Stand: The South and the Agrarian Tradition*. 1930. Baton Rouge, LA: University of Louisiana Press, 1977 ed.
Slotkin, Richard. *No Quarter: The Battle of the Crater, 1864*. New York, NY: Random House, 2009.
Smelser, Marshall. *American Colonial and Revolutionary History*. 1950. New York, NY:

Barnes and Noble, 1966 ed.
———. *The Democratic Republic, 1801-1815*. New York, NY: Harper and Row, 1968.
Smith, Hedrick. *Reagan: The Man, The President*. Oxford, UK: Pergamon Press, 1980.
Smith, Jean Edward. *Grant*. New York, NY: Touchstone, 2001.
Smith, John David (ed.). *Black Soldiers in Blue: African American Troops in the Civil War Era*. Chapel Hill, NC: University of North Carolina Press, 2002.
Smith, Joseph. *The Pearl of Great Price*. Salt Lake City, UT: George Q. Cannon and Sons, 1891.
Smith, Mark M. (ed.). *The Old South*. Oxford, UK: Blackwell Publishers, 2001.
Smith, Page. *Trial by Fire: A People's History of the Civil War and Reconstruction*. New York, NY: McGraw-Hill, 1982.
Smith, Philip D., Jr. *Tartan for Me!: Suggested Tartan for 13,695 Scottish, Scotch-Irish, Irish and North American Names with Lists of Clan, Family, and District Tartans*. Bruceton, WV: Scotpress, 1990.
Smith, Reid. *Majestic Middle Tennessee*. 1975. Gretna, LA: Pelican Publishing Co., 1998 ed.
Smucker, Samuel M. *The Life and Times of Thomas Jefferson*. Philadelphia, PA: J. W. Bradley, 1859.
Snider, Denton J. *Lincoln at Richmond: A Dramatic Epos of the Civil War*. St. Louis, MO: Sigma, 1914.
Sobel, Robert (ed.). *Biographical Directory of the United States Executive Branch, 1774-1898*. Westport, CT: Greenwood Press, 1990.
Sorrel, Gilbert Moxley. *Recollections of a Confederate Staff Officer*. New York, NY: Neale Publishing Co., 1905.
Spaeth, Harold J., and Edward Conrad Smith. *The Constitution of the United States*. 1936. New York, NY: HarperCollins, 1991 ed.
Spence, James. *On the Recognition of the Southern Confederation*. Ithaca, NY: Cornell University Library, 1862.
Spooner, Lysander. *No Treason* (only Numbers 1, 2, and 6 were published). Boston, MA: Lysander Spooner, 1867-1870.
Stampp, Kenneth M. *The Peculiar Institution: Slavery in the Antebellum South*. New York, NY: Vintage, 1956.
Stanford, Peter Thomas. *The Tragedy of the Negro in America*. Boston, MA: published by author, 1898.
Stanton, Elizabeth Cady, Susan B. Anthony, and Matilda Joslyn Gage (eds.). *History of Woman Suffrage*. 2 vols. New York, NY: Fowler and Wells, 1881.
Starr, John W., Jr. *Lincoln and the Railroads: A Biographical Study*. New York, NY: Dodd, Mead and Co., 1927.
Staudenraus, P. J. *The African Colonization Movement, 1816-1865*. New York, NY: Columbia University Press, 1961.
Stebbins, Rufus Phineas. *An Historical Address Delivered At the Centennial Celebration of the Incorporation of the Town of Wilbraham, June 15, 1863*. Boston, MA: George C. Rand and Avery, 1864.
Stedman, Edmund Clarence, and Ellen Mackay Hutchinson (eds.). *A Library of American*

Literature From the Earliest Settlement to the Present Time. 10 vols. New York, NY: Charles L. Webster and Co., 1888.
Steele, Joel Dorman, and Esther Baker Steele. *Barnes' Popular History of the United States of America.* New York, NY: A. S. Barnes and Co., 1904.
Steele, Shelby. *White Guilt: How Blacks and Whites Together Destroyed the Promise of the Civil Rights Era.* New York, NY: Harper Perennial, 2007.
Steers, Edward, Jr. *Lincoln Legends: Myths, Hoaxes, and Confabulations Associated With Our Greatest President.* Lexington, KY: University Press of Kentucky, 2007.
Stein, Ben, and Phil DeMuth. *How To Ruin the United States of America.* Carlsbad, CA: New Beginnings Press, 2008.
Steiner, Bernard. *The History of Slavery in Connecticut.* Baltimore, MD: Johns Hopkins University Press, 1893.
Steiner, Lewis Henry. *Report of Lewis H. Steiner: Inspector of the Sanitary Commission, Containing a Diary Kept During the Rebel Occupation of Frederick, MD, September, 1862.* New York, NY: Anson D. F. Randolph, 1862.
Stephens, Alexander Hamilton. *Speech of Mr. Stephens, of Georgia, on the War and Taxation.* Washington, D.C.: J & G. Gideon, 1848.
——. *A Constitutional View of the Late War Between the States; Its Causes, Character, Conduct and Results.* 2 vols. Philadelphia, PA: National Publishing, Co., 1870.
——. *Recollections of Alexander H. Stephens: His Diary Kept When a Prisoner at Fort Warren, Boston Harbour, 1865.* New York, NY: Doubleday, Page, and Co., 1910.
Stephenson, Nathaniel Wright. *Abraham Lincoln and the Union: A Chronicle of the Embattled North.* New Haven, CT: Yale University Press, 1918.
——. *Lincoln: An Account of His Personal Life, Especially of Its Springs of Action as Revealed and Deepened by the Ordeal of War.* Indianapolis, IN: Bobbs-Merrill, 1922.
Sterling, Dorothy (ed.). *Speak Out in Thunder Tones: Letters and Other Writings by Black Northerners, 1787-1865.* 1973. Cambridge, MA: Da Capo, 1998 ed.
Stern, Philip Van Doren (ed.). *The Life and Writings of Abraham Lincoln.* 1940. New York, NY: Modern Library, 2000 ed.
Stewart, Bruce H., Jr. *Invisible Hero: Patrick R. Cleburne.* Macon, GA: Mercer University Press, 2009.
Stoddard, William O. *Inside the White House in War Times: Memoirs and Reports of Lincoln's Secretary.* Lincoln, NE: University of Nebraska Press, 2000.
Stonebraker, J. Clarence. *The Unwritten South: Cause, Progress and Results of the Civil War - Relics of Hidden Truth After Forty Years.* Seventh ed., n.p., 1908.
Stovall, Pleasant A. *Robert Toombs: Statesman, Speaker, Soldier, Sage.* New York, NY: Cassell Publishing, 1892.
Strain, John Paul. *Witness to the Civil War: The Art of John Paul Strain.* Philadelphia, PA: Courage, 2002.
Strode, Hudson. *Jefferson Davis: American Patriot.* 3 vols. New York, NY: Harcourt, Brace and World, 1955, 1959, 1964.
Strozier, Charles B. *Lincoln's Quest for Union: A Psychological Portrait.* Philadelphia, PA: Paul Dry Books, 2001.
Sturge, Joseph. *A Visit to the United States in 1841.* London, UK: Hamilton, Adams, and

Co., 1842.
Summers, Mark W. *The Plundering Generation: Corruption and the Crisis of the Union, 1849-1861*. New York, NY: Oxford University Press, 1988.
Sumner, Charles. *The Crime Against Kansas: The Apologies for the Crime - The True Remedy*. Boston, MA: John P. Jewett, 1856.
Swanson, James L. *Bloody Crimes: The Chase for Jefferson Davis and the Death Pageant for Lincoln's Corpse*. New York, NY: HarperCollins, 2010.
Swint, Henry L. (ed.) *Dear Ones at Home: Letters From Contraband Camps*. Nashville, TN: Vanderbilt University Press, 1966.
Sword, Wiley. *The Confederacy's Last Hurrah: Spring Hill, Franklin, and Nashville*. New York, NY: HarperCollins, 1992.
——. *Southern Invincibility: A History of the Confederate Heart*. New York, NY: St. Martin's Press, 1999.
Tagg, Larry. *The Unpopular Mr. Lincoln: The Story of America's Most Reviled President*. New York, NY: Savas Beatie, 2009.
Tarbell, Ida Minerva. *The Life of Abraham Lincoln*. 4 vols. New York, NY: Lincoln History Society, 1895-1900.
Tatalovich, Raymond, and Byron W. Daynes. *Presidential Power in the United States*. Monterey, CA: Brooks/Cole, 1984.
Taylor, Richard. *Destruction and Reconstruction: Personal Experiences of the Late War in the United States*. New York, NY: D. Appleton, 1879.
Taylor, Susie King. *Reminiscences of My Life in Camp With the 33rd United States Colored Troops Late 1st S. C. Volunteers*. Boston, MA: Susie King Taylor, 1902.
Taylor, Walter Herron. *General Lee: His Campaigns in Virginia, 1861-1865, With Personal Reminiscences*. Norfolk, VA: Nusbaum Book and News Co., 1906.
Tenney, William Jewett. *The Military and Naval History of the Rebellion in the United States*. New York, NY: D. Appleton and Co., 1865.
Terkel, Studs. *Hard Times: An Oral History of the Great Depression*. New York, NY: Avon, 1970.
Testimony Taken By the Joint Select Committee to Inquire Into the Condition of Affairs in the Late Insurrectionary States. 13 vols. Washington, D.C.: Government Printing Office, 1872.
Thackeray, William Makepeace. *Roundabout Papers*. Boston, MA: Estes and Lauriat, 1883.
Thatcher, Marshall P. *A Hundred Battles in the West: St. Louis to Atlanta, 1861-1865*. Detroit, MI: Marshall P. Thatcher, 1884.
The American Annual Cyclopedia and Register of Important Events of the Year 1861. New York, NY: D. Appleton and Co., 1868.
The American Annual Cyclopedia and Register of Important Events of the Year 1862. New York, NY: D. Appleton and Co., 1869.
The American Annual Cyclopedia and Register of Important Events of the Year 1863. New York, NY: D. Appleton and Co., 1864.
The Congressional Globe, Containing Sketches of the Debates and Proceedings of the First Session of the Twenty-Eighth Congress (Vol. 13). Washington, D.C.: The Globe, 1844.

The Great Issue to be Decided in November Next: Shall the Constitution and the Union Stand or Fall, Shall Sectionalism Triumph? Washington, D.C.: National Democratic Executive Committee, 1860.

The National Almanac and Annual Record for the Year 1863. Philadelphia, PA: George W. Childs, 1863.

The Oxford English Dictionary. Compact edition, 2 vols. 1928. Oxford, UK: Oxford University Press, 1979 ed.

The Quarterly Review (Vol. 111). London, UK: John Murray, 1862.

Thomas, Emory M. *The Confederate Nation: 1861-1865.* New York, NY: Harper and Row, 1979.

Thomas, Gabriel. *An Account of Pennsylvania and West New Jersey.* 1698. Cleveland, OH: Burrows Brothers Co., 1903 ed.

Thompson, Frank Charles (ed.). *The Thompson Chain Reference Bible* (King James Version). 1908. Indianapolis, IN: B. B. Kirkbride Bible Co., 1964 ed.

Thompson, Neal. *Driving With the Devil: Southern Moonshine, Detroit Wheels, and the Birth of NASCAR.* Three Rivers, MI: Three Rivers Press, 2006.

Thompson, Robert Means, and Richard Wainwright (eds.). *Confidential Correspondence of Gustavus Vasa Fox, Assistant Secretary of the Navy, 1861-1865.* 2 vols. 1918. New York, NY: Naval History Society, 1920 ed.

Thorndike, Rachel Sherman (ed.). *The Sherman Letters.* New York, NY: Charles Scribner's Sons, 1894.

Thornton, Brian. *101 Things You Didn't Know About Lincoln: Loves and Losses, Political Power Plays, White House Hauntings.* Avon, MA: Adams Media, 2006.

Thornton, Gordon. *The Southern Nation: The New Rise of the Old South.* Gretna, LA: Pelican Publishing Co., 2000.

Thornton, John. *Africa and Africans in the Making of the Atlantic World, 1400-1800.* 1992. Cambridge, UK: Cambridge University Press, 1999 ed.

Thornton, Mark, and Robert B. Ekelund, Jr. *Tariffs, Blockades, and Inflation: The Economics of the Civil War.* Wilmington, DE: Scholarly Resources, 2004.

Tilley, John Shipley. *Lincoln Takes Command.* 1941. Nashville, TN: Bill Coats Limited, 1991 ed.

———. *Facts the Historians Leave Out: A Confederate Primer.* 1951. Nashville, TN: Bill Coats Limited, 1999 ed.

Tocqueville, Alexis de. *Democracy in America.* 2 vols. 1836. New York, NY: D. Appleton and Co., 1904 ed.

Tourgee, Albion W. *A Fool's Errand By One of the Fools.* London, UK: George Routledge and Sons, 1883.

Tracy, Gilbert A. (ed.). *Uncollected Letters of Abraham Lincoln.* Boston, MA: Houghton Mifflin Co., 1917.

Traupman, John C. *The New College Latin and English Dictionary.* 1966. New York, NY: Bantam, 1988 ed.

Trumbull, Lyman. *Speech of Honorable Lyman Trumbull, of Illinois, at a Mass Meeting in Chicago, August 7, 1858.* Washington, D.C.: Buell and Blanchard, 1858.

Truth, Sojourner. *Sojourner Truth's Narrative and Book of Life.* 1850. Battle Creek, MI:

Sojourner Truth, 1881 ed.
Tucker, St. George. *On the State of Slavery in Virginia, in View of the Constitution of the United States, With Selected Writings*. Indianapolis, IN: Liberty Fund, 1999.
Turner, Edward Raymond. *The Negro in Pennsylvania, Slavery, Servitude, Freedom, 1639-1861*. Washington, D.C.: American Historical Association, 1911.
Tyler, Lyon Gardiner. *The Gray Book: A Confederate Catechism*. Columbia, TN: Gray Book Committee, SCV, 1935.
———. *The Letters and Times of the Tylers*. 3 vols. Williamsburg, VA: N.P., 1896.
———. *Propaganda in History*. Richmond, VA: Richmond Press, 1920.
Upshur, Abel Parker. *A Brief Enquiry Into the True Nature and Character of Our Federal Government*. Philadelphia, PA: John Campbell, 1863.
Vallandigham, Clement Laird. *Speeches, Arguments, Addresses, and Letters of Clement L. Vallandigham*. New York, NY: J. Walter and Co., 1864.
Vanauken, Sheldon. *The Glittering Illusion: English Sympathy for the Southern Confederacy*. Washington, D.C.: Regnery, 1989.
Van Buren, G. M. *Abraham Lincoln's Pen and Voice: Being a Complete Compilation of His Letters, Civil, Political, and Military*. Cincinnati, OH: Robert Clarke and Co., 1890.
Van West, Caroll (ed.). *Tennessee Encyclopedia of History and Culture*. Nashville, TN: Tennessee Historical Society, 1998.
Ver Steeg, Clarence Lester, and Richard Hofstadter. *A People and a Nation*. New York, NY: Harper and Row, 1977.
Villard, Henry. *Memoirs of Henry Villard, Journalist and Financier, 1835-1900*. 2 vols. Boston, MA: Houghton, Mifflin and Co., 1904.
Voegeli, Victor Jacque. *Free But Not Equal: The Midwest and the Negro During the Civil War*. Chicago, IL: University of Chicago Press, 1967.
Wade, Wyn Craig. *The Fiery Cross: The Ku Klux Klan in America*. 1987. New York, NY: Touchstone, 1988 ed.
Wagner, Margaret E., Gary W. Gallagher, and Paul Finkelman (eds.). *The Library of Congress Civil War Desk Reference*. New York, NY: Simon and Schuster, 2002.
Walker, Barbara G. *The Woman's Encyclopedia of Myths and Secrets*. New York, NY: Harper and Row, 1983.
Wallcut, R. F. (pub.). *Southern Hatred of the American Government, the People of the North, and Free Institutions*. Boston, MA: R. F. Wallcut, 1862.
Wallechinsky, David, Irving Wallace, and Amy Wallace. *The People's Almanac Presents The Book of Lists*. New York, NY: Morrow, 1977.
Walsh, George. *"Those Damn Horse Soldiers": True Tales of the Civil War Cavalry*. New York, NY: Forge, 2006.
Ward, John William. *Andrew Jackson: Symbol for an Age*. 1953. Oxford, UK: Oxford University Press, 1973 ed.
Waring, George Edward, Jr. *Whip and Spur*. New York, NY: Doubleday and McClure, 1897.
Warner, Ezra J. *Generals in Gray: Lives of the Confederate Commanders*. 1959. Baton Rouge, LA: Louisiana State University Press, 1989 ed.

——. *Generals in Blue: Lives of the Union Commanders.* 1964. Baton Rouge, LA: Louisiana State University Press, 2006 ed.
Warren, Robert Penn. *Who Speaks for the Negro?* New York, NY: Random House, 1965.
Waugh, John C. *Reelecting Lincoln: The Battle for the 1864 Presidency.* Cambridge, MA: Da Capo Press, 1997.
——. *Lincoln and McClellan: The Troubled Partnership Between a President and His General.* New York, NY: Palgrave Macmillan, 2010.
Washington, Booker T. *Up From Slavery: An Autobiography.* 1901. Garden City, NY: Doubleday, Page and Co., 1919 ed.
Washington, Henry Augustine. *The Writings of Thomas Jefferson.* 9 vols. New York, NY: H. W. Derby, 1861.
Watkins, Samuel Rush. *"Co. Aytch," Maury Grays, First Tennessee Regiment; or, A Side Show of the Big Show.* 1882. Chattanooga, TN: Times Printing Co., 1900 ed.
Watson, Harry L. *Andrew Jackson vs. Henry Clay: Democracy and Development in Antebellum America.* New York, NY: St. Martin's Press, 1998.
Watts, Peter. *A Dictionary of the Old West.* 1977. New York, NY: Promontory Press, 1987 ed.
Waugh, John C. *Surviving the Confederacy: Rebellion, Ruin, and Recovery - Roger and Sara Pryor During the Civil War.* New York, NY: Harcourt, 2002.
Weber, Jennifer L. *Copperheads: The Rise and Fall of Lincoln's Opponents in the North.* New York, NY: Oxford University Press, 2006.
Weintraub, Max. *The Blue Book of American History.* New York, NY: Regents Publishing Co., 1960.
Welles, Gideon. *Diary of Gideon Welles, Secretary of the Navy Under Lincoln and Johnson* (Vol. 1). Boston, MA: Houghton Mifflin, 1911.
Welsh, Jack D. *Medical Histories of Confederate Generals.* Kent, OH: Kent State University Press, 1995.
Wheeler, Joe L. *Abraham Lincoln, a Man of Faith and Courage: Stories of Our Most Admired President.* New York, NY: Howard Books, 2008.
Wheeler, Tom. *Mr. Lincoln's T-Mails: How Abraham Lincoln Used the Telegraph to Win the Civil War.* New York, NY: HarperCollins, 2008.
White, Charles Langdon, Edwin Jay Foscue, and Tom Lee McKnight. *Regional Geography of Anglo-America.* 1943. Englewood Cliffs, NJ: Prentice-Hall, 1985 ed.
White, Henry Alexander. *Robert E. Lee and the Southern Confederacy, 1807-1870.* New York, NY: G. P. Putnam's Sons, 1897.
White, Reginald Cedric. *A. Lincoln: A Biography.* New York, NY: Random House, 2009.
White, Ronald C., Jr. *The Eloquent President: A Portrait of Lincoln Through His Words.* New York, NY: Random House, 2006.
Whitman, Walt. *Leaves of Grass.* 1855. New York, NY: Modern Library, 1921 ed.
——. *Complete Prose Works.* Boston, MA: Small, Maynard, and Co., 1901.
Wilbur, Henry Watson. *President Lincoln's Attitude Towards Slavery and Emancipation: With*

a *Review of Events Before and Since the Civil War.* Philadelphia, PA: W. H. Jenkins, 1914.
Wilder, Craig Steven. *A Covenant With Color: Race and Social Power in Brooklyn.* New York, NY: Columbia University Press, 2000.
Wiley, Bell Irvin. *Southern Negroes: 1861-1865.* 1938. New Haven, CT: Yale University Press, 1969 ed.
———. *The Life of Johnny Reb: The Common Soldier of the Confederacy.* 1943. Baton Rouge, LA: Louisiana State University Press, 1978 ed.
———. *The Plain People of the Confederacy.* 1943. Columbia, SC: University of South Carolina, 2000 ed.
———. *The Life of Billy Yank: The Common Soldier of the Union.* 1952. Baton Rouge, LA: Louisiana State University Press, 2001 ed.
Wilkens, J. Steven. *America: The First 350 Years.* Monroe, LA: Covenant Publications, 1998.
Williams, Charles Richard. *The Life of Rutherford Birchard Hayes, Nineteenth President of the United States.* 2 vols. Boston, MA: Houghton Mifflin Co., 1914.
Williams, George Washington. *History of the Negro Race in America: From 1619 to 1880, Negroes as Slaves, as Soldiers, and as Citizens.* New York, NY: G. P. Putnam's Sons, 1885.
———. *A History of the Negro Troops in the War of the Rebellion 1861-1865.* New York, NY: Harper and Brothers, 1888.
Williams, James. *The South Vindicated.* London, UK: Longman, Green, Longman, Roberts, and Green, 1862.
Williams, William H. *Slavery and Freedom in Delaware, 1639-1865.* Wilmington, DE: Scholarly Resources, 1996.
Wills, Brian Steel. *The Confederacy's Greatest Cavalryman: Nathan Bedford Forrest.* Lawrence, KS: University Press of Kansas, 1992.
Wills, Gary. *Lincoln At Gettysburg: The Words that Remade America.* New York, NY: Touchstone, 1992.
Wills, Ridley, II. *Old Enough To Die.* Franklin, TN: Hillsboro Press, 1996.
Wilson, Charles Reagan, and William Ferris. *Encyclopedia of Southern Culture* (Vol. 1). New York, NY: Anchor, 1989.
Wilson, Clyde N. *Why the South Will Survive: Fifteen Southerners Look at Their Region a Half Century After I'll Take My Stand.* Athens, GA: University of Georgia Press, 1981.
———. (ed.) *The Essential Calhoun: Selections From Writings, Speeches, and Letters.* New Brunswick, NJ: Transaction Publishers, 1991.
———. *A Defender of Southern Conservatism: M.E. Bradford and His Achievements.* Columbia, MO: University of Missouri Press, 1999.
———. *From Union to Empire: Essays in the Jeffersonian Tradition.* Columbia, SC: The Foundation for American Education, 2003.
———. *Defending Dixie: Essays in Southern History and Culture.* Columbia, SC: The Foundation for American Education, 2005.
Wilson, Douglas L. *Honor's Voice: The Transformation of Abraham Lincoln.* New York,

NY: Vintage, 1998.
——. *Lincoln's Sword: The Presidency and the Power of Words*. New York, NY: Vintage, 2006.
Wilson, Henry. *History of the Rise and Fall of the Slave Power in America*. 3 vols. Boston, MA: James R. Osgood and Co., 1877.
Wilson, Joseph Thomas. *The Black Phalanx: A History of the Negro Soldiers of the United States in the Wars of 1775-1812, 1861-'65*. Hartford, CT: American Publishing Co., 1890.
Wilson, Woodrow. *Division and Reunion: 1829-1889*. 1893. New York, NY: Longmans, Green, and Co., 1908 ed.
——. *A History of the American People*. 5 vols. 1902. New York, NY: Harper and Brothers, 1918 ed.
Wood, W. J. *Civil War Generalship: The Art of Command*. 1997. New York, NY: Da Capo Press, 2000 ed.
Woodard, Komozi. *A Nation Within a Nation: Amiri Baraka (LeRoi Jones) and Black Power Politics*. Chapel Hill, NC: University of North Carolina Press, 1999.
Woodburn, James Albert. *The Life of Thaddeus Stevens*. Indianapolis, IN: Bobbs-Merrill, 1913.
Woods, Thomas E., Jr. *The Politically Incorrect Guide to American History*. Washington, D.C.: Regnery, 2004.
Woodson, Carter G. (ed.). *The Journal of Negro History* (Vol. 4). Lancaster, PA: Association for the Study of Negro Life and History, 1919.
Woodward, William E. *Meet General Grant*. 1928. New York, NY: Liveright Publishing, 1946 ed.
Woodworth, Steven E. *Jefferson Davis and His Generals: The Failure of Confederate Command in the West*. Lawrence, KS: University Press of Kansas, 1990.
Wright, John D. *The Language of the Civil War*. Westport, CT: Oryx, 2001.
Wyeth, John Allan. *Life of General Nathan Bedford Forrest*. 1899. New York, NY: Harper and Brothers, 1908 ed.
Young, John Russell. *Around the World With General Grant*. 2 vols. New York, NY: American News Co., 1879.
Zaehner, R. C. (ed.) *Encyclopedia of the World's Religions*. 1959. New York, NY: Barnes and Noble, 1997 ed.
Zall, Paul M. (ed.). *Lincoln on Lincoln*. Lexington, KY: University Press of Kentucky, 1999.
Zavodnyik, Peter. *The Age of Strict Construction: A History of the Growth of Federal Power, 1789-1861*. Washington, D.C.: Catholic University of America Press, 2007.
Zinn, Howard. *A People's History of the United States: 1492-Present*. 1980. New York, NY: HarperCollins, 1995.

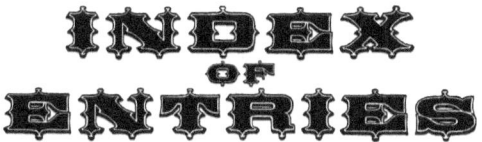

INDEX OF ENTRIES

NOTES
- Only entry headings are listed.
- The illustrations are not included in the Index.
- Auto-indexing may cause ordering irregularities.

abatis	25
Abercrombie, Robert H.	25
Adaire, Thomas N.	26
Adams Street	26
Adams, John	26
Adams' Brigade (CSA)	28
African-Americans	29
American Battlefield Protection Program	30
antebellum houses	30
Armistead, Edward Herbert	31
Armstrong, Frank Crawford	31
Armstrong's Brigade (CSA)	33
Army of Northern Virginia (CSA)	34
Army of Tennessee (CSA)	36
Army of the Cumberland (USA)	33
Army of the Ohio (USA)	35
Army of the Potomac (CSA)	36
Army of the Tennessee (USA)	39
Ashford, Frederick A.	39
Ashwood Hall	39
Athenaeum Rectory	40
Atkins, Thomas M.	41
Badger, Edward	42
Baker, Edward Adams	42
Bald Hill	42
Ballentine's Mississippi Cavalry (CSA)	43
Bate, William Brimage	43
Bate's Division (CSA)	44

Bates, Edward	44
Battle of Columbia	44
Battle of Franklin	45
Battle of Nashville	55
Battle of Spring Hill	56
Beatty, Samuel	57
Beatty's Third Brigade (USA)	57
Beauregard, Pierre Gustave Toutant	57
Beckham, Robert Franklin	59
Beechlawn	59
Bell, Tyree Harris	59
Bell's Brigade (CSA)	60
Belle Meade Plantation	60
Belmont Mansion	61
Biddle, James	62
Biddle's Second Brigade (USA)	62
Biffle, Jacob Barnett	62
Biffle's Brigade (CSA)	63
Bishop, William H.	63
black Confederates	63
blacks	69
Bledsoe's Missouri Battery (CSA)	69
Bostick House	69
Bostick, Joseph	69
Bostick, Rebecca Letitia	70
Bouanchaud's Louisiana Battery (CSA)	70
Boxmere	70
Bradley, Luther Prentice	70
Bradley's Third Brigade (USA)	71
Bragg, Braxton	71
Brantley, William Felix	72
Brantley's Brigade (CSA)	72
Bratton, John C.	73
breastworks	73
Breezy Hill	73
Bridges, Lyman A.	73
Broughton, Edward Thomas, Jr.	73

Brown, John Calvin 74
Brown, John W. 75
Brown's Division (CSA) 75
bucket rings 75
Buell, Don Carlos 75
Buford Street 76
Buford, Abraham 76
Buford's Division (CSA) 77
Bullock, Robert 77
Caldwell House and Cemetery 79
Callahan, Denny 80
Canniff, Patrick 80
Cantley's Brigade (CSA) 80
Capers, Ellison 81
Capron, Horace 82
Carnton Plantation 82
carpetbaggers 85
Carter family cotton gin house 85
Carter House 88
Carter Street 90
Carter, Fountain Branch 86
Carter, Francis Watkins 87
Carter, John Carpenter 87
Carter, Moscow B. 89
Carter, Sallie 90
Carter, Theodrick "Tod" 90
Carter, William F. 92
Carter's Brigade (CSA) 90
Casement, John Stephen 92
Casement's Second Brigade (USA) 93
casualty 93
cavalry 93
Cedar Hill 94
Chalmers, James Ronald 94
Chalmers' Division (CSA) 94
Cheairs, Martin Terrell 95
Cheairs, Nathaniel Francis IV 95

Cheatham, Benjamin Franklin 96
Cheatham's Corps (CSA) 97
Cheatham's Corps Artillery (CSA) 97
Chicago Board of Trade Battery (USA) 97
Civil War 97
Clayton, Henry DeLamar, Sr. 97
Clayton's Division (CSA) 98
Cleburne Street 98
Cleburne, Patrick Ronayne 98
Cleburne's Division (CSA) 100
Cliffe, Cornelia Stith 100
Cliffe, Daniel Bonaparte 100
Clouston, Elizabeth Field 101
Cobb's Battalion (CSA) 102
Cockrell, Francis Marion 102
Cockrell's Brigade (CSA) 103
Coleman Road 104
Coleman, David 103
Collins, William C. 104
Collins' Farm 104
Columbia Turnpike 105
Columbia, Tennessee 105
Confederacy 106
Confederate Cemetery 106
Confederate Flag 106
Confederate Monument 107
Confederate States Army 108
Confederate States of America 110
confederation 111
Conrad, Joseph 113
Coon, Datus Ensign 113
Coon's Second Brigade (USA) 114
Cooper, Joseph Alexander 114
Cooper, Sylvester C. 114
Cooper's First Brigade (USA) 115
Copley, John M. 115
Corput's Georgia Battery (CSA) 115

Courtney, Frances "Fannie" 115
Courtney's Battalion (CSA) 116
Cowan, George Limerick 116
Cowan's Mississippi Battery (CSA) 118
Cox, Aaron A. 118
Cox, Jacob Dolson 118
Cox, Theodore 120
Cox's Third Division (USA) 120
Cox's Third Division Artillery (USA) 120
Crittenden, Robert F. 120
Crossland, Edward 120
Crossland's Brigade (CSA) 121
Croxton, John Thomas 121
Croxton's First Brigade (USA) 122
Cummings' Brigade (CSA) 122
Cunningham, Charles J. L. 122
Cunningham, Sumner Archibald 122
Cuppet, George W. 123
Cuppet, Marcellus 123
Darden's Mississippi Battery (CSA) 125
Davidson, Francis M. 125
Davis, Jefferson 125
Davis, Newton N. 127
Davis' Ford 127
Deas, Zachariah Cantey 127
Deas' Brigade (CSA) 128
Dent's Alabama Battery (CSA) 128
Dibrell's Brigade (CSA) 128
Dixon, M. H. 128
Douglas, James Postell 128
Douglas' Texas Battery (CSA) 129
Dozier, N. B. 129
Duck River 129
Dyer, Samuel M. 129
Ector, Matthew Duncan 130
Ector's Brigade (CSA) 130
Eighteenth Alabama (CSA) 131

Eighteenth Texas Cavalry (CSA)	131
Eighth Arkansas (CSA)	131
Eighth Iowa (USA)	131
Eighth Kansas (USA)	131
Eighth Kentucky Mounted Infantry (CSA)	131
Eighth Michigan Cavalry (USA)	131
Eighth Mississippi (CSA)	131
Eighth Tennessee (CSA)	132
Eighth Tennessee (USA)	132
Eighth Tennessee Cavalry (USA)	132
Eightieth Illinois (USA)	132
Eightieth Indiana (USA)	132
Eighty-eighth Illinois (USA)	132
Eighty-first Indiana (USA)	132
Eighty-fourth Illinois (USA)	132
Eighty-fourth Indiana (USA)	132
Eighty-ninth Illinois (USA)	132
Eighty-sixth Indiana (USA)	133
Eldridge's Battalion (CSA)	133
Eleventh Indiana Cavalry (USA)	133
Eleventh Tennessee (CSA)	133
Elm Springs	133
Emancipation Proclamation	133
enfilade fire	136
entrenchment	136
Eufaula Alabama Battery (CSA)	136
Everbright	136
Ewing, Susan Lee	136
Factory, The	138
Farrell, Mike	138
Featherston, Winfield Scott	138
Featherston's Brigade (CSA)	139
Federal architecture	139
Federal government	141
Fenner, Charles E.	143
Fenner's Louisiana Battery (CSA)	143
Ferguson Hall	143

Ferguson's South Carolina Battery (CSA) 146
field hospital 146
field servant 149
Field, Hume R. 149
Fifteenth Arkansas (CSA) 149
Fifteenth Mississippi (CSA) 150
Fifteenth Missouri (USA) 150
Fifteenth Ohio (USA) 150
Fifteenth Tennessee Cavalry (CSA) 150
Fifteenth Texas (CSA) 150
Fifth Arkansas (CSA) 150
Fifth Confederate (CSA) 150
Fifth Iowa Cavalry (USA) 150
Fifth Mississippi (CSA) 150
Fifth Mississippi Cavalry (CSA) 150
Fifth Missouri (CSA) 151
Fifth Tennessee (CSA) 151
Fifth Tennessee (USA) 151
Fifth Texas Cavalry (CSA) 151
Fiftieth Alabama (CSA) 151
Fiftieth Ohio (USA) 151
Fiftieth Tennessee (CSA) 151
Fifty-eighth Alabama (CSA) 151
Fifty-fifth Alabama (CSA) 151
Fifty-fifth Tennessee (CSA) 151
Fifty-first Illinois (USA) 152
Fifty-first Indiana (USA) 152
Fifty-first Ohio (USA) 152
Fifty-first Tennessee (CSA) 152
Fifty-fourth Georgia (CSA) 152
Fifty-ninth Illinois (USA) 152
Fifty-second Georgia (CSA) 152
Fifty-second Tennessee (CSA) 152
Fifty-seventh Alabama (CSA) 152
Fifty-seventh Georgia (CSA) 152
Fifty-seventh Indiana (USA) 153
Fifty-sixth Georgia (CSA) 153

Fifty-third Tennessee (CSA)	153
Figuers, Harding Perkins	153
Finley, Jesse Johnson	155
Finley's Brigade (CSA)	156
First Alabama (CSA)	156
First Arkansas (CSA)	156
First Arkansas Mounted Rifles (CSA)	156
First Florida (CSA)	156
First Florida Cavalry (CSA)	156
First Georgia Battalion Sharpshooters (CSA)	156
First Georgia Confederate (CSA)	156
First Georgia Volunteers (CSA)	157
First Illinois Artillery, Battery I (USA)	157
First Kentucky Battery (USA)	157
First Louisiana (CSA)	157
First Michigan Battery (USA)	157
First Mississippi (CSA)	157
First Mississippi Battalion Sharpshooters (CSA)	157
First Mississippi Cavalry (CSA)	157
First Missouri (CSA)	157
First Missouri Cavalry (CSA)	157
First Ohio Light, Batteries A and G (USA)	158
First Ohio Light, Battery D (USA)	158
First Tennessee (CSA)	158
First Tennessee Cavalry (USA)	158
First Texas Legion (CSA)	158
Fisher, Rhodes	158
floor cloth	158
Flournoy, Peter C.	159
Forrest Crossing	159
Forrest Street	159
Forrest, Nathan Bedford	159
Forrest's Cavalry Corps (CSA)	165
Forrest's Cavalry Corps Artillery (CSA)	165
Forrest's Regiment Tennessee Cavalry (CSA)	165
Fort Casino	165
Fort Gillem	165

Fort Granger 165
Fort Houston 166
Fort Johnson (Tennessee State Capitol) 166
Fort Morton 167
Fort Negley 168
Fortieth Georgia (CSA) 167
Fortieth Indiana (USA) 167
Fortieth Mississippi (CSA) 167
Forty-eighth Tennessee (CSA) 169
Forty-fifth Alabama (CSA) 169
Forty-fifth Ohio (USA) 169
Forty-first Georgia (CSA) 169
Forty-first Mississippi (CSA) 169
Forty-first Ohio (USA) 169
Forty-first Tennessee (CSA) 169
Forty-fourth Illinois (USA) 169
Forty-fourth Mississippi (CSA) 170
Forty-ninth Alabama (CSA) 170
Forty-ninth Ohio (USA) 170
Forty-ninth Tennessee (CSA) 170
Forty-second Georgia (CSA) 170
Forty-second Illinois (USA) 170
Forty-second Tennessee (CSA) 170
Forty-seventh Tennessee (CSA) 170
Forty-sixth Alabama (CSA) 170
Forty-sixth Georgia (CSA) 170
Forty-sixth Mississippi (CSA) 171
Forty-sixth Tennessee (CSA) 171
Forty-third Georgia (CSA) 171
Forty-third Mississippi (CSA) 171
Foster, Samuel T. 171
Fourteenth Illinois Cavalry (USA) 171
Fourteenth Louisiana Battalion Sharpshooters (CSA) 171
Fourteenth Mississippi (CSA) 171
Fourteenth Ohio Battery (USA) 172
Fourteenth Tennessee Cavalry (CSA) 172
Fourteenth Texas Cavalry (CSA) 172

Fourth Arkansas (CSA) 172
Fourth Army Corps (USA) 172
Fourth Army Corps Artillery (USA) 172
Fourth Florida (CSA) 172
Fourth Georgia Battalion Sharpshooters (CSA) 173
Fourth Kentucky Mounted Infantry (USA) 173
Fourth Louisiana (CSA) 173
Fourth Louisiana Battalion (CSA) 173
Fourth Mississippi (CSA) 173
Fourth Missouri (CSA) 173
Fourth Tennessee (CSA) 173
Fourth Tennessee - Provisional (CSA) 173
Fourth Tennessee Cavalry (USA) 173
Fourth U.S. Regular Artillery, Battery I (USA) 173
Fourth U.S. Regular Battery (USA) 174
Franklin Pike 174
Franklin Railroad Depot 174
Franklin Turnpike Bridge 178
Franklin, Benjamin 174
Franklin, Tennessee 175
French, Samuel Gibbs 179
French, Theodosia 180
French's Division (CSA) 180
Fullerton, Joseph Scott 180
Gale, William Dudley 182
Gardner, A. V. 182
Garland, Hugh Alfred, Jr. 182
Garrett, M. P. 183
Garrity's Alabama Battery (CSA) 183
Garvin, John S. 183
Gates, Elijah 183
Georgian style 183
Gettysburg of the West 184
ghosts 184
Gibson, Randall Lee 186
Gibson's Brigade (CSA) 186
Gist Street 187

Gist, States Rights 187
Gist's Brigade (CSA) 188
Goldthwaite's Alabama Battery (CSA) 189
Gordon, George Washington 189
Gordon's Brigade (CSA) 191
Govan, Daniel Chevillette 191
Govan's Brigade (CSA) 192
Granbury Street 192
Granbury, Hiram Bronson 192
Granbury's Brigade (CSA) 195
Granny White Pike 195
Grant, Ulysses S. 195
Great Seal of the Confederate States 201
Greek Revival architecture 202
Grose, William 203
Grose's Third Brigade (USA) 203
Guibor's Missouri Battery (CSA) 203
Hamilton, A. S. 204
Hammond, John H. 204
Hammond, John W. 204
Hammond's First Brigade (USA) 204
Harding, Selene 204
Harding, William Giles 205
Harlinsdale Farm 205
Harpeth River 206
Harrison House 206
Harrison, Thomas Jefferson 207
Harrison's First Brigade (USA) 207
Hatch, Edward 207
Hatch's Fifth Division (USA) 208
Hatch's Fifth Division Artillery (USA) 208
Haunted Houses 208
Henpeck Lane 208
Hicks, J. M. 208
Hiram Masonic Lodge 208
Holtzclaw, James Thadeus 209
Holtzclaw's Brigade (CSA) 209

Hood, John Bell	209
Hoskin's Mississippi Battery (CSA)	211
Hotchkiss' Battalion (CSA)	211
house servant	211
Howard, Wiley	212
Hoxton's Battalion (CSA)	212
Huey's Kentucky Battalion (CSA)	212
Hughes' Ford	213
Hume, Isaac N.	213
Isola Bella	214
Ives, Samuel Spencer	214
Jackson, Henry Rootes	215
Jackson, William Hicks	216
Jackson's Brigade (CSA)	215
Jackson's Division (CSA)	217
Johnson, Edward	217
Johnson, George D.	218
Johnson, Gilbert Marquis Lafayette	218
Johnson, J. M.	218
Johnson, Richard W.	218
Johnson's Battalion (CSA)	219
Johnson's Division (CSA)	219
Johnson's Second Brigade (USA)	219
Johnson's Sixth Division (USA)	219
Johnson's Sixth Division Artillery (USA)	219
Johnston, John W.	219
Kellar, Andrew J.	221
Kelley, David Campbell	221
Key's Arkansas Battery (CSA)	222
Kimball, Nathan	222
Kimball's First Division (USA)	223
Kirby, Isaac Minor	223
Kirby's First Brigade (USA)	223
Knefler, Frederick	223
Knipe, Joseph Farmer	224
Knipe's Seventh Division (USA)	224
Knipe's Seventh Division Artillery (USA)	224

Knox, Samuel L. 224
Kolb's Alabama Battery (CSA) 224
Lane, John Quincy 225
Lane's Second Brigade (USA) 225
Laurel Hill 225
Lawton, Henry Ware 225
Lee, Stephen Dill 226
Lee's Corps (CSA) 227
Lee's Corps Artillery (CSA) 228
Lewisburg Pike 228
Lincoln, Abraham 228
Loring, William Wing 229
Loring's Division (CSA) 230
Lotz House 230
Lowrey, Mark Perrin 230
Lowrey's Brigade (CSA) 231
Lowry, Robert Gadden Haynes 231
Lumsden, Charles L. 232
Lumsden's Alabama Battery (CSA) 232
MacArthur, Arthur, Jr. 233
Magee, T. D. 234
Magevney, Michael 234
Maney, George Earl 234
Maney's Brigade (CSA) 234
Manigault, Arthur Middleton 235
Manigault's Brigade (CSA) 236
Maplelawn 236
Marshall, Alexander 236
Marshall's Tennessee Battery (CSA) 236
Martin Cheairs House 236
McCook, Edward Moody 236
McCook's First Division (USA) 237
McCook's First Division Artillery (USA) 237
McDonald, Joseph E. 237
McEwen House 237
McGavock Confederate Cemetery 237
McGavock Creek 238

McGavock, Carrie	238
McGavock, Elizabeth Irwin	238
McGavock, Harriet Young	238
McGavock, James Randal	239
McGavock, John W.	239
McGavock, Randal	240
McGavock, Winder	241
McGavock's Ford	240
McGavock's Grove	240
McKissack, Jessie Helen	241
McLemore House	241
McNeilly, James H.	241
McPhail Office	242
McQuaide, John	242
Meek, Alexander T.	242
Merrill Hill	242
Middle Tennessee	242
Midway Plantation	243
Mitchell, George H.	243
Moore, Orlando Hurley	243
Moore's Second Brigade (USA)	244
Morton, John Watson, Jr.	244
Morton's Tennessee Battery (CSA)	245
Motherspaw, Thomas W.	245
Murphey, Virgil S.	245
Music City	245
Myrick's Battalion (CSA)	245
Nashville and Decatur Railroad	246
Nashville and Decatur Railroad Underpass	246
Nashville, Tennessee	246
Negroes	246
Nelson, Noel Ligdon	247
Nineteenth Alabama (CSA)	247
Nineteenth Arkansas (CSA)	247
Nineteenth Louisiana (CSA)	247
Nineteenth Ohio (USA)	247
Nineteenth Ohio Battery (USA)	247

Nineteenth Pennsylvania Cavalry (USA) 247
Nineteenth South Carolina (CSA) 247
Nineteenth Tennessee (CSA) 247
Nineteenth Tennessee Cavalry (CSA) 247
Ninetieth Ohio (USA) 248
Ninety-first Indiana (USA) 248
Ninety-ninth Ohio (USA) 248
Ninety-seventh Ohio (USA) 248
Ninety-sixth Illinois (USA) 248
Ninety-third Ohio (USA) 248
Ninth Arkansas (CSA) 248
Ninth Illinois Cavalry (USA) 248
Ninth Indiana (USA) 248
Ninth Indiana Cavalry (USA) 249
Ninth Mississippi (CSA) 249
Ninth Mississippi Battlalion Sharpshooters (CSA) 249
Ninth Tennessee (CSA) 249
Ninth Tennessee Cavalry (CSA) 249
Ninth Texas (CSA) 249
Ninth Texas Cavalry (CSA) 249
Nixon's Tennessee Cavalry Regiment (CSA) 249
Nutt's Louisiana Cavalry (CSA) 249
Oaklawn Plantation 251
Old Factory Store 251
One hundred eighteenth Ohio (USA) 252
One hundred eighty-third Ohio (USA) 252
One hundred eleventh Ohio (USA) 252
One hundred fifteenth Illinois (USA) 252
One hundred fifty-fourth Tennessee (CSA) 252
One hundred first Ohio (USA) 252
One hundred fourth Ohio (USA) 252
One hundred seventh Illinois (USA) 252
One hundred seventy-fifth Ohio (USA) 253
One hundred third Ohio (USA) 253
One hundred thirtieth Indiana (USA) 253
One hundred twelfth Illinois (USA) 253
One hundred twentieth Indiana (USA) 253

One hundred twenty-eighth Indiana (USA) 253
One hundred twenty-fifth Ohio (USA) 253
One hundred twenty-fourth Indiana (USA) 253
One hundred twenty-fourth Ohio (USA) 253
One hundred twenty-ninth Indiana (USA) 254
One hundred twenty-third Indiana (USA) 254
One hundredth Illinois (USA) 254
One hundredth Ohio (USA) 254
Opdycke, Emerson 254
Opdycke's First Brigade (USA) 254
Osage orange tree 255
Overton Hill 256
Overton, John, Sr. 257
Owen-Cox House 258
Perry's Florida Battery (CSA) 259
Pettus, Edmund Winston 259
Pettus' Brigade (CSA) 260
Phelan's Alabama Battery (CSA) 260
Phillip's Tennessee Battery (CSA) 260
Plain of Franklin 260
Post, Philip Sidney 260
Post's Second Brigade (USA) 260
Presstman, Stephen W. 261
Preston, Sarah Buchanan 261
Privet Knob 261
Quarles, William Andrew 262
Quarles' Brigade (CSA) 263
Quintard, Charles Todd 263
Rally Hill Road 265
Rattle and Snap Plantation 265
Rebel Yell 266
Reconstruction 266
Reeves, Charlotte 268
Reilly, James William 268
Reilly's First Brigade (USA) 269
Rest Haven Cemetery 269
Reynolds, Daniel Harris 269

Reynolds, George W. 270
Reynolds' Brigade (CSA) 270
Rippavilla Plantation 270
Rittenbury, James J. 270
Riverside Plantation 271
Roberts, Deering J. 271
Rodgers, Sarah Dougherty 272
Roper's Knob 272
Rorer, Walter Abram 272
Ross, Lawrence Sullivan 273
Ross' Brigade (CSA) 273
Rousseau, Lawrence H. 273
Rowan, John B. 274
Rucker, Edmund Winchester 274
Rucker's Brigade (CSA) 274
Ruger, Thomas Howard 274
Ruger's Second Division (USA) 275
Ruger's Second Division Artillery (USA) 275
Rutherford's Creek 275
Saint John's Episcopal Church 276
Saint Paul's Episcopal Church 277
scallywag 277
Schofield, John McAllister 278
Scofield, Levi Tucker 279
Scott, Thomas Moore 280
Scott's Brigade (CSA) 280
Scoville, Charles W. 280
Sears, Claudius Wistar 281
Sears' Brigade (CSA) 281
Second Arkansas (CSA) 282
Second Arkansas Mounted Rifles (Csa) 282
Second Georgia Battalion Sharpshooters (CSA) 282
Second Iowa Cavalry (USA) 282
Second Michigan Cavalry (USA) 282
Second Mississippi Cavalry (CSA) 282
Second Missouri (CSA) 282
Second Pennsylvania Battery (USA) 282

Second Tennessee (CSA) 283
Second Tennessee Cavalry (CSA) 283
Second Tennessee Cavalry (USA) 283
Selden's Alabama Battery (CSA) 283
Seventeenth Alabama (CSA) 283
Seventeenth Texas Cavalry (CSA) 283
Seventh Alabama Cavalry (CSA) 283
Seventh Arkansas (CSA) 283
Seventh Florida (CSA) 283
Seventh Illinois Cavalry (USA) 283
Seventh Kentucky Mounted Infantry (CSA) 284
Seventh Mississippi (CSA) 284
Seventh Mississippi Battalion (CSA) 284
Seventh Ohio Cavalry (USA) 284
Seventh Tennessee Cavalry (CSA) 284
Seventh Texas (CSA) 284
Seventy-fifth Illinois (USA) 284
Seventy-first Ohio (USA) 284
Seventy-fourth Illinois (USA) 284
Seventy-ninth Illinois (USA) 284
Seventy-ninth Indiana (USA) 285
Seventy-seventh Pennsylvania (USA) 285
Seventy-third Illinois (USA) 285
Shannon, Isaac N. 285
Sharp, Jacob Hunter 285
Sharp's Brigade (CSA) 286
Shaw, Thomas P. 286
Shellenberger, John K. 286
Shelley, Charles Miller 286
Sherwood, Isaac Ruth 287
Shotwell, Reuben H. 288
Shy's Hill 288
Sims, W. H. 288
Sixteenth Alabama (CSA) 288
Sixteenth Illinois Cavalry (USA) 288
Sixteenth Kentucky (USA) 288
Sixteenth Louisiana (CSA) 289

Sixteenth South Carolina (CSA)	289
Sixteenth Tennessee (CSA)	289
Sixth Arkansas (CSA)	289
Sixth Florida (CSA)	289
Sixth Illinois Cavalry (USA)	289
Sixth Indiana Cavalry (USA)	289
Sixth Mississippi (CSA)	289
Sixth Missouri (CSA)	289
Sixth Ohio Battery (USA)	289
Sixth Tennessee (CSA)	290
Sixth Tennessee (USA)	290
Sixth Texas (CSA)	290
Sixth Texas Cavalry (CSA)	290
Sixty-fifth Georgia (CSA)	290
Sixty-fifth Illinois (USA)	290
Sixty-fifth Indiana (USA)	290
Sixty-fifth Ohio (USA)	290
Sixty-fourth Ohio (USA)	290
Sixty-third Georgia (CSA)	290
Sixty-third Indiana (USA)	291
slaves	291
Slocumb's Louisiana Battery (CSA)	291
Smith, George A.	291
Smith, James Argyle	291
Smith, Melancthon	291
Smith, Thomas Benton	292
Smith's Brigade - 1 (CSA)	291
Smith's Brigade - 2 (CSA)	292
Snodgrass, John	293
Sons of Confederate Veterans	293
Spring Hill Cemetery	293
Spring Hill, Tennessee	293
Stafford, Fountain E. P.	294
Stanford's Mississippi Battery (CSA)	294
Stanley, David Sloane	294
Stephen's Light Artillery (CSA)	295
Stephens, Marcus D. L.	295

Stevens Hill	295
Stevenson, Carter Littlepage	295
Stevenson's Division (CSA)	295
Stewart, Alexander Peter	295
Stewart, Robert R.	297
Stewart's Corps (CSA)	297
Stewart's Corps Artillery (CSA)	297
Stewart's First Brigade (USA)	297
Stiles, Israel Newton	297
Stiles' Third Brigade (USA)	298
Stone Hill	298
Storrs' Battalion (CSA)	298
Stovall, Marcellus Augustus	298
Stovall's Brigade (CSA)	298
Strahl Street	299
Strahl, Otho French	299
Strahl's Brigade (CSA)	299
Streight, Abel D.	300
Streight's First Brigade (USA)	302
Strickland, Silas Allen	302
Strickland's Third Brigade (USA)	302
Tarrant's Alabama Battery (CSA)	303
Taylor, Richard	303
Taylor, William A.	304
Tennessee and Alabama Railroad	304
Tennessee State Capitol	304
Tenth Indiana Cavalry (USA)	304
Tenth Mississippi (CSA)	304
Tenth South Carolina (CSA)	304
Tenth Tennessee (CSA)	304
Tenth Tennessee Cavalry (CSA)	305
Tenth Tennessee Cavalry (USA)	305
Tenth Texas (CSA)	305
Tenth Texas Cavalry (CSA)	305
Third Florida (CSA)	305
Third Illinois Cavalry (USA)	305
Third Kentucky Mounted Infantry (CSA)	305

Third Mississippi (CSA) 305
Third Mississippi Battalion (CSA) 305
Third Missouri (CSA) 306
Third Missouri Cavalry Battalion (CSA) 306
Third Tennessee (USA) 306
Third Tennessee Volunteer Infantry (USA) 306
Thirteenth Arkansas (CSA) 306
Thirteenth Indiana Battery (USA) 306
Thirteenth Indiana Cavalry (USA) 306
Thirteenth Louisiana (CSA) 306
Thirteenth Ohio (USA) 306
Thirteenth Tennessee (CSA) 307
Thirtieth Alabama (CSA) 307
Thirtieth Georgia (CSA) 307
Thirtieth Indiana (USA) 307
Thirtieth Louisiana (CSA) 307
Thirtieth Mississippi (CSA) 307
Thirtieth North Carolina (CSA) 307
Thirty-eighth Alabama (CSA) 307
Thirty-eighth Illinois (USA) 307
Thirty-eighth Tennessee (CSA) 308
Thirty-fifth Alabama (CSA) 308
Thirty-fifth Indiana (USA) 308
Thirty-fifth Mississippi (CSA) 308
Thirty-fifth Tennessee (CSA) 308
Thirty-first Alabama (CSA) 308
Thirty-first Indiana (USA) 308
Thirty-first Mississippi (CSA) 308
Thirty-first Tennessee (CSA) 308
Thirty-fourth Alabama (CSA) 308
Thirty-fourth Mississippi (CSA) 309
Thirty-ninth Alabama (CSA) 309
Thirty-ninth Georgia (CSA) 309
Thirty-ninth Mississippi (CSA) 309
Thirty-second Alabama (CSA) 309
Thirty-second Mississippi (CSA) 309
Thirty-second Texas Cavalry (CSA) 309

Thirty-seventh Georgia (CSA) 309
Thirty-seventh Mississippi (CSA) 309
Thirty-seventh Tennessee (CSA) 310
Thirty-sixth Alabama (CSA) 310
Thirty-sixth Georgia (CSA) 310
Thirty-sixth Illinois (USA) 310
Thirty-Sixth Indiana (USA) 310
Thirty-sixth Mississippi (CSA) 310
Thirty-third Alabama (CSA) 310
Thirty-third Mississippi (CSA) 310
Thirty-third Tennessee (CSA) 310
Thomas, George Henry 310
Tison, William H. H. 312
Toussaint L'Ouverture Cemetery 312
Travellers Rest 312
Truehart's Battalion (CSA) 313
Truett House 313
Turner's Mississippi Battery (CSA) 313
Twelfth Indiana Cavalry (USA) 313
Twelfth Kentucky (USA) 313
Twelfth Kentucky Cavalry (CSA) 314
Twelfth Kentucky Mounted Infantry (CSA) 314
Twelfth Louisiana (CSA) 314
Twelfth Missouri Cavalry (USA) 314
Twelfth Tennessee (CSA) 314
Twelfth Tennessee Cavalry (CSA) 314
Twelfth Tennessee Cavalry (USA) 314
Twentieth Alabama (CSA) 314
Twentieth Louisiana (CSA) 314
Twentieth Mississippi (CSA) 314
Twentieth Ohio Battery (USA) 315
Twentieth Tennessee (CSA) 315
Twentieth Tennessee Cavalry (CSA) 315
Twenty-eighth Alabama (CSA) 315
Twenty-eighth Kentucky (USA) 315
Twenty-eighth Mississippi Cavalry (CSA) 315
Twenty-eighth Tennessee (CSA) 315

Twenty-fifth Alabama (CSA) 315
Twenty-fifth Arkansas (CSA) 315
Twenty-fifth Georgia (CSA) 315
Twenty-fifth Indiana Battery (USA) 316
Twenty-fifth Louisiana (CSA) 316
Twenty-fifth Michigan (USA) 316
Twenty-fifth Texas Cavalry (CSA) 316
Twenty-first Illinois (USA) 316
Twenty-first Kentucky (USA) 316
Twenty-first Tennessee Cavalry (CSA) 316
Twenty-fourth Alabama (CSA) 316
Twenty-fourth Arkansas (CSA) 316
Twenty-fourth Georgia (CSA) 316
Twenty-fourth Mississippi (CSA) 317
Twenty-fourth Missouri (USA) 317
Twenty-fourth South Carolina (CSA) 317
Twenty-fourth Tennessee (CSA) 317
Twenty-fourth Texas Cavalry (CSA) 317
Twenty-fourth Wisconsin (USA) 317
Twenty-ninth Alabama (CSA) 317
Twenty-ninth Georgia (CSA) 317
Twenty-ninth Mississippi (CSA) 317
Twenty-ninth North Carolina (CSA) 318
Twenty-ninth Tennessee (CSA) 318
Twenty-second Alabama (CSA) 318
Twenty-second Mississippi (CSA) 318
Twenty-seventh Alabama (CSA) 318
Twenty-seventh Mississippi (CSA) 318
Twenty-seventh Tennessee (CSA) 318
Twenty-sixth Alabama (CSA) 318
Twenty-sixth Kentucky (USA) 318
Twenty-sixth Ohio (USA) 319
Twenty-third Alabama (CSA) 319
Twenty-third Army Corps (USA) 319
Twenty-third Indiana Battery (USA) 319
Twenty-third Kentucky (USA) 319
Twenty-third Michigan (USA) 319

Twenty-third Mississippi (CSA)	319
Tyler's Brigade (CSA)	319
Union, the	321
United Daughters of the Confederacy	321
Vaughan's Brigade (CSA)	323
Visitors Center	323
Wagner, George Day	325
Wagner's Second Division (USA)	325
Walthall, Edward Cary	326
Walthall's Division (CSA)	326
War Between the States	326
War for Southern Independence	326
Watkins, Elihu P.	330
Watkins, Samuel Rush	330
Watkins, William M.	331
Watkins' Brigade (CSA)	331
Watters, Zachariah L.	331
Weir, John	331
Whitaker, Walter Chiles	332
Whitaker's Second Brigade (USA)	332
William McKissack House	332
William White House	334
Williams, Samuel C.	333
Williamson County Courthouse	333
Williamson County, Tennessee	333
Wilson, James Harrison	334
Wilson, John A.	335
Wilson's Cavalry Corps (USA)	335
Winder, Caroline Elizabeth	335
Winstead Hill	337
Witherspoon, William W.	338
Wood, Thomas John	338
Wood's Third Division (USA)	338
Yankee	339
Young, Robert Butler	339
Zion Presbyterian Church	340

MEET THE AUTHOR

LOCHLAINN SEABROOK, winner of the prestigious Jefferson Davis Historical Gold Medal for his "masterpiece" *A Rebel Born: A Defense of Nathan Bedford Forrest,* is an unreconstructed Southern historian, award-winning author, Forrest scholar, and traditional Southern Agrarian of Scottish, English, Irish, Welsh, German, and Italian extraction. An encyclopedist, lexicographer, musician, artist, graphic designer, genealogist, and photographer, as well as an award-winning poet, songwriter, and screenwriter, he has a thirty year background in historical nonfiction writing and is a member of the Sons of Confederate Veterans, the Civil War Trust, and the National Grange.

Due to similarities in their writing styles, ideas, and literary works, Seabrook is referred to as the "American ROBERT GRAVES," after his cousin, the prolific English writer, historian, mythographer, poet, and author of the classic tomes *The White Goddess* and *The Greek Myths.*

(Illustration © Tracy Latham)

The grandson of an Appalachian coal-mining family, Seabrook is a seventh-generation Kentuckian, co-chair of the Jent/Gent Family Committee (Kentucky), founder and director of the Blakeney Family Tree Project, and a board member of the Friends of Colonel Benjamin E. Caudill. Seabrook's literary works have been endorsed by leading authorities, museum curators, award-winning historians, bestselling authors, celebrities, noted scientists, well respected educators, renown military artists, esteemed Southern organizations, and distinguished academicians from around the world.

Seabrook has authored some thirty popular adult books specializing in the following topics: the American Civil War, pro-South studies, Confederate biography and history, the anthropology of religion, genealogical monographs, Goddess-worship (thealogy), ghost stories, the paranormal, family histories, military encyclopedias, etymological dictionaries, ufology, social issues, comparative analysis of the origins of Christmas, and cross-cultural studies of the family and marriage.

His seven children's books include a Southern children's guide to the Civil War, a dictionary of religion and myth, a rewriting of the King Arthur legend (which reinstates the original pre-Christian motifs), two bedtime stories for preschoolers, a naturalist's guidebook to owls, a worldwide look at the family, and an examination of the Near-Death Experience.

Of blue-blooded Southern stock through his Kentucky, Tennessee, Virginia, West Virginia, and North Carolina ancestors, he is a direct descendant of European royalty via his 6th great-grandfather, the EARL OF OXFORD, after which London's famous Harley Street is named. Among his celebrated male Celtic ancestors is ROBERT THE BRUCE, King of Scotland, Seabrook's 22nd great-grandfather. The 21st great-grandson of EDWARD I "LONGSHANKS" PLANTAGENET), King of England, Seabrook is a thirteenth-generation Southerner through his descent from the colonists of Jamestown, Virginia (1607).

(Photo © Lochlainn Seabrook)

The 2nd, 3rd, and 4th great-grandson of dozens of Confederate soldiers, one of his closest connections to the War for Southern Independence is through his 3rd great-grandfather, ELIAS JENT SR., who fought for the Confederacy in the Thirteenth Cavalry Kentucky under Seabrook's 2nd cousin, Colonel BENJAMIN E. CAUDILL. The Thirteenth, also known as "Caudill's Army," fought in numerous conflicts, including the Battles of Saltville, Gladsville, Mill Cliff, Poor Fork, Whitesburg, and Leatherwood.

Seabrook is also related to the following Confederates and other 19th-Century luminaries: ROBERT E. LEE, MARY ANNA RANDOLPH CUSTIS (General Lee's wife), STEPHEN DILL LEE, JOHN SINGLETON MOSBY, STONEWALL JACKSON, NATHAN BEDFORD FORREST, JAMES LONGSTREET, JOHN HUNT MORGAN, JEB STUART, P. G. T. BEAUREGARD (codesigner of the Confederate Battle Flag), JOHN BELL HOOD, ALEXANDER PETER

STEWART, EDMUND W. PETTUS, ABRAHAM BUFORD, JOHN B. WOMACK, THEODRICK "TOD" CARTER, ARTHUR M. MANIGAULT, JOSEPH MANIGAULT, CHARLES SCOTT VENABLE, THORNTON A. WASHINGTON, JOHN A. WASHINGTON, JOHN H. WINDER, GIDEON J. PILLOW, STATES RIGHTS GIST, EDMUND WINCHESTER RUCKER, HENRY ROOTES JACKSON, JOHN C. BRECKINRIDGE, MARK PERRIN LOWREY, HUGH ALFRED GARLAND JR., TYREE HARRIS BELL, ROBERT FRANKLIN BECKHAM, JESSE JOHNSON FINLEY, WILLIAM ANDREW QUARLES, LEONIDAS POLK, ZACHARY TAYLOR, SARAH KNOX TAYLOR (the first wife of JEFFERSON DAVIS), RICHARD TAYLOR, DAVY CROCKETT, DANIEL BOONE, MERIWETHER LEWIS (of the Lewis and Clark Expedition) ANDREW JACKSON, JAMES K. POLK, ABRAM POINDEXTER MAURY (founder of Franklin, TN), WILLIAM GILES HARDING, ZEBULON VANCE, THOMAS JEFFERSON, GEORGE WYTHE RANDOLPH (grandson of Jefferson), FELIX K. ZOLLICOFFER, FITZHUGH LEE, NATHANIEL F. CHEAIRS, JESSE JAMES, FRANK JAMES, ROBERT BRANK VANCE, CHARLES SIDNEY WINDER, JOHN W. MCGAVOCK, CARRIE (WINDER) MCGAVOCK, DAVID HARDING MCGAVOCK, LYSANDER MCGAVOCK, JAMES RANDAL MCGAVOCK, RANDAL WILLIAM MCGAVOCK, FRANCIS MCGAVOCK, EMILY MCGAVOCK, WILLIAM HENRY F. LEE, LUCIUS E. POLK, MINOR MERIWETHER (husband of noted pro-South author Elizabeth Avery Meriwether), ELLEN BOURNE TYNES (wife of Forrest's chief of artillery, Captain John W. Morton), South Carolina Senators PRESTON SMITH BROOKS and ANDREW PICKENS BUTLER, and famed South Carolina diarist MARY CHESNUT.

Seabrook's modern day cousins include: PATRICK J. BUCHANAN (conservative author), REBECCA GAYHEART (Kentucky-born actress), SHELBY LEE ADAMS (Letcher County, Kentucky, portrait photographer), BERTRAM THOMAS COMBS (Kentucky's fiftieth governor), EDITH BOLLING (wife of President Woodrow Wilson), and actors ROBERT

Duvall, Reese Witherspoon, Lee Marvin, and Tom Cruise.

Born with music in his blood, Seabrook is an award-winning, multi-genre, BMI-Nashville songwriter and lyricist who has composed some 3,000 songs (250 albums), and whose original music has been heard on TV and radio worldwide. A musician, producer, multi-instrumentalist, and renown performer—whose keyboard work has been variously compared to pianists from Hargus Robbins and Vince Guaraldi to Elton John and Leonard Bernstein—Seabrook has opened for groups such as the Earl Scruggs Review, Ted Nugent, and Bob Seger, and has performed privately for such public figures as President Ronald Reagan, Burt Reynolds, and Senator Edward W. Brooke.

Seabrook's cousins in the music business include: Johnny Cash, Elvis Presley, Billy Ray and Miley Cyrus, Patty Loveless, Tim McGraw, Lee Ann Womack, Dolly Parton, Pat Boone, Naomi, Wynonna, and Ashley Judd, Ricky Skaggs, the Sunshine Sisters, Martha Carson, and Chet Atkins.

Seabrook lives with his wife and family in historic Middle Tennessee, the heart of the Confederacy, where his conservative Southern ancestors fought valiantly against liberal Lincoln and the progressive North in defense of Jeffersonianism, constitutional government, and personal liberty.

LochlainnSeabrook.com

MEET THE FOREWORD WRITER

(Photo © Michael Givens)

MICHAEL GIVENS grew up in the rolling hills of Pickens, South Carolina and the gulf coast town of Pascagoula, Mississippi. He attended college at East Tennessee State University in Johnson City, Tennessee, and Brooks Institute in Santa Barbara, California, graduating with a BA in professional photography and cinematography.

He joined the Sons of Confederate Veterans in 1994 after seeing a billboard in Arkansas. He then re-chartered the General Richard H. Anderson, Camp 47 in Beaufort with Commander Brian Canaday. (The Camp still meets in the historic Arsenal, where the original Camp was chartered in 1897.)

Highlights of Givens' SCV achievements include:

- Commander, Camp 47, Beaufort, South Carolina-three years.
- Commander, 5th Brigade, South Carolina Division-four years.
- Lt. Commander, South Carolina Division-two years.
- Commander, South Carolina Division-two years.
- Commander, Army of Northern Virginia-two years.
- Lieutenant Commander-in-Chief, 2008-2010.
- Commander-in-Chief, 2010-present.
- Director, International Development-two years.
- National Committees: Constitutional Review: four years; Recruitment: four years; International Development: four years.

Awards:
- Jefferson Davis Chalice
- Robert E. Lee Award
- Commander-in-Chief's Award
- Meritorious Service (awarded multiple times)
- Distinguished Service (awarded multiple times)

- Stonewall Jackson Award, Dixie Club

Accomplishments (partial list):
- Has reformatted the *Confederate Veteran* magazine into an educational journal.
- Created *The Vision* program to strengthen and grow the SCV in the coming five years.
- Set up the genealogical DNA research program for the SCV through Family Tree DNA as a service for the membership and a fundraiser for the SCV.
- Created the Media Action Committee (MAC), which enables fast and effective response to heritage violations.
- Built the SC Division to over 3,200 members and 69 Camps and increased the coffers to over $100,000.00.
- Persuaded the State of SC to grant proceeds from a special license plate which nets the SCV more than $18,000.00 per year.
- Faced down the US Congress when liberal groups attempted to build a National Park dedicated to Reconstruction.
- Produced two fund raising documentaries for the SCV: *The Hunley Experience* and *Southern Heritage Celebration 2000*.
- Created a Speakers List for the SC Division over sixty pages long.
- Edited a journal of Southern History entitled: *The Richard H. Anderson Review*.
- Helped organize the historic flag rally in Columbia, South Carolina in January of 2000.
- Held speaking engagements all over America (including the Steven D. lee Institute), spreading the word of Southern heritage.
- Director of Photography for *Southern Partisan* magazine.

Givens makes his living as a director and cinematographer of feature films and international commercials. After establishing himself as a renowned photographer in the fashion and music industries, he progressed into the film business when he became the cinematographer of choice for such noted directors as Ridley Scott, Stephen Frears, Philip Borsos, Ron Maxwell and Peter Smillie.

As a screenwriter, director, and cinematographer, Givens has traveled the world shooting feature films and commercials, earning an international reputation for creating memorable images and stories. His film career now spans 30 years and includes more than 35 feature films and over 1000 commercials.

His feature film credits include directing and photographing the second unit for *Coyote Ugly* and cinematographer on *The Celestine Prophecy* (based on the best-selling book by James Redfield). His recent work includes the comedy *Opposite Day*, and the rock and roll drama *Angel Camouflaged*.

Givens' directorial debut came in 1989, while under the tutelage of Ridley Scott while at RSA. Since then he has directed numerous successful, award winning commercial campaigns for large corporations, financial institutions, and manufactures including: UPS, Credit Swiss, Pepsi and Visa. Following his affiliation at RSA, Michael built a successful relationship with the production company GLG and then formed his own company, Michael Givens & Associates. He also joined forces with five time Academy Award nominated director/cinematographer Caleb Deschanel at Dark Light Pictures.

Givens, a member of the First Presbyterian Church and the great-great grandson of Private Peter Harrison Givens, Co. H. Carter's 1st Tennessee Cavalry, currently resides in Beaufort, South Carolina, with his wife Nicole and their two children, Chandler and Olivia.

Givens-SCV.com

918 ~ ENCYCLOPEDIA OF THE BATTLE OF FRANKLIN

If you enjoyed Mr. Seabrook's *Encyclopedia of the Battle of Franklin* you will be interested in his excellent companion works:

THE MCGAVOCKS OF CARNTON PLANTATION: A SOUTHERN HISTORY
&
CARNTON PLANTATION GHOST STORIES:
TRUE TALES OF THE UNEXPLAINED FROM TENNESSEE'S MOST HAUNTED CIVIL WAR HOUSE!

Available from SeaRavenPress.com and wherever fine books are sold.

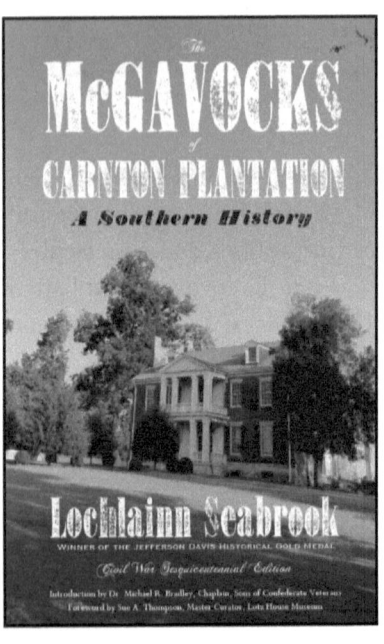

www.ingramcontent.com/pod-product-compliance
Lightning Source LLC
Chambersburg PA
CBHW031932290426
44108CB00011B/523